The 70-305 Cram Sheet

This cram sheet contains the distilled, key facts about developing and implementing Windows-based applications with Microsoft Visual Basic .NET. Review this information as the last thing you do before you enter the testing center, paying special attention to those areas in which you feel that you need the most review. You can transfer any of these facts from your head onto a blank sheet of paper immediately before you begin the exam.

TYPES OF ASP.NET CONTROLS

- **HTML controls**—Standard HTML elements that provide no server-side programmability.

- **HTML server controls**—HTML controls with the `runat="server"` attribute (which adds server-side programmability) that have an easy migration path for classic ASP.

- **Web server controls**—Native ASP.NET controls that render to uplevel and downlevel browsers, and are the best choice for most applications.

- **Validation controls**—Invisible controls that can validate data at both the client side and the server side. Use server-side validation to prevent client spoofing.

- **Templated controls**—Controls whose display is entirely dictated by templates. There are two such controls, the `Repeater` and the `DataList`.

- **Web User control**—A chunk of a user interface packaged for reuse. These are not compiled at design time. They must be copied to each project to reuse.

- **Composite Web custom control**—Controls made up of two or more intrinsic controls. These are a good choice for consistently repeating user interface elements.

- **Derived Web custom control**—Controls that inherit directly from one of the intrinsic controls. These are a good choice for adding functionality to built-in controls.

STATE-MANAGEMENT TECHNIQUES

Client-side techniques:

- **Query strings**—Limited length, not secure from tampering.

- **Cookies**—Limited size, users can block, not secure from tampering.

- **Hidden fields**—Visible in source, makes the page larger.

- **ViewState**—Like hidden fields, but can be encrypted and secured. Makes the page larger. Maintains values across postbacks, enables the `IsPostBack` property. Disable if not needed.

Server-side techniques:

- **Session state**—Depends on cookies or URL modifying. Can be stored in-process, in the Session State service, or in SQL Server.

- **Application state**—Shared by all sessions.

ERROR HANDLING

Following is the typical pattern for using a `Finally` block with a database connection:

```
Dim cnn As SqlConnection = New
SqlConnection(strConn)
Try
    cnn.Open()
    ' Database operations here
Catch ex As Exception
    ' Handle exceptions here
Finally
    cnn.Close()
End Try
```

The `Try` block executes until an error occurs. The `Catch` block executes if an error occurs. The `Finally` block always executes, no matter what.

When an unhandled exception occurs in a Web application, the following events are fired in order:

1. `Page.Error`—page-level event, handled by the `Page_Error` event handler

2. `Application.Error`—application-level event, handled by `Application_Error` event handler

Either of these event handlers can be used to trap and work with unhandled exceptions.

COPY or FTP deployment is simplest, but not suited r all application deployments. Among the factors at can move you to the more complex Installer eployment are: creating IIS sites, allowing users to elect features, adding assemblies to the GAC, config- ring databases, and presenting a UI during setup.

PERFORMANCE TIPS

ollowing are tips for maintaining and improving per- ormance of your applications:

- Use caching to store content.
- Avoid session state and `ViewState`.
- Use Low Cost authentication.
- Use `StringBuilder`.
- Native compilation reduces startup time.
- Don't use exceptions just to manage normal program flow.
- Make fewer calls across processes.
- Use the Release Configuration.
- Use the optimized managed providers.
- Prefer stored procedures over SQL statements.
- Tune the database.
- If you are reading a table sequentially, prefer using `DataReader` over `DataSet`.
- Use Connection Pooling.
- Avoid the `CommandBuilder` and auto-generated commands.

CONFIGURATION

Configuration settings are stored in a hierarchy of XML configuration files. Changes to configuration files are picked up on-the-fly. You can read configuration settings from code with the `ConfigurationSettings.AppSettings` object.

AUTHENTICATION AND AUTHORIZATION

ASP.NET authentication methods include

- **None**—The default, allows anonymous access.
- **Windows**—Uses Windows domain usernames and passwords.
- **Forms-based**—Allows you to authenticate with custom code.
- **Passport**—Depends on Microsoft Passport.

IIS authentication types include

- **Anonymous**—Anyone is allowed access.
- **Basic**—Cleartext Windows username and password.
- **Digest**—Hashed Windows username and password. IE 5.5 and above.
- **Windows integrated**—No passwords on the network. IE 3.01 and above.

Impersonation options include

- `<identity impersonate="false" />`: Uses ASP.NET's own identity.
- `<identity impersonate="true" />`: Uses the identity passed in by IIS.
- `<identity impersonate="true" name="DOMAIN\userName" password="password" />`: Uses the specified identity.

- Can be private or shared. Shared assemblies must have a strong name and be placed in the Global Assembly Cache (GAC).

WEB SERVICES

Web services in .NET are based on three XML protocols:

- **Simple Object Access Protocol (SOAP)**—Encapsulates objects and method calls for transmission across the Internet.
- **Universal Description, Discovery, and Integration (UDDI)**—Allows you to search for Web services filling a particular requirement.
- **Web Services Description Language (WSDL)**—Describes the interface of a Web service.

You create a Web service by decorating classes and methods with the `WebService` and `WebMethod` attributes.

GLOBALIZATION

Steps for preparing a world-ready application:

1. Globalization: Identifying resources to translate.
2. Localizability: Verifying that translation does not require design changes.
3. Localization: Performing the translation.

Resources that should be translated include text; layouts; formats for dates; currency; numbers; shortcut keys; and calendars.

The `CurrentUICulture` property tells the CLR which culture to use when choosing resources for the user interface. The `CurrentCulture` property dictates the format for dates, times, currency, numbers, and other functionality.

USING LEGACY CODE

You can still instantiate late-bound COM components:

```
cnn =
Server.CreateObject("ADODB.Connection")
```

ActiveX controls work on ASP.NET pages, but only if the client is Internet Explorer.

COM components can be used directly by .NET code if you build a Runtime Callable Wrapper (RCW). Use the `tlbimp` tool for this:

```
tlbimp MyCustomer.dll
/out:NETMyCustomer.dll
```

Win32 DLLs can be used via PInvoke.

USER ASSISTANCE

User assistance alternatives: help in a separate browser (might be confusing), help in the search pane (IE only), tooltips, or embedded help (increases download size).

ACCESSIBILITY

Basic principles of accessible design: flexibility, choice of input and output methods, consistency, compatibility with accessibility aids.

Some basic accessibility rules:

- ALT text for all graphics.
- Access keys whenever possible.
- Provide alternatives to frames, tables, and style sheets.
- Don't depend on sound or color.
- Provide captions for audio or video.

TESTING AND DEBUGGING

Types of testing include: unit testing (individual class or method), integration testing (two or more units), regression testing (retest after fixing a bug).

Types of tracing include the following:

- **Using the `System.Web.TraceContext` class**—This class allows you to view diagnostic information and trace messages along with the page output or through a separate trace viewer utility (`trace.axd`).
- **Using the `System.Diagnostics.Trace` and `System.Diagnostics.Debug` classes**—By default, these classes display trace messages in the Output window, but you can use the `TraceListener` class to send output to additional destinations such as text files, event logs, or other custom-defined trace listeners.

Trace switches allow you to control the level of tracing from an XML-based external configuration file.

Debugging Windows in Visual Studio .NET

Debugging Window	Purpose
Watch	Watches the value of a variable or an expression.
Autos	Displays the values of variables in the current statement and in the previous statement.
Locals	Displays the values of all local variables.
Me	Shows the values associated with the current object (normally the current Web Form in an ASP.NET application).
Immediate	Allows you to evaluate expressions and execute commands.
Call Stack	Shows the method call stack, giving you information about the path taken by the code to reach the current point of execution.

DATA BINDING

Simple data binding binds a data element to a property of a control. Complex data binding binds an entire collection of data to a control. Nothing is bound until your code calls the DataBind method.

T-SQL

Essential T-SQL Syntax

Syntax	Meaning
SELECT	Retrieves one or more columns.
FROM Table1, Table2	Cross-joins (usually the wrong thing to do!).
FROM Table 1 INNER JOIN Table 2 ON Table1. Column1 = Table2 .Column2	Retrieves related data.
WHERE Condition	Filters retrieved rows. % wildcard for zero or more characters; _ wildcard for exactly one character.
ORDER BY	Specifies sorting of results (ASC/DESC).
GROUP BY	Creates categories for aggregation.
COUNT(), SUM(), AVG(), MIN(), MAX()	Aggregates functions.
HAVING	Filters on grouped results (use WHERE to filter input).
INSERT	Adds row(s) to a table (must include VALUES clause to target specific columns).
UPDATE	Edits row(s) in a table (must include SET clause).
DELETE	Removes rows from a table.

@@IDENTITY returns the most recent identity value.

Stored procedures are a better choice than ad hoc queries when you know the SQL in advance.

FILE I/O CLASSES

- FileStream treats a file as a stream of bytes.
- StreamReader and StreamWriter are optimized for reading and writing full lines of text.
- BinaryReader and BinaryWriter are optimized for reading and writing binary object data.

ADO.NET CLASSES

ADO.NET classes are divided into two types: data provider classes that are implemented for each source of data, and DataSet classes that are the same for all providers.

Data Provider Classes

- **Connection**—Persistent connection to a database.
- **Command**—Something that can be executed, s as a SQL statement or stored procedure.
- **Parameter**—A parameter for a stored procedure.
- **DataReader**—Fast forward only data source.
- **DataAdapter**—Acts as a bridge between data providers and DataSets.

Data provider classes come in multiple versions depending on the provider; for example, for the Connection class, you can have SqlConnection, OleDbConnection, OdbcConnection, and OracleConnection.

DataSet Classes

- **DataSet**—An entire relational database in memory
- **DataTable**—A single table of data
- **DataRelation**—A relation between two DataTable objects
- **DataRow**—A single row of data
- **DataColumn**—A single column of data
- **DataView**—A view that extracts data from a DataTable

USING THE DATASET

Filling a DataSet:

1. Create a SqlConnection object to connect to the database.
2. Create a SqlCommand object to retrieve the desired data.
3. Assign the SqlCommand to the SelectCommand property of a SqlDataAdapter object.
4. Call the Fill method of the SqlDataAdapter object.

To visit all data in a DataSet, use For Each. To change data, just assign a new value to the appropriate DataRow object. Call the Update method of the SqlDataAdapter object to write the change back to the database.

XML CLASSES

- **XmlDocument**—An entire XML document
- **XmlNode**—A single entity, processing directive, or other part of the XML DOM
- **XmlDataDocument**—An XML document synchronized with a DataSet

ASSEMBLIES

- Are basic units of deployment, scope, security, and versioning.
- All .NET code is executed in assemblies.
- Can contain one file or multiple files.
- Can be used to hold resources.

Developing and Implementing Web Applications with Visual Basic® .NET and Visual Studio® .NET

Mike Gunderloy

Developing and Implementing Web Applications with
Visual Basic® .NET and Visual Studio® .NET
Exam Cram 2 (70-305)

International Standard Book Number: 0-7897-2898-2

Library of Congress Catalog Card Number: 2003100983

Printed in the United States of America

First Printing: July 2003

05   04   03   4   3   2   1

Trademarks

Warning and Disclaimer

Publisher
Paul Boger

Executive Editor
Jeff Riley

Development Editor
Ginny Bess Munroe

Managing Editor
Charlotte Clapp

Project Editor
Tricia Liebig

Copy Editor
Rhonda Tinch-Mize

Indexer
Mandie Frank

Proofreader
Jessica McCarty

Technical Editors
Steve Heckler
Ken Cox

Interior Designer
Gary Adair

Team Coordinator
Pamalee Nelson

Multimedia Developer
Dan Scherf

Page Layout
Cheryl Lynch

Graphics
Tammy Graham

Best Study Guides

CERTIFICATION

Que Certification • 201 West 103rd Street • Indianapolis, Indiana 46290

A Note from Series Editor Ed Tittel

You know better than to trust your certification preparation to just anybody. That's why you, and more than two million others, have purchased an Exam Cram book. As Series Editor for the new and improved Exam Cram 2 series, I have worked with the staff at Que Certification to ensure you won't be disappointed. That's why we've taken the world's best-selling certification product—a finalist for "Best Study Guide" in a CertCities reader poll in 2002—and made it even better.

As a "Favorite Study Guide Author" finalist in a 2002 poll of CertCities readers, I know the value of good books. You'll be impressed with Que Certification's stringent review process, which ensures the books are high-quality, relevant, and technically accurate. Rest assured that at least a dozen industry experts—including the panel of certification experts at CramSession—have reviewed this material, helping us deliver an excellent solution to your exam preparation needs.

We've also added a preview edition of PrepLogic's powerful, full-featured test engine, which is trusted by certification students throughout the world.

As a 20-year-plus veteran of the computing industry and the original creator and editor of the Exam Cram series, I've brought my IT experience to bear on these books. During my tenure at Novell from 1989 to 1994, I worked with and around its excellent education and certification department. This experience helped push my writing and teaching activities heavily in the certification direction. Since then, I've worked on more than 70 certification-related books, and I write about certification topics for numerous Web sites and for *Certification* magazine.

In 1996, while studying for various MCP exams, I became frustrated with the huge, unwieldy study guides that were the only preparation tools available. As an experienced IT professional and former instructor, I wanted "nothing but the facts" necessary to prepare for the exams. From this impetus, Exam Cram emerged in 1997. It quickly became the best-selling computer book series since "...*For Dummies*," and the best-selling certification book series ever. By maintaining an intense focus on subject matter, tracking errata and updates quickly, and following the certification market closely, Exam Cram was able to establish the dominant position in cert prep books.

You will not be disappointed in your decision to purchase this book. If you are, please contact me at etittel@jump.net. All suggestions, ideas, input, or constructive criticism are welcome!

Ed Tittel

For Adam & Kayla
Growing Fast

&

About the Author

Mike Gunderloy pursued his first Microsoft certification the year the program was introduced and has earned the MCP, MCT, MCSE, MCDBA, MCAD, and MCSD credentials in the decade since. As lead developer for Lark Group, Inc., Mike has worked with small businesses and Fortune 500 corporations alike, as well as trained many other developers in the use of Microsoft products. He got hooked on computers when you still had to build your own out of parts, and is still passionately interested in cutting-edge software technology. As a long-time member of the editorial staff of *MCP Magazine*, Mike has remained in close touch with the certification community.

Mike lives on a farm in eastern Washington state, along with his wife and children and an ever changing array of horses, sheep, llamas, geese, turkeys, chickens, ducks, peacocks, cats, dogs, and guinea fowl. When he's not busy testing and writing about software, Mike can usually be found in his garden or greenhouse, trying to persuade recalcitrant vegetables to grow.

You can reach Mike at MikeG1@larkfarm.com or http://www.larkware.com/.

About the Technical Editors

Steve Heckler is president of Accelebrate, an IT training and programming firm based in Atlanta. An avid ASP.NET, Java, and ColdFusion developer and trainer, Steve served more than six years as a senior manager and instructor at a leading East Coast IT training firm prior to founding Accelebrate. He holds bachelor's and master's degrees from Stanford University.

Ken Cox is a technical writer and Web applications programmer in Toronto, specializing in .NET technologies. For the past six years, Microsoft has selected him as a Most Valuable Professional (MVP) for ASP/ASP.NET. Ken is coauthor of several books including *Inside ASP.NET* (New Riders Publishing), *Teach Yourself Object-Oriented Programming with Visual Basic .NET in 21 Days* (Sams), and *.NET Mobile Web Developer's Guide* (Syngress). His software reviews and articles appear frequently in *Visual Studio Magazine*. Ken has a bachelor's degree in Radio and Television Arts and a college certificate in Technical Communication. In a previous life, he was a broadcast journalist in Toronto and Quebec City.

Acknowledgments

As always, thanks to the editorial staff at Que for working with me to create this book. Without their careful checking of my work, you'd find this volume a whole lot less useful. Thanks to Jeff Riley for getting me into this project, and to Ginny Bess Munroe, Tricia Liebig, Rhonda Tinch-Mize, and the rest of the editorial team for turning it into a book. Ken Cox and Steve Heckler offered great advice during the technical review of the book; any remaining errors are my fault, not theirs.

Finishing the manuscript is only half the battle. It's the production staff who actually get this stuff ready to print. So thanks to Mandie Frank, Jessica McCarty, Cheryl Lynch, and Tammy Graham for making an actual physical book out of the final files. I've spent some time in that part of the business and I know how hard they work.

I didn't start out to be a Web developer, but somewhere in the last seven years or so it became inevitable. Along the way, I've been privileged to work with many excellent colleagues and partners, including Steve White, Amit Kalani, Ken Getz, Mary Chipman, Dan Frumin, and Brian Randell. The writers for Hardcore Web Services have also helped shape some of the topics in this book; Chandu Thota, Bill Sempf, and Justin Rudd stand out. On the certification side, I've long enjoyed the support of *MCP Magazine*'s editorial staff, including Dian Schaffhauser, Keith Ward, Michael Domingo, Becky Nagel, and Kris McCarthy. And of course there are all of the folks who post their knowledge to newsgroups and Web sites; in many ways, a book like this reflects the collected experience of hundreds of developers.

When I surface from a long day of writing and coding, my wonderful wife Dana is always there to share real life with me. Of course, these days real life involves as much time as possible with Adam and Kayla, who are growing up fast (and surrounded by computers). Between family and farm, I feel very happy and grounded these days.

We Want to Hear from You!

As the reader of this book, *you* are our most important critic and commentator. We value your opinion and want to know what we're doing right, what we could do better, what areas you'd like to see us publish in, and any other words of wisdom you're willing to pass our way.

As an executive editor for Que Certification, I welcome your comments. You can email or write me directly to let me know what you did or didn't like about this book—as well as what we can do to make our books better.

Please note that I cannot help you with technical problems related to the *topic* of this book. We do have a User Services group, however, where I will forward specific technical questions related to the book.

When you write, please be sure to include this book's title and author as well as your name, email address, and phone number. I will carefully review your comments and share them with the author and editors who worked on the book.

Email: feedback@quepublishing.com

Mail: Jeff Riley
            Executive Editor
            Que Certification
            201 West 103rd Street
            Indianapolis, IN 46290 USA

For more information about this book or another Que title, visit our Web site at www.quepublishing.com. Type the ISBN (excluding hyphens) or the title of a book in the Search field to find the page you're looking for. For information about the Exam Cram 2 Series, visit www.examcram2.com.

Contents at a Glance

Chapter 1   Microsoft Certification Exams   1

Chapter 2   Introducing Web Forms   23

Chapter 3   Controls   57

Chapter 4   Implementing Navigation for the User Interface   89

Chapter 5   Error Handling for the User Interface   123

Chapter 6   Data Binding   143

Chapter 7   Consuming and Manipulating Data   175

Chapter 8   Creating and Managing Components and .NET Assemblies   231

Chapter 9   Web Services   257

Chapter 10   Globalization   271

Chapter 11   Working with Legacy Code   295

Chapter 12   User Assistance and Accessibility   317

Chapter 13   Testing and Debugging a Web Application   333

Chapter 14   Deploying a Web Application   361

Chapter 15   Maintaining and Supporting a Web Application   387

Chapter 16   Configuring a Web Application   407

Chapter 17   Practice Exam #1   431

Chapter 18   Answer Key for Practice Exam #1   467

Chapter 19   Practice Exam #2   483

Chapter 20   Answer Key for Practice Exam #2   517

Table of Contents

. . . .

Introduction..xxv

Self-Assessment xxvii

Chapter 1
Microsoft Certification Exams 1
    Assessing Exam Readiness   2
    What to Expect at the Testing Center   3
    Exam Layout and Design   4
        Multiple-Choice Question Format   5
        Build-List-and-Reorder Question Format   6
        Create-a-Tree Question Format   8
        Drag-and-Connect Question Format   10
        Select-and-Place Question Format   11
        Hot Area   12
    Microsoft's Testing Formats   12
    Strategies for Different Testing Formats   14
        Case Study Exam Strategy   15
        Fixed-Length and Short-Form Exam Strategy   15
        Adaptive Exam Strategy   17
    Question-Handling Strategies   18
    Mastering the Inner Game   19
    Additional Resources   19

Chapter 2
Introducing Web Forms 23
    An Overview of the .NET Framework   24
        The Common Language Runtime   24
        The Framework Class Library   25
    An Overview of .NET Development Tools   25
        The .NET Framework SDK   25
        ASP.NET Web Matrix Project   26
        Visual Studio .NET   26

Understanding Classes, Inheritance, and Namespaces   27
Classes   27
Inheritance   28
Namespaces   28
Introduction to ASP.NET   29
Creating an ASP.NET Page   30
Understanding ASP.NET Page Execution   32
The Page Class   33
Stages in Page Processing   35
ASP.NET Directives   35
Event Handling   38
Elements of Event Handling   39
Event Handling in ASP.NET   41
Separating the User Interface from Business Logic   43
Using Code-Behind   43
Creating a Web Form Using Visual Studio .NET   44
Exam Prep Questions   49
Need to Know More?   56

Chapter 3
Controls **57**
HTML Controls   58
HTML Server Controls   58
Web Server Controls   59
Common Web Server Controls   61
Event Handling with Web Server Controls   64
The List Controls   65
The PlaceHolder and Panel Controls   67
The Table, TableRow, and TableCell Controls   69
The AdRotator Control   70
The Calendar Control   71
User Input Validation   73
The RequiredFieldValidator Control   75
The RegularExpressionValidator Control   75
The RangeValidator Control   76
The CompareValidator Control   76
The CustomValidator Control   76
The ValidationSummary Control   77
Cascading Style Sheets   78
Exam Prep Questions   80
Need to Know More?   88

Chapter 4
Implementing Navigation for the User Interface **89**
Round-Trip and Postback   90
    The IsPostBack Property   91
    The SmartNavigation Property   91
ASP.NET Intrinsic Objects   92
    The HttpRequest Object   93
    The HttpResponse Object   95
    The HttpServerUtility Object   98
ASP.NET Applications   99
    The global.asax File   99
    Global Event Handlers   99
State Management   102
    Client-Side Techniques for State Management   102
    Server-Side Techniques for State Management   108
Navigation Between Pages   113
    The Response.Redirect() Method   113
    The Server.Transfer() Method   113
    The Server.Execute() Method   114
Exam Prep Questions   115
Need to Know More?   121

Chapter 5
Error Handling for the User Interface **123**
Understanding Exceptions   124
Exception Objects   126
Handling Exceptions   127
    The Try Block   127
    The Catch Block   127
    The Finally Block   129
    The Throw Statement   130
Custom Exceptions   131
Managing Unhandled Exceptions   131
    Using Custom Error Pages   132
    Using Error Events   134
Exam Prep Questions   136
Need to Know More?   141

Chapter 6

Data Binding **143**

Binding Data to the UI   144
   Simple Data Binding   144
   Complex Data Binding   146
   The DataBind Method   151
   Using the Data Form Wizard   152
Manipulating Databases   155
   Using Server Explorer   156
   Filtering Data   159
Using Templated Controls to Display Data   160
   The Repeater Control   160
   The DataList Control   163
   Editing Data with a DataList Control   164
Exam Prep Questions   167
Need to Know More?   173

Chapter 7

Consuming and Manipulating Data **175**

Accessing and Manipulating SQL Server Data   176
   Using Ad Hoc Queries   176
   Using Stored Procedures   186
Accessing and Manipulating Data   191
   Working with Disk Files   191
   The ADO.NET Object Model   196
   Using DataSets   205
   Editing Data with ADO.NET   210
   Using XML Data   215
Handling Data Errors   220
Exam Prep Questions   223
Need to Know More?   230

Chapter 8

Creating and Managing Components and .NET Assemblies **231**

Creating and Using .NET Components   232
   Creating a Component   232
Creating and Using Web User Controls   235
   Creating a Web User Control   235
Creating Web Custom Controls   237
   Creating a Composite Control   237
   Creating a Derived Control   240

Creating a Control from Scratch   241
Custom Control Choices   243
Creating and Managing .NET Assemblies   244
Single-File and Multifile Assemblies   245
Static and Dynamic Assemblies   246
Private and Shared Assemblies   246
Satellite and Resource-Only Assemblies   247
Exam Prep Questions   249
Need to Know More?   255

Chapter 9
Web Services 257
Understanding Web Services   258
SOAP   258
Disco and UDDI   259
WSDL   259
Invoking Your First Web Service   259
Discovering Web Services   262
Disco Documents and UDDI's Central Directory of Web Services   262
Using the Web Services Discovery Tool (`disco.exe`)   262
Instantiating and Invoking Web Services   263
Creating Proxy Classes with the Web Services Description Language Tool (`wsdl.exe`)   263
Using Web References   264
Testing a Web Service   264
Exam Prep Questions   266
Need to Know More?   270

Chapter 10
Globalization 271
Understanding Localization and Globalization   272
The Localization Process   273
What Should Be Localized?   273
Understanding Cultures   274
About Culture Codes   275
The `CultureInfo` Class   275
The `CurrentCulture` and `CurrentUICulture` Properties   276
The Invariant Culture   276
Displaying Localized Information   277
Setting Culture Properties   278

Using Localized Calendars   279
Working with Resource Files   281
Converting Existing Encodings   284
Understanding Unicode and Encodings   284
Implementing Mirroring   285
Validating Non-Latin User Input   287
Comparing and Sorting Data   288
Exam Prep Questions   289
Need to Know More?   294

Chapter 11
Working with Legacy Code **295**
Incorporating Existing Code into ASP.NET Applications   296
Running ASP and ASP.NET Together   296
Converting ASP Pages to ASP.NET   297
Using Late-Bound COM Components   297
Using ActiveX Controls   298
Using COM Components   300
Understanding Runtime Callable Wrappers   300
Using TLBIMP   302
Using COM Components Directly   304
Using COM+ Components   305
Using Platform Invoke   306
Exam Prep Questions   309
Need to Know More?   315

Chapter 12
User Assistance and Accessibility **317**
Implementing User Assistance   318
Using a Second Browser Window   318
Using the Search Pane   319
Using ToolTips   320
Embedding Help   321
Other User Assistance Alternatives   321
Implementing Accessibility Features   322
Understanding Accessible Design Guidelines   323
The W3C Guidelines   324
The Section 508 Guidelines   325
Testing Application Accessibility   326
Exam Prep Questions   327
Need to Know More?   332

Chapter 13
Testing and Debugging
a Web Application **333**
 Testing   334
  Creating a Test Plan   334
  Executing Tests   334
  Testing International Applications   336
 Tracing   337
  Using the TraceContext Class   337
  Using the Trace and Debug Classes   341
  Trace Listeners   343
  Trace Switches   345
  Conditional Compilation   347
 Debugging   348
  Setting Breakpoints and Stepping Through Program
  Execution   348
  Analyzing Program State to Resolve Errors   349
  Debugging on Exceptions   350
  Debugging a Running Process   351
  Debugging a Remote Process   352
  Debugging Code in DLL Files   352
  Debugging Client-Side Scripts   353
 Exam Prep Questions   354
 Need to Know More?   359

Chapter 14
Deploying a Web Application **361**
 Deployment Tools   362
  XCOPY Deployment   362
  FTP Deployment   362
  Microsoft Windows Installer   363
 Deploying a Web Application   363
  Creating a Web Setup Project   364
 Customizing Setup Projects   365
  Using the File System Editor   365
  Using the Registry Editor   366
  Using the File Types Editor   366
  Using the User Interface Editor   366
  Using the Custom Actions Editor   366
  Using the Launch Conditions Editor   367

Shared Assemblies   367
Assigning a Strong Name to an Assembly   368
Adding an Assembly to the Global Assembly Cache   369
Delay Signing an Assembly   370
Creating a Setup Project for Distributing Components   370
Creating Installation Components   371
Understanding the Installer Class   372
Working with Predefined Installation Components   372
Deploying an Assembly Containing Installation
Components   374
Working with Installer Classes   375
Scalable and Reliable Deployment   376
Web Gardens   376
Web Farms   377
Clusters   378
Methods of Deployment   378
Deployment via Removable Media   378
Web-Based Deployment   379
Exam Prep Questions   380
Need to Know More?   385

Chapter 15
Maintaining and Supporting a Web Application **387**
Designing a Web Application for Performance   388
Starting and Stopping Processes   392
Working with Event Logs   394
Writing to Event Logs   395
Reading and Monitoring Event Logs   395
Working with Performance Counters   396
Reading Performance Data of Running Processes   397
Publishing Performance Data   399
Exam Prep Questions   401
Need to Know More?   406

Chapter 16
Configuring a Web Application **407**
Configuring a Web Application   408
Anatomy of a Configuration File   409
The Configuration File Hierarchy   410
Reading Configuration Settings from Code   413

Configuring Security   413
   Configuring Authentication   413
   Configuring Authorization   416
Using Caching   419
   Types of Caching   419
   Using the Cache Object   419
   Using a Cache Directive   420
Handling Session State   420
   Using Session State Within a Process   421
   Using Session State Service   421
   Using Microsoft SQL Server to Store Session State   422
Installing and Configuring Server Services   422
   Installing and Configuring IIS   423
   Installing and Configuring FrontPage Server Extensions   423
Exam Prep Questions   425
Need to Know More?   430

Chapter 17
Practice Exam #1 ....**431**
How to Take the Self Tests   432
Exam-Taking Tips   432
Self Test   434

Chapter 18
Answer Key for Practice Exam #1 ....**467**
Answer Key   468
Detailed Answers   469

Chapter 19
Practice Exam #2 ....**483**
Self Test   484

Chapter 20
Answer Key for Practice Exam #2 ....**517**
Answer Key   518
Detailed Answers   519

Appendix A
What's on the CD-ROM **533**
PrepLogic Practice Tests, Preview Edition   533

Appendix B
Using the *PrepLogic Practice Tests, Preview Edition* Software **535**

Exam Simulation   535

Question Quality   535

Interface Design   536

Effective Learning Environment   536

Software Requirements   536

Installing *PrepLogic Practice Tests, Preview Edition*   537

Removing *PrepLogic Practice Tests, Preview Edition* from Your Computer   537

Using *PrepLogic Practice Tests, Preview Edition*   537

Starting a Practice Test Mode Session   538

Starting a Flash Review Mode Session   539

Standard *PrepLogic Practice Tests, Preview Edition* Options   539

Time Remaining   540

Your Examination Score Report   540

Reviewing Your Exam   540

Getting More Exams   540

Contacting PrepLogic   541

Customer Service   541

Product Suggestions and Comments   541

License Agreement   541

Glossary **543**

Index **551**

Introduction

Welcome to the *70-305 Exam Cram 2*! Whether this is your first or your fifteenth *Exam Cram 2* series book, you'll find information here that will help ensure your success as you pursue knowledge, experience, and certification. This introduction explains Microsoft's certification programs in general and talks about how the *Exam Cram 2* series can help you prepare for Microsoft's Certified Application Developer and Certified Solution Developer exams. Chapter 1 discusses the basics of Microsoft certification exams, including a description of the testing environment, and a discussion of test-taking strategies. Chapters 2 through 16 are designed to remind you of everything you'll need to know in order to take—and pass—the 70-305 Microsoft MCAD/MCSD certification exam. The two sample tests at the end of the book should give you a reasonably accurate assessment of your knowledge—and, yes, we've provided the answers and their explanations to the tests. Read the book and understand the material, and you'll stand a very good chance of passing the test.

Exam Cram 2 books help you understand and appreciate the subjects and materials you need to pass Microsoft certification exams. *Exam Cram 2* books are aimed strictly at test preparation and review. They do not teach you everything you need to know about a topic. Instead, I'll present and dissect the questions and problems I've found that you're likely to encounter on a test. I've worked to bring together as much information as possible about Microsoft certification exams.

Nevertheless, to completely prepare yourself for any Microsoft test, I recommend that you begin by taking the Self-Assessment that is included in this book, immediately following this introduction. The Self-Assessment tool will help you evaluate your knowledge base against the requirements for a Microsoft Certified Application Developer (MCAD) or Microsoft Certified Solution Developer (MCSD) under both ideal and real circumstances.

Based on what you learn from the Self-Assessment, you might decide to begin your studies with some classroom training, some practice with Visual Basic .NET, or some background reading. On the other hand, you might decide to pick up and read one of the many study guides available from Microsoft or third-party vendors on certain topics, including the award-winning *MCAD Training Guide* series from Que Publishing. I also recommend that you supplement your study program with visits to www.examcram2.com to receive additional practice questions, get advice, and track the MCAD and MCSD program.

I also strongly recommend that you install, configure, and play around with the software that you'll be tested on, because nothing beats hands-on experience and familiarity when it comes to understanding the questions you're likely to encounter on a certification test. Book learning is essential, but without a doubt, hands-on experience is the best teacher of all! To help you work with the product, I've arranged to include all of the source code from Que's *MCAD 70-305 Training Guide* on the CD in this book. You'll find a variety of examples there that drill into the exam topics in depth. The code listings provide you an opportunity to read, understand, and extend a lot of additional code that demonstrates various concepts related to the 70-305 exam objectives. The readme.txt file on the CD will guide you through the various examples. The CD also contains the *PrepLogic Practice Tests, Preview Edition* exam simulation software. The preview edition exhibits most of the full functionality of the Premium Edition, but offers only questions sufficient for only one practice exam. To get the complete set of practice questions and exam functionality, visit www.preplogic.com.

Taking a Certification Exam

After you've prepared for your exam, you need to register with a testing center. Each computer-based MCP exam costs $125, and if you don't pass, you can retest for an additional $125 for each additional try. In the United States and Canada, tests are administered by Prometric and by VUE. Here's how you can contact them:

➤ **Prometric**—You can sign up for a test through the company's Web site at www.prometric.com. Within the United States and Canada, you can register by phone at 800-755-3926. If you live outside this region, you should check the Prometric Web site for the appropriate phone number.

➤ **VUE**—You can sign up for a test or get the phone numbers for local testing centers through the Web at www.vue.com/ms.

To sign up for a test, you must possess a valid credit card or contact either Prometric or VUE for mailing instructions to send a check (in the United States). Only when payment is verified or your check has cleared can you actually register for the test.

To schedule an exam, you need to call the number or visit either of the Web pages at least one day in advance. To cancel or reschedule an exam, you must call before 7 p.m. Pacific standard time the day before the scheduled test time (or you might be charged, even if you don't show up to take the test).

When you want to schedule a test, you should have the following information ready:

➤ Your name, organization, and mailing address.

➤ Your Microsoft test ID. (Inside the United States, this usually means your Social Security number; citizens of other nations should call ahead to find out what type of identification number is required to register for a test.)

➤ The name and number of the exam you want to take.

➤ A method of payment. (As mentioned previously, a credit card is the most convenient method, but alternate means can be arranged in advance, if necessary.)

After you sign up for a test, you are told when and where the test is scheduled. You should try to arrive at least 15 minutes early. You must supply two forms of identification—one of which must be a photo ID—and sign a nondisclosure agreement to be admitted into the testing room.

All Microsoft exams are completely closed book. In fact, you are not permitted to take anything with you into the testing area, but you are given a blank sheet of paper and a pen (or in some cases an erasable plastic sheet and an erasable pen). I suggest that you immediately write down on that sheet of paper all the information you've memorized for the test. In *Exam Cram 2* books, this information appears on a tear-out sheet inside the front cover of each book. You are given some time to compose yourself, record this information, and take a sample orientation exam before you begin the real thing. I suggest that you take the orientation test before taking your first exam, but because all the certification exams are more or less identical in layout, behavior, and controls, you probably don't need to do this more than once.

When you complete a Microsoft certification exam, the software tells you immediately whether you've passed or failed. If you need to retake an exam, you have to schedule a new test with Prometric or VUE and pay another $125.

 The first time you fail a test, you can retake the test as soon as the next day. However, if you fail a second time, you must wait 14 days before retaking that test. The 14-day waiting period remains in effect for all retakes after the second failure.

Tracking MCP Status

As soon as you pass any Microsoft exam, you attain MCP status. Microsoft generates transcripts that indicate which exams you have passed.

You can view a copy of your transcript at any time by going to the MCP secured site and selecting Transcript Tool. This tool enables you to print a copy of your current transcript and confirm your certification status.

After you pass the necessary set of exams, you are certified. Official certification is normally granted after three to six weeks, so you shouldn't expect to get your credentials overnight. The package for official certification that arrives includes a Welcome Kit that contains a number of elements (see Microsoft's Web site for other benefits of specific certifications):

➤ A certificate that is suitable for framing, along with a wallet card and lapel pin.

➤ A license to use the applicable logo, which means that you can use the logo in advertisements, promotions, and documents, as well as on letterhead, business cards, and so on. Along with the license comes a logo sheet, which includes camera-ready artwork. (Note that before you use any of the artwork, you must sign and return a licensing agreement that indicates you'll abide by its terms and conditions.)

➤ A subscription to *Microsoft Certified Professional Magazine*, which provides ongoing data about testing and certification activities, requirements, and changes to the program.

Many people believe that the benefits of MCP certification go well beyond the perks that Microsoft provides to newly anointed members of this elite group. We're starting to see more job listings that request or require applicants to have MCP, MCAD, and other certifications, and many individuals who complete Microsoft certification programs can qualify for increases in pay and/or responsibility. As an official recognition of hard work and broad knowledge, one of the MCP credentials is a badge of honor in many IT organizations.

How to Prepare for an Exam

Preparing for any MCAD- or MCSD-related test (including Exam 70-305) requires that you obtain and study materials designed to provide comprehensive information about the product and its capabilities that will appear on the specific exam for which you are preparing. The following list of materials can help you study and prepare:

➤ The .NET Framework Software Development Kit (SDK). This SDK, which you can download from `http://msdn.microsoft.com/downloads/sample.asp?url=/msdn-files/027/000/976/msdncompositedoc.xml`, contains full documentation of .NET and should be a primary resource when you are preparing for the test.

➤ The exam preparation materials, practice tests, and self-assessment exams on the Microsoft Training & Services page, at www.microsoft.com/traincert. The Exam Resources link offers examples of the new question types found on the MCAD and MCSD exams. You should find the materials, download them, and use them!

➤ The exam-preparation advice, practice tests, questions of the day, and discussion groups on the www.examcram2.com e-learning and certification destination Web site.

In addition, you might find any or all the following materials useful in your quest for Visual Basic .NET expertise:

➤ **Microsoft training kits**—Microsoft Press offers a training kit that specifically targets Exam 70-305. For more information, visit http://www.microsoft.com/mspress/certification/mcad.asp. This training kit contains information that you will find useful in preparing for the test.

➤ **Microsoft Developer Network CD**—This quarterly CD- or DVD-based publication delivers numerous electronic titles that include coverage of .NET Framework, Visual Basic .NET, and related topics. Its offerings include product facts, technical notes, tools and utilities, sample code, and much more. A subscription to the MSDN Library costs $199 per year, but it is well worth the price. Visit http://msdn.microsoft.com/subscriptions/prodinfo/overview.asp for more details.

➤ **Study guides**—Several publishers—including Que Publishing—offer certification titles. Que Publishing offers the following:

➤ The *Exam Cram 2* series—These books give you information about the material you need to know to pass the tests.

➤ The *MCAD Training Guide* series—These books provide a greater level of detail than the *Exam Cram 2* books and are designed to teach you everything you need to know about the subject covered by an exam. Each book comes with a CD-ROM that contains interactive practice exams in a variety of testing formats.

Together, these two series make a perfect pair.

➤ **Classroom training**—CTECs, online partners, and third-party training companies (such as Wave Technologies, Learning Tree, and Data-Tech) all offer classroom training on Visual Basic .NET. These companies aim to help you prepare to pass Exam 70-305 (or other exams). Although such training runs upward of $350 per day in class, most of the individuals lucky enough to partake find this training to be quite worthwhile.

> ➤ **Other publications**—There's no shortage of materials available about Visual Basic .NET and the .NET Framework. The "Need to Know More?" resource sections at the end of each chapter in this book give you an idea of where we think you should look for further discussion.

This set of required and recommended materials represents an unparalleled collection of sources and resources for Visual Basic .NET and related topics. I hope that you'll find that this book belongs in this company.

What This Book Will Not Do

This book will *not* teach you everything you need to know about computers, or even about a given topic. Nor is this book an introduction to computer technology. If you're new to applications development and looking for an initial preparation guide, check out www.quepublishing.com, where you will find a whole section dedicated to the MCSD/MCAD certifications. This book will review what you need to know before you take the test, with the fundamental purpose dedicated to reviewing the information needed on the Microsoft 70-305 certification exam.

This book uses a variety of teaching and memorization techniques to analyze the exam-related topics and to provide you with ways to input, index, and retrieve everything you'll need to know in order to pass the test. Once again, it is *not* an introduction to application development.

What This Book Is Designed to Do

This book is designed to be read as a pointer to the areas of knowledge you will be tested on. In other words, you might want to read the book one time just to get an insight into how comprehensive your knowledge of computers is. The book is also designed to be read shortly before you go for the actual test and to give you a distillation of the entire field of Windows application development in as few pages as possible. We think you can use this book to get a sense of the underlying context of any topic in the chapters—or to skim read for Exam Alerts, bulleted points, summaries, and topic headings.

I've drawn on material from Microsoft's own listing of knowledge requirements, from other preparation guides, and from the exams themselves. I've also drawn from a battery of third-party test-preparation tools and technical Web sites as well as from my own experience with application development and the exam. My aim is to walk you through the knowledge you will need—looking over your shoulder, so to speak—and point out those things that are important for the exam (Exam Alerts, practice questions, and so on).

The 70-305 exam makes a basic assumption that you already have a strong background of experience with the Windows development platform and its terminology. On the other hand, because the .NET development environment is so new, no one can be a complete expert. I've tried to demystify the jargon, acronyms, terms, and concepts. Also, wherever I think you're likely to blur past an important concept, I've defined the assumptions and premises behind that concept.

About This Book

If you're preparing for the 70-305 certification exam for the first time, I've structured the topics in this book to build upon one another. Therefore, the topics covered in later chapters might refer to previous discussions in earlier chapters.

I suggest that you read this book from front to back. You won't be wasting your time because nothing I've written is a guess about an unknown exam. I've had to explain certain underlying information on such a regular basis that I've included those explanations here.

Once you've read the book, you can brush up on a certain area by using the Index or the Table of Contents to go straight to the topics and questions you want to re-examine. I've tried to use the headings and subheadings to provide outline information about each given topic. After you've been certified, I think that you'll find this book useful as a tightly focused reference and an essential foundation of .NET application development.

Chapter Formats

Each *Exam Cram 2* chapter follows a regular structure, along with graphical cues about especially important or useful material. The structure of a typical chapter is as follows:

➤ **Opening hotlists**—Each chapter begins with lists of the terms you'll need to understand and the concepts you'll need to master before you can be fully conversant with the chapter's subject matter. I follow the hotlists with a few introductory paragraphs, setting the stage for the rest of the chapter.

➤ **Topical coverage**—After the opening hotlists, each chapter covers the topics related to the chapter's subject.

➤ **Exam Alerts**—Throughout the topical coverage section, I highlight material most likely to appear on the exam by using a special Exam Alert layout that looks like this:

This is what an Exam Alert looks like. An Exam Alert stresses concepts, terms, software, or activities that will most likely appear in one or more certification exam questions. For that reason, I think any information found offset in Exam Alert format is worthy of unusual attentiveness on your part.

Even if material isn't flagged as an Exam Alert, *all* the content in this book is associated in some way with test-related material. What appears in the chapter content is critical knowledge.

➤ **Notes**—This book is an overall examination of computers. As such, I'll dip into many aspects of .NET application development. Where a body of knowledge is deeper than the scope of the book, I use notes to indicate areas of concern or specialty training.

Cramming for an exam will get you through a test, but it won't make you a competent IT professional. Although you can memorize just the facts you need in order to become certified, your daily work in the field will rapidly put you in water over your head if you don't know the underlying principles of application development.

➤ **Tips**—I provide tips that will help you to build a better foundation of knowledge or to focus your attention on an important concept that will reappear later in the book. Tips provide a helpful way to remind you of the context surrounding a particular area of a topic under discussion.

You should also read Chapter 1, "Microsoft Certification Exams," for helpful strategies used in taking a test. The introduction to Practice Exam #1 in Chapter 17 contains additional tips on how to figure out the correct response to a question and what to do if you draw a complete blank.

➤ **Practice questions**—This section presents a short list of test questions related to the specific chapter topic. Each question has a following explanation of both correct and incorrect answers. The practice questions highlight the areas we found to be most important on the exam.

➤ **Need to Know More?**—Every chapter ends with a section titled "Need to Know More?" This section provides pointers to resources that we found to be helpful in offering further details on the chapter's subject matter. If you find a resource you like in this collection, use it, but don't feel compelled to use all these resources. I use this section to recommend resources that I have used on a regular basis, so none of the recommendations will be a waste of your time or money. These resources may go out of print or be taken down (in the case of Web sites), so I've tried to reference widely accepted resources.

The bulk of the book follows this chapter structure, but there are a few other elements that we would like to point out:

➤ **Practice exams**—The practice exams, which appear in Chapters 17 and 19 (with answer keys in Chapters 18 and 20), are very close approximations of the types of questions you are likely to see on the current 70-305 exam.

➤ **Answer keys**—These provide the answers to the practice exams, complete with explanations of both the correct responses and the incorrect responses.

➤ **Glossary**—This is an extensive glossary of important terms used in this book.

➤ **The Cram Sheet**—This appears as a tear-away sheet, inside the front cover of this *Exam Cram 2* book. It is a valuable tool that represents a collection of the most difficult-to-remember facts and numbers we think you should memorize before taking the test. Remember, you can dump this information out of your head onto a piece of paper as soon as you enter the testing room. These are usually facts that we've found require brute-force memorization. You only need to remember this information long enough to write it down when you walk into the test room. Be advised that you will be asked to surrender all personal belongings before you enter the exam room itself.

You might want to look at the Cram Sheet in your car or in the lobby of the testing center just before you walk into the testing center. The Cram Sheet is divided under headings, so you can review the appropriate parts just before each test.

➤ **The CD**—The CD includes many helpful code examples that demonstrate all the topics on the exam. If you work through the examples on the CD, you'll understand the techniques that you're likely to be tested on. The CD also contains the *PrepLogic Practice Tests, Preview Edition* exam simulation software. The preview edition exhibits most of the full functionality of the Premium Edition, but offers only questions sufficient for only one practice exam. To get the complete set of practice questions and exam functionality, visit `www.preplogic.com`.

Code and Commands

Limitations of printed pages will, many times, require me to write code with smaller margins than you might use in practice. In these cases, I've used the Visual Basic .NET line continuation character (_) whenever possible, so that the code you see on the printed page is syntactically correct.

In some cases, the margins force me to introduce line continuations into code that's automatically generated by Visual Basic .NET, even though you won't see those continuations when you re-create the code in your own copy.

Contacting the Author

I've tried to create a real-world tool that you can use to prepare for and pass the 70-305 MCAD/MCSD certification exam. I'm interested in any feedback you would care to share about the book, especially if you have ideas about how I can improve it for future test takers. I'll consider everything you say carefully and will respond to all reasonable suggestions and comments. You can reach me via email at MikeG1@larkfarm.com.

Let me know if you found this book to be helpful in your preparation efforts. I'd also like to know how you felt about your chances of passing the exam *before* you read the book and then *after* you read the book. Of course, I'd love to hear that you passed the exam—and even if you just want to share your triumph, I'd be happy to hear from you.

Thanks for choosing me as your personal trainer, and enjoy the book. I would wish you luck on the exam, but I know that if you read through all the chapters and work with the product, you won't need luck—you'll pass the test on the strength of real knowledge!

Self-Assessment

The reason I included a Self-Assessment in this *Exam Cram 2* book is to help you evaluate your readiness to tackle Microsoft certifications. It should also help you understand what you need to know to master the topic of this book—namely, Exam 70-305 "Developing and Implementing Web Applications with Microsoft Visual Basic .NET and Microsoft Visual Studio .NET." But before you tackle this Self-Assessment, let's talk about concerns you might face when pursuing an MCSD (Microsoft Certified Solution Developer) or MCAD (Microsoft Certified Application Developer) for the .NET platform and what an ideal MCSD candidate might look like.

MCSDs in the Real World

In this section, I describe an ideal MCSD candidate, knowing full well that only a few real candidates will meet this ideal. In fact, my description of that ideal candidate might seem downright scary, especially with the changes that have been made to the program to support the .NET development platform. But take heart: Although the requirements to obtain an MCSD might seem formidable, they are by no means impossible to meet. However, be keenly aware that it takes time, involves some expense, and requires real effort to get through the process.

Increasing numbers of people are attaining Microsoft certifications, so the goal is within reach. You can get all the real-world motivation you need from knowing that many others have gone before, so you will be able to follow in their footsteps. If you're willing to tackle the process seriously and do what it takes to obtain the necessary experience and knowledge, you can take—and pass—all the certification tests involved in obtaining an MCSD or MCAD.

Besides MCSD, other Microsoft certifications include the following:

➤ **MCSA (Microsoft Certified Systems Administrator)**—This is the brand-new certification that Microsoft has provided for those Microsoft professionals who are not going to design networks but rather administer them. This certification includes three core exams and a single elective.

➤ **MCAD (Microsoft Certified Application Developer)**—This is aimed at software developers functioning at a departmental level with one to two years of applications-development experience. The MCAD certification requires two specific exams, plus a third elective exam drawn from a limited pool of options. The 70-305 exam is a core exam for the MCAD credential.

➤ **MCDBA (Microsoft Certified Database Administrator)**—This is aimed at database administrators and developers who work with Microsoft SQL Server. The MCDBA certification requires three core exams and one elective exam.

➤ **Other Microsoft certifications**—The requirements for these certifications range from one test (MCP) to several tests (MCSE).

The Ideal MCSD Candidate

The MCSD test is aimed at software developers. The requirements have recently been revised for .NET, and they include one exam on Web application development, one on Windows application development, one on XML and server development, and one on solution architecture, as well as a fifth, elective exam drawn from a different, but limited, pool of options. The 70-305 exam that this book prepares you for fulfills the Web application exam requirement for the MCSD.

Just to give you some idea of what an ideal MCSD candidate is like, here are some relevant statistics about the background and experience such an individual might have:

➤ Academic or professional training in applications-development theory, concepts, and operations. This includes everything from programming and deployment planning through database integration and Web deployment.

➤ Two or more years of lead development experience, including business process analysis, deployment management planning, and solution architecture design within an enterprise.

 NOTE

The .NET platform is somewhat different from previous versions of the Microsoft development languages; therefore, you'll really need some hands-on experience. Due to the structural changes made in creating an object-based development environment built around a Common Language Runtime, the more hands-on experience you have, the better.

➤ Experience in developing applications designed to run within the Windows 2000 Server, Windows 2000/XP Professional, and soon the Windows .NET Server environments. A solid understanding of each system's architecture, installation, configuration, maintenance, and troubleshooting is also helpful when testing your code.

➤ A thorough understanding of the software-development lifecycle is important, including analysis, design, development, testing, deployment, and maintenance of an application.

➤ An understanding of how to implement security for key network data in a Windows 2000/XP environment.

➤ Experience developing XML and server components in the .NET environment.

➤ Working knowledge of the .NET programming environment, preferably with some hands-on experience with the Microsoft Visual Studio .NET development tools. The time you take practicing the use of Visual Studio .NET will be time very well spent!

 Don't worry if you don't meet these qualifications or don't even come that close—this is a far-from-ideal world, and where you fall short is simply where you'll have more work to do.

Fundamentally, this boils down to a bachelor's degree in computer science (or equivalent job experience), plus two years' experience working in a position involving applications design, testing, deployment, and maintenance, with some experience in database integration. I believe that well under half of all certification candidates meet these requirements and that, in fact, most meet less than half of these requirements—at least, when they begin the certification process. But because all the people who already have been certified have survived this ordeal, you can survive it too—especially if you heed what this Self-Assessment can tell you about what you already know and what you need to learn.

Put Yourself to the Test

The following series of questions and observations is designed to help you figure out how much work you must do to pursue Microsoft certification and what kinds of resources you should consult on your quest. Be absolutely honest in your answers; otherwise, you'll end up wasting money on exams you're not yet ready to take. There are no right or wrong answers, only steps along the path to certification. Only you can decide where you really belong in the broad spectrum of aspiring candidates.

Two things should be clear from the outset, however:

➤ Even a modest background in computer science and programming will be helpful.

➤ Hands-on experience with Microsoft products and technologies is an essential ingredient to Microsoft certification success.

Educational Background

Although taking courses in computer science isn't required to become certified, the background you'll gain from formal computer education will certainly help you pass the exams. These questions will help you judge your level of preparation in the classroom.

1. Have you ever taken any computer-related classes? [Yes or No]

   If Yes, proceed to Question 2; if No, proceed to Question 4.

2. Have you taken any classes on computer operating systems? [Yes or No]

   If Yes, you will probably be able to handle Microsoft's architecture and system component discussions. If you're rusty, brush up on basic operating system concepts and general computer security topics.

   If No, consider some basic reading in this area. I strongly recommend a good general operating systems book, such as *Operating System Concepts, 5th Edition*, by Abraham Silberschatz and Peter Baer Galvin (John Wiley & Sons, 1998). If this title doesn't appeal to you, check out reviews for other, similar titles at your favorite online bookstore.

3. Have you taken any programming classes, particularly ones focused on Microsoft development languages and the .NET platform? [Yes or No]

   If Yes, you will probably be able to handle Microsoft's terminology, concepts, and technologies. (Brace yourself for frequent departures from normal usage.) If you're rusty, brush up on basic programming concepts and terminology, with an eye toward the .NET development methodology. Skip to the next section, "Hands-on Experience."

   If No, you might want to read one or two books in this topic area. Good books for detailed knowledge of the .NET Framework include *Essential .NET* (Addison-Wesley), by Don Box and Chris Sells and *Advanced .NET Programming* (Wrox), by Simon Robinson.

4. Have you done any reading on programming? [Yes or No]

   If Yes, review the requirements stated in the first paragraphs after Questions 2 and 3. If you meet those requirements, move on to the next section.

   If No, consult the recommended reading previously discussed in this section for both topics. A strong background will help you prepare for the Microsoft exams better than just about anything else.

Hands-on Experience

The most important key to success on all the Microsoft tests is hands-on experience, especially with the Visual Studio .NET interface. If I leave you with only one realization after taking this Self-Assessment, it should be that there's no substitute for time spent creating, configuring, and deploying applications created using the Visual Basic .NET product, upon which you'll be tested repeatedly and in depth.

 You can download objectives, practice exams, and other data about Microsoft exams from the Training and Certification page at **http://www.microsoft.com/t raincert/**. Use the Microsoft Certifications link to obtain specific exam information.

5. Have you installed, configured, or used Visual Studio .NET and the .NET Framework? [Yes or No]

If Yes, you should be familiar with the main parts of the Visual Studio .NET Integrated Development Environment (IDE), and will be prepared to follow the examples in this book.

If No, you must get some experience. Read on for suggestions on how to do this.

Experience is a must with any Microsoft product exam—be it something as simple as FrontPage 2000 or as challenging as SQL Server 2000. For trial copies of other software, search Microsoft's Web site using the name of the product as your search term. Also, search for bundles such as "BackOffice" or "Small Business Server."

6. Have you developed any Web applications?

If Yes, you will be able to handle the overall architecture that this exam concentrates on.

If No, you must get some experience with these particular types of applications. The best experience is hands-on work in a Web-based environment. You might also choose to work through a study guide such as the Que 70-305 Training Guide.

7. Do you have experience using databases and XML files from Web applications?

If Yes, you're ready to tackle the extensive XML and database content of the 70-305 exam.

If No, you must ensure that you have a basic understanding of XML and databases, as well as how to use them from Web applications, to pass this exam. You'll find reference material for these topics throughout this book, particularly in the suggested readings for Chapters 6, "Data Binding," and 7, "Consuming and Manipulating Data." You might also want to visit the World Wide Web Consortium's Web site at http://www.w3c.org/ to view the many official specifications and documents relating to XML.

If you have the funds, or your employer will pay your way, consider taking a class at a Certified Training and Education Center (CTEC). In addition to classroom exposure to the topic of your choice, you usually get a copy of the software that is the focus of your course, along with a trial version of whatever operating system it needs, with the training materials for that class.

Before you even think about taking any Microsoft exam, make sure that you've spent enough time with the related software to understand how it can be installed, configured, and used. This will help you in the exam and in real life!

Testing Your Exam Readiness

Whether you attend a formal class on a specific topic to get ready for an exam or use written materials to study on your own, some preparation for the Microsoft Certification Exams is essential. At $125 a try, pass or fail, you want to do everything you can to pass on your first try. That's where studying comes in.

I have included two practice exams in this book (Chapters 17 and 19), so if you don't score that well on the first, you can study more and then tackle the second.

For any given subject, consider taking a class if you've tackled self-study materials, taken the test, and failed anyway. The opportunity to interact with an instructor and fellow students can make all the difference in the world if you can afford that privilege. For information about Microsoft classes, visit the Training and Certification page at http://www.microsoft.com/education/partners/ctec.asp for Microsoft Certified Education Centers.

If you can't afford to take a class, visit the Training page at http://www.microsoft.com/traincert/training/find/default.asp anyway because it also includes pointers to free practice exams, Microsoft Certified Professional Approved Study Guides, and other self-study tools. And even if you can't afford to spend much at all, you should still invest in some low-cost practice exams from commercial vendors.

8. Have you taken a practice exam on your chosen test subject? [Yes or No]

If Yes, and you scored 70% or better, you're probably ready to tackle the real thing. If your score isn't above that threshold, keep at it until you break that barrier.

If No, obtain all the free and low-budget practice tests you can find and get to work. Keep at it until you can break the passing threshold comfortably.

 When it comes to assessing your test readiness, there is no better way than to take a good quality practice exam and pass with a score of 70% or better. When I'm preparing myself, I shoot for 80% or more, just to leave room for the unexpected and sometimes nonsensical questions that can show up on Microsoft exams.

Assessing Readiness for Exam 70-305

In addition to the general exam-readiness information in the previous section, there are several things you can do to prepare for the Developing and Implementing Web Applications with Microsoft Visual Basic .NET and Microsoft Visual Studio .NET (70-305) exam. I suggest that you join an active Microsoft Developers mailing list, obtain a Microsoft Developer Network (MSDN) subscription, and regularly visit the MSDN Web site for new information (http://msdn.microsoft.com).

Microsoft exam mavens also recommend checking the Microsoft Knowledge Base (integrated into the MSDN CD-ROM, or on the Microsoft Web site at http://support.microsoft.com/support/) for "meaningful technical support issues" that relate to your exam's topics. Although I'm not sure exactly what the quoted phrase means, I have noticed some overlap between technical support questions on particular products and troubleshooting questions on the exams for those products.

What's Next?

After you've assessed your readiness, undertaken the right background studies, obtained the hands-on experience that will help you understand the products and technologies at work, and reviewed the many sources of information to help you prepare for a test, you'll be ready to take a round of practice tests.

When your scores come back positive enough to get you through the exam, you're ready to go after the real thing. If you follow our assessment regime, you'll not only know what you need to study, but also when you're ready to make a test date at Prometric (www.prometric.com) or VUE (www.vue.com). Good luck!

Microsoft Certification Exams

Terms you'll need to understand:

✓ Case study
✓ Multiple-choice question format
✓ Build-list-and-reorder question format
✓ Create-a-tree question format
✓ Drag-and-connect question format
✓ Select-and-place question format
✓ Fixed-length tests
✓ Simulations
✓ Adaptive tests
✓ Short-form tests

Techniques you'll need to master:

✓ Assessing your exam readiness
✓ Answering Microsoft's varying question types
✓ Altering your test strategy depending on the exam format
✓ Practicing (to make perfect)
✓ Making the best use of the testing software
✓ Budgeting your time
✓ Guessing (as a last resort)

Exam taking is not something that most people anticipate eagerly, no matter how well prepared they might be. In most cases, familiarity helps offset test anxiety. In plain English, this means that you probably won't be as nervous when you take your fourth or fifth Microsoft certification exam as you'll be when you take your first one.

Whether it's your first exam or your tenth, understanding the details of taking the new exam (how much time to spend on questions, the environment you'll be in, and so on) and the new exam software will help you concentrate on the material rather than on the setting. Likewise, mastering a few basic exam-taking skills should help you recognize (and perhaps even outfox) some of the tricks and snares you're bound to find in some exam questions.

This chapter explains the exam environment and software and describes some proven exam-taking strategies that you can use to your advantage.

Assessing Exam Readiness

I strongly recommend that you read through and take the Self-Assessment included with this book. (It appears after the Introduction.) This will help you compare your knowledge base to the requirements for obtaining an MCAD (Microsoft Certified Application Developer) or MCSD (Microsoft Certified Solution Developer), and it will also help you identify parts of your background or experience that might need improvement or enhancement, as well as where you need further learning. If you get the right set of basics under your belt, obtaining Microsoft certification will be that much easier.

After you've gone through the Self-Assessment, you can remedy those topical areas in which your background or experience might be lacking. You can also tackle subject matter for individual tests at the same time, so you can continue making progress while you're catching up in some areas.

After you've worked through an *Exam Cram 2*, have read the supplementary materials, and have taken the practice test, you'll have a pretty clear idea of when you should be ready to take the real exam. Although I strongly recommend that you keep practicing until your scores top the 70% mark, 80% is a better goal because it gives some margin for error when you are in an actual, stressful exam situation. Keep taking practice tests and studying the materials until you attain that score. You'll find more pointers on how to study and prepare in the Self-Assessment. But now, on to the exam itself.

What to Expect at the Testing Center

When you arrive at the testing center where you scheduled your exam, you must sign in with an exam coordinator and show two forms of identification—one of which must be a photo ID. After you've signed in and your time slot arrives, you'll be asked to deposit any books, bags, cell phones, or other items you brought with you. Then, you'll be escorted into a closed room.

All exams are completely closed book. Although you are not permitted to take anything with you into the testing area, you are furnished with a blank sheet of paper and a pen (in some cases, an erasable plastic sheet and an erasable pen). Immediately before entering the testing center, try to memorize as much of the important material as you can so that you can write the information on the blank sheet as soon as you are seated in front of the computer. You can refer to this piece of paper during the test, but you'll have to surrender the sheet when you leave the room. Because your timer does not start until you begin the testing process, it is best to do this first while the information is still fresh in your mind. You will have some time to compose yourself, so write down information on the paper you're given and take a sample orientation exam before you begin the real thing. I suggest that you take the orientation test before taking your first exam. (Because the exams are generally identical in layout, behavior, and controls, you probably won't need to do this more than once.)

Typically, the room has one to six computers, and each workstation is separated from the others by dividers. Most test rooms feature a wall with a large picture window. This permits the exam coordinator to monitor the room, prevent exam takers from talking to one another, and observe anything out of the ordinary. The exam coordinator will have preloaded the appropriate Microsoft certification exam (for this book, Exam 70-305), and you'll be permitted to start as soon as you're seated in front of the computer.

All Microsoft certification exams allow a certain maximum amount of time in which to complete your work. (This time is indicated on the exam by an onscreen counter/clock, so you can check the time remaining whenever you like.) All Microsoft certification exams are computer generated. In addition to multiple choice, you might encounter select and place (drag and drop), create a tree (categorization and prioritization), drag and connect, and build list and reorder (list prioritization) on some exams. The questions are constructed to check your mastery of basic facts and figures about Microsoft Visual Basic .NET Web application development and require you to evaluate one or more sets of circumstances or requirements. Often, you'll be asked to give more than one answer to a question. You might also be asked to select the best or most effective solution to a problem from a range of choices—all of which are technically correct.

Exam Layout and Design

The format of Microsoft exams can vary. For example, many exams consist of a series of case studies, with six types of questions regarding each presented case. Other exams might have the same six types of questions but no complex multiquestion case studies. In this chapter, I'll show you the wide range of questions that you might encounter on Microsoft exams, even though not all of these types of questions will appear on the 70-305 exam.

For the Design exams, each case study presents a detailed problem that you must read and analyze. Figure 1.1 shows an example of what a case study looks like. You must select the different tabs in the case study to view the entire case.

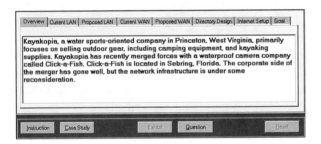

Figure 1.1   This is a typical case study.

Following each case study is a set of questions related to the case study. These questions can be one of several types (which are discussed next). Careful attention to details provided in the case study is the key to success. Be prepared to toggle frequently between the case study and the questions as you work. Some of the case studies also include diagrams (called *exhibits*) that you'll need to examine closely to understand how to answer the questions.

After you complete a case study, you can review all the questions and your answers. However, when you move on to the next case study, you cannot return to the previous case study and make any changes. You probably won't encounter any case studies on the 70-305 exam.

Following are the types of question formats:

➤ Multiple-choice, single answer

➤ Multiple-choice, multiple answers

➤ Build list and reorder (list prioritization)

➤ Create a tree

➤ Drag and connect

➤ Select and place (drag and drop)

➤ Hot area

Multiple-Choice Question Format

Some exam questions require you to select a single answer, whereas others ask you to select multiple correct answers. The following multiple-choice question requires you to select a single correct answer. Following the question is a brief summary of each potential answer and why it is either right or wrong.

Question 1

You have three domains connected to an empty root domain under one contiguous domain name: **tutu.com**. This organization is formed into a forest
arrangement with a secondary domain called **frog.com**. How many Schema
Masters exist for this arrangement?

○ A. One

○ B. Two

○ C. Three

○ D. Four

The correct answer is A. Only one Schema Master is necessary for a forest arrangement. The other answers (B, C, and D) are misleading because you are led to believe that Schema Masters can be in each domain or that you should have one for each contiguous domain namespace.

This sample question format corresponds closely to the Microsoft Certification Exam format. (Of course, questions are not followed by answer keys on the exam.) To select an answer, you position the cursor over the radio button next to the answer and click the mouse button to select the answer.

Let's examine a question in which one or more answers are possible. This type of question provides check boxes rather than radio buttons (circles) for marking all appropriate selections.

Question 2

> How can you seize FSMO roles? [Check all correct answers]
>
> ❑ A. By using the **ntdsutil.exe** utility
>
> ❑ B. By using the Replication Monitor
>
> ❑ C. By using the **secedit.exe** utility
>
> ❑ D. By using Active Directory Domains and Trusts

Answers A and B are correct. You can seize FSMO roles from a server that is still running through the Replication Monitor, or in the case of a server failure, you can seize roles with the ntdsutil.exe utility. The secedit.exe utility is used to force group policies into play; therefore, answer C is incorrect. Active Directory Domains and Trusts is a combination of truth and fiction; therefore, answer D is incorrect.

For this particular question, two answers are required. Microsoft sometimes gives partial credit for partially correct answers. For Question 2, you have to check the boxes next to answers A and B to obtain credit for a correct answer. Notice that picking the right answers also means knowing why the other answers are wrong.

Build-List-and-Reorder Question Format

Questions in the build-list-and-reorder format present two lists of items: one on the left and one on the right. To answer the question, you must move items from the list on the right to the list on the left. The final list must then be reordered into a specific order.

These questions are usually in the form, "From the following list of choices, pick the choices that answer the question. Then arrange the list in a certain order." To give you practice with this type of question, some questions of this type are included in this study guide. Here's an example of how they appear in this book; for an example of how they appear on the test, see Figure 1.2.

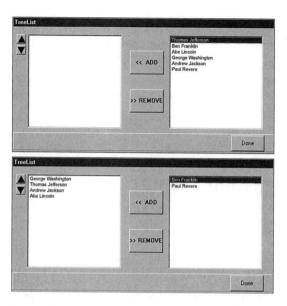

Figure 1.2   This is how build-list-and-reorder questions appear.

Question 3

From the following list of famous people, pick those who have been elected president of the United States. Arrange the list in the order in which they served.

Thomas Jefferson

Ben Franklin

Abe Lincoln

George Washington

Andrew Jackson

Paul Revere

The correct answer is

> George Washington
>
> Thomas Jefferson
>
> Andrew Jackson
>
> Abe Lincoln

On an actual exam, the entire list of famous people would initially appear in the list on the right. You would move the four correct answers to the list on the left and then reorder the list on the left. Notice that the answer to the question did not include all items from the initial list. However, this might not always be the case.

To move an item from the right list to the left list, first select the item by clicking it and then clicking the Add button (left arrow). After you move an item from one list to the other, you can move the item back by first selecting the item and then clicking the appropriate button (either the Add button or the Remove button). After items have been moved to the left list, you can reorder the list by selecting an item and clicking the up or down button.

You're not likely to see this format on the 70-305 exam.

Create-a-Tree Question Format

Questions in the create-a-tree format also present two lists: one on the left and one on the right. The list on the right consists of individual items, and the list on the left consists of nodes in a tree. To answer the question, you must move items from the list on the right to the appropriate node in the tree. You're not likely to see this format on the 70-305 exam, but you should be familiar with it anyhow. Microsoft does change the exam question pool from time to time, and create-a-tree questions could appear in the future.

These questions are basically a matching exercise. Items from the list on the right are placed under the appropriate category in the list on the left. Here's an example of how they appear in this book. For an example of how they appear on the test, see Figure 1.3.

Question 4

The calendar year is divided into four seasons:

Winter

Spring

Summer

Fall

Identify the season when each of the following holidays occurs:

Christmas

Fourth of July

Labor Day

Flag Day

Memorial Day

Washington's Birthday

Thanksgiving

Easter

The correct answer is

Winter   Summer

    Christmas   Fourth of July

    Washington's Birthday   Labor Day

Spring   Fall

    Flag Day   Thanksgiving

    Memorial Day

    Easter

In this case, all the items in the list were used. However, this might not always be the case.

To move an item from the right list to its appropriate location in the tree, you must first select the appropriate tree node by clicking it. Then, you select the item to be moved and click the Add button. If one or more items have been added to a tree node, the node is displayed with a plus sign (+) icon to the left of the node name. You can click this icon to expand the node and view whatever was added. If any item has been added to the wrong tree node, you can remove it by selecting it and clicking the Remove button (see Figure 1.3).

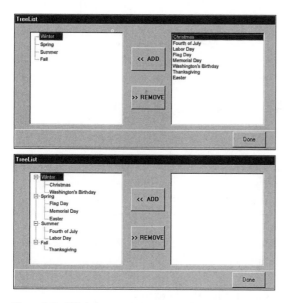

Figure 1.3   This is how create-a-tree questions appear.

Drag-and-Connect Question Format

Questions in the drag-and-connect format present a group of objects and a list of "connections." To answer the question, you must move the appropriate connections between the objects.

This type of question is best described using graphics. Here's an example.

Question 5

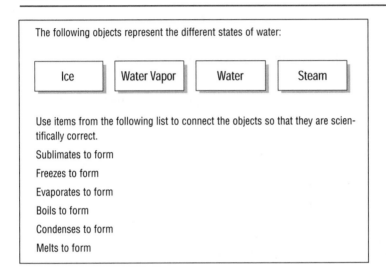

The correct answer is

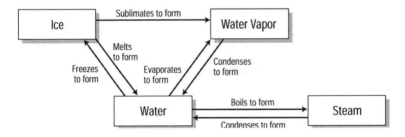

For this type of question, it's not necessary to use every object, but each connection can be used multiple times by dragging the answer to multiple locations. Dragging an answer away from its position removes it. You probably won't see any of these questions on the 70-305 exam.

Select-and-Place Question Format

Questions in the select-and-place (drag-and-drop) format present a diagram with blank boxes and a list of labels that must be dragged to fill in the blank boxes. To answer the question, you must move the labels to their appropriate positions on the diagram.

This type of question is best described using graphics. Here's an example.

Question 6

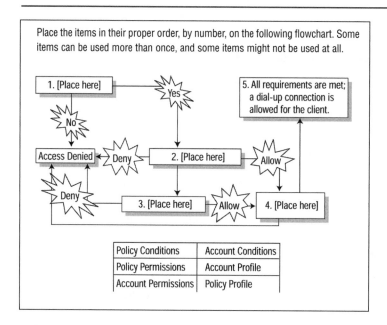

Place the items in their proper order, by number, on the following flowchart. Some items can be used more than once, and some items might not be used at all.

The correct answer is

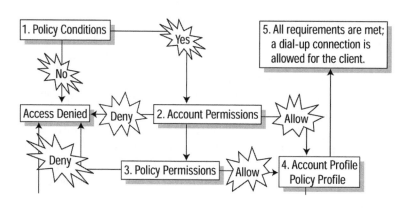

Hot Area

This type of question asks you to select one or more areas on a graphic to indicate the correct answer to a question. The hot spots on the graphic will be shaded when you move the mouse over them, and they are marked with an obvious border. To select or deselect an element, just click it.

A simple hot area question might present a screenshot of the Visual Studio .NET interface and ask you to indicate the tab that allows you to retrieve information on particular databases. In that case, you'd click on the Server Explorer tab to answer the question.

Microsoft's Testing Formats

Currently, Microsoft uses four different testing formats:

➤ Case study

➤ Fixed length

➤ Adaptive

➤ Short form

Currently, the 70-305 exam uses the fixed-length format, but you should be aware of the other formats as well. Microsoft revises popular exams from time to time and sometimes changes their format.

As mentioned earlier, the case study approach is used with many of the newer Microsoft exams. These exams consist of a set of case studies that you must first analyze to answer questions related to the case studies. Such exams include one or more case studies (tabbed topic areas)—each of which is followed by 4 to 10 questions. The question types for exams will be multiple choice, build list and reorder, create a tree, drag and connect, and select and place. Depending on the test topic, some exams are totally case based, whereas others are not at all.

Other Microsoft exams employ advanced testing capabilities that might not be immediately apparent. Although the questions that appear are primarily multiple choice, the logic in *fixed-length tests*, which use a fixed sequence of questions, is more complex than that in older Microsoft tests. Some questions employ a sophisticated user interface (which Microsoft calls a *simulation*) to test your knowledge of particular software and systems in a simulated "live" environment that behaves just like the original. The Testing Innovations article at `http://www.microsoft.com/TRAINCERT/mcpexams/faq/innovations.asp` includes a downloadable series of demonstrations and examples.

For some exams, Microsoft has turned to a well-known technique, called *adaptive testing*, to establish a test taker's level of knowledge and product competence. Adaptive exams look the same as fixed-length exams, but they determine the level of difficulty at which an individual test taker can correctly answer questions. Test takers with differing levels of knowledge or ability see different sets of questions; individuals with a high level of knowledge or ability are presented with a smaller set of more difficult questions, whereas individuals with a lower level of knowledge or ability are presented with a larger set of easier questions. Two individuals might answer the same percentage of questions correctly, but the test taker with a higher knowledge or ability level scores higher because his or her questions are weighted more heavily.

Also, lower-level test takers might answer more questions than more-knowledgeable colleagues. This explains why adaptive tests use ranges of values to define the number of questions and the amount of time needed to complete the tests.

Adaptive tests work by evaluating the test taker's most recent answer. A correct answer leads to a more difficult question and also raises the test software's estimate of the test taker's knowledge and ability level. An incorrect answer leads to a less difficult question and also lowers the test software's estimate of the test taker's knowledge and ability level. This process continues until the test targets the test taker's true ability level. The exam ends when the test taker's level of accuracy meets a statistically acceptable value (in other words, when his or her performance demonstrates an acceptable level of knowledge and ability) or when the maximum number of items has been presented (in which case, the test taker is almost certain to fail).

Microsoft has also introduced a short-form test for its most popular tests. This test consists of 25 to 30 questions, with a time limit of exactly 60 minutes. This type of exam is similar to a fixed-length test because it allows readers to jump ahead or return to earlier questions and to cycle through the questions until the test is done. Microsoft does not use adaptive logic in this test; it claims that statistical analysis of the question pool is such that the 25 to 30 questions delivered during a short-form exam conclusively measure a test taker's knowledge of the subject matter in much the same way as an adaptive test. The short-form test is like a "greatest hits exam" (that is, the most important questions are covered) version of an adaptive exam on the same topic.

 Some of the Microsoft exams might contain a combination of adaptive and fixed-length questions.

Because you won't know in which form the Microsoft exam might be, you should be prepared for an adaptive exam instead of a fixed-length or a short-form exam. The penalties for answering incorrectly are built in to the test itself on an adaptive exam, whereas the layout remains the same for a fixed-length or short-form test no matter how many questions you answer incorrectly. Most likely, you'll see a fixed-length exam for 70-305. But be prepared, just in case!

The biggest difference between adaptive tests and fixed-length or short-form tests is that you can mark and revisit questions on fixed-length and short-form tests after you've read them. On an adaptive test, you must answer the question when it is presented and cannot go back to that question later.

Strategies for Different Testing Formats

Before you choose a test taking strategy, you must determine what type of test it is—case study, fixed length, short form, or adaptive:

➤ Case study tests consist of a tabbed window that allows you to navigate easily through the sections of the case.

➤ Fixed-length tests consist of 50 to 70 questions with a check box for each question. You can return to these questions if you want.

➤ Short-form tests have 25 to 30 questions with a check box for each question. You can return to these questions if you want.

➤ Adaptive tests are identified in the introductory material of the test. Questions have no check boxes and can be visited (and answered) only once.

Some tests contain a variety of testing formats. For example, a test might start with a set of adaptive questions, followed by fixed-length questions. As I mentioned earlier, the initial release of the 70-305 exam is fixed length, so you should concentrate on strategies for that type of exam.

You'll be able to tell for sure whether you are taking an adaptive, fixed-length, or short-form test by the first question. Fixed-length and short-form tests include a check box that allows you to mark the question for later review. Adaptive test questions include no such check box and can be visited (and answered) only once.

Case Study Exam Strategy

Although you won't find this kind of format for the 70-305 test, you might find the test taking strategies beneficial. If you ever take a case study exam, you'll want to review this section. Most test takers find that the case study type of exam is the most difficult to master. When it comes to studying for a case study test, your best bet is to approach each case study as a standalone test. The biggest challenge you'll encounter is that you'll feel you won't have enough time to get through all the cases presented.

Each case provides a lot of material you'll need to read and study before you can effectively answer the questions that follow. The trick to taking a case study exam is to first scan the case study to get the highlights. Make sure that you read the overview section of the case so that you understand the context of the problem at hand. Then, quickly move on and scan the questions.

As you are scanning the questions, make mental notes to yourself or notes on your paper so that you'll remember which sections of the case study you should focus on. Some case studies might provide a fair amount of extra information that you don't really need to answer the questions. The goal with this scanning approach is to avoid having to study and analyze material that is not completely relevant.

When studying a case, read the tabbed information carefully. It is important to answer each and every question. You will be able to toggle back and forth from case to questions, and from question to question within a case testlet. However, after you leave the case and move on, you might not be able to return to it. I suggest that you take notes while reading useful information to help you when you tackle the test questions. It's hard to go wrong with this strategy when taking any kind of Microsoft certification test.

Fixed-Length and Short-Form Exam Strategy

A well-known principle when taking fixed-length or short-form exams is first to read through the entire exam from start to finish. Answer only those questions that you feel absolutely sure you know. On subsequent passes, you can dive into more complex questions more deeply, knowing how many such questions you have left and the amount of time remaining.

There's at least one potential benefit to reading the exam over completely before answering the trickier questions: Sometimes, information supplied in later questions sheds more light on earlier questions. At other times, information you read in later questions might jog your memory about facts, figures, or behavior that helps you answer earlier questions. Either way, you'll come out ahead if you answer only those questions on the first pass that you're absolutely confident about.

Fortunately, the Microsoft exam software for fixed-length and short-form tests makes the multiple-visit approach easy to implement. At the top-left corner of each question is a check box that permits you to mark that question for a later visit.

Marking questions makes later review easier, but you can return to any question by clicking the Forward or Back button repeatedly. Of course, on an adaptive exam, this isn't possible.

Here are some question-handling strategies that apply to fixed-length and short-form tests. Use them if you have the chance:

➤ When returning to a question after your initial read through, read every word again; otherwise, your mind can miss important details. Sometimes, revisiting a question after turning your attention elsewhere lets you see something you missed, but the strong tendency is to see what you've seen before. Try to avoid that tendency at all costs.

➤ If you return to a question more than twice, try to articulate to yourself what you don't understand about the question, why answers don't appear to make sense, or what appears to be missing. If you chew on the subject awhile, your subconscious might provide the missing details, or you might notice a "trick" that points to the right answer.

As you work your way through the exam, another counter that Microsoft provides comes in handy—the number of questions completed and questions outstanding. For fixed-length and short-form tests, it's wise to budget your time by making sure that you've completed roughly one-quarter of the questions one-quarter of the way through the exam period and three-quarters of the questions three-quarters of the way through.

If you're not finished when only five minutes remain, use that time to guess your way through any remaining questions. Remember, guessing is potentially more valuable than not answering. Blank answers are always wrong, but a guess might turn out to be right. If you don't have a clue about any of the remaining questions, pick answers at random or choose all As, Bs, and so on. Questions left unanswered are counted as answered incorrectly, so a guess is better than nothing at all.

At the very end of your exam period, you're better off guessing than leaving questions unanswered.

Adaptive Exam Strategy

This type of exam format will not appear in the 70-305 exam; however, an overview of how to approach adaptive exams might benefit you when taking a future version of the 70-305 exam or if you ever need to take an adaptive exam. If there's one principle that applies to taking an adaptive test, it's "Get it right the first time." You cannot elect to skip a question and move on to the next one when taking an adaptive test because the testing software uses your answer to the current question to select whatever question it plans to present next. You also cannot return to a question because the software gives you only one chance to answer the question. You can, however, take notes as you work through the test. Sometimes, information supplied in earlier questions might help you answer later questions.

Also, when you answer a question correctly, you are presented with a more difficult question next to help the software gauge your level of skill and ability. When you answer a question incorrectly, you are presented with a less difficult question, and the software lowers its current estimate of your skill and ability. This continues until the program settles into a reasonably accurate estimate of what you know and can do.

The good news is that if you know the material, you'll probably finish most adaptive tests in 30 minutes or so. The bad news is that you must really know the material well to do your best on an adaptive test. That's because some questions are so convoluted, complex, or hard to follow that you're bound to miss one or two, at a minimum. Therefore, the more you know, the better you'll do on an adaptive test, even accounting for the occasionally strange or unfathomable questions that appear on these exams.

Because you can't always tell in advance whether a test is fixed length, short form, adaptive, or a combination of these, you should prepare for the exam as if it were adaptive. That way, you will be prepared to pass no matter what kind of test you take. If the test turns out to be fixed length or short form, remember the tips from the preceding section, which will help you improve on what you could do on an adaptive test.

If you encounter a question on an adaptive test that you can't answer, you must guess an answer quickly. (However, you might suffer for your guess on the next question if you guess correctly because the software will give you a more difficult question next!)

Question-Handling Strategies

For those questions that have only one right answer, usually two or three of the answers will be obviously incorrect and two of the answers will be plausible. Unless the answer leaps out at you (if it does, reread the question to look for a trick; sometimes those are the ones you're most likely to get wrong), begin the process of answering by eliminating those answers that are most obviously wrong.

At least one answer out of the possible choices for a question can usually be eliminated immediately because it matches one of these conditions:

➤ The answer does not apply to the situation.

➤ The answer describes a nonexistent issue, an invalid option, or an imaginary state.

After you eliminate all answers that are obviously wrong, you can apply your retained knowledge to eliminate further answers. Look for items that sound correct but refer to actions, commands, or features that are not present or not available in the situation that the question describes.

If you're still faced with a blind guess among two or more potentially correct answers, reread the question. Try to picture how each of the possible remaining answers would alter the situation. Be especially sensitive to terminology; sometimes the choice of words ("remove" instead of "disable") can make the difference between a right answer and a wrong one.

You should guess at an answer only after you've exhausted your ability to eliminate answers and are still unclear about which of the remaining possibilities is correct. An unanswered question offers you no points, but guessing gives you at least some chance of getting a question right; just don't be too hasty when making a blind guess.

If you're taking a fixed-length or a short-form test, you can wait until the last round of reviewing marked questions (just as you're about to run out of time or unanswered questions) before you start making guesses. You will usually have the same option within each case study testlet (but once you leave a testlet, you may not be allowed to return to it). If you're taking an adaptive test, you'll have to guess to move on to the next question if you can't figure out an answer some other way. Either way, guessing should be your technique of last resort!

Numerous questions assume that the default behavior of a particular utility is in effect. If you know the defaults and understand what they mean, this knowledge will help you cut through many Gordian knots. Simple "final" actions might be critical as well. If a utility must be restarted before proposed changes take effect, a correct answer might require this step as well.

Mastering the Inner Game

In the final analysis, knowledge gives confidence, and confidence breeds success. If you study the materials in this book carefully and review all the practice questions at the end of each chapter, you should become aware of those areas where additional learning and study are required.

After you've worked your way through the book, take the practice exam in the back of the book. Taking this test provides a reality check and helps you identify areas to study further. Make sure that you follow up and review materials related to the questions you miss on the practice exam before scheduling a real exam. Don't schedule your exam appointment until after you've thoroughly studied the material and feel comfortable with the whole scope of the practice exam. You should score 80% or better on the practice exam before proceeding to the real thing (otherwise, obtain some additional practice tests so that you can keep trying until you hit this magic number).

If you take a practice exam and don't get at least 70% to 80% of the questions correct, keep practicing. Microsoft provides links to practice exam providers and also self-assessment exams at **http://www.microsoft.com/traincert/mcpexams/ prepare/**.

Armed with the information in this book and with the determination to augment your knowledge, you should be able to pass the certification exam. However, you need to work at it, or you'll spend the exam fee more than once before you finally pass. If you prepare seriously, you should do well.

The next section covers other sources you can use to prepare for the Microsoft Certification Exams.

Additional Resources

A good source of information about Microsoft Certification Exams comes from Microsoft itself. Because its products and technologies—and the exams that go with them—change frequently, the best place to go for exam-related information is online.

If you haven't already visited the Microsoft Certified Professional site, do so right now. The MCP home page resides at http://www.microsoft.com/ traincert/default.asp (see Figure 1.4).

Figure 1.4   The Microsoft Certified Professional Training and Certification home page.

Coping with Change on the Web

Sooner or later, all the information we've shared with you about the Microsoft Certified Professional pages and the other Web-based resources mentioned throughout the rest of this book will go stale or be replaced by newer information. In some cases, the URLs you find here might lead you to their replacements; in other cases, the URLs will go nowhere, leaving you with the dreaded "404 File not found" error message. When that happens, don't give up.

There's always a way to find what you want on the Web if you're willing to invest some time and energy. Most large or complex Web sites (such as the Microsoft site) offer a search engine. On all of Microsoft's Web pages, a Search button appears along the top edge of the page. As long as you can get to the Microsoft site (it should stay at **www.microsoft.com** for a long time), you can use this tool to help you find what you need.

The more focused you can make a search request, the more likely the results will include information you can use. For example, you can search for the string

```
"training and certification"
```

to produce a lot of data about the subject in general, but if you're looking for the preparation guide for Exam 70-305, "Developing Web Applications with Microsoft Visual Basic .NET and Microsoft Visual Studio .NET," you'll be more likely to get there quickly if you use a search string similar to the following:

```
"Exam 70-305" AND "preparation guide"
```

Likewise, if you want to find the Training and Certification downloads, try a search string such as this:

```
"training and certification" AND "download page"
```

Finally, feel free to use general search tools—such as **www.google.com**, **www.altavista.com**, and **www.excite.com**—to look for related information. Although Microsoft offers great information about its certification exams online, there are plenty of third-party sources of information and assistance that need not follow Microsoft's party line. Therefore, if you can't find something immediately, intensify your search.

Introducing Web Forms

Terms you'll need to understand:

✓ ASP.NET
✓ Class
✓ CLR (Common Language Runtime)
✓ Delegate
✓ Event
✓ Event Handling
✓ FCL (Framework Class Library)
✓ Field
✓ Inheritance
✓ IL (Intermediate Language)
✓ JIT (just-in-time) compilation
✓ Managed Code
✓ Namespace
✓ .NET Framework
✓ Property
✓ Structure

Techniques you'll need to master:

✓ Creating ASP.NET pages in Visual Studio .NET
✓ Using **Page** directives to modify the behavior of ASP.NET pages
✓ Separating user interface and business logic by employing code-behind files
✓ Creating event handlers and responding to events

Exam 70-305 focuses on ASP.NET and other Web-related aspects of .NET development. But you'll need to have a solid background in general .NET development as a prerequisite for passing the exam. I'll start this chapter off with a quick overview and review of the .NET Framework. If any of this material is unfamiliar to you, you should consult a general .NET reference (I've listed several at the end of the chapter) before continuing on to the next chapter.

An Overview of the .NET Framework

The Microsoft .NET Framework is a new computing platform for developing distributed applications. The key features of the .NET Framework include a consistent object-oriented development model, a robust execution environment, and support for industry standards such as XML (Extensible Markup Language) and SOAP (Simple Object Access Protocol).

The .NET Framework itself is available as a redistributable file that must be installed on any computer that will run .NET applications—including Web servers that will deliver ASP.NET pages. If you're setting up a server to test ASP.NET, be sure to read the release notes before installing .NET Framework. In particular, you need to configure and install IIS (Internet Information Services) *before* you install the .NET Framework.

 NOTE
Like ASP before it, ASP.NET executes on the server. The output of an ASP.NET application is in the form of HTML pages, which can be displayed in any browser. End users are not required to install the .NET Framework redistributable on their computers to access an ASP.NET Web application.

The .NET Framework has two main components:

➤ The Common Language Runtime (CLR)

➤ The Framework Class Library (FCL)

The Common Language Runtime

The Common Language Runtime (CLR) provides a managed and language-agnostic environment in which .NET applications execute. The CLR provides services to .NET applications such as compilation, code safety verification, code execution, and automatic memory management.

Microsoft provides five language compilers for the .NET Framework: C# .NET, Visual Basic .NET, Managed C++ .NET, JScript .NET, and J# .NET.

Code from any of these compiles is run by the CLR. Although you can use any of these languages for ASP.NET development, the 70-305 exam focuses solely on Visual Basic .NET.

The Framework Class Library

The *Framework Class Library (FCL)* is an extensive collection of reusable types that allows you to develop a variety of applications including

➤ Console applications

➤ Scripted or hosted applications

➤ Desktop applications (Windows Forms)

➤ Web applications (ASP.NET applications)

➤ XML Web services

➤ Windows services

The FCL organizes its classes in hierarchical namespaces so that they are logically grouped and easy to identify. You'll work with these namespaces and classes throughout this book.

An Overview of .NET Development Tools

Several tools are available to support development of Web applications that run on the .NET platform:

➤ The .NET Framework SDK

➤ ASP.NET Web Matrix Project

➤ Visual Studio .NET

The .NET Framework SDK

The Microsoft .NET Framework Software Development Kit (SDK) is available as a free download. You can find the link to download it from http://www.asp.net. When you install the .NET Framework SDK, you get a rich set of resources to help you develop applications for the Microsoft .NET Framework. This includes the Framework itself, command-line compilers, a set of tools, and documentation of the FCL.

Although version 1.1 of the .NET Framework is available, the exam is based on version 1.0.

It is possible to develop all your programs by using just a text editor and the command-line compilers and tools provided by the .NET Framework SDK. However, most developers prefer an Integrated Development Environment (IDE) such as those provided by ASP.NET Web Matrix or Visual Studio .NET.

ASP.NET Web Matrix Project

Microsoft has released a free GUI-based Web application development tool called the Web Matrix Project. This tool itself is completely written using the .NET Framework and the C# programming language. This tool includes a Web page designer, the capability to create and edit SQL Server and MSDE (Microsoft Data Engine) databases, the capability to create data-bound pages, support for application development for mobile devices, support for XML Web services, a development Web server, and an FTP (File Transfer Protocol) tool for uploading the files to the production Web server.

The Web Matrix Project can be downloaded from http://www.asp.net. With all the features listed, its download size is amazingly small at about 1.2MB. To run the Web Matrix Project, the .NET Framework must be installed on your machine.

Visual Studio .NET

Visual Studio .NET provides developers with a full-featured IDE for building ASP.NET Web applications, XML Web services, desktop applications, and mobile applications for the .NET Framework. Visual Studio .NET supports multiple languages and provides transparent development and debugging facilities across these languages in a multi-language solution. The IDE includes modern features such as integrated debugging, a high-end code editor, support for deployment via the Windows Installer service, and support for macros and add-ins.

I'll use Visual Studio .NET 2002, the initial release of the product, for all the examples in this book. This is the version covered by the exam. The more recent Visual Studio .NET, 2003, includes additional features and capabilities that are not a part of the 70-305 exam. You can use either version to learn ASP.NET.

Exam 70-305 requires that you know Visual Studio .NET and the Visual Basic .NET programming language for developing Web applications. You might be asked questions about specific Visual Studio .NET features. The best way to prepare for these questions is to use Visual Studio .NET in your daily work.

Understanding Classes, Inheritance, and Namespaces

The .NET Framework is designed to be object oriented from the ground up. Before taking the exam, you should be familiar with object-oriented basics in .NET including classes, inheritance, and namespaces.

Classes

A *class* represents an abstract idea that you would like to include in your application. For example, the .NET Framework includes a Page class that represents an ASP.NET Web page. The Page class includes properties that dictate such things as the visibility of the page, its HTTP request, session variables, and so on. The Page class also contains a set of methods that defines how a page behaves, such as a DataBind method that binds data to the page and a MapPath method that returns the physical path of the page.

A class functions as the blueprint of a concept. But you can't work with a class directly. When you want to work with a class in your program, you create *instances* of the class. These instances are called objects. *Objects* are created from the blueprint defined by the class, but they physically exist in the sense that memory locations are allocated to them and they will respond to your messages. For example, when you want to create an actual Web page in your program, you create an instance of the Page class. After this instance (an object) is available, you can set its properties and call its methods.

Methods and properties, as well as fields (which store data) and events (which you'll learn more about later in the chapter), are more generally called *members.* The members of an object are accessed using the `ObjectName.MemberName` syntax, where `ObjectName` is the name of the class instance and `MemberName` can be a field, property, method, or event.

A class can have *static members* (properties, methods, and so on). These are the members that belong to the class itself rather than to a particular instance. No instance of a class is required to access its static members. When you access a static member of a class, you do so by prefixing its name with the name of the class, as in ***ClassName.StaticMemberName***.

Inheritance

Object-oriented programming languages such as VB .NET provide another feature called *inheritance*. Inheritance allows you to create new types that are based on already existing types. The original type is called a *base class*, and the inherited class is called a *derived class*. When one class inherits from another class, the derived class gets all the functionality of the base class. The derived class can also choose to extend the base class by introducing new data and behavioral elements, and it can even override the default behavior of the base class.

Every single type (other than the Object class itself) that you create or that is already defined in the framework is implicitly derived from the Object class of the System namespace. This is done to ensure that all classes provide a common minimum functionality. Also note that a VB .NET type can only inherit from a single parent class at a time.

Namespaces

The FCL contains hundreds of classes, and you can also develop your own or purchase them from vendors. Such a large number of classes not only makes organization difficult, but can also create naming conflicts between various vendors. The .NET Framework provides you with a feature called a *namespace*, which allows you to hierarchically organize classes. Namespaces prevent accidental confusion between two classes with the same name. For example, you might use a library of business objects that included a class named Order. The same application could use a statistical library that included a ranking class also named Order. To avoid confusion, the two classes would be placed in different namespaces:

```
BizLibrary.Order
Statistics.Order
```

In this example, the first line of code refers to the Order class within the BizLibrary namespace, whereas the second refers to the Order class within the Statistics namespace.

Namespaces can be arranged in a hierarchy, as shown in the following example:

```
Standards.Corporate.Statistics.Order
```

This example refers to the Order class in the Statistics namespace, which is contained in the Corporate namespace, which is contained in the Standards namespace.

NOTE

A namespace hierarchy does not have to match an inheritance hierarchy. When one class inherits from another, the base class and derived class can belong to the same or to different namespaces.

Introduction to ASP.NET

Active Server Pages .NET (ASP.NET) is the infrastructure built inside the .NET Framework for running Web applications. The ASP.NET infrastructure consists of two main parts. First, there is a set of classes designed for building Web applications, which are located in the System.Web namespace in the FCL. Second, there is a runtime host process that handles ASP.NET requests from an IIS server.

An ASP.NET Web application is executed through a series of Hypertext Transfer Protocol (HTTP) request and response messages between the client browsers and the Web server:

1. A user requests a resource from a Web server by typing a URL in her browser, typically with the ASPX extension. The browser sends an HTTP request to the destination Web server.

2. The Web server analyzes the HTTP request and searches for a process capable of executing this request. For ASPX files, the Web server will invoke the ASP.NET process.

3. The results of the HTTP request are returned to the client browser in the form of an HTTP response.

4. The browser reads the HTTP response and displays it as a Web page to the user.

As a Web programmer, you're probably more interested in knowing what goes on behind the scenes when a Web server executes a Web request for an ASP.NET page. Here's what's going on "under the covers":

1. When the Internet Information Service process (`inetinfo.exe`) receives an HTTP request, it uses the filename extension of the requested resource to determine which Internet Server Application Programming Interface (ISAPI) program to run to process the request. When the request is for an ASP.NET page (`.aspx` file), IIS passes the request to the ISAPI DLL capable of handling the request for ASP.NET pages, which is `aspnet_isapi.dll`.

2. The `aspnet_isapi.dll` process passes the request to the ASP.NET worker process (`aspnet_wp.exe`), which fulfills the request.

3. The ASP.NET worker process compiles the requested .aspx file into an assembly, creates an application domain (an isolated area in memory where .NET code can execute), and instructs the CLR to execute the resulting assembly in the newly created application domain.

4. When the assembly containing the code for an ASP.NET page executes, it uses various classes in the FCL to accomplish its work and to generate response messages for the requesting client.

5. The ASP.NET worker process collects the response generated by the execution of the Web page, creates a response packet, and passes it to the IIS.

6. IIS forwards the response packet to the requesting client machine.

Creating an ASP.NET Page

Creating an ASP.NET page is easy. All you need to do is write the ASP.NET code in a text file with an ASPX extension and place it in a virtual directory on the Web server from which it can be accessed. Although you can write this Web page using any text editor, I recommend using Visual Studio .NET because Visual Studio .NET also sets up the virtual directory required for accessing the Web application. These steps will walk you through the process of creating a Web application that includes a single ASP.NET page:

1. Launch Visual Studio .NET. On the start page, click the New Project button (alternatively, you can select File, New, Project). In the New Project dialog box, select Visual Basic Projects as the project type and Empty Web Project as the template. Specify a location for the project, such as http://localhost/WebApp1, and click OK. This step will set up the project directory (WebApp1) as a virtual directory within the default Web site on the local Web server. The project directory will also be set up as an IIS application—that is, a directory which IIS recognizes as containing a particular set of files. To use a computer other than the one in which you're writing the code as the Web server, just substitute that computer's name in place of localhost.

NOTE | In Visual Studio .NET, a *solution* is used to group one or more projects. If you directly create a project, Visual Studio .NET automatically creates a solution for it. In that case, the name of the solution defaults to the name of the project. For example, the project WebApp1 is automatically created in the solution WebApp1.

2. Right-click the name of the project in the Solution Explorer and select Add, Add New Item from the shortcut menu. In the Add New Item dialog box, select the Text File template and name the file `WebTest1.aspx`.

3. When Visual Studio .NET creates the ASPX page, it detects that it is creating an ASP.NET Web page and displays the page with two available views—the Design view and the HTML view, indicated by tabs at the bottom of the designer. Using the Design view, you can visually design a Web page by placing controls on it from the Visual Studio .NET Toolbox. Using the HTML view, you can view and modify the HTML code for a page. Switch to the HTML view.

4. Add the following code to the HTML view of the new file:

```
<%@ Page Language='vb' %>
<html><head>
<script runat="server">
    Function Factorial(n As Integer) As Integer
        Dim i As Integer
        Dim Result As Integer = 1
        For i = 2 To n
            Result = Result * i
        Next
        Factorial = Result
    End Function
</script></head>
<body>
<h2>Factorial List</h2>
    <table border="2">
        <tr>
        <th>Number</th><th>Factorial</th>
        </tr>
        <%
        Dim i As Integer
        For i = 1 to 10
            ' Sends formatted output to HTTP Response
            Response.Output.Write("<tr><td>{0}</td><td>" & _
                "{1}</td><tr>", i, Factorial(i))
        Next
        %>
    </table>
</body>
</html>
```

NOTE

The **Response** property of the **Page** class gives you access to the HTTP Response object. You can add content to the HTTP Response using the **Response.Write()** and **Response.Output.Write()** methods. The only difference between the two methods is that the latter allows you to format output using placeholders such as {0}, which are replaced with the values of variables in a list after the format string.

5. In the Solution Explorer, right-click the `.aspx` file and select View in Browser from the shortcut menu. A browser window will appear in Visual Studio .NET and display the page output as shown in Figure 2.1.

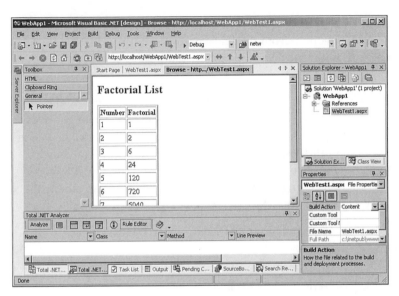

Figure 2.1 The factorial table is created by executing ASP.NET code on the Web server.

Understanding ASP.NET Page Execution

An ASP.NET page is converted dynamically into a class. The Language attribute of the Page directive used in line 1 of the WebTest1.aspx file specifies that the name of the source file for the class has a .vb extension and that the class is compiled using the Visual Basic .NET compiler (vbc.exe). The compiler compiles the source file to a DLL file. When an ASP.NET page is requested, instead of executing the .aspx file directly, the CLR actually executes the code in the compiled DLL file for that ASPX page.

The dynamically generated class inherits from the Page class, which provides the default behavior of an ASP.NET page.

ASP.NET maintains the reference between the source .aspx file and the DLL file. When an .aspx file is requested a second time, ASP.NET matches the timestamp of the .aspx file with that of the generated DLL file. If the .aspx is newer (that is, it has been changed since the last compilation), it is compiled again and the old DLL file is replaced with the new one. If the timestamp is not newer, ASP.NET knows that the .aspx file was not modified since the compilation; therefore, it saves time by skipping the compilation step and directly serves the HTTP request using the already compiled version of the Web page.

The Page Class

The class corresponding to the ASPX page derives most of its functionality from its base class, `System.Web.UI.Page`. If you look at the .NET Framework documentation, you'll see that the `Page` class itself derives from `System.Web.UI.TemplateControl`, `System.Web.UI.Control`, and `System.Object`, as shown in Figure 2.2.

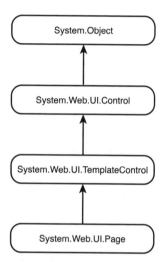

Figure 2.2   The **System.Web.UI.Page** class inherits from **System.Object** through a chain of inheritances.

Because of this inheritance relationship, you can also say that a page is a control, and as the `Page` class derives from the `TemplateControl` class, it includes extended capabilities such as hosting other controls on its surface.

Table 2.1 lists some of the members of the `Page` class with which you should be familiar. You'll see some of these members in this chapter and others throughout the book.

Table 2.1   Important Members of the Page Class

Member	Type	Description
Application	Property	Returns the application state object for the current HTTP request.
Cache	Property	Returns the cache object of the application to which the page belongs.
Controls	Property	Returns a **ControlCollection** object that represents the collection of controls placed on the page.

(continued)

Table 2.1 Important Members of the Page Class *(continued)*

Member	Type	Description
EnableViewState	Property	Indicates whether the view state is maintained for the page and its container controls.
Error	Event	Occurs when an unhandled exception occurs in the page processing.
ErrorPage	Property	Specifies the error page where the user is redirected whenever an unhandled exception occurs in the page processing.
Init	Event	Occurs when the page is initialized. This event is the first step in the page lifecycle.
IsPostBack	Property	Indicates whether the page is loaded in response to a client postback (the browser sending the page back to the server).
IsValid	Property	Indicates whether all the validation controls on a page succeeded.
Load	Event	Occurs when the page is loaded in memory.
MapPath	Method	Returns the actual physical path corresponding to a virtual path.
PreRender	Event	Occurs when a page is about to render its contents.
RenderControl	Method	Outputs content of a page to a provided **HtmlTextWriter** object and stores tracing information about the control if tracing is enabled.
Request	Property	Returns the request object that contains information about the current HTTP request.
Response	Property	Returns the response object for the current HTTP request.
Server	Property	Provides access to the server object associated to the page.
Session	Property	Returns the session state object applicable for the current HTTP request.
SmartNavigation	Property	Indicates whether smart navigation is enabled for the page.
Trace	Property	Returns the trace context object for the current HTTP request.
Unload	Event	Occurs when a page is unloaded from memory.
Validators	Property	Returns a collection of all validation controls contained in a page.
Visible	Property	Indicates whether the page should be displayed.

Stages in Page Processing

When ASP.NET processes a Web page, the page goes through distinct stages.

1. Page Initialization: ASP.NET has done initialization of the page. The Init event is raised to indicate this stage. An Init event handler is the best place for code that you want to be executed before any other page processing. You should not interact with controls during this event.

2. User Code Initialization: The page initialization is complete at this stage. The page object indicates this stage by raising the Load event. A method that handles the Load event is the best place to store initialization code specific to this page.

3. PreRender: The page is just about to render its contents. This stage is indicated by raising the PreRender event. An event handler for the PreRender event has the last chance to modify a page's output before it is sent to the browser.

4. Page Cleanup: The page has finished rendering and is ready to be discarded. The Unload event is raised to indicate this stage.

The Page class raises a distinct event to indicate each processing stage. You can write event-handling methods that respond to these events, as you'll see in the "Event Handling" section later in this chapter.

ASP.NET Directives

ASP.NET pages allow you to specify various compiler options. You can specify these commands and options with the help of directives. A directive name begins with the @ character and is enclosed in <% and %> tags. A directive can be placed anywhere in a Web page, but directives are usually placed at the top of the Web page. Directives contain one or more attribute/value pairs. These attribute/value pairs are not case sensitive, and they need not be placed in quotes.

Table 2.2 lists the different types of directives that can be added to an ASP.NET page.

Table 2.2	ASP.NET Page Directives
Directive	**Description**
Assembly	Links an assembly to the application or a Web page during compilation. It is similar to the **/reference** command-line switch of the VB .NET compiler (**vbc.exe**).
Control	Specifies user-control related attributes that are used by the ASP.NET compiler when the user control (**.ascx** file) is compiled. You will use this directive in Chapter 8, "Creating and Managing Components and .NET Assemblies."
Implements	Indicates that the Web page (**.aspx** file) or the user control (**.ascx** file) implements the interface specified by the **Interface** attribute of the directive.
Import	Imports a namespace into a page, user control, or application. It is similar to the Imports statement in VB .NET.
OutputCache	Controls the output caching of a Web page (**.aspx** file) or user control (**.ascx** file). You will use this directive in Chapter 16, "Configuring a Web Application."
Page	Specifies page-related attributes that are used by the ASP.NET compiler when the Web client requests the ASPX page. Refer to Table 2.4 for a list of attributes allowed in a **Page** directive.
Reference	Indicates a Web page or user control that should be compiled and linked during compilation of the **.aspx** page that contains the **Reference** directive. It can contain either the **Page** attribute (**.aspx** filename) or **Control** attribute (**.ascx** filename).
Register	Registers a custom server control or a user control to be used within an ASP.NET page. You will use this directive in Chapter 7, "Consuming and Manipulating Data."

I discuss these directives as I discuss related topics through the course of this book. For now, I'll only use the Page directive. The Page directive is used to specify page-related attributes that control how an ASP.NET page is compiled and executed. An ASP.NET page can have only one Page directive. Table 2.3 lists the various attributes of the Page directive.

Table 2.3	Attributes of Page Directives
Attributes	**Description**
AspCompat	Indicates whether the page is to be executed on a Single-Threaded Apartment (STA) thread model for backward compatibility. The default value is **False**.

(continued)

Table 2.3   Attributes of Page Directives (continued)

Attributes	Description
AutoEventWireUp	Indicates whether ASP.NET should automatically connect methods with specific names—such as **Page_Init()**, **Page_Load()**, and so on—with the page events. The default value is **True**. However, for Web pages created using Visual Studio .NET, the default value is **False**.
Buffer	Indicates whether the HTTP response buffer is enabled. The default value is **True**.
ClassName	Specifies the name for dynamically generated class files for the ASPX page.
ClientTarget	Represents the target user agent (such as Mozilla/4.0) or alias (such as IE4) according to how the ASP.NET page should be rendered.
CodePage	Indicates the culture codepage value for the ASP.NET page. Supports any valid codepage value. For example, the value **932** specifies a Japanese codepage.
CompilerOptions	Indicates the compiler options and switches to be passed to the language compiler.
ContentType	Indicates the MIME (Multipart Internet Mail Encoding) type for the page response.
Culture	Indicates the culture setting for the page. Supports any valid culture string.
Debug	Indicates whether the compilation should include debug symbols. The default value is **False**.
Description	Represents the description of the page. The page compilers ignore this attribute, so it's strictly for your own reference.
EnableSessionState	Indicates whether the session state is enabled (**True**), read-only (**ReadOnly**), or disabled (**False**) for the page. The default value is **True**.
EnableViewState	Indicates whether the view state is maintained for the page and its container controls. The default value is **True**.
EnableViewStateMac	Indicates whether the encrypted view state should be verified against the Machine Authentication Check (MAC) to ensure that the view state is not tampered with.
ErrorPage	Specifies the error page where the user is redirected whenever an unhandled exception occurs in the page.
Explicit	Indicates whether all variables must be explicitly declared. The default is **False**.

(continued)

Table 2.3 Attributes of Page Directives *(continued)*	
Attributes	**Description**
Inherits	Represents the name of the code-behind class that contains code for the .aspx page and from which the dynamically generated class inherits.
Language	Represents any .NET programming language used for inline coding in the page.
LCID	Defines the 32-bit locale identifier for code in the page.
ResponseEncoding	Defines the response encoding for the page such as UTF7Encoding, UTF8Encoding, ASCIIEncoding, UnicodeEncoding, and so on. You'll learn more about encodings in Chapter 10, "Globalization."
Src	Represents the source filename of the code-behind class that is dynamically compiled when the Web page is requested. Visual Studio .NET does not use this attribute as it precompiles the code-behind class.
SmartNavigation	Indicates whether smart navigation is enabled for the page. The smart navigation feature preserves the scroll position and element focus whenever the page is refreshed. This feature is only supported in IE5 or later browsers. The default value is **False**.
Strict	Indicates whether the page should be compiled using **Option Strict**. The default is **False**.
Trace	Indicates whether page-level tracing is enabled. The default value is **False**.
TraceMode	Indicates how trace messages are to be displayed when tracing is enabled. The default value is **SortByTime**, and the other possible value is **SortByCategory**.
Transaction	Indicates whether transactions are supported on the page. The default value is **Disabled**, and the other possible values are **NotSupported**, **Supported**, **Required**, and **RequiresNew**.
UICulture	Indicates the culture setting for the user interface of a page. Supports any valid culture string.
WarningLevel	Specifies the warning level at which page compilation should be stopped. The possible values are **0** through **4**.

Event Handling

When you perform an action with an object, the object in turn raises events in the application. Clicking a button, for example, generates an event; loading a Web page generates another event. Not all events are triggered by user actions. Changes in the environment—such as the arrival of an email message, modifications to a file, changes in the time, and completion of program execution—can also trigger events.

Events are at the heart of graphical user interface (GUI)–based programming. A significant portion of code for a typical ASP.NET application is devoted to handling various events that are raised in the application. In the following sections, you learn how to raise and handle events in an ASP.NET page.

Elements of Event Handling

Before diving into ASP.NET events, you should understand the event infrastructure of the .NET Framework: event arguments, delegates, event handlers, events, and methods that raise events.

Event Arguments

An event *argument* specifies the data associated with an event. When an event is raised, the event arguments are passed to the event handlers so that they have enough information to handle the event. Event arguments are instances of the EventArgs class or a class that inherits from the EventArgs class.

Event Handlers

An event *handler* is a method that performs some action in response to an event notification provided by the event of a class. An event handler must have a prototype compatible with the event that it is handling. That is, the parameter list of the event handler must exactly match the parameters that the event generates.

By convention, an event handler returns void and takes two arguments. The first argument specifies the object on which the event occurred (that is, the publisher of the event), and the second argument specifies an event argument.

Delegates

A *delegate* is a special class with an object capable of storing references to methods with a particular prototype. If you have a background in C/C++ programming, you can think of delegates as function pointers. The definition of a typical delegate looks like this:

```
Public Delegate Sub EventHandler( _
  ByVal sender As Object, _
  Byval e As EventArgs)
```

Here EventHandler is a delegate whose object is capable of storing references to any method that has a void return type and that accepts two arguments:

the first one of type Object and the other one of type EventArgs. ASP.NET uses delegates to attach code to events.

Events

An *event* enables a class to provide notifications to other objects that something of interest has happened. Events in Visual Basic .NET are based on a publisher-subscriber model. The class that implements an event is called the *publisher* of the event. A *subscriber* class can subscribe to a published event by registering an appropriate event handler with the published event. When an event is raised, the publisher notifies all registered objects about the event by invoking the registered event handlers.

As an example, the Page class notifies other objects that a page is about to render its content using the PreRender event. The definition of the PreRender event in the Page looks like this:

```
'Define the event
Public Event PreRender As EventHandler
```

The type of an event is a delegate. (In this code, the type of the PreRender event is the EventHandler delegate.) You can register an event handler with an event by encapsulating the event handler in a delegate object and adding the delegate to the event. For example within an ASP.NET page, you can code

```
AddHandler Me.PreRender, AddressOf Me.Page_PreRender
```

Here, Page_PreRender is a delegate whose signature is appropriate for the PreRender event. The Me keyword represents the current instance of the Page. Note that there are no method call parentheses () after Me.Page_PreRender; rather, a reference to the address of the method is passed to the event.

An event internally manages a linked list of delegates registered with it. The use of AddHandler in the previous example ensures that if any event handlers are already attached to this event by other objects, they remain in the list. There is also a RemoveHandler keyword that you can use to drop a handler from the list for an event. When an event is raised, all handlers in the list are invoked.

Event Raising Methods

Each class that publishes an event also provides a protected, virtual method that raises the event. When a specific incident occurs in the environment, the publisher class invokes this method. The task of this method is to notify all the event subscribers about the event.

You can easily identify these event-raising methods in a class declaration because their naming convention is the word On followed by the name of the event. For example, OnPreRender() is the method of the Control class that raises the `PreRender` event when the control is about to render its output. If you want to simulate an event, you can call one of these methods directly from your code.

Event Handling in ASP.NET

ASP.NET provides you with three general methods for handling events in a page:

➤ Handling events by overriding the virtual, protected method of the base class

➤ Handling events by attaching a delegate to the event

➤ Handling events of the `Page` class through `AutoEventWireup`

Handling Events by Overriding the Virtual, Protected Method of the Base Class

When an ASP.NET page is dynamically compiled, it inherits from the `Page` class. By virtue of this inheritance, the ASP.NET page also derives a set of events and virtual protected methods for raising those events. For example, `OnInit()` is the method of the `Page` class that raises the `Init` event. When a Web page is first created and initialized, it automatically invokes the `OnInit()` method. The `OnInit()` method in turn raises the `Init` event corresponding to the recently initialized `Page` object and passes any required event-related data to the `Init` event.

You can handle the event yourself by overriding this method in your code, as in this example:

```
Protected Overrides Sub OnLoad(e As EventArgs)
    Response.Write("Handling the Load event.<br>")
    MyBase.OnLoad(e)
End Sub
```

The predefined event handlers `OnInit`, `OnLoad`, and so on have more responsibility than just displaying a message. These methods must also bootstrap the event-handling process for the events (`Init`, `Load`, and so on) of the `Page` class. You need not program this functionality again because it is already programmed in the base class, but to ensure that the base class version of an overridden method is also invoked, you need to explicitly call the base class version of a method by using the `MyBase.MemberName` syntax.

Handling Events by Attaching Delegates

An alternative way of handling an event is by attaching a delegate object to the event. Although this scheme requires additional steps as compared to the event-handling scheme described in the previous section, it offers more flexibility, including the following:

➤ Delegates allow you to attach a single event handler to several events.

➤ Delegates allow you to dynamically add and remove event handlers for an event.

➤ Delegates allow you to associate multiple event handlers with an event.

➤ The subscriber class is not required to derive from the class that publishes an event.

Here's an example of using a delegate to handle an event in an ASPX page:

```
Protected Sub My_Load( _
  o As Object, e As EventArgs)
    Response.Write( _
      "Handling the Load event")
End Sub

Protected Overrides Sub OnInit(e As EventArgs)
    AddHandler Me.Load, AddressOf My_Load
    Mybase.OnInit(e)
End Sub
```

Handling Events of the Page Class Through AutoEventWireup

ASP.NET supports an additional mechanism for handling events raised by the Page class. This technique is called AutoEventWireup.

AutoEventWireup relies on using specific names for the event handlers of Page class events. The name has to be of the type Page_EventName. For example, when handling the Init, Load, and PreRender events, the name of the event handlers should be Page_Init, Page_Load, and Page_PreRender, respectively.

Event handling through AutoEventWireup only works when the AutoEventWireup attribute of the Page directive is True. The AutoEventWireup attribute is True by default, so if you don't specify this attribute in the Page directive, it's assumed to be True by ASP.NET. However, if you create your pages using Visual Studio .NET, it will automatically add AutoEventWireup=False to the Page directive. Here's an example of using AutoEventWireup to handle an event:

```
<%@ Page Language="vb"%>
<html><body>
<script runat=server>
    Protected Sub Page_Load(o As Object, e As EventArgs)
        Response.Write( _
          "Handling the Load event")
    End Sub
</script>
</body>
</html>
```

Convenient as it might sound, this scheme is not as flexible as event handling through delegates because when you use AutoEventWireup, the page event handlers must have specific names. This limits your flexibility in naming the event handlers. Because of this, Visual Studio .NET does not use AutoEventWireup when creating Web Forms.

Separating the User Interface from Business Logic

In the ASP.NET pages created so far in this chapter, you must have noted that the Visual Basic .NET code is interspersed between the HTML code. This is not much of a problem in a simple Web page, but for complex Web pages, this is not a good idea. Mixing HTML and Visual Basic .NET code makes Web pages difficult to understand, maintain, and debug. HTML code represents the user interface (UI) of the application, whereas the ASP.NET code defines the business logic for that page. These are two different ideas that often need to be handled differently.

ASP.NET provides a mechanism to separate the user interface portion of a Web page from the business logic. This mechanism is known as *code-behind*. To implement code-behind, you write all the user interface–related code in one file (.aspx) and the business logic in another file (.vb for VB), and then link these two files using the Page directive in the .aspx file.

Using Code-Behind

When you write both the UI and business logic in separate files, you can link them via the Src and Inherits attributes of the Page directive. For example, you can follow these steps to create a code-behind version of the factorial table that you saw earlier in the chapter:

1. Add a new text file to Web project WebApp1. Name the new file WebTest2.aspx. Switch to its HTML view and add the following code to the Web page:

```
<%@ Page Language="vb"
 Inherits="MathFunctions.Factorial"
 Src="MathFunctions.vb"%>
<html>
<body>
    <h2>Factorial List</h2>
    <table border="2">
        <tr>
            <th>Number</th><th>Factorial</th>
        </tr>
```

```
    <%CreateFactorialTable()%>
  </table>
</body>
</html>
```

2. Right-click the project in the Solution Explorer, and select Add, Add New Item. Select the Code File template and name the file `MathFunctions.vb`.

3. Add the following code to the `MathFunctions.vb` file:

```
' MathFunctions.vb
' Define a namespace
Namespace MathFunctions
    ' Define Factorial class
    Public Class Factorial
        Inherits System.Web.UI.Page

        ' Define MakeFactorial() method
        Function MakeFactorial(ByVal n As Integer) As Integer
            Dim i As Integer
            Dim Result As Integer = 1
            For i = 2 To n
                Result = Result * i
            Next
            MakeFactorial = Result
        End Function

        ' Define CreateFactorialTable() method
        Public Sub CreateFactorialTable()
            Dim i As Integer
            For i = 1 To 10
                ' Sends formatted output to HTTP Response
                Response.Output.Write("<tr><td>{0}</td><td>" & _
                    "{1}</td><tr>", i, MakeFactorial(i))
            Next
        End Sub
    End Class
End Namespace
```

4. View the `WebTest2.aspx` file in the browser. You'll see that the factorial table is created just as it was when you viewed `WebTest1.aspx`.

The `Page` directive in the ASPX file provides the linking mechanism for the UI and the code-behind. The `Inherits` attribute specifies that when the `.aspx` file is dynamically compiled, it inherits its functionality from the `Factorial` class of the `MathFunctions` namespace. The `Src` attribute specifies that the source code for `Factorial` class is stored in the `MathFunctions.vb` file.

Creating a Web Form Using Visual Studio .NET

Web Forms are the preferred way of creating ASP.NET pages using Visual Studio .NET. Web Forms are an integrated way to build ASPX pages within the Visual Studio IDE. Try these steps to practice working with Web Forms:

1. Right-click the project name in Solution Explorer and select Add, Add Web Form. In the Add New Item dialog box, name the file WebTest3.aspx. The Web Form will open in Design view, with a message asking you to select between grid layout mode and flow layout mode.

2. Visual Studio .NET allows you to work with some of the properties of the Page class, and of objects within the page, through the Properties Window, shown in Figure 2.3. If the Properties Window isn't visible, select View, Properties Window. Set the pageLayout property of the DOCUMENT object to FlowLayout.

Figure 2.3   The Properties window shows the properties of an object.

3. In the flow layout mode, type Factorial Table on the page. Select the text and change its block format to Heading 2 using the Block Format combo box on the formatting toolbar.

4. Press Enter to move to a new line on the Web form. Select Table, Insert, Table. In the Insert Table dialog box, select options to make a table of size 1 row and 2 columns. Set the Width attribute to 200 pixels.

5. Switch to the HTML view of the file. Modify the code in the <TABLE> tag as shown here:

```
<TABLE id="Table1" cellSpacing="1" cellPadding="1"
  width="200" border="1">
```

```
<TR>
    <TD>Number</TD>
    <TD>Factorial</TD>
</TR>
<%CreateFactorialTable()%>
</TABLE>
```

6. Go back to Design view, right-click the page, and select View Code. This will open the code-behind file WebTest3.aspx.vb. Add the following code just above the Web Form Designer generated code region:

```
' Define MakeFactorial() method
Function MakeFactorial(ByVal n As Integer) As Integer
    Dim i As Integer
    Dim Result As Integer = 1
    For i = 2 To n
        Result = Result * i
    Next
    MakeFactorial = Result
End Function

' Define CreateFactorialTable() method
Public Sub CreateFactorialTable()
    Dim i As Integer
    For i = 1 To 10
        ' Sends formatted output to HTTP Response
        Response.Output.Write("<tr><td>{0}</td><td>" & _
            "{1}</td><tr>", i, MakeFactorial(i))
    Next
End Sub
```

7. In the Solution Explorer, right-click WebTest3.aspx and select Set As Start Page.

8. Compile the page by selecting Build, Build Solution. Run the page by selecting Debug, Start Without Debugging. A separate browser window will appear with the factorial table.

An ASP.NET Web Form is made up of two distinct pieces:

➤ The user interface piece stored in the .aspx file

➤ The business logic piece stored in a .vb file

Visual Studio keeps the name of the .vb file synchronized with the name of the .aspx file. If you can't find the .vb file corresponding to a Web Form listed in the Solution Explorer, that's because Visual Studio .NET hides it in the default view. To display the code-behind .vb file, select the project and click the Show All Files toolbar button in the Solution Explorer window.

If you inspect the HTML code for the WebTest3.aspx file, you'll see that the Page directive is as follows:

```
<%@ Page Language="vb" AutoEventWireup="false"
Codebehind="WebTest3.aspx.vb"
Inherits="WebApp1.WebTest3"%>
```

This usage of the `Page` directive has two new attributes—`AutoEventWireup` and `Codebehind`. `AutoEventWireup` is used for event handling, and setting it to `False` disables the automatic event naming that you saw earlier. The `Codebehind` attribute is used by Visual Studio .NET to track the location of the source code of the code behind the file. ASP.NET does not understand the `Codebehind` attribute and therefore ignores it. This attribute does not play any role in the execution of the ASP.NET page.

If you are handling events in your program by attaching delegates, you should set the **AutoEventWireup** attribute to **False**. If you keep it **True**, some of the event handlers might be called twice as the page runs. For example, suppose you create a method named **Page_Load** and attach it to the Load event of the Page using a delegate object. Now, if the **AutoEventWireup** attribute is true, the ASP.NET page framework will also automatically attach **Page_Load** as an event handler for the **Load** event of the page. This results in the registration of the same event handler twice; hence, the event handler will also be invoked twice when the event is raised. This is why Visual Studio .NET always keeps **AutoEventWireup** set to **False**.

Analyzing the Business Logic Piece of a Web Form

Take a look at the `WebTest3.aspx.vb` file. The first thing you might notice is that Visual Studio .NET groups code into blocks. This feature is called *code outlining*. You can expand and collapse code blocks by using the + and – signs near the left margin of the window in code view.

The file contains a block of collapsed code named "Web Form Designer generated code." When you expand the block, you'll see a set of statements included between `#region` and `#endregion` directives. These directives mark the beginning and end of a named code block. You can specify a name after the `#region` directive to identify the code block with a name.

The code enclosed in the code block named "Web Form Designer generated code" is required for Designer support, and you should not generally modify it.

The class definition for the `WebTest3` class looks like this:

```
Public Class WebTest3
    Inherits System.Web.UI.Page
    ...
End Class
```

If you prefer, you can also write this definition as

```
Imports System.Web.UI
Public Class WebTest3
    Inherits Page
    ...
End Class
```

How does the compiler locate a class if its full namespace qualified name is not provided? The Imports directive allows you to use classes without typing their fully qualified names. The inclusion of Imports statements directs the VB compiler to search for each class that you are using in the namespaces specified in the Imports statement. The compiler looks up each namespace one by one, and when it finds the given class in one of the namespaces, it internally replaces the reference of the class with *NamespaceName.ClassName* in the code.

Exam Prep Questions

Question 1

You have defined a class whose fully qualified name is **MyApplication.Class1**. Which of these classes could inherit from **MyApplication.Class1** (select all correct answers)?

- ❑ A. **MyApplication.Class2**
- ❑ B. **MyApplication.Details.Class2**
- ❑ C. **System.Object**
- ❑ D. **NewApplication.Class3**

Answers A, B, and D are correct. The namespace hierarchy and the inheritance hierarchy are two separate things. A class can inherit from another class in the same namespace (answer A), from a class in a parent namespace (answer B), or from a class in a completely different namespace (answer D). Answer C is incorrect because the built-in System.Object class is at the root of the inheritance hierarchy and can't inherit from other classes.

Question 2

You use a text editor to create an ASPX file and a matching code-behind file, and then save them in a new directory on your Web server. The new directory is a subdirectory of the Web server's root directory. When you attempt to load the ASPX file, you receive an error instead. What can you do to correct this error?

- ○ A. Install the .NET Framework redistributable on the client computer.
- ○ B. Create a new virtual directory on the Web server that references the new subdirectory.
- ○ C. Insert the code directly into the ASPX file.
- ○ D. Compile the code-behind file before deploying it to the Web server.

Answer B is correct. You must create a virtual directory on the Web server for any Web application. Answer A is incorrect because the .NET Framework is only needed on the server, not on the client. Answer C is incorrect because code-behind and integrated files have the same requirements on the server. Answer D is incorrect because ASP.NET requires the Web application whether the code has been compiled or not.

Question 3

> Which of the following can you specify as part of a **Page** directive on an ASPX page (select all correct answers)?
>
> ❑ A. The caching behavior of the page
>
> ❑ B. The source code language for the page, such as Visual Basic .NET or C#
>
> ❑ C. A namespace that contains classes used by the page
>
> ❑ D. The location of a code-behind file for the page

Answers B and D are correct. The page's language is specified by the Language attribute of the Page directive, and the location of the code-behind file is specified by the Src attribute of the Page directive. Answer A is incorrect because caching behavior is controlled by the OutputCache directive. Answer C is incorrect because namespaces are imported with the Import directive.

Question 4

> You have developed a project management application using ASP.NET. This application will be used by employees on your company's intranet. Which software must the employees install to use the application?
>
> ○ A. The .NET Framework SDK
>
> ○ B. Visual Studio .NET
>
> ○ C. Internet Information Services
>
> ○ D. A modern Web browser

Answer D is correct. Although ASP.NET applications require the .NET Framework on the server, they do not require any .NET pieces on the client. When the Web server calls ASP.NET to fulfill a page request, the resulting page is pure HTML. Thus, the only thing the client computer needs is a Web browser that can display the HTML. Answers A, B, and C are incorrect because the client computer does not require these components to use ASP.NET applications.

Question 5

You are developing a Web Form that will display customer information to sales representatives. When the user requests the Web Form, you need to control the color of specific controls on the form, according to the browser being used, and set the value of some properties that are used for further processing. Where should you put this initialization code?

○ A. In the event handler for the **Init** event of the **Page** class

○ B. In the event handler for the **PreRender** event of the **Page** class

○ C. In the event handler for the **Unload** event of the **Page** class

○ D. In the event handler for the **Load** event of the **Page** class

Answer D is correct. The Load event will happen before the page is displayed but after it has loaded, so the controls will be available. Answer A is incorrect because the controls might not be available during the Init event. Answer B is incorrect because the PreRender event occurs after all the code on the page has been processed, so it's too late to set property values. Answer C is incorrect because the Unload event happens when the page is being cleaned up, not when it's being processed.

Question 6

Your application uses a class named **PieChart**. The **PieChart** class includes a static property named **MaxColors**, a method named **Draw**, and a property named **Slices**. Within your code, you have declared an object named **MyPieChart** that is an instance of the **PieChart** class:

```
Dim MyPieChart As PieChart
```

Which of these lines of code could be valid within your application?

○ A. **Dim S As Integer = PieChart.Slices**

○ B. **Dim I As Integer = PieChart.MaxColors**

○ C. **PieChart.Draw()**

○ D. **Dim I As Integer = MyPieChart.MaxColors**

Answer B is correct. A static member of a class can be used directly from the class, rather than from an instance of the class. Answers A and C are incorrect because regular members of a class are called from an instance of the class. Answer D is incorrect because a static property cannot be referenced from an instance of the class.

Question 7

You have created an ASPX page named **PageOne.aspx**. This page includes both HTML and VB .NET code in a single file; there is no separate code-behind file. When a user requests this page, what happens?

○ A. ASP.NET splits the VB .NET code into a new file named **PageOne.vb**. This class inherits from the **Page** class. ASP.NET then dynamically generates a class named **PageOne_aspx**. This class inherits from the **PageOne** class. The dynamically generated class is compiled, and the CLR executes the code in the dynamically generated class.

○ B. ASP.NET dynamically generates a class named **PageOne_aspx**. This class inherits from the **Page** class. The dynamically generated class is compiled, and the CLR executes the code in the dynamically generated class.

○ C. ASP.NET interprets the statements in the **PageOne.aspx** file, starting at the top and continuing to the bottom, and directly writes any output to the response stream.

○ D. ASP.NET returns the contents of the **PageOne.aspx** file to the browser without changing them.

Answer B is correct. Because the page does not have an associated code-behind file, it is dynamically compiled into a class that inherits directly from the Page class. Answer A is incorrect because it describes the behavior of pages that have an associated code-behind class. Answer C is incorrect because it describes the behavior of classic ASP, which was an interpreted language rather than a compiled one. Answer D is incorrect because it describes the behavior of static HTML pages rather than dynamic pages such as ASPX pages.

Question 8

You want to run the code in a function named **HandleLoad()** to the **Load** event of an ASP.NET page. Which of these code snippets correctly attaches the code to the event (select all correct answers)?

❑ A.
```
<%@ Page Language="vb"%>
<html><body>
<script runat=server>
    Protected Overrides Sub OnLoad(e As EventArgs)
        HandleLoad()
    End Sub
</script>
</body>
</html>
```

❑ B.

```
<%@ Page Language="vb"%>
<html><body>
<script runat="server">
    Protected Sub My_Load( _
      o As Object, e As EventArgs)
        HandleLoad()
    End Sub

    Protected Overrides Sub OnInit(e As EventArgs)
        AddHandler Me.Load, AddressOf My_Load
        MyBase.OnInit(e)
    End Sub
</script>
</body>
</html>
```

❑ C.

```
<%@ Page Language="vb"%>
<html><body>
<script runat=server>
    Protected Overrides Sub OnLoad(e As EventArgs)
        HandleLoad()
        MyBase.OnLoad(e)
    End Sub
</script>
</body>
</html>
```

❑ D.

```
<%@ Page Language="vb" AutoEventWireup="False"%>
<html><body>
<script runat=server>
    Protected Sub Page_Load(o As Object, e As EventArgs)
        HandleLoad()
    End Sub
</script>
</body>
</html>
```

Answers B and C are correct. Answer B handles the event by attaching a delegate, and answer C handles the event by overriding the appropriate method of the parent class. Answer A is incorrect because it neglects to call the event method of the parent class, so it will lead to unpredictable behavior on the part of the page. Answer D is incorrect because it uses the AutoEventWireup syntax to run the code, but has AutoEventWireup disabled.

Question 9

You are using Visual Studio .NET to develop a Web Form for a medical records application. In tracing calls from the application to a SQL Server database, you discover that the initialization code in the **Page_Load()** method of the form is getting executed twice. What should you do to correct this problem?

- ○ A. Set the **AutoEventWireup** attribute of the **Page** directive to **True**.
- ○ B. Write the code in C# instead of Visual Basic .NET.
- ○ C. Set the **AutoEventWireup** attribute of the **Page** directive to **False**.
- ○ D. Merge the code-behind code with the HTML code in a single ASPX file.

Answer C is correct. If you set AutoEventWireup to True, it will add event handlers based on their names, in addition to any AddHandler calls you make in your code. Answer A is incorrect because it is the wrong setting for this attribute. Answer B is incorrect because VB .NET and C# have nearly identical capabilities. Answer D is incorrect because merging the files will lose the benefits of the code-behind programming model.

Question 10

Your code-behind file contains the following code:

```
Imports Corporate
Imports Partners
Dim b As BusinessRules
```

The **Corporate** namespace contains a class named **Corporate.BusinessRules**, and the **Partners** namespace contains a class named **Partners.BusinessRules**. What will happen when this page is loaded?

- ○ A. A compile-time error will occur.
- ○ B. A runtime error will occur.
- ○ C. The variable **b** will be created as an instance of the **Corporate.BusinessRules** class.
- ○ D. The variable **b** will be created as an instance of the **Partners.BusinessRules class**.

Answer C is correct. To resolve a classname, the CLR will look in each namespace listed in an Imports statement, starting at the top of the file. When a matching class is found, that class is instantiated and the search ends. To avoid confusion, you should always fully qualify classnames in cases such as this. Answers A and B are incorrect because the code will run without any error. Answer D is incorrect because the Partners namespace is imported after the Corporate namespace.

Question 11

You are developing an ASPX page that can be reached by several different paths through your application. Depending on the immediately previous page, you want to enable one of three different sets of event handlers on your page. Which event should you use to hook up the appropriate event handlers?

○ A. **Init**

○ B. **Load**

○ C. **PreRender**

○ D. **Unload**

Answer A is correct. The `Init` event is the appropriate event for one-time processing such as hooking up event handlers that might be needed by other code in the page. Answer B is incorrect because the `Load` event occurs when the page is completely initialized. Answers C and D are incorrect because the `PreRender` and `Unload` events come much later in the page's lifecycle. If you wait until those events to hook up event handlers, the event handlers might not be in place when other code tries to use them.

Question 12

You want to implement your Web page using the code-behind technique. Because of budgetary constraints, you're using a text editor to develop your application. You place the user interface in a file named **MyNewPage.aspx** and the business logic in another file named **MyNewPage.aspx.vb**. The **MyNewPage.aspx.vb** file contains the definition for a class that derives from the **Page** class. You want to link the user interface file with the code-behind file. Which of the following attributes will you use for the **Page** directive in **MyNewPage.aspx** file? (Select two.)

❏ A. **ClassName**

❏ B. **Inherits**

❏ C. **CodeBehind**

❏ D. **Src**

Answers B and D are correct. The `Inherits` attribute specifies the class that will provide the business logic for the page, and the `Src` attribute specifies the file where this class is defined. Answer A is incorrect because the `ClassName` attribute specifies the class that will be generated at compilation time. Answer C is incorrect because the `CodeBehind` attribute is just a hint for Visual Studio .NET to use.

Need to Know More?

 David Chappell. *Understanding .NET.* Addison-Wesley, 2001.

 Jones, A. Russell. *Mastering ASP.NET with Visual Basic.NET.* Sybex, 2002.

 Brill, Gregory. *CodeNotes for ASP.NET.* Random House, 2002.

 Burton, Kevin. *.NET Common Language Runtime Unleashed.* Sams, 2002.

 The Official Microsoft ASP.NET site, www.asp.NET.

Controls

. . . .

Terms you'll need to understand:

✓ CSS (cascading style sheets)

✓ HTML controls

✓ HTML server controls

✓ Input validation

✓ Web server controls

Techniques you'll need to master:

✓ Adding controls to ASP.NET pages

✓ Customizing control appearance and behavior by setting properties

✓ Dynamically loading controls at runtime

✓ Using cascading style sheets to customize the look of a Web site

✓ Validating user input

Controls are the building blocks of a graphical user interface (GUI). Visual Studio .NET allows you to work with the following types of controls on Web Forms:

➤ **HTML Controls**—Traditional HTML elements displayed as controls.

➤ **HTML Server Controls**—HTML elements that can be programmed on the server, marked with the `runat="server"` attribute.

➤ **Web Server Controls**—These new controls are specifically designed to integrate well with the ASP.NET programming model. They support data binding and other advanced capabilities and might render as multiple HTML controls.

➤ **Validation Controls**—Validation Controls are Web server controls that contain logic to validate input in other server controls.

➤ **Web User Controls and Web Custom Controls**—These are two types of controls that you can create yourself. You can learn more about these controls in Chapter 8, "Creating and Managing Components and .NET Assemblies."

HTML Controls

HTML controls represent common HTML elements. You can access all the commonly used HTML controls through the HTML tab in the Visual Studio .NET Toolbox. You can drag these controls to a Web Form and set their properties in the Properties window.

Controls from the HTML tab of the Toolbox such as Text Field and Label are converted to their appropriate HTML equivalent such as `<INPUT>` and `<DIV>` elements, respectively, in the source code of the ASPX file. All the HTML controls are automatically placed inside an HTML `<FORM>` element. These controls are saved exactly as they'll appear when they're sent to the user's browser.

You probably won't make much use of HTML controls on ASP.NET Web forms. That's because there's no good way to programmatically interact with these controls from your Visual Basic .NET controls. ASP.NET provides two other sets of controls that are much better suited for server-side programming: HTML Server controls and Web Server controls.

HTML Server Controls

You can mark any HTML control to run as an HTML server control. Unlike regular HTML controls, HTML server controls are programmable on the

Web server. You can access properties and events for the HTML server control just as you do for controls in Windows desktop-based applications.

HTML server controls are not as flexible in code as are Web Server controls. The main reason they exist is that they provide an easy migration path for existing HTML pages. To convert an HTML control to an HTML server control, right-click on it in Visual Studio .NET and select Run As Server Control.

Web Server Controls

Web server controls provide a higher level of abstraction than HTML server controls because their object model matches closely with the .NET Framework, rather than matching with the requirements of HTML syntax. In the HTML source for your page, Web server controls are represented as XML tags rather than as HTML elements. But remember, the browser receives standard HTML in any case.

Web server controls have a number of advanced features:

➤ Web server controls provide a rich object model that closely matches with the rest of the .NET Framework.

➤ Web server controls have built-in automatic browser detection capabilities. They can render their output HTML correctly for both uplevel and downlevel browsers.

➤ Some Web server controls have the capability to cause an immediate postback when users click, change, or select a value.

➤ Some Web server controls (such as the `Calendar` and `AdRotator` controls) provide richer functionality than is available with HTML controls.

 NOTE ASP.NET treats browsers as either uplevel or downlevel. Uplevel browsers support HTML 4.0 or later, the Microsoft Document Object Model (DOM), Cascading Style Sheets, and JavaScript 1.2 or later. Internet Explorer 4.0 or later is an example of an uplevel browser. Browsers with any lesser capabilities are considered to be downlevel browsers.

Web server controls are declared in HTML explicitly by prefixing the classname of the Web server control with `asp:` and of course including the `runat="server"` attribute in its definition, creating an XML tag in the `asp` namespace. For example, a Label Web server control can be declared in code as `<asp:Label runat="server">`. If you are using Visual Studio .NET, you can just drag and drop these controls on a Web Form using the Web Forms tab of the Visual Studio .NET Toolbox.

Most of the Web server controls derive their functionality by inheriting from the WebControl class of the System.Web.UI.WebControls namespace. However, some Web server controls such as the Repeater and XML controls do not get their functionality from the WebControl class; they instead derive directly from the Control class of the System.Web.UI namespace.

Table 3.1 lists some of the common properties that all Web server controls derive from the WebControl class.

Table 3.1	Important Properties of the System.Web.UI.WebControls.WebControl Class
Properties	**Description**
AccessKey	Specifies the single character keyboard shortcut key for quick navigation to the Web server control. The focus is moved to the Web server control when the Alt+AccessKey assigned to this property is pressed.
BackColor	Specifies the background color of the Web server control.
BorderColor	Specifies the border color of the Web server control.
BorderStyle	Specifies the border style of the Web server control.
BorderWidth	Specifies the border width of the Web server control.
Controls	Represents the collection of controls added to the Web server control as child controls.
CssClass	Represents the CSS class with which the Web server control is rendered.
Enabled	Indicates whether the Web server control is allowed to receive the focus.
EnableViewState	Indicates whether view state is enabled for the Web server control.
Font	Specifies a **FontInfo** object that represents the font properties of a Web server control.
ForeColor	Specifies the color of text in the Web server control.
Height	Specifies the height of the Web server control.
ID	Specifies an identifier for the Web server control.
Parent	Represents the parent control of the Web server control.
Style	Specifies the collection of CSS properties applied to the Web server control.
TabIndex	Specifies the tab order of a Web server control.
ToolTip	Specifies the pop-up text displayed by the Web server control when the mouse hovers over it.
Visible	Indicates whether the Web server control is visible.
Width	Specifies the width of the Web server control.

Common Web Server Controls

The following sections discuss some simple but commonly used controls. These controls have a small number of properties, and they are usually rendered as a single HTML element.

The Label Control

A Label control is used to display read-only information to the user. It is generally used to label other controls and to provide the user with any useful messages or statistics. It exposes its text content through the Text property. This property can be used to manipulate its text programmatically. The control is rendered as a `<span>` HTML element on the Web browser.

The TextBox Control

A TextBox control provides an area that the user can use to input text. Depending on how you set the properties of this Web server control, you can use it for single or multiline text input, or you can use it as a password box that masks the characters entered by the user with asterisks or bullets, depending on the browser. Thus, this server control can be rendered as three different types of HTML elements—`<input type="text">`, `<input type="password">`, and `<textarea>`. Table 3.2 summarizes the important members of the TextBox class.

Table 3.2 Important Members of the TextBox Class		
Member	**Type**	**Description**
AutoPostBack	Property	Indicates whether the Web Form should be posted to the server automatically whenever the data in the text box is changed.
Columns	Property	Specifies the width in characters of the text box.
MaxLength	Property	Specifies the maximum number of characters that may be entered by the user. The default value is **0**, which does not impose any limit.
ReadOnly	Property	Indicates whether the contents of the text box are read-only—that is, they cannot be modified. The default value is **False**.
Rows	Property	Specifies the height in characters of a multiline text box. The default value is **0**. Works only if the **TextMode** property is set to **MultiLine**.
Text	Property	Specifies the text contained in the text box.

(continued)

Table 3.2	Important Members of the TextBox Class *(continued)*	
Member	**Type**	**Description**
TextChanged	Event	Occurs when the value of the **Text** property changes. **TextChanged** is the default event for the **TextBox** class.
TextMode	Property	Represents the type of the text box to be rendered in the Web page. It can be displayed in one of the three values of the **TextBoxMode** enumeration—**MultiLine** (text box can accept multiple lines of input), **Password** (single-line text box with each character masked with an asterisk character, *) and **SingleLine** (single-line text box with normal text displayed).
Wrap	Property	Specifies whether the control will automatically wrap words to the next line. The default value is **True**. Works only if the **TextMode** property is set to **MultiLine**.

The Image Control

The Image Web server control can display images from BMP, JPEG, PNG, and GIF files. The control is rendered as an `<img>` HTML element on the Web page. Table 3.3 summarizes the important properties of the Image class.

Table 3.3	Important Members of the Image Class
Properties	**Description**
AlternateText	Specifies the text that is displayed in the place of the **Image** Web server control when the image cannot be displayed.
ImageAlign	Indicates the alignment of the **Image** Web server control with reference to other elements in the Web page.
ImageUrl	Represents the URL of the image that the **Image** Web server control displays. The URL can be relative or absolute.

The CheckBox and RadioButton Controls

A `CheckBox` control allows you to select one or more options from a group of options, and a group of `RadioButton` controls is used to select one out of several mutually exclusive options. The `RadioButton` controls that need to be set mutually exclusive should belong to the same group specified by the `GroupName` property. The check box and radio button Web server controls are rendered as `<input type="checkbox">` and `<input type="radio">` HTML elements on the Web page.

The `RadioButton` class inherits from the `CheckBox` class, and both of them share the same members, except for the `GroupName` property available in the `RadioButton` class.

Table 3.4 summarizes the important members of the CheckBox and RadioButton classes.

Table 3.4	Important Members of the CheckBox and RadioButton Classes	
Member	**Member**	**Description**
AutoPostBack	Property	Indicates whether the Web Form should be posted to the server automatically when the check box is clicked.
Checked	Property	Returns **True** if the check box or radio button has been checked. Otherwise, it returns **False**.
CheckedChanged	Event	Occurs every time a check box is checked or unchecked. **CheckedChanged** is the default event for the **CheckBox** class.
GroupName (RadioButton class only)	Property	Specifies the group to which this control belongs.
Text	Property	Specifies the text displayed along with the check box.
TextAlign	Property	Specifies the alignment of the text displayed along with the check box.

The **Button**, **LinkButton**, and **ImageButton** Controls

There are three types of button Web server controls. Each of these controls is different in its appearance and is rendered differently on the Web page:

➤ Button—The Button control displays as a push button on the Web page and is rendered as an `<input type="submit">` HTML element.

➤ LinkButton—The LinkButton control displays as a hyperlink on the Web page and is rendered as an `<a>` HTML element.

➤ ImageButton—The ImageButton control displays as an image button on the Web page and is rendered as an `<input type="image">` HTML element.

The **LinkButton** control works only if client-side scripting is enabled in the Web browser.

All three of these controls post the form data to the Web server when they are clicked. Table 3.5 summarizes the important members that are applicable to the Button, LinkButton, and ImageButton classes.

Table 3.5	Important Members of the Button, LinkButton, and ImageButton Classes	
Member	Type	Description
CausesValidation	Property	Indicates whether validation should be performed when the button control is clicked.
Click	Event	Occurs when the button control is clicked. **Click** is the default event of all three classes. This event is mostly used for submit buttons.
Command	Event	Occurs when the button control is clicked. This event is mostly used for command buttons. The event handler receives an object of type **CommandEventArgs** that contains both the **CommandName** and **CommandArgument** properties containing event-related data.
CommandArgument	Property	Specifies the argument for a command. Works only if the **CommandName** property is set. The property is passed to the **Command** event when the button is clicked.
CommandName	Property	Specifies the command name for the button. The property is passed to the **Command** event when the button is clicked.
Text	Property	Specifies the text displayed on a button. The **ImageButton** class does not have this property.

All three button controls can behave in two different ways—as a submit button or as a command button. By default, any type of button Web server control is a submit button. If you specify a command name via the CommandName property, the button controls also become a command button.

A command button raises the Command event when it is clicked. The button passes the CommandName and CommandArgument encapsulated in a CommandEventArgs object to the event handlers. A command button is useful when you want to pass some event-related information to the event handler.

Event Handling with Web Server Controls

One key feature of many ASP.NET Web applications is the easy interactivity that they offer to the user. In most cases, handling events plays an important part in this interactivity. Although the user is working with the rendered HTML in his own browser, Web Server controls allow you to handle events with code that's executed on the server.

Web server controls have a set of intrinsic events available to them. The name and number of these events depend on the type of the Web server control.

By convention, all events in the .NET Framework pass two arguments to their event handler—the object that raised the event and an object containing any event-specific information.

Code on the server can't execute until the page is sent back to the server, which is known as *postback*. Some events are cached and are fired on the Web server at a later stage when the page is posted back as a result of a click event. Some Web server controls (for example, the DropDownList) have a property named AutoPostBack. When this property is set to True, it causes an immediate postback of the page when the value of the control is changed.

Some advanced Web server controls such as the DataGrid control can also contain other controls such as a Button. DataGrid controls usually display dynamically generated data, and if each row of DataGrid contains a Button, you might end up having a variable number of Button controls. Writing an individual event handler for each Button control in this case is a very tedious process. To simplify event handling, controls such as DataGrid support bubbling of events in which all events raised at the level of child control are bubbled up to the container control, where the container control can raise a generic event in response to the child events.

For the most part, Web server control events are processed by server code. You can also use client code such as JScript to process Web server control events. To do so, you need to dynamically add the client code method name to the control. For example, the following code fragment attaches the **someClientCode()** client-side method to the **onMouseOver** event of the btnSubmit button.

```
btnSubmit.Attributes.Add("onMouseOver", _
    "someClientCode();")
```

The List Controls

The category of list controls consists of the DropDownList, ListBox, CheckBoxList, and RadioButtonList controls. These controls display a list of items from which the user can select. These controls inherit from the abstract base ListControl class. The class provides the basic properties, methods, and events common to all the list controls. Table 3.6 summarizes the important members of the ListControl class with which you should be familiar.

Table 3.6 Important Members of the ListControl Class		
Member	Member	Description
AutoPostBack	Property	Indicates whether the Web Form should be posted to the server automatically whenever the list selection is changed. Works only if the browser supports client-side scripting.

(continued)

Table 3.6 Important Members of the ListControl Class *(continued)*		
Member	**Member**	**Description**
Items	Property	Specifies a collection of items in the list control.
SelectedIndex	Property	Specifies an index of the currently selected item. The default value is –1, which means that no item is selected in the list control.
SelectedIndexChanged	Event	Occurs when the **SelectedIndex** property changes. **SelectedIndexChanged** is the default event for the list controls.
SelectedItem	Property	Specifies the currently selected item.

Although these controls inherit their basic functionality from the ListControl class, they display the list of items in different styles and support different selection modes.

A DropDownList Web server control allows you to select only a single item from the drop-down list. The DropDownList Web server control is rendered as a <select> HTML element, and its items are added as <option> elements within the HTML <select> element. The default value of the SelectedIndex property is 0, which means that the first item is selected in the drop-down list. This overrides the default of the general ListControl class.

A ListBox Web server control allows you to select single or multiple items from the list of items displayed in the list box. The ListBox Web server control is rendered as a <select> or <select multiple> HTML element, depending on whether single or multiple selections are allowed. The items are added as <option> elements within the HTML <select> element. The ListBox class adds two more properties to enable it to select multiple items:

➤ Rows—This property represents the number of rows to be displayed in the list box. The default value is 4. The value of this property must be between 1 and 2000.

➤ SelectionMode—This property indicates the mode of selection allowed in the list box. It can be one of the ListSelectionMode values—Multiple or Single (default).

The CheckBoxList and RadioButtonList Web server controls display lists of check boxes and radio buttons, respectively, where each check box or radio button represents a CheckBox or RadioButton Web server control. The CheckBoxList control allows you to select multiple check boxes in the list.

The RadioButtonList control allows you to select only a single radio button from the list of radio buttons. CheckBoxList and RadioButtonList render each list item as <input type="checkbox"> and <input type="radio"> HTML elements, respectively. The list items are displayed in a table or without a table structure depending on the layout selected.

The default value of the **SelectedIndex** property in a list control is **–1**, which indicates that no item is selected in the list control. However, the **DropDownList** control overrides this property and sets the default value to **0**, which indicates the first item in the list. This ensures that an item is always selected in the drop-down list.

ListBox and **CheckBoxList** allow you to make multiple selections from the list controls. When these controls allow multiple selections, the **SelectedIndex** and **SelectedItem** properties return the index of the first selected item and the first selected item itself, respectively. You have to iterate through the Items collection and check that each item's **Selected** property is true to retrieve the items selected by the user.

The **IsPostBack** property can be used to ensure that code behind a Web Form only runs when the page is first loaded. **IsPostBack** is **False** when the page is first loaded and **True** whenever it is reloaded (for example, in response to the user clicking a command button) .

The PlaceHolder and Panel Controls

A PlaceHolder Web server control allows you to hold an area on a Web page. The PlaceHolder control allows you to add controls dynamically in a Web page in the area reserved by the PlaceHolder control. This control inherits from the System.Web.UI.Control class and does not share the common properties shared by the Web server controls that inherit from the WebControl class. The control does not define any new properties, events, or methods. It does not render any HTML element for itself.

A Panel Web server control acts as a container for other controls in the Web page. The Panel control can be used to organize controls in the Web page. It can be used to hide or show controls contained in the panel on the Web page. Controls can also be added programmatically to the panel control.

The Panel Web server control is rendered as a <div> HTML element on the Web page. Table 3.7 summarizes the important members of the Panel class with which you should be familiar.

Table 3.7	Important Members of the Panel Class	
Member	**Member**	**Description**
BackImageUrl	Property	Specifies the URL of the background image to be displayed behind the contents of the **Panel** control.
HorizontalAlign	Property	Specifies the horizontal alignment of the contents within the **Panel** control.
Wrap	Property	Indicates whether the contents in the panel can automatically wrap within the panel. The default value is **True**.

The Panel control is especially useful when you want to create controls dynamically. To see how this works, follow these steps:

1. Add a new Web Form to your Web Application.

2. Place a TextBox control, a Button control, and a Panel control on the Web Form. Set the ID property of the TextBox control to txtCount. Set the ID property of the Button control to btnCreate. Set the ID property of the Panel control to pnlDynamic.

3. Double-click the Button control. This will open the code view of the Web Form and display a blank event handler for the Button control's Click event. Add this code to the Click event:

```
Private Sub btnCreate_Click( _
 ByVal sender As System.Object, _
 ByVal e As System.EventArgs) _
 Handles btnCreate.Click
    ' Parse the TextBox contents into an integer
    Dim intControls As Integer = _
     Convert.ToInt32(txtCount.Text)
    ' Create that many TextBox controls
    Dim i As Integer
    Dim txt(intControls) As TextBox
    For i = 1 To intControls
        txt(i) = New TextBox()
        ' Set the id property of the textbox
        txt(i).ID = String.Format("DynamicBox{0}", i)
        ' Add the textbox to the panel
        ' if you omit this step, the textbox is
        ' created but not displayed
        pnlDynamic.Controls.Add(txt(i))
    Next
End Sub
```

4. Click the Save button on the Visual Studio .NET toolbar to save the Web Form.

5. Select Debug, Start to open the Web Form in a browser.

6. Enter a numeral in the TextBox and click the Button control. The form will post back to the server. After a brief delay, the server will deliver the new page with the dynamic controls on it.

When you dynamically create a control, you must remember to add it to one of the container controls on the Web page. If you just create a control but forget to add it to the container control, your control will not be rendered with the page.

The Table, TableRow, and TableCell Controls

You can use the Table, TableRow, and TableCell controls to build a table on the Web page. The Table control is rendered as a `<table>` HTML element on the Web page. Table 3.8 summarizes the important members of the Table class with which you should be familiar.

Table 3.8	Important Members of the Table Class	
Member	**Member**	**Description**
BackImageUrl	Property	Specifies the URL of the background image to be displayed behind the contents of the table.
CellPadding	Property	Specifies the distance in pixels between the border and the contents of a cell in the table control.
CellSpacing	Property	Specifies the width in pixels between the cells of the **Table** control.
GridLines	Property	Indicates which cell borders will be displayed in the **Table** control.
HorizontalAlign	Property	Specifies the horizontal alignment of the table within the Web page.
Rows	Property	Specifies a collection of rows in the **Table** control.

The TableRow class represents a row in a Table control. The TableRow class is rendered as a `<tr>` HTML element on the Web page. Table 3.9 summarizes the important members of the TableRow class with which you should be familiar.

Table 3.9	Important Members of the TableRow Class	
Member	**Member**	**Description**
Cells	Property	Specifies a collection of the table cells contained in a table row.
HorizontalAlign	Property	Specifies the horizontal alignment of the cells within the table row.
VerticalAlign	Property	Specifies the vertical alignment of the cells within the table row.

The TableCell Web server control represents a cell in a Table control. The Table Web server control is rendered as a `<td>` HTML element on the Web page.

Table 3.10 summarizes the important members of the `TableCell` class with which you should be familiar.

Table 3.10	Important Members of the TableCell Class	
Member	**Member**	**Description**
ColumnSpan	Property	Specifies the number of columns occupied by a single table cell.
HorizontalAlign	Property	Specifies the horizontal alignment of the contents of the cells within the table cell.
RowSpan	Property	Specifies the number of rows occupied by a single table cell.
Text	Property	Specifies the text displayed in a table cell.
VerticalAlign	Property	Specifies the vertical alignment of the cells within the table row.
Wrap	Property	Indicates whether the contents in a cell can automatically wrap to the next line.

The AdRotator Control

The `AdRotator` Web server control provides a convenient mechanism for displaying advertisements randomly selected from a list on a Web page. It fetches the images from a list stored in an Extensible Markup Language (XML) file and randomly loads an image in the `AdRotator` control every time the page is loaded. It allows you to specify a Web page whose contents will be displayed in the current window when the `AdRotator` control is clicked. The ad files used by the `AdRotator` control follow this format:

```xml
<?xml version="1.0" ?>
<Advertisements>
    <Ad>
        <ImageUrl>que.gif</ImageUrl>
        <NavigateUrl>http://www.quepublishing.com
        </NavigateUrl>
        <AlternateText>Que Publishing</AlternateText>
        <Impressions>40</Impressions>
        <Keyword>Books</Keyword>
        </Ad>
    <Ad>
    ...
    </Ad>
    ...
</Advertisements>
```

The `AdRotator` control is rendered as an anchor HTML element, `<a>`, with an embedded image HTML element, `<img>`, to display the image on the Web page.

The **Calendar** Control

The `Calendar` Web server control displays a calendar on the Web page. It allows you to select a day, a week, a month, or even a range of days. You can customize the appearance of the control and even add custom content for each day. The control generates events when a selection changes or when the visible month is changed in the `Calendar` control. The `Calendar` control is rendered as a `<table>` HTML element on the Web page.

Tables 3.11 and 3.12 summarize the important properties and events of the `Calendar` class, respectively.

Table 3.11 Important Properties of the Calendar Class	
Properties	**Description**
CellPadding	Specifies the distance in pixels between the border and the contents of a cell in the **Calendar** control.
CellSpacing	Specifies the width in pixels between the cells of the **Calendar** control.
DayHeaderStyle	Specifies the style properties of the section where the days of the week are displayed. Works only if the **ShowDayHeader** property is **True**.
DayNameFormat	Specifies the name format for the days of the week.
DayStyle	Specifies the style properties of the section where the days of the displayed month are displayed.
FirstDayOfWeek	Specifies the day of the week to be displayed in the first column of the **Calendar** control.
NextMonthText	Specifies the text for the navigational element to select the next month. The default value is **>**, the HTML code for the greater-than (>) sign. Works only if the **ShowNextPrevMonth** property is **True**.
NextPrevFormat	Specifies the text format for the navigational elements that select the previous and next months on the **Calendar** control.
NextPrevStyle	Specifies the style properties for the next and previous navigational elements. Works only if the **ShowNextPrevMonth** property is **True**.
OtherMonthDayStyle	Specifies the style properties for the days that do not belong to the displayed month.
PrevMonthText	Specifies the text for the navigational element to select the previous month. The default value is **<**, the HTML code for the less-than (<) sign. Works only if the **ShowNextPrevMonth** property is **True**.

(continued)

Table 3.11 Important Properties of the Calendar Class *(continued)*	
Properties	**Description**
SelectedDate	Specifies the selected date.
SelectedDates	Specifies a collection of selected dates.
SelectedDayStyle	Specifies the style properties for the selected day in the **Calendar** control.
SelectionMode	Specifies the mode of selection in the calendar.
SelectMonthText	Specifies the text for the month selection element in the selector column. The default value is **>>**. Works only if the **SelectionMode** property is **DayWeekMonth**.
SelectorStyle	Specifies the style properties for the week and month selector column. Works only if the **SelectionMode** property is **DayWeek** or **DayWeekMonth**.
SelectWeekText	Specifies the text for the week selection element in the selector column. The default value is **>**. Works only if the **SelectionMode** property is **DayWeek** or **DayWeekMonth**.
ShowDayHeader	Indicates whether the row showing the name of the day of the week should be displayed. The default is **True**.
ShowGridLines	Indicates whether the cells of the **Calendar** control should be separated with grid lines. The default is **False**.
ShowNextPrevMonth	Indicates whether the navigational elements for the next and previous month should be displayed. The default is **True**.
ShowTitle	Indicates whether to show the title of the **Calendar** control.
TitleFormat	Specifies the format of the title of the **Calendar** control. Values are specified by the **TitleFormat** enumeration—**Month** and **MonthYear** (default). Works only if the **ShowTitle** property is **True**.
TitleStyle	Specifies the style properties for the title of the **Calendar** control. Works only if the **ShowTitle** property is **True**.
TodayDayStyle	Specifies the style properties for today's date in the calendar control.
TodaysDate	Specifies today's date. The default is picked up from the system.
VisibleDate	Specifies the month to be displayed on the calendar depending on the value of this property.
WeekendDayStyle	Specifies the style properties for the weekend days in the **Calendar** control.

Table 3.12 Important Events of the Calendar Class	
Event	Description
DayRender	Occurs when each day is created in the **Calendar** control. This event occurs after the control is created but before it is rendered to the Web page.
SelectionChanged	Occurs when the user changes the selection in the **Calendar** control. **SelectionChanged** is the default event for the **Calendar** control.
VisibleMonthChanged	Occurs when the month selection is changed when the user clicks the previous or next month navigational elements.

User Input Validation

ASP.NET provides a set of Web server controls called validation controls. These controls provide sophisticated validation on both the client side and the server side depending on the validation settings and the browser capability.

The client-side validation provided by ASP.NET validation controls works only with Internet Explorer 4.0 or higher.

ASP.NET ensures that validations are performed on the server side even if they were already performed at the client side. This ensures that validations are not bypassed if a malicious user tries to circumvent the client-side validation. Of course, if the client-side validation fails, the server-side validation is never performed.

The validation controls are usually associated with input server controls on which the validation needs to be performed. For validation to work properly, the validation control and the input server control must be placed in the same container control.

All the validation controls derive their basic functionality from the BaseValidator abstract class available in the System.Web.UI.WebControls namespace. Table 3.13 lists some of the important members of the BaseValidator class that are inherited by the validation controls.

Table 3.13	Important Members of the BaseValidator Class	
Member	**Type**	**Description**
ControlToValidate	Property	Specifies the **id** of the input server control that needs to be validated.
Display	Property	Specifies how to display the inline error message contained in the **Text** property. It can be any of the **ValidatorDisplay** values—**Dynamic** (the space is dynamically added), **None** (the message is never displayed), and **Static** (the space is occupied when the validation control is rendered).
EnableClientScript	Property	Indicates whether the client-side validation is enabled. The default is **True**.
Enabled	Property	Indicates whether the validation control is enabled. If **False**, the validation is never performed.
ErrorMessage	Property	Represents the error message to be displayed when the validation fails by the **ValidationSummary** control. If the **Text** property is not set, this message is displayed inline.
ForeColor	Property	Specifies the foreground color in which the message is displayed when the validation fails. The default value is **Color.Red**.
IsValid	Property	Indicates whether the input control passes the validation.
Text	Property	Specifies the text of the error message that is displayed by the validation control inline.
Validate	Method	Performs the validation on the associated input control, and then updates the **IsValid** property with the result of validation.

Each validation control maintains an `IsValid` property that indicates the status of the validation test. The Page control that hosts all the Web controls also contains a property called `IsValid` that indicates the status of the validation for the whole page. When each validation control on the Web Form sets its `IsValid` property to `True`, the `Page.IsValid` property also becomes `True`. If any control has its `IsValid` property set to `False`, `Page.IsValid` will also return `False`.

ASP.NET provides five validation controls that derive their functionality from the `BaseValidator` class:

➤ `RequiredFieldValidator`—Ensures that the data is not empty in the input control.

➤ RegularExpressionValidator—Ensures that the data in the input control matches a specific pattern.

➤ RangeValidator—Ensures that the data is within a specific range in the input control.

➤ CompareValidator—Compares the data against a given value.

➤ CustomValidator—Uses custom logic to validate data.

You can associate any number of validation controls with a single input server control. For example, the Date of Hire input field in an Add Employee form cannot be left empty (validated through the RequiredFieldValidator control) and should be less or equal to the current date (validated through the CompareValidator control) .

The **RequiredFieldValidator** Control

The RequiredFieldValidator control can be used to check whether the input control contains an entry. It makes the associated input control a required field in the Web page and ensures that some input data is passed to it. The control also trims whitespace in order to check for the required field entry.

The RequiredFieldValidator control contains a special property called InitialValue that can be passed the initial value of the associated input control. During validation, if the input control's validation property contains the same initial value or is empty, it sets the IsValid property to False, indicating that the validation failed. For example, a drop-down list may allow users to select a state. When the page loads, the initial value in this control might be *Select a State.* If a RequiredFieldValidator control is associated with the drop-down list control, its InitialValue property can be set to the same initial value as the drop-down list, *Select a State.* When the validation occurs, the validation control will ensure that the item selected in the drop-down list is not the item set in the InitialValue property of the validation control.

The **RegularExpressionValidator** Control

The RegularExpressionValidator control checks whether the associated input control's validation property matches a specified pattern. This pattern is specified by the ValidationExpression property using a regular expression. If you're not familiar with regular expressions, you can find more information in the .NET Framework documentation.

The RangeValidator Control

The RangeValidator control is used to check whether the input control contains a value in a specified range. You can check the range of values against different data types such as String, Date, and Integer.

Table 3.14 shows the important properties of the RangeValidator class.

Table 3.14	Important Properties of the RangeValidator Class
Property	**Description**
MaximumValue	Specifies the upper value of the validation range.
MinimumValue	Specifies the lower value of the validation range.
Type	Specifies the data type to be used when comparing the data.

The CompareValidator Control

The CompareValidator control is used to compare the input server control's value against another value. The CompareValidator control can compare against a value specified to the validator control or against the value of another input control. The comparison can be made with different comparison operators such as equal, greater than, and so on. A special comparison operation can be made to verify that the associated input control's value is of a specified data type. You can make comparisons against different data types such as String, Date, and Integer.

Table 3.15 shows the important properties of the CompareValidator class.

Table 3.15	Important Properties of the CompareValidator Class
Property	**Description**
ControlToCompare	Specifies the input server control against whose value the associated input control is to be validated.
Operator	Specifies the comparison operation to be performed.
Type	Specifies the data type to be used when comparing the data.
ValueToCompare	Specifies the value against which the associated input control is to be validated.

The CustomValidator Control

The validation controls discussed allow you to handle many different types of validations. However, you might want to perform a validation that cannot be achieved by any of these validation controls. The CustomValidator control allows you to build a validation control for a custom specification. You can perform any custom validation both at the server-side and client-side with the help of this validation control.

The validation control exposes a property called ClientValidationFunction that specifies the name of the client script function to be executed for validation on the client side. This custom validation function will be passed two arguments—the first is the custom validator control, and the second argument is an object containing two properties: IsValid and Value. The Value property contains the value that is to be validated and IsValid property is used to return the result of the validation.

At the server side, during the validation on the server, the validation control fires a ServerValidate event. An event handler containing the custom validation code is added to this event to perform validation on the server. The event sends a ServerValidateEventArgs object containing event-related data. This object contains two properties—IsValid and Value. The Value property contains the value of the control that is to be validated, and the IsValid property is used to set the result of the validation.

The **ValidationSummary** Control

As the name implies, the ValidationSummary control is used to display a summary of all the validation errors on a Web page. It displays the ErrorMessage property of the validation controls in the summary. If the ErrorMessage property is not set, the Text property is displayed as error messages for all the validation controls whose validation fails.

Table 3.16 shows the important properties of the ValidationSummary class.

Table 3.16 Important Properties of the ValidationSummary Class	
Property	**Description**
DisplayMode	Specifies the way in which the validation summary will be displayed.
EnableClientScript	Indicates whether the client-side validation is enabled. The default is **True**.
ForeColor	Specifies the foreground color in which the message is displayed when the validation fails. The default value is **Color.Red**.
HeaderText	Specifies the header text of the validation summary control.
ShowMessageBox	Indicates whether the validation summary messages should be displayed in a message box. The default is **False**.
ShowSummary	Indicates whether the validation summary messages should be displayed inline in the validation summary control. The default is **True**.

Cascading Style Sheets

A cascading style sheet (CSS) contains style definitions that are applied to elements in an HTML document. The information inside a CSS defines how HTML elements are displayed and where they are positioned on a Web page. CSS makes it easy to achieve a uniform look and feel across your Web application.

Both HTML server controls and Web server controls provide first-class support for CSS styles. In addition to this, Visual Studio .NET provides GUI-based style-editing tools, which makes it easy to work with CSS files.

 CSS is generally only supported by Web browsers that support HTML 4.0 or higher. Older Web browsers that support only HTML 3.2 or earlier simply ignore CSS styles.

When you create a Web application using Visual Basic .NET, Visual Studio .NET automatically creates a default style sheet named Styles.css for your Web application. You can also add additional style sheets for specific documents. You can modify the built-in styles or add new styles that are then associated with particular controls and elements.

To see how Visual Studio .NET lets you work with cascading style sheets, follow these steps:

1. Add a new Web Form to your Web Application.

2. Add a `Label` control and a `TextBox` control to the Web Form.

3. Type some text in the `Text` property of the `Label` control. Set the `CssClass` property of the `Label` control to `MyLabelClass` and set the `CssClass` property of the `TextBox` control to `MyTextBoxClass`.

4. Switch to the HTML view of the Web Form and add the following code inside of the HTML `<HEAD>` element:

```
<LINK href="Styles.css"
type="text/css" rel="stylesheet">
```

5. Double-click the `Styles.css` file in Solution Explorer to open it. Then click the CSS Outline tab at the bottom of the Toolbox.

6. In the Style Sheet Outline in the Toolbox, right-click on the Classes folder, and select Add Style Rule.

7. In the Add Style Rule dialog box, select the Class Name radio button. Enter `MyLabelClass` as the classname and click the > button. Click OK to create the class. Repeat these steps to create the `MyTextBoxClass` style.

8. Locate the code for `MyLabelClass` in the `Styles.css` file. Right-click inside this code and select Build Style. This will open the Style Builder dialog box, shown in Figure 3.1.

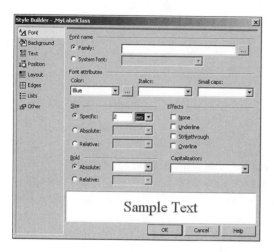

Figure 3.1   The Style Builder dialog box.

9. In the Style Builder dialog box, set the font color to Blue and set the size to 2 em. Click OK to create the style.

10. Locate the code for `MyTextBoxClass`. Right-click inside this code and select Build Style.

11. Select the Background tab and set the background color to Lime. Select the Text tab and set the horizontal alignment to Right. Click OK.

12. Set the Web Form as the start form for the project.

13. Run the project. You'll see your font and color choices applied to the controls on the Web Form.

Exam Prep Questions

Question 1

> You are designing a new page for your ASP.NET Web Application from scratch.
> The page will display statistical information in a series of tables and text fields,
> but will not require any user input. The page will carry out complex calculations
> to determine the validity of the information that it displays. Which controls
> should you use to build the user interface for this page?
>
> ○ A. HTML controls
>
> ○ B. HTML server controls
>
> ○ C. Web server controls
>
> ○ D. Validation controls

Answer C is correct. Web server controls are designed for easy programmability on ASP.NET pages. Answer A is incorrect because you can't use codebehind to easily specify the values to display in HTML controls. Answer B is incorrect because HTML server controls are mainly used to upgrade existing ASP pages, not to create new pages. Answer D is incorrect because validation controls are only useful when there is user input to validate.

Question 2

> You have developed an ASP.NET Web Form that allows users to select from a
> list of replacement parts to order. The Web Form uses the following code to load
> the list into a control:
>
> ```
> Private Sub Page_Load(ByVal sender As System.Object, _
>   ByVal e As System.EventArgs) Handles MyBase.Load
>     lbParts.Items.Add("Flange")
>     lbParts.Items.Add("Motor")
>     lbParts.Items.Add("Bracket")
> End Sub
> ```
>
> As users select parts, you execute code on the Web server to move the select-
> ed parts to a second list. Users report that the page initially displays correctly,
> but after they select one part, the original list reads as follows:
>
> ```
> Flange
> Motor
> Bracket
> Flange
> Motor
> Bracket
> ```
>
> How should you modify the code to prevent this from happening?

○ A.

```
Private Sub Page_Load(ByVal sender As System.Object, _
ByVal e As System.EventArgs) Handles MyBase.Load
    If lbParts.Items.Count < 3 Then
        lbParts.Items.Add("Flange")
        lbParts.Items.Add("Motor")
        lbParts.Items.Add("Bracket")
    End If
End Sub
```

○ B.

```
Private Sub Page_Load(ByVal sender As System.Object, _
ByVal e As System.EventArgs) Handles MyBase.Load
    If Not IsPostBack Then
        lbParts.Items.Add("Flange")
        lbParts.Items.Add("Motor")
        lbParts.Items.Add("Bracket")
    End If
End Sub
```

○ C.

```
Private Sub Page_Load(ByVal sender As System.Object, _
ByVal e As System.EventArgs) Handles MyBase.Load
    If IsPostBack Then
        lbParts.Items.Add("Flange")
        lbParts.Items.Add("Motor")
        lbParts.Items.Add("Bracket")
    End If
End Sub
```

○ D.

```
Private Sub Page_Load(ByVal sender As System.Object, _
ByVal e As System.EventArgs) Handles MyBase.Load
    lbParts.Items.Clear
    lbParts.Items.Add("Flange")
    lbParts.Items.Add("Motor")
    lbParts.Items.Add("Bracket")
End Sub
```

Answer B is correct. You can use the IsPostBack property to tell whether the page is being loaded for the first time and then only perform initializations on the first load. Answers A and D are incorrect because they will reinitialize the ListBox every time that the page is loaded, slowing down the page rendering. Answer C is incorrect because the postback test should be looking for False, not True.

Question 3

You have designed a Web Form that includes a Panel control named **Panel1**. Under some circumstances, you want to dynamically display a **TextBox** control on this Panel control. Your form includes the following code:

```
Dim txtNew As TextBox = New TextBox
txtNew.ID = "txtNew"
txtNew.Text = "Dynamic TextBox"
```

When you run the code, the form does not display the new **TextBox**. You single-step through the code and verify that these lines are being executed. How should you fix this problem?

○ A.
```
Dim txtNew As TextBox = New TextBox
txtNew.ID = "txtNew"
txtNew.Text = "Dynamic TextBox"
txtNew.Enabled = True
```

○ B.
```
Dim txtNew As TextBox = New TextBox
txtNew.ID = "txtNew"
txtNew.Text = "Dynamic TextBox"
txtNew.Visible = True
```

○ C.
```
Dim txtNew As TextBox = New TextBox
txtNew.ID = "txtNew"
txtNew.Text = "Dynamic TextBox"
Panel1.Controls.Add("txtNew")
```

○ D.
```
Dim txtNew As TextBox = New TextBox
txtNew.ID = "txtNew"
txtNew.Text = "Dynamic TextBox"
Panel1.Controls.Add(txtNew)
```

Answer D is correct. To show a dynamically created control on a Web Form, you must add the new control to the Controls collection of a container control such as a Panel. Answers A and B are incorrect because they alter the properties of the control without adding it to a container. Answer C is incorrect because the Add method requires an object reference, not a String with an object name.

Question 4

You are designing a Web page for your corporate intranet. All the users on the intranet are using either Internet Explorer 5.0 or Internet Explorer 6.0 as their browser. When an employee enters his employee number, you need to validate it as a legitimate employee number so that you can audit actions on the Web site. Which type of validation should you perform, if any?

○ A. You should not validate this data.

○ B. You should only perform client-side validation.

○ C. You should only perform server-side validation.

○ D. You should perform both client-side and server-side validation.

Answer D is correct. You should validate the data in this scenario because the correct data is critical to the application. You should use client-side valida-tion because client-side validation is the fastest way to catch accidental errors in the data and can prevent bad data from reaching the server. However, you should also use server-side validation to eliminate the possibility of someone hand-crafting an HTTP request to bypass the client-side validation.

Question 5

You are designing a new home page for your company, using ASP.NET. The home page will have numerous graphics, including the company logo, images used for navigation, and pictures of your company's graphics. You want to make sure that users who cannot view graphics (for example, those browsing with a screen reader) receive a description of each image instead. Which property of the **Image** control should you set to provide this description?

○ A. **Attributes** property

○ B. **ToolTip** property

○ C. **AlternateText** property

○ D. **ImageUrl** property

Answer C is correct. The `AlternateText` property of an `Image` control supplies text that is used by screen readers and by other browsers when an image can-not be displayed. Answer A is incorrect because the `Attributes` property returns an array of attributes of the control. Answer B is incorrect because the `ToolTip` property only supplies text to be seen when the mouse is hovered over the control. Answer D is incorrect because the `ImageUrl` property tells the control which image to display.

Question 6

You are designing a Web Form that will allow the user to specify a date for a dental appointment. You want to allow the user to specify a date by choosing it from a calendar. The users of the application employ a wide variety of Web browsers, including Internet Explorer versions 3.2 through 6.0 and Netscape versions 4.79 through 7.0. How should you proceed to create this page with the least effort?

○ A. Work directly in HTML view of your Web form. Design the calendar using HTML tags.

○ B. Work in Design view of the Web form. Design the calendar by using the **Table**, **TableRow**, and **TableCell** Web server controls.

○ C. Work in Design view of the Web form. Design the calendar by using a single **Calendar** control.

○ D. Work in the code-behind file. Design the calendar by dynamically adding HTML controls to the Web Form at runtime.

Answer C is correct. ASP.NET will render complex controls such as the Calendar control properly for both uplevel and downlevel browsers by detecting the browser and sending the appropriate HTML markup. Answers A, B, and D are incorrect because they all require substantially more work than using a single Calendar control.

Question 7

Your company has an existing classic ASP application that is used to track news on your intranet. You have been tasked with upgrading the application to ASP.NET. As a first step, you want to keep the user interface the same, but move the business logic to code-behind files. How should you proceed?

○ A. Continue to use HTML controls on ASP.NET Web Forms. In the code-behind files, rewrite all business logic using Visual Basic .NET.

○ B. Use ASP.NET Web server controls instead of HTML controls. In the code-behind files, rewrite all business logic using Visual Basic .NET.

○ C. Apply the **runat="server"** attribute to all HTML controls. In the code-behind files, rewrite all business logic using Visual Basic .NET.

○ D. Continue to use HTML controls for labels and textboxes, but convert all button controls to Web server controls. In the code-behind files, rewrite all business logic using Visual Basic .NET.

Answer C is correct. Applying the runat="server" attribute is the only step required to make the controls on the page available to code in a code-behind file. Answers A and D are incorrect because you cannot use code-behind files to manipulate HTML controls. Answer B is incorrect because there is no built-in way to directly convert HTML controls to Web server controls.

Question 8

You are designing a Web Form that includes four **RadioButton** controls named **rb1**, **rb2**, **rb3**, and **rb4**. Users should be able to select either **rb1** or **rb2**, and either **rb3** or **rb4**. How should you configure the controls to achieve this?

- ○ A. Place **rb1** and **rb2** on a **Panel** control named **pnlA**. Place **rb3** and **rb4** on a **Panel** control named **pnlB**.
- ○ B. Set the **GroupName** property of **rb1** and **rb2** to "**Group1**". Set the **GroupName** property of **rb3** and **rb4** to "**Group2**".
- ○ C. Set the **Parent** property of **rb2** to **rb1**. Set the **Parent** property of **rb4** to **rb3**.
- ○ D. Set the **AutoPostBack** property of **rb1** and **rb3** to **True**. Set the **AutoPostBack** property of **rb2** and **rb4** to **False**.

Answer B is correct. RadioButton controls that share a GroupName are mutually exclusive. Answer A is incorrect because placing the controls on different panels organizes them visually, but does not put them in distinct groups. Answer C is incorrect because the Parent property is just a link to the form containing the controls. Answer D is incorrect because AutoPostBack indicates whether the Web Form should be posted when the control is clicked.

Question 9

You want to keep consistent formatting for all the Web Forms in your application. To achieve this, you have created a cascading style sheet named **CompanyStyle.css** and have linked it to all the Web pages. You have defined a style class named **ButtonStyle** in **CompanyStyle.css** to format buttons on the Web Forms. Which of the following property settings would you use with a Button Web server control to use the **ButtonStyle** style class?

- ○ A. **Style="ButtonStyle"**
- ○ B. **Style=".ButtonStyle"**
- ○ C. **CssClass="ButtonStyle"**
- ○ D. **CssClass=".ButtonStyle"**

Answer C is correct. The CssClass property specifies the CSS style class to apply to a particular control. Answers A and B are incorrect because the style property is used to supply CSS attributes directly, rather than the name of a CSS style. Answers B and D are incorrect because styles are referred to without the leading dot, even though you must use the dot when defining them in a CSS file.

Question 10

You are designing a Web Form to collect user registration information for your corporate Web site. You want to ensure that users supply a value for the Age **TextBox** control and that the value supplied is between 18 and 105. Which validation control should you use (select all that apply)?

- ❑ A. RequiredFieldValidator
- ❑ B. RangeValidator
- ❑ C. RegularExpressionValidator
- ❑ D. CustomValidator

Answers A and B are correct. You can use the RequiredFieldValidator control to ensure that the user enters a value and the RangeValidator control to check that the value is in the correct range. Although you could use the RegularExpressionValidator or CustomValidator controls to check the range, doing so would require you to write a complex regular expression or custom business logic, so answers C and D are incorrect.

Question 11

Your Web Form displays a list of State names in a **DropDownList** control. As soon as the user selects a state, you want to update a **Label** control to display the appropriate sales tax rate. You have written custom logic to do so in the **SelectedIndexChanged** event handler for the control. What property should you set to ensure that this event is handled at the correct time?

- ○ A. EnableViewState = True
- ○ B. AutoPostBack = False
- ○ C. EnableViewState = False
- ○ D. AutoPostBack = True

Answer D is correct. By default, selection change events for list controls are not sent to the server until the Web Form is posted by some other means (for example, by the user clicking a Submit button). Setting the AutoPostBack property to True causes the postback to happen as soon as a new item is selected in the list. Answer B is incorrect because it uses the wrong AutoPostBack value. Answers A and C are incorrect because the EnableViewState property has no effect on the timing of postbacks.

Question 12

Your Web Form requires the user to enter an email address. Which control should you use to validate the contents of the **TextBox** containing the email address?

○ A. RequiredFieldValidator

○ B. RegularExpressionValidator

○ C. RangeValidator

○ D. CustomValidator

Answer B is correct. The RegularExpressionValidator control is suited to checking input that conforms to a particular pattern such as a date or an email address (and .NET has a built-in expression for email addresses). Answer A is incorrect because the RequiredFieldValidator ensures that data was entered, but does not check the contents of the data. Answer C is incorrect because the RangeValidator checks to see that data is between a pair of values. Answer D is incorrect because the CustomValidator requires you to write extra code to perform the same tasks that the RegularExpressionValidator has built in.

Need to Know More?

 Liberty, Jesse and Hurwitz, Dan. *Programming ASP.NET.* O'Reilly, 2002.

 Duthie, G. Andrew and MacDonald, Matthew. *ASP.NET in a Nutshell.* O'Reilly, 2002.

 The .NET Framework Community Web site, www.gotdotnet.com.

Implementing Navigation for the User Interface

Terms you'll need to understand:

✓ Postback

✓ Round-trip

✓ **Response** object

✓ **Request** object

✓ **Session** object

✓ **Server** object

✓ **Application** object

✓ ASP.NET application

Techniques you'll need to master:

✓ Managing data during postback events with **ViewState**

✓ Managing data across pages with session state

✓ Using the intrinsic ASP.NET objects, including **Response**, **Request**, **Session**, **Server**, and **Application**

ASP.NET offers a lot of help for the Web application developer. In this chapter, I look at some of the scaffolding that ASP.NET puts into place to help you. This includes state management features (which help mask the fact that HTTP is an inherently stateless protocol) and some of the intrinsic objects that you can use in your ASP.NET code.

Round-Trip and Postback

A typical interactive user session with a Web Form consists of the following steps:

1. The user requests a Web Form from the Web server.

2. The Web server responds back with the requested Web Form.

3. The user enters the data and submits the form to the Web server.

4. The Web server processes the form, and sends the result back to the user.

Step 3, when the user enters the data and submits the form to the Web server, is also referred to as a *page postback*.

Web applications use the HTTP protocol to establish communication between the Web browser and the Web server. The HTTP protocol is stateless. Every time a Web server responds to a page request, it creates the page, sends the page to the requesting client, and then discards the page. The values of page variables and controls are not preserved between page requests.

This model of execution allows a Web server to support a large number of clients because each client request occupies the server resources only for a short duration. However, the disconnected nature of the HTTP protocol provides major challenges to the Web developer. It is difficult to implement the following functionality in Web applications:

➤ Maintain values of controls and variables across page postbacks.

➤ Distinguish the initial request of a page from the page postback.

➤ Provide smart navigation features similar to those of desktop applications.

ASP.NET provides solutions to these problems built right into its framework. By sending and retrieving hidden data in pages, ASP.NET can make it appear as if HTTP is a stateful protocol—that is, one in which pages (and the objects and values that they contain) persist across multiple round-trips between the client and the server.

The **IsPostBack** Property

The IsPostBack property of the Page class returns True when a page is being loaded in response to a client postback. If the page is being requested for the first time (that is, if you've requested the page by navigating to its URL, or by following a link), the value of the IsPostBack property is False.

IsPostBack is useful any time there are one-time initializations for a Web Form. For example, you might like to add some items to a ListBox control the first time that a page is loaded. You could code that this way:

```
Private Sub Page_Load( _
 ByVal sender As System.Object, _
 ByVal e As System.EventArgs) Handles MyBase.Load
    If Not IsPostBack Then
        ListBox1.Items.Add("First Item")
        ListBox1.Items.Add("Second Item")
        ListBox1.Items.Add("Third Item")
    End If
End Sub
```

The **SmartNavigation** Property

ASP.NET has a feature called *smart navigation* that can greatly enhance the user experience of a Web page for the users of Internet Explorer 5.0 or higher browsers. The following list summarizes the enhancements provided by smart navigation:

➤ **Persisting element focus between postbacks**—When a postback occurs, the active control on the Web page loses its focus. Smart navigation prevents this.

➤ **Persisting scroll position between postbacks**—When a postback occurs, the browser loses the record of the scroll position of the page. Smart navigation preserves the scroll position.

➤ **Eliminates page flash caused by page postback**—When users navigate from one page to another, the old page is destroyed and the new one is created on a blank screen. When smart navigation is enabled, ASP.NET uses a technique called double buffering to eliminate the potential onscreen flash.

➤ **Prevents each postback from being saved in the browser history**—Normally, every postback to an ASP.NET page causes an entry to be created in the browser's history. This defeats the purpose of the browser's back button because instead of going back to the previous page, users are taken to the previous state of the current page. Smart navigation prevents this from happening by saving only the latest state of the current page in the browser's history.

NOTE Because smart navigation is limited to recent Internet Explorer versions, it's generally only useful in intranet scenarios. For Internet applications, you can't be sure that any given visitor will see the benefits of smart navigation.

Smart navigation is specified by the SmartNavigation property of the Page class. The default value of this property is False, thereby disabling smart navigation for the Web Form.

You can set the SmartNavigation property to True through the @Page directive on a Web page:

```
<%@ Page Language="vb" AutoEventWireup="false"
Codebehind="MyPage.aspx.vb"
Inherits="MyProject.MyPage"
SmartNavigation="true"%>
```

You can also turn on smart navigation for the complete Web application instead of individual files by adding a directive to the application's Web.config file:

```
<configuration>
    <system.web>
        <pages smartNavigation="true"/>
    </system.web>
</configuration>
```

ASP.NET Intrinsic Objects

ASP.NET provides intrinsic objects to enable low-level access to the Web application framework. With the help of these intrinsic objects, you can work directly with the underlying HTTP streams, server, session, and application objects. These intrinsic objects can be accessed in a Web Form through the properties of the Page class. Table 4.1 lists the important intrinsic objects and the properties of the Page class to which they are mapped.

Table 4.1 Intrinsic Objects and Their Mappings to the Page Class Properties	
Intrinsic Object	**Property of the Page Class**
HttpRequest	Request
HttpResponse	Response
HttpServerUtility	Server
HttpApplicationState	Application
HttpSessionState	Session

I discuss the HttpRequest, HttpResponse, and HttpServerUtility objects in the following sections. The other two objects, HttpApplicationState and HttpSessionState, are discussed later in this chapter in the "State Management" section.

The HttpRequest Object

The HttpRequest object (available through the Request property of the Page class) represents the incoming request from the client to the Web server. Tables 4.2 and 4.3 list the properties and methods of the HttpRequest class. Because the HttpRequest class provides information about the request sent by the client, all the properties are read-only except the Filter property.

Table 4.2 Properties of the HttpRequest Class	
Property	**Description**
AcceptTypes	Specifies the MIME types that the client browser accepts.
ApplicationPath	Represents the application's virtual application root path on the server.
Browser	Provides access to the capabilities and characteristics of the requesting browser.
ClientCertificate	Represents the certificate, if any, sent by the client for secure communications.
ContentEncoding	Represents the character encoding (such as UTF7 or ASCII) for the entity body.
ContentLength	Specifies the length in bytes of the request.
ContentType	Specifies the MIME type of the incoming request.
Cookies	Represents the cookies collection that is sent by the client to the server.
CurrentExecutionFilePath	Specifies the virtual path of the current executing page on the Web server.
FilePath	Specifies the virtual path of the file on the Web server.
Files	Represents the file collection that is posted by the client to the Web server.
Filter	Represents a stream that is applied as a filter on the incoming request.
Form	Specifies the contents of a form posted to the server.
Headers	Represents the HTTP headers passed in with the incoming request.

(continued)

Table 4.2   Properties of the HttpRequest Class *(continued)*

Property	Description
HttpMethod	Represents the method of the HTTP request—for example, **GET**, **POST**, or **HEAD**.
InputStream	Represents the stream that contains the incoming HTTP request body.
IsAuthenticated	Indicates whether the client has been authenticated to the site.
IsSecureConnection	Indicates whether the client connection is over an HTTPS (Secure Hypertext Transfer Protocol) connection.
Params	Represents the form, query string, cookies, and server variables collections of the current request.
Path	Specifies the virtual path of the current request along with additional path information.
PathInfo	Specifies the additional path information of the current request.
PhysicalApplicationPath	Specifies the physical file system path of the application's root directory.
PhysicalPath	Specifies the physical file system path of the current request on the Web server.
QueryString	Represents the querystring collection sent by the client to the Web server through the URL.
RawUrl	Specifies the URL portion of the current request excluding the domain information.
RequestType	Represents the type of request (**GET** or **POST**) made by the client.
ServerVariables	Represents the collection of Web server variables.
TotalBytes	Represents the total number of bytes posted to the server in the current request.
Url	Specifies information about the current URL request.
UrlReferrer	Specifies the URL of the client's previous request that linked to the current URL.
UserAgent	Represents the browser being used by the client.
UserHostAddress	Represents the IP address of the requesting client's machine.
UserHostName	Represents the DNS name of the requesting client's machine.
UserLanguages	Specifies the languages preferred by the client's browser.

The **CurrentExecutionFilePath** property of the **HttpRequest** class returns the file path of the currently executing page. When using the server-side redirection methods—such as **Server.Execute()** and **Server.Transfer()**—the **FilePath** property returns the path to the original page, whereas the **CurrentExecutionFilePath** returns the path to the redirected page.

Table 4.3 Methods of the HttpRequest Class	
Method	**Description**
BinaryRead()	Reads the specified number of bytes from the request stream. This method is provided for backward compatibility. You should use the **InputStream** property instead.
MapImageCoordinates()	Returns the coordinates of a form image that is sent to the server in the current request.
MapPath()	Returns the physical file system path of the file or folder for a specified virtual path of a Web server.
SaveAs()	Saves the current HTTP request to a disk file, with an option to include or exclude headers.

One of the most useful HttpRequest methods for many applications is the MapPath method, which allows you to retrieve (in your server-side code) the actual filename for a Web page. Here's an example of using the MapPath method:

```
Private Sub Page_Load( _
 ByVal sender As System.Object, _
 ByVal e As System.EventArgs) Handles MyBase.Load
    lblInfo.Text = Request.MapPath("MyPage.html")
End Sub
```

Note that the parameter for Request.MapPath can be either an absolute or relative page name. This particular example displays the physical location of a file named MyPage.html, assuming that it exists in the current virtual root.

The **HttpResponse** Object

The HttpResponse object represents the response sent back to the client from the Web server. The Response property of the Page class provides access to the HttpResponse object. Tables 4.4 and 4.5 list the properties and methods of the HttpResponse class.

Table 4.4 Properties of the HttpResponse Class

Property	Description
Buffer	Indicates whether the output to the response stream needs to be buffered and sent to the client after the entire page is processed. This property is provided for backward compatibility. The **BufferOutput** property should be used instead.
BufferOutput	Indicates whether the output to the response stream needs to be buffered and then sent to the client after the entire page is processed. The default is **True**.
Cache	Represents the caching policy of the page. The policy controls where caching can be done, the expiration time, and so on.
CacheControl	Specifies where the caching should be done. The possible values are **Public** and **Private**.
Charset	Represents the character set of the output stream. If set to null, the content-type header will be suppressed.
ContentEncoding	Represents the character set of the response output stream.
ContentType	Represents the MIME type for the outgoing response stream, such as **text/html** or **text/xml**.
Cookies	Represents the cookies collection that is sent by the server to the client.
Expires	Indicates the number of minutes until the page is cached by the client browser.
ExpiresAbsolute	Indicates the specific date and time until the page is cached by the client browser.
Filter	Represents a stream that is applied as a filter to the outgoing response.
IsClientConnected	Indicates whether the client is connected to the server. This property is very helpful when running a lengthy request.
Output	Allows writing text output to the outgoing response.
OutputStream	Allows writing binary output to the outgoing response.
Status	Specifies the status of the HTTP output that is being sent to the client. This property returns both the status code and the text description of the status—for example, **200 OK**.
StatusCode	Specifies the numeric representation of the status of the HTTP output sent to the client—for example, **200** or **302**.
StatusDescription	Specifies the text representation of the status of the HTTP output sent to the client—for example, **OK** or **Redirect**.
SupressContent	Indicates whether the content in the page should be suppressed and not sent to the client.

The **CacheControl**, **Expires**, and **ExpiresAbsolute** properties are provided for backward compatibility. You should instead use the **HttpCachePolicy** object's methods to set caching policy. This object is returned by the **Cache** property. I discuss caching policy in Chapter 16, "Configuring a Web Application."

Table 4.5   Methods of the HttpResponse Class

Method	Description
AddCacheItemDependencies()	Makes the validity of the cache item dependent on the other items in the cache.
AddCacheItemDependency()	Makes the validity of the cache item dependent on another item in the cache.
AddFileDependencies()	Adds a group of files to the collection on which the current response depends.
AddFileDependency()	Adds a file to the collection on which the current response depends.
AddHeader()	Adds an HTTP header to the outgoing response stream. This method is provided for backward compatibility with ASP.
AppendHeader()	Adds an HTTP header to the outgoing response stream.
AppendToLog()	Adds information to the Internet Information Services (IIS) Web log file.
BinaryWrite()	Allows writing binary data such as an image file or an Adobe Acrobat file to the response stream.
Clear()	Clears the entire response stream buffer, including its contents and headers.
ClearContent()	Clears the entire content portion of the response stream buffer.
ClearHeaders()	Clears the headers portion of the response stream buffer.
Close()	Closes the response object and the socket connection to the client.
End()	Stops the execution of the page after flushing the output buffer to the client.
Flush()	Flushes the currently buffered content out to the client.
Pics()	Adds a **PICS-label** HTTP header to the outgoing response.
Redirect()	Redirects the client browser to any URL. This method requires an additional round-trip to the browser.
RemoveOutputCacheItem()	Removes all cache items for the path specified.
Write()	Writes output to the outgoing response.
WriteFile()	Writes a file to the outgoing response.

The **HttpServerUtility** Object

The HttpServerUtility object contains utility methods and properties to work with the Server object. The Server property of the Page class provides access to the HttpServerUtility object. Tables 4.6 and 4.7 list the properties and methods of the HttpServerUtility class.

Table 4.6   Properties of the HttpServerUtility Class

Property	Description
MachineName	Returns the name of the server that hosts the Web application.
ScriptTimeout	Indicates the number of seconds that are allowed to elapse to process the request before a timeout error is sent to the client.

Table 4.7   Methods of the HttpServerUtility Class

Method	Description
ClearError()	Clears the last exception from the memory.
CreateObject()	Creates a COM object on the server.
CreateObjectFromClsid()	Creates a COM object on the server identified by a specified class identifier (CLSID).
Execute()	Executes an ASPX page within the current requested page. This method is discussed later in the chapter.
GetLastError()	Returns the last exception that occurred on the Web server.
HtmlDecode()	Enables decoding a string that has been previously HTML encoded for sending over HTTP to a browser.
HtmlEncode()	Enables HTML encoding a string for sending over HTTP to a browser.
MapPath()	Returns the physical path for a specified virtual path for a Web server.
Transfer()	Allows the transfer of ASPX page execution from the current page to another ASPX page on the same Web server. This method is discussed later in the chapter.
UrlDecode()	Enables decoding a URL string that has been previously HTML encoded for sending over HTTP to a browser.
UrlEncode()	Enables encoding a URL string for safe transmission over HTTP.
UrlPathEncode()	Enables encoding of a path portion of the URL string for safe transmission over HTTP.

ASP.NET Applications

An ASP.NET application is made up of the Web Forms, assemblies, and other files stored within a virtual Web directory marked as an IIS application.

The `HttpApplication` class defines the methods, properties, and events common to all application objects within an ASP.NET application. If you want to customize the behavior of an `HttpApplication` object, you can derive a class from the `HttpApplication` class and override the event handlers of the base class for various application-level events. An easy way to do this is by using the `global.asax` file.

The global.asax File

ASP.NET provides an easy way for application customization through the use of the `global.asax` file. This optional file resides in the root directory of an ASP.NET application. The `global.asax` file defines a class named `Global` that derives from the `HttpApplication` class. ASP.NET creates an instance of the class defined in the `global.asax` file to handle requests for your application. Visual Studio .NET automatically creates a `global.asax` file when you create an ASP.NET Web application project.

 For security reasons, ASP.NET does not allow users to download any file with an extension of **.asax**.

Global Event Handlers

The `global.asax` file is an appropriate place to handle events that are not specific to a Web Form but rather apply to an application as a whole.

Application- and Session-Level Events

Application- and session-level events are fired to signal the start and end of the application or a user session. These events can be handled using event handlers in the `global.asax` file, as shown in Table 4.8.

Table 4.8 Application- and Session-Level Event Handlers in the global.asax File	
Event Handler	**Purpose**
Application_Start()	Called when an application receives its first request.
Application_End()	Called when an application shuts down.

(continued)

Table 4.8   Application- and Session-Level Event Handlers in the global.asax File *(continued)*

Event Handler	Purpose
Session_Start()	Called when an ASP.NET application creates a new session for a user of the application.
Session_End()	Called when the user's session expires. By default, this happens 20 minutes after the last request of a page by a user.

Per-Request Events

Table 4.9 shows the event handlers that are invoked for each individual page request processed by the HttpApplication object.

Table 4.9   Per-Request Event Handlers

Event Handler	Purpose
Application_BeginRequest()	Called at the beginning of each request.
Application_AuthenticateRequest()	Called when a security module has established the identity of the user.
Application_AuthorizeRequest()	Called when a security module has verified user authorization.
Application_ResolveRequestCache()	Called to resolve the current request by providing content from a cache.
Application_AcquireRequestState()	Called to associate the current request with the session state.
Application_PreRequestHandlerExecute()	Called when ASP.NET begins executing a page.
Application_PostRequestHandlerExecute()	Called when ASP.NET finishes executing a page.
Application_ReleaseRequestState()	Called to save the current state data.
Application_UpdateRequestCache()	Called to update a cache with the responses.
Application_EndRequest()	Called at the end of each request.

You can write code in any of these event handlers to modify the default behavior of ASP.NET. For example, you can follow these steps to see the Application_BeginRequest() and Application_EndRequest() methods in action:

1. Open the global.asax file in your Web application. Click the Click here to switch to code view hyperlink to switch to the code view.

2. Add the following code to the `Application_BeginRequest()` event handler:

```
Sub Application_BeginRequest( _
ByVal sender As Object, ByVal e As EventArgs)
    ' Store the begin time of the
    ' request in the HttpContext object
    Me.Context.Items.Add("BeginTime", DateTime.Now)
End Sub
```

3. Add the following code to the `Application_EndRequest()` event handler:

```
Sub Application_EndRequest(ByVal sender As Object, _
ByVal e As System.EventArgs)
    ' Get the begin time from the HttpContext object
    Dim dtBeginTime As DateTime = _
    CType(Me.Context.Items("BeginTime"), DateTime)

    ' Calculate the time span between
    ' the start and end of request
    Dim tsProcessingTime As TimeSpan = _
    DateTime.Now.Subtract(dtBeginTime)

    ' Display the processing
    ' time taken in the response
    Me.Context.Response.Output.Write("<hr>")
    Me.Context.Response.Output.Write( _
      "{0} took {1} milliseconds to execute.", _
      Me.Request.Url, _
      tsProcessingTime.TotalMilliseconds)
End Sub
```

4. Run the project. You should see that the default page shows a message at the bottom indicating the processing time of the request, as shown in Figure 4.1.

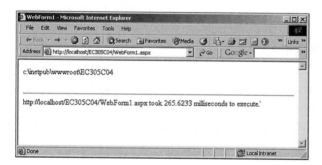

Figure 4.1 The **global.asax** file gives you access to application-level events that affects all the pages in an application.

This modification of the `global.asax` file will affect all Web Forms in the Web application. If you would like to disable the output generated by the global events, just comment the corresponding lines in the `global.asax` file.

State Management

State management is the process of maintaining the state of a Web page across round-trips. For example, if the user fills in a Web Form and clicks a Submit button, you'd probably like to display the information that she filled in if there's a problem. This requires some technique for state persistence.

ASP.NET provides several techniques to preserve state information across page postbacks.

Client-Side Techniques for State Management

Client-side techniques use the HTML code and the capabilities of the Web browser to store state-related information. ASP.NET supports the following techniques for storing state information at the client side: query strings, cookies, hidden fields, and ViewState.

Query Strings

A query string maintains state by appending the state information to a page's URL. The state data is separated from the actual URL with a question mark (?). The data attached to the URL is usually a set of key-value pairs, where each key-value pair is separated using an ampersand (&). For example, here's a URL that embeds two key-value pairs, name and city:

```
http://www.buddy.com/find.aspx?name=Bill+Gates&city=Redmond
```

Because of their simplicity, query strings are widely used for passing small amounts of information to the Web pages. However, query strings suffer from some limitations:

➤ Most browsers restrict the length of the query string to 256 characters; this reduces the amount of data that you can embed to a URL.

➤ Query strings do not provide any support for structured data types.

➤ The information stored in query strings is not secure because these strings are directly visible to the users.

Reading information from a query string in an ASP.NET program is easy. You can use the QueryString property of the current HttpRequest object.

The `QueryString` property returns a `NameValueCollection` object representing the key-value pairs stored in the query string. This makes it easy to pull out a variable from the query string:

```
lblHello.Text = "Hello " & Request.QueryString("Name")
```

Cookies

Cookies are small packets of information, each storing a key-value pair, stored on the client's computer. These packets are associated with a specific domain and are sent along with each request to the associated Web server.

A cookie can be set to expire when a user session ends, or you can request the browser to persist the cookies on the user's computer for a specified period. Cookies are commonly used to store a user's preferences and provide her personalized browsing experience on her repeated visits to a Web page.

Use of cookies suffers from the following limitations:

➤ Most browsers limit the size of information that you can store in a cookie. A typical size is 4,096 bytes with older browser versions and 8,192 bytes with the newer browser versions.

➤ Some users configure their browsers to refuse cookies.

➤ When you request the browser to persist a cookie on the user's computer for a specified period, browsers might override that request by using their own rules for cookie expiration.

➤ Because cookies are stored at the client, they might be tampered with. You cannot trust the data that you receive from a cookie.

To save a cookie, you can create a new `HttpCookie` object, such as this:

```
' Create a cookie called Name
' Set the cookie with the Text of a text box
Dim cName As HttpCookie = New HttpCookie("Name")
cName.Value = txtName.Text
' Set the expiration time of the cookie
' to 15 minutes from the current time
cName.Expires = DateTime.Now.Add( _
  New TimeSpan(0, 0, 15, 0))
' Add the cookie to the response
' cookies collection
' to send it to the client's machine
Response.Cookies.Add(cName)
```

You can use the `Cookies` property of the `HttpRequest` object to get an `HttpCookieCollection` object that represents the cookies sent by the client for the current HTTP request. Here's how you might extract and display a Name cookie:

```
lblHello.Text = "Hello " & Request.Cookies("Name").Value
```

Hidden Fields

Hidden fields contain information that is not visible on the page but is posted to the server along with a page postback. Most browsers support hidden fields on a Web page. However, hidden fields have some limitations:

➤ Although the information stored in a hidden field is not visible on the page, it is still part of the page's HTML code. Users can view them by viewing the HTML source of the page. Hidden fields are therefore not a good choice for storing information that you would like to keep secure.

➤ Hidden fields are part of the HTML for the page. If you store more information in hidden fields, it increases the size of the HTML page, making it slower for users to download.

➤ Hidden fields only allow you to store a single value in a field. If you want to store structured values such as a customer record, you'll have to use several hidden fields or come up with your own encoding standard.

ASP.NET provides an HTML server control, HtmlInputHidden, that maps to the <input type="hidden"> HTML element. You can store values by writing to the Text property of such a field, and later read the stored value back from the same property.

The HtmlInputHidden control is not available as a Web server control. This is mainly because ASP.NET uses a similar but more powerful technique called ViewState.

ViewState

ViewState is the mechanism that ASP.NET uses to maintain the state of controls (such as the text in a TextBox control) across page postbacks. Just like hidden fields and cookies, you can also use ViewState to maintain state for non-control values in a page. You must keep in mind that ViewState works only when a page is posted back to itself. This is the default ASP.NET architecture.

Some server controls such as TextBox or CheckBox post their values as part of the postback operation. These types of controls are known as the postback controls. For postback controls, ASP.NET retrieves their values one-by-one from the HTTP Request and copies them to the control values while creating the HTTP response. Traditionally, Web developers had to write this code manually to maintain state for postback controls, but now ASP.NET does this automatically.

ViewState does not require any additional storage (outside of the Web page) either on the client side or on the server side for maintaining state for postback controls.

In addition to the postback controls, the `ViewState` mechanism of ASP.NET also manages to retain values for non-postback controls (that is, the controls that do not post their values as part of the postback operation, such as `Label` controls). When ASP.NET executes a page, it collects the value of all non-postback controls that are modified in the code and formats them into a single base64-encoded string. This string is then stored in a hidden field in a control named `_VIEWSTATE`. This hidden input field is a postback control, so in the next postback of the page, the encoded string stored in the `_VIEWSTATE` field is also posted. At the Web server, ASP.NET decodes the `ViewState` string at page initialization and restores the controls values in the page.

Maintaining state using this technique does not require many server resources, but it definitely increases the size of the HTML file—therefore increasing the amount of time it takes to load the page.

The `ViewState` property of the `Page` class is a great place to store page-level values. `ViewState` will save these values just prior to rendering that page and restore the values at the time of page initialization after the postback operation. This might sound similar to a cookie or hidden field, but a major improvement is that you are not limited to storing simple values. You can use `ViewState` to store any object as long as it is serializable.

A good practice is to expose a page level value as a property that internally manipulates the `ViewState` of the page, as in this example:

```
Protected Property MyName() As String
    Get
        If ViewState("MyName") Is Nothing Then
            ' The MyName key is not
            ' present in the ViewState
            MyName = 0
        Else
            ' Retrieve the MyName value
            ' from the ViewState
            Return Convert.ToString( _
            ViewState("MyName"))
        End If
    End Get
    Set(ByVal Value As String)
        ' Set the MyName in the ViewState
        ViewState("MyName") = Value
    End Set
End Property
```

You can then refer to this property from other code on the page:

```
lblHello.Text = "Hello " & MyName
```

Disabling **ViewState**

By default, `ViewState` is enabled in an ASP.NET application. But `ViewState` can increase the size of HTML for a Web page. This is especially important when your application contains complex controls such as `DataList` or `DataGrid`. To optimize a Web page size, you might want to disable `ViewState` in the following cases:

➤ When a page does not postback to itself

➤ When there are no dynamically set control properties

➤ When the dynamic properties are set with each request of the page

ASP.NET provides you complete flexibility to disable `ViewState` at various levels:

➤ **At the level of a control**—If you populate the control's state on each request, you may disable `ViewState` at the control level by setting the `EnableViewState` property of the control to `false`:

```
<asp:DataGrid EnableViewState="false" .../>
```

➤ **At the level of a page**—If the page doesn't post back to itself, you may disable `ViewState` at the page level by setting the `EnableViewState` attribute of the `@Page` directive to `false` in the ASPX file:

```
<%@Page EnableViewState="false" %>
```

➤ **At the level of an application**—If no page in an application posts back to itself, you may disable `ViewState` at the application level by adding the following line to the `Web.config` file:

```
<Pages enableViewState="false"/>
```

➤ **At the level of the machine**—In the unlikely case in which you want to disable `ViewState` for all the applications running on a Web server, you can do so by adding the following statement to the `machine.config` file:

```
<Pages enableViewState="false"/>
```

It's good practice to disable **ViewState** when you don't need it. This will improve the response time of your application.

Protecting **ViewState**

By default, the `ViewState` of a page is not protected. Although the values are not directly visible—as in the case of query string or hidden variables—it is not difficult for determined users to decode the storage format.

However, with a few configuration changes, ASP.NET allows you to store ViewState in a much more secure way. ASP.NET provides two ways to increase the security of ViewState:

> ➤ **Tamper-proofing** ViewState—Tamper-proofing does not protect against someone determining the contents of ViewState. It instead provides a way of knowing whether somebody has modified the contents of ViewState to fool your application. Using this technique, ViewState is encoded using a hash code (using the SHA1 or MD5 algorithms) when it is sent to the browser. When the page is posted back, ASP.NET checks the encoded ViewState to verify that it has not been tampered with on the client. This type of check is called machine authentication check (MAC). By default, ASP.NET has the following entry in its machine.config file:

```
<pages enableViewStateMac="true" />
```

This enables tamper-proofing for all the applications running on a Web server. You can also manually enable or disable the tamper-proofing check at a page level by setting the EnableViewStateMac attribute of the @Page directive to true or false in the ASPX file:

```
<%@ Page EnableViewStateMac="true"%>
```

> ➤ **Encrypting** ViewState—This technique instructs ASP.NET to encrypt the contents of ViewState using Triple DES symmetric algorithm (3DES), making it extremely difficult for the client to decode ViewState. This kind of encryption can be applied only at the machine level by specifying the following setting in the machine.config file:

```
<machineKey validation="3DES" />
```

NOTE | Running security algorithms puts additional overhead on your Web server and makes applications slower. Therefore, you should enable security for **ViewState** only when it is a must.

Choosing a Client-Side State Management Technique

Table 4.10 lists the advantages and disadvantages of the various client-side state management techniques. This table will help you make a quick decision about which client-side state management technique to choose in a given scenario.

Table 4.10   Comparing the Client-Side State Management Techniques

Technique	Advantages	Disadvantages
QueryString	Requires no postback operation.	Most browsers limit the length of data that can be included in a query string. No security. No options for persistence. No support for storing structured values.
Cookies	State may be persisted on user's computer. Requires no postback operation.	Some users disable cookies in their browsers. Size restriction by browser (~4 to 8KB). No support for storing structured values. No security.
Hidden fields	Can be used for pages that post to themselves or to other pages.	Increases HTML size. No support for storing structured values. No security. No options for persistence.
ViewState	Support for structured values. Involves less coding. Easy configuration options for security.	Increases HTML size. Only works when a page posts back to itself. No options for persistence.

Server-Side Techniques for State Management

Unlike client-side techniques for state management, server-side techniques (application state and session state) use server resources for storing and managing state. One of the advantages of using server-side techniques for state management is that the possibility of user spoofing or reading the session data is eliminated. But there is a disadvantage, too: Because these techniques use server resources, they raise scalability issues.

Session State

An ASP.NET application creates a session for each user who sends a request to the application. ASP.NET distinctly identifies each of these sessions by sending a unique SessionID to the requesting browser. This SessionID is sent as a cookie or is embedded to the URL, depending on the application's configuration.

When the next request is sent to the server, the server can use the unique SessionID to distinctly identify the repeat visit of the user and both the user visits are considered to belong to the same session.

Comparing ASP.NET Session State with ASP

The concept of SessionID and session state is not new to ASP.NET. ASP.NET's predecessor, ASP, also supported these features. ASP.NET comes with a new implementation of session state that removes all the old problems and provides several enhancements that are equally useful to small and very large Web sites. Table 4.11 compares these improvements.

Table 4.11 Managing the Session State	
The ASP Way	**The ASP.NET Way**
ASP maintains the state in the same process that hosts ASP. If the ASP process somehow fails, the session state is lost.	ASP.NET allows you to store session state out of the process in a state service or in a database.
Each ASP Web server maintains its own session state. This creates a problem in a Web Farm scenario in which a user's request can be dynamically routed to a different server in the Web Farm.	Because ASP.NET can store its session state out-of-process, several computers in a Web Farm can use a common computer as their session state server.
ASP session does not work with browsers that don't support cookies or where the users have disabled the cookies.	ASP.NET supports cookie-less sessions by storing the SessionID in the URL itself (if the application is configured to do so).

You learn more about session state configuration in Chapter 16.

Using Session State

ASP.NET provides access to the session data for the user who originated the request using an instance of the HttpSessionState class. In an ASPX page, this object is accessible through the Session property of the Page class. Tables 4.12 and 4.13 explain the properties and methods of the HttpSessionState class.

Table 4.12   Properties of the HttpSessionState Class

Property	Description
CodePage	Specifies the code page identifier for the current session. This provides compatibility with ASP. **Response.ContentEncoding.CodePage** should be used instead.
Contents	Gets a reference to the session state (**HttpSessionState**) object. This provides compatibility with ASP.
Count	Gets the number of objects in the session state.
IsCookieless	Indicates whether the session is managed using a cookie-less session.
IsNewSession	Indicates whether the session has been created with the current request.
IsReadOnly	Indicates whether the session is read-only.
IsSynchronized	Indicates whether access to the session state is read-only (thread-safe).
Keys	Gets a collection of all session keys.
LCID	Specifies the locale identifier (LCID) of the current session.
Mode	Gets the current session state mode. The values are defined by the **SessionStateMode** enumeration—**Off** (disabled), **InProc** (session state is stored in process with **aspnet_wp.exe**), **SqlServer** (session state is stored in SQL Server) and **StateServer** (session state stored in state service).
SessionID	Represents the unique session identifier used to identify a session.
StaticObjects	Gets a collection of objects declared by **<object runat="server" scope="Session">** tags within the ASPX application file **global.asax**.
SyncRoot	Gets an object that can be used to synchronize access to the collection of session state values.
Timeout	Specifies the timeout period (in minutes) allowed between requests before the session state provider terminates the session.

Table 4.13   Methods of the HttpSessionState Class

Method	Description
Abandon	Cancels the current session.
Add	Adds a new object to the session state.
Clear	Removes all objects from the session state.
CopyTo	Copies the session state values to a single-dimensional array at the specified index.

(continued)

Table 4.13	Methods of the HttpSessionState Class *(continued)*
Method	**Description**
GetEnumerator	Gets an enumerator of all session state values in the current session.
Remove	Removes an object from the session state.
RemoveAll	Removes all the objects from the session state. Calls the **Clear()** method internally.
RemoveAt	Removes an object from the session state at a particular index.

In practice, using session state in your code is pretty easy. You can store an item in the session state just by associating it with a key. This automatically creates the name-value pair in the session state:

```
Session("Name") = txtName.Text
```

Later, you can retrieve the value by supplying the same key:

```
If Not Session("Name") Is Nothing Then
    lblHello.Text = "Hello " & Session("Name").ToString()
End If
```

Application State

Application state is used to store data that is globally used by the application. Application state is stored in memory, and is shared by all sessions of the application.

Application state can be accessed through the `Application` property of the `Page` class. Tables 4.14 and 4.15 discuss the properties and methods of the `HttpApplicationState` class.

Table 4.14	Properties of the HttpApplicationState Class
Property	**Description**
AllKeys	Gets the collection of all the key names in the application state in a string array.
Contents	Gets a reference to the application state (**HttpApplicationState**) object. This provides compatibility with ASP.
Count	Gets the number of objects in the application state.
Keys	Gets the **NameObjectCollectionBase.KeysCollection** collection of all the key names in the application state.
StaticObjects	Gets all objects declared via an **<object runat="server" scope="Application"></object>** tag within the ASP.NET application.

Table 4.15   Methods of the HttpApplicationState Class

Method	Description
Add	Adds a new object to the application state.
Clear	Removes all objects from the application state.
Get	Gets an object from the application state by key name or index.
GetKey	Gets an object from the application state by index.
Lock	Locks access to the application state object. This is used to prevent other clients from changing data stored in the application state.
Remove	Removes an object from the application state.
RemoveAll	Removes all the objects from the application state. Calls the **Clear()** method internally.
RemoveAt	Removes an object from the application state at a particular index.
Set	Updates the value of an object stored in the application state.
Unlock	Unlocks access to the application state.

You can use application state with much the same syntax that you use for session state. For example, this Page_Load event handler will maintain an application-wide hit count for a particular page:

```
Private Sub Page_Load(ByVal sender As System.Object, _
ByVal e As System.EventArgs) Handles MyBase.Load
    ' Lock the Application because the
    ' application state value needs to be modified
    Application.Lock()
    If Not Application("HitCount") Is Nothing Then
        ' Increment the HitCount variable
        ' stored in the application state
        Application("HitCount") = _
            CInt(Application("HitCount")) + 1
    Else
        Application("HitCount") = 1
    End If
    ' Unlock the application now
    ' that the changes are done
    Application.UnLock()
    ' Display the hit count of this page by
    ' fetching the value from the HitCount key
    ' in the application state
    lblInfo.Text = "This page has been accessed " & _
        Application("HitCount").ToString() + " times!"
End Sub
```

Note the use of the **Application.Lock()** and **Application.UnLock()** methods. Locking is important to keep the application state consistent when multiple users might want to modify its content concurrently. While the application is locked, only the current user will be able to change the contents of the application state. This locking mechanism can severely reduce the scalability of a Web application and is one reason not to store any updateable data in the application state.

Navigation Between Pages

A typical Web application is a collection of Web pages linked with each other. In Chapter 3, "Controls," I discussed the Hyperlink control that allows a user to navigate to a different Web page when the hyperlink is clicked. ASP.NET also provides three methods for programmatically navigating between pages—Response.Redirect(), Server.Transfer(), and Server.Execute().

The Response.Redirect() Method

The Response.Redirect() method causes the browser to connect to the specified URL. When the Response.Redirect() method is called, it creates a response whose header contains a 302 (Object Moved) status code and the target URL. When the browser receives this response from the server, it uses the header information to generate another request to the new URL. When using the Response.Redirect() method, the redirection happens at the client side and involves two round-trips to the server.

You should use the Response.Redirect() method in the following cases:

➤ You want to connect to a resource on *any* Web server.

➤ You want to connect to a non-ASPX resource (such as an HTML file).

➤ You want to pass the query string as part of the URL.

The Server.Transfer() Method

The Server.Transfer() method transfers the execution from the current ASPX file to the specified ASPX file. The path specified to the ASPX file must be on the same Web server.

When the Server.Transfer() method is called from an executing ASPX page, the current ASPX page terminates execution and control is transferred to another ASPX page. The new ASPX page still uses the response stream created by the prior ASPX page. When this transfer occurs, the URL in the browser still shows the original page because the redirection occurs on the server side and the browser remains unaware of this transfer.

When you want to transfer the control to an ASPX page residing on the same Web server, you should use Server.Transfer() instead of Response.Redirect() because Server.Transfer() will avoid the unnecessary round-trip to the browser and will provide better performance and a better user experience.

The default use of the Server.Transfer() method does not pass the form data and the query string of the original page request to the transferred page. But, you can preserve the form data and query string of the original page by passing a True value to the optional second argument, preserveForm, of the Server.Transfer() method. This argument takes a Boolean value that indicates whether to preserve the form and query string collections.

When you set the second argument to True, you need to be aware of one thing: The destination page uses the same response stream that was created by the original page; therefore, the hidden _VIEWSTATE field of the original page is also preserved in the form collection. ViewState is valid for a particular page only. This causes the ASP.NET MAC to announce that the ViewState of the new page has been tampered with. Therefore, when you choose to preserve the form and query string collection of the original page, you must set the EnableViewStateMac attribute of the Page directive to False for the destination page.

The Server.Execute() Method

The Server.Execute() method enables the current ASPX page to execute a specified ASPX page. The path to the specified ASPX file must be on the same Web server.

After the specified ASPX page is executed, control returns to the original page from which the Server.Execute() method was called. This technique of page navigation is analogous to making a function call to an ASPX page.

The called ASPX page has access to the form and query string collections of the calling page. Thus, for the reasons explained in the previous section, you need to set the EnableViewStateMac attribute of the Page directive to False on the executed page.

By default, the output of the executed page is added to the current response stream. This method also has an overloaded version in which the output of the redirected page can be fetched in a TextWriter object instead of adding the output to the response stream. This helps you to control where to place the output in the original page.

Exam Prep Questions

Question 1

Which of the following requirements can you address by setting the **SmartNavigation** property of the **Page** class to **True**? (Select all that apply.)

- ❑ A. Initialize data only when a page is first loaded.
- ❑ B. Preserve the vertical scroll position on a Web Form when it is posted back to the server.
- ❑ C. Save session-specific data for use on other pages within the application.
- ❑ D. Keep the focus on the current control when a Web Form is posted back to the server.

Answers B and D are correct. The SmartNavigation property controls a number of IE-specific enhancements to the browsing experience, including persistent focus, persistent scroll position, double-buffered screen painting, and simplified browser history. Answer A is incorrect because the IsPostBack property is used to determine when a page is first loaded. Answer C is incorrect because state management is the job of other techniques such as cookies, query strings, and session state.

Question 2

You have developed an ASP.NET application with a Web Form that stores information about the current user in a **Hashtable** object. You want to preserve the value of this object across page postbacks. You do not need this object in any other page in the application. Which of these state management techniques should you use?

- ○ A. Application state
- ○ B. Query strings
- ○ C. **ViewState**
- ○ D. Cookies

Answer C is correct. Using ViewState is the easiest way to save state across page postbacks. Answer A is incorrect because application state consumes server resources, and does not let you store information on a per-session basis. Answers B and D are incorrect because query strings and cookies cannot easily store structured information such as complex objects. That leaves ViewState as your best choice.

Question 3

> Your ASP.NET application is integrated with an existing set of static HTML pages. At some points in your application, you need to display one of the static HTML pages rather than more ASP.NET content. Which navigation technique could you use? (Select all that apply.)
>
> ❑ A. **Server.Transfer()**
>
> ❑ B. **Response.Redirect()**
>
> ❑ C. Hyperlinks
>
> ❑ D. **Server.Execute()**

Answers B and C are correct. The `Response.Redirect()` method and hyperlinks can be used to transfer control to any page, whether it is an ASP.NET page or not. Answers A and D are incorrect because the `Server.Transfer()` and `Server.Execute()` methods are only suited for ASP.NET pages within the same application.

Question 4

> Which of these types of information would you store in application state? (Select all that apply.)
>
> ❑ A. The time that it took for a particular page to load for a particular user
>
> ❑ B. The **UserID** value of the current user
>
> ❑ C. The last page visited by a user
>
> ❑ D. A counter that tracks the number of currently connected users on your Web site

Answer D is correct. Application state is most useful for information that must be shared by all sessions of an application. Answers A, B, and C are incorrect because these represent information that should be private to a single session; hence they are better served by other state management techniques such as session state or cookies.

Question 5

You would like to initialize a **TextBox** control on a Web Form to show the current time when the user first visits the page. You do not want to update this control when the page is round-tripped to the server. Which code should you use?

○ A.
```
Private Sub Page_Load( _
  ByVal sender As System.Object, _
  ByVal e As System.EventArgs) _
  Handles MyBase.Load
      If IsPostBack Then
          txtDate.Text = DateTime.Now.ToLongTimeString()
      End If
  End Sub
```

○ B.
```
Private Sub Page_Load( _
  ByVal sender As System.Object, _
  ByVal e As System.EventArgs) _
  Handles MyBase.Load
      If Not IsPostBack Then
          txtDate.Text = DateTime.Now.ToLongTimeString()
      End If
  End Sub
```

○ C.
```
Private Sub Page_Init( _
  ByVal sender As System.Object, _
  ByVal e As System.EventArgs) _
  Handles MyBase.Init
      If IsPostBack Then
          txtDate.Text = DateTime.Now.ToLongTimeString()
      End If
  End Sub
```

○ D.
```
Private Sub Page_Init( _
  ByVal sender As System.Object, _
  ByVal e As System.EventArgs) _
  Handles MyBase.Init
      If Not IsPostBack Then
          txtDate.Text = DateTime.Now.ToLongTimeString()
      End If
  End Sub
```

Answer B is correct. By checking the IsPostBack variable, you can perform the initialization only when the page is not being posted back—that is, when it is first loaded. Answers A and C are incorrect because they get the IsPostBack check reversed. Answers C and D are incorrect because the Page_Init event comes before controls are prepared to hold data.

Question 6

You are developing a shopping cart application that tracks item numbers and prices across page postbacks. You want to prevent users from altering the prices that you have assigned to items. Which state management technique should you use for this information?

- O A. Session state
- O B. Query strings
- O C. Hidden fields
- O D. Cookies

Answer A is correct. Session state uses server-side storage, which protects it from malicious client applications. Answers B, C, and D are incorrect because these state management techniques store information on the client where it can be edited before being posted back to the server.

Question 7

You are designing a new Web application to provide real-time inventory information for associates in your company. When an associate first loads the application, you need to store her employee number and the current time in a database. The initial Web Form for the application is named **login.aspx**. Which file should contain the code to perform this task?

- O A. **login.aspx.vb**
- O B. **Web.config**
- O C. **global.asax.vb**
- O D. **machine.config**

Answer C is correct. You can trap the session start event in the `global.asax` file or its `global.asax.vb` code-behind file. This event allows you to perform initialization whenever a new session of your application is launched. Answers B and D are incorrect because the config files do not contain event-handling code. Answer A is incorrect because the page loads after the session has already been initialized.

Question 8

> Your application originally contained a Web Form named Draft1.aspx. You replace Draft1.aspx with Draft2.aspx and use a **Response.Redirect** call to display Draft2.aspx whenever Draft1.aspx is requested. Later, you replace Draft2.aspx with Draft3.aspx and use the **Server.Transfer** method to display Draft3.aspx whenever Draft1.aspx is requested. The Draft3.aspx page uses **Server.Execute** to load Draft4.aspx—from which it extracts some content to combine with the data already on the page.
>
> When the user browses to Draft1.aspx, which page address is displayed in the user's browser after the page has finished loading?
>
> ○ A. Draft1.aspx
>
> ○ B. Draft2.aspx
>
> ○ C. Draft3.aspx
>
> ○ D. Draft4.aspx

Answer B is correct. When the user requests Draft1.aspx, the `Response.Redirect` method performs a client-side redirect. This updates the browser address bar to Draft2.aspx. Then the server-side `Server.Transfer` method performs a server-side redirect; the client is unaware of this redirect, so it does not update the address bar. When Draft4.aspx is used to generate part of the content for Draft3.aspx, this is also done entirely on the server side without any client notification. So the net result is that the page name from the `Response.Redirect` method is the one that remains displayed in the browser.

Question 9

> One of the Web Forms in your ASP.NET application is performing poorly. This Web Form includes several dozen controls, but the contents of those controls are never used when the page is posted back to the server. How can you best disable **ViewState** for this Web Form?
>
> ○ A. Set the **EnableViewStateMac** attribute of the **@Page** directive to **False**.
>
> ○ B. Set the **EnableViewState** property for all the controls on the Web Form to **False**.
>
> ○ C. Set the **EnableViewState** attribute of the **<Pages>** element in the **Web.config** file to **False**.
>
> ○ D. Set the **EnableViewState** attribute of the **@Page** directive to **False**.

Answer D is correct. You can disable ViewState for all controls on the page by disabling it in the @Page directive. Answer A is incorrect because setting EnableViewStateMac to False turns off security checking for ViewState, but does not turn off ViewState itself. Answer B is incorrect because it's more efficient to disable ViewState for the form than for each control individually. Answer C is incorrect because setting the attribute in Web.config will disable ViewState for the entire application instead of only for this Web Form.

Question 10

Your ASP.NET application uses **ViewState** to store the names of session-specific files on the server. These file names are confidential, and you do not want clients to be able to view them. Which setting should you make to protect these filenames?

- ○ A. EnableViewStateMac = True
- ○ B. EnableViewStateMac = False
- ○ C. <machineKey validation="3DES" />
- ○ D. <sessionState cookieless="true" />

Answer C is correct. Setting the validation property in the machine.config file encrypts the ViewState information so that it cannot be easily decoded on the client. Answers A and B are incorrect because EnableViewStateMac controls whether the ViewState is tamper-proofed, not whether it can be decoded. Answer D is incorrect because the cookieless attribute applies to session state, not to ViewState.

Need to Know More?

Onion, Fritz. *Essential ASP.NET.* Addison-Wesley, 2002.

Leinecker, Richard. *Special Edition Using ASP.NET.* Que, 2002.

ASP.NET/Visual Studio .NET Tips, http://www.swarren.net.

Error Handling for the User Interface

Terms you'll need to understand:

✓ Exception
✓ Exception Handling
✓ **Try** block
✓ **Catch** block
✓ **Finally** block
✓ Unhandled Exceptions

Techniques you'll need to master:

✓ Creating custom error pages for an ASP.NET application
✓ Handling errors at the application level
✓ Handling errors at the page level

To pass the 70-305 exam, you'll need to understand exception handling in .NET. In this chapter, you'll review the code that you can use to deal with exceptions in your applications and learn how to create your own exceptions. You'll also learn about the various objects, including the `Page` and `Application` objects, that can trap exceptions.

Understanding Exceptions

An exception occurs when a program encounters any unexpected problems, such as running out of memory, dividing by zero, or attempting to read from a file that no longer exists.

When a program encounters an exception, the default behavior is to stop processing and return an error message. This is not a characteristic of a robust application, and it will not make your program popular among users. Your program should be able to handle exceptional situations and, if possible, gracefully recover from them. How an unhandled exception is presented to the user depends on settings in the `Web.config` file for the application. To see how this works, follow these steps:

1. Create a new Visual Basic .NET ASP.NET Web application.

2. Place three `TextBox` controls (`txtBill`, `txtHours`, and `txtRate`) and one `Button` control (`btnSubmit`) on the default Web Form.

3. Add this code to handle the button's click event:

```
Private Sub btnSubmit_Click( _
 ByVal sender As System.Object, _
 ByVal e As System.EventArgs) _
 Handles btnSubmit.Click
    ProduceReport()
End Sub

Private Sub ProduceReport()
    CalculateRate()
End Sub

Private Sub CalculateRate()
    txtRate.Text = Convert.ToDecimal(txtBill.Text) _
    / Convert.ToDecimal(txtHours.Text)
End Sub
```

4. Open the `Web.config` file for the application. Locate the `customErrors` element and change it as follows:

```
<customErrors mode="On" />
```

5. Run the application. Fill in **5** for the bill and **0** for the hours. Click the button. You'll see a response page as shown in Figure 5.1.

Figure 5.1 Details of runtime errors can be hidden.

6. Stop the application. Open the `Web.config` file and change the `customErrors` element:

```
<customErrors mode="Off" />
```

7. Run the application. Fill in **5** for the bill and **0** for the hours. Click the button. You'll see a response page as shown in Figure 5.2.

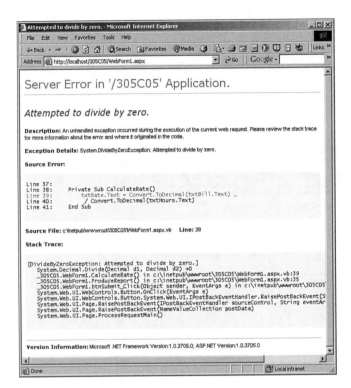

Figure 5.2 With the proper configuration settings, you'll see full details of runtime errors.

As this example demonstrates, you can control whether full error details are returned to the client browser by setting the value of the customErrors element. In addition to the On and Off settings that you saw here, there's a third setting (the default), RemoteOnly. When you set customErrors to RemoteOnly, developers working on the Web server will see the full error, whereas remote users will see the simpler page that hides the details.

Exception Objects

The FCL provides two categories of exceptions:

➤ **ApplicationException**—Represents the exceptions thrown by the user programs.

➤ **SystemException**—Represents the exceptions thrown by the CLR.

Both of these exception classes derive from the base Exception class. Table 5.1 lists the important properties of all three of these classes.

Table 5.1	Important Members of the Exception Class
Property	**Description**
HelpLink	A URL to the help file associated with this exception.
InnerException	Specifies an exception associated with this exception. This property is helpful when a series of exceptions are involved. Each new exception can preserve the information about the previous exception by storing it in the **InnerException** property.
Message	Textual information that specifies the reason for the error and possibly provides a way to resolve it.
Source	The name of the application that causes the error.
StackTrace	Specifies where an error occurred. If the debugging information is available, the stack trace includes the source filename and program line number.
TargetSite	The method that threw the current exception.

Handling Exceptions

Rather than simply displaying the default error page, you can handle exceptions in Visual Basic .NET programs by using a combination of the exception handling statements: Try, Catch, Finally, and Throw.

The Try Block

You should place any code that might cause an exception in a Try block. A typical Try block will look like this:

```
Try
    ' Code that may cause an exception
    ' Catch or Finally block must be included
End Try
```

When an exception occurs within a Try block, the CLR searches for the Try block that encloses this code. The CLR then passes control of the application to a matching Catch block (if any) and then to the Finally block associated with this Try block.

A Try block cannot exist on its own; it must be immediately followed either by one or more Catch blocks or by a Finally block.

The Catch Block

You can have several Catch blocks immediately following a Try block. Each Catch block handles exceptions of a particular type. When an exception occurs in a statement placed inside of a Try block, the CLR looks for a matching Catch block that is capable of handling that type of exception. The formula that CLR uses to match the exception is simple. It looks for the first Catch block with either an exact match for the exception or for any of the exception's base classes. For example, a DivideByZeroException matches with any of these exceptions: DivideByZeroException, ArithmeticException, SystemException, and Exception (progressively more general classes from which DivideByZeroException is derived). In the case of multiple Catch blocks, only the first matching Catch block is executed. All other Catch blocks are ignored.

Exception Handling Hierarchy If there is no matching **Catch** block for a particular exception, that exception becomes an unhandled exception. The unhandled exception is propagated back to the code that called the current method. If the exception is not handled there, it propagates farther up the hierarchy of method calls. If the exception is not handled anywhere, it goes to the CLR for processing. The CLR's default behavior is to terminate the program immediately.

When you write multiple Catch blocks, you need to arrange them from specific exception types to a more general exception type. For example, the Catch block for catching DivideByZeroException should always precede the Catch block for catching ArithmeticException because the DivideByZeroException derives from ArithmeticException and is therefore more specific than the latter. You'll get a compiler error if you do not follow this rule. Here's a sample of a Try block with multiple Catch blocks:

```
Try
    ProduceReport()
Catch fe As FormatException
    Dim msg As String = String.Format( _
    "Message: {0} Stack Trace: {1}", _
        fe.Message, fe.StackTrace)
    lblMessage.Text = fe.GetType().ToString() + _
    "<br>" + msg
Catch dbze As DivideByZeroException
    Dim msg As String = String.Format( _
    "Message: {0} Stack Trace: {1}", _
        dbze.Message, dbze.StackTrace)
    lblMessage.Text = _
    dbze.GetType().ToString() + _
    "<br>" + msg
    ' catches all CLS-complaint exceptions
Catch ex As Exception
    Dim msg As String = String.Format( _
    "Message: {0} Stack Trace: {1}", _
        ex.Message, ex.StackTrace)
    lblMessage.Text = ex.GetType().ToString() + _
    "<br>" + msg
    ' catches all other exception including
    ' the NON-CLS complaint exceptions
Catch
    ' just rethrow the exception to the caller
    Throw
End Try
```

Note that the more specific exception types (FormatException and DivideByZeroException) come before the more general Exception type in the sequence of Catch blocks.

 Languages, such as VB .NET and C#, that follow the Common Language Specification (CLS) throw exceptions with a type of System.Exception or a type that derives from System.Exception. A language that is not CLS-compliant might throw exceptions of other types as well. You can catch those types of exceptions by placing a general **Catch** block (one that does not specify any exception) within a **Try** block. In fact, a general **Catch** block can catch exceptions of all types, so it is the most generic of all **Catch** blocks. This means that it should be the last **Catch** block among the multiple **Catch** blocks associated with a **Try** block.

 A **Try** block need not necessarily have a **Catch** block associated with it, but in that case a **Finally** block must be associated with it.

The Finally Block

The Finally block contains the code that always executes whether or not any exception occurred. You can use the Finally block to write cleanup code that maintains your application in a consistent state and preserves the external environment. As an example, you can write code to close files, database connections, or related I/O resources in a Finally block.

It is not necessary for a Try block to have an associated Finally block. However, if you do write a Finally block, you cannot have more than one, and the Finally block must appear after all the Catch blocks.

 No Code in Between Try, Catch, and Finally Blocks When you write **Try**, **Catch**, and **Finally** blocks, they must be in immediate succession of each other. You cannot write any other code between the blocks, although you can place comments between them.

Here's a typical pattern for using a Finally block with a database connection:

```
Dim cnn As SqlConnection = New SqlConnection(strConn)
Try
    cnn.Open()
    ' Database operations here
Catch ex As Exception
    ' Handle exceptions here
Finally
    cnn.Close()
End Try
```

If you have a **Finally** block associated with a **Try** block, the code in the **Finally** block always executes whether or not an exception occurs. In fact, even if you use a **Goto** statement to try to jump out of the middle of a **Try** block, the associated **Finally** block will still execute.

The `Finally` statement can be used in a `Try` block with no `Catch` block. For example,

```
Try
    ' Write code to allocate some resources
Finally
    ' Write code to Dispose all allocated resources
End Try
```

This pattern ensures that allocated resources are properly disposed of no matter what happens in the `Try` block.

The **Throw** Statement

A `Throw` statement explicitly generates an exception in your code. You can use `Throw` to handle execution paths that lead to undesired results.

You can use the `Throw` statement in two ways. First, in its simplest form, you can simply rethrow an exception that you've caught in a `Catch` block:

```
Catch ex As Exception
    ' Throw the Exception to the calling code
    Throw
```

This usage of the `Throw` statement rethrows the exception that was just caught. It can be useful in situations in which you don't want to handle the exception yourself but would like to take other actions (such as recording the error in an event log or sending an email notification about the error) when the exception occurs. Then you can pass the exception unchanged to the next method in the calling chain.

The second way of using a `Throw` statement is to use it to throw explicitly created exceptions. For example, this code creates and throws an exception:

```
Dim strMessage As String = _
 "EndDate should be greater than the StartDate"
Dim exNew As ArgumentOutOfRangeException = _
 New ArgumentOutOfRangeException(strMessage)
Throw exNew
```

In this example, I first created a new instance of the `Exception` object, associated a custom error message with it, and then threw the newly created exception.

Custom Exceptions

The .NET Framework allows you to define custom exception classes. To make your custom Exception class work well with the .NET exception handling framework, Microsoft recommends that you consider the following when you're designing a custom exception class:

➤ Create an exception class only if no existing exception class satisfies your requirement.

➤ Derive all programmer-defined exception classes from the System.ApplicationException class.

➤ End the name of the custom exception class with the word Exception (for example, MyOwnCustomException).

➤ Implement three constructors with the signatures shown in the following code:

```
Public Class MyOwnCustomException
    Inherits ApplicationException

    ' Default constructor
    Public Sub New()

    End Sub

    ' Constructor accepting a single string message
    Public Sub New(ByVal message As String)
        MyBase.New(message)
    End Sub

    ' Constructor accepting a string message
    '   and an inner exception
    ' that will be wrapped by this
    ' custom exception class
    Public Sub New( _
     ByVal message As String, _
     ByVal inner As Exception)
        MyBase.New(message, inner)
    End Sub

End Class
```

Managing Unhandled Exceptions

Unhandled exceptions are those exceptions that are not caught in a Try/Catch block in an application. Whenever an unhandled exception occurs, ASP.NET displays its default error page to the user. As you saw earlier in this chapter, the default page is not pretty and sometimes (depending on the settings in the Web.config file) can provide enough details to be a security concern. You're usually better off displaying your own custom error messages instead.

ASP.NET stops processing a Web page after it encounters an unhandled exception. However, you can trap an unhandled exception at either the Page or the Application level.

Using Custom Error Pages

Custom error pages are those Web pages that are displayed in the browser when an unhandled exception occurs. You can even display custom error pages whenever an HTTP error occurs (such as Page Not Found, Internal Server Error, and so on) while requesting a Web page from your ASP.NET application.

ASP.NET provides full built-in support to configure custom error pages in a Web application. This configuration information is stored in an XML-based configuration file (Web.config), where you use the <customErrors> element to configure custom error pages. In addition to the mode attribute, you can also set a defaultRedirect attribute for this element. The optional defaultRedirect attribute specifies the custom error page to be displayed when an error occurs. You can use either a static HTML page or a dynamic ASPX page as a custom error page.

You can also display a custom error page for specific HTTP error codes by associating the error codes with the Web page through the <error> element. Multiple <error> elements can be nested inside the <customErrors> element. They consist of the following two attributes:

➤ **statusCode**—HTTP error status code

>   403 (Forbidden)

>   404 (Not Found)

>   500 (Internal Server Error)

>   Other status codes exist, but they aren't listed here for the sake of brevity.

➤ **redirect**—The error page to which the browser should be redirected when the associated HTTP error occurs.

If an error occurs that has no specific page assigned, the custom error page specified by the defaultRedirect attribute of <customErrors> element is displayed.

You can work through this example to see the use of custom error pages in an ASP.NET application:

1. Open the `Web.config` file and modify the `<customErrors>` element as follows:

```
<customErrors mode="On"
 defaultRedirect="ApplicationError.htm">
    <error statusCode="404" redirect="NotFound.htm" />
</customErrors>
```

2. Select Project, Add HTML Page. Create a page with the name `ApplicationError.htm`. Change the page's `pageLayout` property to `FlowLayout` and type the text **An application error has occurred** on the page.

3. Select Project, Add HTML Page. Create a page with the name `NotFound.htm`. Change the page's `pageLayout` property to `FlowLayout` and type the text **The page you requested cannot be found** on the page.

4. Add a Hyperlink control to the default Web Form in your application. Set the `NavigateUrl` property of the control to `Nonexistentpage.aspx`. Make sure that there is no error handler for the page.

5. Run the project. Fill in **5** for the bill and **0** for the hours. Click the button. The application displays the `ApplicationError.htm` page because that page is configured as the default error page for the application.

6. Click the back button, and then click the hyperlink. The application displays the `NotFound.htm` page in response to the 404 error generated by attempting to navigate to a nonexistent page.

The `NotFound.htm` error page is only displayed if the not found page is one that would have been processed by ASP.NET. If you tried to get to `NonExistentPage.htm`, you wouldn't see the custom error page because IIS would never call the ASP.NET processor.

Setting a Custom Error Page for a Specific Page

Sometimes there might be a special need in which a particular Web page in an application should display its own error page. This can be done by setting the `ErrorPage` attribute of the `@Page` directive or the `ErrorPage` property of the `Page` class to the desired custom error page. Settings made for a particular page override settings in the `Web.config` file. For example, you could make any errors on a particular page go to `MyCustomPage.htm` by including this page directive:

```
<%@ Page Language="vb" AutoEventWireup="false"
 Codebehind="NewPage.aspx.vb"
 Inherits="_305c05.NewPage"
 ErrorPage="MyCustomPage.htm" %>
```

Using Error Events

When an unhandled exception occurs in a Web application, the following events are fired in order:

1. Page.Error—Page-level event, handled by the Page_Error event handler

2. Application.Error—Application-level event, handled by the Application_Error event handler

Either of these event handlers can be used to trap and work with unhandled exceptions.

Using the Page.Error Event

The Page_Error event handler can be used to trap unhandled exceptions at a page level. Here's a simple example:

1. Add a new Web Form to your ASP.NET application.

2. Place a single Button control, btnKaboom, on the Web Form.

3. Add this code in the code-behind module:

```
Private Sub btnKaboom_Click( _
ByVal sender As System.Object, _
ByVal e As System.EventArgs) _
Handles btnKaboom.Click
    Dim strMessage As String = _
    "This is a phony exception"
    Dim exNew As Exception = _
    New Exception(strMessage)
    Throw exNew
End Sub

Private Sub Page_Error(ByVal sender As Object, _
ByVal e As System.EventArgs) Handles MyBase.Error
    ' Display error details
    Response.Write("Error Details: <br>")
    Response.Write( _
    Server.GetLastError().Message + "<br>")
    Response.Write( _
    Server.GetLastError().StackTrace + _
    "<br>")
    Server.ClearError()
End Sub
```

4. Set the new Web Form as the default page for the application.

5. Run the application. Click the button. You'll see the error details.

The Page_Error event handler in this example displays the details of the unhandled exception. This is achieved by calling the Server object's

GetLastError method. The method returns an Exception object that is a reference to the last exception that occurred on the server.

The ClearError method of the Server object clears the last exception so that it does not fire subsequent error events (that is, Application.Error) for the exception.

Using the Application.Error Event

You can also choose to trap unhandled exceptions that occur anywhere in the application in the Application.Error event. This event is handled by the Application_Error event handler available in the ASP.NET application file, global.asax. Handling exceptions at the application level can be really helpful if you are planning to handle exceptions from all pages in a similar fashion. For example, application-level error-handling lets you easily log exceptions to a database or email them to the developer no matter where they occur in the application.

To see application-level error handling in action, try these steps:

1. Open the global.asax file in your Web Application and switch to code view.

2. Add this code to handle the Application_Error event:

```
Sub Application_Error(ByVal sender As Object, ByVal e As EventArgs)
    ' Display error details
    Dim UnhandledException As Exception = _
     Server.GetLastError().InnerException
    Response.Write("Application Error Details: <br>")
    Response.Write( _
     UnhandledException.Message + "<br>")
    Response.Write( _
     UnhandledException.StackTrace + _
     "<br>")
    Server.ClearError()
End Sub
```

3. Comment out the page-level error handler in the Web Form that you constructed in the previous example.

4. Run the application. Click the button. You'll see the error details, this time from the Application object.

When ASP.NET propagates the unhandled exception to the Application object (Application.Error event), the exception object is wrapped into an HttpUnhandledException object. To see the original exception at the application level, you need to unpack the Exception object's InnerException property.

Exam Prep Questions

Question 1

A particular Web Form in your application is throwing an exception, and you're not sure why. The Web Form in question includes extensive and complex business logic. When the exception occurs, you'd like to get information on the sequence of method calls and the precise line number where the exception occurred. Which property of the **Exception** class should you inspect?

- ○ A. **Message**
- ○ B. **StackTrace**
- ○ C. **InnerException**
- ○ D. **Source**

Answer B is correct. The `StackTrace` property gives you complete information about the call stack at the time when the exception was thrown. Answer A is incorrect because the `Message` property returns a description of the current exception. Answer C is incorrect because the `InnerException` property returns any wrapped exception object. Answer D is incorrect because the `Source` property returns the application or object that caused the error, but no details as to the error's location.

Question 2

You have deployed an ASP.NET Web Application to a production server. When you're debugging at the server, you want to see full information for any error that occurs. When a client accesses the application over the Internet, you want to prevent him from seeing the stack trace. In the specific case of a permission denied error (403 error), you want to send back a page named **CheckPassword.htm** to the user. Which section should you use in the **Web.config** file?

- ○ A.
```
<customErrors mode="On">
    <error statusCode="403" redirect="CheckPassword.htm" />
</customErrors>
```

- ○ B.
```
<customErrors mode="RemoteOnly"
  defaultRedirect="ApplicationError.htm">
    <error statusCode="403" redirect="CheckPassword.htm" />
</customErrors>
```

○ C.

```
<customErrors mode="RemoteOnly">
    <error statusCode="403" redirect="CheckPassword.htm" />
</customErrors>
```

○ D.

```
<customErrors mode="On"
 defaultRedirect="ApplicationError.htm">
    <error statusCode="403" redirect="CheckPassword.htm" />
</customErrors>
```

Answer C is correct. With these settings, you'll receive full details on errors, and the specified page will be used for 403 errors. Answers A and D are incorrect because with the mode set to On, full details will never be shown. Answers B and D are incorrect because they include a `defaultRedirect`, which will replace the built-in error information.

Question 3

How many **Catch** blocks can be associated with a single **Try** block?

○ A. Only zero or one.

○ B. Exactly one.

○ C. Zero or more.

○ D. One or more.

Answer C is correct. A `Try` block does not have to have any `Catch` blocks, provided that it has a `Finally` block. With or without the `Finally` block, you can have any number of `Catch` blocks arranged in order of increasing generality.

Question 4

Which types of exceptions can you trap with a **Catch** block in Visual Basic .NET (select all correct answers)?

❑ A. Exceptions from Visual Basic .NET code.

❑ B. Exceptions from a component written in C#.

❑ C. Exceptions from a COM component.

❑ D. Exceptions from the Windows API.

Answers A, B, C, and D are correct. A `Catch` block can catch any exception that affects your application. You'll only get full information from exceptions that occur in CLS-compliant languages (such as Visual Basic .NET or C#), but COM and Windows API exceptions can be trapped as well.

Question 5

You have designed an ASP.NET Web Form that uses a database connection to a remote server to retrieve information. Sometimes the server will be unavailable because of network problems. You want to ensure that users do not receive an untrapped error in these cases. Where should you place the code to close and dispose of the connection object?

- ○ A. In a **Try** block.
- ○ B. In a **Catch** block.
- ○ C. In a **Finally** block.
- ○ D. Outside of any **Try/Catch/Finally** blocks.

Answer C is correct. By placing the code to open the connection in a Try block and to close the connection in a Finally block, you can ensure that the connection is properly disposed of regardless of any error. Answer A is incorrect because cleanup code in the Try block won't be executed if an error occurs. Answer B is incorrect because cleanup code in a Catch block won't be executed unless an error occurs. Answer D is incorrect because code outside of any error-handling blocks can cause an unhandled exception.

Question 6

You have created a custom error page for the login page of your ASP.NET Web Application. You want any error on the login page to redirect to this custom page. How should you proceed?

- ○ A. Trap the **Application_Error** event and use **Server.Transfer** to load the custom error page if the error came from the login page.
- ○ B. Trap the **Page_Error** event on the login page and use **Server.Execute** to load the custom error page.
- ○ C. Use a **Try/Catch** block in the **Page_Load** event to load the custom error page in case of any errors.
- ○ D. Include the **ErrorPage** attribute in the **Page** directive for your login page.

Answer D is correct. The ErrorPage attribute provides an easy way to redirect errors from a single Web Form. Answers A, B, and C would all require error-prone custom development to achieve the same effect.

Question 7

Your ASP.NET Web Application includes an application-level error handler in the **Application_Error** procedure in **global.asax**. It also includes a page-level error handler in a Web Form named frmLogin. You discover that when an error occurs on the frmLogin form, the output of both the page-level and application-level error handlers is displayed. How should you modify the application so that only the page-level information is displayed?

- ○ A. Add the line **Server.ClearError()** to the end of the page-level error handler.
- ○ B. Add the line **Server.ClearError()** to the start of the application-level error handler.
- ○ C. Add a **Page** directive specifying a custom error page to frmLogin.
- ○ D. Set **customErrors=RemoteOnly** in the application's **Web.config** file.

Answer A is correct. If you clear the error at the end of the page's error handler, the application's error handler will not be called. Answer B is incorrect because clearing the error at the start of the application handler will prevent the application error handler from ever displaying any information. Answer C is incorrect because the Page directive will override the page-level error handler. Answer D is incorrect because the error handlers will still print information regardless of the customError mode.

Question 8

You have deployed a new ASP.NET Web Application to a production server, but you're concerned that errors will crop up under a heavy load. You want to log any errors to the system event log. Where should you place the code to work with the event log?

- ○ A. In the **Application_End** event handler in the **global.asax** file.
- ○ B. In the **Application_Error** event handler in the **global.asax** file.
- ○ C. In the **Page_Load** event handler in the individual page files.
- ○ D. In the **Page_Error** event handler in the individual page files.

Answer B is correct. The Application_Error event handler will be called any time there is an unhandled error in your application. Answer A is incorrect because Application_End is only called when the application is shutting down. Answers C and D are incorrect because placing the logging code at the page level results in needless duplication of code.

Question 9

Your Web application includes a page that allows the user to submit an email address to subscribe to a mailing list. As part of this page's code, you verify that the email address is correctly formatted. If it is not, you want to throw a custom exception using an instance of the **BadEmailFormatException** class. Which class should you use as the base class for **BadEmailFormatException**?

- ○ A. **Exception**
- ○ B. **SystemException**
- ○ C. **ApplicationException**
- ○ D. **WarningException**

Answer C is correct. Although the Exception, SystemException, and ApplicationException classes all have the same interface, Microsoft recommends that all custom exception classes inherit from the ApplicationException class. Answer D is incorrect because you should not inherit from any of the more specific built-in exception classes.

Question 10

You are using an **Application.Error** event handler to email yourself notification of any errors in an ASP.NET Web Application on a test server. You notice that no matter what error occurs, the email message provides details of an **HttpUnhandledException** object. How should you modify your code?

- ○ A. Unpack the **InnerException** property of the **HttpUnhandledException** object and send the details of the **InnerException**.
- ○ B. Use **Server.LastError** to retrieve the details of the most recent server error and send those details.
- ○ C. Implement **Page.Error** handlers on every page to mail the errors directly from the affected page.
- ○ D. Retrieve the object pointed to by the **Source** property of the **HttpUnhandledException** object and send the details of that object.

Answer A is correct. When ASP.NET invokes the Application.Error event, it wraps the actual exception in an HttpUnhandledException object. To see the actual error details, simply unwrap the inner exception. Answer B is incorrect because Server.LastError will return the HttpUnhandledException object. Answer C is incorrect because, even though it will work, it requires much duplicate effort that you can avoid by working at the application level. Answer D is incorrect because the Source object does not contain full error details.

Need to Know More?

Richter, Jeffrey. *Applied Microsoft .NET Framework Programming.* Microsoft Press, 2001.

Mitchell, Scott, et al. *ASP.NET: Tips, Tutorials, and Code.* Sams, 2001.

Jones, A. Russell. *Mastering ASP.NET with VB.NET.* Sybex, 2002.

Visual Studio .NET Combined Help Collection, "Best Practices for Exception Handling" topic.

Data Binding

Terms you'll need to understand:

✓ Data binding
✓ Relational database
✓ Table
✓ Row
✓ Column
✓ Primary key
✓ Relation
✓ Foreign key
✓ Templated control

Techniques you'll need to master:

✓ Binding data to the user interface
✓ Filtering and transforming data
✓ Using drag-and-drop with Server Explorer
✓ Using simple and complex controls to display data on a Web Form

One of the most important parts of almost any application is to connect the *data model* of the application to the user interface. *Data model* is a general term: It might refer to data stored in a database, to an array of values, or to items contained in an object from the System.Collections namespace. The data model is internal to the application. It contains information that is known to the application.

To be useful for the end users of your application, the data model must somehow be connected to the user interface. One of the easiest ways to make a connection between the data model and the user interface is to bind the data to the user interface. *Data binding* refers to the process of making a link between controls on the user interface and data stored in the data model. As the user views and manipulates controls, the application takes care of translating their actions into reading and writing data from the data model.

Binding Data to the UI

ASP.NET includes extremely flexible data binding capabilities. In this section, you learn about many of those capabilities starting with simple data binding.

Simple Data Binding

Simple data binding means connecting a single value from the data model to a single property of a control. For example, you might bind the product name returned by the ProductName property of an object to text on the user interface of a Web Form this way:

1. Create a new Visual Basic .NET ASP.NET Web application. Set the pageLayout property of the default Web Form to FlowLayout.

2. Switch to HTML view in the designer and add code to the <body> tag:

```
<body>
    <form id="Form1" method="post" runat="server">
        Product Name:
        <%# ProductName %>
    </form>
</body>
```

3. Open the Web Form's module and add code directly after the Web Form Designer Generated Code to create a public property:

```
Public ReadOnly Property ProductName()
    Get
        ProductName = "Green Tea"
    End Get
End Property
```

4. Add code to the Web Form's `Page_Load` event:

```
Private Sub Page_Load( _
  ByVal sender As System.Object, _
  ByVal e As System.EventArgs) Handles MyBase.Load
    DataBind()
  End Sub
```

5. Run the project. The user interface is now bound to the property, and will display the value returned from the property.

The ASP.NET data binding syntax `<%# ... %>` might remind you of the classic ASP syntax `<%= ... %>`, but it works in a different way. The classic ASP version is simply a runtime shortcut for `Response.Write()`. The new ASP.NET version is evaluated when the `DataBind` method is called.

Binding to Public Members

In the example you just saw, the user interface was bound to a property of the Web Form itself. The ASP.NET data binding syntax can accept many other things as a data source. These include

➤ A public member, such as a variable, field, or method of the page

➤ Properties of other controls

➤ An instance of a collection class

➤ The result of an expression

The expression you bind doesn't have to return a constant; it can be anything. For example, you can include this code within a Web Form:

```
<body>
    <form id="Form1" method="post" runat="server">
    The time is:
    <%# CurrentTime() %>
    </form>
</body>
```

Then you could provide a public method to supply the data:

```
Public Function CurrentTime() As String
      CurrentTime = DateTime.Now.ToLongTimeString()
End Function
```

Now each time you refresh the Web Form (assuming that there's a call to the `DataBind` method in the `Page_Load` event), it will show the updated current time.

You can control the point in your code at which the data is bound to the user interface by explicitly calling the **DataBind** method when you want the binding to occur. In fact, if you forget to call the **DataBind** method, the binding will never happen.

You can use simple data binding to any property that you can set in the HTML for a Web Form. For example, you can bind a `DateTime` value to the `SelectedDate` property of a `Calendar` control:

```
<asp:Calendar id="Calendar1" runat="server"
SelectedDate="<%# DateTime.Today.AddDays(1) %>">
</asp:Calendar>
```

When you execute the `DataBind()` method of the containing Web Form, this code will select tomorrow's date on the calendar control.

Binding to Control Properties

You can also bind a property of one server control directly to a property of another server control. This provides you with an easy method to transfer information from one part of a Web Form to another. For example, a `Label` control can pick up the current date from a `Calendar` control this way:

```
<asp:Label id="lblInfo" runat="server">
    <%# Calendar1.SelectedDate.ToShortDateString %>
</asp:Label>
```

Remember, though, that the data won't transfer all by itself. You must call the `DataBind` method, either of the Page or of the individual control, when you want to refresh the bound information. In this case, you might choose to do so when the selection on the `Calendar` control changes:

```
Private Sub Calendar1_SelectionChanged( _
 ByVal sender As System.Object, _
 ByVal e As System.EventArgs) _
 Handles Calendar1.SelectionChanged
    lblInfo.DataBind()
End Sub
```

Complex Data Binding

In complex data binding, you bind a user interface control to an entire collection of data, rather than to a single data item. For example, the `DataGrid` is a single control that displays many pieces of data. Potentially, a `DataGrid` can display all the data from an entire database table at one time. With additional programming, you can add interactivity to the control. For example, you can make it possible to edit the displayed data and then write the changes back to the data model and from there to the underlying database.

Complex data binding is a powerful tool for transferring large amounts of data from a data model to a user interface. ASP.NET offers several controls that support complex data binding:

➤ DropDownList

➤ ListBox

➤ CheckBoxList

➤ RadioButtonList

➤ DataGrid

Binding to a **DropDownList** or **ListBox**

The DropDownList and ListBox controls both provide ways for the user to select one item from a list of data. The difference between the two is that in the ListBox the list is visible at all times, whereas in the DropDownList the list is hidden until the user clicks the drop-down arrow at the end of the box. Either of these controls can be loaded with an entire list of data via complex data binding.

These controls can be bound to any collection that supports the IEnumerable, ICollection, or IListSource interface. This includes the ArrayList, HashTable, DataReader, and DataView classes. Try this example to load a ListBox control with a collection of data:

1. Add a new Web Form to your application and set it to FlowLayout mode.

2. Place a ListBox control on the Web Form. Set the ID of the control to lbExams.

3. Add a new module named Exam.vb to your application. Enter this code in the module:

```
Imports System.Data

Module Exam

    Public Function DataLoad() As ICollection
        Dim dt As DataTable = New DataTable()
        Dim dv As DataView
        Dim dr As DataRow

        ' Add two columns to the DataTable
        dt.Columns.Add(New DataColumn( _
         "ExamNumber", GetType(String)))
        dt.Columns.Add(New DataColumn( _
         "ExamName", GetType(String)))
```

```
' Put some data in
dr = dt.NewRow()
dr(0) = "305"
dr(1) = "Web Applications With VB.NET"
dt.Rows.Add(dr)

dr = dt.NewRow()
dr(0) = "306"
dr(1) = "Windows Applications With VB.NET"
dt.Rows.Add(dr)

dr = dt.NewRow()
dr(0) = "310"
dr(1) = "XML With VB.NET"
dt.Rows.Add(dr)

dr = dt.NewRow()
dr(0) = "315"
dr(1) = "Web Applications With Visual C# .NET"
dt.Rows.Add(dr)

dr = dt.NewRow()
dr(0) = "316"
dr(1) = _
  "Windows Applications With Visual C# .NET"
dt.Rows.Add(dr)

dr = dt.NewRow()
dr(0) = "320"
dr(1) = "XML With Visual C# .NET"
dt.Rows.Add(dr)

' And return the datatable
' wrapped in a dataview
dv = New DataView(dt)
Return dv

End Function

End Module
```

4. Double-click the Web Form and enter code in the form's `Load` event:

```
Private Sub Page_Load( _
ByVal sender As System.Object, _
ByVal e As System.EventArgs) Handles MyBase.Load
    lbExams.DataSource = DataLoad()
    lbExams.DataTextField = "ExamName"
    DataBind()
End Sub
```

5. Set the Web Form as the start page for the project.

6. Run the project. The `ListBox` control will display the `ExamName` property of every object in the `DataView`.

The DataLoad function uses four objects that you might not have seen before: DataRow, DataColumn, DataTable, and DataView. You can just think of these objects in simple terms. The DataTable stores a table. (A table, in this context, is a rectangular array of data.) The DataColumn represents one column in a DataTable, and the DataRow represents one row in a DataTable. The DataView provides a way to deliver all or part of the contents of a DataTable through the bindable ICollection interface. You can also access the contents of a DataView as if it were a two-dimensional array. That is, dv(1)(1) returns the second item in the second row of the DataView. (The subscripts are numbered starting with zero.)

Frequently, you'll use a complex data bound ListBox or DropDownList in conjunction with a simple data bound control such as a TextBox. By selecting a row in the ListBox, the user can choose a value for the TextBox.

You can think of the ListBox as a little pump that moves data from one part of your application to another. To set this up, you create a control that's bound to the ListBox:

```
<asp:Label id="lblSelected" runat="server">
    <%# lbExams.SelectedItem.Value %>
</asp:Label>
```

Then you need to set appropriate properties on the ListBox—for example, when the form is loaded:

```
Private Sub Page_Load(ByVal sender As System.Object, _
ByVal e As System.EventArgs) Handles MyBase.Load
    If Not IsPostBack Then
        lbExams.DataSource = DataLoad()
        lbExams.DataTextField = "ExamName"
        lbExams.DataValueField = "ExamNumber"
        lbExams.DataBind()
    End If
End Sub
```

Finally, bind the control when the user selects an item:

```
Private Sub lbExams_SelectedIndexChanged( _
ByVal sender As System.Object, _
ByVal e As System.EventArgs) _
Handles lbExams.SelectedIndexChanged
    lblSelected.DataBind()
End Sub
```

The following list explains how all the pieces fit together:

➤ The ListBox in this example draws the list of items to display from the DataView of exam information. The list portion of the list box is complex bound to this object. The complex binding is managed by setting the DataSource, DataTextField, and DataValueField properties of the ListBox.

➤ When you first load the form, the data is loaded by calling the DataBind method of the ListBox itself. The check of the IsPostBack form variable makes sure that this only happens once. If you neglected to check, the data would be loaded when the form was posted back, and you'd lose the information on which the ListBox item was selected.

➤ When you click an item in the ListBox, it posts that information back to the server because the AutoPostBack property of the ListBox is set to True.

➤ The SelectedIndexChanged event handles binding the currently selected row of the ListBox to the Label. The code for this calls the DataBind method of the Label control itself.

➤ You can use the DataTextField and DataValueField properties of the ListBox control to cause it to show one value while binding another, as in this example.

Binding to a **CheckBoxList** or **RadioButtonList**

Two other controls in the Web Forms toolbox function like the DropDownList and ListBox controls—the CheckBoxList and RadioButtonList controls. Although the RadioButtonList and CheckBoxList controls are rendered as groups of radio button or check box controls, they're designed as a single control. Just like the other list controls, you can bind to these controls by setting their DataSource and DataTextField properties:

```
Private Sub Page_Load( _
ByVal sender As System.Object, _
ByVal e As System.EventArgs) Handles MyBase.Load
    rblExams.DataSource = DataLoad()
    rblExams.DataTextField = "ExamName"
    DataBind()
End Sub
```

Binding to a **DataGrid**

The DataGrid also provides a way to display many rows from a data model at one time. The DataGrid is designed to let you see an entire collection of data at one time. Here's how you might use a DataGrid to display the exam data you've been working with:

1. Add a new Web Form to your application.

2. Place a DataGrid control on the new Web Form. Set the ID of the control to dgExams.

3. Double-click the form and enter code in the form's Load event:

```
Private Sub Page_Load( _
  ByVal sender As System.Object, _
  ByVal e As System.EventArgs) Handles MyBase.Load
    dgExams.DataSource = DataLoad()
    DataBind()
End Sub
```

4. Set the form as the startup object for the project.

5. Run the project. The DataGrid will display all the information from the exams DataView. Notice that you don't have to do anything to tell the DataGrid what data to display. It takes care of all the details of turning rows and columns from the DataView into rows and columns in an HTML table, as shown in Figure 6.1.

Figure 6.1   The **DataGrid** can use complex binding to display an entire **DataView** at once.

The **DataBind** Method

DataBind is a method of the Page object (which, of course, represents the entire ASP.NET Web Form) and of all server controls. Data binding expressions are not evaluated until you explicitly call the DataBind method. This gives you flexibility to decide when to bind things and lets you run preliminary code to calculate values if necessary.

The DataBind method cascades from parent controls to their children. If you call the DataBind method of the Page, all data binding expressions on the page are evaluated. If you call the DataBind method of a control that has constituent controls, all data binding expressions in any of those controls are evaluated.

In addition to the design-time data binding expressions that you've already seen, you can perform runtime data binding by responding to the DataBinding event of a control. This event is raised by each control when its DataBind method is invoked. For example, suppose that your Page_Load event procedure contains this code:

```
Private Sub Page_Load(ByVal sender As System.Object, _
ByVal e As System.EventArgs) Handles MyBase.Load
    DataBind()
End Sub
```

This will fire the DataBinding event of every control on the page. You can alter control properties in that event:

```
Private Sub lblRuntime_DataBinding( _
ByVal sender As Object, _
ByVal e As System.EventArgs) _
Handles lblRuntime.DataBinding
    lblRuntime.Text = "Runtime data binding"
End Sub
```

Anything you can do with runtime data binding you can also do with design-time data binding. That's because, as you saw earlier in the chapter, you can use design-time data binding with properties of the page. It's a matter of personal style whether you'd like to put code into a public property or into a DataBinding event.

Using the Data Form Wizard

In this section, you see how to use the Data Form Wizard to build both a single-table form and a multiple-table form.

Building a Single-Table Data Form

Start by building a data form that displays data from a single table—the Customers table in the Northwind sample database:

1. Add a new item to your application. In the Add New Item dialog box, select the Data Form Wizard. Name the new form Customers.aspx and click Open.

2. Read the Welcome panel of the wizard and click Next.

3. The next panel helps you choose a Dataset to use with the Data Form. A Dataset is a .NET Framework object that you can think of as representing one or more tables from a database. (It's actually more flexible than that, but that's enough for this example.) Choose to create a new Dataset named dsCustomers. Click Next.

4. The next panel helps you choose or build a Data Connection. A Data Connection tells Visual Basic .NET which database contains the data that you want to retrieve. You haven't set up any Data Connections yet, so click the New Connection button. This will open the Data Link Properties dialog box.

5. Click the Provider tab of the Data Link Properties dialog box and select the Microsoft OLE DB Provider for SQL Server.

6. Click the Connection tab of the Data Link Properties dialog box and enter the information that you need to use the Northwind Database, as shown in Figure 6.2.

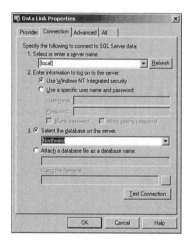

Figure 6.2 Connecting to the Northwind sample database.

You might have to try a few things to connect to the database. For the server name, you can use the name of a computer where SQL Server is running. If SQL Server is installed on the same computer where you're writing the code, you can use the special name "(local)" instead of entering a server name. For logon information, you should first try Windows NT Integrated Security, which logs on to SQL Server using your Windows identity. If that fails, try using the specific user name "sa" and a blank password. If that also fails, you'll need to check with the person responsible for the SQL Server to find out what login information to use. Note the Test Connection button at the bottom of the dialog box. This will come in handy as you're trying to get your login information correct.

7. Click OK on the Data Link Properties dialog box to create the connection and return to the Data Form Wizard. Select the new connection in the combo box (it will have a name such as MACHINENAME.Northwind.dbo) and click Next.

8. On the Choose Tables or Views panel, select the Customers table in the Available Items list and click the > button to move it to the Selected Items list. Click Next.

9. On the Choose Tables and Columns to Display on the Form panel, leave all the columns in the table selected, and click Finish.

10. Set the new form as the start page for the project and run the project to experiment with the Data Form. Figure 6.3 shows the completed Data Form.

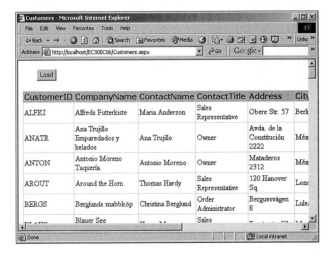

Figure 6.3 The finished Data Form displays all the data from the Customers table. It also provides a button to let you choose when to load the data.

You might want to browse through the code that the wizard created behind this form. As you continue through the book, you'll learn more about database objects and the code that you can use to manipulate them. For now, I'll stick to the relatively easy user interface.

Building a Multiple-Table Data Form

The Data Form Wizard can also build a form that displays data from more than one table. To do this, just choose two tables in the Choose Tables or Views panel of the Data Form Wizard. You'll then see an additional panel to help you create a relationship between the two tables, as shown in Figure 6.4.

Figure 6.5 shows a two-table Data Form in action.

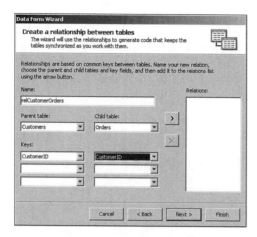

Figure 6.4   Creating a relationship between tables.

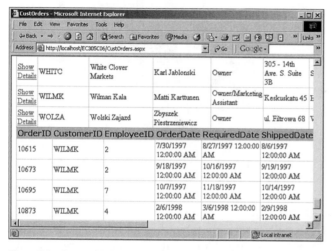

Figure 6.5   A two-table Data Form that uses one **DataGrid** control for each table and uses code to keep the two **DataGrid** controls synchronized.

Manipulating Databases

To pass the exam, you also need to understand techniques for working with databases. You'll need to learn how to connect to databases, as well as how to filter the data that you retrieve to focus on only the necessary data for the task at hand.

Using Server Explorer

By default, the Server Explorer window in Visual Studio .NET is displayed as a small vertical tab to the left of the toolbox. When you hover the mouse over this tab, the Server Explorer will slide out to cover the toolbox. Figure 6.6 shows the two states of the Server Explorer window.

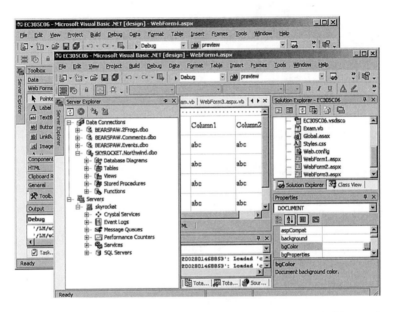

Figure 6.6 The Server Explorer is normally displayed as a small vertical tab. When you hover the mouse over this tab, the window slides out to cover the toolbox.

Adding a Data Connection

You've already seen that you can add a Data Connection to your project from within the Data Form Wizard. Those Data Connections are automatically available in Server Explorer as well. You can also add a Data Connection directly from Server Explorer. To do so, right-click the Data Connections node and select Add Connection. Fill in the Data Link Properties dialog box and click OK.

Visual Studio .NET remembers your Data Connections across sessions and projects. Any Data Connection that you've created will appear in Server Explorer in all of your projects unless you right-click the Data Connection and choose Delete.

Object Design from Server Explorer

Even without bringing SQL Server objects into your Visual Basic .NET projects, you can manipulate them from Server Explorer. Visual Studio .NET provides wide-ranging design options for SQL Server objects. Table 6.1 summarizes your options in this area.

Table 6.1 Manipulating SQL Server Objects from Server Explorer			
Object	**Edit Data?**	**Design?**	**Create New?**
Database	Diagram	N/A	Yes
Table	Yes	Yes	Yes
View	Yes	Yes	Yes
Stored Procedure	Yes	Yes	Yes
Function	Yes	Yes	Yes

To edit one of these objects, right-click the object in Server Explorer and select the appropriate shortcut menu item. Figure 6.7 shows a SQL Server table being designed in Visual Studio .NET.

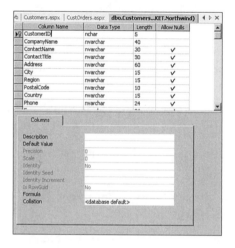

Figure 6.7   Designing a SQL Server table directly within Visual Studio .NET.

Drag-and-Drop from Server Explorer

The Server Explorer can also act as a source for drag-and-drop operations. Different components are created, depending on what sort of object you drag from Server Explorer:

➤ Dragging and dropping a database creates a SqlConnection component.

➤ Dragging and dropping a Table, View, Table Column, or View Column creates a SqlDataAdapter component and a SqlConnection component.

➤ Dragging and dropping a stored procedure or table-valued function creates a SqlCommand component and a SqlConnection component.

These three components encapsulate objects that are members of the System.Data.SqlClient namespace. You'll learn more about this namespace in Chapter 7, "Consuming and Manipulating Data." Even without knowing the details of the code, though, you can work through this example to see how easy Visual Studio .NET makes it to hook up database data to an ASP.NET Web Form:

1. Add a new Web Form to your ASP.NET application.

2. Place a DataGrid control on a new Web Form. Set the ID property of the control to dgCustomers.

3. Open Server Explorer.

4. Expand the tree under Data Connections to show a SQL Server data connection that points to the Northwind sample database, then the Tables node of the SQL Server, and then individual tables.

5. Drag the Customers table from Server Explorer and drop it on the form. This will create two data components in the tray area beneath the form, SqlConnection1 and SqlDataAdapter1.

6. Select the SqlDataAdapter1 object. Click the Generate Dataset link below the Properties window.

7. In the Generate Dataset window, choose to use the existing dsCustomers Dataset.

8. Set the DataSource property of the DataGrid control to DsCustomers1. Set the DataMember property of the DataGrid control to Customers.

9. Double-click the Web Form and enter code in the form's Load event:

```
Private Sub Page_Load(ByVal sender As System.Object, _
ByVal e As System.EventArgs) Handles MyBase.Load
    ' Move the data from the database to the DataGrid
    SqlDataAdapter1.Fill(DsCustomers1, "Customers")
    dgCustomers.DataBind()
End Sub
```

10. Set the Web Form as the start page for the project.

11. Run the project. The DataGrid will display all the data from the Customers table. The code uses the visual data objects that you created on the form to make the connection between the DataGrid and the table.

Filtering Data

Filtering data refers to the process of selecting only some data from a larger body of data to appear on the user interface of a form. This can be a critical part of avoiding information overload for end users of an application. In most cases, users are not going to need to see every row of data in a database or even every row from a specific table. More often, they are only going to need a small subset of the larger data body.

Filtering with a DataView

You've already seen the DataView in action as a way to add the ICollection interface to a DataTable. Now it's time to look at this object in a bit more depth. To understand the DataView, you need to know a little bit about the internal structure of the DataSet object. A DataSet contains two collections. The Tables collection is made up of DataTable objects—each one of which represents data from a single table in the datasource. The Relations collection is made up of DataRelation objects—each one of which represents the relation between two DataTable objects.

The DataView object supplies one more piece of this puzzle: It represents a bindable, customized view of a DataTable. You can sort or filter the records from a DataTable to build a DataView. Then, instead of binding the original DataTable to a control, you can bind the DataView to the control instead. Here's how you might modify the previous example to do this in code:

```
Private Sub Page_Load(ByVal sender As System.Object, _
ByVal e As System.EventArgs) Handles MyBase.Load
    ' Move the data from the database to the DataSet
    SqlDataAdapter1.Fill(DsCustomers1, "Customers")

    ' Create a dataview to filter the Customers table
    Dim dvCustomers As DataView = _
    New DataView(DsCustomers1.Tables("Customers"))
    ' Apply a sort to the dataview
    dvCustomers.Sort = "ContactName"
    ' Apply a filter to the dataview
    dvCustomers.RowFilter = "Country = 'France'"
    ' and bind the results to the grid
    dgCustomers.DataSource = dvCustomers
    dgCustomers.DataBind()
End Sub
```

Filtering at the Server

The DataView class provides a useful way to filter data, but it's inefficient for some purposes. That's because all the data is first retrieved from the database server and stored in memory on the client. So if 10 million rows of data are on the server, a DataView will retrieve all 10 million rows. After that, the DataView can be used to quickly select a subset of the data. But what if you're never going to need all the data? In that case, you're better off filtering on the server, rather than retrieving all that data you'll never need. One way to do this is by basing a SqlDataAdapter object on a view instead of a table. For example, you could create a view on your SQL Server that only retrieves customers from France:

```
SELECT TOP 100 PERCENT dbo.Customers.*
FROM dbo.Customers
WHERE Country='France'
ORDER BY ContactName
```

After doing this, you can use the view in Visual Studio .NET just as you can use a table. For example, you can drop the view on a form and use it to fill a DataSet. It will only retrieve the selected customers instead of all the customers.

Using Templated Controls to Display Data

A *templated control* is one whose display is entirely dictated by templates. These controls have no default rendering. Instead, it's up to you to supply templates for the items in the control. ASP.NET implements two templated controls, the Repeater and the DataList. I start with the simpler of the two, the Repeater control.

The Repeater Control

Following is an example of using the Repeater control with bound data:

1. Add a new Web Form to your application. Place a Repeater control on the new Web Form. Set the ID of the control to rptOrders. The control will initially display a design-time placeholder.

2. Open Server Explorer.

3. Expand the tree under Data Connections to show a SQL Server data connection that points to the Northwind sample database and then the Tables node of the SQL Server.

4. Drag the Orders table from Server Explorer and drop it on the form. This will create two data components, SqlConnection1 and SqlDataAdapter1.

5. Select the SqlDataAdapter1 object. Click the Generate Dataset link below the Properties window.

6. Create a new DataSet named dsOrders. Click OK to close the Generate DataSet dialog box.

7. Set the DataSource property of the Repeater control to DsOrders1. Set the DataMember property of the Repeater control to Orders.

8. Switch to HTML view and enter code to customize the Repeater control:

```
<asp:Repeater id="rptOrders" runat="server"
 DataSource="<%# DsOrders1 %>" DataMember="Orders">
    <HeaderTemplate>
        <table>
            <thead bgcolor=#6699ff>
                <th>Order ID</th>
                <th>Customer ID</th>
                <th>Order Date</th>
                <th>Freight</th>
            </thead>
    </HeaderTemplate>
    <ItemTemplate>
        <tr bgcolor=#ccffff>
            <td><%# DataBinder.Eval(
 Container.DataItem, "OrderID") %></td>
            <td><%# DataBinder.Eval(
 Container.DataItem, "CustomerID") %></td>
            <td><%# DataBinder.Eval(
 Container.DataItem, "OrderDate", "{0:d}") %></td>
            <td><%# DataBinder.Eval(
 Container.DataItem, "Freight", "{0:c}") %></td>
        </tr>
    </ItemTemplate>
    <AlternatingItemTemplate>
        <tr bgcolor=#ffffff>
            <td><%# DataBinder.Eval(
 Container.DataItem, "OrderID") %></td>
            <td><%# DataBinder.Eval(
 Container.DataItem, "CustomerID") %></td>
            <td><%# DataBinder.Eval(
 Container.DataItem, "OrderDate", "{0:d}") %></td>
            <td><%# DataBinder.Eval(
 Container.DataItem, "Freight", "{0:c}") %></td>
        </tr>
    </AlternatingItemTemplate>
    <SeparatorTemplate>
        <tr height=4 bgcolor=#0000ff>
            <td></td><td></td><td></td><td></td>
        </tr>
    </SeparatorTemplate>
    <FooterTemplate>
        </table>
    </FooterTemplate>
</asp:Repeater>
```

9. Double-click the form and enter code in the page's Load event:

```
Private Sub Page_Load(ByVal sender As System.Object, _
 ByVal e As System.EventArgs) Handles MyBase.Load
    'Load the data
    SqlDataAdapter1.Fill(DsOrders1, "Orders")
    DataBind()
End Sub
```

10. Set the form as the start page for the project.

11. Run the project. Repeater will display data from four columns of the Orders table, as shown in Figure 6.8.

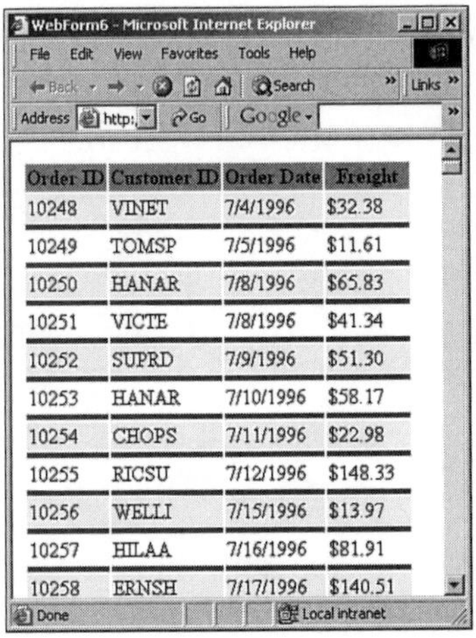

Figure 6.8 The **Repeater** control offers flexible formatting options for tabular data.

If you inspect the HTML, you'll see that the Repeater control allows you to specify five templates:

➤ The HeaderTemplate is rendered once at the start of the control.

➤ The ItemTemplate is rendered once for every row of data in the data source of the control.

➤ The AlternatingItemTemplate is used instead of the ItemTemplate for every other row of data.

➤ The SeparatorTemplate is rendered once between each row of data.

➤ The FooterTemplate is rendered once at the end of the control.

The only one of these templates that you're required to implement for a Repeater control is the ItemTemplate. You can only perform data binding in the ItemTemplate and AlternatingItemTemplate templates.

You'll also see a new object in the HTML code: DataBinder. DataBinder exists to make formatting data in templated controls (and other controls that contain subcontrols) easy. The Eval method of the DataBinder object takes three arguments:

➤ The first argument specifies the source of the data. The templates are contained within the Repeater control, and the Repeater control itself is bound to a collection of data. So in this case, the source of the data is Container.DataItem—a single item of data from the containing control.

➤ The second argument is the name of a column within the data to bind at this position.

➤ The third (optional) argument is a format string of the type that could be supplied to the String.Format method.

The DataBinder control handles all the necessary casting to make string formatting work properly with bound data, regardless of the data type of the underlying data.

The DataList Control

The DataList control is similar to the Repeater control, but it provides more flexible formatting options. The control handles the layout of items in rows and columns, so you don't have to supply <table> tags within its templates. It also lets you build data-editing capabilities into the Web Form. A simple DataList control looks like this in the form's HTML:

```
<asp:DataList id="dlOrders" runat="server"
 DataSource="<%# DsOrders1 %>" DataMember="Orders"
RepeatColumns="2" CellSpacing="10">
    <ItemTemplate>
        <b>Order ID: </b>
        <%# DataBinder.Eval(
➥ Container.DataItem, "OrderID") %>
        <br>
        <b>Customer ID: </b>
        <%# DataBinder.Eval(
➥ Container.DataItem, "CustomerID") %>
        <br>
        <b>Order Date: </b>
        <%# DataBinder.Eval(
➥ Container.DataItem, "OrderDate", "{0:d}") %>
        <br>
        <b>Freight: </b>
        <%# DataBinder.Eval(
➥ Container.DataItem, "Freight", "{0:c}") %>
        <br>
    </ItemTemplate>
</asp:DataList>
```

Figure 6.9 shows what this DataList might look like in action. The number of columns of information on the display is controlled by the RepeatColumns property of the DataList. Each item is rendered according to the HTML code in the ItemTemplate template.

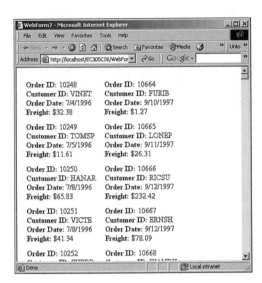

Figure 6.9   The **DataList** control lets you display multiple columns of formatted data.

Editing Data with a **DataList** Control

The DataList control also offers support for editing data. To enable this support, you need to supply an EditItemTemplate as well as code to respond to several events. The HTML, including the editing template, might look like this:

```
<asp:DataList id="dlOrders" runat="server"
 DataSource="<%# DsOrders1 %>" DataMember="Orders"
 RepeatColumns="1" CellSpacing="10">
    <ItemTemplate>
        <B>Order ID: </B>
        <%# DataBinder.Eval(
➥ Container.DataItem, "OrderID") %>
        <BR>
        <B>Customer ID: </B>
        <%# DataBinder.Eval(
➥ Container.DataItem, "CustomerID") %>
        <BR>
        <B>Order Date: </B>
        <%# DataBinder.Eval(
➥ Container.DataItem, "OrderDate", "{0:d}") %>
        <BR>
        <B>Freight: </B>
        <%# DataBinder.Eval(
➥ Container.DataItem, "Freight", "{0:c}") %>
        <BR>
        <asp:Button id="btnEdit"
          runat="server" Text="Edit"
          CommandName="Edit"></asp:Button>
    </ItemTemplate>
    <EditItemTemplate>
        <B>Order ID: </B>
        <%# DataBinder.Eval(
➥ Container.DataItem, "OrderID") %>
```

```
                <BR>
                <B>Customer ID: </B>
                <%# DataBinder.Eval(
➡ Container.DataItem, "CustomerID") %>
                <BR>
                <B>Order Date: </B>
                <%# DataBinder.Eval(
➡ Container.DataItem, "OrderDate", "{0:d}") %>
                <BR>
                <B>Freight: </B><INPUT id=freight type=text
                value='<%# DataBinder.Eval(
➡ Container.DataItem, "Freight") %>' runat="server">
                <BR>
                <asp:Button id="btnUpdate"
runat="server" Text="Update"
                CommandName="Update"></asp:Button>
                <asp:Button id="btnCancel"
runat="server" Text="Cancel"
                CommandName="Cancel"></asp:Button>
            </EditItemTemplate>
        </asp:DataList>
```

In the code behind the page, you can handle editing by supplying appropriate event procedures:

```
Private Sub dlOrders_CancelCommand( _
 ByVal source As Object, _
 ByVal e As System.Web.UI.WebControls. _
 DataListCommandEventArgs) _
 Handles dlOrders.CancelCommand
    ' Turn off the editing controls
    dlOrders.EditItemIndex = -1
    ' Re-bind the data
    SqlDataAdapter1.Fill(DsOrders1, "Orders")
    DataBind()
End Sub

Private Sub dlOrders_EditCommand( _
 ByVal source As Object, _
 ByVal e As System.Web.UI.WebControls. _
 DataListCommandEventArgs) _
 Handles dlOrders.EditCommand
    ' Turn on the editing controls
    dlOrders.EditItemIndex = CInt(e.Item.ItemIndex)
    ' Re-bind the data
    SqlDataAdapter1.Fill(DsOrders1, "Orders")
    DataBind()
End Sub

Private Sub dlOrders_UpdateCommand( _
 ByVal source As Object, _
 ByVal e As System.Web.UI.WebControls. _
 DataListCommandEventArgs) _
 Handles dlOrders.UpdateCommand
    Dim htEdit As HtmlInputText
    ' Get the existing data
    SqlDataAdapter1.Fill(DsOrders1, "Orders")
    ' Get the changed data and put it in the dataase
    htEdit = e.Item.FindControl("freight")
    DsOrders1.Tables("Orders").Rows( _
    e.Item.ItemIndex)(7) = htEdit.Value
```

```
     ' Turn off editing
     dlOrders.EditItemIndex = -1
     ' re-bind the data
     DataBind()
End Sub
```

Figure 6.10 shows how the control looks in edit mode.

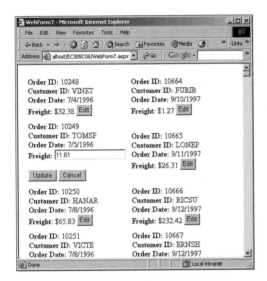

Figure 6.10 Editing data in a **DataList** control.

After you've created a DataList with an EditItemTemplate, you can tell the control to use that template for a specific row by supplying the (zero-based) index of that row. The CommandName tags in the HTML code correspond to the events that DataList will raise in the VB code. For example, the CommandName="Edit" tag in the HTML corresponds to the EditCommand event in the VB .NET code. The Edit, Update, and Cancel commands are hardwired in this fashion. When you raise an EditCommand event, the parameters passed to the event include the data item in which the event was raised. The code uses the index of this item to determine which row to show in the edited state. Note that you need to rebind the data when you do this because, in reality, you're rebuilding the entire page from scratch.

To cancel an edit, you just set the EditItemIndex property back to -1 and rebind the control.

To update the data, the code uses the FindControl method of the data item to find the input control where the freight value was edited. This control can be represented by an HtmlInputText object in the code. The code then uses the Value property of that object to update the corresponding row in the Dataset.

Exam Prep Questions

Question 1

You are designing a Web Form to display a list of the gift baskets that your company sells. You want to show the baskets in two columns in the browser. Each listing will include a name, description, and price. You want to change the background color on alternate listings so that it's easy to tell where one starts and another ends.

Which control should you use to display this information?

- ○ A. **DataList**
- ○ B. **Repeater**
- ○ C. **DataGrid**
- ○ D. **DropDownList**

Answer A is correct. The advanced formatting capabilities of the DataList control, including automatic column support, are perfect for these requirements. Answers B and C are incorrect because the Repeater and DataGrid controls do not support showing records in two parallel columns. Answer D is incorrect because the DropDownList control will only display one item until the list is accessed, and even then it doesn't offer row-by-row formatting.

Question 2

You have developed a Web Form with a **DataList** control that displays product information. Part of the information being displayed is a database column named Price. The Price column is stored as a floating-point value in the database. Which binding expression should you use to display the value of this column on the user interface, formatted as currency?

- ○ A.
  ```
  <%# DataBinder.Eval(Container.DataItem, "Price") %>
  ```

- ○ B.
  ```
  <%# "Price", "{0:c}" %>
  ```

- ○ C.
  ```
  <%# DataBinder.Eval(Container.DataItem, "Price", "{0:c}") %>
  ```

- ○ D.
  ```
  <%# "Price" %>
  ```

Answer C is correct. The `DataBinder.Eval` method takes three parameters: a reference to the data item being evaluated, the name of the column to evaluate, and a formatting expression. Answers A and D are incorrect because they do not include a formatting code. Answers B and D are incorrect because they are using simple data binding syntax rather than `DataBinder.Eval`.

Question 3

Your Web Form displays a list of spare parts in a **ListBox** control. The **Page_Load** event handler uses data binding to place a list of spare parts in this control. The control's **DataTextField** property is set to **PartName**, and its **DataValueField** is set to **PartNumber**. The Web Form also includes a **Label** control named **lblPartNumber** whose **Text** property is bound to **lbParts.SelectedItem.Value**. The Web Form contains this code:

```
Private Sub lbParts_SelectedIndexChanged( _
  ByVal sender As System.Object, _
  ByVal e As System.EventArgs) _
  Handles lbParts.SelectedIndexChanged
      lblPartNumber.DataBind()
End Sub
```

When the user selects a part in the **ListBox**, the corresponding part number is not displayed in the **Label** control. What should you do to fix this problem?

- ○ A. Replace the **Label** control with a **TextBox** control.
- ○ B. Replace the **ListBox** control with a **DropDownList** control.
- ○ C. Set the **AutoPostBack** property of the **ListBox** control to **True**.
- ○ D. Set the control's **DataTextField** property to **PartNumber** and its **DataValueField** to **PartName**.

Answer C is correct. The `ListBox` control does not, by default, post its contents back to the server. Until this postback occurs, event code attached to the `ListBox` won't run. Setting the `AutoPostBack` property to `True` will cause the postback to occur whenever the user selects a new item. Answers A and B are incorrect because swapping controls won't do anything about the missing postback. Answer D is incorrect because it will display the wrong data in the `ListBox`.

Question 4

> Which of these tasks could you perform with simple data binding (select all correct answers)?
>
> ❑ A. Display the date 30 days from now as the selected date on a **Calendar** control.
>
> ❑ B. Enable or disable a control according to the return value of a function.
>
> ❑ C. Display a list of customers together with their orders.
>
> ❑ D. Display a list of order numbers and order dates in a **DropDownList** control.

Answers A and B are correct. Simple data binding lets you assign a value to any one property of a control. Answers C and D are incorrect because displaying multiple pieces of information requires the use of complex data binding.

Question 5

> You have created a Web Form that includes a **Label** control named **lblSupplier**. This control uses simple data binding to display the return value from a function in the Web Form's code-behind module. Which method can you use to update the value displayed by the control (select all correct answers)?
>
> ❑ A. **DataBind()** method
>
> ❑ B. **Page.DataBind()** method
>
> ❑ C. **lblSupplier.DataBind()** method
>
> ❑ D. **lblSupplier.Fill()** method

Answers A, B, and C are correct. A control is data bound when you call its DataBind method or the DataBind method of its container. Because the code is running behind the page, you need not specify the Page object to call its DataBind method, so answer A is correct. Answers B and C are correct because they specify data binding for the page and for the control, respectively. Answer D is incorrect because the Fill method is used with a DataAdapter object to fill a DataSet.

Question 6

You have developed an ASP.NET application for displaying scheduling informa-tion in a busy medical practice. The application represents appointments by delivering a **DataView** containing a collection of **Appointment** objects as the return value of a function. You use simple data binding to display the desired information from the **Appointment** objects on a Web Form. However, at runtime the form does not display any data, even though you have confirmed that the **DataView** is not empty. What should you do to correct this problem?

O A. Create a **DataSet** from the **DataView** and bind the **DataSet** to the controls.

O B. Change the function to return an **ArrayList** instead of a **DataView**.

O C. Call the **DataBind** method of the form to bind the data to the user interface.

O D. Add code to the **Page_Load** event handler to only display the data if **IsPostBack** equals **False**.

Answer C is correct. Bound controls under ASP.NET do not display any data until you explicitly call the DataBind method of the control or of the control's con-tainer. Answers A and C are incorrect because delivering the data in a different object will not remove the requirement to call the DataBind method. Answer D is incorrect because the postback doesn't make a difference to the necessary code.

Question 7

The Orders table in your database contains roughly 500,000 orders. You need to be able to quickly display all orders from a particular customer on a Web Form. The average customer has placed between 3 and 35 orders. Which technique should you use to filter the orders?

O A. Load the Orders table into a **DataSet**. Build a **DataView** that returns the required orders.

O B. Create a view on the server that returns the required orders. Bind the view to the user interface.

O C. Load the Orders table into an array. Use a For Each loop to move through the array, extracting the matching orders to a second array.

O D. Load the Orders table into a **DataSet**. Bind the **DataSet** to a **DataList** control and include buttons to edit the data.

Answer B is correct. To return only a small part of a database, you should always perform the filtering on the database server. Answers A, C, and D are incorrect because they retrieve all the data from the database server and then perform the filtering on the client. This would result in unnecessary network traffic and delays.

Question 8

Your application contains an array of information on endangered species and their population levels. You want to display this information in an HTML table on a Web Form. Which control should you use to hold the data (select all correct answers)?

- ❑ A. **ListBox**
- ❑ B. **Table**
- ❑ C. **DataList**
- ❑ D. **Repeater**

Answers C and D are correct. The ListBox control will display as an HTML ListBox. The Table control does display an HTML table, but you need to write the code for the individual cells rather than using data binding to move the data to the user interface. The DataList and Repeater controls both have the capability to render their contents as a table.

Question 9

You are planning to use the **Repeater** control to display inventory information on a Web Form. Which templates must you supply to the **Repeater** control (select all that apply)?

- ❑ A. **HeaderTemplate**
- ❑ B. **ItemTemplate**
- ❑ C. **AlternatingItemTemplate**
- ❑ D. **FooterTemplate**

Answer B is correct. The only template that you are required to supply for the Repeater control is the ItemTemplate. All other templates are optional, so answers A, C, and D are incorrect.

Question 10

Your application includes a database table named Orders. The Orders table includes columns named OrderNumber and OrderCustomer. You've used drag and drop from Server Explorer to create a **SqlConnection** object and a **SqlDataAdapter** object to access this data. You've also created a **DataSet** named **dsOrders** to hold the data. Your Web Form includes code to fill this **DataSet** when the form is first loaded.

Now you'd like to display the list of orders in a **ListBox** control named **lbOrders**. The **ListBox** should show the order numbers and return the corresponding customer for another control to display. Which of these code snippets should you use?

○ A.

```
With lbOrders
      .DataSource = dsOrders
      .DataTextField = "OrderNumber"
      .DataValueField = "OrderCustomer"
      .DataBind
End With
```

○ B.

```
With lbOrders
      .DataSource = _
      dsOrders.Tables("Orders")
      .DataTextField = "OrderNumber"
      .DataValueField = "OrderCustomer"
      .DataBind
End With
```

○ C.

```
With lbOrders
      .DataSource = _
      dsOrders.Tables("Orders")
      .DataTextField = "OrderNumber"
      .SelectedItem = "OrderCustomer"
End With
```

○ D.

```
With lbOrders
      .DataTextField = "OrderNumber"
      .DataValueField = "OrderCustomer"
      .DataBind
End With
```

Answer B is correct. Answer A is incorrect because it does not specify which data within the DataSet to use. Answer C is incorrect because it does not specify the DataValueField property, which is required to retrieve a value from the ListBox. Answer D is incorrect because it does not set the DataSource property, and hence has no data to bind.

Need to Know More?

 Gunderloy, Mike. *ADO and ADO.NET Programming*. Sybex, 2002.

 Esposito, Dino. *Building Solutions with ASP.NET and ADO.NET*. Microsoft Press, 2002.

 ASP.NET Web site, http://www.asp.net.

 ASP.NET QuickStart Tutorials (installed with the .NET Framework SDK), "Data Binding Server Controls" and "Server-Side Data Access."

Consuming and Manipulating Data

Terms you'll need to understand:

✓ Transact-SQL/SQL-92
✓ Ad hoc query
✓ Stored procedure
✓ Parameter
✓ Stream
✓ Backing store
✓ Data provider
✓ **DataSet** class
✓ Schema
✓ XML (Extensible Markup Language)
✓ XML declaration, element, and attribute
✓ XML namespace
✓ CDATA section
✓ "Last one wins" concurrency control
✓ Optimistic concurrency control

Techniques you'll need to master:

✓ Creating SQL Server queries and stored procedures
✓ Retrieving data from relational databases with ADO.NET
✓ Loading and editing data into a **DataSet** object
✓ Retrieving data from XML documents with the **XmlDocument** class
✓ Retrieving data from flat files using the **System.IO** classes
✓ Handling locking and other errors during data access operations

The 70-305 exam objectives require you know how to manipulate many types of data. You need to know about a broad spectrum of data access methods that you can use to retrieve data from Microsoft SQL Server, from disk files, and from XML files. You also need to know how to handle common database errors.

Accessing and Manipulating SQL Server Data

The Framework Class Library (FCL) includes an entire namespace (System.Data.SqlClient) devoted to efficient communication between .NET applications and SQL Server.

The objects in System.Data.SqlClient, though, won't do you any good unless you understand the language used to communicate with SQL Server. This language is *Transact-SQL (T-SQL)*. T-SQL is Microsoft's implementation of SQL (Structured Query Language), which is defined by a standard from the American National Standards Institute (ANSI).

There are two ways to submit T-SQL to a SQL Server database for processing. You can write *ad hoc queries*, SQL statements that are executed directly. Or, you can write *stored procedures*, SQL statements that are stored on the server as a named object. The .NET Framework includes facilities for running both ad hoc queries and stored procedures.

Using Ad Hoc Queries

Ad hoc T-SQL queries provide you with an extremely flexible way to retrieve data from a SQL Server database or to make changes to that database. This section shows you an easy way to send an ad hoc query to SQL Server, and it explains the basics of the four main T-SQL statements that help you manipulate SQL Server data:

➤ SELECT statements allow you to retrieve data stored in the database.

➤ INSERT statements allow you to add new data to the database.

➤ UPDATE statements allow you to modify data that's already in the database.

➤ DELETE statements allow you to delete data from the database.

You'll usually see SQL keywords (such as **SELECT**, **INSERT**, **UPDATE**, and **DELETE**) formatted entirely in uppercase. I'll follow that convention in this book, but uppercase formatting isn't required by SQL Server. You might see these same keywords in mixed case or lowercase on an exam. As far as SQL Server is concerned, there's no difference between **SELECT**, **Select**, and **select**.

Running Queries

When learning T-SQL, it's useful to be able to send queries to a SQL Server database and to see the results (if any) that the server returns. There are many ways to send queries to SQL Server, including the use of the OSQL or SQL Query Analyzer utilities that are shipped with SQL Server. But for simple SELECT queries, it's just as easy to build your own application in Visual Basic .NET. Here's how:

1. Create a new Visual Basic .NET Web Application project.

2. Open Server Explorer.

3. Expand the tree under Data Connections to show a SQL Server data connection that points to the Northwind sample database. Drag and drop the data connection to the default Web Form in the project.

4. Add a TextBox control with the ID of txtQuery, a Button control with the ID of btnExecute, and a DataGrid control with the ID of dgResults to the form. Set the TextMode property of the TextBox to MultiLine.

5. Double-click the Button control to open the form's module. Enter two statements at the top of the module to make the ADO.NET objects available:

```
Imports System.Data
Imports System.Data.SqlClient
```

6. Enter this code to execute the query when you click the Button control:

```
Private Sub Page_Load(ByVal sender As System.Object, _
    ByVal e As System.EventArgs) Handles MyBase.Load
        ' Process queries when form is posted back
        If IsPostBack Then
            ' Create a SqlCommand to represent the query
            Dim cmd As SqlCommand = _
            SqlConnection1.CreateCommand
            cmd.CommandType = CommandType.Text
            cmd.CommandText = txtQuery.Text
            ' Create a SqlDataAdapter to talk to the database
            Dim da As SqlDataAdapter = New SqlDataAdapter()
            da.SelectCommand = cmd
            ' Create a DataSet to hold the results
            Dim ds As DataSet = New DataSet()
            ' Fill the DataSet
            da.Fill(ds, "Results")
```

```
' And bind it to the DataGrid
dgResults.DataSource = ds
dgResults.DataMember = "Results"
dgResults.DataBind()
    End If
End Sub
```

7. Set the Web Form as the start page for the project.

8. Run the project. Enter a query in the TextBox:

```
SELECT * FROM Employees
```

9. Click the button. This runs the code, retrieving the results to the DataGrid, as shown in Figure 7.1.

Figure 7.1 Running an ad hoc query from a custom Web Form.

The SELECT Statement

It's time to dig into the T-SQL language to see some of the possible queries, starting with the SELECT statement.

You should execute enough of these statements to get a good idea of how the T-SQL langauge works. Just reading the descriptions here is no substitute for actually practicing with T-SQL. You're sure to see some SQL statements on the exam.

The basic SQL statement is the SELECT statement. This statement is used to create a resultset. In skeleton form, a SELECT looks like this:

```
SELECT field_list
FROM table_list
WHERE where_clause
GROUP BY group_by_clause
HAVING having_clause
ORDER BY sort_clause
```

Each of those lines of code is called a *clause*. The SELECT and FROM clauses are required, and the rest are optional. Here's an example of a SQL statement containing only the required clauses:

```
SELECT OrderID, CustomerID
FROM Orders
```

The resultset for this statement contains the values of the OrderID and CustomerID fields from every record in the Orders table.

The * character is a shortcut to refer to all columns in the source:

```
SELECT *
FROM Orders
```

You're also not limited to fields from a single table. For instance, you might try retrieving information from both the Customers and Orders tables with this query:

```
SELECT OrderID, Customers.CustomerID
FROM Orders, Customers
```

Customers.CustomerID is what's known as a *fully qualified name*, specifying both the table name and the field name. This is necessary because both the Customers and the Orders tables contain fields named CustomerID, and you need to tell SQL Server which one you want to display.

If you try the previous query, though, you'll get more than 75,000 records back—many more than the number of orders in the database! That's because the query as written, although it includes all the proper tables, doesn't tell SQL Server how to relate those tables.

The name for this sort of query is a *cross-product* query. SQL Server constructs the resultset by including one row in the output for each row in each combination of input table rows. That is, there's an output row for the first order and the first customer, for the first order and the second customer, and so on. A more useful query, of course, matches each order with the corresponding customer.

That's the job of the INNER JOIN keyword. INNER JOIN tells SQL Server how to match two tables. Here's how the syntax looks for a fixed version of the original query:

```
SELECT OrderID, Customers.CustomerID
FROM Orders INNER JOIN Customers
ON Orders.CustomerID = Customers.CustomerID
```

This rewrite tells SQL Server to look at each row in the Orders table and match it with all rows in the Customers table where the CustomerID of the order equals the CustomerID of the customer. Because CustomerIDs are unique in the Customers table, this is tantamount to including only a single row for each order in the resultset.

The INNER JOIN keyword can appear more than once in a query for more than two tables to join. For example, here's a query to show EmployeeIDs along with Order and CustomerIDs:

```
SELECT Orders.OrderID, Customers.CustomerID,
Employees.EmployeeID
FROM Employees INNER JOIN
(Customers INNER JOIN Orders
ON Customers.CustomerID = Orders.CustomerID)
ON Employees.EmployeeID = Orders.EmployeeID
```

Note the use of parentheses to specify the order in which the joins should be performed.

What if you only want to see some of the rows in the table? That's where the WHERE clause comes into the picture. You can think of a WHERE clause as making a simple, yes-or-no decision for each row of data in the original table, deciding whether to include that row in the resultset.

The simplest form of the WHERE clause checks for the exact contents of a field. For example,

```
SELECT * FROM Orders
WHERE ShipCountry = 'Brazil'
```

This query looks at every row in the Orders table and determines whether the ShipCountry field contains the exact value Brazil. If so, the row is included in the results. If not, it's discarded. However, WHERE clauses need not be exact. This is also a valid SQL statement:

```
SELECT * FROM Orders
WHERE Freight > 50
```

In this case, you'll get all the rows in which the amount in the Freight field is greater than 50.

You're free to combine multiple tests in a single WHERE clause. For example,

```
SELECT * FROM Orders
WHERE ShipCountry = 'Brazil'
 AND Freight > 50
 AND OrderDate <= '12/31/97'
```

This retrieves all orders that went to Brazil, had more than $50 of freight charges, and were shipped before the end of 1997. The key is that the entire WHERE clause must be a single logical predicate. That is, by evaluating all the pieces, the result must be a True or False value. Rows for which the WHERE clause evaluates to True are included in the results; rows for which it evaluates to False are excluded.

You can also use wildcards in a WHERE clause. Consider this simple SELECT statement:

```
SELECT * FROM Customers
WHERE CustomerID = 'BLONP'
```

If you run the query, you'll find that it returns the record for Blondel *pere et fils*, the customer that is assigned the CustomerID BLONP. So far, that's easy. But what if you remember that the CustomerID starts with *B*, but not what it is exactly? That's when you'd use a wildcard:

```
SELECT * FROM Customers
WHERE CustomerID LIKE 'B%'
```

The % wildcard matches zero or more characters, so the result of this query is to retrieve all the customers whose CustomerIDs begin with *B*. Note the switch from = to LIKE when using a wildcard. (If you searched for CustomerID = 'B%', you'd only find a customer with that exact ID.) Now suppose that you almost remember the CustomerID, but not quite: Is it BLOND or BLONP? Try this query:

```
SELECT * FROM Customers
WHERE CustomerID LIKE 'BLON_'
```

The _ wildcard matches precisely one character—so that would match BLONA, BLONB, and so on. If you're sure that it's either *D* or *P*, you can try the following:

```
SELECT * FROM Customers
WHERE CustomerID LIKE 'BLON[dp]'
```

The [dp] is a character set wildcard. The square brackets tell SQL Server to match any one of the characters listed in the set. You can also use a dash in a character set to indicate a range:

```
SELECT * FROM Customers
WHERE CustomerID LIKE 'BLON[D-P]'
```

That matches BLOND, BLONE, and so on, through BLONP. You can also invert a character set with the ^ character. For example,

```
SELECT * FROM Customers
WHERE CustomerID LIKE 'BLON[^A-O]'
```

This matches BLONP, BLONQ, and so on but not BLONA, BLONB, or anything else that would match the character set without the ^ character.

SQL is a set-oriented language; by default, the database engine is free to return the set of results in any order it likes. To guarantee a sort order, include an ORDER BY clause in your SQL statement. For example, to see the customers from Venezuela in Postal Code order, you could use this statement:

```
SELECT * FROM Customers
WHERE Country = 'Venezuela'
ORDER BY PostalCode
```

That's the basic ORDER BY clause: a field name to sort by. You can use two keywords to modify this: ASC, for ascending sort (the default), and DESC, for descending sort. So, you could write the previous SQL statement as

```
SELECT * FROM Customers
WHERE Country = 'Venezuela'
ORDER BY PostalCode ASC
```

You're not limited to sorting by a single field. You can specify on a field-by-field basis the order of the sort:

```
SELECT * FROM Customers
ORDER BY Country ASC, PostalCode DESC
```

That would sort by country in ascending order, and then by postal code in descending order within each country.

It's also possible (and indeed common) to use SQL to return aggregate, summarized information.

For example, suppose that you want to know how many customers you have in each country. This query will give you the answer:

```
SELECT COUNT(CustomerID) AS CustCount, Country
FROM Customers
GROUP BY Country
```

You can think of the GROUP BY clause as creating "buckets" in this case, one for each country. As the database engine examines each record, it is tossed in the appropriate bucket. After this process is done, the database engine counts the number of records that ended up in each bucket and outputs a row for each one.

You can use ORDER BY in conjunction with GROUP BY. In this case, you could sort by the number of customers in each country:

```
SELECT COUNT(CustomerID) AS CustCount, Country
FROM Customers
GROUP BY Country
ORDER BY Count(CustomerID) DESC
```

COUNT() in these SQL statements is an *aggregate function,* one that returns a result based on a number of rows. T-SQL supports a number of aggregate functions. Here are some of the most common:

➤ COUNT()—Number of records

➤ SUM()—Total value of records

➤ AVG()—Average value of records

➤ MIN()—Smallest record

➤ MAX()—Largest record

You can also group on more than one field. For example,

```
SELECT Count(CustomerID) AS CustCount, Region, Country
FROM Customers
GROUP BY Region, Country
```

That statement sets up one bucket for each combination of region and country and categorizes the customers by both fields simultaneously.

So far, the GROUP BY statements you've seen have included all the records in the table. For example, consider this query:

```
SELECT ProductID,
Sum(Quantity) AS TotalSales
FROM [Order Details]
GROUP BY ProductID
ORDER BY Sum(Quantity) DESC
```

This query uses square brackets to quote the name of the Order Details table because the table name has a space in it. Without the quoting, SQL Server would try to interpret it as two names.

That query returns a resultset that has one row for each product found in the Order Details table, with the ProductID and the total quantity of that ordered product.

As stated, that query uses all the rows in the Order Details table to come up with its totals. You can limit this to use only part of the table in two ways.

First, you can use a WHERE clause to limit the rows from the original query that will be included in the totals:

```
SELECT ProductID,
Sum(Quantity) AS TotalSales
FROM [Order Details]
WHERE Quantity > 10
GROUP BY ProductID
ORDER BY Sum(Quantity) DESC
```

That will have the same effect as the first query, except that it will just ignore any row in the Order Details table that has a quantity of 10 or under.

The other way to limit the results is by filtering the totals with a HAVING clause:

```
SELECT ProductID, Sum(Quantity) AS TotalSales
FROM [Order Details]
GROUP BY ProductID
HAVING Sum(Quantity) > 1000
ORDER BY Sum(Quantity) DESC
```

A HAVING clause filters the results, rather than the input. That is, the last query will sum everything from the Order Details table and then show you rows in which the total is greater than 1000.

Note that WHERE and HAVING go in two different places in the SQL statement. The order of clauses is fixed, not optional.

The INSERT Statement

The purpose of the INSERT statement is to add a row or multiple rows to a table through executing a SQL statement. In its simplest form, the insert query lists a target table and a set of values to insert. For example, this query adds a new row to the Order Details table:

```
INSERT INTO [Order Details]
VALUES (10248, 1, 12.00, 5, 0)
```

This simple form of the statement has two drawbacks. First, knowing which field is getting which piece of data is difficult: The values are inserted into the table fields in the order that the fields show up in Design view, but you must remember (in this example) that the quantity is the fourth field. Second, if you use this format, you must supply a value for every field. This is a problem when you want the default value for a field or when a field can't have data inserted into it (for example, an identity field whose values are automatically generated by SQL Server). To get around these problems, a second format explicitly lists the fields for the target table:

```
INSERT INTO [Order Details]
   (OrderID, ProductID, UnitPrice, Quantity, Discount)
VALUES (10248, 2, 12.00, 5, 0)
```

Here, the first set of parentheses holds a column list, and the second set holds the values to insert. If a field has a default value, can store null values, or is an identity field, you can leave it out of the field list:

```
INSERT INTO Products
  (ProductName, SupplierID, CategoryID)
VALUES ('Turnips', 25, 7)
```

This works even though no value is specified for most of the fields in the Products table. Also, you can rearrange the field list as long as you rearrange the value list to match:

```
INSERT INTO Products
  (SupplierID, ProductName, CategoryID)
VALUES (20, 'Lettuce', 7)
```

The UPDATE Statement

Another useful SQL statement is the UPDATE statement. As you can probably guess, the purpose of an UPDATE query is to update data. For example, you could update a field in a record in Northwind with this query:

```
UPDATE Customers
  SET ContactName = 'Maria Anderson'
  WHERE CustomerID = 'ALFKI'
```

In this query, the UPDATE keyword introduces an update query. The SET keyword tells SQL Server what to update. Here it's setting a field equal to a literal value. The WHERE clause tells SQL Server which row in the table to update.

You're not limited to updating a single record. If the WHERE clause selects multiple records, they will all be updated:

```
UPDATE Customers
  SET Country = 'United States'
  WHERE Country = 'USA'
```

You can even update every row in a table by leaving out the WHERE clause:

```
UPDATE Products
  SET Discontinued = False
```

This will update every row in the Products table, even those in which the Discontinued field already has the value False.

You can also update more than one field at a time with an UPDATE query:

```
UPDATE Customers
  SET ContactName = 'Maria Anders', City = 'Berlin'
  WHERE CustomerID = 'ALFKI'
```

And you can update with the result of an expression:

```
UPDATE Products
   SET UnitPrice = UnitPrice * 1.1
```

The DELETE Statement

The DELETE statement removes data from a table.

To avoid destroying existing data, I'll use another query to set the stage. The SELECT INTO statement is used to create a new table. For example, this statement creates a table named BadCustomers with all the data from the existing Customers table:

```
SELECT * INTO BadCustomers
FROM Customers
```

Here's a select query to select a single row from the new table:

```
SELECT * FROM BadCustomers WHERE CustomerID = 'GODOS'
```

Now change the SELECT * clause to DELETE:

```
DELETE FROM BadCustomers WHERE CustomerID = 'GODOS'
```

If you run this query, it will delete the specified row.

There's no need for a WHERE clause if you want to get really extreme:

```
DELETE FROM BadCustomers
```

That statement deletes all the rows from the BadCustomers table.

Using Stored Procedures

When you use an ad hoc query to interact with SQL Server, the SQL statements in the query are completely transient. They vanish as soon as you close whatever tool you've used to execute the query. By contrast, stored procedures are queries stored permanently on the SQL Server itself. Stored procedures have two main benefits. First, you can save complex SQL statements for future execution so that you don't have to re-create them from scratch. Second, SQL Server compiles stored procedures so that they run faster than ad hoc queries.

 In almost every case, stored procedures are preferable to ad hoc queries in production applications. The only time you should consider using ad hoc queries is when you're writing an application that must allow completely free-form querying by the end user. Otherwise, the additional development time required to implement stored procedures will be worth it in the end.

Creating a Stored Procedure

T-SQL includes a CREATE PROCEDURE keyword to create stored procedures. You can run CREATE PROCEDURE statements from any interface that allows you to enter and execute T-SQL. For example, you can create a stored procedure by executing this statement:

```
CREATE PROCEDURE procFranceCustomers
AS
    SELECT * FROM Customers
    WHERE Country = 'France'
```

Now you can execute the new procFranceCustomers stored procedure from any tool that allows you to execute SQL Statements. For example, Figure 7.2 shows the results of executing this stored procedure in the custom Web Form you built earlier in the chapter.

Figure 7.2 The results of running a stored procedure are the same as the results of running the T-SQL statements contained in the stored procedure.

There are two separate executing steps in this process. Executing the CREATE PROCEDURE statement (which is itself an ad hoc query) is necessary to create the stored procedure. After that has been done, you can execute the stored procedure itself to return results.

Running Stored Procedures from .NET

Executing a stored procedure from .NET is very similar to executing an ad hoc query. The difference is that you supply the name of the stored procedure instead of the actual SQL as the CommandText property of a SqlCommand object. For example, this code will execute the stored procedure that you just created:

```
Private Sub Page_Load(ByVal sender As System.Object, _
ByVal e As System.EventArgs) Handles MyBase.Load
    If Not IsPostBack Then
        ' Create a SqlCommand to
        ' represent the stored procedure
        Dim cmd As SqlCommand = _
         SqlConnection1.CreateCommand
        cmd.CommandType = CommandType.StoredProcedure
        cmd.CommandText = "procFranceCustomers"
        ' Create a SqlDataAdapter
        ' to talk to the database
        Dim da As SqlDataAdapter = _
         New SqlDataAdapter()
        da.SelectCommand = cmd
        ' Create a DataSet to hold the results
        Dim ds As DataSet = New DataSet()
        ' Fill the DataSet
        da.Fill(ds, "Customers")
        ' And bind it to a DataGrid
        dgResults.DataSource = ds
        dgResults.DataMember = "Customers"
        dgResults.DataBind()
    End If
End Sub
```

Stored procedures are not limited to containing SELECT statements. You can place any SQL statement inside of a stored procedure. For example, you might use this SQL statement to create a stored procedure to update the Customers table:

```
CREATE PROCEDURE procExpandCountry
AS
UPDATE Customers
 SET Country = 'United States'
 WHERE Country = 'USA'
```

When your stored procedure doesn't return a resultset, you need to use a slightly different code structure to execute it:

```
Private Sub Page_Load(ByVal sender As System.Object, _
ByVal e As System.EventArgs) Handles MyBase.Load
    If IsPostBack Then
        ' Create a SqlCommand to
        ' represent the stored procedure
        Dim cmd As SqlCommand = _
         SqlConnection1.CreateCommand
        cmd.CommandType = CommandType.StoredProcedure
        cmd.CommandText = "procExpandCountry"
        ' Open the connection and
        ' execute the stored procedure
        SqlConnection1.Open()
        cmd.ExecuteNonQuery()
        ' Close the connection
        SqlConnection1.Close()
        ' And notify the user
        lblMessage.Text = "Stored procedure was executed."
        lblMessage.Visible = True
    End If
End Sub
```

The ExecuteNonQuery method of the SqlCommand object can be used to execute any ad hoc query or stored procedure that doesn't return any results.

> When you call the methods of the **SqlDataAdapter** object, the .NET Framework will automatically open and close the associated **SqlConnection** object as necessary. For any other operation (such as using the **SqlCommand.ExecuteNonQuery** method), you must explicitly call the **SqlConnection.Open** and **SqlConnection.Close** methods in your code.

Using Parameters in Stored Procedures

The examples that you've seen so far don't begin to tap the real power of stored procedures. SQL Server supports *parameterized stored procedures*, which allow you to pass information to the stored procedure at runtime. For example, this SQL statement defines a stored procedure that returns the total sales for a particular customer, with the CustomerID specified at runtime:

```
CREATE PROC procCustomerSales
    @CustomerID char(5),
    @TotalSales money OUTPUT
AS
    SELECT @TotalSales = SUM(Quantity * UnitPrice)
    FROM ((Customers INNER JOIN Orders
    ON Customers.CustomerID = Orders.CustomerID)
    INNER JOIN [Order Details]
    ON Orders.OrderID = [Order Details].OrderID)
    WHERE Customers.CustomerID = @CustomerID
```

In this SQL statement, both @CustomerID and @TotalSales are variables (called parameters in T-SQL). To use the stored procedure, you must supply a value for the @CustomerID parameter. The @TotalSales parameter is marked as an OUTPUT parameter; it returns a value from the stored procedure to the calling code.

In the .NET Framework, the SqlCommand object has a collection of parameters to let you manage parameterized stored procedures. You can set parameter values through this collection in code:

```
Private Sub Page_Load(ByVal sender As System.Object, _
    ByVal e As System.EventArgs) Handles MyBase.Load
    If IsPostBack Then
        ' Create a SqlCommand to
        ' represent the stored procedure
        Dim cmd As SqlCommand = _
        SqlConnection1.CreateCommand
        cmd.CommandType = CommandType.StoredProcedure
        cmd.CommandText = "procCustomerSales"
        ' Add the input parameter and set its value
        cmd.Parameters.Add(New SqlParameter( _
        "@CustomerID", SqlDbType.Text, 5))
        cmd.Parameters("@CustomerID").Value = _
        txtCustomerID.Text
```

```
                ' Add the output parameter and set its direction
                cmd.Parameters.Add(New SqlParameter( _
                  "@TotalSales", SqlDbType.Money))
                cmd.Parameters("@TotalSales").Direction = _
                  ParameterDirection.Output
                ' Execute the stored procedure and
                ' display the formatted results
                SqlConnection1.Open()
                cmd.ExecuteNonQuery()
                txtTotalSales.Text = String.Format("{0:c}", _
                  cmd.Parameters("@TotalSales").Value)
                SqlConnection1.Close()
        End If
End Sub
```

In ADO.NET, parameters are represented by SqlParameter objects. This code
uses two different forms of the constructor for SqlParameters. The first takes
the parameter name, the parameter data type, and the size of the parameter;
the second omits the parameter size (because the money type has a fixed
size). The code works by setting the Value property of the @CustomerID parameter, executing the SqlCommand object, and then retrieving the Value property
of the @TotalSales parameter.

The @@IDENTITY Variable

A SQL Server table can have a single *identity* column. An *identity column* is a
column whose value is assigned by SQL Server itself whenever you add a
new row to the table. The purpose of the identity column is to guarantee that
each row in the table has a unique primary key.

If you're working with a table that contains an identity column, you'll often
want to add a new row to the table and then immediately retrieve the value
of the identity column for the new row. SQL Server provides a variable
named @@IDENTITY for just this purpose. The @@IDENTITY variable returns the
most recently assigned identity column value.

For example, you might create a stored procedure to insert a new row in
a table and return the value of the identity column so that your code can
continue to work with the new row:

```
CREATE PROC procInsertShipper
  @CompanyName nvarchar(40),
  @ShipperID int OUTPUT
AS
  INSERT INTO Shippers (CompanyName)
    VALUES (@CompanyName)
  SELECT @ShipperID = @@IDENTITY
```

This stored procedure contains two SQL statements. The first inserts a row into
the Shippers table, and the second retrieves the value of the identity column for
the new row. From code, you can retrieve the return value to a variable:

```
Private Sub Page_Load(ByVal sender As System.Object, _
ByVal e As System.EventArgs) Handles MyBase.Load
    If IsPostBack Then
        ' Create a SqlCommand to
        ' represent the stored procedure
        Dim cmd As SqlCommand = _
        SqlConnection1.CreateCommand
        cmd.CommandType = CommandType.StoredProcedure
        cmd.CommandText = "procInsertShipper"
        ' Add the input parameter and set its value
        cmd.Parameters.Add( _
        New SqlParameter("@CompanyName", _
        SqlDbType.VarChar, 40))
        cmd.Parameters("@CompanyName").Value = _
        txtCompanyName.Text
        ' Add the output parameter
        ' and set its direction
        cmd.Parameters.Add(New SqlParameter( _
        "@ShipperID", SqlDbType.Int))
        cmd.Parameters("@ShipperID").Direction = _
        ParameterDirection.Output
        ' Execute the stored procedure
        ' and display the result
        SqlConnection1.Open()
        cmd.ExecuteNonQuery()
        txtShipperID.Text = cmd.Parameters( _
        "@ShipperID").Value
        SqlConnection1.Close()
    End If
End Sub
```

Accessing and Manipulating Data

The 70-305 exam requires you to know how to work with three types of data:

➤ File-based data

➤ Relational database data

➤ XML data

The .NET Framework includes namespaces and classes optimized for each of these types of data.

Working with Disk Files

The oldest form of data that you're likely to work with in the .NET Framework is the simple disk file.

File-based input and output in the .NET Framework revolves around the twin concepts of *streams* and *backing stores*. A stream represents a flow of raw data.

A backing store represents some place you can put data. A backing store might be a file—but it might also be a network connection, an Internet address, or even a section of memory. The .NET Framework contains classes to let you work with data from any of these backing stores.

You'll find the core classes for working with streams and backing stores in the System.IO namespace.

Using the FileStream Class

The FileStream class treats a file as a stream of bytes. For example, you can use this class as a way to make a backup copy of a file:

```
Private Sub Page_Load(ByVal sender As System.Object, _
ByVal e As System.EventArgs) Handles MyBase.Load
    If IsPostBack Then
        ' Get the physical path of a file
        Dim strFileName = _
        Server.MapPath("XMLFile1.xml")
        ' Open the file for reading as a stream
        Dim fsIn As FileStream = _
        File.OpenRead(strFileName)
        ' Open the file for writing as a stream
        Dim fsOut As FileStream = _
        File.OpenWrite(strFileName & ".bak")
        ' Copy all data from in to out, byte-by-byte
        Dim b As Integer
        b = fsIn.ReadByte()
        Do While (b > -1)
            fsOut.WriteByte(CType(b, Byte))
            b = fsIn.ReadByte()
        Loop
        ' Clean up
        fsOut.Flush()
        fsOut.Close()
        fsIn.Close()
        ' Display the original and backup file names
        lblMessage.Text = "Backed up " & _
        strFileName & _
        " to " & strFileName & ".bak"
        lblMessage.Visible = True
    End If
End Sub
```

You need to give the ASP.NET process permission to write to the server's hard drive for this and other file-based code to work. On the Web server computer, launch Windows Explorer. Locate the folder that contains your Web site. Right-click the folder and select Properties. Click the Security tab. Click the Add Button and select the ASPNET user from the local computer. Click Add, and then click OK. Click the check box to allow the user to write to the folder, and then click OK again.

Unlike previous versions of ASP, ASP.NET is designed to run under a user account with very low privileges. By default, the ASP.NET process cannot write any files to your Web server's hard drive.

The code creates two FileStream objects, one each for the input and output files, by using static methods of the File object (which represents a disk file). It then reads bytes from the input file and writes those bytes to the output file. Note the difference between the ReadByte method, which returns an int, and the WriteByte method, which writes a byte. That's because the ReadByte method uses the special value -1 (which can't be stored in a byte) to indicate that it's reached the end of the data.

When the code is done writing, it calls the Flush method of the output stream. That's necessary to be sure that all the data has actually been written to the disk. Then it closes both the input and output streams.

Table 7.1 shows some of the methods and properties of the FileStream object that you should be familiar with.

Table 7.1	FileStream Object Members	
Member	**Type**	**Description**
CanRead	Property	Indicates whether you can read from this **FileStream**.
CanSeek	Property	Indicates whether you can seek to a particular location in this **FileStream**.
CanWrite	Property	Indicates whether you can write to this **FileStream**.
Close	Method	Closes the **FileStream** and releases associated resources.
Flush	Method	Writes any buffered data to the backing store.
Length	Property	Length of the **FileStream** in bytes.
Position	Property	Gets the position within the **FileStream**.
Read	Method	Reads a sequence of bytes.
ReadByte	Method	Reads a single byte.
Seek	Method	Sets the **FileStream** to a specified position.
Write	Method	Writes a sequence of bytes.
WriteByte	Method	Writes a single byte.

You can optimize the code for copying a file somewhat by using a buffer to transfer the data, rather than doing it byte by byte:

```
' Copy all data from in to out, using a buffer
Dim buf(4096) As Byte
Dim intBytesRead As Integer
intBytesRead = fsIn.Read(buf, 0, 4096)
Do While intBytesRead > 0
    fsOut.Write(buf, 0, intBytesRead)
    intBytesRead = fsIn.Read(buf, 0, 4096)
Loop
```

The `FileStream.Read` method takes three parameters:

➤ A buffer to hold the data being read

➤ An offset in the buffer where newly read bytes should be placed

➤ The maximum number of bytes to read

The `Read` method returns the number of bytes that were actually read. Similarly, the `Write` method takes three parameters:

➤ A buffer to hold the data being written

➤ An offset in the buffer where bytes to write begin

➤ The number of bytes to write

Using the **StreamReader** and **StreamWriter** Classes

The `FileStream` class is your best option when you don't care (or don't know) about the internal structure of the files with which you're working. But in many cases, you have additional knowledge that lets you use other objects. Text files, for example, are often organized as lines of text separated by end of line characters. The `StreamReader` and `StreamWriter` classes provide you with tools for manipulating such files. Here's how you might use these classes to copy a text file:

```
Private Sub Page_Load(ByVal sender As System.Object, _
ByVal e As System.EventArgs) Handles MyBase.Load
    If IsPostBack Then
        ' Create a new file to work with
        Dim fsOut As FileStream = _
        File.Create(Server.MapPath("test.txt"))
        ' Create a StreamWriter to handle writing
        Dim sw As StreamWriter = _
        New StreamWriter(fsOut)
        ' And write some data
        sw.WriteLine("There was a young " & _
        "lady named Bright")
        sw.WriteLine("Whose speed was much " & _
        "faster than light")
        sw.WriteLine("She set out one day")
        sw.WriteLine("In a relative way")
        sw.WriteLine("And returned on the " & _
        "previous night")
        sw.Flush()
        sw.Close()

        ' Now open the file for reading
        Dim fsIn As FileStream = _
        File.OpenRead(Server.MapPath("test.txt"))
        ' Create a StreamReader to handle reading
        Dim sr As StreamReader = New StreamReader(fsIn)
```

```
      ' And read the data
      Do While sr.Peek > -1
          lblLines.Items.Add(sr.ReadLine())
      Loop
      sr.Close()
   End If
End Sub
```

You can think of the StreamWriter and StreamReader classes as forming an additional layer of functionality on top of the FileStream class. The FileStream object handles opening a particular disk file and then serves as a parameter to the constructor of the StreamWriter or StreamReader. This code first opens a StreamWriter and calls its WriteLine method multiple times to write lines of text to the file. It then creates a StreamReader that uses the same text file. The code makes use of the Peek method of the StreamReader to watch for the end of the file. This method returns the next byte in the file without actually reading it, or -1 if no more data is to be read. As long as there's data to read, the ReadLine method of the StreamReader can read it to place in the ListBox.

In addition to the methods that you see in this example, the StreamWriter has a Write method that writes output without adding a new line character. The StreamReader class implements Read and ReadToEnd methods that offer additional functionality for reading data. The Read method reads a specified number of characters. The ReadToEnd method reads all the remaining characters to the end of the stream.

Using the **BinaryReader** and **BinaryWriter** Classes

For files with a known internal structure, the BinaryReader and BinaryWriter classes offer streaming functionality that's oriented toward particular data types. This lets you work easily with very structured data:

```
Private Sub Page_Load(ByVal sender As System.Object, _
ByVal e As System.EventArgs) Handles MyBase.Load
    If IsPostBack Then
        ' Create a new file to work with
        Dim fsOut As FileStream = _
        File.Create(Server.MapPath("test.dat"))
        ' Create a BinaryWriter to handle writing
        Dim bw As BinaryWriter = _
        New BinaryWriter(fsOut)
        ' And write some data
        Dim intData1 As Integer = 7
        Dim dblData2 As Decimal = 3.14159
        Dim strData3 As String = "Pi in the Sky"
        bw.Write(intData1)
        bw.Write(dblData2)
        bw.Write(strData3)
        bw.Flush()
        bw.Close()
```

```
' Now open the file for reading
Dim fsIn As FileStream = _
  File.OpenRead(Server.MapPath("test.dat"))
' Create a BinaryReader to handle reading
Dim br As BinaryReader = New BinaryReader(fsIn)
' And read the data
lbData.Items.Add("Integer: " & br.ReadInt32())
lbData.Items.Add("Decimal: " & _
  br.ReadDecimal())
lbData.Items.Add("String: " & br.ReadString())
br.Close()
    End If
End Sub
```

Like the StreamWriter and the StreamReader, the BinaryWriter and BinaryReader provide a layer on top of the basic FileStream object. BinaryWriter and BinaryReader are oriented toward writing and reading particular types of data. The BinaryWriter.Write method has overloads for many data types, so it can handle writing almost anything to a file. The BinaryReader class has methods for reading all those different data types; this code shows the ReadInt32, ReadDecimal, and ReadString methods in action.

The ADO.NET Object Model

ADO.NET is the overall name for the set of classes (spread across a number of namespaces including System.Data, System.Data.SqlClient, and System.Data.OleDb) that the .NET Framework provides for working with data in relational databases.

The ADO.NET object model is broken up into two distinct sets of classes: data provider classes and DataSet classes. Note that it's traditional to call this an object model, even though it's made up of classes. Two sets of classes exist because the .NET Framework separates the task of using data from the task of storing data. The DataSet classes provide a memory-resident, disconnected set of classes that you can load with data. The data provider classes handle the task of working directly with data sources. One of the provider classes, the DataAdapter class, serves as a conduit between the two sets of classes. By using a DataAdapter, you can load data from a database into a DataSet and later save changes back to the original data source.

Data Providers and Their Classes

The five main data provider classes that you should know about are as follows:

➤ Connection

➤ Command

➤ Parameter

➤ DataReader

➤ DataAdapter

You've actually seen most of these classes already, but not with these names. That's because those are generic names, and each data provider has implementations of these classes with specific names.

A *data provider* is a namespace that implements these five classes (and some other classes and enumerations) for use with a particular database. For example, I've been using the SQL Server data provider, which is implemented in the System.Data.SqlClient namespace. In this namespace, the classnames are as follows:

➤ SqlConnection

➤ SqlCommand

➤ SqlParameter

➤ SqlDataReader

➤ SqlDataAdapter

But the SQL Server data provider is not the only alternative for retrieving data in ADO.NET. The .NET Framework also ships with the OLE DB data provider, implemented in the System.Data.OleDb namespace. In this namespace, the corresponding classnames are as follows:

➤ OleDbConnection

➤ OleDbCommand

➤ OleDbParameter

➤ OleDbDataReader

➤ OleDbDataAdapter

Although the .NET Framework only includes two data providers, there are other alternatives. For example, Microsoft has made an ODBC data provider and an Oracle data provider available for download. Third parties have also released other providers.

The SqlConnection Class

The SqlConnection class represents a single persistent connection to a SQL Server data source. ADO.NET automatically handles connection pooling, which contributes to better application performance. When you call the Close method of a SqlConnection object, it is returned to a connection pool.

Connections in a pool are not immediately destroyed by ADO.NET. Instead, they're available for reuse if another part of your application requests a `SqlConnection` that matches in details a previously closed `SqlConnection`.

Table 7.2 shows the most important members of the `SqlConnection` class.

Table 7.2 SqlConnection Members		
Member	**Type**	**Description**
BeginTransaction	Method	Starts a new transaction on this **SqlConnection**.
Close	Method	Returns the **SqlConnection** to the connection pool.
ConnectionString	Property	Specifies the server to be used by this **SqlConnection**.
CreateCommand	Method	Returns a new **SqlCommand** object that executes via this **SqlConnection**.
Open	Method	Opens the **SqlConnection**.

So far, all the `SqlConnection` objects that you've seen in this book have been created by drag-and-drop from Server Explorer. But it's easy to create them in code yourself:

```
Dim cnn As SqlConnection = New SqlConnection()
cnn.ConnectionString = _
 "Data Source=(local);" & _
 "Initial Catalog=Northwind;" & _
 "Integrated Security=SSPI"
cnn.Open()
' Work with the database
cnn.Close()
```

You should know how to construct a SQL Server connection string for use with the **SqlConnection** object. There are three parts to the string. First is the Data Source, which is the name of the server to which you'd like to connect. You can use **(local)** as a shortcut name for the SQL Server instance running on the same computer as this code. Second is the Initial Catalog, which is the name of the database on the server to use. Third is authentication information. This can either be **Integrated Security=SSPI** to use Windows authentication, or **User ID=*username*; Password=*password*** to use SQL Server authentication. There are other optional parameters, but these three are the most important.

You should know how to construct a SQL Server connection string for use with the **SqlConnection** object. There are three parts to the string:

Data Source—The name of the server to which you'd like to connect. You can use (**local**) as a shortcut name for the SQL Server instance running on the same computer as this code.

Initial Catalog—The name of the database on the server to use.

Authentication Information—This can either be **Integrated Security=SSPI** to use Windows authentication, or **User ID=*username*;Password=*password*** to use SQL Server authentication.

Other optional parameters exist, but these three are the most important.

The **SqlParameter** Class

The `SqlCommand` class represents something that can be executed. This could be an ad hoc query string or a stored procedure name. The associated `SqlParameter` class represents a single parameter to a stored procedure.

Table 7.3 shows the most important members of the `SqlCommand` class.

Table 7.3	SqlCommand Members	
Member	Type	Description
CommandText	Property	Statement to be executed by the **SqlCommand**.
CommandType	Property	Enumeration indicating what type of command this **SqlCommand** represents.
Connection	Property	**SqlConnection** through which this **SqlCommand** executes.
CreateParameter	Method	Creates a new **SqlParameter** for this **SqlCommand**.
ExecuteNonQuery	Method	Executes a **SqlCommand** that does not return a resultset.
ExecuteReader	Method	Executes a **SqlCommand** and places the results in a **SqlDataReader**.
ExecuteScalar	Method	Executes a **SqlCommand** and returns the first column of the first row of the resultset.
ExecuteXmlReader	Method	Executes a **SqlCommand** and places the results in an **XmlReader** object.
Parameters	Property	Collection of **SqlParameter** objects for this **SqlCommand**.

The **SqlDataReader** Object

The `SqlDataReader` object is designed to be the fastest possible way to retrieve a resultset from a database. `SqlDataReader` objects can only be constructed by calling the `ExecuteReader` method of a `Command` object. The resultset contained in a `SqlDataReader` is forward-only, read-only. That is, you can only read the rows in the resultset sequentially from start to finish, and you can't modify any of the data. Any time you just need to retrieve a list that will never be edited by the user, the `SqlDataReader` is a good choice. For example, here's some code to add a list of customers to a `ListBox` control:

```
Private Sub btnGetCustomers_Click( _
  ByVal sender As System.Object, _
  ByVal e As System.EventArgs) _
  Handles btnGetCustomers.Click
    ' Connect to the database
    Dim cnn As SqlConnection = New SqlConnection()
    cnn.ConnectionString = "Data Source=(local);" & _
      "Initial Catalog=Northwind;" & _
      "Integrated Security=SSPI"
```

```
' Create a new ad hoc query
' to retrieve customer names
Dim cmd As SqlCommand = cnn.CreateCommand
cmd.CommandType = CommandType.Text
cmd.CommandText = _
  "SELECT CompanyName FROM Customers " & _
  "ORDER BY CompanyName"
' Dump the data to the user interface
cnn.Open()
Dim dr As SqlDataReader = cmd.ExecuteReader
Do While dr.Read()
    lbCustomers.Items.Add(dr.GetString(0))
Loop
' Clean up
dr.Close()
cnn.Close()
End Sub
```

You can think of the SqlDataReader as a data structure that can contain one row of data at a time. Each call to the SqlDataReader.Read method loads the next row of data into this structure. When there are no more rows to load, the Read method returns False, which indicates that you've reached the end of the data. To retrieve individual columns of data from the current row, the SqlDataReader provides a series of methods (such as the GetString method used in the preceding code) that take a column number and return the data from that column. There's also a GetValue method that you can use with any column, but the typed methods are faster.

The **SqlDataReader** makes exclusive use of its **SqlConnection** object as long as it is open. You won't be able to execute any other **SqlCommand** objects on that connection as long as the **SqlDataReader** is open. Always call **SqlDataReader.Close** as soon as you're done retrieving data.

The SqlDataAdapter Class

The final data provider class that I'll consider, the SqlDataAdapter, provides a bridge between the data provider classes and the DataSet objects that you'll learn about in the next section. You can think of the SqlDataAdapter as a two-way pipeline between the data in its native storage format and the data in a more abstract representation (the DataSet) that's designed for manipulation in your application.

Table 7.4 shows the most important members of the SqlDataAdapter class.

Table 7.4 SqlDataAdapter Members		
Member	**Type**	**Description**
DeleteCommand	Property	**SqlCommand** used to delete rows from the data source.

(continued)

Table 7.4   SqlDataAdapter Members (continued)

Member	Type	Description
Fill	Method	Transfers data from the data source to a **DataSet**.
InsertCommand	Property	**SqlCommand** used to insert rows into the data source.
SelectCommand	Property	**SqlCommand** used to retrieve rows from the data source.
Update	Method	Transfers data from a **DataSet** to the data source.
UpdateCommand	Property	**SqlCommand** used to update rows in the data source.

The DataSet Classes

The second set of ADO.NET classes are the DataSet classes, which are all contained in the System.Data namespace. Unlike the data provider classes, there's only one set of DataSet classes. The DataSet classes represent data in an abstract form that's not tied to any particular database implementation.

The DataSet Class

The DataSet itself is a self-contained, memory-resident representation of relational data. A DataSet object contains other objects, such as DataTables and DataRelations, that hold the actual data and information about the design of the data.

Table 7.5 shows the most important members of the DataSet object.

Table 7.5   DataSet Members

Member	Type	Description
AcceptChanges	Method	Marks all changes in the **DataSet** as having been accepted.
Clear	Method	Removes all data from the **DataSet**.
GetChanges	Method	Gets a **DataSet** that contains only the changed data in this **DataSet**.
GetXml	Method	Gets an XML representation of the **DataSet**.
GetXmlSchema	Method	Gets an XSD representation of the **DataSet**.
Merge	Method	Merges two **DataSets**.
ReadXml	Method	Loads the **DataSet** from an XML file.
ReadXmlSchema	Method	Loads the **DataSet**'s schema from an XSD file.
Relations	Property	A collection of **DataRelation** objects.
Tables	Property	A collection of **DataTable** objects.

(continued)

Table 7.5	DataSet Members *(continued)*	
Member	**Type**	**Description**
WriteXml	Method	Writes the **DataSet** to an XML file.
WriteXmlSchema	Method	Writes the **DataSet**'s schema to an XSD file.

The **DataTable** Class

The DataTable class represents a single table within the DataSet. A single DataSet can contain many DataTable objects. Table 7.6 shows the most important members of the DataTable class.

Table 7.6	DataTable Members	
Member	**Type**	**Description**
Clear	Method	Removes all data from the **DataTable**.
ColumnChanged	Event	Fires when the data in any row of a specified column has been changed.
ColumnChanging	Event	Fires when the data in any row of a specified column is about to be changed.
Columns	Property	A collection of **DataColumn** objects.
Constraints	Property	A collection of **Constraint** objects.
NewRow	Method	Creates a new, blank row in the **DataTable**.
PrimaryKey	Property	An array of **DataColumn** objects that provide the primary key for this **DataTable**.
RowChanged	Event	Fires when any data in a **DataRow** has been changed.
RowChanging	Event	Fires when any data in a **DataRow** is about to be changed.
RowDeleted	Event	Fires when a row has been deleted.
RowDeleting	Event	Fires when a row is about to be deleted.
Rows	Property	A collection of **DataRow** objects.
Select	Method	Selects an array of **DataRow** objects that meet specified criteria.
TableName	Property	The name of this **DataTable**.

The **DataRelation** Class

The DataSet can represent an entire relational database. The DataRelation class stores information on the relations between DataTables within a DataSet. Table 7.7 shows the most important members of the DataRelation class.

Table 7.7	DataRelation Members	
Member	**Type**	**Description**
ChildColumns	Property	Collection of **DataColumn** objects that define the foreign key side of the relation.
ChildKeyConstraint	Property	Returns a **ForeignKeyConstraint** object for the relation.
ChildTable	Property	**DataTable** from the foreign key side of the relation.
ParentColumns	Property	Collection of **DataColumn** objects that define the primary key side of the relation.
ParentKeyConstraint	Property	Returns a **PrimaryKeyConstraint** object for the relation.
ParentTable	Property	**DataTable** from the primary key side of the relation.
RelationName	Property	Name of the **DataRelation**.

The DataRow Class

Continuing down the hierarchy from the DataSet past the DataTable, you come to the DataRow. As you can guess by now, the DataRow represents a single row of data. When you're selecting, inserting, updating, or deleting data in a DataSet, you'll normally work with DataRow objects.

Table 7.8 shows the most important members of the DataRow class.

Table 7.8	DataRow Members	
Member	**Type**	**Description**
BeginEdit	Method	Starts editing the **DataRow**.
CancelEdit	Method	Discards an edit in progress.
Delete	Method	Deletes the **DataRow** from its parent **DataTable**.
EndEdit	Method	Ends an edit in progress, saving the changes.
Item	Property	Returns the data from a particular column in the **DataRow**.
IsNull	Method	Returns **True** if a specified column contains a **Null** value.
RowState	Property	Returns information on the current state of a **DataRow** (for example, whether it has been changed since it was last saved to the database).

The DataColumn Class

The DataTable also contains a collection of DataColumn objects. A DataColumn represents a single column in the DataTable. By manipulating the DataColumn objects, you can determine and even change the structure of the DataTable.

Table 7.9 shows the most important members of the DataColumn class.

Table 7.9	DataColumn Members	
Member	**Type**	**Description**
AllowDbNull	Property	Indicates whether the **DataColumn** can contain Null values.
AutoIncrement	Property	Indicates whether the **DataColumn** is an identity column.
ColumnName	Property	Name of the **DataColumn**.
DataType	Property	Data type of the **DataColumn**.
DefaultValue	Property	Default value of this **DataColumn** for new rows of data.
MaxLength	Property	Maximum length of a text **DataColumn**.
Unique	Property	Indicates whether values in the **DataColumn** must be unique across all rows in the **DataTable**.

The DataView Class

Finally, the DataView class represents a view of the data contained in a DataTable. A DataView might contain every DataRow from the DataTable, or it might be filtered to contain only specific rows.

Table 7.10 shows the most important members of the DataView class.

Table 7.10	DataView Members	
Member	**Type**	**Description**
AddNew	Method	Adds a new row to the **DataView**.
AllowDelete	Property	Indicates whether deletions can be performed through this **DataView**.
AllowEdit	Property	Indicates whether updates can be performed through this **DataView**.
AllowNew	Property	Indicates whether insertions can be performed through this **DataView**.
Count	Property	Number of rows in this **DataView**.
Delete	Method	Deletes a row from this **DataView**.
Find	Method	Searches for a row in the **DataView**.
FindRows	Method	Returns an array of rows matching a filter expression.
Item	Property	Returns a **DataRowView** object representing a particular row in the **DataView**.
Sort	Method	Sorts the data in a **DataView**.

Using DataSets

Now that you've seen the ADO.NET classes, it's time to see what you can do with them. The following sections cover basic operations.

Populating a DataSet from a Database

Before you can do anything with data in a DataSet, you have to get that data into the DataSet somehow. In general, you can follow a four-step pattern to move data from the database to a DataSet object:

1. Create a SqlConnection object to connect to the database.

2. Create a SqlCommand object to retrieve the desired data.

3. Assign the SqlCommand to the SelectCommand property of a SqlDataAdapter object.

4. Call the Fill method of the SqlDataAdapter object.

There are a couple of shortcuts that you can use in your ADO.NET code. First, the constructor for the SqlConnection object has an overloaded form that lets you supply the connection string when you create the object. Second, you don't need to call the Open and Close methods of the SqlConnection explicitly. Instead, you can let the SqlDataAdapter make those calls when it needs the data. Doing this not only cuts down the amount of code that you need to write, it also improves the scalability of your application by keeping the SqlConnection open for the shortest possible period of time.

Moving Around in DataSets and Retrieving Data

DataSets have no concept of a current record pointer. Instead, you move through a DataSet by working with the collections that the DataSet contains. Here's an example that uses these collections to dump a DataSet to a ListBox control:

```
Private Sub btnLoadData_Click( _
 ByVal sender As System.Object, _
 ByVal e As System.EventArgs) _
 Handles btnLoadData.Click
    ' Create a SqlConnection
    Dim cnn As SqlConnection = _
     New SqlConnection("Data Source=(local);" & _
     "Initial Catalog=Northwind;" & _
     "Integrated Security=SSPI")
    ' Create a SqlCommand
    Dim cmd As SqlCommand = cnn.CreateCommand()
    cmd.CommandType = CommandType.Text
    cmd.CommandText = _
     "SELECT * FROM Customers " & _
     "WHERE Country = 'Brazil'"
```

```
' Set up the DataAdapter and fill the DataSet
Dim da As SqlDataAdapter = New SqlDataAdapter()
da.SelectCommand = cmd
Dim ds As DataSet = New DataSet()
da.Fill(ds, "Customers")
' Dump the contents of the DataSet
Dim dt As DataTable
Dim dr As DataRow
Dim dc As DataColumn
lbData.Items.Add("DataSet: " & ds.DataSetName)
For Each dt In ds.Tables
    lbData.Items.Add(" DataTable: " & _
     dt.TableName)
    For Each dr In dt.Rows
        lbData.Items.Add("    DataRow")
        For Each dc In dt.Columns
            lbData.Items.Add("      " & dr(dc))
        Next
    Next
Next
End Sub
```

This example shows how you can visit every piece of data in a DataSet by a proper selection of nested For Each loops. It also shows a general syntax for retrieving data: Locate the DataRow and DataColumn with an intersection containing the data that you're interested in, and use the dr(dc) syntax to retrieve the actual data value. You can use a variety of other syntaxes to retrieve data. Given a DataTable variable named dt that refers to the data from the Customer table, for example, any of these statements will retrieve the value in the first column of the first row of data in the DataTable:

```
dt.Rows(0).Item(0)
dt.Rows(0)(0)
dt.Rows(0).Item("CustomerID")
dt.Rows(0)("CustomerID")
dt.Rows(0)!CustomerID
```

Using Strongly Typed DataSets

All the syntaxes for retrieving data that you saw in the previous section have one thing in common: They're all late-bound. That is, the .NET Framework doesn't know until runtime that "CustomerID" is a valid column name. One of the innovations of ADO.NET is a provision to create strongly typed DataSets. In a strongly typed DataSet, columns actually become properties of the row. This allows you to write an early-bound version of the data-retrieval expression:

```
dt.Rows(0).CustomerID
```

In addition to being faster than the late-bound syntaxes, the early-bound syntax has the added advantage of making column names show up in IntelliSense tips as you type code.

You've already seen quite a few strongly typed DataSets, although I didn't emphasize this while I was using them. Any time that you use the Generate DataSet link in the Properties window for a SqlDataAdapter object on a form, Visual Studio .NET builds a strongly typed DataSet. You can also add a new DataSet class from the Add Item dialog box if you prefer. Once you have such a DataSet, you can instantiate copies of it and use early-binding syntax. Here's an example, using a strongly typed DataSet class named Suppliers:

```
Private Sub Page_Load(ByVal sender As System.Object, _
   ByVal e As System.EventArgs) Handles MyBase.Load
   If IsPostBack Then
      ' Create a SqlConnection
      Dim cnn As SqlConnection = _
      New SqlConnection("Data Source=(local);" & _
      "Initial Catalog=Northwind;" & _
      "Integrated Security=SSPI")
      ' Create a SqlCommand
      Dim cmd As SqlCommand = cnn.CreateCommand()
      cmd.CommandType = CommandType.Text
      cmd.CommandText = "SELECT * FROM Suppliers"
      ' Set up the DataAdapter and fill the DataSet
      Dim da As SqlDataAdapter = _
      New SqlDataAdapter()
      da.SelectCommand = cmd
      Dim ds As Suppliers = New Suppliers()
      da.Fill(ds, "Suppliers")
      ' Dump the contents of the DataSet
      Dim suppRow As Suppliers.SuppliersRow
      For Each suppRow In ds.Suppliers
         lbData.Items.Add(suppRow.SupplierID & _
            " " & suppRow.CompanyName)
      Next
   End If
End Sub
```

Using the Suppliers class to define the DataSet in this case gives you several syntactical benefits. You can refer to the Suppliers DataTable as a property of the DataSet. You can also refer to the columns in the DataRows in this DataTable as properties of the DataRow. The strongly typed DataSet automatically defines a class named SuppliersRow to represent one DataRow with strong typing.

DataSets with Multiple Tables

DataSets are not limited to a single DataTable; in fact, there's no practical limit on the number of DataTables that a DataSet can contain. By using multiple DataAdapter objects, you can connect a single DataSet to more than one table in the SQL Server database. You can also define DataRelation objects to represent the relationship between the DataTables in the DataSet, as in this code sample:

```
Private Sub LoadData()
   ' Create a SqlConnection and a DataSet
   Dim cnn As SqlConnection = _
   New SqlConnection("Data Source=(local);" & _
   "Initial Catalog=Northwind;" & _
   "Integrated Security=SSPI")
```

```
' Add the customers data to the DataSet
Dim cmdCustomers As SqlCommand = _
cnn.CreateCommand()
cmdCustomers.CommandType = CommandType.Text
cmdCustomers.CommandText = _
"SELECT * FROM Customers"
Dim daCustomers As SqlDataAdapter = _
New SqlDataAdapter()
daCustomers.SelectCommand = cmdCustomers
daCustomers.Fill(mds, "Customers")

' Add the Orders data to the DataSet
Dim cmdOrders As SqlCommand = cnn.CreateCommand()
cmdOrders.CommandType = CommandType.Text
cmdOrders.CommandText = "SELECT * FROM Orders"
Dim daOrders As SqlDataAdapter = _
New SqlDataAdapter()
daOrders.SelectCommand = cmdOrders
daOrders.Fill(mds, "Orders")

' Add Relation
Dim relCustOrder As DataRelation = _
mds.Relations.Add("CustOrder", _
mds.Tables("Customers"). _
Columns("CustomerID"), _
mds.Tables("Orders").Columns("CustomerID"))

End Sub
```

The `Add` method of the `DataSet.Relations` collection takes three parameters:

➤ A name for the `DataRelation` object to be created

➤ The `DataColumn` object representing the primary key side of the relationship

➤ The `DataColumn` object representing the foreign key side of the relationship

Finding and Sorting Data in DataSets

The `Select` method of the `DataTable` object is a convenient way to find particular `DataRow` objects within the `DataTable`. This method extracts an array of
`DataRow` objects that you can work with. This is useful when you're selecting
data from a large `DataTable` that's already been returned to your code. If you
know in advance which rows you want to work with, it's more efficient to do
the selection in the WHERE clause of your SQL statement. But when you
already have the data, you might use the `Select` method like this:

```
Private Sub Page_Load(ByVal sender As System.Object, _
ByVal e As System.EventArgs) Handles MyBase.Load
    If IsPostBack Then
        ' Create a SqlConnection
        Dim cnn As SqlConnection = _
        New SqlConnection("Data Source=(local);" & _
        "Initial Catalog=Northwind;" & _
        "Integrated Security=SSPI")
```

```
    ' Create a SqlCommand
    Dim cmd As SqlCommand = cnn.CreateCommand()
    cmd.CommandType = CommandType.Text
    cmd.CommandText = "SELECT * FROM Customers"
    ' Set up the DataAdapter and fill the DataSet
    Dim da As SqlDataAdapter = _
     New SqlDataAdapter()
    da.SelectCommand = cmd
    Dim ds As DataSet = New DataSet()
    da.Fill(ds, "Customers")
    ' Use the Select method to get
    ' a sorted array of DataRows
    Dim adr() As DataRow = _
     ds.Tables("Customers").Select( _
     "Country = '" & txtCountry.Text & _
     "'", "ContactName ASC")
    ' Dump the result to the user interface
    lbSelected.Items.Clear()
    Dim dr As DataRow
    For Each dr In adr
        lbSelected.Items.Add(dr(0) & " " & _
        dr(1) & " " & dr(2))
    Next
  End If
End Sub
```

The `Select` method of the `DataTable` constructs an array of `DataRows`, based on up to three factors: a filter expression, a sort expression, and a state constant.

Filter expressions are essentially SQL WHERE clauses constructed according to these rules:

➤ Column names containing special characters should be enclosed in square brackets.

➤ String constants should be enclosed in single quotes.

➤ Date constants should be enclosed in pound signs.

➤ Numeric expressions can be specified in decimal or scientific notation.

➤ Expressions can be created using AND, OR, NOT, parentheses, IN, LIKE, comparison operators, and arithmetic operators.

➤ The + operator is used to concatenate strings.

➤ Either * or % can be used as a wildcard to match any number of characters. Wildcards may be used only at the start or end of strings.

➤ Columns in a child table can be referenced with the expression `Child.Column`. If the table has more than one child table, use the expression `Child(RelationName).Column` to choose a particular child table.

➤ The `Sum`, `Avg`, `Min`, `Max`, `Count`, `StDev`, and `Var` aggregates can be used with child tables.

➤ Supported functions include CONVERT, LEN, ISNULL, IIF, and SUBSTRING.

If you don't specify a sort order in the Select method, the rows are returned in primary key order or in the order of addition if the table doesn't have a primary key. You can also specify a sort expression consisting of one or more column names and the keywords ASC or DESC to specify ascending or descending sorts. For example, this is a valid sort expression:

```
Country ASC, CompanyName DESC
```

The expression will sort first by country in ascending order and then by company name within each country in descending order.

Finally, you can also select DataRows according to their current state by supplying one of the DataViewRowState constants. Table 7.11 shows these constants.

Table 7.11	DataViewRowState Constants
Constant	Meaning
Added	New rows that have not yet been committed
CurrentRows	All current rows, whether unchanged, modified, or new
Deleted	Deleted rows
ModifiedCurrent	Modified rows
ModifiedOriginal	Original data from modified rows
None	No rows
OriginalRows	Original data, including rows that have been modified or deleted
Unchanged	Rows that have not been changed

You can also sort and filter data by using a DataView. The DataView has the same structure of rows and columns as a DataTable, but it also lets you specify sorting and filtering options. Typically you'll create a DataView by starting with a DataTable and specifying options to include a subset of the rows in the DataTable. Refer back to Chapter 6, "Data Binding," for an example of using the DataView to filter data.

Editing Data with ADO.NET

ADO.NET supports all the normal database operations of updating existing data, adding new data, and deleting existing data.

As you read this section, you need to keep in mind the distinction between the data model and the database. As you work with data in the DataSet and its subsidiary objects, you're altering the data in the data model. These changes will not be reflected in the underlying database until and unless you call the Update method of the DataAdapter object. So far, I've only been using the SqlDataAdapter to move data from the database to the data model; in this section, you'll see how it works to move data back from the data model to the database.

If you make changes to a **DataSet** and forget to call the **DataAdapter's Update** method, those changes will be lost when you exit the application.

Updating Data

Updating data is easy: Just assign a new value to the item in the DataRow that you want to change. But there's more to finishing the job. In order for the Update method of the SqlDataAdapter to write changes back to the database, you need to set its UpdateCommand property to an appropriate SqlCommand object. Here's an example:

1. Add a new Web Form to your Visual Basic .NET Web project.

2. Place a Button control with the ID of btnUpdate, three Label controls (one of which should have the ID of lblResults), and two TextBox controls (txtCustomerID and txtContactName) on the form. Figure 7.3 shows the layout of this form in design mode.

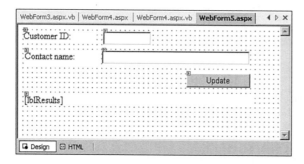

Figure 7.3   Designing a form to update contact information in the database.

3. Double-click the form to open the form's module. Enter these statements at the top of the module:

```
Imports System.Data
Imports System.Data.SqlClient
```

4. Enter this code to load and update data when the button is clicked:

```
Private Sub Page_Load(ByVal sender As System.Object, _
   ByVal e As System.EventArgs) Handles MyBase.Load
    If IsPostBack Then
        ' Create some ADO.NET objects
        Dim cnn As SqlConnection = _
        New SqlConnection("Data Source=(local);" & _
        "Initial Catalog=Northwind;" & _
        "Integrated Security=SSPI")
        Dim ds As DataSet = New DataSet()
        Dim da As SqlDataAdapter = _
        New SqlDataAdapter()
```

```
' Create a SqlCommand to select data
Dim cmdSelect As SqlCommand = _
  cnn.CreateCommand()
cmdSelect.CommandType = CommandType.Text
cmdSelect.CommandText = _
  "SELECT CustomerID, ContactName " & _
  "FROM Customers"
' Create a SqlCommand to update data
Dim cmdUpdate As SqlCommand = _
  cnn.CreateCommand()
cmdUpdate.CommandType = CommandType.Text
cmdUpdate.CommandText = _
  "UPDATE Customers SET " & _
  "ContactName = @ContactName " & _
  "WHERE CustomerID = @CustomerID"
cmdUpdate.Parameters.Add("@ContactName", _
  SqlDbType.NVarChar, _
  30, "ContactName")
cmdUpdate.Parameters.Add("@CustomerID", _
  SqlDbType.NChar, _
  5, "CustomerID")
cmdUpdate.Parameters("@CustomerID"). _
  SourceVersion = _
  DataRowVersion.Original
' Set up the DataAdapter and fill the DataSet
da.SelectCommand = cmdSelect
da.UpdateCommand = cmdUpdate
da.Fill(ds, "Customers")
' Get the DataRow to edit
Dim adrEdit() As DataRow = _
  ds.Tables("Customers").Select( _
    "CustomerID = '" & _
    txtCustomerID.Text & "'")
' Make sure there's some data
If UBound(adrEdit) > -1 Then
    ' Put in the edited data
    adrEdit(0)("ContactName") = _
    txtContactName.Text
    ' Save the changes
    da.Update(ds, "Customers")
    ' And make a note on the UI
    lblResults.Text = "Row has been updated"
End If
    End If
End Sub
```

5. Set the Web Form as the start page for the project.

6. Run the project. Enter a customer ID (such as ALFKI) and a new contact name, and click OK. The code writes the change back to the database and shows the Row has been updated text on the form.

The Update method of the SqlDataAdapter is syntactically similar to the Fill method. It takes as its parameters the DataSet to be reconciled with the database and the name of the DataTable to be saved. You don't have to worry about which rows or columns of data were changed. The SqlDataAdapter automatically locates the changed rows. It executes the SqlCommand specified in its UpdateCommand property for each of those rows.

Adding Data

To add data to the database, you must supply a SqlCommand for the InsertCommand property of the SqlDataAdapter. Otherwise, the code follows the same pattern for adding data as for updating data. Here's how you might add a row to a DataSet and then to the underlying database:

```
Private Sub Page_Load(ByVal sender As System.Object, _
ByVal e As System.EventArgs) Handles MyBase.Load
    If IsPostBack Then
        ' Create some ADO.NET objects
        Dim cnn As SqlConnection = _
        New SqlConnection("Data Source=(local);" & _
        "Initial Catalog=Northwind;" & _
        "Integrated Security=SSPI")
        Dim ds As DataSet = New DataSet()
        Dim da As SqlDataAdapter = _
        New SqlDataAdapter()
        ' Create a SqlCommand to select data
        Dim cmdSelect As SqlCommand = _
        cnn.CreateCommand()
        cmdSelect.CommandType = CommandType.Text
        cmdSelect.CommandText = _
        "SELECT CustomerID, CompanyName, " & _
        "ContactName FROM Customers"
        ' Create a SqlCommand to insert data
        Dim cmdInsert As SqlCommand = _
        cnn.CreateCommand()
        cmdInsert.CommandType = CommandType.Text
        cmdInsert.CommandText = _
        "INSERT INTO Customers " & _
        "(CustomerID, CompanyName, ContactName) " & _
        "VALUES(@CustomerID, @CompanyName, " & _
        "@ContactName)"
        cmdInsert.Parameters.Add("@CustomerID", _
        SqlDbType.NChar, _
        5, "CustomerID")
        cmdInsert.Parameters.Add("@CompanyName", _
        SqlDbType.NVarChar, _
        40, "CompanyName")
        cmdInsert.Parameters.Add("@ContactName", _
        SqlDbType.NVarChar, _
        30, "ContactName")
        cmdInsert.Parameters("@CustomerID"). _
        SourceVersion = _
        DataRowVersion.Original
        ' Set up the DataAdapter and fill the DataSet
        da.SelectCommand = cmdSelect
        da.InsertCommand = cmdInsert
        da.Fill(ds, "Customers")
        ' Create a new DataRow
        Dim dr As DataRow = ds.Tables( _
        "Customers").NewRow()
```

```
                    ' Set values
                    dr(0) = txtCustomerID.Text
                    dr(1) = txtCompanyName.Text
                    dr(2) = txtContactName.Text
                    ' And append the new row to the DataTable
                    ds.Tables("Customers").Rows.Add(dr)
                    ' Now save back to the database
                    da.Update(ds, "Customers")
                    lblResults.Text = "Row added!"
            End If
    End Sub
```

As you can see, adding a new DataRow to a DataTable is a process that has several steps. First, you call the NewRow method of the DataTable. This returns a DataRow object that has the proper schema for that particular DataTable. Then you can set the values of the individual items in the DataRow. Finally, call the Add method of the DataTable to actually append this DataRow to the DataTable.

Deleting Data

The Rows collection of the DataTable object supports a Remove method that deletes an entire DataRow from the DataTable. As you can guess, to persist the changes to the database, you'll need to call the Update method of the SqlDataAdapter. You must supply an appropriate value for the DeleteCommand property of the DataAdapter:

```
Private Sub Page_Load(ByVal sender As System.Object, _
    ByVal e As System.EventArgs) Handles MyBase.Load
    If IsPostBack Then
        ' Create some ADO.NET objects
        Dim cnn As SqlConnection = _
            New SqlConnection("Data Source=(local);" & _
            "Initial Catalog=Northwind;" & _
            "Integrated Security=SSPI")
        Dim ds As DataSet = New DataSet()
        Dim da As SqlDataAdapter = _
            New SqlDataAdapter()
        ' Create a SqlCommand to select data
        Dim cmdSelect As SqlCommand = _
            cnn.CreateCommand()
        cmdSelect.CommandType = CommandType.Text
        cmdSelect.CommandText = _
            "SELECT CustomerID, ContactName " & _
            "FROM Customers"
        ' Create a SqlCommand to delete data
        Dim cmdDelete As SqlCommand = _
            cnn.CreateCommand()
        cmdDelete.CommandType = CommandType.Text
        cmdDelete.CommandText = _
            "DELETE FROM Customers " & _
            "WHERE CustomerID = @CustomerID"
        cmdDelete.Parameters.Add("@CustomerID", _
            SqlDbType.NChar, _
            5, "CustomerID")
        cmdDelete.Parameters("@CustomerID"). _
            SourceVersion = _
            DataRowVersion.Original
```

```
' Set up the DataAdapter and fill the DataSet
da.SelectCommand = cmdSelect
da.DeleteCommand = cmdDelete
da.Fill(ds, "Customers")
' Find the specified row and delete it
Dim dr As DataRow
For Each dr In ds.Tables("Customers").Rows
    If dr(0) = txtCustomerID.Text Then
        ds.Tables("Customers").Rows.Remove(dr)
        Exit For
    End If
Next
' Save the changes
da.Update(ds, "Customers")
lblResults.Text = "Row deleted!"
    End If
End Sub
```

Using XML Data

The final type of data that you'll learn about in this chapter is XML data. XML (Extensible Markup Language) is an entire family of closely related standards. For example, an XSD file is a special type of XML file optimized for storing schema information.

XML Basics

You'll need to understand basic XML terminology to pass the exam. Here's a concrete example to start with. This XML file represents data for two customers:

```
<?xml version="1.0" encoding="UTF-8"?>
<!-- Customer list for Bob's Tractor Parts -->
<Customers>
    <Customer CustomerNumber="1">
        <CustomerName>Lambert Tractor Works
        </CustomerName>
        <CustomerCity>Millbank</CustomerCity>
        <CustomerState>WA</CustomerState>
    </Customer>
    <Customer CustomerNumber="2">
        <CustomerName><![CDATA[Joe's Garage]]>
        </CustomerName>
        <CustomerCity>Doppel</CustomerCity>
        <CustomerState>OR</CustomerState>
    </Customer>
</Customers>
```

XML consists of *tags* (which are contained within angle brackets) and data. Tags come in pairs, with each opening tag matched by a closing tag. The closing tag has the same text as the opening tag, prefixed with a forward slash. Tags without content can use a special syntax that combines the opening and closing tags:

```
<Customer />
```

The first thing that you'll find in an XML file is the *XML declaration*:

```
<?xml version="1.0" encoding="UTF-8"?>
```

The declaration tells you three things about this document:

➤ It's an XML document.

➤ It conforms to the XML 1.0 specification.

➤ It uses the UTF-8 character set (a standard set of characters for the western alphabet) .

Tags in an XML document contain the names of elements. You can make up any name you like for an element, subject to some simple naming rules:

➤ Names can contain any alphanumeric character.

➤ Names can contain underscores, hyphens, and periods.

➤ Names must not contain any whitespace.

➤ Names must start with a letter or underscore.

A start tag together with an end tag and the content between them defines an *element*. For example, here's a single element from the sample document:

```
<CustomerState>OR</CustomerState>
```

This defines an element with a name of `CustomerState` and with a value of `OR`.

Elements can be nested, but they cannot overlap. Every XML document contains a single root element. The root element in the sample document is named Customers. The effect of these rules (nesting is okay, overlapping is not, and there is a single root element) is that any XML document can be represented as a tree of nodes.

Elements can contain *attributes*. An attribute is a piece of data that further describes an element. For example, the sample document includes this opening tag for an element:

```
<Customer CustomerNumber="1">
```

That declares an element named `Customer`. The `Customer` element includes an attribute with a name of `CustomerNumber` and with a value of `1`.

XML documents can contain one or more *namespace* declarations. The sample document does not declare a namespace. Here's the syntax for a namespace declaration:

```
<Customers xmlns:tr="urn:schemas-tractor-repair">
```

The namespace is declared as part of the root tag for the document. In this particular case, the namespace (introduced with the special xmlns characters) defines a prefix of tr for tags within the namespace. The urn (Uniform Resource Name) is an arbitrary string, the purpose of which is to distinguish this namespace from other namespaces.

XML namespaces serve the same purpose as .NET namespaces: They help cut down on naming collisions. After declaring the tr namespace, an XML document could use a tag such as

```
<tr:CustomerState>OR</tr:CustomerState>
```

This indicates that this CustomerState tag is from the tr namespace, and it should not be confused with any other CustomerState tag.

XML offers two ways to deal with special characters in data. First, for individual characters, you can use entity references. Five entity references are defined in the XML standard:

➤ <—Translates to < (opening angle bracket)

➤ >—Translates to > (closing angle bracket)

➤ &—Translates to & (ampersand)

➤ '—Translates to ' (apostrophe)

➤ "—Translates to " (quotation mark)

You can also use a CDATA section to hold any arbitrary data, whether the data contains special characters or not. The sample document uses this approach to store a customer name containing an apostrophe:

```
<CustomerName><![CDATA[Joe's Garage]]></CustomerName>
```

Finally, an XML document can contain comments. Comments are set off by the opening string <!-- and the closing string -->. Here's an example:

```
<!-- Customer list for Bob's Tractor Parts -->
```

A great deal more complexity is available in XML than I've covered in this section. But these basics are more than enough to understand most of the XML that you're likely to run across until you start working with XML in depth.

Using the **XmlDocument** Class

To understand the .NET Framework representation of an XML document, you can start with the concept of a node. A node is one item in an XML document: It might be an attribute, a comment, an element, or something else. In the System.Xml namespace, nodes are represented by XmlNode objects. Table 7.12 shows the most important members of the XmlNode class.

Table 7.12   XmlNode Members

Member	Type	Description
AppendChild	Method	Adds a new child node to the end of this node's list of children.
Attributes	Property	A collection of the attributes of this node.
ChildNodes	Property	A collection of child nodes of this node.
FirstChild	Property	The first child node of this node.
InnerText	Property	The value of this node and all its children.
InnerXml	Property	XML representing just the children of this node.
InsertAfter	Method	Inserts a new node after this node.
InsertBefore	Method	Inserts a new node before this node.
LastChild	Property	The last child node of this node.
Name	Property	The name of the node.
NextSibling	Property	The next child node of this node's parent node.
NodeType	Property	The type of this node. The **XmlNodeType** enumeration includes values for all possible node types.
OuterXml	Property	XML representing this node and all its children.
ParentNode	Property	The parent of this node.
PrependChild	Method	Adds a new child node to the start of this node's list of children.
PreviousSibling	Method	The previous child node of this node's parent node.
RemoveAll	Method	Removes all children of this node.
RemoveChild	Method	Removes a specified child of this node.
ReplaceChild	Method	Replaces a child node with a new node.
Value	Property	Value of the node.

XmlNode objects are collected into an XmlDocument object. As you can probably guess, XmlDocument is the class in the System.Xml namespace that represents an entire XML document. Table 7.13 shows the most important members of the XmlNode class.

Table 7.13   XmlNode Members

Member	Type	Description
CreateAttribute	Method	Creates a new attribute node.
CreateElement	Method	Creates a new element node.
CreateNode	Method	Creates a new **XmlNode** object.

(continued)

Table 7.13   XmlNode Members *(continued)*

Member	Type	Description
DocumentElement	Property	Returns the **XmlElement** object that represents the root node of this document.
GetElementsByTagName	Method	Returns a list of all elements with the specified tag name.
Load	Method	Loads an XML document.
LoadXml	Method	Loads a string of XML.
Save	Method	Saves the **XmlDocument** as a file or stream.
WriteTo	Method	Saves the **XmlDocument** to an **XmlWriter**.

To see how these classes work together, try this simple example of displaying XML in a ListBox control:

Attribute nodes are not included in the ChildNodes collection of a node in the XmlDocument. Instead, you can use the Attributes property of the XmlNode object to get a collection of attribute nodes only.

You can also modify an XML document through the XmlDocument object. To do so, you need to modify the individual XmlNode objects by changing their Value properties, and then write the file back out to disk.

```
' Write the modified file to disk
Dim xtw As XmlTextWriter = _
 New XmlTextWriter(Server.MapPath( _
  "BobsTractors.new.xml"), _
  System.Text.Encoding.UTF8)
xd.WriteTo(xtw)
xtw.Flush()
xtw.Close ()
```

Treating XML as Relational Data

You can also treat an XML document as relational data. To do this, you can use an XmlDataDocument class, which inherits from XmlDocument. The key feature of the XmlDataDocument class is that it can be synchronized with a DataSet:

```
Private Sub Page_Load(ByVal sender As System.Object, _
 ByVal e As System.EventArgs) Handles MyBase.Load
    If IsPostBack Then
        ' Hook up to the disk file
        Dim xtr As New XmlTextReader( _
         Server.MapPath("BobsTractors.xml"))
        Dim xdd As XmlDataDocument = _
         New XmlDataDocument()
        ' Get the DataSet
        Dim ds As DataSet = xdd.DataSet
```

```
        ' Read the schema of the file
        ' to initialize the DataSet
        ds.ReadXmlSchema(xtr)
        xtr.Close()
        xtr = New XmlTextReader( _
         Server.MapPath("BobsTractors.xml"))
        xtr.WhitespaceHandling = _
         WhitespaceHandling.None
        ' Load the file into the XmlDataDocument
        xdd.Load(xtr)
        xtr.Close()
        ' And display it on the DataGrid
        dgXML.DataSource = ds
        dgXML.DataBind()
    End If
End Sub
```

For the DataSet to properly represent the XML, it must have the same schema (structure) as the XML file. In this example, I've ensured that by using the ReadXmlSchema method of the DataSet to load the schema from the same XML file that the XmlDataDocument holds. The XmlTextReader has to be closed and reopened after reading the schema because it's a forward-only object.

The synchronization between the XmlDataDocument and the DataSet is two way. If you derive a DataSet from an XmlDataDocument, modify the DataSet, and then write the XmlDataDocument back to disk, the changes that you made in the DataSet will be reflected in the XML file.

You can also go in the other direction. If you've already got a DataSet in your code, you can create the equivalent XML document by calling an overloaded constructor of the XmlDataDocument class:

```
Dim xdd As XmlDataDocument = New XmlDataDocument(ds)
```

Handling Data Errors

Many things can go wrong when you're working with a database. You might try to add a duplicate value to a column that only allows unique values, or you might try to write to a table that you don't have permission to modify. In serious cases, the database server itself might run out of disk space. These are just a few of the thousands of specific conditions that can trigger SQL Server errors.

The System.Data.SqlClient namespace includes two objects to help you handle SQL Server–specific errors. These are the SqlException class, which inherits from System.Exception, and the SqlError class, which represents a single SQL Server error. You can use the SqlException class to trap an error, and then retrieve details with the SqlError class:

```
Try
    ' Database code here
Catch SqlEx As SqlException
    ' Handle SQL Server specific errors
    Dim err As SqlError
    For Each err In SqlEx.Errors
        lbErrors.Items.Add("SQL Error " & _
        err.Number & ": " & err.Message)
    Next
Catch Ex As Exception
    ' Handle general errors
    lbErrors.Items.Add( _
    "Non-SQL Exception " & Ex.Message)
End Try
```

There's a second class of errors that you need to be aware of when you're writing database code—although actually, these are better thought of as "potentially unexpected outcomes" than as errors. Whenever you have more than one user updating the same data, concurrency issues can arise. The basic question is who wins in case of multiple updates.

Here's how the problem arises: Suppose that both Alice and Bob are working with data from the Customers table in a SQL Server database. They've both downloaded a DataSet containing the table to their local computers, and both are making edits in a DataGrid control. Alice changes the address of the first customer in the table because she's working on a stack of change of address requests. Meanwhile, Bob changes the contact name for the first customer because he's updating the sales records. So now there are three versions of the row: the original one that's still on the SQL Server, the one with a new address that's on Alice's computer, and the one with the new contact name that's on Bob's computer. Now Bob saves his changes by calling the Update method of the SqlDataAdapter, so the SQL Server database contains the new contact name.

What happens when Alice saves her changes?

The answer is, "It depends." When you're creating the SqlCommand object that will be used for the UpdateCommand property of a SqlDataAdapter, it's up to you to choose between two different strategies for dealing with such conflicts:

➤ With optimistic concurrency control, an update to a row will succeed only if no one else has changed that row after it was loaded into the DataSet.

➤ With "last one wins" concurrency control, an update to a row always succeeds, whether another user has edited the row or not (as long as the row still exists).

You've already seen how to implement "last one wins" concurrency control, when I talked about updating the database. Consider the SQL statement that I used to update the database:

```
UPDATE Customers
SET ContactName = @ContactName
WHERE CustomerID = @CustomerID
```

The key thing to look at here is the WHERE clause. The only column that it looks at is the CustomerID column. CustomerID is the primary key of this table, a value that should never change. As long as that one column has not been changed, the UPDATE statement will succeed, no matter what might have changed about other columns in the same table. To use optimistic concurrency control, you just implement a different UPDATE statement:

```
UPDATE Customers
SET ContactName = @ContactName
WHERE CustomerID = @CustomerID AND
ContactName = @ContactNameOrig
```

In this case, of course, @ContactNameOrig needs to be attached to a SqlParameter object that retrieves the original value of the ContactName column.

Exam Prep Questions

Question 1

Your application uses a **SqlDataReader** object to retrieve information on product inventory levels. When you find a product with low inventory, you want to write a new entry to an ordering table by executing a stored procedure in the same database. You have used a **SqlCommand** object to represent the stored procedure. Calling the **ExecuteNonQuery** method of the **SqlCommand** object is causing an error. What is the most likely cause of this error?

- ○ A. You must use a **SqlDataAdapter** object to execute the stored procedure.
- ○ B. You are using the **ExecuteNonQuery** method of the **SqlCommand** object, but you should be using the **ExecuteScalar** method instead.
- ○ C. You must use an ad hoc SQL statement rather than a stored procedure to insert new rows in a database.
- ○ D. You are using the same **SqlConnection** object for both the **SqlDataReader** object and the **SqlCommand** object, and the **SqlDataReader** is still open when you try to execute the **SqlCommand**.

Answer D is correct. The SqlDataReader object demands exclusive use of the underlying SqlConnection as long as SqlDataReader is open. Answer A is incorrect because SqlDataAdapter is only used to execute queries when writing DataSet changes back to the database. Answer B is incorrect because ExecuteScalar is used to retrieve single-value results from the database. Answer C is incorrect because ad hoc SQL statements and stored procedures are equivalent in functionality.

Question 2

Your SQL Server database contains a table named Orders with these columns:

OrderID (int, identity)

ProductNumber (int)

Quantity (int)

You want to create a stored procedure that accepts as inputs the product number and quantity, inserts a new row in the table with this information, and returns the new **OrderID** value. Which SQL statement should you use?

○ A.
```
CREATE PROCEDURE procInsertOrder
   @ProductNumber int,
   @Quantity int,
   @OrderID int
AS
   INSERT INTO Orders (
   ProductNumber, Quantity)
   VALUES (@ProductNumber, @Quantity)
   SELECT @OrderID = @@IDENTITY
```

○ B.
```
CREATE PROCEDURE procInsertOrder
   @ProductNumber int,
   @Quantity int,
   @OrderID int OUTPUT
AS
   INSERT INTO Orders (
   OrderID, ProductNumber, Quantity)
   VALUES (@OrderID, @ProductNumber,
   @Quantity)
```

○ C.
```
CREATE PROCEDURE procInsertOrder
   @ProductNumber int,
   @Quantity int,
   @OrderID int OUTPUT
AS
   INSERT INTO Orders (
   OrderID, ProductNumber, Quantity)
   VALUES (0, @ProductNumber, @Quantity)
   SELECT @OrderID = @@IDENTITY
```

○ D.
```
CREATE PROCEDURE procInsertOrder
   @ProductNumber int,
   @Quantity int,
   @OrderID int OUTPUT
AS
   INSERT INTO Orders (ProductNumber,
   Quantity)
   VALUES (@ProductNumber, @Quantity)
   SELECT @OrderID = @@IDENTITY
```

Answer D is correct. The stored procedure needs to insert the ProductNumber and Quantity, and then retrieve the @@IDENTITY variable to get the new OrderID. Answer A is incorrect because @OrderID is not marked as an OUTPUT parameter. Answers B and C are incorrect because they attempt to insert values into OrderID, which is an identity column.

Question 3

> Your application allows the user to edit customer data on a **DataGrid** control. The **DataGrid** is bound to a **DataSet**. The **DataSet** is filled through a **SqlDataAdapter** object. The **InsertCommand**, **UpdateCommand**, and **DeleteCommand** properties of **SqlDataAdapter** are set to **SqlCommand** objects, and you have tested the SQL in those **SqlCommand** objects.
>
> Users report that none of their changes are saved to the database when they exit the application, and they do not receive any errors. What could be the problem?
>
> ○ A. You have neglected to call the **SqlDataAdapter.Update** method in your code.
>
> ○ B. The users do not have permission to write to the database.
>
> ○ C. You have neglected to fill the **DataSet** from the **DataGrid** after the users finish editing the data.
>
> ○ D. The **DataSet** is a read-only object.

Answer A is correct. Calling the Update method is essential to transmit changes from the data model back to the database. Answer B is incorrect because a permissions problem would generate an error message. Answer C is incorrect because the DataGrid and the underlying DataSet are automatically synchronized by ASP.NET. Answer D is incorrect because DataSet is a read-write object.

Question 4

Your SQL Server database contains a table, Orders, with these columns:

OrderID (int, identity)

ProductNumber (int)

Quantity (int)

You want to see a list of each product, with its total quantity sold. The list should be filtered to only include products with a total quantity sold of more than 10. Which SQL statement should you use?

- ○ A. SELECT ProductNumber, Quantity FROM Orders WHERE Quantity > 10
- ○ B. SELECT ProductNumber, SUM(Quantity) FROM Orders WHERE Quantity > 10 GROUP BY ProductNumber
- ○ C. SELECT ProductNumber, SUM(Quantity) FROM Orders GROUP BY ProductNumber HAVING SUM(Quantity) > 10
- ○ D. SELECT ProductNumber, SUM(Quantity) FROM Orders WHERE Quantity > 10 GROUP BY ProductNumber HAVING SUM(Quantity) > 10

Answer C is correct. The GROUP BY clause dictates the aggregation of the results, and the HAVING clause filters after aggregating. Answer A is incorrect because it doesn't add up the Quantity values. Answers B and D are incorrect because the WHERE clause will limit the results to products with a quantity over 10 on a single order.

Question 5

Users of your application can edit customer information on a **DataGrid** that is bound to a **DataSet**. When the user clicks the Update button on the Web Form, your code calls the **SqlDataAdapter.Update** method to persist the changes from the **DataSet** to the underlying database.

Users report that new records and changes to existing records are properly saved. However, when they return to the application, rows that were deleted previously are reappearing. What could be the problem?

- ○ A. The users do not have permission to update the customers table.
- ○ B. The **Update** method does not delete existing data.
- ○ C. The database is being restored from a backup.
- ○ D. The **DeleteCommand** property of the **SqlDataAdapter** is not properly initialized.

Answer D is correct. When you call the Update method, it uses the SqlCommand object pointed to by the DeleteCommand property to delete rows. If this command is missing or improperly written, the rows won't actually be deleted.

Answer B is incorrect because Update will delete rows when everything is set up properly. Answers A and C are incorrect because in those scenarios, insertions and updates would also fail.

Question 6

Your application recursively calls the **FirstChild** and **NextChild** methods of **XmlNode** objects to visit every node in an XML file that you've loaded into an **XmlDocument**. When you find a node that includes product information, you store the information. The application is not returning all the product information that you know is in the file. What could be the problem?

- ○ A. The XML file is not well-formed.
- ○ B. The XML file has more than on root node.
- ○ C. Some of the product information is stored in attributes.
- ○ D. The **HasChildNodes** property on the **XmlNode** object is not reliable.

Answer C is correct. Using FirstChild and NextChild will visit every node in the DOM, but attributes are not considered nodes. Answers A and B are incorrect because you can't load an ill-formed XML document into an XmlDocument object. Answer D is incorrect because HasChildNodes is a reliable way to determine whether a node has child nodes.

Question 7

Your SQL Server database contains a table, Orders, with these columns:

OrderID (int, identity)

ProductNumber (int)

Quantity (int)

You want to see a list of each product, with its total quantity sold. The list should be filtered to only include orders with a quantity of more than 10. Which SQL statement should you use?

- ○ A. SELECT ProductNumber, Quantity FROM Orders WHERE Quantity > 10
- ○ B. SELECT ProductNumber, SUM(Quantity) FROM Orders WHERE Quantity > 10 GROUP BY ProductNumber
- ○ C. SELECT ProductNumber, SUM(Quantity) FROM Orders GROUP BY ProductNumber HAVING SUM(Quantity) > 10
- ○ D. SELECT ProductNumber, SUM(Quantity) FROM Orders WHERE Quantity > 10 GROUP BY ProductNumber HAVING SUM(Quantity) > 10

Answer B is correct. The WHERE clause ensures that only orders having a quantity larger than 10 are included in the sum. Answer A is incorrect because it doesn't include the SUM operator to total the quantity. Answers C and D are incorrect because the HAVING clause will remove result rows, rather than filtering input rows.

Question 8

You have designed your application to use optimistic concurrency control. Mary and Joe each retrieve the inventory table to the application at 10:00 a.m. The initial inventory of widgets is 37. At 10:05 a.m. Mary changes the inventory of widgets to 35 and saves her changes to the database. At 10:10 a.m. Joe changes the inventory of widgets to 42 and saves his changes to the database. What will be the inventory of widgets in the database at 10:11 a.m. if no one makes any other changes?

○ A. 37

○ B. 35

○ C. 42

○ D. 87

Answer B is correct. With optimistic concurrency control, an update will succeed only when the data in the database completely matches the original state of the row being saved. In this case, Mary's change is saved to the database, but then Joe's change fails because the row has been changed.

Question 9

Your application stores a file of decimal numbers retrieved from lab equipment. The file should be stored in the minimum possible disk space. It is not important that the file be human-readable. Which object should you use to write this file?

○ A. **FileStream**

○ B. **StreamWriter**

○ C. **BinaryWriter**

○ D. **XmlTextWriter**

Answer C is correct. The BinaryWriter class is a good choice for writing data types to a disk file with minimal overhead. The FileStream class is oriented toward byte-by-byte writing, which is a poor choice for structured data, so answer A is incorrect. Answers B and D are incorrect because text and XML files are normally larger than the equivalent binary file.

Question 10

Your application needs to retrieve the total number of products in the Products table in your database. What is the fastest way to do this?

- O A. Create a stored procedure to return the total number of products. Use the **SqlCommand.ExecuteScalar** method to execute the stored procedure.

- O B. Write ad hoc SQL to return the total number of products. Use the **SqlDataAdapter.Fill** method to execute the SQL statement.

- O C. Write ad hoc SQL to return the total number of products. Use the **SqlCommand.ExecuteScalar** method to execute the SQL statement.

- O D. Create a stored procedure to return the total number of products. Use the **SqlDataAdapter.Fill** method to execute the stored procedure.

Answer A is correct. A stored procedure will execute faster than an ad hoc SQL statement. Answers B and C are incorrect because they use ad hoc SQL statements. Answer D is incorrect because the `SqlDataAdapter.Fill` method adds overhead to the data retrieval process that isn't necessary if you just need to retrieve a single value.

Need to Know More?

Gunderloy, Mike. *ADO and ADO.NET Programming*. Sybex, 2002.

Esposito, Dino. *Building Solutions with ASP.NET and ADO.NET*. Microsoft Press, 2002.

Vaughn, Bill. *ADO.NET and ADO Examples and Best Practices for VB Programmers*. Apress, 2002.

Delaney, Kalen. *Inside SQL Server 2000*. Microsoft Press, 2000.

Wildermuth, Shawn. *Pragmatic ADO.NET*. Addison-Wesley, 2003.

Harold, Eliotte Rusty & Means, W. Scott. *XML in a Nutshell*. O'Reilly, 2001.

Microsoft SQL Server Books Online.

Creating and Managing Components and .NET Assemblies

Terms you'll need to understand:

✓ Component class
✓ Web user control
✓ Web custom control
✓ Derived control
✓ Assembly
✓ Assembly manifest
✓ Assembly metadata
✓ Global Assembly Cache (GAC)
✓ Metadata
✓ Private assembly
✓ Resource-only assembly
✓ Satellite assembly
✓ Shared assembly
✓ Strong name

Techniques you'll need to master:

✓ Deriving a component from the Component class
✓ Creating a Web user control
✓ Creating a composite custom control
✓ Creating a derived custom control
✓ Creating a .NET assembly

In this chapter, you learn about several types of components supported by .NET. You begin by exploring components that derive from the Component class within the .NET Framework. Then I discuss Web user controls and Web custom controls, which provide two different reuse models for ASP.NET applications. Finally, I discuss assemblies, which can be used to group components together for security, deployment, and versioning.

Creating and Using .NET Components

There are many ways to reuse code. For example, you might simply cut and paste code from one application to another. For more organized code reuse, you might create a class library that can be referenced from many different applications.

Although you can refer to any piece of reusable code as a *component*, the .NET Framework has formalized the notion of a component as a class that implements the IComponent interface (normally by inheriting from the base Component class). In this sense, components have advanced capabilities, including a specified architecture for managing resources and support for use on containers such as forms.

Creating a Component

To create a component, you derive a class from the System.ComponentModel.Component base class. But to effectively program with components, you need to set up a class library to contain the component and a project to test the component. Follow these steps to get started with a basic component:

1. Create a new blank solution in Visual Studio .NET.

2. Add to the solution a new Visual Basic Class Library project named CramComponents.

3. Right-click the new project in Solution Explorer. Select Add, Add Component. Name the new component RandomNumber.vb and click Open.

4. Delete the default Class1.vb class from the project.

5. The new component opens, with a blank designer where you can drop other components. Click the hyperlink to view the source code. Expand the Component Designer generated code region. Modify the New and Dispose methods as follows (by adding the code shown in bold):

```
Public Sub New()
    MyBase.New()

    'This call is required by
    'the Component Designer.
    InitializeComponent()

    'Add any initialization after
    ' the InitializeComponent() call
    StartRandom()
End Sub

'Component overrides dispose to clean
'up the component list.
Protected Overloads Overrides Sub Dispose( _
 ByVal disposing As Boolean)
    If disposing Then
        If Not (components Is Nothing) Then
            components.Dispose()
        End If
    End If
    mRandom = Nothing
    MyBase.Dispose(disposing)
End Sub
```

6. Add this code after the Component Designer generated code region:

```
Private mRandom As System.Random

Private Sub StartRandom()
    mRandom = New System.Random()
End Sub

Protected Overrides Sub Finalize()
    Dispose(False)
    MyBase.Finalize()
End Sub
```

7. Add a new Visual Basic ASP.NET Web Application project named RandomTest to the solution.

8. Right-click the References folder in the new project and select Add Reference. Click the Projects tab of the Add Reference dialog box and select the CramComponents project. Click OK.

9. Switch to Code view of the default Web Form. Enter this code at the top of the module:

```
Imports CramComponents
```

10. Enter this code to handle the Web Form's Load event:

```
Private Sub Page_Load( _
ByVal sender As System.Object, _
ByVal e As System.EventArgs) Handles MyBase.Load
    Dim rt As RandomNumber = New RandomNumber()
    Response.Write("Created RandomNumber component")
End Sub
```

11. Set RandomTest as the startup project for the solution. Run the project. The Web Form appears, with the message "Created RandomNumber component."

At this point, all the component does is create and destroy an instance of the System.Random class. Most components require properties and methods in order to be truly useful. Here's a version of the implementation code for the RandomNumber.vb class that demonstrates the syntax for properties and methods:

```
Private mRandom As System.Random
Private mMinValue As Integer
Private mMaxValue As Integer
Private mResult As Integer

Private Sub StartRandom()
    mRandom = New System.Random()
    mMaxValue = 1000
    mResult = mRandom.Next()
End Sub

Protected Overrides Sub Finalize()
    Dispose(False)
    MyBase.Finalize()
End Sub

Public Property minValue() As Integer
    Get
        minValue = mMinValue
    End Get
    Set(ByVal Value As Integer)
        Value = mMinValue
    End Set
End Property

Public Property maxValue() As Integer
    Get
        maxValue = mMaxValue
    End Get
    Set(ByVal Value As Integer)
        mMaxValue = Value
    End Set
End Property

Public ReadOnly Property Result() As Integer
    Get
        Result = mResult
    End Get
End Property
```

```
Public Function GetRandom() As Integer
    mResult = mRandom.Next(mMinValue, mMaxValue)
    GetRandom = mResult
End Function

Public Function GetRandom(ByVal minValue As Integer, _
 ByVal maxValue As Integer) As Integer
    mResult = mRandom.Next(minValue, maxValue)
    GetRandom = mResult
End Function
```

Creating and Using Web User Controls

A Web user control provides more specialized reuse than does the basic component class. Web user controls are designed to let you reuse common user interface functionality in a Web application. You can think of a Web user control as a chunk of an application's user interface packaged for easy reuse.

Creating a Web User Control

The process of creating a Web user control is very similar to the process of creating a Web Form, as the following steps demonstrate:

1. Right-click the RandomTest project in Solution Explorer and select Add, Add Web User Control. Name the new Web user control ComboLabel.ascx.

2. Add a LinkButton control with the ID lbMain and a Label control with the ID lblNotes to the Web user control. Set the Text property of the LinkButton control to Resources. Set the Text property of the Label control to Click the link for more information.

3. Right-click the Web user control and select View Code.

4. Add the following code after the Web Form Designer generated code region:

```
Public TargetUrl As String

Public WriteOnly Property ForeColor() As String
    Set(ByVal Value As String)
        lblNotes.ForeColor = _
        ColorTranslator.FromHtml(Value)
        lbMain.ForeColor = _
        ColorTranslator.FromHtml(Value)
    End Set
End Property
```

5. Add the following code to handle the `click` event of the `LinkButton` control:

```
Private Sub lbMain_Click( _
  ByVal sender As System.Object, _
  ByVal e As System.EventArgs) _
  Handles lbMain.Click
    Response.Redirect(TargetUrl)
End Sub
```

6. Add a new Web Form to the project. Switch the new Web Form to flow layout.

7. Drag `ComboLabel.ascx` from Solution Explorer and drop it on the new Web Form. Figure 8.1 shows the Web Form in the designer. The Web user control is shown on the Web Form as a placeholder image. That's because the user control is not compiled until the project itself is compiled, so ASP.NET can't know how large the final control will be.

Figure 8.1 A Web user control on a Web Form.

8. Switch to the HTML view of the Web Form. Alter the tag for `ComboLabel1` so that it looks like this:

```
<uc1:ComboLabel id="ComboLabel1"
runat="server"
ForeColor="Red" TargetUrl="http://www.larkware.com/">
</uc1:ComboLabel>
```

9. Set the Web Form as the start page for the project.

10. Run the project. Click the `LinkButton` control when the page is displayed. The code in the `LinkButton` control's event handler runs and redirects the browser to the Larkware Web site.

Note that the properties of the Web user control are set in the HTML, rather than in code. That's because the control is not compiled at design time, so its properties are not available to the code.

Creating Web Custom Controls

Web custom controls provide a more flexible (and more complex) alternative to Web user controls for reusing user interface functionality on Web Forms. With a Web custom control, you can provide complete design-time support, event handling, data binding, and other advanced features. However, you need to do quite a bit of work to properly implement a Web custom control. This section shows the basics of three different ways to create a Web custom control:

➤ By combining two or more controls into a composite control

➤ By inheriting from a specific server control

➤ By inheriting from the generic `System.Web.Ui.Control` class

Creating a Composite Control

A *composite control* is a Web custom control that is composed of two or more standard Web server controls. Here's how you create a new composite control consisting of a `Label` control and a `Button` control:

1. Launch a new instance of Visual Studio .NET.

2. Create a new Visual Basic .NET Web Control Library project named `WebCustomControls`.

NOTE

You can add a Web Control Library project to an existing solution, but I've found that Visual Studio .NET can become confused as to which version of the controls to use in that case. Creating the Control Library as a separate solution seems to be more reliable.

3. Right-click the project in Solution Explorer and select Add, Add Class. Name the new class `CompositeControl.vb`.

4. Enter the following code for the `CompositeControl.vb` class:

```
Imports System.Web.UI
Imports System.Web.UI.WebControls
Imports System.ComponentModel

Public Class CompositeControl
    Inherits Control
    Implements INamingContainer

    Public Sub New()
        ' Set default values for persisted properties
        ViewState("MinValue") = 0
        ViewState("MaxValue") = 1000
    End Sub
```

```
Protected Overrides Sub CreateChildControls()
    ' Create the constituent controls
    Dim lbl As System.Web.UI.WebControls.Label = _
    New Label()
    Dim btn As _
    System.Web.UI.WebControls.Button = _
    New Button()
    ' Set initial properties
    With lbl
        .Height = Unit.Pixel(25)
        .Width = Unit.Pixel(75)
        .Text = "0"
    End With
    With btn
        .Height = Unit.Pixel(25)
        .Width = Unit.Pixel(75)
        .Text = "Go"
    End With
    ' Add them to the controls to be rendered
    Controls.Add(lbl)
    Controls.Add(btn)
    ' Hook up an event handler
    AddHandler btn.Click, AddressOf btnClick
End Sub

' Public properties to display
' in the Properties Window
<Category("Behavior"), _
Description("Minimum value")> _
Public Property MinValue() As Integer
    Get
        MinValue = _
        CType(ViewState("MinValue"), Integer)
    End Get
    Set(ByVal Value As Integer)
        ViewState("MinValue") = Value
    End Set
End Property

<Category("Behavior"), _
Description("Maximum value")> _
Public Property MaxValue() As Integer
    Get
        MaxValue = _
        CType(ViewState("MaxValue"), Integer)
    End Get
    Set(ByVal Value As Integer)
        ViewState("MaxValue") = Value
    End Set
End Property

' Handle the constituent control event
Public Sub btnClick(ByVal sender As Object, _
ByVal e As EventArgs)
    Dim r As System.Random = New System.Random()
    Dim Value As Integer
    ' Generate a new random value based
    ' on the minimum and
    ' maximum stored in the state
    Value = CType(r.Next( _
    CType(ViewState("MinValue"), Integer), _
    CType(ViewState("MaxValue"), _
    Integer)), String)
```

```
' Find the constituent label control
Dim lbl As Label = Controls(0)
' Make sure the controls really exist
Me.EnsureChildControls()
' And set the text to display
lbl.Text = Value.ToString
End Sub

End Class
```

5. Save and build the WebCustomControls project.

6. Switch back to the solution that contains your test project.

7. Add a Web Form named WebForm1.aspx to the project.

8. Select the Components tab in the Visual Studio .NET Toolbox. Right-click the tab and select Customize Toolbox. Select the .NET Framework Components tab in the Customize Toolbox dialog box. Click the Browse button and browse to the WebCustomControls.dll file in the bin directory under the WebCustomControls project. Click OK. Both the CompositeControl control and the WebCustomControl1 control (which is a default part of the library template) are added to the Toolbox.

9. Drag the CompositeControl control from the Toolbox and drop it on the Web Form. Figure 8.2 shows the resulting Web Form.

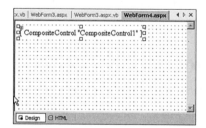

Figure 8.2 A composite control on a Web Form at design time.

10. Set the MinValue property of the new control to 500 and the MaxValue property of the new control to 1500 by changing the values in the Properties window.

11. Set the Web Form as the start page for the project.

12. Run the solution. The composite control renders as a label and a button in the browser. Click the button to display a random number between 500 and 1500.

The composite control uses the ViewState container to store property values that need to be persisted across round-trips to the browser. Recall that ViewState allows you to automatically read existing values from a hidden value that is sent as part of a postback. Using ViewState is a necessity for values that are required for postback processing (such as the minimum and maximum values in this case).

ASP.NET automatically calls the CreateChildControls method when it's time to render the control. In this procedure, the composite control creates new instances of the server controls that it will contain, sets their properties, and adds them to its own Controls collection. This is also the point at which any event handlers can be hooked up.

Public properties of the composite control are displayed in the Properties window. The attributes of the properties control some Visual Studio .NET–specific behaviors. For example, the attributes on the MinValue property set the control to be displayed in the Behavior category and specify descriptive text to show when the property is selected.

Finally, the event handler in this example demonstrates how you can retrieve a control from the collection of constituent controls to continue working with it. Controls in the collection are numbered starting at zero, in the order in which they were added to the collection. Note also the call to the EnsureChildControls method. This method should be used to protect any access to properties of the child controls; it causes the code to exit if the control does not exist for some reason.

Creating a Derived Control

Another way to create a Web custom control is to subclass an existing Web server control. As an example, you can create a TextBox control that has a green, grooved border by following these steps:

1. Open the WebCustomControls project.

2. Add a new class, CustomTextbox.vb, to the project.

3. Enter the following code for the CustomTextbox.vb class:

```
Imports System.Web.UI
Imports System.Web.UI.WebControls
Imports System.ComponentModel

Public Class CustomTextBox
    Inherits System.Web.UI.WebControls.TextBox

    Public Sub New()
        Me.BorderColor = System.Drawing.Color.Green
        Me.BorderStyle = BorderStyle.Groove
    End Sub
End Class
```

4. Save and build the WebCustomControls project.

5. Switch back to the test project.

6. Add a new Web Form to the project.

7. Select the Components tab in the Visual Studio .NET Toolbox. Delete the existing custom controls from the WebCustomControls project by selecting each one in the Toolbox and clicking Delete. Delete the reference to the WebCustomControls project from the references node in Solution Explorer.

8. Select the Components tab in the Visual Studio .NET Toolbox. Right-click the Components tab and select Customize Toolbox. Select the .NET Framework Components tab in the Customize Toolbox dialog box. Click the Browse button and browse to the WebCustomControls.dll file in the bin directory under the WebCustomControls project. Click OK.

9. Drag the CustomTextbox control from the Toolbox and drop it on the Web Form. Figure 8.3 shows the resulting Web Form.

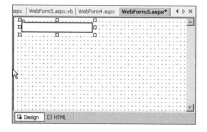

Figure 8.3 A derived control on a Web Form at design time.

10. Set the Web Form as the start page for the project and set the project as the startup project for the solution.

11. Run the solution. The derived control behaves like any other TextBox control at runtime.

Creating a Control from Scratch

The third way to create a Web custom control is to create the control "from scratch," by deriving it from the WebControl class and writing code to handle rendering and other tasks, rather than depending on existing controls. You probably noticed the WebCustomControl class that's automatically created as part of the Web Control Library project type. This class handles its own rendering. The following steps describe how to modify this default control:

1. Open the WebCustomControls project.

2. Open the WebCustomControl class and modify its code so that it looks like this:

```
Imports System.ComponentModel
Imports System.Web.UI

<DefaultProperty("Text"), _
 ToolboxData("<{0}:WebCustomControl1 " &  _
 "runat=server>" & _
 "</{0}:WebCustomControl1>")> _
Public Class WebCustomControl1
    Inherits System.Web.UI.WebControls.WebControl

    Dim _text As String
    Dim _bold As Boolean

    <Bindable(True), Category("Appearance"), _
    DefaultValue("")> _
    Property [Text]() As String
        Get
            Return _text
        End Get

        Set(ByVal Value As String)
            _text = Value
        End Set
    End Property

    <Category("Appearance")> _
    Property Bold() As Boolean
        Get
            Return _bold
        End Get

        Set(ByVal Value As Boolean)
            _bold = Value
        End Set
    End Property

    Protected Overrides Sub Render( _
    ByVal output As System.Web.UI.HtmlTextWriter)
        If _bold Then
            output.RenderBeginTag(HtmlTextWriterTag.B)
            output.Write([Text])
            output.RenderEndTag()
        Else
            output.Write([Text])
        End If
    End Sub

End Class
```

3. Save and build the WebCustomControls project.

4. Switch back to the test project.

5. Add a new Web Form named WebForm2.aspx to the project.

6. Delete the existing set of components and add the WebCustomControls project back to the Toolbox, just as you did in the previous set of steps.

7. Drag the WebCustomControl control from the Toolbox and drop it on the Web Form.

8. Set the Bold property of the control to True. Set the Text property of the control to This is my custom control.

9. Set the Web Form as the start page for the project and set the project as the startup project for the solution.

10. Run the solution. You should see the text from the control displayed in bold on the resulting HTML page.

The Render method gets called to draw text in both design and run modes. Because this control implements its own version of Render, it can display text easily in either mode. Note also the use of the RenderBeginTag and RenderEndTag methods to add HTML markup to the control's output.

You can also see some new attributes at both the class level and the property level here:

➤ The DefaultProperty attribute of the class specifies the name of a property that is the default property for the control.

➤ The ToolboxData attribute of the class provides the default HTML that the control will generate when it is dropped on a form.

➤ The Bindable attribute of a property specifies whether the property can participate in data binding.

➤ The DefaultValue attribute of a property specifies the default value for the property on a new instance of the control.

Custom Control Choices

As you've seen, there are quite a few choices when you want to build a control for use in ASP.NET applications. Here are some points to keep in mind as you decide which architecture to implement for a particular control:

➤ Web user controls can be used only in the same project where their .ascx file is contained. So they're not well suited for controls that need to be used across many projects.

➤ Web user controls are much easier to create than Web custom controls.

➤ Web user controls don't support a good representation at design time. Web custom controls can be represented more precisely at design time, although you might need to write additional code to do this.

➤ Web user controls cannot be added to the Visual Studio .NET Toolbox. Web custom controls can be added to the Toolbox.

➤ Web custom controls are better suited than Web user controls to dynamic layout tasks where constituent controls must be created at runtime.

➤ Using composite custom controls is a good choice when a group of controls must be repeated consistently on the user interface of an application.

➤ Using derived custom controls is a good choice when you want most of the functionality of an existing server control with only a few changes.

➤ Writing a Web custom control from scratch provides you with the most flexibility and control over the generated HTML.

Creating and Managing .NET Assemblies

A Web application usually consists of several different files; it typically includes the DLL files that contain the application code; the GIF, BMP, or JPG files that contain graphics; and other data files such as those that store strings in several languages for multilingual support. A Web application created using the .NET Framework groups together a logical collection of such files into what is called an *assembly*.

One of the files in the assembly contains a special piece of information called the *assembly manifest*. The manifest contains the metadata for the assembly. When the Common Language Runtime (CLR) loads an assembly, it first reads the manifest to get the following information:

➤ The name and version of the assembly

➤ The files that make up the assembly, including their names and hash values

➤ The compile-time dependency of the assembly on other assemblies

➤ The culture or language that an assembly supports

➤ The set of permissions required for the assembly to run properly

An assembly is the basic unit of deployment, scoping, versioning, and security in the .NET Framework. Microsoft uses assemblies to deliver the following benefits to .NET:

➤ Each assembly has a version number. All the types and resources in an assembly share the same version number, to make it easy for applications to refer to the correct version of files and avoid problems like the infamous "DLL hell," in which installing a new version of a shared library breaks older applications.

➤ The self-describing nature of assemblies makes it possible to deploy applications by using the zero-impact XCOPY installation. There's nothing to register, and there are no system files to change.

➤ Assemblies define a security boundary, allowing the CLR to restrict a set of operations to be executed, depending on the identity and origin of the assembly.

All .NET code executes as part of an assembly. When a user browses to a page on your ASP.NET Web site, the compiled class for the page is part of an assembly.

Assemblies exist in different forms, depending on how they are used. One way to classify assemblies (which was used by the exam developers) is with these categories:

➤ Single-file and multifile assemblies

➤ Static and dynamic assemblies

➤ Private and shared assemblies

➤ Satellite and resource-only assemblies

The following sections discuss each of these categories.

Single-File and Multifile Assemblies

A *single-file assembly* consists of a single EXE or DLL file. This file consists of code, any embedded resources, and the assembly manifest of the assembly.

The assemblies that ASP.NET creates are always single-file assemblies. The .NET Framework can also handle multifile assemblies. A *multifile assembly* can include multiple files in one assembly. You should have at least one DLL or EXE file among these files. You can choose to attach the assembly manifest with any of these files, or you can keep it in a separate file of its own. Because multifile assemblies aren't used in ASP.NET, I don't cover the details of their creation here.

Static and Dynamic Assemblies

When you compile programs using Visual Studio .NET or through the command-line compiler, they emit the files that make up an assembly. These files are physically stored on disk. Such an assembly is called a *static assembly*.

However, it is also possible to create and execute assemblies on-the-fly (that is, while a program is still under execution). Such assemblies are called *dynamic assemblies*. In fact, dynamic assemblies are used extensively by ASP.NET. While you're executing ASPX files, the ASP.NET process creates the corresponding assemblies at runtime. That's how ASP.NET automatically uses new files when you upload them, even if you don't supply the compiled version of the assemblies. If needed, dynamic assemblies can be saved to disk to be later loaded again. The classes used to create dynamic assemblies are available in the System.Reflection.Emit namespace. The System.Reflection.Emit namespace is not covered on the exam.

Private and Shared Assemblies

You can deploy assemblies by using two different approaches:

➤ You can deploy an assembly for use with a single application. When an assembly is deployed this way, it is called a *private assembly*.

➤ You can deploy an assembly for use with several applications. When an assembly is deployed in the shared mode, it is called a *shared assembly*.

Here are some fast facts about private assemblies:

➤ Private assemblies are intended to be only used by the application they are deployed with.

➤ Private assemblies are deployed in the directory (or a subdirectory) where the main application is installed.

➤ Typically, a private assembly is written by the same company that writes the main application that uses the private assembly.

Because of the limited nature of a private assembly, the CLR does not impose a strict versioning policy with them. How the application developers version and name their assemblies is more or less left to them.

On the other hand, a shared assembly can be used by more than one application. All the shared assemblies on a computer are stored in a special place called the *Global Assembly Cache (GAC)* in order to be accessible by all applications. Because of the shared nature of the GAC, the CLR imposes special security and versioning requirements on any assembly installed in the GAC.

As a general rule, you should always deploy assemblies as private assemblies. You should install the assemblies in the GAC only if you are explicitly required to share them with other applications. One common use for shared assemblies in ASP.NET is to allow Web custom controls to be shared by multiple applications.

Here are some fast facts about shared assemblies and the GAC:

➤ Each assembly that is installed in the GAC must have a strong name. A *strong name* consists of an assembly's name, a version number, a culture, a public key, and a digital signature. Having a strong name ensures an assembly's identity.

➤ The CLR checks for an assembly's integrity before installing it in the GAC and ensures that an assembly has not been tampered with by checking the strong name of the assembly.

➤ The GAC is capable of maintaining multiple copies of an assembly with the same name but different versions.

➤ You can view the contents of the GAC by opening Windows Explorer and navigating to the `Assembly` folder under the `Windows` folder of the computer.

➤ The CLR can determine what version of an assembly to load based on the information in an application's configuration file or the machinewide configuration file (`machine.config`). You'll learn more about this in Chapter 16, "Configuring a Web Application."

Satellite and Resource-Only Assemblies

A Web application typically contains resources such as images and strings in addition to code. These resources can be translated into various cultures and languages. When you add these files to a Visual Studio .NET project, their default `Build Type` is `Content`. When you compile the project, the assemblies contain just code, metadata, and links to files that exist externally. This means that the resource files will be distributed with the application as separate files, and all these files must be available at runtime in order for the application to function correctly.

Another way to package the resource files with an application is to embed them into the assembly itself. To achieve this, when you add the resource files to a project, you set their `Build Type` to `Embedded Resources`. You can do this through the Properties window by accessing the properties of these files.

When the Build Type is set to Embedded Resources, the contents of the resource file will be included in the assembly itself at compile time. Visual Studio .NET does this in the following three steps:

1. It creates an XML resource file with the extension .resx. This file stores the resources as key-value pairs (for example, the name of a resource file and its location).

2. At the time of compilation, all resources referenced by the .resx file are embedded into a binary file with the extension .resources.

3. The binary resource file is embedded into the code assembly.

These steps can be done manually. The .resx file is an XML file, so you can manually create it by using any text editor. You can compile it into a resource file by using the Resource Generator tool (resgen.exe). You can embed a resource file into an assembly by using the VBC compiler's /resource option.

These steps create an assembly that contains both code and resources. Assemblies created in such a way are not dependent on external resource files but have all necessary information stuffed into themselves.

Another way to attach resources in an application is by creating *resource-only assemblies*. These assemblies just contain resources, without any code.

Resource-only assemblies that store culture-specific information are also known as *satellite assemblies*. Visual Studio .NET offers user interface support for creating and using satellite assemblies for Windows forms but not for Web Forms. To use a satellite assembly for a Web Form, you need to build your own resource-only assembly and use custom code to retrieve the resources. I cover the topic of satellite assemblies and globalization of applications in Chapter 10, "Globalization."

Exam Prep Questions

Question 1

You are creating an ASP.NET Web application to serve as the Web site for a small business client of yours. Each page in the site will have the same text and images as a sidebar menu. You won't need to reuse these controls for any other project. What sort of control should you create to represent the menu?

- ○ A. A composite Web custom control
- ○ B. A Web custom control that inherits directly from the **Label** control
- ○ C. A Web custom control that inherits directly from the **WebControl** control
- ○ D. A Web user control

Answer D is correct. Using a Web user control is the easiest way to group several controls for reuse, if the controls do not need to be reused outside a single project. Answer A is incorrect because building a Web custom control is much more work than building a Web user control in this case. Answers B and C are incorrect because inheriting from a single control does not let you create a control with multiple constituent controls.

Question 2

Which type of information is contained in the assembly manifest of a .NET assembly (select all correct answers)?

- ❑ A. The name of the assembly
- ❑ B. The version of the assembly
- ❑ C. The source code of the assembly
- ❑ D. The preferred installation location of the assembly

Answers A and B are correct. An assembly manifest contains the name and version of the assembly, a list of the files in the assembly, together with their hash values, dependency information, culture and language information, and permissions required for the assembly to run. Answer C is incorrect because an assembly contains MSIL (Microsoft intermediate language) code rather than source code. Answer D is incorrect because you can choose where to install assemblies.

Question 3

The **CreateChildControls** method of your composite custom control uses this code to add four controls to its **Controls** collection:

```
Protected Overrides Sub _
  CreateChildControls()
    Dim lbl As System.Web.UI. _
    WebControls.Label = _
    New Label()
    Dim btn As System.Web.UI. _
    WebControls.Button = _
    New Button()
    Dim txt As System.Web.UI. _
    WebControls.TextBox = _
    New TextBox()
    Dim img As System.Web.UI. _
    WebControls.Image = _
    New Image()
    Controls.Add(lbl)
    Controls.Add(btn)
    Controls.Add(txt)
    Controls.Add(img)
End Sub
```

In an event handler within the composite control class, you need to refer to the **Button** control. Which of the following can you use to retrieve this control?

O A. **Dim btn As Button = ViewState(btn)**

O B. **Dim btn As Button = New Button()**

O C. **Dim btn As Button = Controls(1)**

O D. **Dim btn As Button = Controls(2)**

Answer C is correct. The constituent controls in a composite control are numbered in the order in which they were added to the Controls collection, starting at zero. Answer A is incorrect because the ViewState collection contains information you put in it but not entire controls. Answer B is incorrect because this creates a new control rather than a reference to an existing control. Answer D is incorrect because it uses the wrong index to refer to the control.

Question 4

You are creating a specialized control that will ensure consistency in your company's logo across many Web pages. This control must be installed into the Visual Studio .NET Toolbox so that it can be used in many projects. The control's user interface will be a single **Image** control that can be customized with several properties. What sort of control should you create?

- ○ A. A composite Web custom control
- ○ B. A Web custom control that inherits directly from the **Image** control
- ○ C. A Web custom control that inherits directly from the **WebControl** control
- ○ D. A Web user control

Answer B is correct. By inheriting directly from the Image control, you can build on the default Image control behavior with a minimum of code. Answer A is incorrect because you don't need a composite control to hold a single image. Answer C is incorrect because inheriting from WebControl requires you to provide your own rendering logic. Answer D is incorrect because Web user controls are not well suited to sharing between projects.

Question 5

You have created a Web custom control named **sidebar.vb** that encapsulates a standard sidebar to be used on all your company's Web sites. You now want to use this control in Web applications other than the one where you built the control. What should you do?

- ○ A. Install the control in the GAC.
- ○ B. Include the control's project in the solution that contains all the applications.
- ○ C. Copy the control's files into each application.
- ○ D. Compile the control and copy the compiled assembly into each application's **bin** folder.

Answer A is correct. A Web custom control can be used by any application that can set a reference to the compiled version of the control. If you install a Web custom control in the GAC, it can be used by any application on the computer. Answers B, C, and D are incorrect because they require managing multiple copies of the control code when a single copy in the GAC would suffice.

Question 6

You are building a new control that will monitor a SQL Server database by issuing queries from the browser and listening for results. The control will not have a runtime user interface. What sort of control should you create?

- ○ A. A composite Web custom control
- ○ B. A Web custom control that inherits directly from the **Label** control
- ○ C. A Web custom control that inherits directly from the **WebControl** control
- ○ D. A Web user control

Answer C is correct. If you don't need a user interface, the simplest choice is to inherit directly from WebControl, which does not have a default runtime user interface. Answers A and B are incorrect because each automatically provides a user interface. Answer D is incorrect because a Web user control is a collection of user interface controls.

Question 7

You have created a Web user control named **sidebar.ascx** that encapsulates a standard sidebar to be used on all your company's Web sites. You now want to use this control in Web applications other than the one where you built the control. What should you do?

- ○ A. Install the control in the GAC.
- ○ B. Include the control's project in the solution that contains all the applications.
- ○ C. Copy the control's files into each application.
- ○ D. Compile the control and copy the compiled assembly into each application's **bin** folder.

Answer C is correct. A Web user control can be used only by a project that contains the control's files. Answer A is incorrect because the GAC is for sharing assemblies, not Web user controls. Answer B is incorrect because just having the control in the same solution is not sufficient. Answer D is incorrect because you can compile the code-behind file, but the .ascx file must still be copied to every application.

Question 8

You have created a Web custom control by inheriting directly from the **WebControl** class. At design time, you want a specific HTML string to represent this control on the Web Form's user interface. How should you supply this HTML string?

○ A. As the value of the **DefaultProperty** attribute of the class

○ B. As a public property named **DesignHTML**

○ C. As the value of the **ToolboxData** attribute of the class

○ D. As a separate file that is stored in the same folder as the Web custom control

Answer C is correct. At design time, the page designer reads the value of the ToolboxData attribute and uses this attribute to render HTML to the page being designed.

Question 9

You have a standard set of controls that you use to implement a company identity section in a variety of Web applications. These controls include a series of **LinkButton**, **Image**, and **Label** controls. You've decided that you would like to encapsulate these controls for easy reuse. What sort of control should you create?

○ A. A composite Web custom control

○ B. A Web custom control that inherits directly from the **Panel** control

○ C. A Web custom control that inherits directly from the **WebControl** control

○ D. A Web user control

Answer A is correct. A composite Web custom control lets you group a set of controls together as a single reusable piece. Answers B and C are incorrect because they do not provide an easy way to encapsulate multiple controls. Answer D is incorrect because Web user controls are not well suited to use across multiple applications.

Question 10

Which type of custom control can you add to the Visual Studio .NET Toolbox (select all correct answers)?

- ❑ A. A Web user control
- ❑ B. A composite Web custom control
- ❑ C. A Web custom control derived directly from the **WebControl** control
- ❑ D. A Web custom control derived directly from the **Label** control

Answers B, C, and D are correct. All types of Web custom controls can be added to the Toolbox. Answer A is incorrect because Web user controls cannot be added to the Toolbox.

Need to Know More?

 Liberty, Jesse, and Hurwitz, Dan. *Programming ASP.NET.* O'Reilly, 2002.

 Ahmed, Mesbah, et al. *ASP.NET Web Developer's Guide.* Syngress, 2002.

 Visual Studio .NET Combined Help Collection, "Developing ASP.NET Server Controls" section.

 The Code Project, http://www.codeproject.com.

Web Services

Terms you'll need to understand:

✓ Web service
✓ SOAP (Simple Object Access Protocol)
✓ Disco
✓ UDDI (Universal Description, Discovery, and Integration)
✓ WSDL (Web Services Description Language)
✓ Web method
✓ Web reference

Techniques you'll need to master:

✓ Creating a Web service
✓ Discovering a Web service
✓ Instantiating a Web service
✓ Invoking a Web method

You might also run across a lot of complex and confusing explanations of the architecture of these Web services. But at their most basic level, Web services are simple: They are a means for interacting with objects over the Internet. In this chapter, you'll learn about the fundamentals of Web services and learn to build and use them.

Understanding Web Services

Web services in .NET are based on three protocols:

➤ SOAP

➤ UDDI

➤ WSDL

By default, all communication between Web services servers and their clients is through XML messages transmitted over the HTTP protocol. This has two benefits. First, because Web services messages are formatted as XML, they're reasonably easy for human beings to read and understand. Second, because those messages are transmitted over the pervasive HTTP protocol, they can normally reach any machine on the Internet without worrying about firewalls.

SOAP

For Web services to manipulate objects through XML messages, there has to be a way to translate objects (as well as their methods and properties) into XML. This translation method is called SOAP, the Simple Object Access Protocol. SOAP is a way to encapsulate object calls as XML sent via HTTP. In theory, it can travel over other protocols as well, but .NET uses HTTP exclusively.

There are two major advantages to using SOAP to communicate with Web services. First, because HTTP is so pervasive, it can travel to any point on the Internet, regardless of intervening hardware or firewalls. Second, because SOAP is XML based, it can be interpreted by a wide variety of software on many operating systems. Although you'll only work with the Microsoft implementation of Web services for the exam, numerous Web services tools from other vendors can interoperate with Microsoft-based Web services.

Disco and UDDI

Before you can use a Web service, you need to know where to find the service. Handling such requests is the job of several protocols, including Disco and UDDI. These protocols allow you to communicate with a Web server to discover the details of the Web services that are available at that server.

WSDL

The other prerequisite for using a Web service is knowledge of the SOAP messages that it can receive and send. You can obtain this knowledge by parsing WSDL files. WSDL is a standard by which a Web service can tell clients what messages it accepts and which results it will return.

WSDL files define everything about a Web service: the data types that it can process, the methods that it exposes, and the URLs through which those methods can be accessed.

Although UDDI and WSDL files make it possible to interact with Web services without any prior knowledge, these files are not required for a Web service to function. You can make a Web service available on the Internet without any UDDI or WSDL file. In that case, only clients who already know the expected message formats and location of the Web service will be able to use it.

Invoking Your First Web Service

The easiest way to understand Web services is to start working with them.

Most of the examples in this chapter assume that you're working on a computer that is connected to the Internet. It's okay if there's a proxy server between you and the Internet, as long as you can connect to Web sites.

If the Airport Weather Web service doesn't seem to be available, one good way to find other examples is to use your favorite search engine to look for the term "Web service examples."

Follow these steps to use the public Airport Weather Web Service on the Internet.

1. Create a new Visual Basic .NET ASP.NET Web Application in the Visual Studio .NET IDE.

2. Right-click the References folder in Solution Explorer and select Add Web Reference. This opens the Add Web Reference dialog box.

3. Type `http://live.capescience.com/wsdl/AirportWeather.wsdl` into the Address bar of the Add Web Reference dialog box and press Enter. This connects to the Airport Weather Web service and downloads the information shown in Figure 9.1.

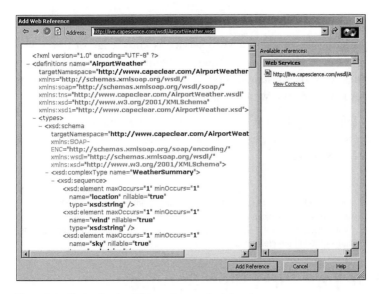

Figure 9.1 Connecting to a Web service over the Internet.

4. Click the Add Reference button.

5. Place a `Label` control, a `TextBox` control with the ID of `txtCode`, a `Button` control with the ID of `btnGetSummary`, and a `ListBox` control with the ID of `lbResults` on the default Web Form in the project. Figure 9.2 shows this form.

6. Double-click the `Button` control to open the form's module. Enter this code to invoke the Web service when the user clicks the button:

```
Private Sub btnGetSummary_Click( _
    ByVal sender As System.Object, _
    ByVal e As System.EventArgs) _
    Handles btnGetSummary.Click
    ' Connect to the Web service by declaring
    ' a variable of the appropriate type
    Dim aw As com.capescience.live.AirportWeather = _
        New com.capescience.live.AirportWeather()
```

```
' Call the Web service to get the summary
' for the entered airport
Dim ws As com.capescience.live.WeatherSummary = _
aw.getSummary(txtCode.Text)

' Display some of the properties
' filled in by the Web service
With lbResults.Items
    .Clear()
    .Add(ws.location)
    .Add("Temperature: " & ws.temp)
    .Add("Visibility: " & ws.visibility)
    .Add("Wind: " & ws.wind)
End With
End Sub
```

7. Run the project and fill in a value such as KSEA for the airport code. Click the button. After a brief pause while the Web service is invoked, you'll see some information in the ListBox control, as shown in Figure 9.2. This information is delivered from the server where the Web service resides, as properties of the WeatherSummary object.

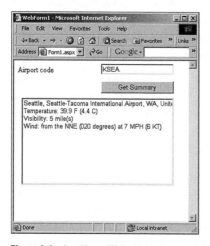

Figure 9.2   Invoking a Web service from a Web Form.

In one sense, there's not much new here, compared to invoking any other object. After you've set a reference to the server, you can create objects from that server, invoke their methods, and examine the results. You could do the same with objects from a .NET library on your own computer.

But in another sense, a lot of revolutionary work is going on here, even though you don't see most of it happening. When you create the Web reference, for example, Visual Studio .NET reads the appropriate WSDL file to determine which classes and methods are available from the remote server.

When you call a method on an object from that server, the .NET infrastructure translates your call and the results into SOAP messages and manages them without any intervention on your part.

Discovering Web Services

One of the problems with Web services is simply finding them. Because Web services aren't installed on your computer, you need some way to determine the messages that they accept and the services that they provide. The usual term for this process is *discovery*, which encompasses both finding Web services and determining their interfaces.

Disco Documents and UDDI's Central Directory of Web Services

Disco is a Microsoft standard for the creation of discovery documents. A Disco document is kept at a standard location on a Web services server and contains paths and other information for retrieving other useful information, such as the WSDL file that describes a service.

UDDI (Universal Description, Discovery, and Integration) is a method for finding services by referring to a central directory. These can be Web services, URLs for information, or any other online resource. UDDI registries are sites that contain information available via UDDI; you can search such a registry to find information about Web services.

UDDI registries come in two forms—*public* and *private*. A public UDDI registry is available to all comers via the Internet, and it serves as a central repository of information about Web and other services for businesses. A private UDDI registry follows the same specifications as a public UDDI registry, but is located on an intranet for the use of workers at one particular enterprise.

Using the Web Services Discovery Tool (disco.exe)

When you set a Web reference inside of Visual Studio .NET, the software automatically handles the details of discovery for you. But you can also execute the process using the Web Services Discovery Tool, `disco.exe`. Follow these steps to see how this tool works:

1. Select Start, Programs, Microsoft Visual Studio .NET, Visual Studio .NET Tools, Visual Studio .NET Command Prompt.

2. Enter the following command to discover the details of the Airport Weather Web service:

```
disco http://live.capescience.com/wsdl/AirportWeather.wsdl
```

As you can see, you need to know the base address of the Web service to use this tool.

3. The tool contacts the Web service and (in this case) creates two files of results: `AirportWeather.wsdl` and `results.discomap`.

4. Open the files in Visual Studio .NET or your favorite text editor to see the results of the discovery process.

5. The `results.discomap` file is an XML file that shows you the name of the other file and the URL from which its contents were retrieved.

6. The `AirportWeather.wsdl` file is an XML file that contains information on the interface of the Web service. This includes details of the messages, parameters, and objects with which you can interact. This file gives Visual Studio .NET the details that it needs to let you use a Web service from your code.

Instantiating and Invoking Web Services

After you've discovered a Web service and retrieved information about its interface, you can instantiate an object representing that Web service and then invoke its methods.

Creating Proxy Classes with the Web Services Description Language Tool (wsdl.exe)

The .NET Framework SDK includes the Web Services Description Language Tool, `wsdl.exe`. This tool can take a WSDL file and generate a corresponding proxy class that you can use to invoke the Web service. To use this tool, just run it from the command line, as in this example:

```
wsdl /language:VB /out:aw.vb AirportWeather.wsdl
```

Table 9.1 shows some of the command-line options that you can use with `wsdl.exe`. You can use either the path to a local WSDL or Disco file or the URL of a remote WSDL or Disco file with this tool.

Table 9.1 Command-Line Options for wsdl.exe	
Option	Meaning
/domain:*DomainName*	Domain name to use when connecting to a server that requires authentication.
/language:*LanguageCode*	Specifies the language for the generated class. The **LanguageCode** parameter can be CS (for C#), VB (for VB .NET), or JS (for JScript).
/namespace:*Namespace*	Specifies a namespace for the generated class.
/out:*Filename*	Filename for the generated output. If not specified, the filename will be derived from the Web service name.
/password:*Password*	Password to use when connecting to a server that requires authentication.
/server	Generates a class to create a server based on the input file. By default, the tool generates a client proxy object.
/username:*Username*	Username to use when connecting to a server that requires authentication.
/?	Displays full help on the tool.

Using Web References

As an alternative to using the Web Service Discovery Tool and the Web Service Description Language Tool to create explicit proxy classes, you can simply add a Web reference to your project to enable the project to use the Web service. In fact, there's no difference in the end result between using the tools to create a proxy class and adding a Web reference. That's because, behind the scenes, the Web reference creates its own proxy class. To see this, click the Show All Files toolbar button within Solution Explorer, and then expand the Solution Explorer node for a Web reference. You'll find the generated .vb file defining the proxy beneath the Web reference.

The major benefit of using a Web reference (as compared to constructing proxy classes with the command-line tools) is that it's easier to update the proxy classes if the Web service changes. All you need to do in that case is right-click the Web Reference node in Solution Explorer and select Update Web Reference.

Testing a Web Service

If you'd like to test a Web service without building an entire client application, you can use a testing tool. Several such tools are easily available:

➤ NetTool is a free Web services proxy tool from CapeClear. You can get a copy from http://capescience.capeclear.com/articles/using_nettool/.

➤ The .NET WebService Studio tool comes from Microsoft. You can download a free copy from http://www.gotdotnet.com/team/tools/web_svc/default.aspx.

➤ Mindreef SOAPScope is a general proxy and debugging tool for SOAP communications. You can download a trial copy from http://www.mindreef.com/.

➤ XML Spy includes a SOAP debugger that can be used to test Web services. You can download a trial copy of this XML editor and toolkit from http://www.xmlspy.com/default.asp.

All four of these tools work in the same basic way: They intercept SOAP messages between Web services clients and servers so that you can inspect and, if you like, alter the results.

Exam Prep Questions

Question 1

> One of your trading partners has informed you that he is making pricing infor-
> mation available via a Web service. You do not know the URL of the Web serv-
> ice. How can you discover the URL of the Web service?
>
> ○ A. Use the Web Service Discovery Tool to download the information.
>
> ○ B. Use the Web Service Description Language Tool to create a proxy
> class.
>
> ○ C. Use a UDDI Registry to locate the Web service.
>
> ○ D. Use a search engine to explore your partner's Web site.

Answer C is correct. The purpose of a UDDI Registry is to locate Web services based on criteria such as the industry or company that makes the Web
service available. Answers A and B are incorrect because they require you to
already know where the Web service is located. Answer D is incorrect
because most search engines do not index Web service discovery documents.

Question 2

> You are invoking a Web service that returns a **DataSet** object. Your client appli-
> cation is written in Visual Basic .NET, whereas the Web service itself is written
> in C#. The Web service is outside of your corporate firewall. You receive an
> "object not found" error when you call the method that returns the **DataSet**.
> What could be the problem?
>
> ○ A. Objects supplied by a Web service cannot cross a firewall.
>
> ○ B. The client project does not contain a reference to the **System.Data**
> **namespace**.
>
> ○ C. The client project and the Web service project must use the same language.
>
> ○ D. Web services cannot properly serialize a complex object such as the
> **DataSet** object.

Answer B is correct. Web service servers and clients must agree on the objects
that they exchange, which means that both are required to have a reference to
any namespace that defines an object returned by a Web method. Answer A
is incorrect because Web services use SOAP, which crosses most firewalls, to
transmit messages. Answer C is incorrect because the protocols used by Web
services are platform and language independent. Answer D is incorrect
because any object that can be serialized can be used by a Web service.

Question 3

You have used the Web Services Discovery Tool to retrieve information about a Web service named HolidayService. Which file will contain the URL for any documentation of the HolidayService Web service?

○ A. **disco.exe**

○ B. **results.discomap**

○ C. **HolidayService.wsdl**

○ D. **HolidayService.disco**

Answer D is correct. The .disco file is the file that contains pointers to non-XML resources. Answer A is incorrect because disco.exe is the tool itself. Answer B is incorrect because the .discomap file just lists the other files retrieved. Answer C is incorrect because the .wsdl file contains the XML description of the Web service's interface.

Question 4

You have used the Web Services Description Language Tool to create a proxy class for a Web service. When you add the proxy class to your VB.NET project, you discover that it is coded in the C# language. What should you do to get the proxy class coded in VB.NET instead of C# with the least effort?

○ A. Manually convert the C# code to VB .NET code.

○ B. Select File, Save As and give the new file a **.vb** extension.

○ C. Rerun the tool, specifying the **/language:VB** option.

○ D. Rerun the tool, specifying the **/namespace:VB** option.

Answer C is correct. The /language switch to the tool specifies the output language. Answer A is incorrect because, even though it would work, it is much more effort than just running the tool again. Answer B is incorrect because saving the file with a new extension will not change its language. Answer D is incorrect because the /namespace switch specifies the namespace of the proxy class, not its language.

Question 5

> You need to create a proxy class in order to use a Web service named ScheduleService in your Visual Basic .NET application. Which methods can you use to create the proxy class (select all that apply)?
>
> ❑ A. Run the **wsdl.exe** tool.
>
> ❑ B. Set a Web reference to the Web service.
>
> ❑ C. Run the **disco.exe** tool.
>
> ❑ D. Use File, Add Existing Item to add the Web service's **.asmx** file to your project.

Answers A and B are correct. The wsdl.exe tool allows you to create a proxy class from the command line, whereas setting a Web reference creates a proxy class from within Visual Studio .NET. Answer C is incorrect because disco.exe is a tool for locating documents published by the Web service. Answer D is incorrect because you won't use the actual code of the Web service in your client projects.

Question 6

> You want to encapsulate an object for transmission over HTTP as an XML message. Which protocol will help you do this?
>
> ○ A. SOAP
>
> ○ B. Disco
>
> ○ C. WSDL
>
> ○ D. UDDI

Answer A is correct. SOAP is a protocol for converting objects and method calls into XML messages. Answer B is incorrect because Disco is Microsoft's method for discovering information about a Web service. Answer C is incorrect because WSDL describes the interface of a Web service. Answer D is incorrect because UDDI is a standard for discovering Web services and other resources on the Internet.

Question 7

You have created a Web service to return inventory information. One of the methods in your Web service is defined with this code:

```
Public Function InvLevel (ProductID As Integer) As Integer
    ' Details omitted
End Function
```

Users of your Web service report that although they can set a Web reference to the Web service, the **InvLevel** method is not available. What could be the problem?

○ A. The **.asmx** file for the Web service is not available on your Web server.

○ B. The Web service class is not marked with the **<WebService>** attribute.

○ C. The **InvLevel** method is not marked with the **<WebMethod>** attribute.

○ D. Web services cannot return integer values.

Answer C is correct. Only public functions decorated with the WebMethod attribute will be available to clients of a Web service. Answers A and B are incorrect because in those cases the client would be unable to set a reference to the Web service. Answer D is incorrect because a Web service can return any type that can be described in WSDL.

Question 8

Your application consumes a Web service named Northwind. The Northwind Web service includes a Web method named **Products** that returns a **System.Data.DataSet** object. What data type should you use for an object to hold the results of the **Products** method?

○ A. **System.Data.DataSet**

○ B. **Northwind.DataSet**

○ C. **Northwind.Products.DataSet**

○ D. **Products.DataSet**

Answer A is correct. Variables used in a Web service call must exactly match the type of the variables defined by the server in the Web method signature. Because Answer A is the only one that matches exactly, it is the only correct answer.

Need to Know More?

 Jennings, Roger. *Visual Basic .NET Web Services Developer's Guide.* McGraw-Hill/Osborne, 2002.

 Scribner, Kenn and Stiver, Mark C. *Applied Soap: Implementing .NET XML Web Services.* Sams, 2001.

 Short, Scott. *Building XML Web Services for the Microsoft .NET Platform.* Microsoft Press, 2002.

 WebServices.org, `http://www.webservices.org/index.php`.

 Microsoft   UDDI   Business   Registry   Node,   `http://uddi.microsoft.com/`.

Globalization

Terms you'll need to understand:

✓ Globalization
✓ Localization
✓ Localizability
✓ Culture
✓ Resource file
✓ Culture code
✓ Unicode
✓ Encoding

Techniques you'll need to master:

✓ Localizing an application
✓ Using culture information at runtime
✓ Using character encodings to present information
✓ Mirroring a user interface

You need to think from the beginning of a project about translating a user interface into multiple languages—a process known as *localization*. If your application runs on the Internet (as many ASP.NET applications will), this is even more true.

The .NET Framework provides excellent capabilities for localizing applications. Localization goes far beyond simply translating the text on a user interface. Some of the topics you need to consider include

➤ Translating user interface text, message boxes, and so on

➤ Using encodings to translate characters from one representation to another

➤ Using mirroring to change the direction of text in controls on the user interface

➤ Formatting things, such as currency and dates, that are presented in different ways in different locales

➤ Managing data sorts to take different alphabets into account

Understanding Localization and Globalization

There are two basic ways to prepare an application for multiple locales (say, the United States, France, and Germany):

➤ Write three completely different sets of source code—one for each location where the application will be used.

➤ Write one set of source code and build in the capability to customize the application for different locations.

The first of these alternatives is likely to be prohibitively expensive. Using three different sets of source code will require three times as many developers, testers, and managers as building a single version of the application. Perhaps worse, a bug that's found and fixed in one version might slip through the cracks and ship in another version. If you later needed to ship a version for a fourth location, you'd have to repeat the entire process again.

Not surprisingly, Visual Basic .NET encourages you to take the second approach. An application built from a single code base can be easily customized for multiple locations by using techniques such as locale-aware formatting functions and resource files. You don't have to worry about different versions getting "out of synch" (because they're all built from the same source code), and building a new version requires no work beyond translating strings into a new language.

The Localization Process

The technical term for the entire process of preparing an application for shipment in a new location-specific version is *localization*. Microsoft divides this process of preparing a "world-ready application" into three phases:

1. Globalization

2. Localizability

3. Localization

Globalization is the first step in the process. In the globalization stage, you identify all the localizable resources in the application and separate them from the executable code so that they can be modified easily. Ideally, you'll perform the globalization step during the design phase so that the resources will always remain separate from the code.

Localizability is the second step in the process. In the localizability stage, you check to make sure that translating the application for a new location won't require design changes. If you've planned for localization from the beginning, localizability will typically be part of your quality assurance (QA) process.

Localization is the final step in the process. In the localization phase, you customize your application for new locales. This consists primarily of translating resources that you identified during the globalization phase.

 Although, in theory, the terms *globalization*, *localizability*, and *localization* are precise and distinct, in practice they tend to be used interchangeably. Indeed, even the objectives for the certification exam are not careful in the way that they use these terms.

What Should Be Localized?

Obviously, you must modify text that shows on the user interface when you're localizing an application. This includes text on Web Forms, in error messages, and any other text that is shown to the user. But there are many other things that you might need to localize in any given application.

Here's a list of resources that are commonly localized, depending on the target locale:

➤ Menu item text.

➤ Form layouts. Text in German, for example, averages nearly twice as long as the same text in English. You might need to move and resize controls to accommodate this.

➤ The display format for dates and times.

➤ The display format for currency.

➤ The display format for numbers. (For example, some countries use commas as the thousands separator in long numbers.)

➤ Data input fields. (What if you're asking for a ZIP Code in a country other than the United States?)

➤ Maps, road signs, photos, or other graphics with local content.

➤ Shortcut keys. Not every character you know appears on every keyboard.

➤ Calendars. Countries such as Korea or Saudi Arabia use calendars completely different from each other.

➤ Alphabetical order.

You'll need to use some judgment in deciding which of these things really need to be localized in your application. You might decide, for example, that a set of general-purpose data entry fields can serve your needs for collecting addresses, rather than trying to research address formats worldwide.

Understanding Cultures

A culture, in .NET terms, is a more precise identifier than a location or a language. A *culture* identifies all the things that might need to be localized in an application, which requires you to know more than just the language. For example, just knowing that an application uses English as its user interface language doesn't give you enough information to completely localize it: Should you format dates and currency amounts in that application in a way appropriate to the United States, the United Kingdom, Canada, Australia, or New Zealand (among other possibilities)? Similarly, just knowing the location isn't enough: If an application will be used in Switzerland, there are four possibilities for the user interface language. Each combination of location and language identifies a culture.

About Culture Codes

Cultures are identified by abbreviations called *culture codes*. A full culture code consists of a neutral culture code (written in lowercase), followed by one or more subculture codes (written in mixed case or uppercase). Here are a few culture codes as examples:

➤ **de**—Identifies the German culture. This is a neutral culture—a culture that does not specify a subculture code. Neutral cultures generally do not provide sufficient information to localize an application.

➤ **en-GB**—Identifies the English (United Kingdom) culture. This is a specific culture—a culture that provides enough information to localize an application (in this case, for English speakers in Great Britain).

➤ **az-AZ-Cyrl**—Is an example of a specific culture with two subculture codes. This particular culture refers to the Azeri language in Azerbaijan, written with Cyrillic characters.

The CultureInfo Class

The .NET Framework represents cultures with the `System.Globalization.CultureInfo` class. This class lets you retrieve a wide variety of information about any particular culture. For example, you might use this code to dump information about the en-GB culture to a `ListBox` control on a Web Form:

```
Private Sub btnGetInfo_Click( _
  ByVal sender As System.Object, _
  ByVal e As System.EventArgs) Handles btnGetInfo.Click
    ' Create a CultureInfo object
    ' for the specified culture
    Dim ci As CultureInfo = _
      New CultureInfo("en-GB")
    ' Dump information about the culture
    With lbInfo.Items
        .Clear()
        .Add("Display Name: " & ci.DisplayName)
        .Add("English Name: " & ci.EnglishName)
        .Add("Native Name: " & ci.NativeName)
        ' Get day names
        .Add("Day Names:")
        Dim strDayNames() As String = _
          ci.DateTimeFormat.DayNames
        Dim strDay As String
        For Each strDay In strDayNames
            .Add("  " & strDay)
        Next
        ' Get the current year
        .Add("Current year: " & ci.Calendar. _
          GetYear(DateTime.Today))
```

```
' And the currency symbol
.Add("Currency symbol: " & _
   ci.NumberFormat.CurrencySymbol)
   End With
End Sub
```

The static `CultureInfo.GetCultures` method returns an array of `CultureInfo` objects that you can enumerate to get the entire list of cultures supported by .NET.

The **CurrentCulture** and **CurrentUICulture** Properties

The .NET Framework handles localization on a thread-by-thread basis. Each thread has two properties that are used for determining the culture to use: `CurrentCulture` and `CurrentUICulture`. You can set or view these properties on the `Thread.CurrentThread` object.

The `CurrentUICulture` property tells the CLR which culture to use when choosing resources for the user interface. The `CurrentCulture` property is also used by the CLR to manage localization, but in a different way. The `CurrentCulture` property dictates the format for dates, times, currency, and numbers, as well as other culture-specific functionality, such as string comparison rules and casing rules.

The Invariant Culture

There's one more culture that you should know about: the invariant culture. This is a special culture that doesn't have an abbreviation. The invariant culture has two purposes:

➤ Interacting with other software, such as system services, where no user is directly involved

➤ Storing data in a culture-independent format that won't be displayed directly to end users

There are two ways to create a `CultureInfo` object that represents the invariant culture, as shown in the following:

```
Dim ciInv As CultureInfo = New CultureInfo("")
Dim ciInv As CultureInfo = CultureInfo.InvariantCulture
```

Displaying Localized Information

Now that you know how culture information is stored in the .NET Framework, you're ready to see its use in code. Here's an example that lets you select a culture at runtime and formats information accordingly:

1. Create a new Visual Basic .NET ASP.NET Web Application project.

2. Place a `Label` control, a `DropDownList` control (`ddlSelectCulture`), and four `TextBox` controls (`txtCulture`, `txtDate`, `txtCurrency`, and `txtNumber`) on the default Web Form. Set the `AutoPostBack` property of the `DropDownList` control to `True`.

3. Double-click the `DropDownList` control to open the form's module. Enter references at the top of the code module:

```
Imports System.Globalization
Imports System.Threading
```

4. Enter code to handle events in the form's module:

```
Private Sub Page_Load(ByVal sender As System.Object, _
ByVal e As System.EventArgs) Handles MyBase.Load
    ' Stock the combo box
    If Not IsPostBack Then
        Dim ci As CultureInfo
        For Each ci In CultureInfo.GetCultures( _
        CultureTypes.SpecificCultures)
            ddlSelectCulture.Items.Add(ci.Name)
        Next
    End If
End Sub

Private Sub ddlSelectCulture_SelectedIndexChanged( _
ByVal sender As System.Object, _
ByVal e As System.EventArgs) _
Handles ddlSelectCulture.SelectedIndexChanged
    ' Create an appropriate CultureInfo
    ' object for the thread
    Thread.CurrentThread.CurrentCulture = _
    New CultureInfo(ddlSelectCulture.SelectedItem.Text)
    ' Display the name of the culture
    txtCulture.Text = Thread.CurrentThread. _
    CurrentCulture.EnglishName
    ' Refresh the display of the data
    DisplayData()
End Sub

Private Sub DisplayData()
    Dim dtNow As Date = DateTime.Now
    Dim dblcurrency As Double = 13472.85
    Dim dblnumber As Double = 1409872.3502

    txtDate.Text = dtNow.ToLongDateString()
    txtCurrency.Text = dblcurrency.ToString("c")
    txtNumber.Text = dblnumber.ToString("n")
End Sub
```

5. Run the project. Select a culture from the combo box. The form refreshes to display localized information, as shown in Figure 10.1.

Figure 10.1   Displaying localized information.

Setting Culture Properties

When you're setting the `CurrentCulture` and `CurrentUICulture` properties, you have two choices. You can set them based on information stored in the user's operating system, or you can provide a user interface to let the user choose a culture for formatting.

To use the culture of the operating system, you don't have to do anything. If the application is being executed on the Multiple User Interface (MUI) version of Windows 2000 or Windows XP, the .NET Framework automatically defaults to the culture that's currently selected. If the application is being executed on another version of Windows, the .NET Framework automatically defaults the culture to the language used by the operating system.

Although letting the .NET Framework choose the appropriate culture is the easy way to handle things, this strategy does not work well in ASP.NET applications. That's because the culture that the .NET Framework detects will be the culture on the Web server, not the culture on the user's computer! Remember, ASP.NET applications execute entirely on the server, and only the resulting HTML is sent to the client.

You can also code your ASP.NET application to sense the culture from the user's browser. To do this, you can retrieve the value of `Request.UserLanguages(0)` when you're processing a page. The ASP.NET `Request` object returns an array of strings specifying the language that the user's browser has set. The first member of this array will be the default language of the browser, in the standard culture code format. You can use this

value to create an appropriate `CultureInfo` object for the current thread. For
example,

```
Thread.CurrentThread.CurrentCulture = _
New CultureInfo(Request.UserLanguages(0))
```

Attractive though this strategy sounds, there are several reasons why it
doesn't work well in practice:

➤ Web browsers aren't required to specify a user language when sending
an HTTP request for a Web page.

➤ Even if a Web browser specifies one or more acceptable languages,
there's no guarantee that any of those languages will exactly match a
culture that the .NET Framework makes available.

➤ The user might be using a Web browser whose language doesn't match
the user's own preferred language.

I think the best bet is generally to let the user choose the culture that the
application should use. If you want to let the user choose the culture to use,
you can follow a strategy similar to the one you just saw: Provide a control
to select a culture and update the `CurrentCulture` property when the user
makes a selection from this control.

Using Localized Calendars

The `CultureInfo` class can supply localized calendars for different cultures. In
this set of steps, you'll see how you can retrieve culture-specific calendar
information.

1. Add a new Web Form to the application.

2. Place a `Label` control, a `DropDownList` control with the ID of `ddlCultures`,
   and a `ListBox` control with the ID of `lbInfo` on the form. Set the
   `AutoPostBack` property of the `DropDownList` control to `True`.

3. Double-click the `DropDownList` control to open the form's module. Add a
   line of code to the top of the module:

```
Imports System.Globalization
```

4. Add code to handle the `Load` event of the Form and the
   `SelectedIndexChanged` event of the `DropDownList` control:

```
Private Sub Page_Load( _
  ByVal sender As System.Object, _
  ByVal e As System.EventArgs) _
  Handles MyBase.Load
    If Not IsPostBack Then
```

```
      ' Fill the combo box with cultures
      Dim ci As CultureInfo
      For Each ci In CultureInfo. _
       GetCultures( _
       CultureTypes.SpecificCultures)
           ddlCultures.Items.Add(ci.Name)
      Next
    End If
End Sub

Private Sub _
 ddlCultures_SelectedIndexChanged( _
 ByVal sender As System.Object, _
 ByVal e As System.EventArgs) _
 Handles ddlCultures.SelectedIndexChanged
      ' Get the selected CultureInfo
      ' and some other objects
      Dim ci As CultureInfo = _
       New CultureInfo(ddlCultures. _
       SelectedItem.Text)
      Dim cal As Calendar = ci.Calendar
      Dim dtfi As DateTimeFormatInfo = _
       ci.DateTimeFormat
      lbInfo.Items.Clear()
      Dim dt As DateTime = DateTime.Today
      ' List the culture and the calendar
      With lbInfo.Items
          .Add("The culture is " & _
           ci.EnglishName)
          .Add("The calendar is " & _
           cal.GetType.ToString)
          ' Get the current day,
          ' month, and year
          .Add("Today is day " & _
           cal.GetDayOfMonth(dt))
          .Add(" of month " & _
           cal.GetMonth(dt))
          .Add(" of year " & cal.GetYear(dt))
          .Add("This is day " & _
           cal.GetDayOfWeek(dt) &  _
           "of the week")
          .Add("The day name is " & _
           dtfi.DayNames( _
           cal.GetDayOfWeek(dt)))
          .Add("The month name is " & _
           dtfi.MonthNames( _
           cal.GetMonth(dt) - 1))
          .Add("There are " & _
           cal.GetMonthsInYear( _
           cal.GetYear(dt)) & _
           " months in this year")
      End With
End Sub
```

5. Set the Web Form as the start page for the project.

6. Run the project. Select cultures from the combo box to see some of their calendar information in the ListBox control. You might try ar-SA, he-IL, and th-TH to get some sense of the calendars that the .NET Framework supports.

Working with Resource Files

So far you've seen how to use the CurrentCulture property to handle localized formatting of things such as currency, dates, and numbers. But localizing the text displayed on the user interface is perhaps even more important. The .NET Framework offers support for user interface localization through its capability to select a set of user interface resources at runtime.

The resources that you select at runtime will be contained in assembly resource files. *Assembly resource files* are specially formatted XML files that contain localized text. Visual Studio .NET allows you to work directly with assembly resource files.

The following steps demonstrate how to use Visual Studio .NET to localize the user interface of a simple application.

1. Add a new Web Form to your Visual Basic ASP.NET Web Application project.

2. Place a Label control with the ID of lblFolder, three RadioButton controls (rbMyDocuments, rbDesktop, and rbNewFolder), a DropDownList control with the ID of ddlCulture, and a Button control with the ID of btnSave on the form. Set the AutoPostBack property of the DropDownList control to True. Give the RadioButton controls a common GroupName such as Folders. Figure 10.2 shows this Web Form in design view.

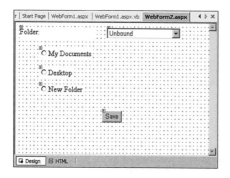

Figure 10.2 A Web Form to be localized at runtime.

3. Select Project, Add New Item. Select the Assembly Resource File template. Name the new item **AppStrings.resx** and click Open to create the file.

4. The new file opens in the Visual Studio IDE with a grid-based editing interface. Enter names and values to identify all the text strings on the

user interface, as shown in Figure 10.3. (Note that the column widths hide some of the English strings.) You can optionally enter a comment for each string. The `Type` and `Mimetype` columns are not used for localizing strings.

Data for data

name	value	comment	type	mimetype
Folder	Folder	(null)	(null)	(null)
My_Documen	My Document	(null)	(null)	(null)
Desktop	Desktop	(null)	(null)	(null)
New_Folder	New Folder	(null)	(null)	(null)
*				

Figure 10.3   Entering invariant resources.

5. Add two more Assembly resource files to your project. The first, named `AppStrings.en-US.resx`, should contain another copy of the strings in English. The second, named `AppStrings.fr-FR.resx`, should contain the strings in French, as shown in Figure 10.4. Note that the `Name` column is the same in the English and French version; only the value column changes.

Data for data

name	value	comment	type	mimetype
Folder	Dossier	(null)	(null)	(null)
My_Documents	Mes documents	(null)	(null)	(null)
Desktop	Bureau	(null)	(null)	(null)
New_Folder	Nouveau Dossier	(null)	(null)	(null)
Save	Enregistrer	(null)	(null)	(null)
(null)	(null)	(null)	(null)	(null)

Figure 10.4   Entering French resources.

6. Double-click the `DropDownList` control to open the form's module. Enter references at the top of the code module:

```
Imports System.Globalization
Imports System.Resources
Imports System.Threading
```

7. Enter code to handle events in the form's module:

```
Private Sub Page_Load(ByVal sender As System.Object, _
ByVal e As System.EventArgs) Handles MyBase.Load
    If Not IsPostBack Then
        ' Put language choices in the combo box
        ddlCulture.Items.Add("English")
        ddlCulture.Items.Add("French")
        ' Initialize the UI text
        SetUIText()
    End If
End Sub
```

```
Private Sub ddlCulture_SelectedIndexChanged( _
ByVal sender As System.Object, _
ByVal e As System.EventArgs) _
Handles ddlCulture.SelectedIndexChanged
    ' When the user selects a language,
    ' change the UI culture
    Select Case ddlCulture.SelectedItem.Text
        Case "English"
            Thread.CurrentThread.CurrentUICulture = _
            New CultureInfo("en-US")
        Case "French"
            Thread.CurrentThread.CurrentUICulture = _
            New CultureInfo("fr-FR")
    End Select
    ' Initialize the UI text
    SetUIText()
End Sub

Private Sub SetUIText()
    Dim rm As ResourceManager = _
    New ResourceManager("EC305C10.AppStrings", _
    GetType(WebForm2).Assembly)
    lblFolder.Text = rm.GetString("Folder")
    rbMyDocuments.Text = rm.GetString("My_Documents")
    rbDesktop.Text = rm.GetString("Desktop")
    rbNewFolder.Text = rm.GetString("New_Folder")
    btnSave.Text = rm.GetString("Save")
End Sub
```

NOTE This code assumes that your VB .NET project is named EC305C10. If it has another name, you'll need to alter the first parameter to the constructor for the **ResourceManager** object. This parameter is the root namespace of your project. You can find the name of the root namespace by right-clicking the project node in Solution Explorer. Select Properties, and you'll find the root namespace in the General section. The second parameter to the **ResourceManager** constructor is the specific type of the executing code, as determined by the **GetType** method.

8. Set the Web Form as the start page for the project.

9. Run the project. As you select languages in the combo box, the user interface is refreshed with the appropriate resources.

The naming of the resource files in this example follows a required pattern. The .NET Framework looks for several specific files when it's loading resources, depending on the base name of the resources and the selected culture. The base name is the second part of the first parameter to the ResourceManager constructor— in this case, AppStrings. When the CurrentUICulture is set to a CultureInfo object representing the fr-FR (French in France) culture, the .NET Framework checks for resources in three possible files, in this order:

1. A specific culture file—in this case, AppStrings.fr-FR.resx.

2. A neutral culture file—in this case, AppStrings.fr.resx.

3. An invariant culture file—in this case, AppStrings.resx.

In other words, the .NET Framework falls back on increasingly more general resources in trying to load resources for a form.

Localizing Resources at Runtime

Runtime user interface resources are actually loaded by an instance of the System.Resources.ResourceManager class. After you've initialized a ResourceManager object by calling one of the class's constructors, there are two methods that you can use to retrieve localized resources:

➤ GetObject—Returns an object from the appropriate resource file.

➤ GetString—Returns a string from the appropriate resource file.

Converting Existing Encodings

Many different schemes have been developed for representing the characters in a language as numeric codes within a computer. These schemes are referred to as encodings. For example, the venerable ASCII encoding represents common Latin characters as numeric codes ranging from 0 to 127. The .NET Framework provides support for encodings through the System.Text.Encoding class.

Understanding Unicode and Encodings

Internally, the .NET Framework's preferred encoding for characters is 16-bit Unicode—otherwise known as UTF-16. This encoding represents characters as 16-bit numbers, giving it the capability to represent approximately 65,000 distinct characters. That's enough to represent every character commonly in use.

Over time, Windows has been moving toward Unicode as the basis for encoding characters, but that wasn't always the case. Earlier versions of Windows used code pages to represent character sets. A code page could hold 256 characters, and the system supplied different code pages for different character sets such as Greek characters or Latin characters.

Although Unicode is the native character encoding for .NET, the .NET Framework supports conversion to and from older encodings, such as ASCII or code pages, for compatibility with other applications. For example, Web services constructed with tools other than .NET might not be able to accept the full range of Unicode characters. In that case, you might want to use a more restrictive encoding, such as ASCII, for communication with the Web service, while retaining the Unicode strings for internal processing in your own application.

The System.Text namespace contains classes such as ASCIIEncoding that are designed to let you convert characters from the UTF-16 Unicode encoding to other encodings, and vice versa. For example, this code converts a Unicode string to an array of ASCII bytes, which it then displays in a ListBox control:

```
Private Sub btnConvert_Click( _
 ByVal sender As System.Object, _
 ByVal e As System.EventArgs) Handles btnConvert.Click
    ' Get an encoding object for ascii
    Dim encASCII As ASCIIEncoding = _
     New ASCIIEncoding()
    ' Convert the string to an array of ASCII bytes
    Dim bytEncodedCharacters() As Byte
    bytEncodedCharacters = _
     encASCII.GetBytes(txtUnicode.Text)
    Dim i As Integer
    For i = 0 To bytEncodedCharacters.Length - 1
        lbASCII.Items.Add(bytEncodedCharacters(i))
    Next
End Sub
```

This code example uses the GetBytes method of the ASCIIEncoding object to convert a Unicode string into an array of ASCII bytes. Although I didn't use it in this example, there's a matching GetChars method that converts ASCII bytes into Unicode text.

The ASCIIEncoding class is a subclass of System.Text.Encoding. Table 10.1 lists the other available subclasses that help you convert to and from other encodings.

Table 10.1 Encoding Classes in the System.Text Namespace	
Class	**Use**
ASCIIEncoding	Converts characters between Unicode and ASCII.
Encoding	General-purpose class. The **Encoding.GetEncoding** static method returns encodings that can be used for legacy code page compatibility.
UnicodeEncoding	Converts characters to and from Unicode encoded as consecutive bytes in either big-endian or little-endian order.
UTF7Encoding	Converts characters to and from 7-bit Unicode encoding.
UTF8Encoding	Converts characters to and from 8-bit Unicode encoding.

Implementing Mirroring

There are many differences between human languages. Of course different languages use different character sets, but there are differences beyond that. One of the most important differences is whether the language reads from left-to-right (like English) or from right-to-left (like Arabic). The .NET Framework supports both reading directions.

The process of switching a user interface between a left-to-right language such as German or English and a right-to-left language such as Hebrew or Arabic is called mirroring. Mirroring in the Windows environment involves changes beyond simply reversing the order of text strings. Figure 10.5, for example, shows part of the user interface from Arabic Windows.

Figure 10.5 Mirroring in the Windows user interface.

As you can see, the entire format of the Windows user interface is reversed when you use mirroring. The Close, Minimize, and other buttons appear at the upper left of the window. Menus appear to the right of the menu bar. Combo box arrows are located to the left of the combo box, and check box text appears to the left of the text box.

ASP.NET offers partial support for mirroring through the HTML `dir` attribute. To render a Web Form in right-to-left mode, switch to HTML view and modify the HTML tag of the document as follows:

```
<HTML dir="rtl">
```

Setting the HTML `dir` attribute (which can also be set on individual controls) handles most of the facets of the mirroring process automatically. Controls fill from right-to-left as you enter text. `DropDownList`, `RadioButton`, and `CheckBox` controls reverse their appearance as well.

But the mirroring support is imperfect. The system menu and the other window buttons (such as the Close and Minimize buttons) don't switch positions. Controls are not mirrored to the opposite position on the form from their initial design. (Although, of course, you can manage that by manipulating the control properties at runtime from VB. NET code.)

Validating Non-Latin User Input

Another area in which world-ready applications might require code changes is in handling character strings. I'll look at two areas in which different alphabets might require you to implement code changes: string indexing and data sorting. These areas require the most coding attention for non-Latin characters (such as Arabic, Hebrew, or Cyrillic characters), but can be important when dealing with Latin characters as well.

String indexing refers to the process of extracting single characters from a text string. You might think that you could simply iterate through the data that makes up the string 16 bits at a time, treating each 16 bits as a separate character. But it turns out that things aren't that simple in the Unicode world.

Unicode supports surrogate pairs and combining character sequences. A *surrogate pair* is a set of two 16-bit codes that represent a single character from the extended 32-bit Unicode character space. A *combining character sequence* is a set of more than one 16-bit codes that represents a single character. Combining character sequences are often used to combine diacritical marks such as accents with base characters.

This presents a problem: If characters in a string aren't all the same length, how can you move through a string one character at a time? Because of the surrogate pairs and combining characters, you can't just assume that each 16 bits represents a single character. The answer, of course, is to use a class from the .NET Framework that knows how to perform this task. The System.Globalization.StringInfo class is designed to be able to iterate through the elements in a string. Here's how you can move through any string, character by character, writing the characters to a ListBox:

```
Private Sub btnIterate_Click( _
 ByVal sender As System.Object, _
 ByVal e As System.EventArgs) Handles btnIterate.Click
    lbIterate.Items.Clear()
    ' Get an iterator for the entered text
    Dim iter As TextElementEnumerator = _
     StringInfo.GetTextElementEnumerator(txtText.Text)
    ' The iterator starts before
    ' the string, have to move
    ' it forward once to reach the first element
    iter.MoveNext()
    Do
        lbIterate.Items.Add("Element " & _
         iter.ElementIndex & _
         ": " & iter.Current)
    Loop While (iter.MoveNext)
End Sub
```

This code uses the static GetTextElementEnumerator method of the StringInfo class. Given any Unicode string, this method returns an iterator that you can use to move through the string one character at a time, properly handling surrogate pairs and combining characters. The iterator has a MoveNext method that returns True when there are more characters to be read or False when it has exhausted the characters in the string. The Current property of the iterator returns a single character from the current position of the iterator.

Comparing and Sorting Data

Another area in which you might need to alter code to produce a world-ready application is in working with strings. Different cultures use different alphabetical orders to sort strings, and different cultures compare strings differently. For example, the single-character ligature "AE" is considered to match the two characters "AE" in some cultures but not in others.

For the most part, you don't have to do any special programming to account for these factors in the .NET Framework. To make your application world ready, you're more likely to need to remove old code—for example, code that assumes that characters are properly sorted if you sort their ASCII character numbers. Specifically, the .NET Framework provides these culture-aware features:

➤ The String.Compare method compares strings according to the rules of the CultureInfo referenced by the CurrentCulture property.

➤ The CultureInfo.CompareInfo object can search for substrings according to the comparison rules of the current culture.

➤ The Array.Sort method sorts the members of an array by the alphabetical order rules of the current culture.

➤ The SortKey.Compare method also compares strings according to the rules of the current culture.

Exam Prep Questions

Question 1

> You are localizing a Web Form for use in Israel (the he-IL culture). You must make certain that dates and currencies are displayed correctly and that the text reads right-to-left. Which of these steps should you perform as part of the process (select two)?
>
> ❑ A. Set the **Text** property to **he-IL**.
>
> ❑ B. Add the **dir="rtl"** attribute to the page's HTML tag.
>
> ❑ C. Set the **CurrentUICulture** property of the thread that displays the form to **he-IL**.
>
> ❑ D. Set the **Tag** property to **he-IL**.

Answers B and C are correct. The `dir` property of the HTML tag controls the direction of display, and the `CurrentUICulture` property controls formatting for dates and currencies. Answers A and D are incorrect because the `Text` and `Tag` properties are not part of the localization process.

Question 2

> A **Label** control in your application reports the number of characters in a particular data entry field. You're dividing the number of bits taken up by the data by 16 to arrive at this figure. Users of the localized version in Korea complain that the number of characters is persistently overestimated. What should you do?
>
> ○ A. Use a **GetTextElementEnumerator** object to enumerate the characters.
>
> ○ B. Use the **String.Length** method to get the actual length of the data.
>
> ○ C. Divide the number of bits by 32.
>
> ○ D. Divide the number of bits by 16.

Answer A is correct. In double-byte and Unicode languages, you cannot depend on characters having a fixed width. Using the `GetTextElementEnumerator` object allows you to move through the string one character at a time, regardless of how many bytes each character occupies. Answers B, C, and D are incorrect because they all assume that characters have a fixed width.

Question 3

> Your ASP.NET application displays course registration information including the cost per credit hour of each course. You are beginning to resell this application to universities around the world. How should you ensure that the correct currency symbol is displayed in all cases?
>
> O A. Allow the user to select a currency symbol from a list of supported symbols.
>
> O B. Prompt the user for a currency symbol and store it in the registry.
>
> O C. Allow the user to select a culture from a list. Create a **CultureInfo** object based on the user's selection and assign it to the **Thread.CurrentThread.CurrentCulture** property. Use the **ToString** method to format currency amounts.
>
> O D. Accept the **Thread.CurrentThread.CurrentCulture** property as it is set when you run your application. Use the **ToString** method to format currency amounts.

Answer C is correct. The `CultureInfo` object includes many pieces of localized information, including the local currency symbol. Answer A is incorrect because this would force you to maintain your own list of currency symbols instead of using the one that's already built in to the .NET Framework. Answer B is incorrect because there is no good way to store information in the user's registry from ASP.NET. Answer D is incorrect because the `CurrentCulture` property will return the culture of the Web server, not of the client.

Question 4

> Your application's users would like to see dates displayed with the months and years of their local calendar, without affecting the user interface language. How can you accomplish this?
>
> O A. Retrieve a **DateTime** object from **Thread.CurrentThread.CurrentCulture**, and use its methods to format the dates.
>
> O B. Retrieve a **DateTime** object from **Thread.CurrentThread.CurrentUICulture**, and use its methods to format the dates.
>
> O C. Retrieve a **Calendar** object from **Thread.CurrentThread.CurrentCulture**, and use its methods to format the dates.
>
> O D. Retrieve a **Calendar** object from **Thread.CurrentThread.CurrentUICulture**, and use its methods to format the dates.

Answer C is correct. `CurrentCulture` holds the culture appropriate for formatting date information. The `Calendar` object includes arrays with information on month names and year numbering. Answers A and B are incorrect because the `DateTime` object can help you format dates, but does not localize the parts of the date. Answers B and D are incorrect because `CurrentUICulture` controls text translation rather than formatting.

Question 5

You are developing an application on a system that uses U.S. English Windows (culture code en-US). The application will run on a system that uses French Windows (culture code fr-FR). The application will exchange information with Windows services on the French system, but will not display any user interface. Which culture should you use to format the messages that your application sends to the services?

○ A. en-US

○ B. en

○ C. fr-FR

○ D. Invariant Culture

Answer D is correct. The invariant culture is designed for exchanging information with Windows services and other pieces of the operating system. These services are not culture aware, so answers A, B, and C are incorrect.

Question 6

Your application needs to search for substrings in longer strings. This searching should work properly no matter what user interface language is in use. What should you use to perform these searches?

○ A. **InStr**

○ B. **Array.Sort**

○ C. **IndexOf**

○ D. **CultureInfo.CompareInfo**

Answer D is correct. The `CompareInfo` method is designed to work across all character encodings and languages. Answer A is incorrect because `InStr` is obsolete. Answer B is incorrect because `Array.Sort` does not locate substrings. Answer C is incorrect because `IndexOf` is not culture aware.

Question 7

The user would like to see French dates and currencies displayed in your application, but wants the user interface to remain in English. How can you accomplish this?

○ A. Set the **CurrentCulture** property to a **CultureInfo** representing the fr-FR culture, and set the **CurrentUICulture** property to a **CultureInfo** representing the fr-FR culture.

○ B. Set the **CurrentCulture** property to a **CultureInfo** representing the en-US culture, and set the **CurrentUICulture** property to a **CultureInfo** representing the en-US culture.

○ C. Set the **CurrentCulture** property to a **CultureInfo** representing the fr-FR culture and set the **CurrentUICulture** property to a **CultureInfo** representing the en-US culture.

○ D. Set the **CurrentCulture** property to a **CultureInfo** representing the en-US culture, and set the **CurrentUICulture** property to a **CultureInfo** representing the fr-FR culture.

Answer C is correct. The `CurrentCulture` property controls the formatting of information such as dates and currencies, whereas the `CurrentUICulture` property controls the formatting of the user interface. Answers A and D are wrong because they result in a French user interface. Answers B and D are wrong because they result in U.S. English dates and currencies.

Question 8

Your application includes three Assembly resource files: **Strings.resx** contains the default (English) resources; **Strings.en-US.resx** contains the English resources; **Strings.France.resx** contains the French resources. Users report that they are getting the default English user interface when they've selected the option for a French user interface. What should you do?

○ A. Delete the **Strings.en-US.resx** file from the project.

○ B. Instruct users to close their browsers and relaunch the application after setting their user interface language.

○ C. Add French resources to the **Strings.resx** file.

○ D. Rename the French resource file to **Strings.fr-FR.resx**.

Answer D is correct. The .NET Framework only searches for resources in files that follow the proper naming convention. Strings for a specific culture must be in a file with that culture as part of its name. Answer A is incorrect because this will break the English interface of the application. Answer B is incorrect because the relaunched application will still be unable to find the resources. Answer C is incorrect because a single file should only contain one set of strings.

Question 9

Which of these culture codes could be used to specify the **CurrentUICulture** property of an application (select all correct answers)?

❑ A. en

❑ B. en-GB

❑ C. en-NZ

❑ D. FR-FR

Answers B and C are correct. These culture codes include a neutral code and a subculture code; hence, they specify enough information to localize an application. Answer A is incorrect because it only includes a neutral code and does not supply enough information. Answer D is incorrect because it is not properly formatted as a culture.

Question 10

Your application contains Unicode strings encoded in the UTF-16 format. You'd like to save a copy of those strings to disk in the UTF-8 format. What should you do?

○ A. Use the **Unicode.GetBytes** method to perform the conversion.

○ B. Use the **Unicode.GetChars** method to perform the conversion.

○ C. Use the **UTF8Encoding.GetBytes** method to perform the conversion.

○ D. Use the **UTF8Encoding.GetChars** method to perform the conversion.

Answer C is correct. The GetBytes method translates from Unicode to the specified encoding. Answer A is incorrect because the Unicode.GetBytes method also translates to Unicode. Answers B and D are incorrect because the GetChars method returns Unicode.

Need to Know More?

 Symmonds, Nick. *Internationalization and Localization Using Microsoft .NET.* Apress, 2002.

 Visual Studio .NET Combined Help Collection, "Developing World Ready Applications topic."

Working with Legacy Code

Terms you'll need to understand:

✓ Runtime Callable Wrapper (RCW)
✓ Managed code
✓ Unmanaged code
✓ Platform invoke

Techniques you'll need to master:

✓ Using an ActiveX control from ASP.NET
✓ Instantiating a COM component from .NET code

.NET makes it easy to mix new code with existing code. Classic ASP and ASP.NET pages can coexist on the same server. Also, from .NET components, you can easily instantiate and call COM components such as ActiveX controls or COM libraries. (In fact, interoperability works in the other direction too, with COM components able to call .NET code, though I won't cover those techniques here.) This chapter discusses how to work with legacy code.

Incorporating Existing Code into ASP.NET Applications

Many organizations will be implementing ASP.NET on the same servers that already host existing ASP applications. Fortunately, ASP and ASP.NET work fine together. You can continue to run existing ASP pages on your ASP.NET servers, convert the pages to the new format, or move COM components from ASP pages to ASP.NET pages.

Running ASP and ASP.NET Together

ASP and ASP.NET run perfectly well together on the same server. That's a fundamental consequence of the architecture of the two systems. When you install Internet Information Services (IIS), it associates each file extension that the server understands with a particular application. For example, on a Windows 2000 system, ASP pages are handled by `c:\WINNT\System32\inetsrv\asp.dll`, whereas ASP.NET pages are handled by `C:\WINNT\Microsoft.NET\Framework\v1.0.3705\aspnet_isapi.dll`. Thus there's no confusion on the part of the server between the two file types and no need to worry that old pages will be executed incorrectly after you install ASP.NET.

ASP pages and ASP.NET pages can even be incorporated into the same ASP.NET application. If you add a text file to your ASP.NET application and give it the extension `.asp`, it will be handled by the `asp.dll` application. However, session and application state is not shared between the two types of pages. If you set a session or application variable in ASP.NET code, there's no easy way to retrieve it from ASP code, and vice versa.

Being able to run both types of pages on the same server is a useful technique, but in the long run you'll probably want to migrate all of your ASP code to ASP.NET code. That will allow you to make use of the improved features of ASP.NET in your applications.

Converting ASP Pages to ASP.NET

One strategy for migrating an existing ASP application to ASP.NET is to rename the existing files so that they have the .aspx extension instead of the .asp extension. As soon as you do this, the pages will be delivered by ASP.NET instead of ASP.

The syntax of ASP.NET pages is very close to the syntax of ASP pages, but it's not identical. Here's a partial list of things you might need to change if you want to convert an existing ASP page to run as an ASP.NET page:

➤ In ASP, you could declare global variables and procedures in <%...%> blocks, which would be visible to all code on the page. In ASP.NET, such variables and procedures should be declared inside of a <script runat=server> block. ASP.NET will still execute code inside of <%...%> blocks, but such code is executed at render time after all the code behind the page has already finished executing.

➤ In ASP, you could mix programming languages within a single page. ASP.NET requires each page to use a single programming language on the server.

➤ ASP used scripting languages such as VBScript. ASP.NET uses the .NET languages such as Visual Basic .NET and C#. Although VBScript syntax is close to Visual Basic .NET syntax, it is not identical.

➤ ASP used the Variant data type for all variables. ASP.NET uses strong data types. You can use the Object data type when you do not know the exact type for a variable.

➤ ASP defaulted to passing all parameters by reference. ASP.NET defaults to passing simple parameters by value.

➤ The Set keyword, the Let keyword, and default properties have been removed from ASP.NET.

➤ The arguments of a method in ASP.NET must be enclosed in parentheses, even if there is no return value.

➤ ASP would allow you to use nondeclared variables. ASP.NET requires you to declare all variables by default.

Using Late-Bound COM Components

The ASP.NET processor understands nearly all the syntax and all the objects that ASP itself supported. In particular, ASP.NET still supports the Server.CreateObject method for creating late-bound COM components.

For example, you can create an ADO Connection object in either an ASP page with this line of code:

```
Set cnn = Server.CreateObject("ADODB.Connection")
```

The corresponding line of code for an ASP.NET page omits the now obselete Set keyword, but is otherwise the same.

Not all COM components can be instantiated in ASP.NET this way. In particular, components that use the Single-Threaded Apartment (STA) threading model will not function properly in ASP.NET pages unless you add a compatibility directive to the page:

```
<%@Page aspcompat=true%>
```

Using ActiveX Controls

Many ActiveX controls exist that can supply functionality to Internet Explorer because IE is an ActiveX container. By means of a GUID, a Web page can specify an ActiveX control that should be instantiated and displayed in the browser.

But in the .NET world, an ActiveX control is useless. Web Forms can only contain instances of controls derived from the System.Web.UI.Control class. ActiveX controls, being built using previous technologies, do not derive from this class. So how can you possibly use an ActiveX control on a Web Form?

The answer is that ActiveX controls are a client-side technology, not a server-side technology. Unlike a regular ASP.NET Server control, which is compiled into HTML before the page is sent to the client, an ActiveX control is actually instantiated on the client. It doesn't matter whether the original page was HTML, ASP, or ASP.NET; in every case, it's up to the browser to handle the ActiveX control.

 NOTE Internet Explorer functions as an ActiveX host, but other browsers offer little or no support for ActiveX controls. You should only consider ActiveX controls a solution for situations in which you control the choice of browser. Usually, this means that ActiveX controls are only suitable for intranet applications.

This set of steps shows you how to use ActiveX controls in ASP.NET:

1. Create a new Visual Basic ASP.NET Web application.

2. Right-click the Toolbox and select Customize Toolbox.

3. Select the COM components tab in the Customize Toolbox dialog box.

4. Scroll down the list of components, which will include all the ActiveX controls that are registered on your computer, until you find the Microsoft Forms 2.0 `CommandButton` control.

5. Click OK to add the control to the Toolbox.

6. The new control will show up at the bottom of the Toolbox. You can click and drag the control to a form just like any native .NET control. Place an instance of the `CommandButton` control on your form. Set the `id` property of the `CommandButton` control to `cmd1`.

7. Switch the form to HTML view in the designer. You'll find that the ActiveX control is represented as a collapsed region with an `OBJECT` tag. Expand the region. Modify the `PARAM` tag for the control's caption as follows:

```
<PARAM NAME="Caption" VALUE="Click Me">
```

8. Add a client-side script section to the HTML, just above the `</HEAD>` tag:

```
    <script language="vbscript">
Sub cmd1_Click()
    MsgBox "Hello Client World"
End Sub
    </script>
```

9. Run the project. Your browser will instantiate and display the ActiveX control. Click the button to display the message box.

When you run this example, ASP.NET sends the `classid` value for the ActiveX control to the browser. It's up to the browser to check the registry on the computer where it is running and to create the corresponding ActiveX control (which, of course, must be installed on the client). The VBScript procedure that's tied to the control's click event is also sent to the browser. When the user clicks the control, the VBScript is executed on the client. This code doesn't interact with the server at all.

There are a few things you should consider before you use ActiveX controls in your ASP.NET applications:

➤ ActiveX controls impose a performance penalty, particularly if the control must be downloaded to the client.

➤ ActiveX controls are not managed code, so they do not benefit from the memory management and garbage collection facilities of the Common Language Runtime (CLR) .

➤ Some companies block ActiveX controls at the firewall.

➤ ActiveX controls will only function in Internet Explorer.

Because of these drawbacks, you should use ActiveX controls sparingly (if at all). Before importing an ActiveX control into your project, you should consider whether a native .NET control can fill your requirements.

Using COM Components

If you're migrating a project that uses COM components to ASP.NET, you don't have to do a "big bang" migration all at once. .NET components can call COM components, and COM components can call .NET components. This means that you can migrate one component (a control, a class library, and so on) at a time and still keep all of your code working together.

Why might you want to undertake such a gradual migration? There are four basic reasons for maintaining part of a system in COM components while moving other parts to .NET components:

➤ It takes time to learn enough about Visual Basic .NET, ASP.NET, and the .NET Framework to be productive.

➤ You might have components that can't be easily moved to .NET because they use language features that are no longer supported or because of other implementation quirks.

➤ It takes time to move code from one system to the other.

➤ Your application might depend on third-party controls or libraries for which you do not have the source code.

Understanding Runtime Callable Wrappers

Managed code (which includes all VB .NET code) expects that all the code with which it interacts will use the CLR. This is an obvious problem for COM components. How can you take a component that was developed before the advent of .NET and make it look like a .NET component to other .NET components? The answer is to use a proxy. In general terms, a proxy accepts commands and messages from one component, modifies them, and passes them to another component. The particular type of proxy that allows you to use COM components within a .NET application is called a *Runtime Callable Wrapper*. That is, it's a proxy that can be called by the CLR.

Figure 11.1 shows schematically how the pieces fit together.

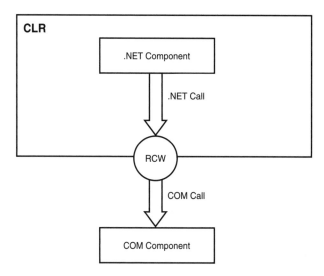

Figure 11.1   The architecture of a Runtime Callable Wrapper.

To see how COM interoperability works, you'll need a COM library. There are probably a variety of COM components on your computer, including Office and ADO components. But to demonstrate the code, I start with a simple COM DLL built using Visual Basic 6.0:

1. Launch Visual Basic 6.0. Create a new ActiveX DLL project.

2. Select the Project1 node in the Project Explorer window and rename it MyCustomer.

3. Select the Class1 node in the Project Explorer window and rename it Balances.

4. Add this code to the Balances class:

```
Option Explicit

Private mintCustomerCount As Integer
Private macurBalances(1 To 10) As Currency

' Create a read-only CustomerCount property
Public Property Get CustomerCount() As Integer
    CustomerCount = mintCustomerCount
End Property

' Create a GetBalance method
Public Function GetBalance(CustomerNumber As Integer) _
    As Currency
    GetBalance = macurBalances(CustomerNumber)
End Function
```

```
' Initialize the data
Private Sub Class_Initialize()
    Dim intI As Integer

    mintCustomerCount = 10

    For intI = 1 To 10
        macurBalances(intI) = Int(Rnd(1) _
            * 100000) / 100
    Next intI

End Sub
```

5. Save the Visual Basic project.

6. Select File, Build MyCustomer.dll to create the COM component.

Using TLBIMP

The .NET Framework includes a tool, the Type Library Importer (TLBIMP), that can create an RCW from COM metadata contained in a type library. You run this tool from a Visual Studio .NET command prompt. For example, you could create an RCW for MyCustomer.dll with this command:

```
tlbimp MyCustomer.dll /out:NETMyCustomer.dll
```

After creating the RCW, you can use the component from .NET code:

1. Add a new Web Form to your Visual Basic ASP.NET application.

2. Place three labels on the form: a TextBox control with the ID of txtCustomerCount, a TextBox control with the ID of txtCustomerNumber, a Button control with the ID of btnGetBalance, and a TextBox control with the ID of txtBalance. Figure 11.2 shows the design of this form.

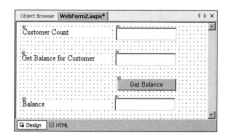

Figure 11.2 A form to test the use of a COM component.

3. Right-click the References node in Solution Explorer and select Add Reference.

4. Select the COM tab in the Add reference dialog box. Click the Browse button. Browse to the NETMyCustomer.dll file. Click OK to add the reference to the project.

5. Double-click the Button control to open the form's module. Enter this line of code at the top of the module:

```
Imports NETMyCustomer
```

6. Enter this code within the module:

```
Dim B As Balances

Private Sub Page_Load(ByVal sender As System.Object, _
ByVal e As System.EventArgs) Handles MyBase.Load
    B = New Balances()
    txtCustomerCount.Text = B.CustomerCount
End Sub

Private Sub btnGetBalance_Click( _
ByVal sender As System.Object, _
ByVal e As System.EventArgs) _
Handles btnGetBalance.Click
    txtBalance.Text = B.GetBalance( _
    txtCustomerNumber.Text)
End Sub
```

7. Set the Web Form as the start page for the project.

8. Run the project. The form will display the customer count in the first TextBox control. Enter a number between 1 and 10 in the customer number TextBox control and click the Button control to see that customer's balance.

This example uses the Type Library Importer to create a Runtime Callable Wrapper for the COM type library. The RCW is a library that you can add to your .NET project as a reference. After you've done that, the classes in the COM component can be used just like native .NET classes. When you use a class from the COM component, .NET makes the call to the RCW, which in turn forwards the call to the original COM component and returns the results to your .NET managed code.

The Type Library Importer supports a set of command-line options. Table 11.1 shows the available options.

Table 11.1 Options for the Type Library Importer	
Option	Meaning
/asmversion:*versionNumber*	Specifies the version number for the created assembly.
/delaysign	Prepares the assembly for delay signing.
/help	Displays help on command-line options.
/keycontainer:*containerName*	Signs the assembly with the strong name from the specified key container.
/keyfile:*filename*	Signs the assembly with the strong name from the specified key file.
/namespace:*namespace*	Specifies the namespace for the created assembly.
/out:*filename*	Specifies the name of the created assembly.
/primary	Produces a primary **interop** assembly.
/publickey:*filename*	Specifies the file containing a public key used to sign the resulting file.
/reference:*filename*	Specifies a file to be used to resolve references from the file being imported.
/silent	Suppresses information that would otherwise be displayed on the command line during conversion.
/strictref	Refuses to create the assembly if one or more references cannot be resolved.
/sysarray	Imports COM **SafeArrays** as instances of the **System.Array.Class** type.
/unsafe	Creates interfaces without net security checks.
/verbose	Displays additional information on the command line during conversion.
/?	Displays help on command-line options.

Using COM Components Directly

As with ActiveX controls, the Visual Studio .NET interface provides a streamlined way to use a COM component from your .NET code. You don't need to use the Type Library Importer at all. Instead, select the COM tab in the Add Reference dialog box. Scroll down the list of COM components until you come to the MyCustomer library. Select the MyCustomer library, click Select, and then click OK.

When you directly reference a COM library from the Visual Studio .NET IDE, the effect is almost the same as if you had used the Type Library Importer to import the same library. Visual Studio .NET creates a new namespace with the name of the original library and then exposes the classes from the library within that namespace.

Although you can use either of the two methods you've seen to call a COM component from a .NET component, there are reasons to prefer one method over the other:

➤ For a COM component that will only be used in a single Visual Basic .NET project and that you wrote yourself, use the easiest method: direct reference from your .NET project. This method is only suitable for a truly private component that does not need to be shared.

➤ If a COM component is shared among multiple projects, use the Type Library Importer so that you can sign the resulting assembly and place it in the Global Assembly Cache. Shared code must be signed.

➤ If you need to control details of the created assembly, such as its name, namespace, or version number, you must use the Type Library Importer. The direct reference method gives you no control over these details.

 You should not use either one of these methods on code written by another developer. That's because you are not allowed (according to Microsoft's recommendations on how to proceed) to sign code written by someone else. If you need to use a COM component from another developer, you should obtain a Primary Interop Assembly (PIA) from the original developer of the component. Microsoft supplies PIAs for all of its common libraries.

Using COM+ Components

COM+ is the Component Services layer of Windows 2000 and later operating systems. COM+ supplies a number of services to components running under Windows. These include

➤ Role-based security

➤ Object pooling and reusability

➤ Queued components for asynchronous calls

➤ Transactional processing

➤ A publish-and-subscribe events model

Despite the significant differences between COM+ and straight COM, you don't have to do anything different to use a COM+ component than if you use a COM component. To the consumer, a COM+ component looks much like a COM component. The Type Library Importer and Visual Studio .NET can both create wrappers for COM+ components using the same procedures that they use for COM components.

Using Platform Invoke

There's a second way that .NET can interoperate with unmanaged code, though: through functional calls to unmanaged libraries. The *platform invoke* (often abbreviated as PInvoke) feature of .NET enables .NET code to call functions from unmanaged libraries such as the Windows API. The easiest way to understand PInvoke is to work through an example:

1. Add a new module to your Visual Basic ASP.NET application. Name the new module API.vb.

2. Add this code to the API.vb module:

```
Public Module API

    Declare Auto Function GetComputerName _
    Lib "kernel32" ( _
    ByVal lpBuffer As String, _
    ByRef nSize As Integer) As Integer

End Module
```

3. Add a new Web Form to your Visual Basic ASP.NET application.

4. Place a Label control named lblComputerName on the form.

5. Double-click the Form to open its module. Enter this line of code at the top of the module:

```
Imports System.Text
```

6. Enter this code within the module:

```
Private Sub Page_Load(ByVal sender As System.Object, _
ByVal e As System.EventArgs) Handles MyBase.Load
    Dim buf As String = New String(CChar(" "), 128)
    Dim len As Integer = buf.Length
    Dim ret As Integer
    ret = GetComputerName(buf, len)
    lblComputerName.Text = _
    "This computer is named " & _
    buf.ToString.Substring(0, len)
End Sub
```

7. Set the Web Form as the start page for the project.

8. Run the project. The Web Form will display the name of the computer where the code is run. Remember, if you're using a client on one computer and a server on another, the ASP.NET code executes on the server. So in that case, the browser will display the name of the server, not the name of the client.

If you've used the Windows API from Visual Basic 6.0, PInvoke will look very familiar. The Declare statement (which must be contained in a module or a class module) tells the CLR where to find an API function by specifying the name of the library (in this case, kernel32.dll) and the name of the function (in this case, GetComputerName). After the function is declared, you can use it within Visual Basic .NET just like any other function.

Note the use of the Auto modifier in the function declaration. You might know that many Windows API calls come in two versions, depending on the character set that you're using. For example, GetComputerName really exists as GetComputerNameA (for ANSI characters) and GetComputerNameW (for Unicode characters). The Auto modifier instructs the .NET Framework to use the appropriate version of the API call for the platform where the code is running.

The code can be improved somewhat by using a StringBuilder object (found in the System.Text namespace) instead of a String as the API parameter:

```
Declare Auto Function _
 GetComputerName Lib _
 "kernel32" ( _
 ByVal lpBuffer As StringBuilder, _
 ByRef nSize _
 As Integer) As Integer
```

When you use a StringBuilder object as a buffer for a Windows API call, you don't have to worry about the length of the returned string. The .NET Framework automatically truncates the returned string at the first null character. Thus, the code to use PInvoke becomes this:

```
Dim buf As StringBuilder = _
 New StringBuilder(128)
Dim len As Integer = buf.Capacity
Dim ret As Integer

 ret = GetComputerName(buf, len)

lblComputerName.Text = _
 "This computer is named " & _
 buf.ToString
```

PInvoke can also handle API calls that require structures as parameters. For example, many API calls require a Rect structure, which consists of four longs that are filled in with the coordinates of a rectangle. In Visual Basic .NET, you can declare a structure with explicit byte offsets for each member, which lets you define any structure that the Windows API requires, as shown here:

```
<StructLayout(LayoutKind.Explicit)> _
Public Structure Rect
    <FieldOffset(0)> Public left As Integer
    <FieldOffset(4)> Public top As Integer
    <FieldOffset(8)> Public right As Integer
    <FieldOffset(12)> Public bottom As Integer
End Structure
```

The StructLayout attribute tells the VB .NET compiler that you'll explicitly specify the location of the individual fields within the structure. The FieldOffset attribute specifies the starting byte of each field within the structure. By using these attributes, you can ensure that .NET constructs the same structure that the API function expects to receive.

Exam Prep Questions

Question 1

> You have created your own COM component to perform statistical analysis of
> captured data. Objects supplied by this component are used in several applica-
> tions that you also wrote. You are moving the applications to .NET, but you
> intend to leave the COM component untouched. How should you proceed?
>
> ○ A. Use the Type Library Importer to create an unsigned RCW for the COM
>   component. Place a copy of this RCW in each application's directory.
>
> ○ B. Set a direct reference from each application to the existing COM com-
>   ponent.
>
> ○ C. Use **PInvoke** to call functions from the existing COM component in
>   each application.
>
> ○ D. Use the Type Library Importer to create a signed RCW for the COM
>   component. Place this RCW in the Global Assembly Cache.

Answer D is correct. The easiest and most efficient way to share a COM
component among multiple .NET applications is to create a signed RCW in
the GAC (Global Assembly Cache). Answer A is incorrect because it requires
duplicating the RCW, which can cause maintenance issues. Answer B is
incorrect because it also creates one RCW for each application. Answer C is
incorrect because PInvoke cannot be used for object creation.

Question 2

> You are declaring the **GetComputerName** API call in your application for use by
> PInvoke. Which declaration is preferable?
>
> ○ A.
> ```
> Declare Auto Function _
> GetComputerName Lib _
> "kernel32" ( _
> ByVal lpBuffer As String, _
> ByRef nSize _
> As Integer) As Integer
> ```
>
> ○ B.
> ```
> Declare Function _
> GetComputerNameA Lib _
> "kernel32" ( _
> ByVal lpBuffer As StringBuilder, _
> ByRef nSize _
> As Integer) As Integer
> ```

○ C.
```
Declare Function _
GetComputerNameW Lib _
"kernel32" ( _
ByVal lpBuffer As StringBuilder, _
ByRef nSize _
As Integer) As Integer
```

○ D.
```
Declare Auto Function _
GetComputerName Lib _
"kernel32" ( _
ByVal lpBuffer As StringBuilder, _
ByRef nSize _
As Integer) As Integer
```

Answer D is correct. Answer A is incorrect because it uses String instead of StringBuilder, which results in more complex programming. Answers B and C are incorrect because they use platform-specific versions of the declaration.

Question 3

You are using a COM component that performs Internet searches in your application. This component was purchased from a third-party developer. You are migrating your application to .NET. What should you do to continue to use the classes and methods within the searching library?

○ A. Use the Type Library Importer to create an unsigned Runtime Callable Wrapper for the library. Install the RCW in the Global Assembly Cache.

○ B. Obtain a Primary Interop Assembly from the developer of the library. Install the PIA in the Global Assembly Cache.

○ C. Use the Type Library Importer to create a signed Runtime Callable Wrapper for the library. Install the RCW in the Global Assembly Cache.

○ D. Create wrapper code that uses **PInvoke** to call functions from the library. Import this wrapper code into your application.

Answer B is correct. Because this component was purchased from an outside developer, you should obtain a PIA from that developer. Answers A and C are incorrect because these will create your own private RCW instead of using a PIA. Answer D is incorrect because PInvoke is not used with COM components.

Question 4

You're moving a legacy ASP application that uses Single-Threaded Apartment ADO objects to ASP.NET. The application uses **CreateObject** to instantiate the objects. The pages containing these objects will not load. What must you do to use the ADO objects in your ASP.NET application?

- ○ A. Build a Runtime Callable Wrapper for the ADO objects.
- ○ B. Convert the ADO objects to ADO.NET.
- ○ C. Use a **Page** directive to set ASP compatibility mode.
- ○ D. Use a **Page** directive to set the page language to VBScript.

Answer C is correct. To use STA objects in ASP.NET, you must use a `Page` directive to set ASP compatibility mode. Answer A is incorrect because you can instantiate objects using `CreateObject` without an RCW. Answer B is incorrect because ASP.NET can use ADO (although using ADO.NET will improve performance). Answer D is incorrect because the choice of scripting language does not affect object creation.

Question 5

Your application uses the **GetComputerName** API function. This function exists in **kernel32.dll** in both ANSI and Unicode versions. Your declaration is as follows:

```
Declare Function GetComputerName _
  Lib "kernel32" ( _
  ByVal lpBuffer As String, _
  ByRef nSize As Integer) As Integer
```

Your code is failing with a **System.EntryPointNotFoundException** exception whenever you call this function. What should you do to fix this failure?

- ○ A. Declare the function as **GetComputerNameA** instead of **GetComputerName**.
- ○ B. Add the **Auto** modifier to the declaration.
- ○ C. Declare the function as **GetComputerNameW** instead of **GetComputerName**.
- ○ D. Supply the full path for **kernel32.dll**.

Answer B is correct. The `Auto` modifier instructs .NET to choose the ANSI or Unicode version of the function as appropriate. Answer A is incorrect because it will fail on Unicode platforms. Answer C is incorrect because it will fail on ANSI platforms. Answer D is incorrect because `kernel32.dll` is in a known location that does not require an explicit path.

Question 6

You are using three classes from a COM component, which you wrote in your Visual Basic ASP.NET application. You'd like to give the Runtime Callable Wrapper for the COM component the same version number as the rest of your components when you ship your application. What should you do?

- ○ A. Use the Type Library Importer with the **/asmversion** option to explicitly set the version of the RCW.

- ○ B. Directly import the COM component into the References list. Right-click the reference and select Properties to set the version number.

- ○ C. Recompile the existing COM library with the desired version number before creating the RCW.

- ○ D. Use **PInvoke** to call functions from the COM component, thus eliminating the RCW.

Answer A is correct. The Type Library Importer allows you to explicitly specify a version for the RCW. Answer B is incorrect because the reference does not include a version number. Answer C is incorrect because the RCW version does not depend on the COM version. Answer D is incorrect because PInvoke is not used with COM components.

Question 7

Your application will use functions from a COM+ component that uses COM+ for transaction support and object pooling. Which of these methods can you use to access the classes in the COM+ component (select two)?

- ❑ A. Set a direct reference to the COM+ component.

- ❑ B. Add the COM+ component directly to the Visual Basic .NET Toolbox.

- ❑ C. Use the Type Library Importer to create a Runtime Callable Wrapper for the COM+ component.

- ❑ D. Use **PInvoke** to declare the functions within the COM+ component.

Answers A and C are correct. You can use COM+ components like any other COM component by creating an RCW (either automatically or manually). Answer B is incorrect because the Toolbox does not store generic COM+ components. Answer D is incorrect because PInvoke is not used with COM+.

Question 8

Your company supplies a COM component that manages file transfers over dedicated lines. Some customers of your company are moving to .NET and require a Runtime Callable Wrapper for your component. How should you proceed?

- ○ A. Create a class that uses PInvoke to call functions from your component.
- ○ B. Use the Visual Basic Migration Wizard to bring the code into .NET and recompile it.
- ○ C. Set a reference to your component from any Visual Basic .NET project to create the Runtime Callable Wrapper for your component.
- ○ D. Use the Type Library Importer to create and sign a Primary Interop Assembly for your component.

Answer D is correct. Because you are the original producer of the component, supplying a PIA is the correct approach here. Answers A and B are incorrect because they do not result in the creation of an RCW. Answer C is incorrect because the direct reference method does not create a redistributable RCW.

Question 9

You have an existing COM component that contains shared classes. These classes encapsulate functionality that you want to use in your ASP.NET application. How can you use these classes while maintaining the benefits of managed code such as type safety and automatic garbage collection?

- ○ A. Rewrite the COM component as a .NET component.
- ○ B. Use the Type Library Importer with the **/strictref** option to create a Runtime Callable Wrapper for the COM component.
- ○ C. Add a direct reference to the COM component.
- ○ D. Call the methods from the COM component directly via Platform Invoke.

Answer A is correct. The benefits of managed code are only available to components that are themselves written in managed code. Answers B, C, and D are incorrect because they include COM code, which will not gain the benefits of managed code.

Question 10

You wrote a COM component to monitor an analog-to-digital (A/D) interface. The COM component is used in a single application that you also wrote. Now you're moving that client application to .NET. The COM component is used nowhere else, and you have not shipped copies to anyone else. You want to call the objects in the COM server from your new .NET client. How should you proceed?

○ A. Set a direct reference from your .NET client to the COM server.

○ B. Use the Type Library Importer to create an unsigned RCW for the COM component.

○ C. Use the Type Library Importer to create a signed RCW for the COM component.

○ D. Use **PInvoke** to instantiate classes from the COM component.

Answer A is correct. Because you own the component and only use it in a single application, the simplest and easiest approach is best. Answers B and C are incorrect because they require extra effort. Answer D is incorrect because PInvoke is used with API calls, not with classes.

Need to Know More?

 Nathan, Adam. *.NET AND COM: The Complete Interoperability Guide.* Sams, 2002.

 Visual Studio .NET Combined Help Collection, "Interoperating with Unmanaged Code" topic.

User Assistance and Accessibility

Terms you'll need to understand:

✓ User assistance
✓ Accessibility
✓ Search pane
✓ ToolTip
✓ W3C (World Wide Web Consortium)
✓ WAI (Web Accessibility Initiative)

Techniques you'll need to master:

✓ Implementing user assistance
✓ Ensuring accessibility for users with disabilities

User assistance refers to the type of help that you get from the traditional help file: a set of short topics designed to teach you what you need to know to effectively use the capabilities of an application. Although there is no standard for user assistance with Web applications, you can make assistance available in a number of ways. For example, you can display help topics in a separate browser window or within a pane in the main browser window.

Accessibility refers to making sure that users with disabilities can work with your application. Windows and the .NET Framework include a variety of tools and techniques to help you make your application accessible to these users.

Implementing User Assistance

User assistance refers to the techniques used to deliver helpful information to the users of an application. For Windows applications, there are well-defined standard ways to do this. For example, help files are written using HTML Help, a Microsoft standard for combining a set of HTML pages into a single file that can be browsed in a help viewer.

With Web applications, things are considerably less standardized. Even though HTML Help starts with HTML topics, it's not suitable for Web applications. The entire HTML Help file must be present on the client computer, which must also have a help viewer installed, for HTML Help to function properly. This poses a problem if you can't guarantee that all of your application's clients will be using the Windows platform, or if the entire help file is prohibitively large to download.

For Web applications, you'll need to get creative to deliver user assistance. Alternatives include

➤ Help in a separate browser window

➤ Help in a browser pane

➤ Using ToolTips

➤ Embedding Help

Using a Second Browser Window

The simplest way to provide help for a Web application is to just show the user instructions on Web pages. After all, if he is running a Web application, he certainly has a Web browser available.

To use this technique, you just need to add links to the main pages of your application. These links will open other pages that contain the help. In ASP.NET, you can do this conveniently by adding a hyperlink control to the main page. Set the NavigateUrl property of the hyperlink control to the name of the page containing the help, and set the Target property to _blank.

Setting this property uses the target="_blank" attribute to open help pages in a second browser window. Although this method should work with nearly any browser, it has some problems. Users might become confused with multiple browser windows open, and it can be annoying to have the help window overlap the window where you are trying to do work.

Using the Search Pane

One way to address the problems of using a separate browser window for user assistance is to use the Internet Explorer search pane instead. You can do this by setting the Target property to _search instead of _blank. This will open your user assistance pages in the Internet Explorer search pane, as shown in Figure 12.1.

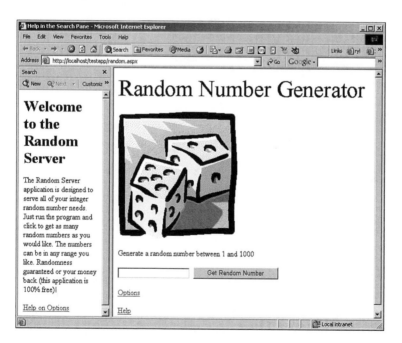

Figure 12.1 An application displaying user assistance in the search pane.

Although using the search pane does address the problem of keeping the help with the application, it raises other issues. If your users are sophisticated enough to actually use the search pane (for search, history, or favorites, for example), they might not be pleased at having it hijacked by your application's help pages. Worse, though, is the fact that the _search target is specific to Internet Explorer. This technique won't work properly in other browsers including some versions of Netscape, Mozilla, or Opera; instead, your help content will replace the page that the user was looking at. This makes using the Search pane a reasonable technique only if you have a captive audience that you know is using Internet Explorer for Web browsing.

Using ToolTips

ASP.NET offers a variety of properties for server controls. One of these, the ToolTip property, can be used to display brief help strings to the user when they hover their mouse pointer over a control. To use ToolTips for help, put help text applicable to a control in the ToolTip property of that control. When the application is running and you hover your mouse over the control, the tooltip text will appear after a short delay, as shown in Figure 12.2.

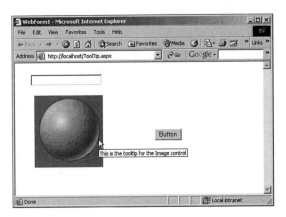

Figure 12.2 ToolTip on a Web Form.

ASP.NET renders ToolTips by using the TITLE attribute of HTML control tags. This solution is portable among all reasonably current browsers, although some older browsers (such as Netscape Communicator 4.79) will not display this information. In addition, some controls (notably the DropDownList control) do not support ToolTips.

Embedding Help

To avoid the problems with extra browser windows or with the search pane, you might choose to embed the user assistance directly in your Web pages. For example, you could add a Label control named lblHelp with its Visible property set to False. Type help for the page as the Text property of the Label control. Then add a LinkButton control named lbtnHelp with a Click event handler:

```
Private Sub lbtnHelp_Click(ByVal sender As System.Object, _
ByVal e As System.EventArgs) Handles lbtnHelp.Click
    lblHelp.Visible = True
End Sub
```

When you click the Help hyperlink on the main page, it will display the help directly on the page. Embedding user assistance directly in the Web page is a good solution in many ways. It's compatible with all browsers (because the .NET Framework is delivering pure HTML when you show the Label control), and doesn't require opening a new browser window. Unfortunately, it does require a round-trip to the server to redraw the page when the user clicks the link.

NOTE If you want, you can ship the user assistance embedded on the page and use DHTML behaviors to hide and show the information that's already in the user's browser. However this technique is not widely compatible with all browsers, and it increases the size of your Web pages by sending the help to the browser whether it's needed or not.

Other User Assistance Alternatives

Although I'm focusing on the mechanics of providing user assistance in code, you should consider this just one facet of an overall user assistance strategy. Depending on your organization and the applications involved, user assistance can include any or all of the following:

➤ A Readme file or other introductory material for the user to refer to even before installing the application.

➤ Printed, online, or electronic documentation.

➤ Email, telephone, or onsite support from a product specialist.

➤ Wizards, builders, and other user interface components designed to guide the user through a process.

Implementing Accessibility Features

According to Microsoft, more than 30 million people in the United States alone have disabilities that can be affected by the design of computer hardware and software. From both ethical and economic standpoints, as well as to comply with the law, designing software for accessibility simply makes sense. In fact, Microsoft has made accessibility a key feature of the Windows logo certification program, which allows applications to display the "designed for Windows" logo.

There are five basic principles to accessible design:

➤ **Flexibility**—The user interface should be flexible and customizable so that users can adjust it to their own individual needs and preferences.

➤ **Choice of Input Methods**—Different users have different abilities and preferences when it comes to choosing the mouse or keyboard to perform tasks. All operations in your application should be accessible to the keyboard, and basic operations should be available via the mouse as well. In the future, voice and other types of input might also be considered here.

➤ **Choice of Output Methods**—You should not depend on a single method of output (such as sound, color, or text) for important information.

➤ **Consistency**—Your application should be consistent with the Windows operating system and other applications to minimize difficulties in learning and using new interfaces.

➤ **Compatibility with Accessibility Aids**—Windows includes a number of accessibility aids such as the Magnifier (which can blow up text or graphics to a larger size) and the On-Screen Keyboard (which enables keyboard input via the mouse). Users might also be using specialized browsers that render pages as pure text, read the text aloud, or assist in other ways. Your application should not circumvent these accessibility aids.

As an example of implementing these principles, the Windows logo certification requirements include these items:

➤ Support the standard system size, color, font, and input settings.

➤ Ensure compatibility with the High Contrast display setting. With this setting, the application can only use colors from the Control Panel or colors explicitly chosen by the user.

➤ Provide documented keyboard access to all features.

➤ It must always be obvious to both the user and to software tools where the keyboard focus is located. This is necessary for the Magnifier and Narrator accessibility aids to function properly.

➤ Do not convey information by sound alone.

Understanding Accessible Design Guidelines

Table 12.1 lays out some of the important accessibility guidelines that you should consider for any application.

Table 12.1 Accessibility Guidelines for Web Application Design	
Area	**Guidelines**
ALT text	Every graphic should have **ALT** text. **ALT** text should convey the important information about an image. For large and complex images, you might want to include a link to a page that explains the image in text.
Imagemaps	Do not depend on imagemaps for navigation; also include a set of text links for those who cannot use the images.
Link Text	Link text should be useful in isolation because some accessible browsers present a list of links with no context for fast navigation. If this isn't possible, use the **TITLE** attribute of the link to provide a more descriptive string.
Keyboard Navigation	The tab key will move between all links and imagemap areas in the order that they're defined in the HTML. Use the **TABINDEX** attribute where appropriate to override this.
Access Keys	All controls and links that act as controls should have an **ACCESSKEY** attribute. Underline the access key in the control's label.
Control Identification	Use the **TITLE** attribute or **LABEL** tags to associate a caption with every control.
Frames and Tables	Provide alternative pages that do not use frames or tables.
Support Formatting Options	Do not assume that text will be in a specific font, color, or size. Do not assume that things will line up because the width may change. Use heading tags such as **<TH>** rather than specially formatted text.
Style Sheets	Make sure that the page works even if the style sheet is turned off. Otherwise, offer an alternative page that is designed to work without a style sheet.
Audio and Video	Provide captions or transcripts for audio and video content.

The W3C Guidelines

The World Wide Web Consortium (better known as the W3C) is the body that governs standards for the Internet. The W3C has invested considerable effort in defining accessibility guidelines. You can find the home page of the W3C Web Accessibility Initiative at http://www.w3.org/WAI/. From that page, you can navigate through the W3C WAI's extensive list of resources, which should be required reading if you're concerned about Web site accessibility.

Here's a summary of the W3C's priority 1 guidelines, which it says that Web content developers *must* satisfy:

➤ Provide a text equivalent for every non-text element (for example, using ALT, LONGDESC, or in-element content). Non-text elements include images, graphical representations of text (including symbols), imagemap regions, animations (for example, animated GIFs), applets and programmatic objects, ASCII art, frames, scripts, images used as list bullets, spacers, graphical buttons, sounds (played with or without user interaction), standalone audio files, audio tracks of video, and video.

➤ Don't use color as the sole means to convey information. Always provide an alternative in content or markup.

➤ Clearly identify any changes in the document's natural language.

➤ Make sure that documents are still readable in the absence of any style sheet.

➤ Ensure that equivalents for dynamic content are updated when the dynamic content changes.

➤ Avoid causing the screen to flicker.

➤ Use the clearest and simplest language appropriate to the site's content.

➤ Provide redundant text links for each active region of a server-side imagemap.

➤ Provide client-side imagemaps instead of server-side imagemaps except where the regions cannot be defined with an available geometric shape.

➤ Identify row and column headers in tables.

➤ Use markup to associate data cells and header cells.

➤ Use TITLE tags for all frames.

➤ Ensure that pages are usable when scripts, applets, or other programmatic objects are turned off or not supported. If this is not possible, provide equivalent information on an alternative accessible page.

➤ Provide an auditory description of any important video information.

➤ Synchronize captions with movies or animations.

➤ If, after best efforts, you cannot create an accessible page, provide a link to an alternative page that uses W3C technologies, is accessible, has equivalent information (or functionality), and is updated as often as the inaccessible (original) page.

The Section 508 Guidelines

Section 508 of the Rehabilitation Act sets standards for all U.S. agencies that maintain Web sites. This gives accessibility the force of law for federal Web sites (and serves to emphasize that it's a good idea for all Web sites).

An excellent discussion of the Section 508 standards can be found at `http://www.access-board.gov/sec508/guide/1194.22.htm`. Here's a summary of the guidelines that Web sites must comply with. You'll see that there is considerable overlap with the Microsoft and W3C guidelines.

➤ A text equivalent for every non-text element shall be provided (for example, using `alt`, `longdesc`, or in-element content).

➤ Equivalent alternatives for any multimedia presentation shall be synchronized with the presentation.

➤ Web pages shall be designed so that all information conveyed with color is also available without color—for example, from context or markup.

➤ Documents shall be organized so that they are readable without requiring an associated style sheet.

➤ Redundant text links shall be provided for each active region of a server-side imagemap.

➤ Client-side imagemaps shall be provided instead of server-side imagemaps except where the regions cannot be defined with an available geometric shape.

➤ Row and column headers shall be identified for data tables.

➤ Markup shall be used to associate data cells and header cells for data tables that have two or more logical levels of row or column headers.

➤ Frames shall be titled with text that facilitates frame identification and navigation.

➤ Pages shall be designed to avoid causing the screen to flicker with a frequency greater than 2Hz and lower than 55Hz.

➤ A text-only page, with equivalent information or functionality, shall be provided to make a Web site comply with the provisions of these standards, when compliance cannot be accomplished in any other way. The content of the text-only page shall be updated whenever the primary page changes.

➤ When pages use scripting languages to display content or to create interface elements, the information provided by the script shall be identified with functional text that can be read by assistive technology.

➤ When a Web page requires that an applet, plug-in, or other application be present on the client system to interpret page content, the page must provide a link to a plug-in or applet that complies with [the standards of the Act].

➤ When electronic forms are designed to be completed online, the form shall allow people using assistive technology to access the information, field elements, and functionality required for completion and submission of the form, including all directions and cues.

➤ A method shall be provided that permits users to skip repetitive navigation links.

➤ When a timed response is required, the user shall be alerted and given sufficient time to indicate whether more time is required.

Testing Application Accessibility

Before shipping an application, you should test the accessibility features. Here are some tests that you should perform:

➤ Navigate your user interface using only the keyboard. Make sure that all functionality is accessible by using the keyboard alone. Test all access keys. Press Enter to follow a selected link.

➤ View the page with graphics turned off to make sure that the ALT tags are a good substitute. In Internet Explorer, you can turn off graphics from Tools, Internet Options, Advanced.

➤ Use the application with sound turned off to make sure that no important information is lost.

➤ Turn on the High Contrast option under Control Panel, Display and make sure that the page is still readable.

➤ Alter the page's font size (you can do this with View, Text Size in Internet Explorer) and make sure that the page is still readable.

➤ Resize the browser window and check for readability.

Exam Prep Questions

Question 1

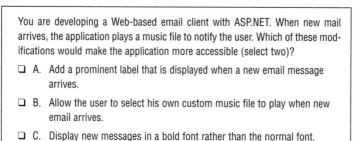

You are developing a Web-based email client with ASP.NET. When new mail arrives, the application plays a music file to notify the user. Which of these modifications would make the application more accessible (select two)?

❑ A. Add a prominent label that is displayed when a new email message arrives.

❑ B. Allow the user to select his own custom music file to play when new email arrives.

❑ C. Display new messages in a bold font rather than the normal font.

❑ D. Allow the user to select the volume at which the music file is played.

Answers A and C are correct. These two answers add visual cues to the audio cue for new email, which makes the application more accessible to users with hearing disabilities. Answers B and D are incorrect because they continue to rely entirely on audio notification.

Question 2

You'd like to highlight some information on a Web page. Which of these tags might you choose for accessible highlighting (select two)?

❑ A. **<MARQUEE>**

❑ B. **<B>**

❑ C. **<BLINK>**

❑ D. **<U>**

Answers B and D are correct. Making text bold or underlined is useful for all users. Answers A and C are incorrect because moving or blinking text might cause problems for some users or browsers.

Question 3

You are deploying an ASP.NET application to manage travel vouchers on your company's intranet. Users would like to have detailed online help, including the corporate travel policies, available for the application. They do not want to manage additional windows, and they do not want to download the help if they don't need it. Your company uses Internet Explorer 6.0 as its only browser. How should you implement user assistance for this application?

○ A. Display help by using DHTML to hide and show.

○ B. Display help by loading a separate HTML page with **target=_blank**.

○ C. Display help by showing normally invisible **Label** controls.

○ D. Display help by loading a separate HTML page with **target=_search**.

Answer D is correct. The `target=_search` tag will display the help in IE's search pane. The help will not be downloaded unless it is needed. Answers A and C are incorrect because the help will always be downloaded, whether it is needed or not. Answer B is incorrect because this would open the help in a separate browser window.

Question 4

Your company is preparing to deploy a new ASP.NET Web application to the Internet. The CTO in the company proposes to use Microsoft's HTML Help for user assistance in this application because the company has experience shipping HTML Help files with desktop applications. Do you agree with this proposal?

○ A. No, because HTML Help is limited to just a small set of HTML tags.

○ B. Yes, because HTML Help is the standard for Visual Studio .NET applications.

○ C. No, because HTML Help is only available on the Microsoft Windows operating system.

○ D. Yes, because HTML Help is viewable in any Web browser.

Answer C is correct. HTML Help is a Windows-specific technology that is not suitable for Internet applications that might be accessed from a variety of browsers and operating systems. Answer A is incorrect because HTML Help can use all HTML 4.01 tags. Answer B is incorrect because you're not writing a VS .NET application. Answer D is incorrect because HTML Help uses its own shell to display help rather than using a browser.

Question 5

Your ASP.NET Web application uses a frame set to organize multiple panes of information at one time. What must you do to comply with the Section 508 accessibility guidelines?

○ A. Provide a link to an alternative, non-framed page.

○ B. Add an **ALT** text tag to the **FRAMESET** tag.

○ C. Provide Title text for each frame.

○ D. Replace the frame set with a table.

Answer C is correct. Frames can be used in accessible sites as long as the frames are titled with text that makes it easy to identify and navigate between frames. Answer A is incorrect because there is no need to provide an alternative site. Answer B is incorrect because ALT tags are for graphics, not frames. Answer D is incorrect because frames do not have to be replaced for accessibility.

Question 6

Your ASP.NET application uses a set of **ImageButton** controls to implement a navigation menu. Users with visual disabilities report difficulties in using the application because their screen readers will not read the text on the button images. What should you do to make your application more accessible?

○ A. Ensure that the graphics on the **ImageButton** controls are saved in PNG format rather than GIF or JPG.

○ B. Use the **AccessKey** property of the **ImageButton** controls to create key shortcuts for the links.

○ C. Use the **AlternateText** property of the **ImageButton** controls to indicate their purpose.

○ D. Provide an alternative version of the page that uses hyperlinks instead of **ImageButton** controls.

Answer C is correct. Supplying alternative text for visual controls is important for users who work with screen reader software, which can only display textual information. Answer A is incorrect because graphics in general are not interpreted by such software. Answer B is incorrect because AccessKey can make it easier to trigger the link, but not to know where it leads. Answer D is incorrect because you should not degrade to an alternative version of a page unless no alternative is available.

Question 7

> Your ASP.NET site is extremely complex and frequently updated. In order to comply with accessible guidelines, the main page features a prominent link to a text-only version of the page. How often must you update the text-only version of the page?
>
> ○ A. Every time that the regular main page is changed.
>
> ○ B. Every time five or more changes accumulate on the main page.
>
> ○ C. Within two weeks of every change to the main page.
>
> ○ D. Within six months of every change to the main page.

Answer A is correct. Text-only versions are meant to be a way for users with disabilities to access all the information on your Web site. Thus, they must remain synchronized with the non-accessible versions. Answers B, C, and D are incorrect because they allow the two versions to get out of synch.

Question 8

> Which of the following techniques might be part of your user assistance strategy for an ASP.NET application (select all correct answers)?
>
> ❑ A. Supply **ALT** text for all graphical elements.
>
> ❑ B. Use ToolTips to display quick help for form fields.
>
> ❑ C. Use a normally hidden **Label** control to display extensive help.
>
> ❑ D. Use proper markup to indicate the semantic content of tables.

Answers B and C are correct. User assistance encompasses all the techniques that help convey information to the user about the proper functioning of your application. Answers A and D are incorrect because these are accessibility techniques, not user assistance techniques.

Question 9

You are deploying an ASP.NET Web application that will be used by international college students to register for courses. The students will be using a variety of browsers and operating systems. Some might be connected to your server via very slow and expensive links. Which of these would be the best alternative for user assistance for this application?

○ A. Help links to the search pane

○ B. HTML Help

○ C. Help links to a separate browser window

○ D. DHTML help

Answer C is correct. Any browser should be able to open a second window and download the help to that window only when it is needed. Answer A is incorrect because the search pane is Internet Explorer–specific technology. Answer B is incorrect because HTML Help is Windows-only technology. Answer D is incorrect because DHTML will not work in older browsers and because it would require downloading the help every time the application was loaded.

Need to Know More?

 W3C WAI Web site, http://www.w3.org/WAI/.

 Section 508 Web site, http://www.section508.gov/.

 Visual Studio .NET Combined Help Collection, "Designing Accessible Applications" topic.

Testing and Debugging a Web Application

Terms you'll need to understand:

✓ Debugging
✓ Testing
✓ Tracing
✓ **TraceContext** class
✓ **Trace** class
✓ **Debug** class
✓ Trace listener
✓ Trace switch
✓ Conditional compilation

Techniques you'll need to master:

✓ Creating a test plan
✓ Tracing application execution
✓ Adding trace listeners and trace switches to an application
✓ Displaying trace output
✓ Configuring and using the debugging environment

Building a quality Web application requires thorough testing and the ability to figure out what's going on when something goes wrong. The goal of testing and debugging your applications is to make sure that end users never encounter an error. Although it's hard to achieve this ideal, having a formal test plan and a good grasp of the debugging tools in Visual Studio .NET can help you approach it.

In this chapter, I discuss test plans and various common testing techniques. I also show you how to put tracing code in a program to monitor its execution. Finally, I talk about the debugging capabilities of Visual Studio .NET.

Testing

Testing is the process of executing a program with the intention of finding errors (bugs). The process of testing can be manual, automated, or a mix of both techniques.

 NOTE *Correctness* refers to the capability of a program to produce expected results when the program is given a set of valid input data. *Robustness* is the capability of a program to cope with invalid data or operation. *Reliability* is the capability of a program to produce consistent results on every use.

Creating a Test Plan

A *test plan* is a document that guides the whole process of testing. A good test plan will typically include answers to the following questions:

➤ Which software component needs to be tested?

➤ What parts of a component's specification are to be tested?

➤ What parts of a component's specification are not to be tested?

➤ What approach needs to be followed for testing?

➤ Who will be responsible for each task in the testing process?

➤ What is the schedule for testing?

➤ What are the criteria for a test to fail or pass?

➤ How will the test results be documented and disseminated?

Executing Tests

Incremental testing (sometimes also called evolutionary testing) is a modern approach to testing that has proven very useful for Rapid Application

Development (RAD). The idea here is to test the system as you build it. The three levels of testing involved are as follows:

➤ **Unit testing**—Involves testing an elementary unit of the application (usually a class or a method).

➤ **Integration testing**—Tests the integration of two or more units or integration between subsystems of those units.

➤ **Regression testing**—Usually involves the process of repeating the unit and integration tests whenever a bug is fixed to ensure that no old bugs have recurred and that no new bugs have been introduced. You should also run your regression tests when you have modified or added code to make sure that the new code does not have unintended consequences.

Unit Testing

Units are the smallest building blocks of an application. In Visual Basic .NET, these building blocks are often a component or a class definition. Unit tests involve performing basic tests at the component level to ensure that each unique execution path in the component behaves exactly as documented in its specifications.

Often the same person who writes the component also does unit testing for it. Unit testing typically requires writing special programs that use the component or class under test. These programs are called *test drivers*. They are used throughout the testing process, but are not part of the final product.

NUnit is a simple framework that enables you to write repeatable tests in any .NET language. For more information, visit **http://www.nunit.org/**.

Some of the major benefits of unit testing are as follows:

➤ It allows you to test parts of an application without waiting for the other parts to be available.

➤ It allows you to test those exceptional conditions that are not easily reached by external inputs in a large integrated system.

➤ It simplifies the debugging process by limiting the search for bugs to a small unit when compared to the complete application.

➤ It avoids lengthy compile-build-debug cycles when debugging difficult problems.

> It enables you to detect and remove defects at a much lower cost compared to other, later stages of testing.

Integration Testing

Integration testing verifies that the major subsystems of an application work well with each other. The objective of integration testing is to uncover the errors that might result because of the way units integrate or interface with each other. Integration testing can be performed in a variety of ways, including

> **Bottom-up approach**—Testing progresses from the smallest subsystem and then gradually progresses up the hierarchy to cover the whole system.

> **Top-Down approach**—Testing progresses from the top-level interfaces and gradually comes down and tests smaller subsystems.

> **Umbrella approach**—Testing starts with those modules that have a high degree of user interaction. This approach enables you to release GUI-based applications early, allowing you to gradually increase functionality.

Regression Testing

Regression testing should be performed any time a program is modified, either to fix a bug or to add a feature. The process of regression testing involves running all the previous tests plus any newly added test cases to test the added functionality. Regression testing has two main goals:

> Verify that all known bugs are corrected.

> Verify that the program has no new bugs.

Testing International Applications

Testing an application designed for international usage involves checking the country and language dependencies of each locale for which the application has been designed. Here are some guidelines for testing international applications:

> Test the application's data and user interface to make sure that they conform to the locale's standards for date and time, numeric values, currency, list separators, and measurements.

> Test your application on as many language and culture variants as necessary to cover your entire market.

> Use Unicode whenever possible.

➤ Carefully test your application's logic for setting an appropriate language. It might be difficult to determine the user's preferred language from her Web browser settings. You might want to allow the user to select a language instead.

➤ While testing a localized version of an application, make sure that you use input data in the language supported by the localized version.

For more information on support for globalization in a Window application, refer to Chapter 10, "Globalization."

Tracing

The process of collecting information about a program's execution is called *tracing*. This section discusses two different methods of tracing:

➤ Using the `System.Web.TraceContext` class—This class allows you to view diagnostic information and trace messages along with the page output or through a separate trace viewer utility (trace.axd).

➤ Using the `System.Diagnostics.Trace` and `System.Diagnostics.Debug` classes—By default, these classes display trace messages in the Output window, but you can use the `TraceListener` class to send output to additional destinations such as text files, event logs, or other custom-defined trace listeners.

Using the TraceContext Class

The `TraceContext` class is responsible for gathering the execution details of a Web request. You can access the `TraceContext` object for the current request through the `Trace` property of the `Page` object. Once you have the `TraceContext` object, you can invoke its member methods to write trace messages to the trace log. Table 13.1 lists some of the important members of the `TraceContext` class.

Table 13.1   Important Members of TraceContext Classes

Member	Type	Description
IsEnabled	Property	Specifies whether tracing is enabled for a request.
TraceMode	Property	Indicates the sort order in which the messages should be displayed. It can have one of three values—Default, **SortByCategory**, and **SortByTime**.

(continued)

Table 13.1 Important Members of TraceContext Classes *(continued)*		
Member	**Type**	**Description**
Warn	Method	Writes messages to the trace log in red, which indicates warnings. It has three overloads—one with message, the second one with category and message, and the last one with category, message, and exception object.
Write	Method	Writes the messages to the trace log. It has the same three overloads as the **Warn** method.

By default, tracing is not enabled. Thus, trace messages are not displayed. You can enable tracing for a Page by using the Trace attribute of the Page directive. When the Trace attribute is set to True, the page appends the tracing information of the current Web request to its output. You can also enable tracing by setting the DOCUMENT object's Trace property to True. This gives you both automatic tracing and the ability to insert your own messages in the trace output:

1. Create a new Visual Basic ASP.NET Web Application project.

2. Set the default Web Form to FlowLayout mode. Add a Button control named btnTrace to the Web Form.

3. Switch to HTML view of the form in the designer. Add the Trace="True" attribute to the Page directive:

```
<%@ Page Language="vb" AutoEventWireup="false"
Codebehind="WebForm1.aspx.vb"
Inherits="EC305C13.WebForm1" Trace="True"%>
```

4. Switch back to design view of the form. Double-click the button control and add the following code to the event handler to handle the Click event:

```
Private Sub btnTrace_Click( _
ByVal sender As System.Object, _
ByVal e As System.EventArgs) _
Handles btnTrace.Click
    Trace.Write("Sent by the Trace.Write method")
    Trace.Warn("Sent by the Trace.Warn method")
End Sub
```

5. Run the project. ASP.NET will display a wide range of information after rendering the controls on the page. Click the Trace button. The page will be reloaded with the output from the Trace.Write and Trace.Warn statements, as shown in Figure 13.1.

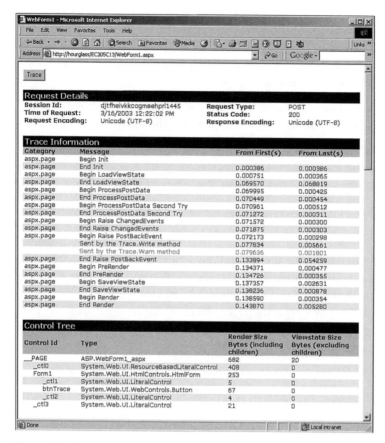

Figure 13.1   Tracing information.

Here's a summary of the information that tracing adds to the page:

➤ **Request Details**—Includes the session identifier, the time the request was made, the request character encoding, the type of HTTP request (GET or POST), the HTTP response status code, and the response character encoding.

➤ **Trace Information**—Includes the messages and warnings generated internally by the ASP.NET engine or by explicit calls to the Write or Warn methods of the TraceContext class.

➤ **Control Tree**—Includes information on the entire collection of controls in the ASP.NET page hierarchically.

➤ **Session State**—Includes the session state (only if any data is stored in the session).

➤ **Cookies Collection**—Includes the cookies associated with the application.

➤ **Headers Collection**—Includes the HTTP headers passed to the Web page. It displays the name of the header and its value.

➤ **Form Collection**—Includes the form collection. It is displayed only if there is a Web Form defined in the page and the form is posting back from the server.

➤ **Querystring Collection**—Includes the querystring collection only if any querystring parameters are passed while requesting the page.

➤ **Server Variables**—Includes all the server variables associated with the page.

You can enable tracing for the entire Web application using the application configuration Web.config file in the application's root directory. Enabling tracing through the Web.config file allows you to view the trace information using trace viewer in a separate page instead of displaying it with the page output. The <trace> element is used to configure tracing for an application. The attributes of the <trace> element are

➤ enabled—Indicates whether tracing is enabled for an application. If enabled, trace information can be viewed using trace viewer.

➤ localOnly—Indicates whether trace viewer can be viewed by only the local client (running on the Web server itself) or by any client.

➤ pageOutput—Indicates whether the trace information should be displayed along with the page output.

➤ requestLimit—Indicates the number of requests whose trace information should be stored on the server. Tracing gets disabled when the request limit is reached.

➤ traceMode—Indicates the order in which the trace messages should be displayed in the Trace Information section. It can be either SortByCategory (sorted by the Category column) or SortByTime (sorted by the First(s) column) .

The page-level trace setting overrides the trace setting for the application. For example, if **pageOutput** is set to **False** in the **Web.config** file and if the trace attribute is enabled at page level, the trace information is still displayed along with the page output.

Follow these steps to use the trace viewer and application tracing instead of page tracing:

1. Open the Web.config file from Solution Explorer. Modify the <trace> element defined in the <system.web> element as follows:

```
<trace
    enabled="true"
    requestLimit="10"
    pageOutput="false"
    traceMode="SortByTime"
    localOnly="true"
/>
```

2. Remove the Trace="True" attribute from the Page directive of the default Web Form.

3. Run the project. Click the button. You will notice that there is no trace information along with the page display.

4. Now navigate to trace.axd under your application directory. This is not a real page, but is intercepted by ASP.NET to show trace information. Click the View Details link to see the details of a particular request.

5. Set the enabled attribute of the trace element to False in the Web.config file.

Using the Trace and Debug Classes

The Trace and Debug classes have several things in common—both send their output to Visual Studio .NET, both belong to the System.Diagnostics namespace, they have members with the same names, all their members are static, and they are conditionally compiled (that is, their statements will be included in the object code only if a certain symbol is defined). The only difference between the Debug and Trace classes is that the members of the Debug class are conditionally compiled only when the DEBUG symbol is defined. On the other hand, members in the Trace class are conditionally compiled only if the TRACE symbol is defined.

 Don't confuse the **Page.Trace** property, which returns an instance of the **TraceContext** class, with the Trace class from the **System.Diagnostics** namespace.

Visual Basic .NET provides two basic configurations for a project—Debug and Release. Debug is the default configuration. When you compile a program using the Debug configuration, both the TRACE and DEBUG conditional compilation symbols are defined. When you compile a program in the Release configuration, only the TRACE symbol is defined. You can switch between Debug and Release configurations by using the Solution Configurations combo box on the standard toolbar or by using the Configuration Manager from the project's property pages.

When you compile a program in the Debug configuration, it will send output through both the Trace and the Debug classes.

Table 13.2 summarizes the members of both the Trace and Debug classes.

Table 13.2	Members of Debug and Trace Classes	
Member	**Type**	**Description**
Assert	Method	Checks for a condition and displays a message if the condition is **False**.
AutoFlush	Property	Specifies whether Flush should be called on the Listeners after every write.
Close	Method	Flushes the output buffer and then closes the Listeners.
Fail	Method	Displays an error message.
Flush	Method	Flushes the output buffer and causes buffered data to be written to the Listeners.
Indent	Method	Increases the current **IndentLevel** by one.
IndentLevel	Property	Specifies the indent level.
IndentSize	Property	Specifies the number of spaces in an indent.
Listeners	Property	Collection of listeners that monitors the trace output.
Unindent	Method	Decreases the current **IndentLevel** by one.
Write	Method	Writes the given information to the trace listeners in the Listeners collection.
WriteIf	Method	Writes the given information to the trace listeners in the Listeners collection only if a condition is true.
WriteLine	Method	Same as **Write**, but appends the information with a newline character.
WriteLineIf	Method	Same as **WriteIf**, but appends the information with a newline character.

To see the Trace and Debug classes in action, try adding this code to an ASP.NET Web Form:

```
Private Sub btnTest_Click( _
 ByVal sender As System.Object, _
 ByVal e As System.EventArgs) _
 Handles btnTest.Click
    ' Demonstrate the Debug class
    Debug.WriteLine("Simple message")
    Debug.IndentSize = 4
    Debug.Indent()
    Debug.WriteLineIf(Rnd(1) > 0.5, _
      "Conditional message")
    Debug.Assert(Rnd(1) > 0.5, _
      "Assertion failed")
    Debug.Unindent()

    ' Demonstrate the Trace class
    System.Diagnostics.Trace.WriteLine("Simple message")
    System.Diagnostics.Trace.IndentSize = 4
    System.Diagnostics.Trace.Indent()
    System.Diagnostics.Trace.WriteLineIf(Rnd(1) > 0.5, _
      "Conditional message")
    System.Diagnostics.Trace.Assert(Rnd(1) > 0.5, _
      "Assertion failed")
    System.Diagnostics.Trace.Unindent()
End Sub
```

When you run the project, you'll see messages from both the Debug and Trace classes in the Output window (View, Other Windows, Output).

NOTE — Note the use of the fully qualified name for the **System.Diagnostics.Trace** class to avoid conflicts with the **Page.Trace** property.

Trace Listeners

Listeners are the classes responsible for forwarding, recording, or displaying the messages generated by the Trace and Debug classes. You can have multiple listeners associated with the Trace and Debug classes by adding multiple Listener objects to their Listeners property. The Listeners property is a collection capable of holding objects of any type derived from the TraceListener class. The TraceListener class is an abstract class that belongs to the System.Diagnostics namespace, which has three implementations in the FCL:

➤ **DefaultTraceListener**—An object of this class is automatically added to the Listeners collection of Trace and Debug classes. Its behavior is to write messages on the Output window. You've already seen this class in action.

➤ **TextWriterTraceListener**—Writes the messages to any class that derives from Stream class. That includes a console window or a file.

➤ **EventLogTraceListener**—Writes the messages to the Windows Event Log.

You can also create your own class that inherits from the TraceListener class. When doing so, you must at least implement the Write and WriteLine methods.

Messages sent through the Debug and Trace objects are directed through each Listener in the Listeners collection. Debug and Trace share the same Listeners collection, so any Listener defined in the **Trace.Listeners** collection will also be defined in the **Debug.Listeners** collection.

To see the effect of adding a second Listener to the collection, modify the code from the previous example. First, add an Imports statement for the System.IO namespace. Then modify the Click event handler:

```
Private Sub btnTest_Click( _
 ByVal sender As System.Object, _
 ByVal e As System.EventArgs) _
 Handles btnTest.Click
    ' Add a trace listener
    Dim fs As FileStream = File.OpenWrite(Server.MapPath("TraceFile.txt"))
    Dim tl As TextWriterTraceListener = _
     New TextWriterTraceListener(fs)
    Debug.Listeners.Add(tl)

    ' Demonstrate the Debug class
    Debug.WriteLine("Simple message")
    Debug.IndentSize = 4
    Debug.Indent()
    Debug.WriteLineIf(Rnd(1) > 0.5, _
     "Conditional message")
    Debug.Assert(Rnd(1) > 0.5, _
     "Assertion failed")
    Debug.Unindent()

    ' Demonstrate the Trace class
    System.Diagnostics.Trace.WriteLine("Simple message")
    System.Diagnostics.Trace.IndentSize = 4
    System.Diagnostics.Trace.Indent()
    System.Diagnostics.Trace.WriteLineIf(Rnd(1) > 0.5, _
     "Conditional message")
    System.Diagnostics.Trace.Assert(Rnd(1) > 0.5, _
     "Assertion failed")
    System.Diagnostics.Trace.Unindent()

    tl.Close()

End Sub
```

Run the project and click the button. Close the Web Form and click the Show All Files toolbar button in Solution Explorer. You'll find that the TraceFile.txt file has been created in the project's folder (click the Refresh button if it doesn't appear immediately). If you open it, it will contain a copy of the trace output.

Trace Switches

Trace switches allow you to control the level of tracing from an XML-based external configuration file. This is especially useful when the application is in production mode. You may instruct the application to write a particular type of trace information by just changing the configuration file. There's no need to recompile the application. The application will automatically pick up the changes from the configuration file the next time you run the application.

There are two predefined classes for creating trace switches: the BooleanSwitch class and the TraceSwitch class. Both classes derive from the abstract Switch class. You can also define your own trace switch class by deriving a class from the Switch class.

The BooleanSwitch class differentiates between two modes of tracing: trace-on or trace-off. Its default value is 0. This corresponds to the trace-off state. If the value of the class is set to any non-zero value, this corresponds to a trace-on state.

Unlike the BooleanSwitch class, the TraceSwitch class provides you with five different levels of tracing switches. These levels are defined by the TraceLevel enumeration, listed in Table 13.3. The default value of TraceLevel for a TraceSwitch is 0 (Off).

Table 13.3   The TraceLevel Enumeration

Enumerated Value	Integer Value	Type of Tracing
Off	0	None
Error	1	Only error messages
Warning	2	Warning messages and error messages
Info	3	Informational messages, warning messages, and error messages
Verbose	4	Verbose messages, informational messages, warning messages, and error messages

Table 13.4 displays the important properties of the TraceSwitch class.

Table 13.4   Important Properties of the TraceSwitch Class

Property	Description
Description	Description of the switch (inherited from Switch).
DisplayName	A name used to identify the switch (inherited from Switch).

(continued)

Table 13.4	Important Properties of the TraceSwitch Class *(continued)*
Property	**Description**
Level	Specifies the trace level that helps in selecting which trace and debug messages will be processed. Its value is one of the **TraceLevel** enumeration values (refer to Table 13.3).
TraceError	Returns **True** if the Level is set to Error, Warning, Info, or Verbose; otherwise a false value.
TraceInfo	Returns **True** if the Level is set to Info or Verbose; otherwise a false value.
TraceVerbose	Returns **True** if the Level is set to Verbose; otherwise a false value.
TraceWarning	Returns **True** if the Level is set to Warning, Info, or Verbose; otherwise a false value.

Here's a simple demonstration of the `TraceSwitch` class. This code depends on the value of a trace switch to determine whether to print messages:

```
Private Sub btnTest_Click( _
ByVal sender As System.Object, _
ByVal e As System.EventArgs) _
Handles btnTest.Click
    Dim ts As TraceSwitch = New TraceSwitch( _
    "MySwitch", "Demonstration Trace Switch")
    If ts.TraceError Then
        Debug.WriteLine("Error message")
    End If
    If ts.TraceWarning Then
        Debug.WriteLine("Warning message")
    End If
    If ts.TraceInfo Then
        Debug.WriteLine("Info message")
    End If
    If ts.TraceVerbose Then
        Debug.WriteLine("Verbose message")
    End If
End Sub
```

To define the trace switch, you can insert the `<system.diagnostics>` element after the `<system.web>` element definition in the `<configuration>` element (that is, in between the `</system.web>` and `</configuration>` element) as shown here:

```
<configuration>
  <system.web>
  ...
  </system.web>
  <system.diagnostics>
      <switches>
          <add name="MySwitch" value="4" />
      </switches>
  </system.diagnostics>
</configuration>
```

Conditional Compilation

The Visual Basic .NET programming language provides a set of preprocessing directives. Table 13.5 summarizes the preprocessing directives available in Visual Basic .NET

Table 13.5	Visual Basic .NET Preprocessing Directives
Directives	**Description**
#If, **#Else**, **#ElseIf**, and **#End If**	These directives conditionally skip sections of code. The skipped sections are not the part of compiled code.
#Const	This directive defines a preprocessor constant. This constant can only be used within a conditional compilation directive, not in regular code.
#ExternalSource and **#End ExternalSource**	These directives are used by the compiler to track line numbers for compiler error messages. You won't use them in your own code.
#Region and **#End Region**	These directives mark sections of code. A common example of these directives is the code generated by Windows Forms Designer. This marking can be used by visual designers such as Visual Studio .NET to show, hide, and format code.

In addition to the preprocessing directives, Visual Basic .NET also provides you with the `ConditionalAttribute` class. A method can be marked as conditional by applying the `Conditional` attribute to it. The `Conditional` attribute takes one argument that specifies a symbol. A symbol is just an arbitrary name that conditional compilation can use to make decisions. The conditional method is either included or omitted from the compiled code depending on the definition of the specified symbol at that point. If the symbol definition is available, the call to that method is included; otherwise, the method call is excluded from the compiled code. For example, this code will only be compiled if the DEBUG symbol is defined:

```
<Conditional("DEBUG")> _
Public Sub InitializeDebugMode()
    lblMode.Text =_
    " Debug Mode"
End Sub
```

A method must be a **Sub** rather than a **Function** to have the **Conditional** attribute applied to it.

Debugging

Debugging is the process of finding the cause of errors in a program, locating the lines of code causing the error, and then fixing those errors. Visual Studio .NET comes loaded with a large set of tools to help you with various debugging tasks.

Because of the compiled nature of ASP.NET applications, the process of debugging Web applications is almost the same as the process of debugging any other managed application. To enable debugging in an ASP.NET application, make sure that the debug attribute of the `<compilation>` element in the `Web.config` file is set to `True`.

```
<compilation
    debug="true">
</compilation>
```

Setting Breakpoints and Stepping Through Program Execution

A common technique for debugging is the step-by-step execution of a program, sometimes called *stepping*. The Debug menu provides three options for step execution of a program, as listed in Table 13.6. The Keyboard shortcuts listed in the table correspond to the Visual Basic settings of the Visual Studio IDE (Integrated Development Environment). If you have personalized the keyboard scheme either through the Tools, Options, Environment, Keyboard menu or through the VS .NET Start Page, you might have a different keyboard mapping. You can check out the keyboard mappings available for your customization through VS .NET's context-sensitive help.

Table 13.6	Debug Options for Step Execution	
Debug Menu Item	**Keyboard Shortcut**	**Purpose**
Step Into	F8	Executes the code in step mode. If a method call is encountered, the program execution steps into the code of the function and executes the method in step mode.
Step Over	Shift+F8	Use this key combination when a method call is encountered and you do not want to step in to the method code. When this key is pressed, the debugger will execute the entire method without any step-by-step execution (interruption) and then step to the next statement after the method call.

(continued)

Table 13.6 Debug Options for Step Execution *(continued)*		
Debug Menu Item	Keyboard Shortcut	Purpose
Step Out	Ctrl+Shift+F8	Use this key combination inside a method call to execute the rest of the method without stepping and resume step execution mode when the control reaches back to the calling method.

Breakpoints are markers in the code that signal the debugger to pause execution as soon as it encounters one. Once the debugger pauses at a breakpoint, you can inspect the program state and then choose to execute the program in step mode from this point onward.

If you have placed a breakpoint in the Click event handler of a button, the program will be paused when you click the button and the execution reaches to the point at which you have marked the breakpoint. You can now step through the execution for the rest of the event handler. Once the handler code is over, control will be transferred back to the form under execution. Be sure to insert breakpoints wherever you want execution to pause for debugging.

NOTE

Breakpoints and other debugging features are only available when you run your project using the Debug configuration.

You can choose to create a new breakpoint by selecting this option from the context menu of the code or from the toolbar in the Breakpoints window. The New Breakpoint dialog box has four different tabs that allow you to set a breakpoint in a function, in a file, at an address in the object code, and when the data value (value of a variable) changes.

Analyzing Program State to Resolve Errors

When you break the execution of a program, you have a program at a particular state in its execution cycle. You can use various debugger tools to analyze the values of variables, the result of expressions, the path of execution, and so on, to help you identify the cause of error that you are debugging. Table 13.7 lists the various windows that Visual Studio .NET provides to help you analyze program state.

Table 13.7 Debugging Windows in Visual Studio .NET

Debugging Window	Purpose
Watch	Watches the value of a variable or an expression.
Autos	Displays the values of variables in the current statement and in the previous statement.
Locals	Displays the values of all local variables.
Me	Shows the values associated with the current object (normally the current Web Form in an ASP.NET application).
Immediate	Allows you to evaluate expressions and execute commands.
Call Stack	Shows the method call stack, giving you information about the path taken by the code to reach the current point of execution.

Debugging on Exceptions

You can control the way the debugger behaves when it encounters a line of code that throws an exception. You can control this behavior through the Exceptions dialog box shown in Figure 13.2, which is invoked from the Debug, Exceptions menu option. The Exception dialog box allows you to control the debugger's behavior for each different type of exception defined in the system. If you have defined your own exceptions, you can also add them to this dialog box.

Figure 13.2 The Exceptions dialog box.

The two levels at which you can control behavior of the debugger for exceptional code are as follows:

➤ **When the exception is thrown**—You can instruct the debugger to either continue or break the execution of the program when an exception is thrown. The default setting for CLR exceptions is to continue the execution—possibly in anticipation that there will be an exception handler.

➤ **If the exception is not handled**—If the program that you are debugging fails to handle an exception, you can instruct the debugger to either ignore it and continue or break the execution of the program. The default setting for CLR exceptions is to break the execution, alarming the programmer of a possible problematic situation.

Debugging a Running Process

The Visual Studio .NET debugging environment also allows you to debug processes running outside the debugging environment. This feature can be quite helpful for debugging already deployed applications.

When a Web page is requested from the Web server, the ASP.NET worker process (`aspnet_wp.exe`) serves the request. To debug a running page, you need to attach the VS .NET debugger to the `aspnet_wp.exe` process running on the Web server. In addition to this, you also need to open the source files for the Web page in VS .NET and set a breakpoint in it at the desired location. Once this debugging setup is done, when you interact with the already running Web page, it will break into the debugger whenever the breakpoint is hit. Try these steps to see how this works:

1. Launch Internet Explorer. Navigate to a Web Form in your application.

2. Start a new instance of Visual Studio .NET. Select Tools, Debug Processes. You will now see the Processes dialog box. Change the Name field to point to the Web server used in step 1. Make sure that you check the Show System Processes option. Look for a process named `aspnet_wp.exe`.

3. Select the process named `aspnet_wp.exe` and click the Attach button. This will invoke an Attach to Process dialog box. Select the Common Language Runtime as your program type. Click the OK button. You will now see the selected process in the Debugged Processes section of the Processes dialog box. Click the Close button to close the Processes dialog box for now.

4. Now open the VB source code file for the Web Form file in the instance of VS .NET where you started debugging. If you set a breakpoint in this code, you'll discover that the running application will stop when the breakpoint is reached.

Debugging a Remote Process

The process of debugging a Remote process is almost the same as debugging an already running process. The only difference is that, prior to selecting a running process from the Processes dialog box, you must select the remote machine name from the Name list in the Processes dialog box.

Before you can debug a process remotely, you need to perform a one-time configuration on the remote machine (where the processes are running). You can do this in either of two ways:

➤ Install Visual Studio .NET on the remote machine. This installs much more software than you need for remote debugging, but it includes the remote debugging components.

➤ Install the Remote Components Setup on the remote machine. (You can start this from the Visual Studio .NET Setup Disc 1.)

The previous step will set up Machine Debug Manager (mdm.exe) on the remote computer. Mdm.exe will run as a background service on the computer and will provide remote debugging support. In addition to this, the previous step will also add the logged-on user to the Debugger Users group. You need to be a member of this group if you want to remotely access this computer. If the name is not added directly, you can always add a username to this group by using the Computer Management MMC Snap-in. By default, aspnet_wp.exe runs as a MACHINE process, so you must also have Administrator privileges on the remote machine to debug it.

If you get a DCOM configuration error while debugging, it is possible that you are not a member of the Debugger Users group on the remote machine.

Debugging Code in DLL Files

The process of debugging a DLL file for which you have the source code is similar to debugging a Web Form. There is one difference though; the code in a DLL file cannot be directly invoked, so you need to have a Web Form that calls various methods from the DLL files.

You typically need to take the following steps for debugging code in a DLL file:

1. Launch the Web Form that uses the methods in the DLL file.

2. Launch Visual Studio .NET and attach the debugger on the Web Form. Set a breakpoint where the method in the DLL file is called. Continue with the execution.

3. The execution will break when the breakpoint is reached. At this point, select Step Into from the Debug menu to step in to the source code of the DLL file. Execute the code in the DLL file in step mode while you watch the value of its variables.

In addition to this, if the code files are executing on a remote machine, make sure that the remote machine is set up with Remote Debugging support as explained in the previous section.

Debugging Client-Side Scripts

Visual Studio .NET also allows you to debug client-side scripts. The process is similar to the process for ASP.NET Web Forms that was discussed earlier. However, you must note the following points for client-side scripting:

➤ Client-side debugging only works with Microsoft Internet Explorer.

➤ You have to enable script debugging in Internet Explorer.

➤ Attach the debugger to the `iexplore.exe` process displaying the Web Form.

Exam Prep Questions

Question 1

> You want to debug an ASP.NET Web Application that is installed on a remote computer. Which of these steps should you take to enable debugging (select all correct answers)?
>
> ❑ A. Install Visual Studio .NET on your local computer.
>
> ❑ B. Install Visual Studio .NET on the remote computer.
>
> ❑ C. Run the Remote Components setup on your local computer.
>
> ❑ D. Run the Remote Components setup on the remote computer.

Answers A, B, and D are correct. Visual Studio .NET provides the user interface tools that you need to debug a process, while the Remote Components setup puts into place the components that are needed to attach to a running process. Answer C is incorrect because there is no need for a local copy of the Remote Components in this scenario. Note that Answer B installs more software than you'll really need on the remote computer unless you plan to do actual development there.

Question 2

> You are debugging a complex process in the code-behind file of a Web Form. You want to keep an eye on the variable values that apply to the current statement. Which debugging window should you keep open for this purpose?
>
> ○ A. Locals
>
> ○ B. Watch
>
> ○ C. Autos
>
> ○ D. Immediate

Answer C is correct. The Autos window automatically shows the values of variables in the current statement and in the previous statement. Answer A is incorrect because the Locals window shows the values of all local variables. Answer B is incorrect because the Watch window shows the value of expressions that you enter. Answer D is incorrect because the Immediate window is used to evaluate expressions and enter commands.

Question 3

You want to view the trace output for your Web application. The Web application root directory is at **http://localhost/bizapp**. Which of the following URLs would you type in the Internet Explorer to view the trace result for this application?

- ○ A. **http://localhost/bizapp/trace.axd**
- ○ B. **http://localhost/bizapp/trace**
- ○ C. **http://localhost/bizapp?trace=true**
- ○ D. **http://localhost/bizapp?trace=ON**

Answer A is correct. The .axd extension is intercepted by ASP.NET and directs ASP.NET to display the stored tracing information for the specified application. Answers B, C, and D are incorrect because the URLs are incorrect for tracing.

Question 4

You have just fixed a bug in your company's Web Application, which has already been deployed. You are certain that your bug fix is correct because you have tested it in isolation. Which sort of testing should you perform before making the fix on the live Web site?

- ○ A. Unit Testing
- ○ B. Integration Testing
- ○ C. Top-Down Testing
- ○ D. Regression Testing

Answer D is correct. The purpose of regression testing is to ensure that changes to code do not break code that was previously working. Answer A is incorrect because you have already performed unit testing when you tested the fix in isolation. Answer B is incorrect because integration testing is used when an application is being assembled from components. Answer C is incorrect because top-down testing is a special case of integration testing.

Question 5

Your application's **Web.config** file contains the following directive:

```
<trace
    enabled="true"
    requestLimit="10"
    pageOutput="true"
    traceMode="SortByTime"
    localOnly="true"
/>
```

The **Form1.aspx** file in this application has this **Page** directive:

```
<%@ Page Language="vb" AutoEventWireup="false"
 Codebehind="Form1.aspx.vb"
 Inherits="MyApp.Form1" Trace="False"%>
```

The **Form2.aspx** file in this application has this **Page** directive:

```
<%@ Page Language="vb" AutoEventWireup="false"
 Codebehind="Form2.aspx.vb"
 Inherits="MyApp.Form2" Trace="True"%>
```

You run your application and navigate to Form1 and then Form2. What is the result?

- ○ A. Trace output appears on Form1 only.
- ○ B. Trace output appears on Form2 only.
- ○ C. Trace output appears on both Form1 and Form2.
- ○ D. Trace output does not appear on Form1 or Form2.

Answer B is correct. The page-level directive overrides the trace setting for the application, so Form1 does not display trace output. The page-level directive on Form2 and the application setting both direct the application to display trace output on Form2. Answers A and C are incorrect because Form1 will not display trace output. Answer D is incorrect because Form2 will display trace output.

Question 6

You want your application to display a warning in the Output window whenever a particular variable has the value of zero at a certain point in your program. Which method could you use?

- ○ A. **TraceContext.Warn**
- ○ B. **Debug.Assert**
- ○ C. **Trace.Flush**
- ○ D. **TraceSwitch.TraceWarning**

Answer B is correct. The Debug.Assert method can be used to send output to the Output window if a particular expression (such as var<>0) evaluates to false. Answer A is incorrect because the TraceContext class places its output on the Web Form rather than in the Output window. Answer C is incorrect because the Flush method writes pending output. Answer D is incorrect because the TraceWarning property of the TraceSwitch is used to check the settings of the TraceSwitch object.

Question 7

Your Web Form includes the following statement in its Load event handler:

```
Trace.Listeners.Add( _
  New TextWriterTraceListener( _
  Server.MapPath("TraceLog.txt")))
```

You run the application in the default Release configuration. With this setting, which of these statements is true (select all that apply)?

- ❑ A. Messages from the **System.Diagnostics.Debug** class will be written to the Output window.
- ❑ B. Messages from the **System.Diagnostics.Trace** class will be written to the Output window.
- ❑ C. Messages from the **System.Diagnostics.Debug** class will be written to the **TraceLog.txt** file.
- ❑ D. Messages from the **System.Diagnostics.Trace** class will be written to the **TraceLog.txt** file.

Answers B and D are correct. In Release configuration, the TRACE symbol is defined, but the DEBUG symbol is not defined. This prevents the Debug class from generating output. Trace messages are always written to the Output window. Adding a Listener to the Listeners collection causes messages to be written to that listener (in this case, the text file) as well. Answers A and C are incorrect because the Debug class will not generate output in this configuration.

Question 8

You place a breakpoint at the first statement in the Click event handler of btnTest on a Web Form. You run the application, click the button, and then single-step through the code until you reach the End Sub statement in the Click event handler. Then you click a different button, btnCheck. There is no breakpoint in btnCheck's event handler. What happens?

- ○ A. The application enters single-step mode on the first statement in btnCheck's event handler.
- ○ B. The application begins to execute btnCheck's event handler and stops at the first subroutine call.
- ○ C. The application executes btnCheck's event handler without stopping.
- ○ D. The application enters single-step mode on the first statement in btnCheck's event handler.

Answer C is correct. When you reach the End Sub statement in the first event handler, the application exits single-step mode. It won't return to single-step mode until it hits another breakpoint.

Question 9

Your Visual Basic .NET program includes the following lines of code:

```
Dim myTraceSwitch As TraceSwitch = _
  New TraceSwitch("MySwitch", _
  "Switch Set in code")
myTraceSwitch.Level = TraceLevel.Info
```

Which of the following expressions in your program will evaluate to **True** (select all correct answers)?

- ❑ A. **myTraceSwitch.TraceInfo**
- ❑ B. **myTraceSwitch.TraceError**
- ❑ C. **myTraceSwitch.TraceVerbose**
- ❑ D. **myTraceSwitch.TraceWarning**

Answers A, B, and D are correct. When you set the switch level to info, it responds to all error, warning, and info trace messages. Answer C is incorrect because only verbose trace messages are suppressed.

Need to Know More?

 Burton, Kevin. *.NET Common Language Runtime Unleashed.* Sams, 2002.

 ASP.NET QuickStart Tutorial, "The Microsoft .NET Framework SDK Debugger."

Deploying a Web Application

Terms you'll need to understand:

✓ Delayed signing
✓ Deployment
✓ Merge module
✓ Native compilation
✓ Native Image Cache
✓ Web Garden
✓ Web Farm
✓ Cluster

Techniques you'll need to master:

✓ Creating setup and deployment projects for Web applications
✓ Adding assemblies to the Global Assembly Cache
✓ Deploying a Web application
✓ Deploying an application to a Web garden, Web farm, or cluster

Once you have developed and tested a Web application, the next step is to deploy the application so that the end user can run it. The complexity and requirements of the application should be kept in mind in order to choose the right deployment tool. Depending on the application, a simple XCOPY deployment might be sufficient, or you might have to build a Windows Installer–based setup application.

The .NET Framework and Visual Studio .NET offer tools to support a wide variety of deployment scenarios.

Deployment Tools

A deployment tool helps you to set up an application on the user's computer. Choosing the right deployment tool is important to minimize costs and to optimize the experience of your users.

XCOPY Deployment

The .NET Framework simplifies deployment by making zero-impact install and XCOPY deployment feasible. Many .NET applications can be installed simply by using the XCOPY command to copy all their files to the target computer. But some things cannot be done with this simple means of deployment, such as creating IIS sites, adding assemblies to the Global Assembly Cache (GAC), or adding custom event logs to the target machine.

FTP Deployment

When you're deploying a Web application to a Web server to which you don't have a direct network connection, you can still achieve a simple file copy deployment by using FTP. ASP.NET's design lets you upgrade an application by using FTP to replace files. This is because ASP.NET monitors the source code of your Web applications and automatically recompiles any files that are replaced.

FTP deployment is logically the same as XCOPY deployment; both are merely ways to move a file or set of files to a deployment location. FTP deployment suffers from the same lack of advanced features as XCOPY deployment. To satisfy advanced requirements, you'll still need to use the Windows Installer.

Microsoft Windows Installer

The Microsoft Windows Installer is an installation and configuration service built in to the Windows operating system. It gives you complete control over installation of an application, a component, or an update.

The Windows Installer includes many built-in actions for performing the installation process. Among the actions that the Installer can perform are the following:

➤ Install files.

➤ Create shortcuts.

➤ Create registry keys.

➤ Run SQL scripts and other programs during installation.

➤ Provide "on-demand" installation of features.

➤ Manage repairs, updates, and uninstallations.

When you create an installation program for the Windows Installer service, the end result is a Windows Installer (.msi) package. When this package is executed on the target machine, the Windows Installation service will install the program by reading the installation information stored in the Windows Installer package.

You can create a Windows Installer package by using the Setup and Deployment Visual Studio .NET projects, or by using installation tools from vendors such as ActiveInstall, InstallShield, or Wise Solutions.

Deploying a Web Application

Microsoft Visual Studio .NET allows you to create Windows Installer–based installation packages. It offers four types of deployment project templates:

➤ **Setup Project**—Used to create installation packages for deploying Windows-based applications.

➤ **Web Setup Project**—Used to create installation packages for deploying Web-based applications. This is the most important type for this exam.

➤ **Merge Module Project**—Used to create installation packages for components that may be shared by multiple applications.

➤ **Cab Project**—Used to package ActiveX components so that they can be downloaded over the Internet. This type of project is largely obsolete.

Creating a Web Setup Project

Visual Studio .NET provides a Setup project template to create an installer for a Web application. It also provides a Setup Wizard that helps you in creating different types of setup and deployment projects using an interactive interface. Typically, you run this Wizard to create a setup project in the same solution that contains the Web application that you wish to deploy. Here's an outline of the steps involved:

1. In the Solution Explorer window, right-click the Solution and select Add, New Project. Select Setup and Deployment projects from the Project Types tree and then select Setup Wizard from the list of templates on the right.

2. Name the project and click OK. This will launch the Setup Wizard. The first screen that will appear is the Welcome screen. Click Next.

3. The second page will show the Choose a Project Type screen. Choose Create a Setup for a Web Application in the first group of options as shown in Figure 14.1. Click Next.

4. The third page will show the Choose Project Outputs to Include screen. Generally you should select Primary Output from *ProjectName* and Content Files from *ProjectName*. Click Next.

5. The fourth page will show the Choose Files to Include screen. Click the Add button to include any additional files such as readme files, licensing agreements, or help files. Click Next.

6. The fifth and last page will show a summary of your choices. Click Finish to create the setup project.

When a setup project is compiled, the output files are placed in the Release or Debug folder, depending on the active configuration. The contents of the folder are an installer package (.msi), executables (.exe), and initialization (.ini) files. The .msi file is the installation package in the Microsoft Windows Installer format. If the Windows Installer Service is installed on your computer, you can directly start the installation by double-clicking this file. The executable files consist of Setup.exe, InstMsiA.exe, and InstMsiW.exe. Setup.exe (also called the *Windows Installer Bootstrapper*) bootstraps the installation process by first testing for the presence of the Windows Installer service on the target machine. If the Windows Installer service is not installed, the bootstrapper will first install it using either InstMsiA.exe (for Windows 9x and Me) or InstMsiW.exe (for Windows NT/2000/XP/.NET) and then will instruct the Windows Installer service to execute the installation based on the information stored in the installation package (.msi file).

The setup.ini file stores the initialization settings, such as the name of the installation database, for the bootstrap file setup.exe.

 Setup projects created with Visual Studio .NET will only work on the computers where the .NET Framework runtime has been already installed. For a setup that can be installed from scratch, you should consider using a third-party tool.

The output files generated can be deployed (copied) to any target machine and then be installed and later uninstalled. When an application is uninstalled, all the actions performed by the installer application during the installation on the target machine are undone, leaving the target machine to its original state. You can also choose to repair or reinstall the application installed by clicking the Change button in the Add/Remove Programs dialog box.

Customizing Setup Projects

Visual Studio .NET provides several different editors to customize various aspects of the installation process. These are discussed in the following sections.

You can view an editor by either choosing its icon from the Solution Explorer or selecting the Project in Solution Explorer and choosing View and the respective editor option from its shortcut menu.

Using the File System Editor

The File System Editor provides a mapping of the file system on the target machine. The folders are referred to by special names that are converted to represent the folder on the target machine during the installation process. For example, the special folder User's Desktop will be converted to the actual desktop path on the target machine at the time of installation.

You can add special folders by selecting the File System on the Target Machine node in the left pane and choosing the Add Special Folder option from its context menu. Many types of special folders exist such as Application Folder, Common Files Folder, Program Files Folder, User's Desktop, System Folder, User's Startup Folder, and others—each of which represents a particular folder on the target machine.

You can use the context menus in the File System Editor to select additional files to deploy or to create shortcuts on the target computer.

Using the Registry Editor

The Registry Editor allows you to specify registry keys, subkeys, and values that are added to the registry in the target machine during installation. You can also import registry files to the Registry Editor.

Using the File Types Editor

The File Types Editor provides the facility to associate file extensions and actions with an application. For example, files with the extension .doc are normally associated with Microsoft Word or WordPad. I'm mentioning this editor only for the sake of completeness. You're unlikely to need the File Types Editor for an ASP.NET application because all the file types that your application uses will be processed by ASP.NET.

Using the User Interface Editor

The User Interface Editor allows you to customize the user interface that is provided to the user during the installation process. The user interface is nothing but the various dialog boxes that appear during the installation process. The user interface provided to the user is divided into three stages—Start, Progress, and End. You can add different types of dialog boxes at each stage. Each stage allows only certain types of dialog boxes to be added. For example, you might choose to add a license agreement dialog box to the Start stage.

The User Interface Editor displays the user interface applicable to both end-user installation and administrative. You can customize the user interface for both types of installations. The administrative installation occurs when you run the msiexec command line tool with the /a option. This is the type of installation you can use to make an application available for installation over a network.

Using the Custom Actions Editor

The Custom Actions Editor allows you to run compiled .dll or .exe files or assemblies at the end of the installation. These files can be used to perform custom actions that are vital but were not carried out during the installation. If the custom action fails, the entire installation process is rolled back. For example, you might have to install the database required by your application during the installation process.

You can add custom actions to be performed when an application is installed, when the install is completed, when a failed install is rolled back, or when an application is uninstalled.

Using the Launch Conditions Editor

The Launch Conditions Editor allows you to set conditions to be evaluated when the installation begins on the target machine. If the conditions are not met, the installation stops. For example, you would like to install your Visual Basic .NET application only if the .NET Framework runtime exists on the target machine. By default, this condition is added by Visual Studio .NET. You might also need to perform other checks such as whether a particular file exists on the target machine or verify a particular registry key value on the target machine.

The Launch Conditions Editor allows you to perform searches on the target machine for a file, registry key, or Windows Installer components. For example, you can determine whether the Microsoft Data Access Components package (MDAC) is installed on the target machine by making a search in the registry for a particular registry key value. If the search fails, you can abort the installation.

Setup and Deployment Project Editor elements such as folders, files, registry keys, custom actions, launch conditions, and so on have a Condition property. The Condition property consists of a valid conditional statement in the form of a string that evaluates to either True or False. Such strings can refer to any Launch Condition that is part of the setup project.

The conditional statement is executed during installation, and if it returns True, the action associated with that particular element is performed on the target machine. For example, a condition is applied to a registry key value, and if it evaluates to False during installation, the particular key value will not be entered in the registry on the target machine.

Shared Assemblies

A *shared assembly* is shared among multiple applications on a machine. It is therefore stored at a central location called the Global Assembly Cache (GAC) and enjoys special services such as file security, shared location, and side-by-side versioning.

Because shared assemblies are all installed at a central location, distinguishing them with just a filename is not enough. You would not like your application to break when some other vendor installs an assembly with the same name in the GAC. To avoid this possibility, Microsoft requires you to assign a strong name to each assembly before placing it in the GAC.

Assigning a Strong Name to an Assembly

An assembly is identified by its text name (usually the name of the file without the file extension), version number, and culture information. However, these pieces of information do not guarantee that an assembly will be unique. There might be a case in which two software publishers end up using the same identity for an assembly, thereby causing applications using those assemblies to behave abnormally. This problem can be greatly reduced by assigning a strong name to an assembly. A strong name strengthens an assembly's identity by qualifying it by the software publisher's identity. The .NET Framework uses a standard cryptography technique known as digital signing to ensure uniqueness of an assembly.

The process of digital signing involves two related pieces of binary data known as the *public key* and *private key*. The public key represents the software publisher's identity and is freely distributed. While creating a strong named assembly, the public key is stored in the assembly manifest along with other identification information such as the name, version number, and culture of the assembly. This scheme does not look foolproof because after all the public key is available freely and nobody can stop a software publisher from using some other company's public key. To verify that only the legitimate owner of the public key has created the assembly, an assembly is signed using the publisher's private key. The private key is assumed to be known only to the publisher of the assembly. The process of signing an assembly and verifying its signature works like this:

> ➤ **Signing an assembly**—A signature is created by computing a cryptographic hash from the contents of the assembly. The hash is encoded with the private key. This signature is then stored within the assembly.

> ➤ **Verifying the signature**—Later when the CLR (Common Language Runtime) verifies an assembly's identity, it will read its public key from the assembly manifest and use it to decrypt the cryptographic hash stored in the assembly. It will then recalculate the hash for the current contents of the assembly. If the two hashes match, it ensures two things: First, the contents of the assembly were not tampered with after it was signed, and, second, only the person having a private key associated with the public key stored in the assembly has signed the assembly.

To sign an assembly, you must first generate a public/private key pair by using the Strong Name tool (sn.exe) available in the .NET Framework SDK. Then you can specify that key pair by using the AssemblyKeyFile attribute in the AssemblyInfo.vb file, as in this example:

```
<Assembly: AssemblyVersion("1.0")>
<Assembly: AssemblyKeyFile( _
 "..\..\RandNumCorpKeys.snk")>
```

Adding an Assembly to the Global Assembly Cache

Once you have associated a strong name with an assembly, you can place it in the GAC. There are several ways in which you can add an assembly to the Global Assembly Cache. Using the Windows Installer is the recommended approach, but there are some quick alternatives too. However, these quick approaches should be used only for development purposes and are not recommended for installing assemblies on the end user's computer.

NOTE You need to have administrative privileges on a computer to manage its Global Assembly Cache.

Using Windows Installer

Using Microsoft Windows Installer is the preferred way of adding assemblies to the Global Assembly Cache. It maintains a reference counting for assemblies in the GAC and provides uninstallation support. To add an assembly to the GAC with the Windows Installer, you can place the assembly in the Global Assembly Cache within the File System Editor in a Setup and Deployment project.

Using Windows Explorer

When the .NET Framework is installed, it also installs the Assembly Cache Viewer Shell Extension (`shfusion.dll`). This extension allows you to view the complex structure of the GAC folder in a much more navigable and understandable manner. Because it is integrated with Windows Shell, you can view and manage GAC contents with the help of Windows Explorer. Dragging and dropping a file to the Assembly Cache folder (usually `c:\WINNT\assembly` or `C:\Windows\assembly`) will add it to the GAC.

If you want to remove a file from the GAC that you added this way, just delete it from the Windows Explorer by selecting the delete option from the File menu or the shortcut menu.

Using the .NET Framework Configuration Tool

You can also use the .NET Framework Configuration Tool (`mscorcfg.msc`) to manage an assembly in the GAC. You can launch this tool from the Administrative Tools menu on your computer. The Assembly Cache folder in the tool allows you to add an assembly to the GAC by clicking a link and following instructions.

Using the Global Assembly Cache Tool (GacUtil.exe)

GacUtil.exe is a command-line tool that is especially useful to add or remove assemblies from the GAC from a program script or a batch file. To install an assembly to the GAC, call the tool with the /i switch:

```
gacutil /i RandomNumberGenerator.dll
```

You can list all the assemblies in the GAC using the gacutil.exe tool with the /l option. You can use the /u option with the name of the assembly (without the file extension) to uninstall the assembly from the GAC.

```
gacutil /u RandomNumberGenerator
```

Delay Signing an Assembly

Normally, when you sign an assembly, you use a key file that contains both the public key and the private key for a company. But the private key ensures that the assembly is signed only by its advertised publisher. Thus in most companies, the private key is stored securely, and only a few people have access to it.

If the keys are highly protected, it might be difficult to frequently access the private key when multiple developers of a company are building assemblies several times a day. To solve this problem, the .NET Framework uses a technique of delay signing an assembly.

Using delay signing, you will use only the public key to build an assembly. Associating public keys with an assembly will allow you to place the assembly in the GAC and complete most of the development and testing tasks with the assembly. Later, when you are ready to package the assembly, someone who is authorized will sign the assembly with the private key. Signing with the private key will ensure that the CLR will provide tamper protection for your assembly.

Creating a Setup Project for Distributing Components

When you have a component that will be shared among multiple applications, you should package it as a merge module (.msm file). A merge module will include the actual component such as a .dll along with any related setup logic, such as adding resources, registry entries, custom actions, and launch conditions.

When you modify a component to release new versions, you will create a new merge module for each of its new versions. A new merge module should be created for each successive version of a component in order to avoid version conflicts.

Merge modules cannot be directly installed. They need to be merged with installers of applications that use the component packed into a merge module.

Here are the general steps for creating a merge module:

1. In the Solution Explorer window, right-click the Solution and select Add, New Project. Select Setup and Deployment projects from the Project Types tree and then select Setup Wizard from the list of templates on the right. Name the project.

2. The first screen that will appear is the Welcome screen. Click Next. The second page will show the Choose a Project Type screen. Choose the Create a Merge Module for Windows Installer option in the second group. (Do you want to create a redistributable package?) Click Next.

3. The third page will show the Choose Project Outputs to Include screen. Select Primary Output from `ComponentProjectName`. Click Next. Click Next on the fourth page, and then click Finish.

4. Build the project to create the merge module.

If you want to distribute this component later with a Windows application, you can just add the merge module to your application's setup project like any other project output.

Creating Installation Components

When you develop an application using Visual Studio .NET, you may use several resources at the time of development, such as databases, event logs, performance counters, message queues, and so on. However, when you install the program on a user's machine, these resources might not be present there. A good installation program ensures that all necessary resources required by an application exist on the target machine.

The .NET Framework provides you with an `Installer` class that is defined in the `System.Configuration.Install` namespace. This class is specifically designed to help you perform customized installation actions like those mentioned previously. Visual Studio .NET supplies some predefined installation classes, and you can also create your own custom installation classes.

Understanding the Installer Class

The System.Configuration.Install.Installer class works as a base class for all the custom installers in the .NET Framework. Table 14.1 lists some of the important members of the Installer class.

Table 14.1 Important Members of the Installer Class

Member Name	Type	Description
Commit	Method	The code in the **Commit()** method is executed if the **Install()** method executes successfully.
Install	Method	Performs the specified actions during an application's installation.
Installers	Property	Collection of **Installer** objects that are needed for this **Installer** instance to successfully install a component.
Rollback	Method	If the **Install()** method fails for some reason, the code in the **Rollback()** method is called to undo any custom actions performed during the **Install** method.
Uninstall	Method	Performs the specified actions when a previously installed application is uninstalled.

You can derive a class from the Installer class and override the methods given in Table 14.1 to perform any custom actions.

If you want the derived Installer class to execute when an assembly is installed using a Setup project or by using the Installer tool (InstallUtil.exe), you need to decorate the class with RunInstallerAttribute set to True, as shown here:

```
<RunInstaller(true)>
```

Working with Predefined Installation Components

Most of the components available through the Server Explorer have a predefined installation component associated with them. For example, creating an instance of the EventLog component in your project allows you to add an installer corresponding to it with your project. When you set the properties of an EventLog object in your program, those properties will be stored by the Installer component and will be reproduced on the target machine when the application is deployed.

These steps will show you how to include an Installer component in your project:

1. Create a new Visual Basic ASP.NET Web application project.

2. Rename `WebForm1.aspx` to `EventLogApplication.aspx` in the project.

3. Open Server Explorer. Expand the tree under Event Logs. Drag and drop the Application event log to the Web Form. This will create an `EventLog1` object that you will see in the component tray.

4. Change the `Source` property of `EventLog1` to `EventLogApplication`. Change the `MachineName` property to . (a single dot) so that it will refer to the local computer no matter what computer the application is installed on. Click the Add Installer link just above the description area in the Properties window. This will add a new class named `ProjectInstaller.vb` to the project. You will see that in design mode, `ProjectInstaller.vb` contains an object named `EventLogInstaller1`. This is the installation component for the event log.

5. Switch to the code view of `ProjectInstaller.vb`. You will note the use of the following attribute within the code for the `ProjectInstaller` class.

```
<RunInstaller(true)>
```

This attribute specifies that this code should be invoked during the installation of an assembly. View the component designer–generated code for this class. You will find all the necessary coding for installing an event log or event source on the target machine.

6. Switch to the design view of `EventLogApplication.aspx`, and add a `TextBox` (`txtMessage`) and a `Button` (`btnWrite`) control to the Form. Double-click the `Button` control to attach an event handler to its `Click` event. Add the following code to the event handler:

```
Private Sub btnWrite_Click( _
  ByVal sender As System.Object, _
  ByVal e As System.EventArgs) Handles btnWrite.Click
    EventLog1.WriteEntry(txtMessage.Text)
End Sub
```

Allowing an event log to access ASP.NET forms can be a security risk. If you're running ASP.NET as the untrusted machine account, this code won't run. You'll need to configure ASP.NET to use the trusted System account to complete this example. See Chapter 16, "Configuring a Web Application," for more details.

7. Build your project using the `Release` mode. This project is now ready for deployment. If you create a Setup project for this project and run the setup project, it will install the `EventLog` component.

Deploying an Assembly Containing Installation Components

The two ways in which an assembly containing installation components can be deployed are as follows:

➤ Using a setup and deployment project

➤ Using the Installer tool (InstallUtil.exe)

Deploying an Installation Component Using a Setup Project

To deploy an application that consists of installation components, you will create a setup project as you would do normally. But this time, you will use the Custom Actions Editor to deploy the additional resources needed for the application. At the time of deployment, the deployment project will execute the ProjectInstaller class as a part of its custom installation action to create component resources. Here's how to do this for the example you just created:

1. Add a New Web Setup project to the solution. Name the project EventLogApplicationSetup.

2. Right-click the EventLogApplicationSetup project in the Solution Explorer. Select Add, Project Output from its shortcut menu. In the Add Project Output Group dialog box, select Primary Output and Content Files of the EventLogApplication project. Click OK.

3. Open the Custom Actions Editor for the EventLogApplicationSetup project. Select the Custom Actions node, and select Add Custom Action from its shortcut menu. This will open the Select Item in Project dialog box. Look in the Web Application Folder and select Primary Output from EventLogApplication(Active). Click OK. The primary output will be added to all the four nodes under Custom actions Install, Commit, Rollback, and Uninstall.

4. Select the EventLogApplicationSetup project in the Solution Explorer. Activate the Properties window. Set the Manufacturer to EventLog Application and the ProductName to EventLogApplication.

5. Build the EventLogApplicationSetup project. Take the project's output to a computer that does not already have an event source for the EventLogApplication. Alternatively, clear out the event log to wipe out previous traces of the program. Run the installation. You will note that the setup program will install the EventLogApplication along with the required event source.

6. Run the application's executable from the installation folder. Enter some text and click the button. Launch the Event Viewer from the Administrative Tools section of the Windows Control Panel. Select the Application log under the Event Viewer node. You will notice your event log entries in the right pane of the event viewer.

Deploying an Installation Component Using the Installer Tool (Installutil.exe)

You can also use the command-line Installer tool (`Installutil.exe`) to install assemblies that contain additional component resources.

To install the resources contained in an assembly named `Assembly1.dll`, you can use the following form of the `Installutil.exe` command:

```
Installutil.exe Assembly1.dll
```

You can also install resources contained in multiple assemblies together:

```
InstallUtil.exe Assembly1.dll Assembly2.dll Assembly3.dll
```

If you instead want to launch the uninstaller for installation classes stored in an assembly, you will use the `/u` or `/uninstall` option with the command:

```
InstallUtil.exe /u Assembly1.dll
```

If you are installing components from multiple assemblies using the **InstallUtil.exe** command, and any of the assemblies fails to install, **InstallUtil.exe** will roll back the installations of all the assemblies.

Working with Installer Classes

You can add your own `Installer` classes to a project to perform custom actions during installation, such as compiling the code to native image or creating a database on a target computer. These compiled `Installer` classes from your project are then added to the deployment project as custom actions that are run at the end of the installation. The following are typical actions you would perform while creating a Custom Installer class:

➤ Inherit a class from the `Installer` class.

➤ Make sure that the `RunInstallerAttribute` is set to `True` in the derived class.

➤ Override the `Install()`, `Commit()`, `Rollback()`, and `Uninstall()` methods to perform any custom actions.

➤ In a Setup project, use the Custom Action Editor to invoke this derived class to do the required processing.

➤ If needed, pass arguments from the Custom Actions Editor to the custom `Installer` class using the `CustomActionData` property.

Scalable and Reliable Deployment

Web applications can be subject to considerable traffic. A popular Web site might have to support hundreds or thousands of simultaneous users. To handle this load reliably, designers have developed several server architectures. You should be aware of the differences between these architectures and their uses:

➤ Web garden

➤ Web farm

➤ Cluster

 Although Web gardens and Web farms offer increased scalability for your application, they can involve other trade-offs. In particular, if your application is distributed across multiple processors or multiple computers, you can't use simple session state to store user-related information; you'll need to move to using the State Service or a SQL Server database to store session state. See Chapter 16 for more details on session state.

Web Gardens

A *Web garden* is a Web application that is distributed across more than one processor on a multiprocessor computer. Web gardening is the default behavior for ASP.NET. For example, suppose that you install an ASP.NET application on a computer with eight CPUs. In this case, ASP.NET will automatically launch eight worker processes to handle incoming Web requests and assign one of these processes to each CPU (a procedure known as setting the affinity of the process).

Web gardens offer the benefit of faster response times on a multiple CPU computer. In particular, if one worker process hangs or slows down because of programming errors or unexpected input, the Web garden can continue serving requests from the other worker processes.

Because ASP.NET enables this behavior automatically, you don't have to do anything to gain the benefit of a Web garden. However, you might want to configure your Web server to not use every processor for Web gardening.

To do this, you can set the value of two attributes within the `processModel` element of the `Web.config` file:

➤ `webGarden`—When set to `True`, this attribute directs Windows to schedule processes to CPUs (thus enabling the default behavior of Web gardening). When set to `False`, this attribute uses the `cpuMask` attribute to determine which processors should participate in a Web garden.

➤ `cpuMask`—This attribute is a bitmask indicating which processors should participate in a Web garden. For example, setting `cpuMask` to 7 would indicate that processors 0, 1, and 2 (and no others) should participate in a Web garden.

Changes to the `processModel` element only take effect when IIS is restarted and are only effective in the top-level `Web.config` file. For these reasons, Web gardening is best customized by the system administrator rather than as part of a setup package.

Web Farms

A *Web farm* takes the concept of a Web garden and extends it to multiple computers. In a Web farm, your application runs on multiple Web servers at the same time. Some mechanism outside of the Web servers is used to distribute requests to the individual servers.

Web farms offer the benefits of both scalability and reliability. Your application is more scalable because you can increase its capacity by adding more computers to the Web farm. Your application is more reliable because a failure of any one server does not affect the other servers. Although requests that were in process at the failing server might not receive responses, the other computers in the Web farm can continue running despite the failure.

Web farms are typically enabled by a technique known as *Network Load Balancing (NLB)*. NLB can be implemented in either hardware or software. Hardware devices, such as Cisco LocalDirector or F5 Networks' BIG-IP, distribute incoming HTTP requests among a pool of Web servers. Software NLB is built in to the Windows 2000 Advanced Server operating system and is available for the Windows 2000 Server operating system as part of Microsoft Application Center. Software NLB, although not supporting quite as many computers as hardware NLB, is less expensive to implement.

Provided that you've chosen an appropriate option for storing session state, you do not need to change your application at all for deployment on a Web farm. Your system administrator can simply run the setup program for your application on each server in the Web farm, and then configure the Web farm using the tools built in to Windows 2000 or Application Center.

Clusters

Clustering provides a second method of combining multiple computers for a single purpose. The goal of clustering is not to provide additional scalability, but to provide additional reliability. In a cluster, multiple computers are configured using the same software, but only one of these computers is active at any given time. The active server handles all requests unless it experiences a hardware or software failure. At that point, the clustering software automatically directs requests to the standby server, which becomes the new active server.

Clustering solutions are typically implemented with hardware that includes shared storage. You might, for example, have two computers sharing the same external array of hard drives to store information. If the active server fails, the standby server can pick up where the active server left off, using the same disks for storing application data.

Clustering is a built-in feature of the Windows server operating systems. You can also use products such as Microsoft Application Center to make it easier to manage software on a cluster. But like Web farms, clusters have no impact on the coding of your Visual Basic .NET applications.

Methods of Deployment

After you have created a setup package, you can deploy your application from any location that's accessible to all its potential users. The Web-based applications exam requires you to know about two types of deployment:

➤ Deployment via removable media

➤ Web-based deployment

Deployment via Removable Media

The most common examples of removable media are floppy disks, CD-ROMs, and DVDs. Deployment via removable media is suitable under the following conditions:

➤ Users are in many locations without any common central connection.

➤ Not all users have access to the Internet.

➤ Application size is huge and not all users have access to a high-speed Internet connection.

Deployment via removable media is becoming more outdated with every new day. It involves costs for media, replication, and distribution that can be easily eliminated by other deployment options. But deployment via removable media is still the "lowest common denominator" solution and will cover the maximum number of users.

Deployment projects in Visual Studio .NET can be used to create packages divided across multiple files—each with a small size as specified by the developer. These small-sized files then can be copied to floppy disks or CD-ROM and distributed to the users.

To create a setup project for removable media, create a setup project as you would normally. Right-click the project in the Solution Explorer window and select Properties from its shortcut menu. In the Properties page, change Package files to "In cabinet file(s)." This will enable the CAB size option. Set the CAB size to custom and set the size depending on your media size.

Web-Based Deployment

Web-based deployment is the most popular form of deployment, especially for small-sized applications. With the growth of high-speed Internet connections, you will see this form of deployment in higher demand as compared to removable media. It offers several advantages over other forms of application deployment:

➤ It reduces the cost of media, replication, and distribution.

➤ Management of software updates is simple. You can program an application so that it can check for updates automatically on the Web or you can instruct users to download the setup from a Web page.

Creating a setup package for Web-based deployment is the same as creating a setup package for direct deployment, just as you did earlier in this chapter. Once the setup files are created, rather than copying them to a network share or directly to the target computer, you will copy them to a virtual directory on a Web server. You might also want to password protect the deployment Web site so that only authorized users are able to download your application. You can then install the application by navigating to the virtual directory and executing the Setup.exe program that you find there.

Exam Prep Questions

Question 1

> Which of the following setup requirements would force you to use the Windows Installer service rather than FTP or XCOPY deployment? (Select all correct answers.)
>
> ❑ A. Copying new files to the target computer
>
> ❑ B. Adding a file to the Global Assembly Cache
>
> ❑ C. Replacing an existing Web Form in a deployed Web application
>
> ❑ D. Adding a performance counter to the target computer

Answers B and D are correct. Although the GAC is represented as a folder within Windows Explorer, you cannot place files in this folder simply by copying them. Performance counter creation also requires running code on the target machine, instead of just copying files. Answer A is incorrect because XCOPY or FTP can copy files. Answer C is incorrect because ASP.NET is designed to allow you to replace a Web Form simply by copying the new version to the target computer.

Question 2

> You need to deploy an ASP.NET application to a production server. As part of this deployment, you need to create a virtual root in IIS and set up a database. Which type of project should you create?
>
> ○ A. Setup Project
>
> ○ B. Web Setup Project
>
> ○ C. Merge Module Project
>
> ○ D. Cab Project

Answer B is correct. A Web Setup Project is designed to perform all the tasks needed for an ASP.NET application to function, including the creation of a virtual root. You can add a custom action to create the database. Answer A is incorrect because a regular Setup Project is intended to deploy Windows applications. Answer C is incorrect because a Merge Module Project supplies a component to other setup projects. Answer D is incorrect because a Cab Project is designed to download ActiveX controls over the Internet.

Question 3

You have created a Web Setup Project using Visual Studio .NET. The project installs your ASP.NET Web application. Which of these components must already be present on the target computer when you run your application?

- O A. The Windows Installer Service 2.0
- O B. The .NET Framework Class Library
- O C. The Windows Installer Bootstrapper
- O D. The virtual root for your application

Answer B is correct. Setup projects created by Visual Studio .NET depend on the Framework being present before they can run. Answer A is incorrect because the Setup Project will install or upgrade the framework if necessary. Answer C is incorrect because the bootstrapper is automatically included in the setup. Answer D is incorrect because the Web Setup will create the virtual root itself.

Question 4

You are using the **installutil.exe** tool to install three server resources by executing this command line:

```
installutil R1.exe R2.exe R3.exe
```

The installation of **R2.exe** fails because a library that it depends on is not present. What will be the outcome of the entire operation?

- O A. Only R1 will be installed.
- O B. Only R3 will be installed.
- O C. Both R1 and R3 will be installed.
- O D. None of the assemblies will be installed.

Answer D is correct. The installutil tool treats its entire command line as a single transaction. If any assembly in the command fails to install, installutil rolls back the entire operation. Answers A, B, and C are wrong because they leave at least one assembly installed.

Question 5

You need to ensure that purchasers of your software agree to a license agreement as part of the setup process. Which specialized editor should you use to implement this?

- ○ A. Launch Conditions Editor
- ○ B. Custom Actions Editor
- ○ C. User Interface Editor
- ○ D. File Types Editor

Answer C is correct. The User Interface Editor can insert a license agreement dialog box into the setup process. Answer A is incorrect because the Launch Conditions Editor is used to determine whether a setup should proceed based on software installed on or missing from the target computer. Answer B is incorrect because custom actions are used to perform additional setup chores. Answer D is incorrect because the File Types Editor is used to associate file extensions with the programs that handle them.

Question 6

Which of these assemblies requires a strong name?

- ○ A. An assembly that will be installed in the same folder as your application and used only by that application
- ○ B. An assembly that will be installed in the Global Assembly Cache to be shared by all applications on the computer
- ○ C. An assembly that will be installed in a folder and used by several applications located within that folder
- ○ D. An assembly that will be downloaded over the Internet

Answer B is correct. Any assembly that will be installed in the GAC must have a strong name. Answers A, C, and D are incorrect because in these situations, assemblies without a strong name will work just as well. The strong name is used to guarantee assembly integrity and to distinguish between assemblies that coincidentally have the same name.

Question 7

> You want to create a component and then install it to the Global Assembly Cache (GAC) on your computer. Which tools will you use to achieve this? (Select two.)
>
> ❑ A. **installutil.exe**
>
> ❑ B. **sn.exe**
>
> ❑ C. **gacutil.exe**
>
> ❑ D. **ngen.exe**

Answers B and C are correct. The `sn.exe` tool will create a strong name, which is required to sign the assembly before it can be installed in the GAC. The `gacutil.exe` tool will install an assembly into the GAC. Answer A is incorrect because `installutil.exe` is used to run custom installation class components. Answer D is incorrect because `ngen.exe` is used to precompile an assembly into native code.

Question 8

> You are deploying a mission-critical Web application for your company. Which of these configurations will enable your application to continue functioning even if a critical hardware component, such as a power supply, fails? (Select two.)
>
> ❑ A. Single-server deployment
>
> ❑ B. Web garden deployment
>
> ❑ C. Web farm deployment
>
> ❑ D. Cluster deployment

Answers C and D are correct. A Web farm uses multiple servers active at the same time to serve an application, and a cluster uses one of a redundant group of servers to serve the application. Either is proof against a single critical hardware failure. Answers A and B are incorrect because they place the entire site on a single server that could be removed by a single failure.

Question 9

You have developed a Web application that stores its information in a SQL Server database. When the application is installed on the user's computer, it must also install the required database. The execution of the program cannot continue without the database. Therefore, if the setup of the database fails, you would like to roll back the installation process. Which of the following editors would you use in the Setup project to ensure that the database is properly installed on the target machine?

○ A. File System Editor

○ B. Launch Conditions Editor

○ C. Custom Actions Editor

○ D. Registry Editor

Answer C is correct. To perform extra operations such as installing a database, you must write a custom action. If the custom action fails, the Installer service will automatically roll back the entire installation. Answer A is incorrect because the File System Editor can deploy files and folders, but not perform the extra steps to initialize a database. Answer B is incorrect because the Launch Conditions Editor is used to determine whether an installation should proceed at all. Answer D is incorrect because the Registry Editor is limited to registry operations.

Need to Know More?

 Jeffery Ritcher. *Applied Microsoft .NET Framework Programming.* Microsoft Press, 2002.

 Version 1 Security Changes for the Microsoft .NET Framework, `http://msdn.microsoft.com/library/en-us/dnnetsec/html/ v1securitychanges.asp`.

Maintaining and Supporting a Web Application

....

Terms you'll need to understand:

✓ Boxing
✓ **EventLog** Class
✓ **PerformanceCounter** Class
✓ **Process** Class
✓ Unboxing

Techniques you'll need to master:

✓ Optimizing the performance of a Web application
✓ Locating and resolving errors in a Web application
✓ Reading and writing event log data
✓ Reading and monitoring performance data

A critical part of building a Web application is ensuring that it delivers satisfactory performance. Many things in your code can help or hinder performance. In the first part of this chapter, I'll round up some tips for improving application performance.

You should also know how to monitor performance. The System.Diagnostics namespace provides various classes that help in managing and monitoring applications. In this chapter, I'll briefly review the Process, EventLog, and PerformanceCounter classes.

Many of the techniques in this chapter require the ASP.NET process to have access to system resources that are ordinarily secured. The easiest way to ensure this in testing is to configure ASP.NET to use the system account rather than the machine account. Alternatively, you can use .NET's security facilities to grant permissions on an assembly-by-assembly basis. For more details on these topics, see Chapter 16, "Configuring a Web Application."

Designing a Web Application for Performance

You should design and develop an application for performance early in its development cycle. Removing any performance glitches early in the development cycle is the cheapest solution. The cost of rewriting modules, modifying code, or redistributing applications goes up as the application moves beyond design and into implementation.

Performance tuning is as much art as science. To get you started, I have listed some of the commonly acknowledged best practices for writing high performing applications using the .NET Framework here.

Watch for performance issues on the exam. Any time a question asks for the "best," "fastest," or "optimal" way to perform a task, you should consider runtime performance in choosing your answer.

➤ **Use caching to store content**—ASP.NET allows you to cache entire pages, fragments of pages, or controls. You can also cache variable data by specifying the parameters that the data depends on. Using caching makes it quicker for the ASP.NET engine to return data in response to repeated requests for the same page.

➤ **Avoid session state**—Whether you store it in-process, in State Server, or in a SQL Server database, session state takes memory and requires processing time to store and receive. If your application doesn't depend on session state, disable it with the <@% EnableSessionState="False" %> directive.

➤ **Avoid `ViewState`**—`ViewState` lets you persist the contents of a control across trips to a server. This comes at the cost of additional bytes traveling in each direction and hence imposes a speed hit. You can avoid this penalty by setting the `EnableViewState` property of controls to `False` when you don't need their contents to persist.

➤ **Use low-cost authentication**—Passport authentication is slower than forms-based authentication, which is slower than Windows authentication. Not authenticating users at all is the fastest choice.

➤ **Boxing and unboxing**—When a value type (such as a structure) is copied to a reference type (such as a class), the compiler needs to create an object on the heap and copy the value of the value type from the stack to this newly created object on the heap. This process is called *boxing* and requires more overhead than a simple copy from value type to value type. On the other hand, when you copy a reference type to a value type, the value of object from the heap is copied to the value type in stack. This process is called *unboxing*. You should be aware of this overhead involved in boxing and unboxing, and while designing the application, choose data types to minimize this overhead.

➤ **Use `StringBuilder`**—The `string` type is immutable. This means that once a string is created, it can't be modified. When you modify a string, the runtime will, in fact, create a new string based on your modifications and return it. The original string still hangs around in memory waiting to be garbage collected. If your application is extensively modifying strings, you should consider using the `System.Text.StringBuilder` class. The `StringBuilder` class stores the string as an array of characters. The `StringBuilder` object is mutable and does in-place modification of strings. Using `StringBuilder` might help you achieve noticeable performance gains in an application using extensive string manipulations.

➤ **Use `AddRange` with collections**—A large number of collection classes provide an `AddRange` method to add an array of items to the collection. Using `AddRange` is much faster than adding elements by repeatedly calling the `Add` method inside a loop.

➤ **Native compilation reduces startup time**—When you compile a program using the VB .NET compiler, it generates the MSIL (Microsoft Intermediate Language) code. When the program is loaded, this MSIL code is compiled into the native code by the just-in-time (JIT) compiler as it executes. When a method is called for the first time, it will be slower because of the additional step of compilation. Successive calls to the method will be faster because the code is already converted to the native code.

Although this behavior will meet your requirements most of the time, you might want to optimize your application's performance even when the functions are loaded for the first time. In these cases, you should consider using the native code compilation tool (`ngen.exe`) to convert an application to native code before deploying it on the target machine. This way, you will get maximum performance at all times. As an example, Microsoft precompiles several libraries of the .NET Framework, including `mscorlib.dll`, `System.Drawing.dll`, `System.Windows.Forms.dll`, and others, before deploying them on your machine because these classes are used by most applications.

➤ **Throw exceptions**—Throwing exceptions is a costly operation. You should be very careful when you throw exceptions from programs; use them only to signify exceptional error cases. Don't use exceptions just to manage normal program flow.

➤ **Unmanaged code**—Calls to unmanaged components involve costly marshaling operations; therefore, these programs might see deteriorated performance. For maximum performance, rewrite the unmanaged components using one of the languages supported by the CLR. If a rewrite is not possible, monitor the use of an unmanaged component and see whether you can reduce the number of calls between the managed and unmanaged code, possibly by doing more work in each call rather than making frequent calls for doing small tasks.

➤ **Make fewer calls across processes**—Working with distributed applications involves the additional overhead of negotiating network and application level protocols. Network speed might also be a bottleneck. The best approach is to get more done with fewer calls across the network. Reducing the number of calls is critical in the creation of high-performance distributed applications.

➤ **Compile the application using the Release configuration**—When you are ready to deploy your application, compile it in Release mode rather than the default Debug mode. Deploying an application compiled using Debug mode may cause it to run slowly because of the presence of extra debugging code.

➤ **Use the optimized managed providers**—`System.Data.OleDb` is a generic provider that can access data exposed by any OLE DB provider. For some databases, managed providers are specifically optimized. For example, when you use `System.Data.OleDb` to connect to the SQL Server database, it first passes your request to the OLE DB COM components that, in turn, translate the requests to SQL Server's native Tabular Data Stream (TDS) format. When you use `System.Data.SqlClient`, it directly constructs the TDS packets and communicates with SQL Server.

The removal of the extra translation step significantly increases data access performance. So if you are connecting to a SQL Server database, use System.Data.SqlClient instead of the generic System.Data.OleDb. Similarly, use System.Data.OracleClient for connecting to an Oracle database.

The Oracle managed provider is an add-on to the .NET Framework 1.0. You can download it from **http://www.microsoft.com/downloads/ release.asp?releaseid=40032**.

➤ **Prefer stored procedures over SQL statements**—When working with SQL Server, use stored procedures instead of a set of SQL statements given as a text command. This is because stored procedures are highly optimized for server-side data access, and their use will usually significantly improve the data access performance.

➤ **Tune the database**—Keeping up-to-date indexes also greatly helps in improving performance for a database-intensive Web application. You can run SQL Server's Profiler and Index Tuning Wizard to avoid any bottlenecks because of indexing. Also, use SQL Server Query Analyzer to optimize a query's performance.

➤ **DataReader versus DataSet**—If you are reading a table sequentially, use DataReader instead of DataSet. DataReader is a read-only, forward-only stream of data. This increases application performance and reduces system overhead because only one row is in memory at a time.

➤ **Connection pooling for the SQL Server .NET Data provider**—The slowest database operation is establishing a connection with the database. The SQL Server .NET Data provider furnishes connection pooling to improve performance when connecting to a database. This stores old connection information in a connection pool and reuses this information when connecting the next time, thereby allowing significant performance gains. A connection pool is created based on the connection string in the connection. Each connection pool is associated with a distinct connection string. When a new connection is opened, a new pool is created if the connection string is not an exact match to an existing pool.

For connection pooling to work, multiple connections to a database must use the same connection strings. If you are including user identity and password information in the connection string, the connection string for user Mahesh will not match with user Mary. This will instead form two separate connection pools. To gain maximum performance gains, you must use a single identity and password in the connection string to a database.

> ➤ **Auto-generated commands**—The `SqlCommandBuilder` and `OleDbCommandBuilder` classes provide a means of automatically generating commands used to reconcile changes made to a `DataSet`. Although the automatic generation of `INSERT`, `UPDATE`, and `DELETE` statements for changes to the `DataSet` makes database updates very convenient, it makes extra trips to the server to get the schema information.

> ➤ **Use transactions**—Distributed transactions might have significant performance overhead. As a rule of thumb, use transactions only when required and keep transactions as short-lived as possible. If a transaction is limited to a single database, it should be implemented in a stored procedure rather than in application logic.

> ➤ **Improve perceived performance**—This last technique has more to do with human behavior than the actual performance of the application. Studies have shown that showing an active splash screen at the application startup might make your application appear as if it is loading faster. Similarly, showing a progress bar for a long operation keeps users informed and in communication with the application. Use these techniques to improve the perceived performance of your application.

Starting and Stopping Processes

The `System.Diagnostics` namespace provides several classes that help you with process management. The key to working with processes is the `Process` class. This class represents an instance of a process.

To start a process, you can call the `Start` method of the `Process` class. This method is available in both static and non-static versions. To use the non-static version of the `Start` method, you must first create an instance of the `Process` class, set its `StartInfo` property to specify the necessary startup information (such as the executable filename, arguments, environment variables, working directory, and so on), and finally call the `Start` method of this instance. The static version of the `Start` method returns an instance of a created process. You pass the static version a `ProcessStartupInfo` object or other arguments such as the application's filename and environment.

Two methods exist that can stop a process: `CloseMainWindow` and `Kill`. The `CloseMainWindow` method requests a normal shutdown of the program. This is equivalent to closing an application by clicking on the close icon in its main window. `CloseMainWindow` can only stop processes that participate in the Windows message loop and that have a user interface. On the other hand, the `Kill` method causes an abnormal program termination by forcibly killing

an application. Kill is the way to stop processes that do not have a user interface, or those that do not participate in the Windows message loop (such as
MS-DOS-based programs).

The **Process** class only allows you to start and stop processes on the local
machine where the code is running. For ASP.NET applications, this will be the Web
server. Although you can access process information for remote machines, you
cannot start or stop a process on a remote machine using this class.

Table 15.1 lists the members of the Process class that are useful for starting
or stopping processes.

Table 15.1 Members of the Process Class That Are Useful for Starting or Stopping Processes		
Member	**Type**	**Description**
CloseMainWindow	Method	Closes a process that has a user interface by sending a close message to its main window.
EnableRaisingEvents	Property	Specifies whether the **Exited** event should be raised when the process terminates.
ExitCode	Property	Value specified by a process when it exits.
Exited	Event	Occurs when a process exits.
ExitTime	Property	Time at which the process exited.
GetProcessById	Method	Returns a **Process** object that represents an already running process with the given Process Identifier (PID).
GetProcesses	Method	Returns an array of **Process** objects, where each element represents an already existing process.
GetProcessesByName	Method	Returns an array of Process objects where each element represents an already running process with the specified process name.
HasExited	Property	Indicates whether the process has been terminated.
Id	Property	The unique identifier of the process.
Kill	Method	Immediately stops the process.
Start	Method	Starts a new process.
StartInfo	Property	Specifies the properties to pass to the **Start** method of the process.
WaitForExit	Method	Sets the period to wait for the process to exit and blocks the current thread of execution until the time has elapsed or the process has exited.
WaitForInputIdle	Method	Causes a **Process** object to wait for the process to enter an idle state.

NOTE

You're unlikely to need to manipulate processes in ASP.NET applications because the only process on the server that the client communicates with is the ASP.NET process.

Working with Event Logs

Event logging is the standard way in Windows for applications to leave a record of their activities. A system administrator can easily monitor the behavior of an application by analyzing its messages in the event log with the Event Viewer utility. You can also view events from within the Visual Studio .NET environment. You can access event logs through Server Explorer.

The Framework Class Library provides you with a set of classes designed to work with event logs. With the help of these classes, you can programmatically read from or write to the event logs. Programmatic access might even allow you to automate some of the administrative tasks associated with the application.

By default, three event logs are available: Application, Security, and System. Other applications (including .NET applications) or operating system components such as Active Directory might add other event logs. Table 15.2 lists the important members of the EventLog class.

Table 15.2   Important Members of the EventLog Class

Member	Type	Description
CreateEventSource	Method	Opens an event source for an application to write event information.
Delete	Method	Removes a log resource.
DeleteEventSource	Method	Removes an application's event source from the event log.
EnableRaisingEvents	Property	Specifies whether the **EventLog** object receives notifications for the **EntryWritten** event.
Entries	Property	Gets the contents of the event log.
EntryWritten	Event	Occurs when an entry is written to an event log on the local computer.
Exists	Method	Determines whether the specified log exists.
GetEventLogs	Method	Creates an array of the event logs.
Log	Property	Specifies the name of the log to read from or write to.

(continued)

Table 15.2 Important Members of the EventLog Class *(continued)*		
Member	**Type**	**Description**
LogDisplayName	Property	An event log's friendly name.
LogNameFromSourceName	Method	Gets the name of the log to which the specified source is registered.
MachineName	Property	Name of the computer on which to read or write events.
Source	Property	Specifies the source to register and use when writing to the event log.
SourceExists	Method	Finds whether a given event source exists.
WriteEntry	Method	Writes an entry in the event log.

Each application that is interested in interacting with an event log must register an event source with it. Once an event source is registered, its information is stored in the system registry and is available across application restarts.

Writing to Event Logs

The WriteEntry method of the EventLog object allows you to write messages to the event log specified by the event source. If you haven't called CreateEventSource, WriteEntry will create the event source for you.

You can write different type of messages (information, error, and so on) to an event log. These types are specified by the values in EventLogEntryType enumeration. For example, this code checks to see whether a particular source exists, and if so, writes a warning from that source to the event log:

```
If EventLog.SourceExists(strSourceName) Then
    ' Write an entry into event log
    EventLog.WriteEntry(strSourceName, _
    "Warning Message", _
    EventLogEntryType.Warning)
End If
```

The Security log is read-only.

Reading and Monitoring Event Logs

To read the contents of an event log, you can access the Entries property of the EventLog object. The Entries property returns an EventLogEntryCollection object—each of whose elements gives you access to an individual event log entry, as shown in the following code:

```
Dim el As EventLog = New EventLog( _
  "Application", _
  ".")

Dim ele As EventLogEntry
For Each ele In el.Entries
    ' Add the entry in to a list view
    AddEntryToList(ele)
Next
```

You can also monitor an event log by registering an event handler for its `EntryWritten` event. Before that, you will have to set the `EnableRaisingEvents` property of the `EventLog` object to `True`. If you do this, your event handler will be called each time a new entry is written to the specified event log.

 You can easily refer to the local machine in all event log-related classes by using a single dot "." as the name.

Working with Performance Counters

Performance counters are the Windows way of collecting performance data from running processes. Microsoft Windows itself provides several hundred performance counters—each monitoring a particular system parameter. In addition to this, the various .NET server products, such as SQL Server and Exchange Server, and applications, such as the .NET Framework, also publish their own custom performance counters.

Windows organizes performance counters in categories. Each category defines a specific set of performance counters. For example, there are categories such as Memory, Process, Processor, and PhysicalDisk. The Memory category has various counters such as Available Bytes, Cache Bytes, Committed Bytes, and so on.

Some categories are further divided into instances. For example, the Process category is divided into several instances—each representing a running process on the computer. A new instance is added to the category whenever a new process is started and removed when a process is killed. Each instance can have performance counters such as I/O Read Bytes/sec that specify the activity of that particular process. Usually all instances in a category will have the same list of performance counters. Of course, each of the performance counters will have separate performance data associated with it.

The `PerformanceCounter` class allows you to read performance samples for processes running on the local computer or remote machines. By using this class, an application can even publish its own performance counters, informing the world about its performance level.

Table 15.3 lists the important members of the `PerformanceCounter` class.

Table 15.3	Important Members of the PerformanceCounter Class	
Member	**Type**	**Description**
CategoryName	Property	Performance Counter category name.
Close	Method	Closes the performance counter and frees all the resources.
CounterHelp	Property	Performance counter description.
CounterName	Property	Performance counter name.
CounterType	Property	Performance counter type.
Decrement	Method	Decrements the performance counter value by one.
Increment	Method	Increments the performance counter value by one.
IncrementBy	Method	Increments or decrements the value of the performance counter by a specified amount.
InstanceName	Property	Instance name.
MachineName	Property	Computer name.
NextSample	Method	Gets a sample for the performance counter and returns the raw, or uncalculated, value for it.
NextValue	Method	Gets a sample for the performance counter and returns the calculated value for it.
RawValue	Property	Gets a sample for the performance counter and returns its raw or uncalculated value.
ReadOnly	Property	Indicates whether the **PerformanceCounter** is in read-only mode.
RemoveInstance	Method	Deletes an instance from the **PerformanceCounter** object.

Reading Performance Data of Running Processes

The process of reading a performance counter value is also referred to as *sampling* the performance counter. The performance monitors installed on a computer can be easily accessed through Server Explorer in Visual Studio .NET.

You can drag and drop the performance counter of your choice to create an instance of the PerformanceCounter component. This example shows how you might use such a component:

1. Create a new Visual Basic ASP.NET Web application.

2. Place a Label control, a Button control (btnSample), and a ListBox control (lbPerformance) on the default Web Form.

3. Open Server Explorer and select the server from the Servers node. Select the Available Bytes performance counter by navigating to Performance Counters, Memory, Available Bytes from the server node (see Figure 15.1; the counters available on your computer might differ). Drag the Available Bytes counter to the form. Name the counter pcMemory. Change the MachineName property of the counter to a single dot (.) to refer to the Web server where the code is running.

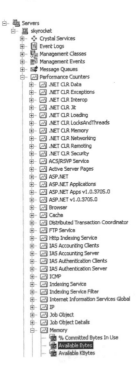

Figure 15.1   The Available Bytes performance counter in Server Explorer.

4. Switch to code view. Add the following code to the top of the form's module:

```
Imports System.Diagnostics
```

5. Attach an event handler to the `Click` event of the `Button` control and add the following code in the event handler:

```
Private Sub btnSample_Click( _
ByVal sender As System.Object, _
ByVal e As System.EventArgs) Handles btnSample.Click
    ' Get the next performance data
    ' Add the data to the listview
    Dim csSample As CounterSample = _
    pcMemory.NextSample()
    lbPerformance.Items.Add( _
    pcMemory.CounterName & ": " & _
    csSample.RawValue.ToString() & " at " & _
    csSample.TimeStamp.ToString())
End Sub
```

6. Run the project. Each time you click the button, a new performance value will be added as a new row to the `ListBox` control.

Publishing Performance Data

The .NET Framework also enables applications to create their own custom performance counters and publish their performance data. This performance data can be then monitored from Performance Monitor (`perfmon.exe`) or can be monitored through any other application, such as the one you just created.

To create a performance counter, you must first build an array of `CounterCreationData` objects. The array can have a single member to create one performance counter, but you can use a larger array to create more than one counter at the same time. This array is used as input to the constructor for a `CounterCreationDataCollection` object. This object, in turn, goes to the constructor for a `PerformanceCounterCategory` object, which also takes as parameters the name of the new category and a description of the category that other tools can use:

```
Dim ccd(0) As CounterCreationData
ccd(0) = New CounterCreationData()
ccd(0).CounterName = "Performance"
Dim ccdcoll As New _
CounterCreationDataCollection(ccd)
PerformanceCounterCategory.Create( _
"CategoryName", _
"Category description", ccdcoll)
Dim pc As PerformanceCounter = _
New PerformanceCounter( _
"CategoryName", _
"CounterName", "", False)
```

After you've created a performance counter, you can set its value by creating the appropriate PerformanceCounter object and manipulating its RawValue property:

```
Dim pc As PerformanceCounter = _
 New PerformanceCounter()
pc.CategoryName = "CategoryName"
pc.CounterName = "CounterName"
pc.ReadOnly = False
pc.RawValue = 500
```

Exam Prep Questions

Question 1

You have created a data-entry application in ASP.NET. The main form of your application contains approximately 40 controls. The contents of 10 of these controls are required by the server-side code that processes the page; the other controls are only accessed by client-side JavaScript code. What should you do to improve performance on this page?

- ○ A. Set the **Enabled** property of the controls that are only used by client-side code to **False**.
- ○ B. Set the **Enabled** property of the controls that are used by server-side code to **False**.
- ○ C. Set the **EnableViewState** property of the controls that are only used by client-side code to **False**.
- ○ D. Set the **EnableViewState** property of the controls that are used by server-side code to **False**.

Answer C is correct. Turning off ViewState on controls that are only used by client-side code will lower the overall size of the page and hence increase performance. Answers A and B are incorrect because setting Enabled to False would prevent the user from interacting with those controls at all. Answer D is incorrect because turning off ViewState for controls prevents their contents from being uploaded to the server.

Question 2

You have designed an intranet application using ASP.NET. It is important that you authenticate users and track their usage of the application. Each user has an account on the Windows servers for your domain. Which form of authentication should you use for best performance while still meeting the requirements?

- ○ A. Default authentication
- ○ B. Windows authentication
- ○ C. Forms-based authentication
- ○ D. Passport authentication

Answer B is correct. The default authentication for ASP.NET is no authentication at all, which does not satisfy the requirements. Of the remaining alternatives, Passport authentication is slower than forms-based authentication, which is slower than Windows authentication. Therefore, Windows authentication is the correct answer.

Question 3

You have deployed an inventory application for your corporate intranet as an ASP.NET application with a SQL Server backend database. All the employees of the company have the same access to the data. When a user logs on to the system, her account name and password are used to dynamically construct a connection string for the database. Users report that the system is very slow at peak loads. What step should you take to speed up the data access?

- ○ A. Use **ngen.exe** to compile the ASP.NET assemblies to native code.
- ○ B. Add a **PerformanceMonitor** component to the main page of the application.
- ○ C. Assign all users to a single SQL Server application role and share the same connection string among all users.
- ○ D. Increase the maximum size of the connection pool.

Answer C is correct. With every user having a unique connection string, the application does not benefit from connection pooling. By switching to a shared connection string, you lower the overhead of connecting and speed up the application. Answer A is incorrect because the ASP.NET application will be compiled to native code when it is first loaded already. Answer B is incorrect because monitoring the performance will not speed it up. Answer D is incorrect because there is no point in increasing the size of the connection pool if there is no connection pooling in the application.

Question 4

You are designing an ASP.NET application that must retrieve a list of employees from a large SQL Server database. After the list is retrieved, the application will move through it once and write the results to a table on a Web page. Which of these code segments will meet the requirements and give you the best performance?

- ○ A.
```
Dim conn As SqlConnection = _
  New SqlConnection(connStr)
conn.Open()
Dim ds As DataSet = New DataSet()
Dim ad As SqlDataAdapter = _
  New SqlDataAdapter( _
  "SELECT * FROM authors", conn)
ad.Fill(ds)
End Sub
```

○ B.

```
Dim conn As OleDbConnection = _
  New OleDbConnection(connStr)
conn.Open()
Dim ds As DataSet = New DataSet()
Dim ad As OleDbDataAdapter = _
  New OleDbDataAdapter( _
  "SELECT * FROM authors", conn)
ad.Fill(ds)
```

○ C.

```
Dim conn As SqlConnection = _
  New SqlConnection(connStr)
Dim cmd As SqlCommand = _
  New SqlCommand("SELECT * FROM authors", _
  connStr)
conn.Open()
Dim rdr As SqlDataReader
rdr = cmd.ExecuteReader()
```

○ D.

```
Dim conn As OleDbConnection = _
  New OleDbConnection(connStr)
Dim cmd As OleDbCommand = _
  New OleDbCommand( _
  "SELECT * FROM authors", connStr)
conn.Open()
Dim rdr As OleDbDataReader
rdr = cmd.ExecuteReader()
```

Answer C is correct. When dealing with SQL Server data, the native SQL Server data classes are faster than the general OLE DB classes. If you only want to go through a set of data once, a DataReader is faster than a DataSet. Answers A and B are incorrect because they store the data in a DataSet. Answers B and D are incorrect because they use OLE DB data classes.

Question 5

Your ASP.NET application displays customers and their order information to sales representatives over the Internet. The data is stored in a SQL Server on a different computer than the one where ASP.NET is installed. Which architecture will lead to the best performance?

○ A. Use **OleDbDataConnection** to connect to the SQL Server. Retrieve the customers and orders using a single stored procedure.

○ B. Use **SqlDataConnection** to connect to the SQL Server. Retrieve the customers and orders using a single stored procedure.

○ C. Use **OleDbDataConnection** to connect to the SQL Server. Retrieve the customers and orders using different stored procedures.

○ D. Use **SqlDataConnection** to connect to the SQL Server. Retrieve the customers and orders using different stored procedures.

Answer B is correct. `SqlDataConnection` can retrieve data more efficiently from SQL Server than `OleDbDataConnection` can. When working with a remote server, it's important to minimize the number of round trips, so retrieving all necessary information with a single stored procedure is the best architecture. Answers A and C are incorrect because they use `OleDbDataConnection`. Answers C and D are incorrect because they require an additional round trip between servers.

Question 6

You have developed a pair of ASP.NET applications that work together to deliver stock quotes. The first application is responsible for authenticating users, and it must reject them if they are not properly authenticated. The second application accepts users from the first application and shows them pages customized according to their portfolios. Which configurations should you use for these applications to obtain the best performance?

- ○ A. Compile both applications in Debug mode.
- ○ B. Compile the first application in Debug mode and the second in Release mode.
- ○ C. Compile the first application in Release mode and the second in Debug mode.
- ○ D. Compile both applications in Release mode.

Answer D is correct. Release mode is faster than Debug mode because it does not contain extra debugging code. Answers A, B, and C are all incorrect because they include debugging code in at least one of the applications.

Question 7

Your application allows the user to edit project data in a **DataGrid** control on an ASP.NET Web Form. When the user is done editing the data, you must persist her changes to the database. How should you do this?

- ○ A. Store the data in a **DataSet** and use a **CommandBuilder** class to automatically provide the proper statements to update the database.
- ○ B. Store the data in a **DataSet** and use stored procedures to update the data in the database.
- ○ C. Store the data in a **DataReader** and use ad hoc SQL statements to update the data in the database.
- ○ D. Store the data in a **DataSet** and use ad hoc SQL statements to update the data in the database.

Answer B is correct. Stored procedures generally represent the best way to update data because they can be precompiled and optimized by the database engine. Answer A is incorrect because CommandBuilder requires additional round trips to the database to generate the updating statements. Answers C and D are incorrect because ad hoc SQL statements are generally slower than the equivalent stored procedures. Answer C is also incorrect because a DataReader does not allow you to edit the data that it contains.

Question 8

Your Web application displays up-to-the-minute inventory information from your company's warehouses. Each time a new page is loaded, it makes entirely new calculations to determine which information to display. No page in the application passes any information to another page in the application. Which alternative should you use for session state in this application to maximize performance?

○ A. Disable session state

○ B. In-process session state

○ C. State Server session state

○ D. SQL Server session state

Answer A is correct. If you do not need to share information between pages in your application, disabling session state is the best alternative. Answers B, C, and D are incorrect because any means of storing session state imposes overhead on the application.

Question 9

Your application must create its own event log, and then write data to the event log. Which method of the **EventLog** class must you call?

○ A. **CreateEventSource**

○ B. **LogNameFromSourceName**

○ C. **WriteEntry**

○ D. **SourceExists**

Answer C is correct. The WriteEntry method is the only way to write data to an event log. If the event source does not already exist, WriteEntry will create it.

Need to Know More?

 Burton, Kevin. *.NET Common Language Runtime Unleashed*. Sams, 2002.

Configuring a Web Application

Terms you'll need to understand:

✓ Configuration file
✓ Authentication
✓ Authorization
✓ Role-based security
✓ Impersonation
✓ Caching
✓ Session state

Techniques you'll need to master:

✓ Changing settings within the **Web.config** and **machine.config** files
✓ Using application configuration files
✓ Configuring authentication and authorization for a Web application
✓ Configuring impersonation for a Web application
✓ Using caching to hold data
✓ Using session state to hold data
✓ Installing and configuring a Web server

The .NET Framework offers substantial control of many types of configuration for ASP.NET applications. A few of the types of options you can change include

➤ ASP.NET options

➤ Caching options

➤ Security options

In this chapter, you learn how you can configure your ASP.NET environment for your own needs, both as a developer and as an administrator.

Configuring a Web Application

ASP.NET stores many settings in a set of external XML configuration files. These files offer several advantages:

➤ Because they're XML files, they can be modified by any editor that understands the XML file format.

➤ Because XML files are also plain-text files, configuration files can even be modified with a text editor such as Notepad (as long as you know what you're doing).

➤ There's no need for direct access to the server to change configuration; you can just apply a new configuration file via FTP or any other means that you have for transferring files to the server.

ASP.NET automatically monitors configuration files for changes. If you change a configuration file, the new settings automatically take effect. There's no need to stop and restart the ASP.NET process or to reboot the computer.

There's an exception to the general rule: If you change the **processModel** element in the **machine.config** file, you must restart Internet Information Services (IIS) to have the changes take effect. This element controls internal IIS settings such as which processors to use on a multiprocessor computer and the number of threads to allocate to ASP.NET.

Although changes to configuration files are picked up automatically by ASP.NET, it doesn't mean that you can change things without consequences. When you change a configuration file, ASP.NET clears all the application state and session state variables for the affected site. If you change the **machine.config** file, you'll lose all the state settings for every site on the Web server.

Anatomy of a Configuration File

The master configuration file that controls ASP.NET's operations is named machine.config, and you'll find it in a directory underneath your Windows installation directory. For example, on a Windows 2000 computer with the initial release of the .NET Framework installed, this file is at

```
C:\WINNT\Microsoft.NET\Framework\
➡v1.0.3705\CONFIG\machine.config
```

 Because the **machine.config** file is critical to the workings of ASP.NET, I recommend that you explore a copy of this file rather than the actual file. Any changes to **machine.config** should be made very cautiously, and you should always keep a copy of the unchanged file in case you need to reverse the changes.

Like any other XML file, the machine.config file starts with an XML declaration. Then comes a root element named <configuration> that brackets the entire contents of the XML file. Then comes a single <configSections> element. This element contains entries that identify all the types of configuration settings that the file can manage. Here's a portion of the <configSections> element (I've reformatted this a bit to fit on the page; ellipses indicate where I've omitted sections of the file):

```
<configSections>
    <!-- tell .NET Framework to ignore CLR sections -->
    <section name="runtime"
    type="System.Configuration.IgnoreSectionHandler,
    System, Version=1.0.3300.0,
    Culture=neutral,
    PublicKeyToken=b77a5c561934e089"
    allowLocation="false"/>
...
    <section name="appSettings"
    type="System.Configuration.
    NameValueFileSectionHandler,
    System, Version=1.0.3300.0,
    Culture=neutral,
    PublicKeyToken=b77a5c561934e089"/>
    <sectionGroup name="system.net">
        <section name="authenticationModules"
        type="System.Net.Configuration.
        NetAuthenticationModuleHandler,
        System, Version=1.0.3300.0,
        Culture=neutral,
        PublicKeyToken=b77a5c561934e089"/>
...
    </sectionGroup>
...
</configSections>
```

The   element purpose of the <configSections> element is to tell the .NET Framework what sorts of settings are contained within the rest of the file. As you can see, there are both <sectionGroup> and <section> elements within this section of the file. The <sectionGroup> element defines a namespace within the configuration file. This allows you to keep section names from conflicting with one another. For example, in the part of the file shown here, the system.net section group contains an authenticationModules section. You could also have an authenticationModules section in another section group.

The <section> element defines a section of the configuration file. Each section has an arbitrary name and a type. The type of a section defines a class within the .NET Framework that will be used to read settings from the specified section. As you can see, types are specified with complete information, including a public key token, to ensure their identity.

Two optional attributes exist that you can add to the section tag. The allowDefinition attribute specifies which configuration files can contain a particular section. The values for this attribute are Everywhere (the default), MachineOnly (which allows defining the section in the machine.config file only), or MachineToApplication (which allows defining the section in the machine.config file or application configuration files). The other optional attribute is allowLocation, which can be set to True or False. If you set allowLocation to False, it prevents this section from appearing farther down in the configuration file hierarchy. In the section of the file shown previously, this setting is used to prevent other files from defining a section that might substitute a malicious .NET runtime file.

After the <configSections> element, you'll find the actual sections themselves. For example, <configSections> defines a section named appSettings: Farther down in the file, you'll find the corresponding <appSettings> element. Within that element, you would place any configuration settings defined for applications.

If you browse through the machine.config file on your computer, you'll get a sense of what you can configure in this fashion.

The Configuration File Hierarchy

As I mentioned previously, configuration files are arranged in a hierarchy. This means that individual applications can supplement or even override the configuration defined in the machine.config file. Here's a demonstration:

1. Create a new Visual Basic ASP.NET application. Add a new Web Form to the application.

2. Add a HyperLink control to the Web Form and set its NavigateUrl property to NonexistentPage.aspx. Set this form as the start page for the application.

3. Open the machine.config file on your Web server and scroll down until you find the <customErrors> section. If you have not edited this section since the file was installed, it will contain the following setting:

```
<customErrors mode="RemoteOnly"/>
```

This setting tells ASP.NET to display any custom errors to remote clients and to use ASP.NET native errors if the application is running on the local host.

4. Double-click the Web.config file in Solution Explorer. This is the configuration file that contains settings for the local application. By default, it has the same custom error setting that the machine.config file contains. Change the setting in the Web.config file so that it reads

```
<customErrors mode="On">
    <error statusCode="404" redirect="404.aspx" />
</customErrors>
```

This tells ASP.NET to display custom errors regardless of whether you're executing the application from a remote client or a local client and to display a page named 404.aspx in response to 404 (page not found) errors.

5. Add a new Web Form to the application. Name the new form 404.aspx. Change the pageLayout property of the page to FlowLayout. Type this text directly on the page:

```
The page you were trying to open was not found.
```

6. Run the project. Click the HyperLink control. Your custom error page will appear in the browser window.

7. Stop the project. Right-click the project in Solution Explorer and select Add, New Folder. Name the new folder SubDir.

8. Right-click the SubDir folder and select Add, Add New Item. Add a new Web Form to this folder.

9. Add a HyperLink control to the Web Form and set its NavigateUrl property to NonexistentPage.aspx. Set this form as the start page for the application.

10. Run the project. Click the HyperLink control. Your custom error page will once again appear in the browser window.

11. Stop the project. Right-click the SubDir folder and select Add, Add New Item. Add a Web configuration file with the default name of Web.config to the folder. The new file will be created with the default customErrors setting. Open the new Web.config file and edit it so that it contains only the customErrors setting:

```
<?xml version="1.0" encoding="utf-8" ?>
<configuration>
  <system.web>
    <customErrors mode="Off" />
  </system.web>
</configuration>
```

12. Run the project again. Click the HyperLink control. Instead of your custom error page, you'll see the default error message for a nonexistent file.

This example demonstrates the essentials of hierarchical configuration files. When you ran the project in step 6, ASP.NET found the default machine.config file, but it also found the Web.config file in the same folder as the Web page that you were displaying. The more specific custom error setting in the Web.config file overrides the setting in the general machine.config file, so the custom 404 page was displayed.

When you ran the project the second time, in step 10, ASP.NET did not find a Web.config file in the same folder as the Web page that you were working with. Therefore, the page inherited the settings from the Web.config file in the parent folder, and the custom error page was displayed again.

The third time, the Web.config file in the SubDir folder overrode the machine.config file and the Web.config file in the parent folder, so the default error message came up in the browser instead.

At any time, the Web.config file closest in the folder chain to the page being displayed controls the settings used by ASP.NET. Note that not every setting comes from the same file. For example, in the final part of the previous example, only the custom error setting comes from the most specific Web.config file. Other settings, such as the tracing and session state settings, come from the parent Web.config file or even from the machine.config file.

Several other factors complicate this simple picture of how things work:

➤ The parent folder that matters is not the physical folder on the hard drive, but the virtual folder in IIS.

➤ A setting in a configuration file can be marked with a location element to limit it to a particular subdirectory.

➤ ASP.NET configuration files only apply to ASP.NET resources.

➤ Any configuration file can mark a section with the allowOverride="false" attribute. In this case, more specific configuration files cannot override this setting.

Reading Configuration Settings from Code

All the settings that you've seen so far in the ASP.NET configuration files are used by ASP.NET itself. Your code can also use the configuration files to store information. The .NET Framework provides you with programmatic access to these files via the `ConfigurationSettings` object. For example, suppose that you had a configuration file with this section:

```
<appSettings>
  <add key="Custom"
    value="Custom configuration value" />
</appSettings>
```

You could read the value by accessing the `ConfigurationSettings.AppSettings("Custom")` object.

Configuring Security

When you're developing ASP.NET applications, you need to configure two aspects of security: *authentication* and *authorization*. Authentication refers to the process of obtaining credentials from a user and verifying his identity. After an identity has been authenticated, it can be authorized to use various resources.

ASP.NET supports a number of methods of authentication. These methods of authentication include

➤ None

➤ Windows

➤ Forms-based

➤ Passport

➤ IIS authentication

After you've authenticated a user, you can use his identity to authorize access to resources. One way to do this is by using .NET's own role-based security, which allows you to dictate in code which users should have access to which resources. As an alternative, you can allow the ASP.NET process to imper-sonate the authenticated user and rely on the security mechanisms in Windows to determine access to resources.

Configuring Authentication

ASP.NET provides you with flexible alternatives for authentication. You can per-form authentication yourself in code or delegate authentication to other authorities.

Settings in the `Web.config` file control the method of authentication that will be used for any given request.

No Authentication

The simplest form of authentication is no authentication at all. To enable an application to execute without authentication, add the following section to its configuration file:

```
<authentication mode="None" />
```

Setting the mode to `None` tells ASP.NET that you don't care about user authentication. The natural consequence of this, of course, is that you can't base authorization on user identities because users are never authenticated.

IIS and ASP.NET Authentication

One thing that trips up some developers is that there are actually two separate authentication layers in an ASP.NET application. That's because all requests flow through IIS before they're handed to ASP.NET, and IIS can decide to deny access before the ASP.NET process even knows about the request. Here's a rundown on how the process works:

1. IIS first checks to make sure that the incoming request comes from an IP address that is allowed access to the domain. If not, the request is denied.

2. Next, IIS performs its own user authentication, if it's configured to do so. I'll talk more about IIS authentication later in the chapter. By default, IIS allows anonymous access, so requests are automatically authenticated.

3. If the request is passed to ASP.NET with an authenticated user, ASP.NET checks to see whether impersonation is enabled. If impersonation is enabled, ASP.NET acts as though it were the authenticated user. If not, ASP.NET acts with its own configured account.

4. Finally, the identity from step 3 is used to request resources from the operating system. If all the necessary resources can be obtained, the user's request is granted; otherwise, it is denied.

Authentication Providers

So what happens when a request gets to ASP.NET? The answer depends on the site's configuration. The ASP.NET architecture delegates authentication to an authentication provider—a module whose job it is to verify credentials and provide authentication. ASP.NET ships with three authentication providers:

➤ The Windows authentication provider allows you to authenticate users based on their Windows accounts.

➤ The Passport authentication provider uses Microsoft's Passport service to authenticate users.

➤ The Forms authentication provider uses custom HTML forms to collect authentication information and allows you to use your own logic to authenticate users. Credentials are then stored in a cookie.

To select an authentication provider, you make an entry in the `Web.config` file for the application. You can use any of these entries to select one of the built-in authentication providers:

```
<authentication mode="Windows" />

<authentication mode="Passport" />

<authentication mode="Forms" />
```

Configuring IIS Authentication

If you decide to use Windows authentication within your applications, you'll need to consider how to configure IIS authentication. That's because the Windows identities are actually provided by IIS. IIS offers four different authentication methods:

➤ **Anonymous authentication**—IIS does not perform any authentication. Anyone is allowed access to the ASP.NET application.

➤ **Basic authentication**—Users must provide a Windows username and password to connect. However, this information is sent across the network in clear text, making basic authentication dangerously insecure on the Internet.

➤ **Digest authentication**—Users must still provide a Windows username and password to connect. However, the password is hashed (scrambled) before being sent across the network. Digest authentication requires that all users be running Internet Explorer 5 or later and that Windows accounts are stored in Active Directory.

➤ **Windows integrated authentication**—Passwords never cross the network. Users must still have a Windows username and password, but either the Kerberos or challenge/response protocols are used to authenticate the user. Windows-integrated authentication requires that all users be running Internet Explorer 3.01 or later.

You can set the type of IIS authentication from the Properties page for your Web site in Internet Services Manager (Start, Programs, Administrative Tools, Internet Services Manager) .

Passport Authentication

ASP.NET has built-in connections to Microsoft's Passport authentication service. If your users have signed up with Passport, and you configure the authentication mode of the application to be Passport authentication, all authentication duties are offloaded to the Passport servers.

To use Passport authentication, you'll need to download the Passport Software Development Kit (SDK) and install it on your server. The SDK can be found at `http://msdn.microsoft.com/library/default.asp?url=/downloads/list/websrvpass.asp`.

You'll also need to license Passport authentication. Currently, the license fees are $10,000 per year plus a periodic $1,500 testing fee. You can get details on licensing Passport at `http://www.microsoft.com/net/services/passport/`.

Forms Authentication

Forms authentication provides you with a way to handle authentication using your own custom logic within an ASP.NET application. (Note that this is different from custom authentication using an ISAPI filter, which takes place before the request ever gets to ASP.NET.) With forms authentication, the logic of the application goes like this:

1. When a user requests a page from the application, ASP.NET checks for the presence of a special cookie. If the cookie is present, the request is processed.

2. If the cookie is not present, ASP.NET redirects the user to a Web Form that you provide.

3. You can carry out whatever authentication checks you like in your form. When the user is authenticated, you indicate this to ASP.NET, which creates the special cookie to handle subsequent requests.

Configuring Authorization

After your application has authenticated users, you can proceed to authorize their access to resources. But there's a question to answer first: Just who is the user to whom you are granting access? It turns out that there are different answers to that question, depending on whether you implement *impersonation*. With impersonation, the ASP.NET process can actually take on the identity of the authenticated user.

After a user has been authenticated and you've decided whether to use impersonation, you can proceed to grant access to resources. ASP.NET uses the role-based authorization features of the .NET Framework for this purpose.

Implementing Impersonation

ASP.NET impersonation is controlled by entries in the applicable web.config file. The default setting is no impersonation. You can also explicitly specify this setting by including this element in the file:

```
<identity impersonate="false"/>
```

With this setting, ASP.NET will always run with its own privileges. By default, ASP.NET runs as an unprivileged account named ASPNET. You can change this by making a setting in the processModel section of the machine.config. This setting can only be changed in machine.config, so any change automatically applies to every site on the server. To use a high-privilege system account instead of a low-privilege account, set the userName attribute of the processModel element to SYSTEM.

So when impersonation is disabled, all requests will run in the context of the account running ASP.NET, either the ASPNET account or the system account. This is true whether you're using anonymous access or authenticating users in some fashion.

The second possible setting is to turn on impersonation:

```
<identity impersonate="true"/>
```

In this case, ASP.NET takes on the identity passed to it by IIS. If you're allowing anonymous access in IIS, it means that ASP.NET will impersonate the IUSR_ComputerName account that IIS itself uses. If you're not allowing anonymous access, ASP.NET will take on the credentials of the authenticated user and make requests for resources as if it were that user.

Finally, you can specify a particular identity to use for all authenticated requests:

```
<identity impersonate="true"
   name="DOMAIN\userName" password="password"/>
```

With this setting, all requests are made as the specified user (assuming that the password is correct in the configuration file).

Using Role-Based Authorization

If you prefer, you can use the security mechanisms in Windows to authorize access to resources after you've authenticated a user. For example, you can give a Windows account permissions to log on to a SQL Server or to open a particular file.

These permissions can be granted to the ASPNET user (if you're not using imperson-ation) or to individual domain users or groups (if you are using impersonation).

But you can also control access to resources directly in your .NET code. Within the Visual Basic .NET Windows application, authorization is han-dled by the role-based security system. Role-based security revolves around two interfaces: IIdentity and IPrincipal. For applications that use Windows accounts in role-based security, these interfaces are implemented by the WindowsIdentity and WindowsPrincipal objects, respectively.

The WindowsIdentity object represents the Windows user who is running the current code. The properties of this object allow you to retrieve such infor-mation as the username and his authentication method.

The WindowsPrincipal object adds functionality to the WindowsIdentity object. The WindowsPrincipal object represents the entire security context of the user who is running the current code, including any roles to which he belongs. When the CLR decides which role-based permissions to assign to your code, it inspects the WindowsPrincipal object.

You can retrieve the current WindowsPrincipal object this way:

```
' Tell the CLR which principal policy is in use
AppDomain.CurrentDomain.SetPrincipalPolicy( _
  PrincipalPolicy.WindowsPrincipal)
Dim wi As WindowsIdentity = _
  WindowsIdentity.GetCurrent()
Dim prin As WindowsPrincipal = _
  New WindowsPrincipal(wi)
```

One way to manage role-based security is to use the IsInRole method of the WindowsPrincipal object to determine whether the current user is in a specific Windows group:

```
Dim fAdmin As Boolean = _
  prin.IsInRole(WindowsBuiltInRole.Administrator)
```

The three available overloaded forms of the IsInRole method are as follows:

➤ IsInRole(WindowsBuiltInRole)—Uses one of the WindowsBuiltInRole constants to check for membership in the standard Windows groups.

➤ IsInRole(String)—Checks for membership in a group with the specified name.

➤ IsInRole(Integer)—Checks for membership in a group with the specified Role Identifier (RID). RIDs are assigned by the operating system and provide a language-independent way to identify groups.

Using Caching

Caching refers to storing information for later retrieval, rather than generating it anew every time it's requested. For instance, a Web page can be cached so that it's quicker to deliver when requested a second time. ASP.NET supplies detailed control over caching in Web applications. You can control what should be cached, how long it should be cached, and whether the cached item depends on particular data.

Types of Caching

ASP.NET implements the following three types of caching:

➤ **Output caching**—Refers to caching the entire output of a page request. When you cache a page's output, there are two things that you need to specify. The first is an expiration policy for the cache; you can choose how long a cached page is considered valid before ASP.NET will generate a new version of the page instead of returning the cached page. The second thing to specify is any parameter dependence of the page. For example, suppose that your application includes a Web page that generates statistics for voter registrations by state. You could specify that the output varies by state, so pages for California and Connecticut (and any other states) will be cached separately.

➤ **Fragment caching**—Refers to caching part of a page. ASP.NET enables fragment caching by allowing you to specify cache rules for Web Forms user controls. You can encapsulate a portion of a page into a user control and cache that portion of the page, while still making the rest of the page dynamically generated for each request. The @OutputCache directive will also cache user controls.

➤ **Application data caching**—Refers to caching arbitrary data. You can cache any object you like in ASP.NET by calling the Add or Insert methods of the Cache object. Later, you can retrieve the object programmatically by supplying its key. Cached data can be set to expire in a fixed amount of time, but it can also be made dependent on an external resource. For example, you could cache a connection string with instructions to invalidate the cache if a particular XML file were ever changed.

Using the Cache Object

One way to manage caching is to use the Cache object, which is a static class that's always available to your code. For example, you could configure your page to be cached for 15 seconds with this code:

```
Private Sub Page_Load(ByVal sender As System.Object, _
   ByVal e As System.EventArgs) Handles MyBase.Load
   Response.Cache.SetExpires( _
   DateTime.Now.AddSeconds(15))
   Response.Cache.SetCacheability( _
   HttpCacheability.Public)
   Response.Cache.SetValidUntilExpires(True)
End Sub
```

The SetExpires method specifies an expiration time for the cached version of the page; in this case, 15 seconds from the time the page is generated.

The SetCacheability method specifies where the output can be cached:

NoCache—Indicates no caching at all.

Private—Allows caching only on the client (the default value).

Public—Allows caching on any proxy server, as well as on the client.

Server—Caches the document on the server only.

Finally, the SetValidUntilExpires(true) method tells the server to ignore client-side attempts to refresh the cached content until it expires.

Using a Cache Directive

Alternatively, you can specify the cacheability of a page by using the @OutputCache directive. In your page's HTML, you can specify a 15-second caching time this way:

```
<%@ OutputCache Duration="15" VaryByParam="None" %>
```

In this case, the @OutputCache directive has exactly the same effect as manipulating the cache object did in the previous example. Note that the @OutputCache directive requires the VaryByParam attribute. If the page output doesn't depend on any input parameters, you can use None as the value of this attribute; otherwise, use the name of the parameter to cause caching to be done on a per-parameter-value basis. You can programmatically get the same effect with the cache object by using the Cache.VaryByParams property.

Handling Session State

You probably already know about the use of Session variables to store information in an ASP.NET application. HTTP is, of course, a stateless protocol—meaning that the browser has no way of associating information from one page to another of an ASP.NET application. With Session variables, you store this information on the server. The server sends a cookie or a specially munged URL to the browser with each request, and then uses this value to retrieve session state information when the browser returns a new request.

ASP.NET offers several choices for storing Session variables:

➤ In-process storage

➤ Session state service

➤ SQL Server

Using Session State Within a Process

The default location for session state storage is in the ASP.NET process itself. This enables the server to retrieve the information quickly, but it has a drawback: If you stop the WWW server (or if it crashes for some reason), all this information is lost.

Using Session State Service

As an alternative to using in-process storage for session state, ASP.NET provides the ASP.NET State Service. To use the State Service, you must make an entry in the application's `Web.config` file:

```
<sessionState
    mode="StateServer"
    stateConnectionString="tcpip=127.0.0.1:42424"
    sqlConnectionString=
      "data source=127.0.0.1;user id=sa;password="
    cookieless="false"
    timeout="20"
/>
```

There are two main advantages to using the State Service. First, it does not run in the same process as ASP.NET, so a crash of ASP.NET will not destroy session information. Second, the `stateConnectionString` used to locate the State Service includes the TCP/IP address of the service, which need not be running on the same computer as ASP.NET. This allows you to share state information across a *Web garden* (multiple processors on the same computer) or even across a *Web farm* (multiple servers running the application). With the default in-process storage, you can't share state information between multiple instances of your application.

The major disadvantage of using the State Service is that it's an external process, rather than part of ASP.NET. This means that reading and writing session state is slower than it would be if you kept the state in-process.

Using Microsoft SQL Server to Store Session State

The final choice for storing state information is to save it in a Microsoft SQL Server database. To use SQL Server for storing session state, follow these steps:

1. Run the `InstallSqlState.sql` script from your .NET folder on the Microsoft SQL Server where you intend to store session state. This script will create the necessary database and database objects.

2. Edit the `sessionState` element in the `Web.config` file for your application as follows:

```
<sessionState
        mode="SQLServer"
        stateConnectionString="tcpip=127.0.0.1:42424"
        sqlConnectionString=
        "data source=SERVERHAME;user id=sa;password="
        cookieless="false"
        timeout="20"
/>
```

3. Supply the server name, username, and password for a SQL Server account in the `sqlConnectionString` attribute.

Like the State Service, SQL Server lets you share session state among the processors in a Web garden or the servers in a Web farm. But you also get the additional benefit of persistent storage. Even if the computer hosting SQL Server crashes and is restarted, the session state information will still be present in the database and will be available as soon as the database is running again.

Like the State Service, SQL Server is slower than keeping session state in process. You also need to pay additional licensing fees to use SQL Server for session state in a production application.

Installing and Configuring Server Services

Finally, the exam requires you to understand the basic installation of the server software that ASP.NET depends on. This includes Internet Information Services (IIS) and the Microsoft FrontPage Server Extensions.

Installing and Configuring IIS

Ordinarily, installing IIS is simple: It's installed as part of the operating system. Although you can run some .NET code on Windows NT 4.0 using IIS 4.0, you'll lose substantial functionality that way; in particular, ASP.NET applications or Web Services won't run on that platform. The recommended platform is IIS 5.0 or higher on Windows 2000 or Windows XP.

As of this writing, IIS 6.0 is in beta and is expected to ship as part of Windows Server 2003 in 2003. IIS 6.0 supports ASP.NET excellently out of the box.

To check the status of an IIS installation on Windows 2000 (Windows XP is similar), follow these steps:

1. Select Start, Settings, Control Panel, Add/Remove Programs.

2. Click the Add/Remove Windows Components button on the left side bar of the dialog box.

3. In the Windows Component Wizard, check the check box for Internet Information Services (IIS). You can also click the Details button and select individual components. Make sure that you install at least the common files, FrontPage 2000 Server Extensions, Internet Information Services Snap-In, and World Wide Web Server component.

4. Click Next to install the selected components.

5. Click Finish.

Installing and Configuring FrontPage Server Extensions

Visual Studio .NET also depends on the FrontPage Server Extensions for access to ASP.NET projects on remote servers. If you're working with a server across the Internet, you need to be sure that FrontPage Server Extensions are installed and configured on that server. Even if the server is on the local intranet, you can still use this method of access.

If you install IIS on a hard drive formatted with the NTFS file system, the FrontPage Server Extensions will automatically be installed and configured for you. If you install IIS on a hard drive formatted with the FAT16 or FAT32 file system, you need to follow these steps to configure the FrontPage Server Extensions:

1. Select Start, Settings, Control Panel, Administrative Tools, Computer Management.

2. Drill down into the tree via the Services and Applications node and expand the Internet Information Services node.

3. Right-click the Default Web Server Site node and select All Tasks, Configure Server Extensions.

4. Complete the Server Extensions Wizard by clicking Next, Yes, Next, and then Finish.

Exam Prep Questions

Question 1

> Your ASP.NET application includes this section in its **Web.config** file:
>
> ```
> <identity impersonate="true"
> userName="ADMIN\Megan"
> password="MegansPassword" />
> ```
>
> Your IIS server allows only Windows integrated authentication. What identity will ASP.NET use to authorize resources if a user with the Windows account **Joe** in the **SALES** domain logs in?
>
> ○ A. **ADMIN\Megan**
>
> ○ B. **SALES\Joe**
>
> ○ C. **ASPNET**
>
> ○ D. **IUSR_ComputerName**

Answer A is correct. Because IIS is only allowing Windows integrated authentication, Joe will be forced to log in with his Windows identity. However, ASP.NET will then take the identity explicitly specified in the Web.config file and impersonate that user for all resource requests. Answer B is wrong because impersonation will override the user's login identity. Answer C is wrong because ASPNET is only used when impersonation is off. Answer D is wrong because the server isn't allowing anonymous authentication.

Question 2

> Your ASP.NET application runs on a two-processor computer in a Web garden configuration. Requests are randomly assigned to one of the two processors. If the computer crashes, it's acceptable to lose state information. However, session state information must be available no matter which processor handles the next request. Which alternative should you use for storing state information?
>
> ○ A. Isolated storage
>
> ○ B. In-process storage
>
> ○ C. Session State service
>
> ○ D. SQL Server

Answer C is correct. The Session State service allows you to share state among multiple processors. Answer A is incorrect because isolated storage is a high-overhead disk-based form of storage that is not suitable for ASP.NET applications. Answer B is incorrect because in-process storage is not shared between processors. Answer D is incorrect because the scenario does not require the capabilities of SQL Server, which would just add cost and overhead.

Question 3

Your IIS authentication policy allows anonymous or Windows-integrated authentication. Your ASP.NET application uses role-based security with impersonation enabled. Which account will ASP.NET use when a user attempts to retrieve a page from the application?

- ○ A. The user's own Windows account
- ○ B. The **ASPNET** account
- ○ C. The **IUSR_ComputerName** account
- ○ D. The local Administrator account

Answer C is correct. Because the IIS server allows anonymous authentication, the user will never be prompted for his Windows logon information. ASP.NET will then impersonate the identity of IIS itself: the IUSR_ComputerName account. Thus, Answers A, B, and D are incorrect.

Question 4

You have adjusted a setting in one of your ASP.NET application's configuration files by copying the file to your client computer, editing it with a text editor, and using FTP to copy the changed file over the original file. What must you do to have the new setting take effect?

- ○ A. Restart the WWW service on the computer.
- ○ B. Restart the ASP.NET service on the computer.
- ○ C. Reboot the computer.
- ○ D. Continue to use the application.

Answer D is correct. ASP.NET monitors your application's configuration files for changes and immediately applies the changes when any are detected. You don't have to take any special action to have changed settings take effect. Thus, answers A, B, and C are incorrect.

Question 5

Your Web application is installed on a Web farm to provide scalability. The application maintains critical medical records information in session state until several pages have finished processing the information. This session state must be maintained even if the server crashes. Which alternative should you use for storing state information in this application?

- ○ A. In-process storage
- ○ B. Session State service
- ○ C. SQL Server
- ○ D. Configuration files

Answer C is correct. SQL Server provides secure, transactional, logged storage for session state information that will even survive server reboots. Answer A is incorrect because in-process storage cannot be shared across servers in a Web farm. Answer B is incorrect because state in the Session State service will not survive a reboot. Answer D is incorrect because configuration files are used for storing administrative information, not state information.

Question 6

Your application requires the user to be in the Debugger Users group to ensure proper functionality. Which ASP.NET security feature can you use to check the user's group membership?

- ○ A. Role-based security
- ○ B. Encryption
- ○ C. Passport authentication
- ○ D. Impersonation

Answer A is correct. Role-based security lets you make decisions in your application logic based on the user's Windows identity, including his group memberships. Answer B is incorrect because encryption is used to protect sensitive data. Answer C is incorrect because Passport provides authentication, but does not tie the authenticated user to your Windows domain. Answer D is incorrect because impersonation controls which set of credentials ASP.NET presents for a user, but does not allow you to verify the user's group membership.

Question 7

> You require users of your ASP.NET application to provide a strong identity to the application. You must allow users with any version 4.x or higher browser, and you must ensure that any passwords that cross the network are encrypted. Which form of authentication should you use?
>
> ○ A. Windows authentication with basic IIS authentication
>
> ○ B. Windows authentication with digest IIS authentication
>
> ○ C. Windows authentication with integrated IIS authentication
>
> ○ D. Passport authentication with anonymous IIS authentication

Answer D is correct. Answer A is incorrect because basic IIS authentication does not use encryption for passwords. Answer B is incorrect because digest authentication requires Internet Explorer as a browser. Answer C is incorrect because integrated authentication requires Internet Explorer as a browser. Only Passport authentication, as specified in answer D, fulfills the requirements.

Question 8

> Your ASP.NET application will run on your company's intranet, where all users have Internet Explorer 6.0 as their browser, and all users are authenticated by a Windows domain. You need to track which user accesses certain critical resources. Which form of authentication should you use?
>
> ○ A. None
>
> ○ B. Forms
>
> ○ C. Windows
>
> ○ D. Passport

Answer C is correct. In this situation, all users are already authenticated by a Windows domain, so using Windows authentication avoids an extra authentication step while still identifying each user. Answer A is incorrect because with no authentication, you cannot track users. Answers B and D are incorrect because these forms of authentication will require additional programming and user effort.

Question 9

You need to add a configuration section to the **machine.config** file on your Web server so that it is shared by all applications on the server. You want to ensure that this section cannot be defined in any other configuration file. Which declaration should you use?

○ A.
```
<section name="customSection"
      type="CustomConfiguration Handler"
      allowDefinition=
      "MachineToApplication"/>
```

○ B.
```
<section name="customSection"
      type="CustomConfiguration Handler"
      allowLocation="false"/>
```

○ C.
```
<section name="customSection"
      type="CustomConfiguration Handler" />
```

○ D.
```
<section name="customSection"
      type="CustomConfiguration Handler"
      allowOverride="false"/>
```

Answer B is correct. The `allowLocation` attribute lets you specify that this section should not appear beneath the file where it is defined. Answer A is incorrect because setting the `allowDefinition` attribute to `MachineToApplication` allows defining this section on the application level. Answer C is incorrect because omitting all attributes allows it to be defined everywhere. Answer D is incorrect because the `allowOverride` attribute applies to actual configuration data, not to section declarations.

Need to Know More?

 Jones, A. Russell. *Mastering ASP.NET with VB.NET.* Sybex, 2002.

 Liberty, Jesse and Hurwitz, Dan. *Programming ASP.NET.* O'Reilly, 2002.

 Leinecker, Richard. *Special Edition Using ASP.NET.* Que, 2002.

 ASP.NET Web, `http://www.asp.net`.

17

Practice Exam #1

Do not read Chapters 17–20 until you've learned and practiced all the material presented in the chapters of this book. These chapters serve a special purpose; they are designed to test whether you are ready to take the exam 70-305. In these chapters, you will find two self tests. Each self test is followed by an answer key and brief explanation of correct answers, along with an explanation for why the other answers are incorrect. Reading these chapters prior to other chapters is like reading the climax of a story and then going back to find out how the story arrived at that ending. Of course, you don't want to spoil the excitement, do you?

How to Take the Self Tests

Each self test in this book consists of 60 questions, and you should complete each test within 120 minutes. The number of questions and the time duration in the actual exam might vary, but it should be close to this number.

Once you have prepared the material presented in the chapters of this book, you should take Practice Exam #1 to check how much you are prepared. After the self test is complete, evaluate yourself using the answer key in Chapter 18, "Answer Key for Practice Exam #1." When you evaluate yourself, note the questions that you answered incorrectly, identify the corresponding chapters in the book, and then read and understand that material before taking the Practice Exam #2. After taking the second exam, evaluate yourself again and reread the material corresponding to any incorrect answers. Finally, retake both tests again until you have correctly answered all the questions. The information presented in the following sections should help you prepare for the exams.

Exam-Taking Tips

Take these sample exams under your own circumstances, but I strongly suggest that when you take them, you treat them just as you would treat the actual exam at the test center. Use the following tips to get maximum benefit from the exams:

➤ Before you start, create a quiet, secluded environment in which you are not disturbed for the duration of the exam.

➤ Provide yourself with a few blank sheets of paper before you start. Use some of these sheets to write your answers, and use the others to organize your thoughts. At the end of the exam, use your answer sheet to evaluate your exam with the help of the answer key that follows the sample exam.

➤ Don't use any reference material during the exam.

➤ Some of the questions might be vague and require you to make deductions to come up with the best possible answer from the possibilities given. Others might be verbose, requiring you to read and process a lot of information before you reach the actual question.

➤ As you progress, keep track of the elapsed time and make sure that you'll be able to answer all the questions in the given time limit.

Self Test

Question 1

You are developing an ASP.NET application using Visual Basic .NET. In your ASPX page, you want to invoke and display a Visual Basic .NET method named **DisplayProductNames()** when the page is rendered to the client. Which of the following code blocks should you choose to call the **DisplayProductNames()** method?

O A.
```
<script language="VB" runat="server">
    Response.Write(DisplayProductNames())
</script>
```

O B.
```
<script language="VB" runat="client">
    Response.Write(DisplayProductNames())
</script>
```

O C.
```
<script language="VB">
    Response.Write(DisplayProductNames())
</script>
```

O D.
```
<%= DisplayProductNames()%>
```

Question 2

You use Visual Basic .NET to develop an ASP.NET Web Form named **Login.aspx**. This Web Form allows users to enter their credentials for accessing the Web site. You have defined a code-behind class named **Login** under the **MyCompany** namespace in a file named **Login.aspx.vb** that contains the business logic. You now want to link the user interface file with the code-behind file; you do not want to pre-compile the code-behind class each time you make modifications. Which of the following **Page** directives would you use in **Login.aspx** file?

O A.
```
<%@ Page Language="vb"
Codebehind="Login.aspx.vb"
ClassName="MyCompany.Login"%>
```

O B.
```
<%@ Page Language="vb"
Codebehind="Login.aspx.vb"
Inherits="MyCompany.Login"%>
```

○ C.
```
<%@ Page Language="vb"
Src="Login.aspx.vb"
Inherits="MyCompany.Login"%>
```

○ D.
```
<%@ Page Language="vb"
Src="Login.aspx.vb"
ClassName="MyCompany.Login"%>
```

Question 3

Your Web Form allows the user to enter a telephone number into a **TextBox** ASP.NET Web server control named **txtPhone**. You use the **RegularExpressionValidator** control to ensure that the phone number is in the correct format.

The Web Form also includes a **Button** ASP.NET Web server control, **btnReset**, to reset the data entry values. You do not want the validations to occur when the button is clicked. What should you do to ensure this?

○ A. Set the **CausesValidation** property of the **TextBox** control to **True**.

○ B. Set the **CausesValidation** property of the **Button** control to **True**.

○ C. Set the **CausesValidation** property of the **TextBox** control to **False**.

○ D. Set the **CausesValidation** property of the **Button** control to **False**.

Question 4

You have designed a Web Form that uses a **DropDownList** control to allow the user to select his state of residence to complete his shipping address. You've implemented an event handler for the **SelectedIndexChanged** event to update the sales tax amount displayed on the Web Form when a new state is changed.

Users report that the sales tax amount is not updated no matter which state they choose in the **DropDownList** control. What must you do to fix this problem?

○ A. Move the code to the **PreRender** event of the **DropDownList** control.

○ B. Set the **AutoPostBack** property of the **DropDownList** control to **True**.

○ C. Replace the **DropDownList** control with a **ListBox** control.

○ D. Set the **EnableViewState** property of the **DropDownList** control to **True**.

Question 5

You have designed a Web Form that includes a **DropDownList** control with the **ID** of **ddlSize**. The **Items** property of the **ddlSize** control contains the following items:

-
1
2
3
4

The Web Form also contains a **RequiredFieldValidator** control named **rfvSize**. You have set the **ControlToValidate** property of **rfvSize** to **ddlSize**. Your goal is to make sure that a non-default value is chosen from **ddlSize** before the Web Form is posted back to the server. What other property setting must you make on the **rfvSize** control?

○ A.
```
rfvSize.InitialValue = "-"
```

○ B.
```
rfvSize.Display = ValidatorDisplay.Dynamic
```

○ C.
```
rfvSize.Visible = True
```

○ D.
```
rfvSize.EnableClientScript = False
```

Question 6

You have developed an ASP.NET Web page that consists of several Web server controls for data entry. You have placed validation controls to validate the data entered in the Web server controls. You have used the **Text** property of the validation controls to display the error messages inline within the validation control. You have deployed the Web page to the testing Web server so that the testers can test your Web page. One of the testers who uses Internet Explorer 4.0 reports that the Web page does not display the error message when he tabs from the control after providing an invalid value. The error messages are only displayed when he clicks the Submit button. How can you solve this problem?

○ A. Set the **Enabled** attribute of the validation controls to **True**.

○ B. Set the **SmartNavigation** attribute to **True** in the **Page** directive.

○ C. Ask the tester to enable client-side scripting before accessing the Web page.

○ D. Ask the tester to upgrade to Internet Explorer 6.0 before accessing the Web page.

Question 7

When a page is restricted in your ASP.NET application (that is, when a 403 error occurs), you want to display a page named **Forbidden.aspx**. For all other errors, you want to display a page named **GeneralError.aspx** to the user. Which settings should you make in the **Web.config** file to ensure this?

○ A.
```
<customErrors mode="On"
 defaultRedirect="GeneralError.aspx">
    <error statusCode="403" redirect="Forbidden.aspx" />
</customErrors>
```

○ B.
```
<customErrors mode="RemoteOnly"
 defaultRedirect="GeneralError.aspx">
    <error statusCode="403" redirect="Forbidden.aspx" />
</customErrors>
```

○ C.
```
<customErrors mode="On">
    <error statusCode="403" redirect="Forbidden.aspx" />
    <error statusCode="all" redirect="GeneralError.aspx" />
</customErrors>
```

○ D.
```
<customErrors mode="RemoteOnly">
    <error statusCode="403" redirect="Forbidden.aspx" />
    <error statusCode="all" redirect="GeneralError.aspx" />
</customErrors>
```

Question 8

You have written a Visual Basic .NET method that opens a database connection using a **SqlConnection** object, which retrieves some information from the database and then closes the connection. The information is retrieved using a stored procedure that might not always be available because of the maintenance schedules. You have wrapped the code to call the stored procedure in a **Try-Catch-Finally** block. You use two Catch blocks, one to catch the exceptions of type **SqlException** and the second to catch the exceptions of type **Exception**. Which of the following places should you choose to call the **Close()** method of the **SqlConnection** object?

○ A. Inside the **Try** block, before the first **Catch** block

○ B. Inside the **Catch** block that catches **SqlException** objects

○ C. Inside the **Catch** block that catches **Exception** objects

○ D. Inside the **Finally** block

Question 9

Your ASP.NET application includes a Web page named **Errors.htm** that is displayed in response to any error. This page is configured using this code in the **Web.config** file:

```
<customErrors mode="Off"
 defaultRedirect="Errors.htm">
</customErrors>
```

The application includes a detail page named **AccountSummary.aspx**. When an error occurs on the account summary page, you want to log those errors in the custom log file **Custom.txt**. What should you do?

○ A. Add an **<error>** element as a child of the **<customErrors>** element in **Web.config**. Specify the page name **AccountSummary.aspx** and the redirect page **Custom.txt** in the new element.

○ B. Add an **ErrorPage** attribute to the **Page** directive for **AccountSummary.aspx**. Set the value of this attribute to **Custom.txt**.

○ C. Implement the logic in the **Page_Error()** event handler in **AccountSummary.aspx** to store errors into **Custom.txt**.

○ D. Implement the logic in the **Application_Error()** event handler in **AccountSummary.aspx** to store errors into **Custom.txt**.

Question 10

You are developing an application to take orders over the Internet. When the user posts back the order form, you first check to see whether he is a registered customer of your company. If not, you must transfer control to the **Register.html** page. Which method should you use to transfer?

○ A.
```
Response.Redirect("Register.html")
```

○ B.
```
Server.Transfer("Register.html")
```

○ C.
```
Server.Execute("Register.html")
```

○ D.
```
Server.CreateObject("Register.html")
```

Question 11

You have deployed an ASP.NET application on your company's intranet. Your company has standardized on Internet Explorer 6.0 as the corporate browser. Users complain that when they use the Submit button to send in their expense reports via the application, the focus moves to the first control on the reporting form. This makes it difficult for users to edit their expense reports.

What is the easiest way to maintain focus across postback operations in this application?

- O A. Store the name of the current control in session state when the page is posted back, and use this name to set the focus when the page is re-created.

- O B. Store the name of the current control in view state when the page is posted back, and use this name to set the focus when the page is re-created.

- O C. Write client-side code that stores the focus control in a hidden field and retrieves this information when the page is re-created.

- O D. Set the **SmartNavigation** attribute of the **Page** directive to **True**.

Question 12

Your ASP.NET Web application makes use of session state to track the username and other user specific details. Your Web application contains a Web page that displays the greetings to the user "Welcome *<UserName>*" and the product catalog from a SQL Server database. The product catalog is displayed in a **DataGrid** control that is populated at every page load. Which of the following options should you use in this application to maximize performance? (Select two.)

- ❑ A. Disable view state for the page.
- ❑ B. Disable session state for the page.
- ❑ C. Make the session state read-only for the page.
- ❑ D. Store the session state in SQL Server.

Question 13

Your ASP.NET application stores sensitive data in the session state. You need to maintain the session state even if the Web server crashes and needs to be restarted. Which mode attribute should you use to configure the **<sessionState>** element for this application?

○ A.

```
mode="Inproc"
```

○ B.

```
mode="StateServer"
```

○ C.

```
mode="SqlServer"
```

○ D.

```
mode="Off"
```

Question 14

You are developing an online bookstore application in Visual Basic .NET. Your application needs to store the most recent book viewed by the user. You show the recently viewed book's details in the lower part of the Web pages whenever the user accesses the Web site. You do not want to use server-side resources to store the book's ISBN. Which of the following state management techniques will help you accomplish this?

○ A. Hidden fields

○ B. **ViewState**

○ C. Cookies

○ D. Session

Question 15

You have created an ASP.NET Web page named **Catalog.aspx** that allows the user to purchase products from the catalog. The catalog displays the previously selected item in the lower part of the Web page. This product detail is encapsulated in a **Product** object and is not accessed outside the Web page. The **Product** class is defined as

```
<Serializable>Public Class Product
    Public ProductCode As Int32
    Public ProductName As String
End Class
```

Which of the following objects should you use to store the **Product** object?

○ A. Application state

○ B. Session state

○ C. **ViewState**

○ D. Cache object

Question 16

You have developed an ASP.NET Web Form that displays product information from a SQL Server 2000 database. The database contains information for about 100 products. Each time the page is displayed, it retrieves information on one product specified by the user. These pages are requested very frequently by the users.

What type of caching can you use to speed up the delivery of this page?

○ A. Output

○ B. Varying Output

○ C. Application Data

○ D. Fragment Output

Question 17

You are creating an ASP.NET Web page that reads data from a large XML file, **CustomerInformation.xml**, processes and loads the data in a **DataSet** object, and displays the results to the browser in a **DataGrid** control. The processing of the file data consumes server resources and delays loading of the Web page. The Web page displays the same data at every request unless the data in the file changes. Which of the following code segments should you use for caching to improve performance?

○ A.
```
<%@ OutputCache VaryByCustom="CustomerInformation.xml" %>
```

○ B.
```
<%@ OutputCache VaryByParam="CustomerInformation.xml" %>
```

○ C.
```
Cache("FileData") = dsCustomers
```

○ D.
```
Cache.Insert("CacheValue", dsCustomers, _
    New CacheDependency(Server.MapPath( _
    "CustomerInformation.xml")))
```

Question 18

You are an ASP.NET developer of a company that has a chain of stores selling leather products in the United States. You have developed a user control named **StoreLocator.ascx** that is placed in the main page of the company's Web site. The user control contains a text box named **txtState** that accepts a state name from the user and displays the list of stores in the state. You want to cache different versions of the user control for 600 seconds for each state. Which of the following **OutputCache** directives should you choose to enable caching on the user control?

○ A.
```
<%@ OutputCache Duration="600" VaryByControl="txtState" %>
```

○ B.
```
<%@ OutputCache Duration="600" VaryByParam="txtState" %>
```

○ C.
```
<%@ OutputCache Duration="600" VaryByControl="*" %>
```

○ D.
```
<%@ OutputCache Duration="600" VaryByParam="*" %>
```

Question 19

In your ASP.NET application, you use the data cache to store a **DataSet** object containing a single **DataTable** object named **Customers**. The **Customers DataTable** has all the rows and columns from the **Customers** table in your database. You would like to bind only selected columns from the **Customers** table to a **DataGrid** control. You want a solution that requires minimum programming, and you want to have minimum impact on the functionality and performance of other applications accessing the same SQL Server database. How should you proceed?

○ A. Create a second **DataTable** in the **DataSet**. Copy the desired data to the second **DataTable**. Bind the second **DataTable** to the **DataGrid**.

○ B. Create a **Command** object to retrieve the desired columns from the **DataTable**. Bind the **Command** object to the **DataGrid**.

○ C. Delete the undesired columns from the **DataTable**.

○ D. Create a **DataView** that retrieves only the desired columns from the **DataTable**. Bind the **DataGrid** to the **DataView**.

Question 20

Your ASP.NET Web application includes a **SqlDataAdapter** object named **sqlDataAdapter1** that was created by dragging and dropping the Customers table from a database to your form. Your application also includes a **DataSet** named **dsCustomers1**, based on this **SqlDataAdapter**. What line of code should you use to load the data from the database into the **DataSet**?

○ A.
```
dsCustomers1= sqlDataAdapter1.Fill("Customers")
```

○ B.
```
sqlDataAdapter1.Fill("dsCustomers1", "Customers")
```

○ C.
```
sqlDataAdapter1.Fill(dsCustomers1, "Customers")
```

○ D.
```
sqlDataAdapter1.Fill(dsCustomers1)
```

Question 21

You have recently deployed an ASP.NET expense reporting system in your company. The application relies heavily on its SQL Server database. All employees in the company have similar access permissions to the database. You have created the application in such a way that it uses an employee's logon name and password in the connection string to connect to SQL Server. Users of the application are consistently reporting slow performance of the application. Your task is to optimize the performance of this application. You noted that another application, which uses the same SQL Server database, is having good performance. Which of the following steps will you take?

○ A. Compile the application to native code using **ngen.exe**.

○ B. Run the SQL Server Index Tuning Wizard.

○ C. Increase the maximum size of the connection pool.

○ D. Use the same connection string for all users.

Question 22

You are developing an ASP.NET Web application named **VerifyOrders**. The **VerifyOrders** application receives data from the Orders application in XML format. The **VerifyOrders** application enables its users to review the orders and make any changes if required. When the users are done reviewing the orders, the **VerifyOrders** application must create an output XML file, which is returned to the Orders application. The output XML file must contain the original as well as the changed values. Which of the following options will you choose to create such an output XML file?

○ A. Call the **DataSet.WriteXmlSchema()** method and pass an **XmlWriter** object as a parameter.

○ B. Call the **DataSet.WriteXml()** method and set the value for the **XmlWriteMode** parameter to **IgnoreSchema**.

○ C. Call the **DataSet.WriteXml()** method and set the value for the **XmlWriteMode** parameter to **WriteSchema**.

○ D. Call the **DataSet.WriteXml()** method and set the value for the **XmlWriteMode** parameter to **DiffGram**.

Question 23

You are writing a Visual Basic .NET Web application that executes several stored procedures to update a SQL Server database. You use database transactions to ensure that either all updates to the database succeed or the changes are rolled back in case of an error. You used the following code segment to create the database connection and the transaction object in your program:

```
Dim sqlConnection1 As SqlConnection = _
    New SqlConnection(strConnString)
sqlConnection1.Open()

Dim sqlCommand1 As SqlCommand = New SqlCommand()
Dim sqlTrans As SqlTransaction
```

You need to prevent other users from updating or inserting rows into the database until the transaction is complete. Which of the following statements enables you to fulfill this requirement?

○ A.
```
sqlTrans = sqlConnection1.BeginTransaction( _
    IsolationLevel.ReadCommitted)
```

○ B.
```
sqlTrans = sqlConnection1.BeginTransaction( _
    IsolationLevel.Serializable)
```

○ C.
```
sqlTrans = sqlCommand1.BeginTransaction( _
    IsolationLevel.ReadCommitted)
```

○ D.
```
sqlTrans = sqlCommand1.BeginTransaction( _
    IsolationLevel.Serializable)
```

Question 24

You need to develop a Web application that exports the content of the **Customers** table to an XML file. The exported XML file will be used by a marketing company for various customer relation programs. The marketing company requires that customer data should be exported to the XML file in the following format:

```
<Customers CustomerID="ALFKI" ContactName="Maria Anders"
    Phone="030-0074321" />
<Customers CustomerID="ANATR" ContactName="Ana Trujillo"
    Phone="(5) 555-4729" />
```

Which of the following code segment would you use to export the Customers table to the XML format in the specified format?

○ A.

```
Dim c As DataColumn
For Each c in dataSet1.Tables("Customers").Columns
    c.ColumnMapping = MappingType.Attribute
Next
dataSet1.WriteXml("Customers.xml")
```

○ B.

```
Dim c As DataColumn
For Each c in dataSet1.Tables("Customers").Columns
    c.ColumnMapping = MappingType.Element
Next
dataSet1.WriteXml("Customers.xml")
```

○ C.

```
Dim c As DataColumn
For Each c in dataSet1.Tables("Customers").Columns
    c.ColumnMapping = MappingType.Attribute
Next
dataSet1.WriteXml("Customers.xml", XmlWriteMode.WriteSchema)
```

○ D.

```
Dim c As DataColumn
For Each c in dataSet1.Tables("Customers").Columns
    c.ColumnMapping = MappingType.Element
Next
dataSet1.WriteXml("Customers.xml", XmlWriteMode.WriteSchema)
```

Question 25

You are developing a Web application that processes data from a SQL Server 7.0 database. The application reads the data from the database in a forward-only way and does not perform any update operations. You use the **System.Data.SqlClient.SqlConnection** object to connect to the SQL Server database. You then use a **System.Data.SqlClient.SqlCommand** object to run a stored procedure and retrieve the results into a **System.Data.SqlClient.SqlDataReader** object. The data returned by the **SqlCommand** object consists of 1,000 rows and 1 column; the column is defined as **nvarchar(20)** in the database. You have written the following code to concatenate the column values of the returned result set into a string variable. What can you do to optimize this portion of the application? (Select two.)

```
Dim dr As SqlDataReader = cmd.ExecuteReader()
Dim s As String
While(dr.Read())
    s = s & dr.GetValue(0)
End While
```

- ❑ A. Replace the stored procedure with a SQL statement.
- ❑ B. Replace the **SqlDataReader** object with a **DataSet** object.
- ❑ C. Replace the **While** loop with a **For Each** loop.
- ❑ D. Replace the **String** variable with a **StringBuilder** object.
- ❑ E. Replace the **GetValue()** method with the **GetString()** method.

Question 26

Your application uses a **SqlDataReader** object to retrieve patient information from a medical records database. When you find a patient who is currently hospitalized, you want to read the names of the patient's caregivers from the same database. You have created a second **SqlDataReader** object, based on a second **SqlCommand** object, to retrieve the caregiver information. When you call the **ExecuteReader()** method of the **SqlCommand** object, you get an error. What is the most likely cause of this error?

- ○ A. You are using the same **SqlConnection** object for both the **SqlDataReader** objects, and the first **SqlDataReader** is still open when you try to execute the **SqlCommand**.
- ○ B. You must use a **SqlDataAdapter** object to retrieve the caregiver information.
- ○ C. You must use the **OleDbDataReader** object to retrieve information instead of the **SqlDataReader** object.
- ○ D. You are using the **ExecuteReader()** method of the **SqlCommand** object, but you should be using the **ExecuteScalar()** method instead.

Question 27

You use Visual Basic .NET to develop an ASP.NET Web application that will be used by the customer service department. Your application receives data from the Orders application. Users of your application get calls from the customers to make changes to their orders. You write the code that allows them to make the changes to the data, but now you want to write code that sends the changed records back to the Orders application. Which of the following methods should you use to accomplish this requirement?

○ A. **DataSet.Clone()**

○ B. **DataSet.Copy()**

○ C. **DataSet.GetChanges()**

○ D. **DataSet.Merge()**

Question 28

You are a .NET developer for a large warehousing company. You need to develop a Web application that helps users in managing the inventory. Inventory data is stored in a SQL Server 2000 named **WareHouse2** in a database named Inventory. You use the **SqlConnection** object and Windows Integrated authentication to connect with the **Inventory** database. Which of the following connection strings should you choose in your Visual Basic .NET program?

○ A.

```
"Provider=SQLOLEDB;Data Source=WareHouse2;
➥Initial Catalog=Inventory;
➥Integrated Security=SSPI;"
```

○ B.

```
"Provider=SQLOLEDB;Data Source=WareHouse2;
➥Initial Catalog=Inventory;
➥User Id=sa;Password=Ti7uGf1;"
```

○ C.

```
"Data Source=WareHouse2;
➥Initial Catalog=inventory;
➥Trusted_Connection=True;"
```

○ D.

```
"Data Source=WareHouse2;User Id=sa;
➥Password=Ti7uikGf1;
➥Initial Catalog=inventory;"
```

Question 29

You need to develop a database application that interacts with a Jet database. You need to write code to return the total number of customers from the database. You need to create the fastest solution. Which of the following actions should you take?

- ❑ A. Write an ad hoc SQL query to return the total number of customers.
- ❑ B. Create a stored procedure to return the total number of customers.
- ❑ C. Use the **OleDbCommand.ExecuteScalar()** method.
- ❑ D. Use the **OleDbCommand.ExecuteReader()** method.
- ❑ E. Use the **OleDbDataAdapter.Fill()** method.

Question 30

A Web Form in your ASP.NET application includes a **ListBox** control named **lbCustomers** that displays a list of customers. The **DataTextField** property of the **ListBox** is bound to the **CompanyName** column of the **Customers** database table. The **DataValueField** property of the **ListBox** is bound to the **CustomerID** column of the **Customers** database table.

Your form also contains a **TextBox** control named **txtCustomerID**. This control uses simple data binding to display the **SelectedItem.Value** from the **ListBox** control.

When the user selects a new company name in the **ListBox**, you want to display the corresponding **CustomerID** value in the **txtCustomerID** control. What should you do?

- ○ A. Call the **DataBind()** method of the **ListBox** control in the **SelectedIndexChanged** event of the **ListBox**.
- ○ B. Create a public property named **CustomerID** and return the **SelectedItem.Value** property of the **ListBox** as the value of the public property.
- ○ C. Use simple data binding to bind the **SelectedItem.Value** property of the **ListBox** to the **CustomerID** column of the Customers table.
- ○ D. Call the **DataBind()** method of the **TextBox** control in the **SelectedIndexChanged** event of the **ListBox**.

Question 31

You are developing a sales analysis Web page that displays monthly sales in a **DataGrid** control. Whenever the sales amount increases average sales, you want to display the sales amount underlined. Which of the following events should you choose to display the sales amount underlined?

- ○ A. **ItemCreated**
- ○ B. **ItemCommand**
- ○ C. **ItemDataBound**
- ○ D. **DataBinding**

Question 32

You have to develop an ASP.NET Web application that will be used by the order tracking system of your company. The application contains a form that displays a list of orders placed by the customers for the past one year. When an employee selects an order from the list box, you need to display the order status and other information of the selected order in a **DataList** control. You have retrieved the order details in a **DataSet** object named **dsOrders**. The **dsOrders** contains a table Order that contains the order status and other information. You have set the **DataSource** property of the **DataList** control to **dsOrders** and **DataMember** property to Order. Which line of code would you use to bind the text box control to the field named **OrderID** in the Order table?

- ○ A.
```
<ItemTemplate>
    <asp:TextBox id="txtOrderID" runat="server"
     text='<%# dsOrders.Order.OrderID %>'>
    </asp:TextBox>
</ItemTemplate>
```

- ○ B.
```
<SelectedItemTemplate>
    <asp:TextBox id="txtOrderID" runat="server"
     text='<%# dsOrders.Order.OrderID %>'>
    </asp:TextBox>
</SelectedItemTemplate>
```

○ C.
```
<ItemTemplate>
    <asp:TextBox id="txtOrderID" runat="server"
        text='<%# DataBinder.Eval(
            Container.DataItem, "OrderID") %>'>
    </asp:TextBox>
</ItemTemplate>
```

○ D.
```
<SelectedItemTemplate>
    <asp:TextBox id="txtOrderID" runat="server"
        text='<%# DataBinder.Eval(
            Container.DataItem, "OrderID") %>'>
    </asp:TextBox>
</SelectedItemTemplate>
```

Question 33

You are designing an application that will allow the user to read an XML file from an orders system and convert the XML file into an HTML file using the style sheet **DisplayOrders.xsl**. Which object should you use to implement this requirement?

○ A. **XPathNavigator**

○ B. **XslTransform**

○ C. **XmlSchema**

○ D. **XmlNode**

Question 34

You need to develop an ASP.NET Web application that accesses the Orders XML Web service provided by your company's business partner. You know the URL of the Web service. How can you generate client-side proxy classes for a Web service? (Select two.)

❑ A. Use a proxy tool such as the .NET Web Service Studio tool.

❑ B. Use the Web Services Description Language tool.

❑ C. Use the Web Services Discovery tool.

❑ D. Add a Web Reference to point to the Web service.

Question 35

You work as a Visual Basic .NET programmer for a multinational marketing company. You have been given a task to create a localized version of a Web Form for use in countries where the text is read from right to left. You need to make sure that all the controls in the form are aligned properly for the ease of local users. You need to make minimum changes. Which of the following options should you choose to accomplish this task?

○ A. Set the **dir** attribute of each control on the Web Form to **rtl**.

○ B. Set the **rtl** attribute of each control on the Web Form to **True**.

○ C. Set the **dir** attribute of the **<HTML>** element to **rtl**.

○ D. Set the **rtl** attribute of the **<HTML>** element to **True**.

Question 36

You are converting an existing ASP application to an ASP.NET application. The ASP application uses ADO extensively for data access. You do not yet want to convert the ADO code to ADO.NET code. You should ensure that the ADO objects continue to function properly on the ASP.NET pages. You want to achieve the best possible performance from your application. Which of the following solutions should you choose?

○ A. Build a Runtime Callable Wrapper for each ADO object that you use.

○ B. Use a **Page** directive to set ASP compatibility mode on the ASP.NET pages:

```
<%@ Page AspCompat="True" %>
```

○ C. Use a **Page** directive to set the ASP.NET page language to **VBScript**:

```
<%@ Page Language="VBScript" %>
```

○ D. Use the Type Library Importer tool to create a Primary Interop Assembly for the ADO objects.

Question 37

You are responsible for maintaining a COM component that is used by numerous applications throughout your company. You are not yet ready to convert this COM component to .NET managed code, but you need to make it available to an increasing number of other projects that are being developed under the .NET Framework. What should you do?

○ A. Set a direct reference to the existing COM component from each .NET project.

○ B. Use the Type Library Importer tool to create and sign an assembly that will use the COM component. Place the created assembly in the Global Assembly Cache.

○ C. Use the Type Library Importer tool to create an assembly that will use the COM component. Place the created assembly in the Global Assembly Cache.

○ D. Obtain a Primary Interop Assembly for the COM component.

○ E. Set a direct reference from a single .NET project to the COM component. Include this project in each solution that must make use of the component.

Question 38

You are developing your company's Web site using a Visual Basic .NET Web application. The product demo page of the Web site uses PNG graphics to represent the steps involved in using the product. Your company has a strict policy to make Web pages accessible to all the readers. What should you do to make this page more accessible?

○ A. Use JPG graphics instead of PNG graphics for maximum browser compatibility.

○ B. Use the **AccessKey** property for all graphical controls to make them more accessible.

○ C. Add ALT text to all graphics to indicate their purpose through the **AlternateText** property.

○ D. Add ALT text to all graphics to indicate their purpose through the **ToolTip** property.

Question 39

You use Visual Studio .NET to create an ASP.NET Web application that interacts with a Microsoft SQL Server database. You create a stored procedure to calculate the monthly wireless Internet access charges for the customers. You name the stored procedure **CalculateAccessCharges**. When you run the program, you observe that the results from the stored procedure are not as expected. You want to debug the **CalculateAccessCharges** stored procedure to find the error. You want to minimize the time and efforts involved in debugging; which of the following actions should you take?

- ○ A. Use the Tools, Debug Processes menu to attach a debugger to the SQL Server and then step in to the **CalculateAccessAcharges** stored procedure.

- ○ B. Place a breakpoint in the **CalculateAccessCharges** stored procedure and then use the Debug, Step Into menu item to step in to the Visual Basic .NET program that calls the stored procedure.

- ○ C. Use the SQL Server **Print** command to print the calculated values in the stored procedure.

- ○ D. Use the **Debug.WriteLine()** method to print the calculated values in the stored procedure.

Question 40

You develop a customer contact management application using a Visual Basic ASP.NET Web application. You use the methods of the **Trace** and **Debug** classes to log serious error messages encountered during program execution. You want to record all such errors in the Windows event log. You do not want any duplicate entries for error messages in the event log. In what two ways can you add a listener to the Windows event log?

- ❑ A.
```
Dim traceListener As EventLogTraceListener = _
    New EventLogTraceListener("CustomEventLog")
Trace.Listeners.Add(traceListener)
```

- ❑ B.
```
Dim traceListener As EventLogTraceListener = _
    New EventLogTraceListener("CustomEventLog")
Trace.Listeners.Add(traceListener)
Debug.Listeners.Add(traceListener)
```

❑ C.
```
Dim traceListener As EventLogTraceListener = _
    New EventLogTraceListener("CustomEventLog")
```

❑ D.
```
Dim traceListener As EventLogTraceListener = _
    New EventLogTraceListener("CustomEventLog")
Debug.Listeners.Add(traceListener)
```

Question 41

Your Web application is failing when a particular variable equals 117. Unfortunately, you cannot predict when this will happen. You want to write minimum code; which debugging tool should you use to investigate the problem?

○ A. Locals window

○ B. Output window

○ C. Immediate window

○ D. Conditional Breakpoint

Question 42

You develop a Visual Studio .NET application that helps the shipping department in creating mix-and-match pallets. Users of the application complain that the numbers of cases in the pallet are not displayed correctly. To find the location of the error, you place a breakpoint on the **GetCasesInPallet()** method. However, when you execute the program from the Visual Studio .NET environment, the execution does not break at the breakpoint. Which of the following actions should you take to resolve this problem?

○ A. Select Exceptions from the Debug menu.

○ B. Select Enable All Breakpoints from the Debug menu.

○ C. Select Build, Configuration Manager and set the project's configuration to Debug.

○ D. Select Build, Configuration Manager and set the project's configuration to Release.

Question 43

You are debugging your ASP.NET Web application; you are concerned about the amount of time it's taking to render a particular page. Which class can you use to obtain detailed timing information for the events on the page as it is rendered by the ASP.NET engine?

- ○ A. **System.Diagnostics.Trace**
- ○ B. **System.Diagnostics.Debug**
- ○ C. **System.Web.TraceContext**
- ○ D. **System.Web.UI.Page**

Question 44

You have developed an online shipment tracking a Visual Basic ASP.NET application. The **ShipmentStatus.aspx** page in your application is displaying incorrect shipping status for shipments. You want to view the tracing information for the page. What should you do?

- ○ A. Set the **<trace>** element in the **Web.config** configuration file of the application to
  ```
  <trace enabled="False" />
  ```

- ○ B. Set the **<trace>** element in the **Web.config** configuration file of the application to
  ```
  <trace enabled="True" />
  ```

- ○ C. Set the **<trace>** element in the **Web.config** configuration file of the application to
  ```
  <trace enabled="ShipmentStatus.aspx" />
  ```

- ○ D. Set the **Trace** attribute in the **Page** directive of the **ShipmentStatus.aspx** page to
  ```
  <%@ Page Trace="True" />
  ```

- ○ E. Set the **Trace** attribute in the **Page** directive of the **ShipmentStatus.aspx** page to
  ```
  <%@ Page Trace="False" />
  ```

Question 45

You develop an intranet ASP.NET Web application, which helps manage production schedules for a manufacturing company. This application uses a library named **Production.dll**. You anticipate that in the future, some other applications might use classes from the **Production.dll** library. You might also need to maintain multiple versions of **Production.dll**. Which of the following options should you choose to deploy **Production.dll**?

- ❑ A. Sign **Production.dll** with **sn.exe**
- ❑ B. Sign **Production.dll** with **signcode.exe**
- ❑ C. Install **Production.dll** in the Windows system directory
- ❑ D. Install **Production.dll** in the application's bin directory
- ❑ E. Install **Production.dll** in the Global Assembly Cache

Question 46

You are a programmer for a popular gaming software publishing company. The company has recently designed a series of games using the .NET Framework. All these new game applications share some components. Some of these components are shipped in the box with the application, and others are deployed over the Internet. Which of the following commands will you use for these components before packaging them for deployment?

- ○ A. Use **sn.exe** to sign the components.
- ○ B. Use **signcode.exe** to sign the components.
- ○ C. Use **sn.exe** followed by **signcode.exe** to sign your components.
- ○ D. Use **signcode.exe** followed by **sn.exe** to sign your components.

Question 47

You use Visual Basic .NET to develop an assembly that allows developers in your company to create pie charts in their Web applications. You name the assembly **PieChart.dll** and package it as version 1.0.0.0, which is deployed into the GAC. After two months, you discover that there is a bug in the assembly. You fix the bug by releasing a new version 1.0.1.0 of the assembly. You place the newly created assembly in the GAC. What will happen to the application written by other developers who use **PieChart.dll**?

- ○ A. The applications using the **PieChart.dll** assembly will break because the applications will notice two versions of the assembly in the GAC and won't know which one to execute.

- ○ B. The applications using the **PieChart.dll** assembly will notice a new version of the assembly and will load the new version of the assembly and cause no problems.

- ○ C. The applications using the **PieChart.dll** assembly will not bother about the new version of the assembly in the GAC and will continue to use the older buggy version of the assembly.

- ○ D. The applications using the **PieChart.dll** assembly will be requested to select the desired assembly version to run for their application.

Question 48

You use Visual Basic .NET to develop a component that allows developers to create bar graphs in their applications. You name the component **BarGraph**. The developers need to deploy the **BarGraph** component with each application that uses the component. How should you package the **BarGraph** component for deployment?

- ○ A. Use a Cab project to package the **BarGraph** component.
- ○ B. Use a Setup project to package the **BarGraph** component.
- ○ C. Use a Web Setup project to package the **BarGraph** component.
- ○ D. Use a Merge Module project to package the **BarGraph** component.
- ○ E. Use a Primary Interop Assembly to package the **BarGraph** component.

Question 49

You have created a database-driven Web application. Using Microsoft SQL Server, you have also generated an installation script for your database. This script is stored in a file named **InstData.sql**. You create a Web Setup project using Visual Studio .NET to deploy this application on your production Web server. Which of the following editors should you choose to create the database when deploying your application on the client's machine?

○ A. Custom Actions Editor

○ B. Launch Conditions Editor

○ C. File System Editor

○ D. User Interface Editor

Question 50

Your ASP.NET application contains this setting in the **Web.config** file:

```
<identity impersonate="True"
    userName="CORP\Auditing"
    password="Auditing" />
```

You are allowing only digest or Windows integrated authentication in IIS. ASP.NET is running under the **SYSTEM** account. What identity will ASP.NET use to authorize resources if a user with the Windows account Shirley in the CORP domain logs in via digest authentication?

○ A. **CORP\Shirley**

○ B. **ASPNET**

○ C. **SYSTEM**

○ D. **IUSR_ComputerName**

○ E. **CORP\Auditing**

Question 51

You would like to give target Web servers the capability to customize your application. In particular, you want to let them specify the file path where the output files, which are generated by the application, need to be placed. You want to write minimum code; how should you add this capability to your application?

- ○ A. Let the user edit the text in the Registry and use the **Microsoft.Win32.Registry** class to retrieve the value that he saves.

- ○ B. Add another **customconfiguration.xml** file to store the output file path for the application.

- ○ C. Add an **<outputFilePath>** element to the application configuration file, **Web.config**, to store the output file path for the application.

- ○ D. Add an **<add>** element to the **<appSettings>** element of the application configuration file, **Web.config**, to store the output file path for the application.

Question 52

Your ASP.NET application requires users to be authenticated with a strong identity. You must allow users with any version 4.*x* or better browser, and you want passwords to cross the network only with secure encryption. Which authentication should you use?

- ○ A. Passport authentication with anonymous IIS authentication

- ○ B. Windows authentication with Basic IIS authentication

- ○ C. Windows authentication with digest IIS authentication

- ○ D. Windows authentication with integrated IIS authentication

Question 53

You have developed an intranet ASP.NET application for your company that uses Microsoft Windows authentication to authenticate the users of the application. Once the employee is authenticated, he can access all the Web pages of the intranet application. However, your application contains an **Accounting** directory that contains details of the salaries and paychecks of the employees. You want only users of the **Accounting** role to access the pages in this directory. Which of the following pieces of code should you write in the **Web.config** file of your application?

☐ A. Add the following **<authorization>** element in the **Web.config** file of the application directory:

```
<authentication mode="Windows"/>
<authorization>
    <deny users="?" />
</authorization>
```

☐ B. Add the following **<authorization>** element in the **Web.config** file of the application directory:

```
<authentication mode="Windows"/>
<authorization>
    <deny roles="?" />
</authorization>
```

☐ C. Add the following **<authorization>** element in the **Web.config** file of the **Accounting** directory:

```
<authorization>
    <allow roles="Accounting" />
    <deny users="*" />
</authorization>
```

☐ D. Add the following **<authorization>** element in the **Web.config** file of the **Accounting** directory:

```
<authorization>
    <allow roles="Accounting" />
    <deny users="?" />
</authorization>
```

Question 54

You use Visual Studio .NET to develop an ASP.NET Web application for your state university. You want only members of **Faculty** or **Admins** role to have access to the **GradesManagement.aspx** Web page of your application. Which of the following options should you choose to implement the security?

○ A.

```
If Thread.CurrentPrincipal.IsInRole("Faculty") = True  Or _
    Thread.CurrentPrincipal.IsInRole("Admins") = True
    Transfer()
End If
```

○ B.

```
If Thread.CurrentPrincipal.IsInRole("Faculty") = True  And _
    Thread.CurrentPrincipal.IsInRole("Admins") = True
    Transfer()
End If
```

○ C.

```
<PrincipalPermissionAttribute( _
    SecurityAction.Demand, Role:="Faculty"), _
    PrincipalPermissionAttribute( _
    SecurityAction.Demand, Role:="Admins")> _
Public Sub Transfer()
...
End Sub
```

○ D.

```
Dim permCheckFaculty As PrincipalPermission  = _
        New PrincipalPermission(Nothing, "Faculty")
Dim permCheckAdmins As PrincipalPermission = _
        New PrincipalPermission(Nothing, "Admins")
permCheckAdmins.Demand()
```

Question 55

One of your colleagues is designing a **Changed** event for his control. He complains to you that his code behaves quite abnormally because it runs fine some of the time and generates exceptions at other times. Part of his event handling code is as listed here (line numbers are for reference purpose only):

```
01: Public Delegate Sub ChangedEventHandler(ByVal sender
➥As Object, _
 ByVal args As ColorMixerEventArgs)

02: Public Event Changed As ChangedEventHandler

03: Protected Sub OnChanged(ByVal e As ColorMixerEventArgs)
04:     RaiseEvent Changed()
05: End Sub
```

Which of the following suggestions will solve his problem?

- ○ A. The code in line 4 should be replaced with the following:
  ```
  RaiseEvent Changed(Me)
  ```

- ○ B. The code in line 4 should be replaced with the following:
  ```
  RaiseEvent ChangedEventHandler(Me)
  ```

- ○ C. The code in line 4 should be replaced with the following:
  ```
  RaiseEvent ChangedEventHandler(Me, e)
  ```

- ○ D. The code in line 4 should be replaced with the following:
  ```
  RaiseEvent Changed(Me, e)
  ```

Question 56

You are building a custom control for your company's ASP.NET Web applications. The control will contain the company's privacy policy and copyright notices in a standard set of labels. This control should be shared by multiple applications. Which type of control should you create?

- ○ A. Web user control
- ○ B. Composite Web custom control
- ○ C. Web custom control that inherits from the **Label** control
- ○ D. Web custom control that inherits from the **WebControl** control

Question 57

Your department is responsible for maintaining the accounting application of your company. You've been assigned the task of creating a standard control to represent credit and debit accounts that will be placed in the Web Forms of the accounting application. The control will be made up of a collection of **TextBox** and **ComboBox** controls. You want to write minimum code. Which of the following options should you choose to create such a custom control?

○ A. Add a Web custom control to the project and inherit the custom control from the **WebControl** class.

○ B. Add a Component class to the project and inherit the custom control from the **Component** class.

○ C. Add a Web user control to the project and inherit the custom control from the **UserControl** class.

○ D. Add a Web Form to the project and inherit the custom control from the **Form** class.

Question 58

You are creating a specialized control that will display text rotated at an angle specified at design time. This control must be installed into the Visual Studio .NET toolbox so that it can be used in many projects. The control's user interface will resemble that of a **Label** control, with one additional property named **RotationAngle**. What sort of control should you create?

○ A. Web user control

○ B. Composite Web custom control

○ C. Web custom control that inherits from the **WebControl** control

○ D. Web custom control that inherits from the **Label** control

Question 59

Your colleague has developed a user control in a file named **LogIn.ascx** to prompt the username and password from the user. He wants to display the **LogIn** control, defined in the **CMI** namespace in the Welcome Web page. Which of the following options would you recommend to your colleague to make the **LogIn** user control available in the Welcome Web page?

O A.
```
<%@ Register TagPrefix="CMI" TagName="LogIn"
    Src="LogIn.ascx" %>
```

O B.
```
<%@ Control Namespace="CMI" ClassName="LogIn"
    Src="LogIn.ascx" %>
```

O C.
```
<%@ Register Namespace="CMI" TagName="LogIn"
    Src="LogIn.ascx" %>
```

O D.
```
<%@ Control Namespace="CMI" Inherits="LogIn"
    Src="LogIn.ascx" %>
```

Question 60

You are creating a composite control for your ASP.NET Web application that consists of a set of **Label**, **TextBox**, and **DropDownList** Web server controls. Which of the following methods should you override to enable custom rendering for the composite control?

O A. **CreateControl()**

O B. **CreateChildControls()**

O C. **RenderControl()**

O D. **Render()**

Answer Key for Practice Exam #1

Answer Key

1. D	**21.** D	**41.** D
2. C	**22.** D	**42.** C
3. D	**23.** B	**43.** C
4. B	**24.** A	**44.** D
5. A	**25.** D and E	**45.** A and E
6. C	**26.** A	**46.** C
7. A	**27.** C	**47.** C
8. D	**28.** C	**48.** D
9. C	**29.** B and C	**49.** A
10. A	**30.** D	**50.** E
11. D	**31.** C	**51.** D
12. A and C	**32.** C	**52.** A
13. C	**33.** B	**53.** A and C
14. C	**34.** B and D	**54.** A and C
15. C	**35.** C	**55.** D
16. B	**36.** B	**56.** B
17. D	**37.** B	**57.** C
18. A	**38.** C	**58.** D
19. D	**39.** B	**59.** A
20. C	**40.** A and D	**60.** B

Detailed Answers

1. Correct answer is **D**. When an ASPX page is dynamically compiled, the statements placed inside the `<% %>` code blocks are translated into a method that renders the user interface of an ASPX page. The `<%= %>` construct is used to display values from an ASP.NET code. Answer A is incorrect because the `<script runat="server"></script>` code block is used to define class-level methods, properties, and variables. When an ASPX page is dynamically compiled, the code in these code blocks is directly placed in the class definition of the resulting class file. Answer B is incorrect because the `runat` attribute of the `<script>` element should have the value "server". Answer C is incorrect because the `<script>` element without the `runat="server"` attribute is not executed on the server and is directly passed to the browser.

2. Correct answer is **C**. The `Inherits` attribute in the `Page` directive specifies a fully qualified name of a code-behind class from which the page should inherit. The `Src` attribute specifies the source filename of the code-behind class; this attribute is used when the code-behind class is not pre-compiled. Answers A and B are incorrect because the `CodeBehind` attribute is not used by the ASP.NET runtime; it is used internally by Visual Studio .NET to link the ASPX page with the code-behind file. Answer D is incorrect because the `ClassName` attribute specifies the classname for the page that will be dynamically compiled when the page is requested; it does not play any role in linking the ASP.NET page with the code-behind class or file.

3. Correct answer is **D**. You should set the `CausesValidation` property of the `Button` control to `False` because setting the `CausesValidation` property of a button to `False` prevents the validation to occur when the button is clicked. Answer A and C are incorrect because the `TextBox` Web server control does not contain a `CausesValidation` property. Answer B is incorrect because setting the `CausesValidation` property of the `Button` control to `True` will cause validation when the button is clicked.

4. Correct answer is **B**. By default, the `SelectedIndexChanged` event of the `DropDownList` control is only fired when the page is posted back to the server. By setting the `AutoPostBack` property of the control to `True`, you cause the page to post back as soon as a selection is changed in the list. Answer A is incorrect because the `PreRender` event will not cause a post-back when a selection is changed in the drop-down list. Answer C is incorrect because the `ListBox` control also does not post back immediately when the selection is changed. Answer D is incorrect because the `EnableViewState` property only indicates whether the view state should be maintained for the drop-down list.

5. Correct answer is **A**. The RequiredFieldValidator control ensures whether a value is entered or selected in the control. It can also ensure that the value in a control is different from the original value in the control, if the original value is supplied to the InitialValue property of the RequiredFieldValidator control. Answer B is incorrect because the Display property specifies how to display the inline error message; the ValidatorDisplay.Dynamic ensures that the space for the validation control is dynamically added only when the validation fails. Answer C is incorrect because by default, the Visible property is set to True. The Visible property has no control over the validation; it only indicates whether the control should be rendered on the page. Answer D is incorrect because the EnableClientScript property specifies whether the client-side validation should occur. By setting it to False, the validation will occur only on the server side.

6. Correct answer is **C**. The ASP.NET validation server controls require client-side scripting support in order to perform validation on the client side. If the browser does not support scripting, the validation occurs only on the server side when the page is posted. Answer A is incorrect because if the Enabled attribute had been set to False, the validation would have not occurred on either the client or server sides. Answer B is incorrect because the SmartNavigation attribute is used to enable smart navigation between postbacks and has no control on validation. Answer D is incorrect because client-side validation works with Internet Explorer 4.0 or higher.

7. Correct answer is **A**. To display custom error pages to all the users, the mode attribute of the <customErrors> element must be set to On. The defaultRedirect attribute of the customErrors element specifies the page to be displayed for any errors not listed. Answers B and D are incorrect because the mode attribute of the <customErrors> element is set to RemoteOnly; this would disable custom error pages for the local computer. Answer C is incorrect because the <error> element specifies an error status code and the resulting page to display.

8. Correct answer is **D**. The database connection should be closed whether the information can be retrieved or not. The code in the Finally block will be executed regardless of whether an exception is thrown. Answer A is incorrect because if an exception occurs before the code that closes the SqlConnection object in the Try block, the code will not be executed. Answer B is incorrect because in this case the SqlConnection object will only be closed when a SqlException occurs. Answer C is incorrect because in this case the SqlConnection object will only be closed when an exception other than SqlException occurs.

9. Correct answer is **C**. In a page, to log errors in to a custom log file, you need to provide an event handler for the `Page.Error` event. The `Page.Error` event occurs whenever an unhandled exception occurs in the page. Answer A is incorrect because the `<error>` element specifies an error HTTP status code and the redirect page for the HTTP status code. Answer B is incorrect because the `ErrorPage` attribute specifies the custom error page for an individual page. Answer D is incorrect because the `Application_Error()` event handler is generated whenever an unhandled exception occurs in the application rather than a page. The `Application_Error()` event handler should be placed in the `global.asax` file.

10. Correct answer is **A**. To transfer execution to a page that is not processed by the ASP.NET process, you must use the `Response.Redirect()` method. Answer B and C are incorrect because these methods are used to redirect control to ASPX pages. Answer D is incorrect because the `CreateObject()` method creates instances of COM components.

11. Correct answer is **D**. The `SmartNavigation` attribute offers several benefits to users running Internet Explorer 5.0 or higher, including focus persistence, minimized screen flashing, persistent scroll positioning, and better history management. Answers A, B, and C require more efforts because they involve writing code to implement the logic. Thus, none of these answers is "the easiest way."

12. Correct answers are **A** and **C**. If the Web page loads the data for the controls at every page load, disabling the view state will make the page size much smaller and maximize performance. If the Web page only reads the data but does not update data in the session state, you can make the session state for the page read-only. This will eliminate the time taken by ASP.NET to store the data in the session state for the Web page. Answer B is incorrect because by disabling the session state, the Web page will not be able to display the username from the session in the greeting to the user. Answer D is incorrect because storing the session state in the SQL Server creates extra overhead.

13. Correct answer is **C**. When you store session state data in SQL Server, you can take advantage of the robustness and data protection qualities of SQL Server. This includes the capability to preserve data even across server crashes. Answers A and B are incorrect because storing the session state in the ASP.NET worker process or `StateServer` process would not be able to recover data if the Web server is restarted. Answer D is incorrect because it disables session state.

14. Correct answer is **C**. You want the information to be available across Web pages and browser restarts. Therefore, you should choose cookies because they allow you to store a small amount of information on the user's computer. Answers A, B, and D are incorrect because none of these options (hidden fields, ViewState, and sessions) can store information across browser restarts.

15. Correct answer is **C**. You should use ViewState to store page-specific values. ViewState can store any type of object as long as it is serializable. Answers A and D are incorrect because both these techniques store data global to the application and should not be selected for storing user-specific data. Answer B is incorrect because although the session state is suitable for storing user-specific data, it is not required until the data is used across pages and is too sensitive to be stored on the client side.

16. Correct answer is **B**. By using varying output caching, you can store the output of the page for each product in the database. These pages then can quickly deliver information on the individual products without requiring a round-trip to the database and creating output for each request. Answer A is incorrect because only Varying output caching enables you to save information on each product. Answer C is incorrect because even though it would save a round-trip to the database, it would require the response to be created at each request that can be easily avoided by using varying output caching. Answer D is incorrect because fragment caching is used to cache output of user controls rather than ASPX pages.

17. Correct answer is **D**. The processing of the file data takes time to load the Web page. Further, the output only changes when the data in the XML file changes; therefore, the best solution is to cache the DataSet object. This way, you can eliminate the consumption of server resources to create the DataSet object from scratch at every request. Answer A and B are incorrect because output caching cannot be made dependent on a file. Only data stored in the Cache object can be made dependent on other items in the data cache or on an external resource such as a file or directory. Answer C is incorrect because it only adds the DataSet object to the cache but does not set any dependencies.

18. Correct answer is **A**. You need caching based on the state entered by the user; therefore, you need to set the VaryByControl attribute to txtState to cache different versions of the user control output by state. Answer B and D are incorrect because the VaryByParam attribute specifies the parameters of the Web page rather than user control for which the output cache is varied. Answer C is incorrect because the VaryByControl attribute does not work if * is passed; it needs a list of controls in the user control for which the output cache is to vary.

19. Correct answer is **D**. The DataView object represents a databindable, customized view of a data table, which is optimized for sorting, filtering, searching, editing, and navigation. Answers A and C are incorrect because they would involve additional programming. Answer B is incorrect because it will impact the SQL Server database with additional hits.

20. Correct answer is **C**. Although Answers C and D both use the correct syntax of the Fill() method, the question clearly states the name of the table; therefore, it is recommended to use the name of the table when filling the DataSet. Therefore, Answer D is incorrect. Answer A is incorrect because there is no overload of the Fill() method that accepts a single string parameter. Answer B is incorrect because there is no overload of the Fill() method that accepts two string parameters.

21. Correct answer is **D**. Using the same connection string enables ADO.NET to reuse existing pooled database connections instead of creating new ones. This improves performance because creating a new database connection is a costly operation. Answer B is incorrect because another application that uses the same database is already performing well. Answer C is incorrect because if different connection strings are used, each request for the connection will create a new connection pool anyway; therefore, increasing the maximum size of the pool will not matter. Answer A is incorrect because users are facing slow performance consistently and not just during the first execution.

22. Correct answer is **D**. When you set the XmlWriteMode parameter of the DataSet.WriteXml() method to DiffGram, the output contains both the original and current values. Answer A is incorrect because the DataSet.WriteXmlSchema() method writes the DataSet structure as an XML Schema instead of writing XML data. Answers B and C are incorrect because setting XmlWriteMode parameter to IgnoreSchema or WriteSchema writes only the current value of the data to the XML file.

23. Correct answer is **B**. IsolationLevel.Serializable places a range lock on the database, preventing other users from updating or inserting rows into the database until the transaction is complete. Answer A is incorrect because IsolationLevel.ReadCommitted holds the lock while the data is being read, but data can be changed before the transaction is complete. Answers C and D are incorrect because the BeginTrasaction() method should be called on the SqlConnection object rather than the SqlCommand object.

24. Correct answer is **A**. The ColumnMapping property determines how a column's values will be written when the WriteXml() method is called on a DataSet to write output to an XML document. When you set the ColumnMapping property of a column to MappingType.Attribute, that column of the table is mapped to an XML attribute. Answer B is incorrect because setting the ColumnMapping property of the column to MappingType.Element maps that column of the table to an XML element. Answers C and D are incorrect because XmlWriteMode.WriteSchema instructs the WriteXml() method to write the current contents of the DataSet as XML data along with the relational structure as an inline XSD schema. Writing an additional schema is not required in the question.

25. Correct answers are **D** and **E**. Strings in Visual Basic .NET are immutable, so concatenating multiple values into a string requires deleting and recreating the string many times. The StringBuilder object is optimized for changing textual data. The GetString() method should be used rather than the GetValue() method to retrieve data because the typed methods are faster than the GetValue() method. Answer A is incorrect because stored procedures have much higher performance as compared to SQL statements. Answer B is incorrect because for a forward-only, read-only operation, the SqlDataReader object provides the best performance. Answer C is incorrect because the while loop provides better performance when compared to the for each loop.

26. Correct answer is **A**. You can only have a single SqlDataReader object open on a single SqlConnection object. If you need a second SqlDataReader object, you'll need to open a second SqlConnection object. Answers B and C are incorrect because the question asks for the likely cause for the error and not just an alternative approach. Answer D is incorrect because you want to retrieve multiple values from the database and the ExecuteScalar() method only retrieves the first column of the first row in the resultset.

27. Correct answer is **C**. Calling the GetChanges() method of a DataSet returns a new DataSet that contains only records that have been changed. Answer A is incorrect because the DataSet.Clone() method copies the structure of the DataSet but does not copy any data. Answer B is incorrect because the DataSet.Copy() method copies all the data instead of only the changed data. Answer D is incorrect because you do not want to merge two DataSet objects.

28. Correct answer is **C**. To create a connection string for a SqlConnection object that uses Windows Integrated authentication, you need to specify the data source, the initial catalog, and indicate that it is a secure connection.

You can indicate it is a secure connection by setting the `Trusted_Connection` or `Integrated Security` parameters to `True` or `sspi`. Answers A and B are incorrect because you do not specify the provider in the connection string when connecting through the `SqlConnection` object. Answer D is incorrect because you need to use Windows authentication instead of SQL Server authentication.

29. Correct answers are **B** and **C**. To return a single value from the database, you should use the `ExecuteScalar()` method of the `OleDbCommand` object. The `ExecuteScalar()` method executes the query and retrieves the first column of the first row of the resultset. You should always prefer to use stored procedures rather than the ad hoc SQL statements for speedy delivery. Answer A is incorrect because it uses a SQL query rather than the stored procedure. Answers D and E are incorrect because these solutions involve extra overhead when only a single value needs to be returned from the database.

30. Correct answer is **D**. The controls already contain all the necessary property settings to transfer the data from the `ListBox` control to the `TextBox` control. However, you must call the `DataBind` method to actually perform the transfer. Answer A is incorrect because you want to bind the value with a textbox and therefore you should call the `DataBind()` method on the `TextBox` control instead of the `ListBox` control. Answers B and C are incorrect because they do not present a solution that binds the value of the `TextBox` control.

31. Correct answer is **C**. The best place to display the data underlined is when the sales amount is data bound with the control and before it is rendered. The `ItemDataBound` event is generated when an item is data bound, and it always occurs before it is rendered for display. The `ItemDataBound` event passes a `DataGridItemEventArgs` object to the event handler containing the details about the data bound item. Answer A is incorrect because the `ItemCreated` event is generated when an item is created in the `DataGrid` control. Answer B is incorrect because the `ItemCommand` event is generated when any of the buttons are clicked in the `DataGrid` control. Answer D is incorrect because the `DataBinding` event is generated when the `DataGrid` control binds to the data source rather than when individual items are data bound to the data in the data source.

32. Correct answer is **C**. You have to bind the text box control with a single column of data in the data source control. You have already set the data source and the data member to bind. Therefore, you specify the row to bind using the `Container.DataItem` and then specify the column to bind.

Answer A is incorrect because you have already set the `DataSource` and `DataMember` properties; now, you just have to bind to the specific column in the data. Answers B and D are incorrect because `SelectedItemTemplate` only applies to the selected row in the `DataList` control.

33. Correct answer is **B**. You should use `XslTransform` object to transform XML data using an XSLT style sheet. Answer A is incorrect because the `XPathNavigator` object enables you to explore the structure of the XML file. Answer C is incorrect because the `XmlSchema` object provides the schema definition. Answer D is incorrect because the `XmlNode` object represents a single node in the document.

34. Correct answers are **B** and **D**. Either of these options can generate proxy classes for use in a client application. Answer A is incorrect because the .NET Web Service Studio tool is used to invoke a Web service for testing. Answer C is incorrect because the Web Services Discovery Tool can locate files related to a Web service, but it does not generate any proxy classes.

35. Correct answer is **C**. When the `dir` attribute is set to `rtl`, the horizontal alignment of the control's elements is reversed. Answer A is incorrect because you need to make minimum changes. Answers B and D are incorrect because there is no `rtl` attribute.

36. Correct answer is **B**. The ADO library and other components developed with Microsoft Visual Basic 6.0 use STA as their threading model. By setting `AspCompat` attribute to `True`, the .NET Framework allows the page to call STA components. Answer A is incorrect because STA (Single-Threaded Apartment) COM components can be directly used only from ASP.NET pages and not from the compiled .NET assemblies. Answer C is incorrect because the `Language` attribute should be set to any .NET supported language such as C# and VB. Answer D is incorrect because if you convert the STA component to an assembly using the type library importer tool, your application can suffer from poor performance and possible deadlocks.

37. Correct answer is **B**. Using the Type Library Importer tool (`tlbimp.exe`) enables you to generate a RCW assembly. To place the RCW assembly in the GAC so that it can be shared by all projects on the computer, you need to sign the assembly using the `tlbimp.exe` tool. Answers A and E are incorrect because you need to use the component in more than one project. Answer C is incorrect because you also need to sign the RCW assembly while generating it from the Type Library Importer tool. Answer D is incorrect because a Primary Interop Assembly is for code from other vendors, not for your own code.

38. Correct answer is **C**. To make the demo page more accessible, you should ensure that you supply all graphics with an `alt` attribute that conveys the important information about the image. The `alt` text information is displayed in place of the image when the image is being downloaded, the image is unavailable, the graphics are turned off in the browser, or the browser doesn't support images. Answer A is incorrect because PNG graphics are widely supported. Answer B is incorrect because providing the short key for the graphics is not as important as providing the `alt` attribute for the image. Answer D is incorrect because the `AlternateText` property is rendered to the browser as an `alt` attribute unlike the `ToolTip` property.

39. Correct answer is **B**. You can step into a stored procedure execution directly from within Visual Studio .NET. Answer A is incorrect because the Tools, Debug Processes menu item is useful for debugging running processes and not the stored procedures. Answer C is incorrect because this option will take more time and effort. The questions require minimal effort and time. Answer D is incorrect because the `Debug.WriteLine()` method cannot directly access the stored procedure values.

40. Correct answers are **A** and **D**. The `Debug` and `Trace` classes share the same `Listeners` collection. Therefore, you should add a listener object either to the `Trace.Listeners` collection or to the `Debug.Listeners` collection. Answer B is incorrect because this solution will generate double entries in the event log. Answer C is incorrect because the newly created listener object is not attached to the `Listeners` collection of the `Trace` and `Debug` classes.

41. Correct answer is **D**. A conditional breakpoint lets you pause your code only when a particular condition is true. In this case, you can use that capability to break into the code when the variable has the value of 117. Answers A, B, and C (Locals window, Output windows, and Immediate window) are incorrect because they do not work conditionally.

42. Correct answer is **C**. Breakpoints are invoked only when the project's configuration is in Debug mode. Answer A is incorrect because the Exceptions dialog box is used to configure the breakpoint only in case of an exception. Answer B is incorrect because when you place a breakpoint, it is enabled by default. Answer D is incorrect because the project's configuration should be Debug instead of Release for debugging to occur (for breakpoints to be executed).

43. Correct answer is **C**. The TraceContext class is responsible for providing detailed timing and other information in the browser window when you activate ASP.NET tracing. Answer A and B are incorrect because the Debug and Trace classes can be used to display messages about a program's execution but they can't provide detailed timing and other information about a program's execution. Answer D is incorrect because the Page class cannot provide timing information for the events on the Web page.

44. Correct answer is **D**. To enable tracing for a particular page, you should set the Trace attribute of the Page directive to True. Answers A and B are incorrect because the <trace> element in Web.config enables or disables tracing for all the Web pages of the application rather than just a single page. Answer C is incorrect because the enabled attribute takes a Boolean value rather than the name of the Web page. Answer E is incorrect because it disables tracing for the Web page.

45. Correct answers are **A** and **E**. You need to sign a shared assembly with the strong name and then install the assembly in the Global Assembly Cache. Answer B is incorrect because you use sn.exe instead of signcode.exe to sign an assembly with a strong name. Answer C is incorrect because the Windows system directory does not allow multiple versions of an assembly to be maintained. Answer D is incorrect because an assembly that needs to be shared by multiple applications should be stored in a common place like the GAC rather than the bin directory of the Web application. Further, multiple versions of the assembly can only be placed in the GAC.

46. Correct answer is **C**. Because the components are being used between several games published by your company, they are good candidates to be placed in the Global Assembly Cache of the target machine. But before a component can be placed in GAC, it must be signed using a Strong Name Tool (sn.exe). Your company is also deploying software over the Internet; in this case, it is a good idea to digitally sign your code with a software publisher's certificate obtained by a respected certification authority. Once you obtain the certificate, you can use signcode.exe to sign your component. When you are using both sn.exe and signcode.exe with your assembly, you should always use sn.exe before using signcode.exe. Answers A and B are incorrect because you need to use both the tools instead of just one of them. Answer D is incorrect because sn.exe must be used before signcode.exe.

47. Correct answer is **C**. The applications always bind to the assemblies with which they are compiled. Therefore, if you want to execute a new version of the assembly, you either should recompile the application with the new version of the assembly or should modify the application configuration file to redirect to a new version of the assembly. Answers A and B are incorrect because the application will still request for the old version of the assembly. Answer D is incorrect because applications will not be requested to choose a particular version of the assembly; instead the applications themselves will request the common language runtime to locate a specific aseembly.

48. Correct answer is **D**. The Merge Module projects allow you to create reusable setup components by packaging all the required files, resources, Registry entries, and setup logic necessary to install a component. Answer A is incorrect because the Cab project creates a cabinet file for downloading from a Web browser. Answer B is incorrect because the Setup project creates an installer for a Windows application. Answer C is incorrect because the Web Setup project creates an installer for a Web application. Answer E is incorrect because the Primary Interop Assembly is used for packaging legacy components.

49. Correct answer is **A**. You can use the Custom Actions editor to take custom actions such as database installation during the application setup. If you have an installer class or program that can create a database, you must override the Install() method of the base class and add the installer program to the Install node of the Custom Actions editor. Answer B is incorrect because the Launch Conditions editor is used to specify the prerequisite conditions that must be met in order to successfully run an installation; it cannot be used to execute custom actions. Answer C is incorrect because the File System Editor only provides a mapping of the file system on the target machine and allows you to place files or folders on specific locations on the target machine. However, the File System Editor cannot be used to execute code to create the database. Answer D is incorrect because the User Interface Editor allows you to customize the user interface displayed during the installation process.

50. Correct answer is **E**. When you enable impersonation providing a name and password for impersonation, any authenticated user takes on the credentials of the specified account for the purposes of authorizing resources. Answer A is incorrect because the name and password that ASP.NET will use to authorize resources is already defined by the <identity> element. Answer B and C are incorrect because a username and password for impersonation is provided in the <identity> element.

Answer D is incorrect because the IUSR_ComputerName account, the identity of the IIS, will be used by the ASP.NET to make requests if the application allows anonymous access.

51. Correct answer is **D**. You can store your custom settings in the <appSettings> element of the application configuration file. The .NET Framework provides the AppSettings property of the System.Configuration.ConfigurationSettings class to access the value of the custom key added to the <appSettings> element. Answer A is incorrect because asking the user to modify the Windows Registry might have undesirable effects. Answers B and C are incorrect because they would involve writing additional code.

52. Correct answer is **A**. Passport authentication enables users to be authenticated with a strong identity using any browser or version. Answer B is incorrect because Basic IIS authentication does not securely encrypt passwords. Answers C and D are incorrect because Digest and Windows integrated authentication require Internet Explorer as the browser.

53. Correct answers are **A** and **C**. You should deny all unauthenticated users with the ? wildcard character at the application level so that only authenticated users can access the application. In the Web.config file of the Accounting directory, you should allow only members of the Accounting role and deny all other users (authenticated as well as unauthenticated) with the * wildcard character. Answer B is incorrect because you should disallow all unauthenticated users. The roles attribute should not contain wildcard characters; it should contain only the names of the Windows roles separated by commas. Answer D is incorrect because the <deny> element denies only unauthenticated users and provides access to the authenticated users.

54. Correct answers are **A** and **C**. Both code segments will allow access to the user if he belongs to either the Admins or Faculty role. Answer B is incorrect because it allows access only for those users who are in both the Admins and Faculty roles. Answer D is incorrect because to give access to the users in the Faculty role, you must call the permCheckFaculty.Demand() method.

55. Correct answer is **D**. The RaiseEvent statement raises the specified event. RaiseEvent checks whether any event handlers are registered for the event and passes the parameter list to the event handlers.

Therefore, if the event handler expects to receive any arguments, you must supply them while invoking this statement. Answer A is incorrect because the argument list does not match the signature defined by the Delegate ChangedEventHandler. Answers B and C are incorrect because the name of the event is Changed rather than ChangedEventHandler.

56. Correct answer is **B**. The composite control can encapsulate multiple Label controls into a single control easily. Because it's a custom control, it can be installed into the GAC and shared by multiple applications. Answer A is incorrect because the custom control needs to be used in multiple applications. If you create a Web user control, the user control files will need to be included in each application. Answer C is incorrect because the control consists of multiple Label controls. Answer D is incorrect because your control needs to combine existing Web server controls and the WebControl class is used to create Web controls from scratch.

57. Correct answer is **C**. Web user controls are the best way to reuse common user interface functionality in a Web application. Web user controls are easy to create, just like ASPX pages, and they inherit from the System.Web.UI.UserControl class. They can be easily dragged from the Solution Explorer into the Web Form. Answer A is incorrect because Web custom controls are precompiled and are best suited for creating custom controls to be used by multiple applications. Answer B is incorrect because using the Component class to create reusable visual components requires additional programming and is therefore better suited for creating non-visual components. Answer D is incorrect because a Web Form cannot be placed inside another Web Form.

58. Correct answer is **D**. Because this control is an extension of the Label control, it's easiest to create it by subclassing the existing Label control. Answer A is incorrect because a Web user control cannot be added to the Visual Studio .NET toolbox. Answer B is incorrect because composite controls contain more than one control. Answer C is incorrect because if you derive from the WebControl class you have to write more code.

59. Correct answer is **A**. The Register directive is used to register a Web user control within an ASP.NET Web Form. To register a Web user control, you need to specify three attributes: TagPrefix to provide an alias to a namespace to which the user control belongs, TagName to provide an alias to the user control, and Src to provide the path to the user control. Answer B and D are incorrect because the Control directive is used to define user-control specific attributes in the user control file (.ascx). Answer C is incorrect because the Namespace attribute is used to associate with the tag prefix and is not a required attribute to register a user control.

60. Correct answer is **B**. You should override the `CreateChildControls()` method to create new controls that the composite control will contain. This method is automatically called by ASP.NET when the control is supposed to be rendered. Answers A and C are incorrect because they are not defined as `Overridable` methods and cannot be overridden to create child controls. Answer D is incorrect because the `Render()` method is overridden to provide the complete rendering of a Web control; it is used when you are designing a Web custom control from scratch rather than by combining existing controls.

19

Practice Exam #2

Self Test

Question 1

You are developing an accounting application that includes a class named **Transaction**. The **Transaction** class is inherited by subclasses such as **DepositTransaction** and **PaymentTransaction**. The **Transaction** class includes a method named **VerifyChecksum()**. The **VerifyChecksum()** method should be available to the **Transaction** class and to all classes derived from the **Transaction** class, but not to any other classes in the application. Which access modifier should you use in the declaration of the **VerifyChecksum()** method?

- ○ A. **Protected**
- ○ B. **Public**
- ○ C. **Private**
- ○ D. **Friend**

Question 2

You have developed an ASP.NET page that contains the following code:

```
<%@ Page Language="vb"
        AutoEventWireUp="True"
        EnableViewState="True"
        SmartNavigation="False"%>
<html>
    <script runat="server">
    Private Sub Page_Load(ByVal sender As System.Object, _
    ByVal e As System.EventArgs) Handles MyBase.Load
        If Not Page.IsPostBack Then
            ' Populate the color drop-down list
            ddlColor.Items.Add("Blue")
            ddlColor.Items.Add("Red")
            ddlColor.Items.Add("Green")
        End If
    End Sub

    </script>
    <body>
        <form runat="server">
                Select a Color:
                <asp:DropDownList id="ddlColor"
                                  runat="server">
                </asp:DropDownList>
                <asp:Button id="btnSubmit"
                            runat="server">
                </asp:Button>
        </form>
    </body>
</html>
```

When you view the page in the browser, you find that the color names are displayed twice in the drop-down list. Which of the following options should you choose to solve this problem?

○ A. Modify the **Page** directive to

```
<%@ Page Language="vb"
        AutoEventWireUp="True"
        EnableViewState="False"
        SmartNavigation="False"%>
```

○ B. Modify the **Page** directive to

```
<%@ Page Language="vb"
        AutoEventWireUp="True"
        EnableViewState="True"
        SmartNavigation="True"%>
```

○ C. Modify the **Page** directive to

```
<%@ Page Language="vb"
        AutoEventWireUp="False"
        EnableViewState="True"
        SmartNavigation="False"%>
```

○ D. Change the **Page_Load()** method to

```
Private Sub Page_Load(ByVal sender As System.Object, _
    ByVal e As System.EventArgs) Handles MyBase.Load
        If Page.IsPostBack Then
            ' Populate the color drop-down list
            ddlColor.Items.Add("Blue")
            ddlColor.Items.Add("Red")
            ddlColor.Items.Add("Green")
        End If
    End Sub
```

Question 3

You are designing a Visual Basic ASP.NET Web Form with a variety of controls on its user interface. Some controls will be infrequently used. For these controls, you do not want the user to be able to tab into the control, but the user should still be able to activate the control by clicking in it. Which of the following options should you use?

○ A. Set the **TabIndex** property of the control to **0**.

○ B. Set the **TabIndex** property of the control to **-1**.

○ C. Set the **AccessKey** property of the control to empty string.

○ D. Set the **Enabled** property of the control to **False**.

Question 4

You have developed a Web page that uses the **Image** ASP.NET Web server controls to display images from various sources on the Internet. Sometimes an image might not be available because a Web site might be temporarily down for maintenance. For these situations, you are required to display a description for the image. Which of the following properties of **Image** would you use?

- ○ A. **ToolTip**
- ○ B. **Attributes**
- ○ C. **AlternateText**
- ○ D. **ImageUrl**

Question 5

You are designing a Web site that is used by your suppliers to quote their pricing for a product that your company will buy over the next quarter. The Web site will use data to calculate the best possible purchase options. Your application displays three text boxes to the suppliers. The first text box (**txtPrevQtrMax**) allows suppliers to enter the maximum value they charged for this product the previous quarter. The second text box (**txtPrevQtrMin**) allows suppliers to enter the minimum value they charged the previous quarter. The third text box (**txtQuote**) is for entering the proposed product pricing for the next quarter. You want suppliers to restrict the value of the **txtQuote** field between **txtPrevQtrMin** and **txtPrevQtrMax**. The validation technique you use should use the minimum amount of code. Which of the following validation controls would you use to perform the validation?

- ○ A. **CompareValidator**
- ○ B. **RangeValidator**
- ○ C. **CustomValidator**
- ○ D. **RegularExpressionValidator**

Question 6

Your ASP.NET application allows the user to input the URL of a Web page, and then applies an XSLT file to show how that Web page looks on a mobile device. What sort of control should you use to validate the **TextBox** control where the user inputs the URL? (Select two options; each option presents part of the complete answer.)

❑ A. **RequiredFieldValidator**

❑ B. **RangeValidator**

❑ C. **RegularExpressionValidator**

❑ D. **CompareValidator**

Question 7

You are assisting your colleague in solving the compiler error that his code is throwing. Following is the problematic portion of his code:

```
Try
    Dim success As Boolean = GenerateNewtonSeries(500, 0)
    ' more code here
Catch dbze As DivideByZeroException
    ' exception handling code
Catch nfne As NotFiniteNumberException
    ' exception handling code
Catch ae As ArithmeticException
    ' exception handling code
Catch e As OverflowException
    ' exception handling code
End Try
```

To remove the compilation error, which of the following ways would you modify the code?

○ A.

```
Try
    Dim success As Boolean = GenerateNewtonSeries(500, 0)
    ' more code here
Catch dbze As DivideByZeroException
    ' exception handling code
Catch ae As ArithmeticException
    ' exception handling code
Catch e As OverflowException
    ' exception handling code
End Try
```

○ B.

```
Try
    Dim success As Boolean = GenerateNewtonSeries(500, 0)
    ' more code here
Catch dbze As DivideByZeroException
    ' exception handling code
Catch ae As Exception
    ' exception handling code
Catch e As OverflowException
    ' exception handling code
End Try
```

○ C.

```
Try
    Dim success As Boolean = GenerateNewtonSeries(500, 0)
    ' more code here
Catch dbze As DivideByZeroException
    ' exception handling code
Catch nfne As NotFiniteNumberException
    ' exception handling code
Catch e As OverflowException
    ' exception handling code
Catch ae As ArithmeticException
    ' exception handling code
End Try
```

○ D.

```
Try
    Dim success As Boolean = GenerateNewtonSeries(500, 0)
    ' more code here
Catch dbze As DivideByZeroException
    ' exception handling code
Catch nfne As NotFiniteNumberException
    ' exception handling code
Catch ae As Exception
    ' exception handling code
Catch e As OverflowException
    ' exception handling code
End Try
```

Question 8

You develop an ASP.NET Web application that retrieves data from a SQL Server database named Customers. You use the **System.Data.SqlClient** data provider to connect with the database. You need to log the severity level of any error returned from the SQL Server .NET data provider. Which of the following options should you choose?

○ A. Catch the **SqlException**, which is thrown by the SQL Server .NET data provider. Examine the **Class** property of the **SqlException** object.

○ B. Catch the **SqlException**, which is thrown by the SQL Server .NET data provider. Examine the **Source** property of the **SqlException** object.

○ C. Catch the **SqlException**, which is thrown by the SQL Server .NET data provider. Examine the **Server** property of the **SqlException** object.

○ D. Catch the **SqlException**, which is thrown by the SQL Server .NET data provider. Examine the **State** property of the **SqlException** object.

Question 9

The **machine.config** file on your computer contains this setting:
```
<customErrors mode="RemoteOnly"/>
```

Your application's root directory contains a **Web.config** file with this setting:
```
<customErrors mode="On">
    <error statusCode="404" redirect="404.htm" />
</customErrors>
```

Your application's **/custom** directory contains a **Web.config** file with this setting:
```
<customErrors mode="Off" />
```

Your application's **/custom/local** directory contains a **Web.config** file with this setting:
```
<customErrors mode="On">
    <error statusCode="404" redirect="404.aspx" />
</customErrors>
```

A user at a remote computer requests the file **/custom/remote/ NonExistingPage.aspx**, which does not exist. What is the result?

○ A. The **404.aspx** file is displayed.

○ B. The default ASP.NET error page is displayed.

○ C. The **404.htm** file is displayed.

○ D. The stack trace information for the error is displayed.

Question 10

Your ASP.NET application contains a Web Form named **login.aspx**. When this page is posted back to the server, you check the entered username and password against your corporate database. If the username and password match, you want to display the **accountdetails.aspx** Web Form as the result in the user's browser. Execution of the application will proceed from the **accountdetails.aspx** page. How should you transfer control in this case?

○ A. **HyperLink** ASP.NET Web server control

○ B. **Response.Redirect()** method

○ C. **Server.Transfer()** method

○ D. **Server.Execute()** method

Question 11

You are creating an ASP.NET Web application that reads a text file and displays its data in the browser. You set the **BufferOutput** property of the **HttpResponse** object to **True**. You execute the **CreateHeaders.aspx** page using the **Server.Execute()** method to display heading information to the browser. After this, you read and display the file in the browser. If the file is not found, you want to remove any heading information created for the output and you want the page to continue execution further. How can you achieve this?

- ○ A.
  ```
  Response.Flush()
  ```

- ○ B.
  ```
  Response.Clear()
  ```

- ○ C.
  ```
  Response.Close()
  ```

- ○ D.
  ```
  Response.End()
  ```

Question 12

Your ASP.NET Web Form displays ordering information for 50 products in **DataGrid** and other controls. Your company is unable to accept Web orders, so there are no controls on the page to post the data back to the server. What can you do to optimize the delivery of this page?

- ○ A. Set the **EnableViewState** attribute to **True** for the **DataGrid** control.
- ○ B. Set the **EnableViewState** attribute to **True** for the **Page** directive.
- ○ C. Set the **EnableViewState** attribute to **False** for the **DataGrid** control.
- ○ D. Set the **EnableViewState** attribute to **False** for the **Page** directive.

Question 13

Your ASP.NET shopping application is deployed and running on your production server. Your Web site hits have increased recently, so you are planning to deploy your ASP.NET Web application to a Web farm, which consists of four servers handling the requests of your shopping application. Which of the following steps should you perform before you move your Web application to a Web farm?

○ A. Disable session state for the application.

○ B. Use either the State Service or SQL Server to store session state.

○ C. Use View state rather than using session to maintain state.

○ D. Remove all references to the Request, Response, and Server objects from your code.

Question 14

You are in the process of upgrading an existing ASP application to ASP.NET by converting pages one by one to the new architecture. The application currently uses an ASP.NET page to request the user's first name, which is stored in a session variable with this line of code:

```
Session("FirstName") = txtFirstName.Text
```

You run the application and enter a first name on the ASP.NET page. When you browse to an existing ASP page that uses the **FirstName** session variable, the first name is blank. What could be the problem?

○ A. You must explicitly use the **Page.Session** property to store shared session state.

○ B. The ASP page needs to explicitly retrieve the **Value** property of the Session item.

○ C. The ASP and ASP.NET engines do not share session state or application state.

○ D. You do not have cookies enabled on your computer.

Question 15

You are designing an ASP.NET Web application for a multinational company. When users access the Web site, you want them to be automatically redirected to a page specific to their country. Your colleague has developed a method that determines the user's country from the HTTP Request and does the redirection. Where should you call this method in your application?

- ○ A. The **Session_Start()** event handler of the **global.asax** file
- ○ B. The **Application_BeginRequest()** event handler of the **global.asax** file
- ○ C. The **Page_Load()** event handler of the **default.aspx** file
- ○ D. The **Application_Start()** event handler of the **global.asax** file

Question 16

You have created an ASP.NET Web page **Catalog.aspx** that allows users to purchase products from a catalog. The product details are fetched in a **DataSet** object from a legacy database over a slow link. The details are displayed in the **Catalog.aspx** page in a **DataGrid** control, as per the preferences of the user. The user preferences are maintained in the session state. The product details do not change very often; you only need to reload the **DataSet** object every two hours. Which of the following options should you use to store the **DataSet** object?

- ○ A. Application state
- ○ B. Session state
- ○ C. View state
- ○ D. **HttpCachePolicy** object
- ○ E. **Cache** object

Question 17

You are creating an ASP.NET Web page that performs complex mathematical and scientific calculations and displays the results to the user. The complex calculations use server resources extensively. The calculations change once every 30 minutes. Which of the following **OutputCache** directives should you choose to enable caching on the Web page?

○ A.
```
<%@ OutputCache Duration="30" VaryByParam="None" %>
```

○ B.
```
<%@ OutputCache Duration="1800" VaryByParam="None" %>
```

○ C.
```
<%@ OutputCache Duration="30" %>
```

○ D.
```
<%@ OutputCache Duration="1800" %>
```

Question 18

You have developed an ASP.NET Web Form that displays information on parks by fetching the data from a SQL Server 2000 database. The database contains information on approximately 2,500 parks. The user can select a state from the **ddlStates** control and select a park from the **ddlParks** control to get information on the desired park. The page also accepts other information from the user but this information does not influence the results. The users request these pages very frequently. Which of the following **OutputCache** directives should you use to maximize performance?

○ A.
```
<%@ OutputCache Duration="120" VaryByParam="*" %>
```

○ B.
```
<%@ OutputCache Duration="120"
    VaryByParam="ddlStates;ddlParks" %>
```

○ C.
```
<%@ OutputCache Duration="120" VaryByParam="ddlParks" %>
```

○ D.
```
<%@ OutputCache Duration="120" VaryByControl="ddlParks" %>
```

○ E.
```
<%@ OutputCache Duration="120"
    VaryByControl="ddlStates;ddlParks" %>
```

○ F.
```
<%@ OutputCache Duration="120" VaryByControl="*" %>
```

Question 19

You develop a Visual Basic ASP.NET Web application that displays supplier data in a **DataGrid** control. The supplier data is stored in a data cache in a table named Suppliers within the **dsSuppliers DataSet** object. The primary key for the Suppliers table is the **SupplierID** column. You need to display the supplier data in the **DataGrid** control in the ascending order of the primary key. You write the following code segment to accomplish this task:

```
Dim dvSuppliers As DataView = _
    New DataView(dsSuppliers.Tables("Suppliers"))
dvSuppliers.Sort = "ASC"
dvSuppliers.ApplyDefaultSort = True
dataGrid1.DataSource = dvSuppliers
dataGrid1.DataBind()
```

However, when you run the program, the results are not as expected. How should you change the previous code segment to get the intended results?

- ○ A. Set the **Sort** property of the **DataView** object to an empty string.
- ○ B. Set the **ApplyDefaultSort** property of the **DataView** object to **False**.
- ○ C. Set the **RowFilter** property of the **DataView** object to **SupplierID**.
- ○ D. The code segment is correct. You need to ensure that the data in the Suppliers table is already sorted on the primary key.

Question 20

Your new project is to write a Visual Basic ASP.NET Web application that allows professors to maintain the scores of students. You place a **DataGrid** control on the Web Form and bind the data grid to a **DataView** object. You allow professors to make changes in the data grid by adding new rows, by modifying existing rows, and by deleting existing rows. You now want to place a command button that allows professors to view the deleted rows from the original data. How should you program the **Click** event of the command button?

- ○ A. In the event handler for the **Click** event, set the **RowFilter** property of the **DataView** object to **DataViewRowState.Deleted**.
- ○ B. In the event handler for the **Click** event, set the **RowFilter** property of the **DataView** object to **DataViewRowState.OriginalRows**.
- ○ C. In the event handler for the **Click** event, set the **RowStateFilter** property of the **DataView** object to **DataViewRowState.Deleted**.
- ○ D. In the event handler for the **Click** event, set the **RowStateFilter** property of the **DataView** object to **DataViewRowState.OriginalRows**.

Question 21

You have created an array of **Project** objects named **aProjects**. Each **Project** object has a **Name** and a **Number** property. You want to display all the **Name** values in a **ListBox** Web server control named **lbProjects**. Which code snippet should you use for this purpose?

○ A.

```
lbProjects.DataSource = aProjects
lbProjects.DataValueField = Name
lbProjects.DataBind()
```

○ B.

```
lbProjects.DataSource = aProjects
lbProjects.DataTextField = Name
lbProjects.DataBind()
```

○ C.

```
lbProjects.DataSource = aProjects
lbProjects.DataValueField = "Name"
lbProjects.DataBind()
```

○ D.

```
lbProjects.DataSource = aProjects
lbProjects.DataTextField = "Name"
lbProjects.DataBind()
```

Question 22

You use Visual Studio .NET to develop an ASP.NET Web application that queries data from a SQL Server database. You use the **SqlConnection** object to connect to the database. As soon as the database operation is completed, you want to make sure that any pending database transactions are rolled back and connection is returned to the connection pool. You need to reuse the same **SqlConnection** object when your program needs to query the database again. Which of the following actions should you take?

○ A. Call the **Dispose()** method on the **SqlConnection** object.

○ B. Call the **Finalize()** method of the **SqlConnection** object.

○ C. Call the **Close()** method on the **SqlConnection** object.

○ D. Set the **SqlConnection** object to **Nothing**.

Question 23

> You develop an ASP.NET Web application that allows the users to view and modify recently placed orders. Your application needs to display data from **OrderHeader** and **OrderDetails** data tables. Information from **OrderHeader** is displayed in a **ListBox** control; the information from **OrderDetails** is displayed in a **DataGrid** control. Your program must ensure that as soon as a different order is selected in the **ListBox** control, the **DataGrid** control should display the details corresponding to that order. Which of the following actions will you take to implement this functionality?
>
> ○ A. Define primary keys on the **OrderHeader** and **OrderDetails** tables.
>
> ○ B. Create a foreign key constraint in the **OrderDetails** table.
>
> ○ C. Add a **DataRelation** object to the Relations collection of the **DataSet** object.
>
> ○ D. Use the **DataSet.Merge()** method.

Question 24

> You need to develop an ASP.NET Web application named **ProcessOrders**. This application receives XML data files from various customers, reads the files, and stores them in a SQL Server database for further processing. The **ProcessOrders** application uses an XML schema file to define the format and data types of the XML data files. However, not all customers send the XML data file using the same schema. Your application should parse the incoming data files to ensure that they conform to the XML schema. Which of the following actions should you take to accomplish this requirement?
>
> ○ A. Implement an **XmlDocument** object to load the document. Pass the schema file to this object to validate and parse the XML document.
>
> ○ B. Implement an **XmlValidatingReader** object and program an event handler for the **ValidationEventHandler** event to parse the data file that does not conform to the XML schema.
>
> ○ C. Read the XML file into a **DataSet** object and set its **EnforceConstraints** property to **True**.
>
> ○ D. Read the XML file and schema into a **DataSet** object. Program the **DataSet.MergeFailed** event handler to parse the data file that does not conform to the XML schema.

Question 25

You are developing a Visual Basic ASP.NET Web application to query product information from a SQL Server database. The application specification requires that the users of your application should be able to search for a product just by entering the first few characters. You store the characters entered by the user in a variable name **ProdName**. Which of the following SQL statements should you use to retrieve the data from the database?

○ A.
```
sqlStatement = "SELECT Name, Description, Price FROM " & _
    "Product WHERE Name IN '" & ProdName & "%'"
```

○ B.
```
sqlStatement = "SELECT Name, Description, Price FROM " & _
    "Product WHERE Name LIKE '" & ProdName & "%'"
```

○ C.
```
sqlStatement = "SELECT Name, Description, Price FROM " & _
    "Product WHERE Name IN '" & ProdName & "*'"
```

○ D.
```
sqlStatement = "SELECT Name, Description, Price FROM " & _
    "Product WHERE Name LIKE '" & ProdName & "*'"
```

Question 26

Your Visual Basic .NET application needs to read data from a SQL Server 6.5 database and write it to a flat file once every 12 hours. A legacy application accesses this file to update its data. Because the data you will read from the database is huge, you want to retrieve the data with little impact on the server resources and maximize the performance. Which object should you use to load the data from the database?

○ A. **DataSet**

○ B. **DataTable**

○ C. **SqlDataReader**

○ D. **OleDbDataReader**

Question 27

You allow users to edit product information on a **DataGrid** control that is bound to a **DataSet** object. When the user clicks the Update button on the form, you call the **SqlDataAdapter.Update()** method to cause the changes from the **DataSet** object to persist to the underlying database. Users report that new records and updated rows are saved properly but that deleted rows are reappearing the next time they run the application. What could be the problem?

- ○ A. The users do not have permission to update the underlying table.
- ○ B. The **Update()** method does not delete rows.
- ○ C. Someone is restoring an old version of the database between the two executions of the program.
- ○ D. You forgot to set the **DeleteCommand** property of the **SqlDataAdapter** object.

Question 28

Your ASP.NET Web application has two **FileStream** objects. The **fsIn** object is open for reading, and the **fsOut** object is open for writing. Which code snippet would copy the contents of **fsIn** to **fsOut** using a 2KB buffer?

○ A.
```
Dim buf(2048) As Integer
Dim intBytesRead As Integer
Do While ((intBytesRead = fsIn.Read(buf, 0, 2048)) > 0)
    fsOut.Write(buf, 0, intBytesRead)
Loop
' Clean up
fsOut.Flush()
fsOut.Close()
fsIn.Close()
```

○ B.
```
Dim buf(2048) As Integer
Dim intBytesRead As Integer
Do While ((intBytesRead = fsIn.Read(buf, 0, 2048)) > 1)
    fsOut.Write(buf, 0, intBytesRead)
Loop
' Clean up
fsOut.Flush()
fsOut.Close()
fsIn.Close()
```

○ C.

```
Dim buf(2048) As Byte
Dim intBytesRead As Integer
Do While ((intBytesRead = fsIn.Read(buf, 0, 2048)) > 0)
    fsOut.Write(buf, 0, intBytesRead)
Loop
' Clean up
fsOut.Flush()
fsOut.Close()
fsIn.Close()
```

○ D.

```
Dim buf(2048) As Byte
Dim intBytesRead As Integer
Do While ((intBytesRead = fsIn.Read(buf, 0, 2048)) > 1)
    fsOut.Write(buf, 0, intBytesRead)
Loop
' Clean up
fsOut.Flush()
fsOut.Close()
fsIn.Close()
```

Question 29

Your SQL Server database contains a table, Sales, with these columns:

```
SalesID (int, identity)
StoreNumber (int)
Sales (int)
```

You have created a stored procedure that accepts as inputs the store number
and sales, inserts a new row in the table with this information, and returns the
new identity value:

```
CREATE PROCEDURE procInsertSales
   @StoreNumber int,
   @Sales int,
   @SalesID int OUTPUT
AS
   INSERT INTO Sales (StoreNumber, Sales)
   VALUES (@StoreNumber, @Sales)
   SELECT @SalesID = @@IDENTITY
```

Which statement should you use to define the **SqlParameter** object for the **@SalesID** parameter for the previous stored procedure?

○ A.
```
Dim paramSalesID As SqlParameter = New SqlParameter( _
    "@SalesID", SqlDbType.Int)
paramSalesID.Direction = ParameterDirection.Output
```

○ B.
```
Dim paramSalesID As SqlParameter = New SqlParameter( _
    "@SalesID", SqlDbType.Int)
paramSalesID.Direction = ParameterDirection.ReturnValue
```

○ C.
```
Dim paramSalesID As SqlParameter = New SqlParameter( _
    "@SalesID", Int32)
paramSalesID.Direction = ParameterDirection.Output
```

○ D.
```
Dim paramSalesID As SqlParameter = New SqlParameter( _
    "@SalesID", Int32)
paramSalesID.Direction = ParameterDirection.ReturnValue
```

Question 30

You have defined a method named **DataLoad** that makes a list of suppliers available by returning an **ICollection** interface. You have an ASP.NET Web Form with a **ListBox** control named **lbCustomers**. The **Page_Load()** event handler for the Web Form contains this code:

```
Private Sub Page_Load(ByVal sender As System.Object, _
    ByVal e As System.EventArgs) Handles MyBase.Load
    lbCustomers.DataSource = DataLoad()
    lbCustomers.DataTextField = "CustomerName"
End Sub
```

The Web Form opens without error, but no customer names are displayed. What is the problem?

○ A. You have neglected to call the **DataBind()** method of the page.

○ B. You have neglected to set the **DataValueField** property of the **ListBox** control.

○ C. A **ListBox** control cannot be bound to an **ICollection** interface.

○ D. The code should be placed in the **Page_Init()** event handler.

Question 31

You are designing a Web Form that will use a **Repeater** Web server control to display information from several columns of the Orders table in your database. You want to display the column names at the top of the control in **Label** Web server controls. Which template should you include with the column names?

- ○ A. **ItemTemplate**
- ○ B. **AlternatingItemTemplate**
- ○ C. **HeaderTemplate**
- ○ D. **SeparatorTemplate**

Question 32

You are creating a user control that displays employee names whose birthdays fall within the current quarter. The user control is displayed in the activities page of your company's intranet. You have placed a **Repeater** control in the user control. You are using data binding to display values from the **dsEmployees DataSet** object into the **Repeater** control. The **Repeater** control contains the following definition:

```
<asp:Repeater id="rptProducts" runat="server"
DataSource="<%# dsEmployees %>" DataMember="Employees">
```

You want to display the employee name, as well as the month and day of his birthday, in the **Repeater** control. Which of the following options would you choose to maximize performance?

- ○ A.
```
<ItemTemplate>
    <tr>
        <td><%# DataBinder.Eval(
            Container.DataItem, "Name") %></td>
        <td><%# DataBinder.Eval(
            Container.DataItem, "Date", "{0:m}") %></td>
    </tr>
</ItemTemplate>
```

- ○ B.
```
<ItemTemplate>
    <tr>
        <td><%# DataBinder.Eval(
            Container.DataItem, "Name") %></td>
        <td><%# DataBinder.Eval(
            Container.DataItem, "Date") %></td>
    </tr>
</ItemTemplate>
```

○ C.

```
<ItemTemplate>
    <tr>
        <td><%#
        (CType(Container.DataItem, DataRowView)("Name"))
        %></td>
        <td><%# String.Format("{0:m}",
            (CType(Container.DataItem, DataRowView)("Date")))
        %></td>
    </tr>
</ItemTemplate>
```

○ D.

```
<ItemTemplate>
    <tr>
        <td><%#
        (CType(Container.DataItem, DataRowView)("Name"))
        %></td>
        <td><%#
        (CType(Container.DataItem, DataRowView)("Date"))
        %></td>
    </tr>
</ItemTemplate>
```

Question 33

You develop an ASP.NET Web application named **ProcessOrder** using Visual Basic .NET. Your application receives orders from customers in an XML file named **Orders.xml**. The **Orders.xml** file does not include a schema. Which of the following methods can you use to load the data from **Orders.xml** into a **DataSet** object? (Select two.)

❑ A.

```
Dim ds As DataSet = New DataSet("Orders")
ds.ReadXml("Orders.xml", XmlReadMode.Auto)
```

❑ B.

```
Dim ds As DataSet = New DataSet("Orders")
ds.ReadXml("Orders.xml", XmlReadMode.DiffGram)
```

❑ C.

```
Dim ds As DataSet = New DataSet("Orders")
ds.ReadXml("Orders.xml", XmlReadMode.Fragment)
```

❑ D.

```
Dim ds As DataSet = New DataSet("Orders")
ds.ReadXml("Orders.xml", XmlReadMode.InferSchema)
```

❑ E.

```
Dim ds As DataSet = New DataSet("Orders")
ds.ReadXml("Orders.xml", XmlReadMode.ReadSchema)
```

Question 34

You create an ASP.NET Web Service project using Visual Studio .NET. The project includes a class named **RefLibrary**. The **RefLibrary** class contains this method:

```
Public Function Version() As String
    Version = "1.6"
End Function
```

You note that you are able to instantiate the **RefLibrary** class from a Web service client project, but the **Version()** method is not available. What could be the problem?

- ○ A. Only properties can be part of the public interface of a Web service.
- ○ B. You must mark the method with the **WebService** attribute.
- ○ C. The methods of a Web service can only return Object data.
- ○ D. You must mark the method with the **WebMethod** attribute.

Question 35

Your ASP.NET application performs various mathematical calculations. You are beginning to sell this application in multiple countries. How should you ensure that the correct numeric formatting is used in all cases?

- ○ A. Allow the user to select a culture from a list. Create a **CultureInfo** object based on the user's selection and assign it to the **Thread.CurrentThread.CurrentCulture** property. Use the **ToString()** method to format numeric amounts.
- ○ B. Retrieve the value of **Request.UserLanguages(0)** when you're processing the page and assign it to the **Thread.CurrentThread.CurrentCulture** property. Use the **ToString()** method to format numeric amounts.
- ○ C. Allow the user to select a culture from a list. Create a **CultureInfo** object based on the user's selection and assign it to the **Thread.CurrentThread.CurrentUICulture** property. Use the **ToString()** method to format numeric amounts.
- ○ D. Retrieve the value of **Request.UserLanguages(0)** when you're processing the page and assign it to the **Thread.CurrentThread.CurrentUICulture** property. Use the **ToString()** method to format numeric amounts.

Question 36

Your ASP.NET application needs to search for text within longer text passages. You have been assigned to implement this culture-aware feature using Visual Basic .NET. What should you use to perform this search?

○ A. **CultureInfo.CompareInfo**

○ B. **Array.Sort()**

○ C. **String.IndexOf()**

○ D. **String.IndexOfAny()**

Question 37

You wrote a COM component to supply weather information from the weather database to the Weather Web page of your Web application. You are porting the Web application to .NET. You now want to call the methods of the COM component from your ASP.NET Web application. The COM component is not used by any other application. Which of the following is the quickest way to use the COM component in the ASP.NET Web application?

○ A. Set a direct reference from your .NET client to the COM server.

○ B. Use the Type Library Importer to create an unsigned RCW for the COM component.

○ C. Use the Type Library Importer to create a signed RCW for the COM component.

○ D. Use **PInvoke** to instantiate classes from the COM component.

Question 38

You have designed an ASP.NET Web Form that displays inventory information. When a product falls below the reorder level, you need to highlight product information within a table so that it stands out to the user. Which method of highlighting is most accessible?

○ A. **<BGCOLOR>**

○ B. **<BLINK>**

○ C. **<B>**

○ D. **<MARQUEE>**

Question 39

You need to debug an ASP.NET Web application by using Visual Studio .NET installed on your local machine. The Web application is deployed on a remote server. When you attempt to debug the application, you get a DCOM configuration error. Which of the following steps should you take to resolve this problem?

○ A. Add your account to the Main Users group on the local computer.

○ B. Add your account to the Main Users group on the remote computer.

○ C. Add your account to the Debugger Users group on the local computer.

○ D. Add your account to the Debugger Users group on the remote computer.

Question 40

You develop a supplier evaluation system using Visual Studio .NET. While testing the program, you notice that the value of the **TotalShipments** variable sometimes becomes zero and causes an exception within the **CalculateAvgShipDelay()** method. You want your program to check the value of the **TotalShipments** variable and display an error message when the value of **TotalShipments** is zero. You want the program to display this error message irrespective of how you compile the program. Which of the following code segments should you write before making a call to the **CalculateAvgShipDelay()** method?

○ A.

```
Trace.Assert(TotalShipments = 0, "TotalShipments is zero")
```

○ B.

```
Trace.Assert(TotalShipments <> 0, "TotalShipments is zero")
```

○ C.

```
Debug.Assert(TotalShipments = 0, "TotalShipments is zero")
```

○ D.

```
Debug.Assert(TotalShipments <> 0, "TotalShipments is zero")
```

Question 41

You develop an ASP.NET Web application that enables the users to generate shipping labels. The program needs to generate thousands of shipping labels each day. You use the **Trace** object to monitor the application and log the results in the Windows event log. You need to monitor errors, warnings, and other informational messages generated by the **Trace** object. You should have flexibility of controlling the amount of information logged for your application, and you want to do this with minimum administrative efforts. What should you do?

- ○ A. Compile the application using the **/d:TRACE** switch.

- ○ B. Define an environment variable named **TRACE** and set its value to **True** or **False**. In the program, check the value of the environment variable to indicate the amount of information you want for your application to log.

- ○ C. Declare a compilation constant named **TRACE** and set its value to **Error**, **Warning**, or **Info**. In your program, use **#if**, **#else**, and **#endif** directives to check the level of tracing you want.

- ○ D. Use the **TraceSwitch** class in your program and use the **TraceSwitch.Level** property to check if you need to log the performance or not. Set the level of the **TraceSwitch** by using the application's configuration file.

Question 42

The configuration file of a Web application has the following contents:

```
<system.diagnostics>
   <switches>
      <add name="BooleanSwitch" value="-1" />
      <add name="TraceLevelSwitch" value="33" />
   </switches>
</system.diagnostics>
```

You are using the following statements to create switch objects in your code:

```
Dim booleanSwitch As BooleanSwitch = _
   New BooleanSwitch("BooleanSwitch", "Boolean Switch")
Dim traceSwitch As TraceSwitch = _
   New TraceSwitch("TraceLevelSwitch", "Trace Switch")
```

Which of the following options is correct regarding the values of these switch objects?

- ○ A. The **booleanSwitch.Enabled property** is set to **False**, and **traceSwitch.Level** is set to **TraceLevel.Verbose**.

- ○ B. The **booleanSwitch.Enabled** property is set to **True**, and **traceSwitch.Level** is set to **TraceLevel.Verbose**.

- ○ C. The **booleanSwitch.Enabled** property is set to **False**, and **traceSwitch.Level** is set to **TraceLevel.Error**.

- ○ D. The **booleanSwitch.Enabled** property is set to **False**, and **traceSwitch.Level** is set to **TraceLevel.Info**.

Question 43

You are debugging an ASP.NET Web application that you wrote using Visual Studio .NET. Your code uses the **Trace** class to produce the debugging output. In which configuration(s) will this output be enabled?

- ○ A. In the default Release configuration only
- ○ B. In the default Debug configuration only
- ○ C. In both the default Release and the default Debug configurations
- ○ D. In neither the default Release nor the default Debug configuration

Question 44

You are testing a huge Web application running on the main testing server, and you have enabled tracing in the application. You find it difficult to test the application from your desktop because the Web application is storing tracing information for only a few requests. You want the Web application to record tracing information for a larger number of requests, and you also want the tracing information to be displayed in the Web page along with the trace viewer. Which of the following options should you choose?

- ○ A. Set the **<trace>** element in the **Web.config** application configuration file of the application to
  ```
  <trace enabled="True" pageOutput="True" localOnly="False" />
  ```

- ○ B. Set the **<trace>** element in the **Web.config** application configuration file of the application to
  ```
  <trace enabled="True" pageOutput="True" localOnly="True" />
  ```

- ○ C. Set the **<trace>** element in the **Web.config** application configuration file of the application to
  ```
  <trace enabled="False" pageOutput="True" localOnly="True" />
  ```

- ○ D. Set the **<trace>** element in the **Web.config** application configuration file of the application to
  ```
  <trace enabled="True" pageOutput="True"
     requestLimit="50" localOnly="False" />
  ```

- ○ E. Set the **<trace>** element in the **Web.config** application configuration file of the application to
  ```
  <trace enabled="True" pageOutput="True"
     requestLimit="50" localOnly="True" />
  ```

- ○ F. Set the **<trace>** element in the **Web.config** application configuration file of the application to
  ```
  <trace enabled="False" pageOutput="True"
     requestLimit="50" localOnly="True" />
  ```

Question 45

You use Visual Basic .NET to create an assembly named **Tracker.dll**. **Tracker.dll** contains classes for tracking a shipment and is used by several applications including both managed applications and unmanaged COM applications. The COM applications are already compiled, and they use late binding to invoke methods from the assembly. What actions should you take to ensure that the assembly is properly deployed on the target machine? (Select all that apply.)

- ❑ A. Create a strong name for the assembly by using the Strong Name tool (**sn.exe**).
- ❑ B. Register the assembly using the Assembly Registration tool (**regasm.exe**).
- ❑ C. Create a type library for the application using the Type Library Exporter tool (**tlbexp.exe**).
- ❑ D. Import the COM type library definition into an assembly by using the Type Library Importer tool (**tlbimp.exe**).
- ❑ E. Deploy the assembly to the Global Assembly Cache (GAC).
- ❑ F. Deploy the assembly to the application's bin directory.
- ❑ G. Deploy the assembly to the Windows system directory.

Question 46

You use Visual Basic .NET to develop a component named **ReplicateWarehouseData**. This component replicates the data used by the Warehousing application that is developed by the Warehouse Development team of your company. The Warehouse Development team needs to deploy the Warehousing application to its first three customers. How should they deploy the application? (Select two best answers.)

- ❑ A. Create a Merge module for the **ReplicateWarehouseData** component.
- ❑ B. Create a Setup project that deploys the application and includes the Merge module containing the component into the Setup project.
- ❑ C. Copy the **ReplicateWarehouseData** component into the directory of the Warehousing application.
- ❑ D. Create a Web Setup project to deploy the application that contains the code for the component.

Question 47

You use Visual Basic .NET to create an assembly named **Tracker.dll**. **Tracker.dll** contains classes for tracking a shipment. You need to deploy the assembly on the target computer in such a way that it can be accessed by multiple .NET applications. Which of the following actions should you take? (Select all that apply.)

- ❑ A. Create a strong name for the assembly by using the Strong Name tool (**sn.exe**).

- ❑ B. Register the assembly using the Assembly Registration tool (**regasm.exe**).

- ❑ C. Use XCOPY to deploy the assembly to the Global Assembly Cache.

- ❑ D. Use FTP to deploy the assembly to the Global Assembly Cache.

- ❑ E. Use the Setup and Deployment project to deploy the assembly to the Global Assembly Cache.

Question 48

You have created and tested an ASP.NET application on your local development server. The application makes heavy use of Web server controls, along with static HTML text. Now you have deployed the application to your company's production server via FTP. The production server has IIS 5.0 installed. The pages in the application are displaying in a jumbled fashion, with text present but none of the Web server controls. What could be the problem?

- ○ A. Applications containing Web server controls cannot be deployed via FTP.

- ○ B. Web server controls will not function properly on a page that also contains static HTML text.

- ○ C. The ASP.NET worker process is not properly installed on the production server.

- ○ D. ASP.NET requires IIS 6.0 to function properly.

Question 49

You are creating a Web Setup project for a Web application. In the Property Pages for the Web Setup project, you have set the compression property to **Optimized for speed**. Which of the following options will be **True** as a result of this configuration option? (Choose two.)

- ❑ A. All assemblies in the application will be pre-compiled to native code so that they run faster.
- ❑ B. Resulting assemblies will be of a larger size.
- ❑ C. The setup package will be larger.
- ❑ D. The setup project will run faster.

Question 50

Your application requires the user to be a member of Accounting role to access a **BalanceSheet** object. Which .NET security feature should you use to ensure that your code has this capability?

- ○ A. Role-based security
- ○ B. Code access security
- ○ C. SSL Encryption
- ○ D. Type Safety

Question 51

You design a Visual Basic .NET application that uses the following code to check for membership in the Developers group:

```
Private Sub frmSecure_Load(ByVal sender As System.Object, _
ByVal e As System.EventArgs) Handles MyBase.Load
    ' Get the current principal object
    Dim prin As WindowsPrincipal = Thread.CurrentPrincipal
    ' Determine whether the user is an admin
    Dim fAdmin As Boolean = prin.IsInRole("Developers")
    ' Display the results on the UI
    If fAdmin Then
        lblMembership.Text = _
            "You are in the Developers group"
    Else
        lblMembership.Text = _
            "You are not in the Developers group"
    End If
End Sub
```

Users report that the code claims they are not in the Developers group even when they are. What must you do to fix this problem?

- ○ A. Use imperative security to make sure that your code has access to the Windows environment variables.

- ○ B. Create a **WindowsIdentity** object by using the **WindowsIdentity.GetCurrent()** method, and then use this object to construct the **WindowsPrincipal** object.

- ○ C. Use the **WindowsPrincipal.Name** property to retrieve the user's name, and then use that name to call the **IsInRole()** method.

- ○ D. Call **AppDomain.CurrentDomain.SetPrincipalPolicy(PrincipalPolicy. WindowsPrincipal)** to specify the authentication mode.

Question 52

You developed a project management system for your company that will be accessed through the company's intranet. The project management system provides an interface to be used by all employees to manage their projects in spite of their diverse nature. All the employees must log on using their Windows domain accounts to access this application. The **Web.config** file of the project management application contains the following definition for the **<authentication>** element:

```
<authentication mode="Windows">
```

The Web application runs on IIS 5.0 on Windows 2000 Advanced server. IIS is configured to use Basic authentication to authenticate the users. When you run the application, you notice that all users are allowed access to the application. Which of the following options should you take in order to allow access to only authenticated users?

- ❑ A. Add the following code in the **Web.config** file of the Web application:
  ```
  <authentication mode="Windows">
  <identity impersonate="True" />
  ```

- ❑ B. Add the following code in the **Web.config** file of the Web application:
  ```
  <authentication mode="Windows">
  <authorization>
      <deny users="?" />
  </authorization>
  ```

- ❑ C. Configure IIS to Enable Windows Integrated authentication rather than the Basic authentication for the Web application.

- ❑ D. Configure IIS to Disable Anonymous Access for the Web application.

Question 53

You have deployed an ASP.NET application in your company's intranet to manage the timesheet of the associates in your company. ASP.NET is running using the default settings and impersonation is not enabled. The application uses Windows integrated authentication to authenticate its users. You allow only authenticated users to access the application. What account will ASP.NET use to access resources?

- ○ A. The **ASPNET** account
- ○ B. The **SYSTEM** account
- ○ C. The **IUSR_ComputerName** account
- ○ D. The authenticated user's account

Question 54

You are developing a proof-of-concept program to evaluate role-based security for your .NET Framework application. You write the following code:

```
Dim pp1 As PrincipalPermission = _
     New PrincipalPermission("User1", "Role1")
Dim pp2 As PrincipalPermission = _
     New PrincipalPermission("User2", "Role2")
Dim pp3 As PrincipalPermission = _
     New PrincipalPermission("User3", "Role3")

Dim perm1 As PrincipalPermission = _
     CType(pp1.Union(pp2), PrincipalPermission)
Dim perm2 As PrincipalPermission = _
     CType(pp3.Union(perm1), PrincipalPermission)
```

Which of the following statements is correct with respect to the preceding code? (Select all that apply.)

- ❑ A. The expression **perm1.IsSubsetOf(perm2)** will evaluate to **True**.
- ❑ B. The expression **perm1.IsSubsetOf(perm2)** will evaluate to **False**.
- ❑ C. The expression **perm2.IsSubsetOf(perm1)** will evaluate to **True**.
- ❑ D. The expression **perm2.IsSubsetOf(perm1)** will evaluate to **False**.

Question 55

You have deployed an ASP.NET application that displays the company's product catalog. The customers can select the product desired from the catalog and place orders. The application has been running successfully, but—as orders increase—you gradually notice that the application performs slowly because it is not capable of managing the load. The application also becomes unreachable whenever there is a hardware failure. This is causing serious side effects in the business of your company. You want to resolve this problem, so which of the following options should you select to deploy your Web application?

- ○ A. Single-server deployment
- ○ B. Web garden deployment
- ○ C. Cluster deployment
- ○ D. Web farm deployment

Question 56

You have created a Web user control named **signup.ascx** that encapsulates the controls used within your company for newsletter signup forms. Now you want to use this control in other Web applications. What must you do?

- ○ A. Install the control in the Global Assembly Cache (GAC).
- ○ B. Copy the control's files into each application.
- ○ C. Include the control's project in the solution containing each application.
- ○ D. Compile the control and copy the compiled assembly into each application's bin folder.

Question 57

You are designing a new control for use in ASP.NET applications. The new control will be used to load an image from a disk file to an **Image** control at runtime. The control needs to provide a customized user interface at runtime. Which type of control should you create?

- ○ A. A Web custom control that inherits directly from the **WebControl** control
- ○ B. A Web custom control that inherits directly from the **Label** control
- ○ C. A Composite Web custom control
- ○ D. A Web user control

Question 58

You have created a custom component for your application that monitors a bidi-rectional parallel port for error messages. This component raises an event named **PortError** whenever an error message is detected. At that point, you must make the error code available to the control container. You want to use the best coding practices. Which of the following options should you choose to make the error code available to the container?

○ A. Place the error code in a property of the component for the container to retrieve.

○ B. Pass the error code as a parameter to the **PortError** event handler.

○ C. Define a global variable in a separate class and place the value in that variable.

○ D. Define a custom **PortErrorEventArgs** class that inherits from the **EventArgs** class to contain the error code, and pass an instance of the class as a parameter of the **PortError** event handler.

Question 59

Your application contains a Web user control **LogIn**, which you have defined, in the **LogIn.ascx** file. You want to load this control in the Web page programmat-ically only if the user is not currently logged in to the Web site. The user control contains the following **Control** directive:

```
<%@ Control
    ClassName="LogIn"
    Language="vb"
    AutoEventWireup="False"
    Codebehind="LogIn.ascx.vb"
    Inherits="LogIn" %>
```

You have added the reference to the user control in the Home Web page, as shown here:

```
<%@ Reference Control="LogIn.ascx" %>
```

Which of the following options should you use to load the user control and set its properties in the Web page?

○ A.
```
Dim c As Control = New Control("LogIn.ascx")
CType(c, LogIn).ShowForgotPassword = True
```

○ B.
```
Dim c As Control = New Control("LogIn.ascx")
CType(c, LogIn).ShowForgotPassword = True
Controls.Add(c)
```

○ C.
```
Dim c As Control = LoadControl("LogIn.ascx")
CType(c, LogIn).ShowForgotPassword = True
```

○ D.
```
Dim c As Control = LoadControl("LogIn.ascx")
CType(c, LogIn).ShowForgotPassword = True
++
```

Question 60

You are designing a custom control for monitoring usage patterns of the Web pages. This control will log specific user actions in to a SQL Server table. You will place this control on the Web Forms, but the control does not require any visual representation at runtime. From which class should you derive this control?

○ A. **Control**

○ B. **UserControl**

○ C. **Form**

○ D. **Component**

Answer Key for Practice Exam #2

Answer Key

1. A	21. D	41. D
2. C	22. C	42. B
3. B	23. C	43. C
4. C	24. B	44. D
5. A	25. B	45. A, B, and E
6. A and C	26. D	46. C and D
7. C	27. D	47. A and E
8. A	28. C	48. C
9. B	29. A	49. C and D
10. C	30. A	50. A
11. B	31. C	51. D
12. D	32. C	52. B and D
13. B	33. A and D	53. A
14. C	34. D	54. A and D
15. A	35. A	55. D
16. E	36. A	56. B
17. B	37. A	57. A
18. B	38. C	58. D
19. A	39. D	59. D
20. C	40. B	60. D

Detailed Answers

1. Correct answer is **A**. The `Protected` modifier limits member access to the class containing the member and to subclasses of that class. Answer B is incorrect because the `Public` modifier allows any class to call the member. Answer C is incorrect because the `Private` modifier limits access to the defining class only. Answer D is incorrect because the `Friend` modifier limits access to classes within the same project, whether they are derived from the defining class or not.

2. Correct answer is **C**. When the `AutoEventWireup` attribute is set to `True`, ASP.NET automatically registers the `Page_Load()` method as an event handler for the `Load` event of the `Page` class. You also explicitly attach the `Page_Load()` method to the `Load` event of the page with the `Handles` keyword. Therefore, the drop-down list is populated twice because the `Page_Load()` method is executed twice. Setting the `AutoEventWireup` to `False` will avoid auto event wiring for Page event handlers. Answer A is incorrect because the `EnableViewState` attribute is used to indicate whether the view state should be enabled and has no control on executing the event handlers. Answer B is incorrect because the `SmartNavigation` attribute is used to remember the control focus on a postback and implement other navigation features on a Web page. Answer D is incorrect because if the drop-down list control is populated on page postback, the drop-down list will not display any values when the page is first displayed, and also, multiple postbacks will add multiple values in the drop-down list.

3. Correct answer is **B**. Setting the `TabIndex` property of the control to a negative value removes the control from the tab order. Answer A is incorrect because controls with a `TabIndex` of `0` also participate in the tab order. Answer C is incorrect because `AccessKey` only provides a shortcut key for quick navigation to the control. Setting it to an empty string will have no impact on the tab order. Answer D is incorrect because if you set the `Enabled` property of the control to `False`, it cannot get the focus under any circumstances.

4. Correct answer is **C**. The `AlternateText` property specifies the text that is displayed in place of the `Image` Web server control when the image is being downloaded, the image is unavailable, or the browser doesn't support images. Answer A is incorrect because the `ToolTip` property is only used to display ToolTips for the image. Answer B is incorrect because the `Attributes` property represents a collection of name/value pairs that is rendered to the browser in the opening tag of the control. Answer D is incorrect because the `ImageUrl` property is used to specify the URL of the image.

5. Correct answer is **A**. You would use two `CompareValidator` controls—one control to compare that the value in control `txtQuote` is greater than or equal to `txtPrevQtrMin` and the other control to compare that `txtQuote` is less than or equal to `txtPrevQtrMax`. Answer B is incorrect because the `RangeValidator` control is used to perform range validations only on the fixed values set to its `MinimumValue` and `MaximumValue` properties. Only the `CompareValidator` control enables you to compare and validate controls based on the values of other controls. Answer C is incorrect because the `CustomValidator` control would involve writing more code. Answer D is incorrect because the `RegularExpressionValidator` control is used to ensure that the input control's value is in a specified pattern.

6. Correct answers are **A** and **C**. The `RequiredFieldValidator` control lets you check that the URL is entered in the input control, and the `RegularExpressionValidator` control lets you check that the URL is in the proper format. Answer B is incorrect because `RangeValidator` control lets you check that the data is within a specific range in the input control. Answer D is incorrect because `CompareValidator` lets you compare the data against a given value or another input control's value.

7. Correct answer is **C**. When you have multiple `Catch` blocks associated with a `Try` block, you must write them in order from specific to general. The `Catch` block corresponding to `ArithmeticException` should come at the end because it is more general compared to the other three. In fact, the `DivideByZeroException`, `NotFiniteNumberException`, and the `OverFlowException` classes are derived from `ArithmeticException`. Answers A, B, and D are incorrect because they do not place `Catch` blocks in order of specific to general exceptions.

8. Correct answer is **A**. The `SqlException.Class` property gets a value from `1` to `25` that indicates the severity level of the error. Answer B is incorrect because the `SqlException.Source` property gets the name of the provider that generated the error. Answer C is incorrect because the `SqlException.Server` property gets the name of the computer running an instance of SQL Server that generated the error. Answer D is incorrect because the `SqlException.State` property gets a numeric error code from SQL Server that represents an error, warning, or "no data found" message.

9. Correct answer is **B**. The configuration settings most local to the requested page control the response of ASP.NET. In the case of `/custom/remote/NonExistingPage.aspx`, the configuration file in the `/custom` directory will be applied, which disables custom error pages. Therefore, answers A, C, and D are incorrect.

10. Correct answer is **C**. The `Server.Transfer()` method provides a quick way to switch to ASPX pages within the ASP.NET application. Answer A is incorrect because the `HyperLink` control cannot be used to transfer control to other pages programmatically. Answer B is incorrect because the `Response.Redirect()` method causes an extra round-trip between the server and the client to transfer control to another page. Answer D is incorrect because the `Server.Execute()` method executes the specified ASPX page and returns back the control to the calling ASPX page.

11. Correct answer is **B**. Setting the `BufferOutput` property to `True` enables the output to the response stream to be buffered until the entire page is processed. Therefore, you should call the `Clear()` method to clear the entire response stream buffer created until the file was not found. Answer A is incorrect because the `Flush()` method flushes the currently buffered content out to the client. Answer C is incorrect because the `Close()` method closes the HTTP response object and the socket connection to the client. Answer D is incorrect because the `End()` method stops the execution of the page after flushing the output buffer to the client.

12. Correct answer is **D**. By default, When ASP.NET executes a page, it saves a copy of all non-postback controls in the hidden `__VIEWSTATE` control. Because the page will not be posted back, you don't need this information. Therefore, you can disable view state for the entire page and make the page smaller so that it can be delivered more quickly. Answers A and B are incorrect because they enable the view state, which would store the data of controls in the `__VIEWSTATE` control and make the page bulky. Answer C is incorrect because it disables view state only for the `DataGrid` control rather than the whole page.

13. Correct answer is **B**. Because different computers within a Web farm might serve multiple page requests during a session, you need to store any session state information in a shared repository outside of the ASP.NET worker process. Answer A is incorrect because you can use session state in a Web farm configuration. Answer C is incorrect because view state is used to store data related to a page rather than a user session. Answer D is incorrect because `HttpRequest`, `HttpResponse`, and `HttpServerUtility` objects can be used in a Web farm configuration.

14. Correct answer is **C**. Session and application state are not shared between the ASP and ASP.NET pages. If you set a session or application variable in ASP.NET code, there's no way to retrieve it from ASP code, and vice versa. Answer A is incorrect because the Session property need not explicitly refer to Page.Session in the given context. Answer B is incorrect because the ASP.NET Session object is not available in the ASP pages. Answer D is incorrect because cookies are required not just for ASP but are required for ASP.NET as well.

15. Correct answer is **A**. When a user visits the site, the browser establishes a new session with the Web server. At that time, the Session_Start() event handler is executed. This method is executed only once for the user session and is an appropriate choice for the case in question. Answer B is incorrect because Application_BeginRequest() works for every HTTP request and not just the first request. Answer C is incorrect because the Page_Load() event handler of default.aspx might not work in all cases. For example, the user might enter the Web site through a page other than default.aspx. Answer D is incorrect because the Application_Start() event handler will only redirect the first user of the application.

16. Correct answer is **E**. The DataSet object contains product details that are global to the application and need to be expired every two hours. The best place to store application data is the application data cache, the Cache object. The data cached in the data cache can be set to expire in a fixed amount of time, or by using sliding expiration. Answer A is incorrect because application state is used to store data global to the application, but it cannot expire after a fixed amount of time or offer other features of the Cache object. Answer B is incorrect because session state is used to store user-specific data; if session state is used to store the DataSet object, multiple copies of the DataSet object will be created for each user, hindering the performance. Further, the data in session state cannot expire in a fixed amount of time. Answer C is incorrect because it is used to store only page-specific data on the client side. Answer D is incorrect because the HttpCachePolicy object is used to store the HTML output of Web pages rather than the data.

17. Correct answer is **B**. The Duration and VaryByParam attributes must be specified when an OutputCache directive is applied to an ASPX page. The Duration attribute specifies the period in seconds for which the page should be cached. If the output does not vary by any parameters, None should be passed to the VaryByParam attribute. Answers A and C are incorrect because the Duration attribute specifies the time in seconds. Answer D is incorrect because the required VaryByParam attribute is missing.

18. Correct answer is **B**. Because the page accepts other information and the output changes for every state and park selected by the user, you should supply the VaryByParam attribute with ddlStates;ddlParks to cache different versions of pages for every state and park selected. Answer A is incorrect because the page accepts other information and it would cache all the possible versions of the Web page. Answer C is incorrect because it would cache only on the basis of the park irrespective of the state. Therefore, if two states have parks with the same name, the cache will contain output on only the first park selected by the user.

Answers D, E, and F are incorrect because the VaryByControl attribute is only applied in user controls rather than the ASPX pages.

19. Correct answer is **A**. The ApplyDefaultSort property is used to automatically create a sort order, in ascending order, based on the primary key of the table. The ApplyDefaultSort property only applies when the table has a primary key defined and the Sort property is Nothing or an empty string. Answer B is incorrect because you want to sort using the primary key; for that, you should set the ApplyDefaultSort property to True. Answer C is incorrect because you need to sort instead of filtering the data. Answer D is incorrect because the given code segment is incorrect. You must specify the name of a column in the Sort property along with ASC or DESC.

20. Correct answer is **C**. Setting the RowStateFilter property of the DataView object to DataViewRowState.Deleted specifies that you want to view the deleted rows from the original data. Answer A and B are incorrect because the RowFilter property is used to filter rows based on an expression rather than their state. Answer D is incorrect because setting the RowStateFilter property to DataViewRowState.OriginalRows displays the original data of all the rows including deleted rows.

21. Correct answer is **D**. To display values from an array in a ListBox control, set the DataTextField property of the control to a string containing the name of the field. Answers A and C are incorrect because they use the DataValueField property instead of the DataTextField property. The DataValueField property is used to set the value associated with the items in the ListBox control, but this property is not displayed in the control. Answer B is incorrect because the property name of the data source must be specified as a string.

22. Correct answer is **C**. When you use the Close() method on an SqlConnection object, the connection is closed, all pending database transactions are rolled back, and the connection is returned back to the connection pool. Answer A is incorrect because reusing an instance after you have called the Dispose() method might result into undesirable effects. In general, you should use Close() rather than Dispose() if you think you might want to reuse the connection instance. Answer B is incorrect because you should generally call the Finalize() method only when you need to release unmanaged resources. Answer D is incorrect because setting the SqlConnection object to Nothing will not actually close the connection, but the object will continue to exist in memory waiting for garbage collection.

23. Correct answer is **C**. A `DataRelation` object is used to relate two `DataTable` objects to each other. Once you create a `DataRelation` object, you can call the `GetChildRows()` and `GetParentRows()` methods of the `DataRow` object to fetch the child or parent rows, respectively. Answers A and B are incorrect because just defining primary or foreign keys on the table will not relate the tables. Answer D is incorrect because the `DataSet.Merge()` method is use to merge two `DataSet` objects, which is not a requirement in this case.

24. Correct answer is **B**. The `XmlValidatingReader` object allows you to validate an XML document. You use its `ValidationEventHandler` event to set an event handler for receiving information about the schema validation errors. Answer A is incorrect because the `XmlDocument` object cannot validate the XML document on its own. Answer C is incorrect because the `EnforceConstraints` property of the `DataSet` is used to specify whether the database constraint rules are followed when attempting any update operation. Answer D is incorrect because the `DataSet.MergeFailed` event occurs only when a target and source `DataRow` have the same primary key value and `EnforceConstraints` is set to `True`.

25. Correct answer is **B**. The `LIKE` clause determines whether or not a given character string matches a specified pattern. You use the % character to work as the wildcard character. Answer A is incorrect because you need to use the `LIKE` clause instead of the `IN` clause for pattern searching. Answers C and D are incorrect because you need to use % as the wildcard character for matching instead of the * character.

26. Correct answer is **D**. `OleDbDataReader` allows you to read the data one row at a time in a forward-only fashion; therefore, it occupies less memory and improves the performance of your application. The question requires you to read the data in a sequential fashion and write it to the flat file; the `OleDbDataReader` object is the best option. Answer A is incorrect because a `DataSet` object loads the entire retrieved data in the memory. Answer B is incorrect because you cannot retrieve the data directly in a `DataTable` object. Answer C is incorrect because the `SqlDataReader` object is optimized to work with SQL Server 7.0 and later versions.

27. Correct answer is **D**. Because other operations on the database, such as add and update, are working fine, chances are that the `DeleteCommand` property is not set. The `DeleteCommand` property should be set to a command that deletes rows from the database. Answers A and C are incorrect because if that were the case, none of the changes would be saved. Answer B is incorrect because if the `DeleteCommand` property is correctly set, the `Update()` method will delete rows.

28. Correct answer is **C**. The Read() method returns the number of bytes read, so Answers B and D fail when there is 1 byte in the file. The Read() method reads to a byte array, so Answers A and B fail because the buffer is of the incorrect data type.

29. Correct answer is **A**. While creating a SqlParameter object, you specify SQL Server data types using the SqlDbType enumeration rather than specify the .NET Framework data types. The @SALESID parameter is defined as an output parameter in the stored procedure; therefore, the Direction property of the SqlParameter object should be set to Output. Answers B and D are incorrect because the Direction property is set to ReturnValue, which specifies that the parameter represents a return value from a stored procedure. Answers C and D are incorrect because you should specify SQL Server data types when creating a SqlParameter object.

30. Correct answer is **A**. You must explicitly call the DataBind method of the page or of the particular control to bind the data. Answer B is incorrect because you can display data in a ListBox control even without setting any value for the DataValueField property. Answer C is incorrect because a ListBox control can be bound to the ICollection interface. Answer D is incorrect because you should write data-binding code in the Page_Load() event handler rather than Page_Init().

31. Correct answer is **C**. The controls in the HeaderTemplate template are rendered once at the start of the Repeater control. Answer A is incorrect because the controls in ItemTemplate are rendered once for every row of data in the data source of the control. Answer B is incorrect because the controls in AlternatingItemTemplate are rendered once for every other row instead of ItemTemplate. Answer D is incorrect because SeparatorTemplate is rendered once between each row of data in the data source of the control.

32. Correct answer is **C**. You should prefer using type-casting to display data as the data is early bound. You should avoid using the DataBinder.Eval() method because the data is late bound and causes a performance penalty. To display the month and day, you need to format the date. Answers A and B are incorrect because they use the DataBinder.Eval() method and cause a performance penalty. Answer D is incorrect because it does not format the date returned from the database in the desired format.

33. Correct answers are **A** and **D**. In the current scenario, the XmlReadMode.Auto and XmlReadMode.InferSchema options will infer schema from the data. Answer B is incorrect because the data in the Orders.xml file is not a DiffGram. Answer C is incorrect because when XmlReadMode is set to Fragment, the default namespace is read as the inline schema. Answer E is incorrect because the XML file does not include a schema.

34. Correct answer is **D**. Adding the WebMethod attribute to a public method makes it callable from remote Web clients. Answer A is incorrect because methods can be part of the public interface of a Web service. Answer B is incorrect because the WebService attribute is applied to the Web service class and not Web methods. Answer C is incorrect because Web service methods can return any data type.

35. Correct answer is **A**. The CurrentCulture property specifies which culture to use for formatting dates, numbers, currencies, and so on. Answer B is incorrect because allowing the user to choose a culture is better than accepting the value of the UserLanguages string. The UserLanguages property of the HttpRequest object is not a reliable indicator of the end user's preferred language because Web browsers are not required to set this property. Answers C and D are incorrect because the CurrentUICulture property specifies which culture to use when choosing resources for the user interface. The CurrentCulture property specifies which culture to use for formatting dates, numbers, currencies, and so on.

36. Correct answer is **A**. Only the CompareInfo object can correctly handle the search in all character sets, including those that use multiple bytes per character. Answer B is incorrect because Array.Sort() does not locate substrings. Answers C and D are incorrect because the String.IndexOf() and the String.IndexOfAny() methods can find substrings, but are not culture aware.

37. Correct answer is **A**. Because only one application is using the COM component, the quickest way to create the Runtime Callable Wrapper (RCW) and have the COM component available in your Visual Basic .NET project is to use the Add Reference dialog box to add a direct reference to the COM component. Answers B and C are incorrect because the COM component is not shared by multiple applications; therefore, you need not use the Type Library Importer tool to generate RCW for the COM component. Answer D is incorrect because the PInvoke feature is used to call functions from unmanaged libraries such as Win 32 API libraries rather than the COM component libraries.

38. Correct answer is **C**. For compatibility with the largest number of accessibility aids, you should use bold or underlining to highlight information. Answer A is incorrect because you shouldn't depend on only color to convey information in an accessible application. Answers B and D are incorrect because they are not accessible ways to highlight information and are not compatible with most of the accessibility aids and Web browsers.

39. Correct answer is **D**. If you get a DCOM configuration error while debugging, you might not be a member of the Debugger Users group on the remote machine. To resolve this, add your account on the remote machine to the Debugger Users group. Answers A and B are incorrect because to debug a program remotely using Visual Studio .NET, you should be a member of the Debugger Users group rather than the Main Users group. Answer C is incorrect because you should be a member of the Debuggers group on the remote computer rather than the local computer.

40. Correct answer is **B**. The `Assert()` method checks for the given condition and generates an error when the condition evaluates to `False`. Answer A is incorrect because this code segment will only generate an error when the value of `TotalShipments` is not equal to zero. Answers C and D are incorrect because the `Debug.Assert()` method is invoked only when the program is complied using the Debug configuration.

41. Correct answer is **D**. The `TraceSwitch` class provides a multilevel switch to control tracing output without recompiling your code. Answer A is incorrect because the `/d:TRACE` option just enables the tracing but does not allow multilevel control over tracing output. Answer B is incorrect because modifying environmental variables requires much more administrative efforts when compared to a configuration file. Answer C is incorrect because this option requires the program to be recompiled each time the value of `TRACE` is modified.

42. Correct answer is **B**. For `BooleanSwitch`, a value of `0` corresponds to `Off`, and any nonzero value corresponds to `On`. For `TraceSwitch` any number greater than 4 is treated as Verbose. From the given values in the configuration file, the `booleanSwitch` object will have its `Enabled` property set to `True` and the `traceSwitch` object will have its `Level` property set to `TraceLevel.Verbose`. Answers A, C, and D are incorrect because the `booleanSwitch.Enabled` property is set to `False` instead of `True`.

43. Correct answer is **C**. Answers A, B, and D are incorrect because the `TRACE` symbol is defined in both the default Debug and the default Release configurations. In the default Debug configuration, only the `DEBUG` symbol is defined.

44. Correct answer is **D**. To enable tracing for all the pages of the Web application, you should enable tracing in the application configuration file, `Web.config`. To view the tracing information in the Web page, you should set the `pageOuput` attribute to `True`. To store tracing information for more requests, you should set the `requestLimit` attribute to a larger number.

Finally, to be able to access the tracing information from the trace viewer in the tester's desktop, the `localOnly` attribute should be set to `False`. Answers A and B are incorrect because the tester wants to view tracing information for a larger number of requests. Answers C and F are incorrect because they disable tracing for the entire Web application. Answer E is incorrect because the `localOnly` attribute is set to `True`. The `localOnly` attribute indicates whether the tracing information should be available only in hosting the Web server or all the clients (local as well as remote).

45. Correct answers are **A**, **B**, and **E**. Because multiple applications are using this assembly, you need to install the assembly in the GAC (Global Assembly Cache). To install the assembly into the GAC, you need to sign the assembly with a strong name before deploying it to the GAC. Finally, to enable COM applications to use the assembly, you need to register the assembly in the Windows registry. Answer C is incorrect because the COM applications need not be compiled. Answer D is incorrect because you do not need to use a COM DLL in a .NET application. Answers F and G are incorrect because shared assemblies should be deployed in the GAC. When an assembly is registered in the Windows Registry, COM applications are capable of locating shared assemblies from the GAC.

46. Correct answers are **C** and **D**. Because Warehousing is the only application using the component, you should copy the component to the Warehousing application. You can now create a Web Setup project to deploy the application and component. Answers A and B are incorrect because the Merge Module projects are only useful for creating reusable setup components.

47. Correct answers are **A** and **E**. If you want multiple applications to use an assembly, you need to sign the assembly with a strong name and place the assembly into the global assembly cache. Answer B is incorrect because no COM applications are using the assembly. Answers C and D are incorrect because assemblies cannot be deployed into the global assembly cache with XCOPY or FTP.

48. Correct answer is **C**. You must install the ASP.NET software on the Web server before accessing ASPX pages. If ASP.NET is not installed, the pages are rendered by IIS as HTML pages, and the Web server controls will not be displayed. Answer A is not correct because Web server controls do not require registration in Windows Registry and can be simply deployed by using the FTP command. Answer B is not correct because the Web server controls can easily co-exist with static HTML. Answer D is incorrect because even the most basic Web browsers can render ASP.NET pages successfully.

49. Correct answers are **C** and **D**. By optimizing the compression of the Web Setup project for speed, the setup program will compress the assemblies using a compression algorithm optimized for speed. As a result, you will have a lower compression ratio resulting in a large size setup package but that will execute faster. Answers A and B are incorrect because modifying the Web setup project's properties will not affect the size or the speed of the installed assemblies.

50. Correct answer is **A**. When you want to check whether a particular user belongs to a particular role or whether the user has a particular privilege, you need to perform role-based security. Answer B is incorrect because the application requires access to the BalanceSheet object for specific users. Answer C is incorrect because encryption makes the data more difficult to read but does not restrict the code from performing certain operations. Answer D is incorrect because type safety only allows code to access the primary memory locations that it is authorized to access. Type safety has no control over the application-specific operations.

51. Correct answer is **D**. You must tell the Common Language Runtime (CLR) how users are authenticated, even when you are using a Windows application that automatically employs Windows authentication. Answers A, B, and C are incorrect because they do not specify the authentication mode.

52. Correct answers are **B** and **D**. You should configure IIS to disable anonymous access to keep anonymous employees from accessing the system. You can use any of the Windows authentication methods for authenticating the employees. You can also disallow unauthenticated access in the application by using the <deny> element. Answer A is incorrect because it allows access to all users. Answer C is incorrect because you can use any of the Windows authentication methods to implement Windows authentication in your Web application.

53. Correct answer is **A**. By default, ASP.NET runs under a low privilege account, the ASPNET account. If impersonation is not enabled, all requests are made by ASP.NET using the ASPNET account. Answer B is incorrect because by default ASP.NET does not run under a high privilege account, the SYSTEM account. Answers C and D are incorrect because impersonation is not enabled.

54. Correct answers are **A** and **D**. The object perm2 is a union of all three PrincipalPermission objects (pp1, pp2, and pp3). The object perm1 is the union of two PrincipalPermission objects (pp1 and pp2). As a result, perm1 is a subset of perm2 and not vice versa. Answer B is incorrect because perm1 is a subset of perm2. Answer C is incorrect because perm2 is not a subset of perm1.

55. Correct answer is **D**. To manage the load of your Web application and make the application accessible, you should select a Web farm configuration to deploy your application. A Web farm configuration makes your application scalable and reliable because it allows you to run multiple Web servers to process the requests of the application. Therefore, the load is balanced, and failure of one server does not affect other servers to process the requests. Answer A is incorrect because the existing deployment is single server and it is not capable of balancing the load of the application or managing a hardware failure in the Web server. Answer B is incorrect because although Web garden deployment can balance the load of your application by running the application in a multiple-processor computer, it cannot provide a solution in case of server failure. Answer C is incorrect because cluster deployment can make the application more reliable, but it cannot help in making an application scalable.

56. Correct answer is **B**. Web user controls can only be shared by copying their files into each application in which you want to use the control. Answers A and D are incorrect because user controls cannot be pre-compiled into an assembly and cannot be shared by multiple applications by placing the assembly in the GAC. Answer C is incorrect because the user control files should be included in each application project in which they are needed.

57. Correct answer is **A**. Because you need to provide a customized user interface, you should create a Web custom control. Answer B is incorrect because inheriting from the Label control will restrict the functionality of the new control. Answers C and D are incorrect because these options are useful when you need to design a control based on one or more existing controls.

58. Correct answer is **D**. Using a class derived from EventArgs to pass event parameters is preferable to using individual arguments because it's more readily extended in case you need to pass additional parameters in the future. Answers A and C are incorrect because event-related data should be passed as an argument to the event handler. Answer B is incorrect because, by convention, event handlers only accept two arguments—the first is the object that received the event and the second is the object containing the event argument. According to good programming practices, classes containing event data should derive from the EventArgs class and their names should end with the suffix EventArgs.

59. Correct answer is **D**. The LoadControl method of the Page class is used to load a user control programmatically from an .ascx file. Because you want to set the user control properties programmatically, you need to typecast the control to the user control. Answers A and B are incorrect because you cannot create a user control using the constructor of the Control class. Answer C is incorrect because it does not add the user control to the ControlCollection of the parent control.

60. Correct answer is **D**. When a custom control does not require a run-time user interface, the Component class provides the lowest overhead. Answers A, B, and C are incorrect because they are suitable for designing controls with a user interface.

Appendix A
What's on the CD-ROM

This appendix is a brief rundown of what you'll find on the CD-ROM that comes with this book. For a more detailed description of the *PrepLogic Practice Tests, Preview Edition* exam simulation software, see Appendix B, "Using the *PrepLogic Practice Tests, Preview Edition* Software." In addition to the *PrepLogic Practice Tests, Preview Edition*, the CD-ROM includes the electronic version of the book in Portable Document Format (PDF), and the complete sample code from Que's *MCAD 70-305 Training Guide*.

PrepLogic Practice Tests, Preview Edition

PrepLogic is a leading provider of certification training tools. Trusted by certification students worldwide, PrepLogic is, we believe, the best practice exam software available. In addition to providing a means of evaluating your knowledge of the Exam Cram 2 material, *PrepLogic Practice Tests, Preview Edition* features several innovations that help you to improve your mastery of the subject matter.

For example, the practice tests allow you to check your score by exam area or domain to determine which topics you need to study more. Another feature allows you to obtain immediate feedback on your responses in the form of explanations for the correct and incorrect answers.

PrepLogic Practice Tests, Preview Edition exhibits most of the full functionality of the *Premium Edition* but offers only a fraction of the total questions. To get the complete set of practice questions and exam functionality, visit

PrepLogic.com and order the Premium Edition for this and other challenging exam titles.

Again, for a more detailed description of the *PrepLogic Practice Tests, Preview Edition* features, see Appendix B.

Appendix B

Using the *PrepLogic Practice Tests, Preview Edition* Software

This Exam Cram 2 includes a special version of *PrepLogic Practice Tests*—a revolutionary test engine designed to give you the best in certification exam preparation. PrepLogic offers sample and practice exams for many of today's most in-demand and challenging technical certifications. This special Preview Edition is included with this book as a tool to use in assessing your knowledge of the Exam Cram 2 material while also providing you with the experience of taking an electronic exam.

This appendix describes in detail what *PrepLogic Practice Tests, Preview Edition* is, how it works, and what it can do to help you prepare for the exam. Note that although the Preview Edition includes all the test simulation functions of the complete, retail version, it contains only a single practice test. The Premium Edition, available at PrepLogic.com, contains the complete set of challenging practice exams designed to optimize your learning experience.

Exam Simulation

One of the main functions of *PrepLogic Practice Tests, Preview Edition* is exam simulation. To prepare you to take the actual vendor certification exam, PrepLogic is designed to offer the most effective exam simulation available.

Question Quality

The questions provided in the *PrepLogic Practice Tests, Preview Edition* are written to highest standards of technical accuracy. The questions tap the content of the Exam Cram 2 chapters and help you review and assess your knowledge before you take the actual exam.

Interface Design

The *PrepLogic Practice Tests, Preview Edition* exam simulation interface provides you with the experience of taking an electronic exam. This enables you to effectively prepare for taking the actual exam by making the test experience a familiar one. Using this test simulation can help eliminate the sense of surprise or anxiety you might experience in the testing center because you will already be acquainted with computerized testing.

Effective Learning Environment

The *PrepLogic Practice Tests, Preview Edition* interface provides a learning environment that not only tests you through the computer, but also teaches the material you need to know to pass the certification exam. Each question comes with a detailed explanation of the correct answer and often provides reasons the other options are incorrect. This information helps to reinforce the knowledge you already have and also provides practical information you can use on the job.

Software Requirements

PrepLogic Practice Tests requires a computer with the following:

➤ Microsoft Windows 98, Windows Me, Windows NT 4.0, Windows 2000, or Windows XP

➤ A 166MHz or faster processor is recommended

➤ A minimum of 32MB of RAM

➤ As with any Windows application, the more memory, the better your performance.

➤ 10MB of hard drive space

Installing *PrepLogic Practice Tests, Preview Edition*

Install *PrepLogic Practice Tests, Preview Edition* by running the setup program on the *PrepLogic Practice Tests, Preview Edition* CD. Follow these instructions to install the software on your computer.

1. Insert the CD into your CD-ROM drive. The Autorun feature of Windows should launch the software. If you have Autorun disabled, click Start and select Run. Go to the root directory of the CD and select setup.exe. Click Open, and then click OK.

2. The Installation Wizard copies the *PrepLogic Practice Tests, Preview Edition* files to your hard drive, adds *PrepLogic Practice Tests, Preview Edition* to your Desktop and Program menu, and installs test engine components to the appropriate system folders.

Removing *PrepLogic Practice Tests, Preview Edition* from Your Computer

If you elect to remove the *PrepLogic Practice Tests, Preview Edition* product from your computer, an uninstall process has been included to ensure that it is removed from your system safely and completely. Follow these instructions to remove *PrepLogic Practice Tests, Preview Edition* from your computer:

1. Select Start, Settings, Control Panel.

2. Double-click the Add/Remove Programs icon.

3. You are presented with a list of software installed on your computer. Select the appropriate *PrepLogic Practice Tests, Preview Edition* title you want to remove. Click the Add/Remove button. The software is then removed from your computer.

Using *PrepLogic Practice Tests, Preview Edition*

PrepLogic is designed to be user friendly and intuitive. Because the software has a smooth learning curve, your time is maximized because you start practicing almost immediately. *PrepLogic Practice Tests, Preview Edition* has two major modes of study: Practice Test and Flash Review.

Using Practice Test mode, you can develop your test-taking abilities as well as your knowledge through the use of the Show Answer option. While you are taking the test, you can expose the answers along with a detailed explanation of why the given answers are right or wrong. This gives you the ability to better understand the material presented.

Flash Review is designed to reinforce exam topics rather than quiz you. In this mode, you will be shown a series of questions but no answer choices. Instead, you will be given a button that reveals the correct answer to the question and a full explanation for that answer.

Starting a Practice Test Mode Session

Practice Test mode enables you to control the exam experience in ways that actual certification exams do not allow:

➤ **Enable Show Answer Button**—Activates the Show Answer button allowing you to view the correct answer(s) and full explanation(s) for each question during the exam. When not enabled, you must wait until after your exam has been graded to view the correct answer(s) and explanation.

➤ **Enable Item Review Button**—Activates the Item Review button, allowing you to view your answer choices, marked questions, and to facilitate navigation between questions.

➤ **Randomize Choices**—Randomize answer choices from one exam session to the next. Makes memorizing question choices more difficult, therefore keeping questions fresh and challenging longer.

To begin studying in Practice Test mode, click the Practice Test radio button from the main exam customization screen. This enables the options detailed in the preceding list.

To your left, you are presented with the option of selecting the preconfigured Practice Test or creating your own Custom Test. The preconfigured test has a fixed time limit and number of questions. Custom Tests allow you to configure the time limit and the number of questions in your exam.

The Preview Edition included with this book includes a single preconfigured Practice Test. Get the complete set of challenging PrepLogic Practice Tests at PrepLogic.com and make certain you're ready for the big exam.

Click the Begin Exam button to begin your exam.

Starting a Flash Review Mode Session

Flash Review mode provides you with an easy way to reinforce topics covered in the practice questions. To begin studying in Flash Review mode, click the Flash Review radio button from the main exam customization screen. Select either the preconfigured Practice Test or create your own Custom Test.

Click the Best Exam button to begin your Flash Review of the exam questions.

Standard *PrepLogic Practice Tests, Preview Edition* Options

The following list describes the function of each of the buttons you see. Depending on the options, some of the buttons will be grayed out and inaccessible or missing completely. Buttons that are appropriate are active. The buttons are as follows:

➤ **Exhibit**—This button is visible if an exhibit is provided to support the question. An exhibit is an image that provides supplemental information necessary to answer the question.

➤ **Item Review**—This button leaves the question window and opens the Item Review screen. From this screen you will see all questions, your answers, and your marked items. You will also see correct answers listed here when appropriate.

➤ **Show Answer**—This option displays the correct answer with an explanation of why it is correct. If you select this option, the current question is not scored.

➤ **Mark Item**—Check this box to tag a question you need to review further. You can view and navigate your Marked Items by clicking the Item Review button (if enabled). When grading your exam, you will be notified if you have marked items remaining.

➤ **Previous Item**—View the previous question.

➤ **Next Item**—View the next question.

➤ **Grade Exam**—When you have completed your exam, click to end your exam and view your detailed score report. If you have unanswered or marked items remaining, you will be asked if you would like to continue taking your exam or view your exam report.

Time Remaining

If the test is timed, the time remaining is displayed on the upper-right corner of the application screen. It counts down minutes and seconds remaining to complete the test. If you run out of time, you will be asked if you want to continue taking the test or if you want to end your exam.

Your Examination Score Report

The Examination Score Report screen appears when the Practice Test mode ends—as the result of time expiration, completion of all questions, or your decision to terminate early.

This screen provides you with a graphical display of your test score with a breakdown of scores by topic domain. The graphical display at the top of the screen compares your overall score with the PrepLogic Exam Competency Score.

The PrepLogic Exam Competency Score reflects the level of subject competency required to pass this vendor's exam. Although this score does not directly translate to a passing score, consistently matching or exceeding this score does suggest you possess the knowledge to pass the actual vendor exam.

Reviewing Your Exam

From Your Score Report screen, you can review the exam that you just completed by clicking on the View Items button. Navigate through the items, viewing the questions, your answers, the correct answers, and the explanations for those questions. You can return to your score report by clicking the View Items button.

Getting More Exams

Each *PrepLogic Practice Tests, Preview Edition* that accompanies your book contains a single PrepLogic Practice Test. Certification students worldwide trust PrepLogic Practice Tests to help them pass their IT certification exams the first time. Purchase the Premium Edition of *PrepLogic Practice*

Tests and get the entire set of all new challenging Practice Tests for this exam. PrepLogic Practice Tests—because you want to pass the first time.

Contacting PrepLogic

If you would like to contact PrepLogic for any reason including information about our extensive line of certification practice tests, we invite you to do so. Please contact us online at www.preplogic.com.

Customer Service

If you have a damaged product and need a replacement or refund, please call the following phone number:

800-858-7674

Product Suggestions and Comments

We value your input! Please email your suggestions and comments to the following address:

feedback@preplogic.com

License Agreement

YOU MUST AGREE TO THE TERMS AND CONDITIONS OUTLINED IN THE END USER LICENSE AGREEMENT ("EULA") PRESENTED TO YOU DURING THE INSTALLATION PROCESS. IF YOU DO NOT AGREE TO THESE TERMS, DO NOT INSTALL THE SOFTWARE.

Glossary

Accessibility
The process of making an application more readily available to users who may have disabilities that interfere with their use of computer hardware or software.

Ad hoc query
A set of SQL statements that are executed immediately.

ASP.NET
The portion of the Microsoft .NET Framework that enables you to develop applications for the Web.

ASP.NET application
A set of ASP.NET pages that are contained in a single Internet Information Services virtual directory.

Assembly
An assembly is a logical unit of functionality that can contain one or more files. Every type loaded in the Common Language Runtime belongs to precisely one assembly.

Assembly manifest
The assembly manifest stores the assembly's metadata. The metadata provides self-describing information such as the name and version of the assembly, the files that are part of the assembly and their hash values, the files' dependencies on other assemblies, and so on. This subset of information in the manifest makes assemblies self-sufficient.

Attribute
A property of an XML object.

Authentication
Determining the identity of a user from his or her credentials.

Authorization
Allowing a user to use specific resources based on his or her authenticated identity.

Backing store
A place where you can store a file.

Boxing
The process of conversion of a value type to a reference type.

Caching

Caching refers to storing information for later retrieval, rather than generating it anew every time it's requested.

CDATA section

Raw data within an XML file.

Class

A reference type that encapsulates its data (constants and fields) and behavior (methods, properties, indexers, events, operators, instance constructors, static constructors, and destructors).

CLR (Common Language Runtime)

The program that executes all managed code and provides code with various services at runtime, such as automatic memory management, cross-language integration, code access security, and debugging and profiling support.

Code access security

Security based on the identity of the running code.

Column

A part of a database table containing one particular type of information.

Component

A package of reusable code that implements the IComponent interface.

Conditional compilation

A process for determining at compile time whether or not particular sections of code should be included in a project.

Configuration files

XML files that ASP.NET reads at runtime to determine configuration options.

CSS (cascading style sheets)

A cascading style sheet defines the styles that are applied to elements in an HTML document. The CSS styles define how the HTML elements are displayed and where they are rendered in the Web browser.

Culture

A combination of language and location that is sufficient to dictate the formatting of resources.

Culture code

An abbreviation that identifies a particular culture.

Data binding

The process of making a link between controls on the user interface and data stored in the data model.

Data provider

A server-specific ADO.NET class that supplies data.

DataSet class

A server-independent store that can hold multiple tables and their relations.

Debugging

The process of locating logical or runtime errors in an application. It involves finding the cause of the errors and fixing them.

Delayed signing

A process that allows an assembly to be given a strong name while withholding the signing keys until after the assembly is compiled.

Delegate

A reference type that stores references to a method with a specific signature. A delegate object can be used to dynamically invoke a method at runtime.

Deployment

A process by which a Windows application or component is distributed in the form of installation package files to be installed on the other computers.

Derived control

A control that inherits directly from a specific server control such as the `TextBox` or `Label` control.

Disco

A Microsoft standard for Web service discovery.

Element

An XML tag together with its contents.

Encoding

A scheme for representing textual characters as numeric codes.

Event

A message that is sent by an object to signal an action. The action can be a result of user interaction, such as a mouse click, or it can be triggered by any other program.

Event handling

The act of responding to an event. Event handling can be accomplished by writing methods called event handlers that are invoked in response to events.

Exception

An exception indicates a problem that occurred during normal execution of the program.

Exception handling

The process of handling exceptions that are raised when a program executes. You can choose to ignore an exception or respond to it by running your own code.

FCL (Framework Class Library)

A library of classes, interfaces, and value types that are included in the Microsoft .NET Framework. This library provides access to the system functionality and is the foundation on which the .NET Framework applications, components, and controls are built.

Field

A variable that is associated with an object or a class.

Foreign key

The foreign key in a database table stores values from the primary key in another table. These values indicate which row in the primary table each row in the other table is related to.

GAC (Global Assembly Cache)

The Global Assembly Cache is an area for the storage of assemblies that can be shared by many applications on the computer.

Globalization

The process of identifying the resources to be localized in a particular application.

HTML controls

Standard HTML elements. These controls are only used for client-side rendering and are not directly accessible in the ASP.NET programs.

HTML server controls

HTML elements that are marked with `runat="server"` attribute. These controls can be directly used in ASP.NET programs.

Identity

An identity column in a database is one with a value that is automatically assigned by the server when a new row is entered.

IL (Intermediate Language)

The language into which compilers that support the .NET Framework compile a program. IL has been ratified as an ECMA standard that calls IL common intermediate language (CIL). The Microsoft implementation of CIL is called Microsoft IL (MSIL).

Impersonation

ASP.NET uses impersonation to make requests for resources as if those requests were made by the authenticated user.

Inheritance

The process through which you create a new type based on an existing type.

In an inheritance relationship, the existing type is called the base type and the new type is called the derived type.

Input validation

The process by which an application examines user input to determine whether it is acceptable for the application.

JIT (just-in-time) compilation

The process of converting IL code into machine code at runtime, just when it is required.

Localizability

The process of verifying that all localizable resources have been separated from code.

Localization

The process of translating resources for another culture.

Managed code

Code that runs under the CLR.

Merge Module

A Merge Module allows you to create reusable components that help in deploying shared components. Merge Modules cannot be directly installed. They need to be merged with installers of applications that use the component packed into a merge module.

Namespace

A naming scheme that provides a way to logically group related types. Namespaces have two benefits: They are used to avoid naming conflicts and they make it easier to browse and locate classes.

Native compilation

The process of pre-compiling assemblies in the processor-specific machine code is called Native compilation.

.NET Framework

A platform for building, deploying, and running XML Web services and applications. The .NET Framework consists of three main parts: the CLR, the FCL, and a set of language compilers.

Parameter

A piece of information that is passed to a stored procedure at runtime.

PInvoke (Platform Invoke)

The feature of the .NET Framework that allows you to call Windows API and other DLL procedures from managed code.

Postback

A postback occurs when the user submits a Web Form to the server.

Primary key

The unique identifier for a row in a database table.

Private assembly

A private assembly is an assembly available only to clients in the same directory tree as the assembly.

Property

A class member that is like a public field but that can also encapsulate additional logic within its Get and Set accessor methods.

RCW (Runtime Callable Wrapper)

A proxy that allows .NET code to make use of COM classes and members.

Relation

A connection between two tables in a database.

Relational database

A relational database stores multiple tables and the relations between them.

Resource file

A file containing string, bitmap, or other resources that can differ between cultures.

Resource-only assembly

An assembly that only contains resources and no executable code.

Role-based security

Security based on the authenticated identity of the user running the code.

Round trip

The combination of a Web page request and a postback operation.

Row

All of the values in a table that describe one instance of an entity.

Satellite assembly

A resource-only assembly that contains culture-specific information.

Schema

The structure of a database or XML file.

Session

A sequence of interaction between a client browser and a Web server. Each session is uniquely identified using a SessionID.

Session State

Information that is persisted between individual stateless HTTP requests.

Shared assembly

A shared assembly can be referenced by more than one application. An assembly must be explicitly built to be shared by giving it a cryptographically strong name. Shared assemblies are stored in the machinewide Global Assembly Cache.

Signing

The process of assigning a cryptographically strong name to an assembly.

SOAP (Simple Object Access Protocol)

A standard for transmitting objects as XML over HTTP.

SQL-92

The official ANSI specification for Structured Query Language.

Stored procedure

A set of SQL statements that are stored on the server for later execution.

Stream

A file viewed as a stream of bytes.

Strong name

The combination of a simple text name, a version number, and culture information (if provided) that is signed by a digital signature and contains a public key of the assembly.

Structure

A user-defined value type. Like a class, a structure has constructors, fields, methods, properties, and so on. However, structures do not support inheritance.

Table

A collection of data about instances of a single entity.

Templated control

A control whose display is entirely dictated by templates.

Testing

The process of executing programs and determining whether they worked as expected.

Trace listener

A class that can receive trace messages.

Trace switch

A class that dictates whether trace messages should be emitted by an application being executed.

Tracing

The process of displaying informative messages in an application at the time of execution.

T-SQL (Transact-SQL)

The SQL-92 dialect used in Microsoft SQL Server.

UDDI (Universal Description, Discovery, and Integration)

A standard for discovering details of Web services and other business services available via the Internet.

Unboxing

The process of converting a reference type to a value type.

Unicode

A universal character set that can represent over a million characters. Unicode is the default internal language of .NET.

Unmanaged code

Code written in a non-.NET environment that does not benefit from the services of the CLR.

User assistance

Any means of providing information about your application to the user.

W3C (World Wide Web Consortium)

The body that develops and ratifies the standards for the Internet.

WAI (Web Accessibility Initiative)

A W3C initiative to make Web sites accessible to disabled users.

Web custom control

A control that inherits from the WebControl class. Web custom controls can be compiled and support advanced features in Visual Studio .NET.

Web method

A method of a Web service that can be invoked by client applications.

Web reference

Information in a Visual Studio .NET project that allows you to use objects supplied by a Web service.

Web server controls

Native ASP.NET controls that provide rich functionality and a consistent programming model.

Web service

A Web service allows you to instantiate and invoke objects over the Internet.

Web user control

A composite control implemented as an ascx file with an associated vb file.

WSDL (Web Services Description Language)

An XML language that describes the interface of a Web service.

XML

Extensible Markup Language.

XML declaration

The line in an XML file that identifies the file as XML.

XML namespace

A set of XML tags that is private to an application.

Index

Symbols

& (ampersand), 102
& (ampersand) entity reference, 217
' (apostrophe) entity reference, 217
> (closing angle bracket) entity reference, 217
< (opening angle bracket) entity reference, 217
/? option (Type Library Importer), 304
+ (plus sign), 47
? (question mark), 102
"" (quotation mark) entity reference, 217
- (subtract sign), 47

A

Abandon method, 110
AcceptChanges method, 201
AcceptTypes property, 93
access keys (accessibility guidelines), 323
accessibility
  authorization, 416-418
  design guidelines, 323
  input methods, 322
  output methods, 322
  Section 508 standards, 325-326
  testing, 326
  W3C Web Accessibility Initiative guidelines, 324-325
AccessKey property, 60
Active Server Pages. See ASP.NET
ActiveX controls, 300
  adding to Toolbox, 299
  browser support, 298
  packaging, 363
ad hoc queries, 176
  DELETE statement, 186
  INSERT statement, 184-185

  running, 177-178
  SELECT statement, 178-184
  UPDATE statement, 185-186
adaptive exams, 12-14, 17
Add Class command (Add menu), 237
Add Component command (Add menu), 232
Add HTML Page command (Project menu), 133
Add Installer link, 373
Add Item dialog box, 207
Add menu commands
  Add Class, 237
  Add Component, 232
  Add New Item, 44
  Add Web Form, 45
  New Project, 364
  Project Output, 374
Add method, 111-112
Add New Item command
  Add menu, 44
  Project menu, 281
Add New Item dialog box, 31, 45, 152
Add Project Output Group dialog box, 374
Add Reference dialog box, 233, 303-304
Add Style Rule dialog box, 79
Add Web Form command (Add menu), 45
Add Web Reference dialog box, 260
Add/Remove Programs dialog box, 365
AddCacheItemDependencies() method, 97
AddCacheItemDependency() method, 97
AddFileDependencies() method, 97
AddFileDependency() method, 97
AddHeader() method, 97
AddNew method, 204
AddRange method, 389
ADO.NET
  data, 210-215
  data providers, 196

SqlConnection object, 197-198
SqlDataAdapter object, 200-201
SqlDataReader object, 199-200
SqlParameter object, 199
DataSet classes, 201
DataColumn class, 203-204
DataRelation class, 202-203
DataRow class, 203
DataView class, 204
finding data, 208-210
multiple tables, 207-208
populating, 205
retrieving data, 205-206
sorting data, 208-210
strongly typed, 206-207
DataSet objects, DataTable, 202
AdRotator control, 70
Airport Weather Web service, 259-261
All Tasks menu commands, Configure
Server Extensions, 424
AllKeys property, 111
AllowDbNull property, 204
allowDefinition attribute, 410
AllowDelete property, 204
AllowEdit property, 204
allowLocation attribute, 410
AllowNew property, 204
ALT text (accessibility guideline), 323
Altavista Web site, 21
AlternateText property, 62
AlternatingTemplate, 162
ampersand (&), 102
ampersand (&) entity reference, 217
anonymous authentication, IIS, 415
AppendChild method, 218
AppendHeader() method, 97
AppendToLog() method, 97
application data caching, 419
Application event logs, 394
Application property, 33, 111
application state, 111-112
application-level global event handling,
99-100
application-level tracing, 341
Application.Error event, 134-135
Application_AcquireRequestState() event
handler, 100
Application_AuthenticateRequest() event
handler, 100
Application_AuthorizeRequest() event
handler, 100
Application_BeginRequest() event handler,
100
Application_End() event handler, 99
Application_EndRequest() event handler,
100
Application_PostRequestHandlerExecute()
event handler, 100

Application_PreRequestHandlerExecute()
event handler, 100
Application_ReleaseRequestState() event
handler, 100
Application_ResolveRequestCache() event
handler, 100
Application_Start() event handler, 99
Application_UpdateRequestCache() event
handler, 100
ApplicationException, 126
ApplicationPath property, 93
applications, international, 336-337.
See also Web applications
<appSettings> element, 410
arguments, event handling, 39, 65
ArithmeticException, 128
ASC keyword, 210
ASCII, 284
ASCIIEncoding class, 285
/asmversion option (Type Library
Importer), 304
.asp file extension, 296-297
ASP.NET, 24, 99
browsers, 59
classes, 29
converting ASP pages to, 297
culture properties, setting, 278
event handling
attached delegates, 41-42, 47
AutoEventWireup attribute, 42-43
base class, 41
global.asax file, global event handling,
99-102
intrinsic objects, 92
HttpApplicationState, 111
HttpRequest, 93-95
HttpResponse, 95-97
HttpServerUtility, 98
Page class, 33-34
pages
code, 297
creating, 30-31
directives, 35-38
executing, 32
inheritance, 41
processing, 35
running together with ASP, 296
syntax, 297
virtual protected methods, 41
runtime hosts, 29
UI (user interface), business logic, 43-48
Web requests, 29-30
ASP.NET Web Matrix Project, 26
AspCompat attribute, 36
.aspx file extension, 297
assemblies, 244
benefits, 245
categories, 245

deploying, 246, 374-375
dynamic assemblies, 246
multifile assemblies, 245
private assemblies, 246-247
resource-only assemblies, 247-248
shared, 367
    delay signing, 370
    GAC (Global Assembly Cache),
    369-370
    merge modules, 370-371
    strong names, 368
shared assemblies, 246-247
single-file assemblies, 245
static assemblies, 246
strong names, 247
Assembly Cache Viewer Shell Extension
    (shfusion.dll), 369
Assembly directive, 36
assembly manifest, 244
Assembly Resource File template, 281
assembly resource files, 281-284
Assert method, 342
attributes. *See* properties
Attributes property, 218
audio (accessibility guidelines), 323
authentication
    configuring, 413-416
    passport, 389
    providers, 414
authentication information (connection
    strings), 198
authorization, configuring, 416-418
Auto modifier, 307
AutoEventWireUp attribute, 37, 42-43, 47
AutoFlush property, 342
AutoIncrement property, 204
AutoPostBack property, 61-65
Autorun, 536
AVG() function, 183

B

BackColor property, 60
Background tab, 79
BackImageUrl property, 68-69
backing stores, 191
backing up files, 192
base classes, 28, 41
BaseValidator class, 73-74
basic authentication, IIS, 415
Begin Exam button, 538
BeginEdit method, 203
BeginTransaction method, 198
Best Exam button, 539
BinaryRead() method, 95
BinaryReader class, 195-196
BinaryWrite() method, 97
BinaryWriter class, 195-196
Bindable attribute, 243

binding. *See* data binding
blocks
    Catch, 127-129
    code
        Visual Studio .NET, 47
        writing, 129
    Finally, 129-130
    Try, 127
BooleanSwitch class, 345
bootstrapper (Setup.exe), 364
BorderColor property, 60
BorderStyle property, 60
BorderWidth property, 60
bottom-up integration testing, 336
boxes, check boxes, 66. *See also* dialog boxes
boxing, 389
breakpoints, setting, 349
Browse button, 239
Browser property, 93
browser windows, second, 318
browsers
    ActiveX support, 298
    ASP.NET, 59
    CSS (cascading style sheets), 78
Buffer property, 37, 96
BufferOutput property, 96
bugs. *See* testing, Web applications
Build menu commands, Build Solution, 46
Build MyCustomer.dll command (File
    menu), 302
Build Solution command (Build menu), 46
build-list-and-reorder questions, exam for-
    mat, 6-8
business logic
    UI (user interface), separating, 43-48
    Web Forms, analyzing, 47-48
Button control, 63-64
buttons
    Begin Exam, 538
    Best Exam, 539
    Browse, 239
    Exhibit, 539
    Grade Exam, 539
    Item Review, 538-539
    Mark Item, 539
    New Connection, 153
    New Project, 30
    Next Item, 539
    Previous Item, 539
    radio
        Class Name, 79
        Flash Review, 539
        Practice Test, 539
        selecting, 67
    Save, 68
    Show Answer, 538-539
    toolbars, Show All Files, 264
    View Items, 539

How can we make this index more useful? Email us at indexes@quepublishing.com

C

CAB projects, 363
Cache directive, 420
Cache object, 419-420
Cache property, 33, 96
CacheControl property, 96-97
caching, 388, 419-420
Calendar class, 71-73
Calendar control, 71-73, 146
calendars, localized, 279-280
calling COM components, 304-305
calls, reducing (performance considerations), 390
CancelEdit method, 203
CanRead property, 193
CanSeek property, 193
CanWrite property, 193
cascading style sheet (CSS), 78-79
case studies, 4, 12-15
casing rules, localization, 276
Catch block, 127-129
CategoryName property, 397
CausesValidation property, 64
CD-ROMs, deploying Web applications, 378
CDATA section, XML files, 217
CDs, *PrepLogic Practice Tests, Preview Edition*, 537
CellPadding property, 69-71
Cells property, 69
CellSpacing property, 69-71
certification exams
    adaptive exams, strategies, 17
    build-list-and-reorder questions, 6-8
    case studies, 4, 15
    create-a-tree questions, 8-9
    drag-and-connect questions, 10
    fixed-length, strategies, 15-16
    formats, 12-14
    hot area questions, 12
    multiple-choice questions, 5-6
    practice exams, taking, 19
    question handling, strategies, 18
    readiness, assessing, 2
    resources, 19-21
    select-and-place questions, 11
    short-form, strategies, 15-16
    testing centers, 3-4
character strings, 287-288
CharSet property, 96
check boxes, multiple, 66
CheckBox control, 62-63
CheckBoxList control, 65-67, 150
Checked property, 63
CheckedChanged event, 63
ChildColumns property, 203
ChildKeyConstraint property, 203

ChildNodes property, 218
ChildTable property, 203
Class Name radio button, 79
classes
    ASCIIEncoding, 285
    ASP.NET, 29
    base, 28, 41
    BaseValidator, 73-74
    BinaryReader, 195-196
    BinaryWriter, 195-196
    BooleanSwitch, 345
    Calendar, 71-73
    CompareValidator, properties, 76
    ConditionalAttribute, 347
    CultureInfo, 275-276, 279
    custom installer classes, 375
    DataAdapter, 196
    DataColumn, 203-204
    DataRelation, 202-203
    DataRow, 203
    DataSet, 201
        DataColumn class, 203-204
        DataRelation class, 202-203
        DataRow class, 203
        DataView class, 204
        finding data, 208-210
        multiple tables, 207-208
        populating, 205
        retrieving data, 205-206
        sorting data, 208-210
        strongly typed, 206-207
    DataView, 204
    Debug, 341-343
    DefaultTraceListener, 343
    derived, 28
    Encoding, 285
    EventLog, 394-396
    EventLogTraceListner, 343
    Exception, properties, 127
    FileStream, 192-194
    Global, 99
    HttpApplication, 99
    HttpApplicationState, 111-112
    HttpRequest, 93-95
    HttpResponse, 95-97
    HttpServerUtility, 98
    HttpSessionState, 110-111
    Installer, 372
    ListControl, 65-66
    listener classes, 343-344
    members, 27
    namespaces, 28
    .NET Framework, members, 27
    objects, 27
    OleDbCommandBuilder, 392
    Page, 27, 33-34
    PerformanceCounter, 397-399
    Process, 392-393
    ProjectInstaller, 374

proxy, 263-264
RangeValidator, properties, 76
ResourceManager, 284
SqlCommandBuilder, 392
SqlError, 220
SqlException, 220
StreamReader, 194-195
StreamWriter, 194-195
StringBuilder, 389
StringInfo, 287-288
Table, properties, 69
TableCell, properties, 70
TableRow, properties, 69
TextWriterTraceListener, 343
Trace, 341-343
TraceContext, 337-341
TraceSwitch, 345
UnicodeEncoding, 285
UTF7Encoding, 285
UTF8Encoding, 285
ValidationSummary, properties, 77
WebControl, properties, 60
WebCustomControl, 241-243
XmlDataDocument, 219-220
XmlDocument, 218-219
XmlNode, 217-219
ClassName attribute, 37
clauses, WHERE, 222
cleanup code, writing, 129
Clear method, 111-112, 201-202
Clear() method, HttpResponse class, 97
ClearContent() method, 97
ClearError() method, 98, 135
ClearHeaders() method, 97
Click event, 64
client code, Web server controls, 65
client-side scripts, debugging, 353
client-side state management
    choosing, 108
    cookies, 103-104
    hidden fields, 104
    query strings, 102-103
    ViewState, 104-108
client-side validations, 73, 77
ClientCertificate property, 93
ClientTarget attribute, 37
ClientValidationFunction property, 77
Close method, 193, 198, 342, 397
CloseMainWindow method, 392-393
CLR (Common Language Runtime), 24
clustering, 378
code. *See also* legacy code
    Airport Weather Web service, invoking, 260-261
    application state, server-side state management, 112
    ASP.NET pages, 31, 297
    BinaryReader class, 195-196
    BinaryWriter class, 195-196

blocks, writing, 129
cleanup, writing, 129
client, Web server controls, 65
CompositeControl.vb, 237-239
cookies, saving, 103
CultureInfo class, 275-276
cultures, 275
CustomTextbox.vb, 240
data, 135-166, 211-215
DataList control, 163
DataSets, multiple tables, 207-208
Debug class, 342-343
EditItemTemplate, 164-165
event handling, attached delegates, 42
exceptions, generating, 130
FileStream class, 192
@@IDENTITY variable, 190-191
localized calendars, 279-280
localized information, displaying, 277
parameterized stored procedures, 189-190
RandomNumber.vb, 234-235
Repeater control, customizing, 161
resource files, 282-283
Select method, 208-209
server, Web server controls, 65
stored procedures, running, 187-188
StreamReader class, 194-195
StreamWriter class, 194-195
strongly typed DataSets, 207
Trace class, 342-343
TraceSwitch class, 346
Try blocks, multiple Catch blocks, 128
unmanaged, performance considerations, 390
ViewState page-level values, 105
WebCustomControl class, 242
XmlDataDocument class, 219-220
Code File template, 44
code outlining, 47
code-behind, UI (user interface), 43-44
Codebehind attribute, 47
CodePage attribute, 37
CodePage property, 110
collections, 159
ColumnChanged event, 202
ColumnChanging event, 202
ColumnName property, 204
columns, identity (SQL Server), 190
Columns property, 61, 202
ColumnSpan property, 70
COM components
    calling, 304-305
    late-bound, 297-298
    runtime-callable wrappers, 300-302
    TLBIMP (Type Library Importer), 302-304
COM components tab, 298
COM libraries, 301, 305

COM+ components, 305
combining character sequence, Unicode, 287
Command event, 64
Command object, 157, 196-197
command-line options, Web Services Description Language Tool (wsdl.exe), 264
CommandArgument property, 64
CommandName property, 64
CommandName tags, 166
commands
  Add menu
    Add Class, 237
    Add Component, 232
    Add New Item, 44
    Add Web Form, 45
    New Project, 364
    Project Output, 374
  All Tasks menu, Configure Server Extensions, 424
  Build menu, Build Solution, 46
  Debug menu
    Start, 68
    Start Without Debugging, 46
    Step Into, 348
    Step Out, 349
    Step Over, 348
  File menu
    Build MyCustomer.dll, 302
    New, Project, 30
  FTP, 362
  Project menu
    Add HTML Page, 133
    Add New Item, 281
  Table menu, Insert, Table, 45
  Tools menu, Debug Processes, 351
  View menu, Other Windows, Output, 343
  XCOPY, 362
CommandText property, 199
CommandType property, 199
comments, XML, 217
Commit() method, 372
Common Language Runtime (CLR), 24
Compare method, 288
CompareInfo object, 288
CompareValidator class, properties, 76
CompareValidator control, 76
comparing data, 288
Compentecy Score, *PrepLogic Practice Tests, Preview Edition*, 540
<compilation> element, 348
CompilerOptions attribute, 37
complex data binding, 146-150
components, .NET components, 232-235
Components tab, 239
composite controls, creating, 237-240

Condition property, 367
conditional compilation, 347
ConditionalAttribute class, 347
<configSections, 409-410
configuration errors, DCOM, 352
configuration files
  hierarchy, 410
  machine.config, 408-412
  settings, reading, 413
  web.config
    authentication providers, selecting, 415
    impersonation settings, 417
    modifying, 411-412
    processModel element, 376-377
configurations
  caching, 419-420
  custom error pages, 132
  Debug, 341
  Release, 341
  security
    authentication, 413-416
    authorization, 416-418
    role-based, 413
  server services, 422-424
ConfigurationSettings object, 413
Configure Server Extensions command (All Tasks menu), 424
Connection object, 157, 196-198
connection pooling (SQL Server), 197-198, 391
Connection property, 199
connection strings, 198
Connection tab, 153
connections, Data Connections
  building, 153
  Server Explorer, 156
ConnectionString property, 198
#Const preprocessing directive, 347
constants, 210
Constraints property, 202
container controls, 69
containers
  controls, Web pages, 67
  ViewState, 240
ContentEncoding property, 93, 96
ContentLength property, 93
Contents property, 110-112
ContentType property, 37, 93, 96
Control directive, 36
control identification (accessibility guidelines), 323
Control Library, 237
control properties, simple data binding, 146
Control Tree table (ASP.NET), 339
controls
  ActiveX, 298-300
  AdRotator, 70

Button, 63-64
Calendar, 71-73, 146
CheckBox, 62-63
CheckBoxList, 65-67, 150
CompareValidator, 76
composite, creating, 237-240
containers, 67-69
CustomValidator, 76-77
DataGrid, 65, 146, 150
DataList, 163-166
derived, creating, 240-241
DropDownList, 65-67, 147-150
dynamic, creating, 68-69
HTML controls, 58
HTML server controls, 58
HtmlInputHidden, 104
Image, properties, 62
ImageButton, 63-64
input, entries, 75
input servers, 73, 76
Label, 61, 146
LinkButton, 63-64
List, 65-67
ListBox, 65-67, 147-150
non-postback controls, 105
Page, 74
Panel, 67-69
PlaceHolder, 67-69
postback controls, 104-105
RadioButton, 62-63
RadioButtonList, 65-66, 150
RangeValidator, 76
RegularExpressionValidator, 75
Repeater, 160-163
RequiredFieldValidator, 75
Table, 69-70
TableCell, 69-70
TableRow, 69-70
templated, data displays, 160-166
TextBox, members, 61-62
validation controls, 73-77
ValidationSummary, 77
Web custom controls
    choosing, 243-244
    composite controls, 237-240
    creating, 237, 241-243
    derived controls, 240-241
Web pages, adding dynamically, 67
Web server controls
    AdRotator controls, 70
    Button control, 63-64
    Calendar controls, 71-73
    CheckBox control, 62-63
    client code, 65
    DataGrid control, 65
    declaring, 59
    event handling, 64-65
    Image control, 62

ImageButton control, 63-64
Label control, 61
LinkButton control, 63-64
List controls, 65-67
Panel controls, 67-69
PlaceHolder controls, 67-69
RadioButton control, 62-63
server code, 65
Table controls, 69-70
TableCell controls, 69-70
TableRow controls, 69-70
TextBox control, 61-62
WebControl class, 60
Web user controls, 235-236
Controls property, 33, 60
ControlToCompare property, 76
ControlToValidate property, 74
cookies, 103-104
Cookies Collection table (ASP.NET), 340
Cookies property, 93, 96, 104
CopyTo method, 111
Count property, 110-112, 204
COUNT() function, 183
CounterCreationData object, 399
CounterCreationDataCollection object, 399
CounterHelp property, 397
CounterName property, 397
CounterType property, 397
cpuMask attribute, 377
CREATE PROCEDURE keyword, 187
create-a-tree questions, exam format, 8-9
CreateAttribute method, 218
CreateChildControls method, 240
CreateCommand method, 198
CreateElement method, 218
CreateEventSource method, 394
CreateNode method, 218
CreateObject() method, 98, 297
CreateObjectFromClsid() method, 98
CreateParameter method, 199
cross-product query, 179
CSS (cascading style sheet), 78-79
CssClass property, 60
Culture attribute, 37
culture codes, 275
CultureInfo class, 275-276, 279
cultures, 274
    CultureInfoclass, 275-276
    CurrentCulture property, 276
    CurrentUICulture property, 276
    invariant, 276
    localized calendars, 279-280
    localized information, displaying, 277-278
    properties, setting, 278-279
    resource files, 281-284
    text strings, sorting, 288
currency, formatting, 276-279
Current property, 288

CurrentCulture property, 276-281
CurrentExecutionFilePath property, 93-95
CurrentUICulture property, 276-279
Custom Actions Editor, 366
custom error pages, 132-133
custom exceptions, 131
custom installer classes, 375
custom specifications, validation controls, 76
custom Web Forms, ad hoc queries, 178
CustomActionData property, 376
Customize Toolbox dialog box, 239-241, 298
CustomValidator control, 76-77

D

data
  accessing/manipulating, 202
  ADO.NET object model
    adding data, 213-214
    data editing, 210
    data providers, 196-201
    data updates, 211-212
    DataSet classes, 201-210
    deleting data, 214-215
    DELETE statement, 186
    editing (DataList control), 164-166
    filtering, 159
    finding (DataSets), 208-210
    flat files, 191-196
    INSERT statement, 184-185
    retrieving (DataSet class), 205-206
    running, 177-178
    SELECT statement, 178-184
    sorting (DataSets), 208-210
    SQL Server, ad hoc queries, 176
    UPDATE statement, 176, 185-191
    XML, 215-220
  data binding
    complex data binding, 146-150
    data displays, templated controls, 160-166
    Data Form Wizard, 152-154
    databases, 155
      data filtering, 159
      Server Explorer, 156-158
    DataBind method, 151-152
    expressions, 151
    simple data binding, 144-146
  data caching, 419
  Data Connections, 153, 156
  data displays, templated controls
    DataList control, 163-166
    Repeater control, 160-163
  data errors, 220-222
  Data Form Wizard, 152-154
  data forms, 152-154

Data Link Properties dialog box, 153, 156
data models, versus databases, 210
data providers, 196
  ODBC, 197
  OLE DB data provider, 197
  Oracle, 197
  SqlConnection object, 197-198
  SqlDataAdapter object, 200-201
  SqlDataReader object, 199-200
  SqlParameter object, 199
data sorting, 288
Data Source (connection strings), 198
data types, 297
DataAdapter class, 196
DataAdapter object, 157, 196-197, 200-201
databases, 155
  connecting to, 153
  data filtering, 159
  MSDE (Microsoft Data Engine), 26
  relational. See ADO.NET
  resultsets, retrieving, 199
  Server Explorer, 156-158
  versus data models, 210
DataBind() method, 146, 151-152
DataBinder object, Eval method, 162-163
DataBinding event, 152
DataColumn class, 203-204
DataColumn object, 149
DataGrid control, 65, 146, 150
DataList control, 163-166
DataLoad function, 149
DataReader, versus DataSet, 391
DataReader object, 196-200
DataRelation class, 202-203
DataRelation object, 159
DataRow class, 203
DataRow object, 149
DataSet, versus DataReader, 391
DataSet classes, 201
  DataColumn class, 203-204
  DataRelation class, 202-203
  DataRow class, 203
  DataView class, 204
  finding data, 208-210
  multiple tables, 207-208
  populating, 205
  retrieving data, 205-206
  sorting data, 208-210
  strongly typed, 206-207
DataSet objects
  DataTable, 202
  members of, 201
  reading XML documents into, 220
  synchronization, 220
DataTable object, 149-159, 202
DataType property, 204
DataView class, 204
DataView object, 149, 159

DataViewRowState constants, 210
dates, formatting, 276-279
DayHeaderStyle property, 71
DayNameFormat property, 71
DayRender event, 73
DayStyle property, 71
DCOM configuration errors, 352
Debug attribute, 37
Debug class, 341-343
Debug configurations, 341
Debug menu
  commands
    Start, 68
    Start Without Debugging, 46
    Step Into, 348
    Step Out, 349
    Step Over, 348
  step execution of programs, 349
Debug Processes command (Tools menu), 351
DEBUG symbol, 341
Debugger Users group, 352
debugging Web applications
  breakpoints, setting, 349
  client-side scripts, 353
  DCOM configuration errors, 352
  displaying debugging information with Trace and Debug classes, 343
  DLL files, 352-353
  exceptions, 350-351
  program state, analyzing, 349-350
  remote processes, 352
  running processes, 351-352
  stepping, 348-349
  TraceContext, 338
declarations, XML, 216
Declare statement, 307
declaring
  global procedures, 297
  global variables, 297
  Web server controls, 59
Decrement method, 397
Default Web Server Site node, 424
DefaultProperty attribute, 243
DefaultTraceListener class, 343
DefaultValue property, 204, 243
delay signing, shared assemblies, 370
/delaysign option (Type Library Importer), 304
delegates, event handling, 39-42, 47
Delete method, 203-204, 394
DELETE statement, 186
DeleteCommand property, 200
DeleteEventSource method, 394
deploying assemblies, 246, 374-375
deploying Web applications
  deployment planning, 376-379
  deployment tools, 362-363

installation components, 371-375
setup and deployment projects, 363-367
shared assemblies, 367-371
derived classes, 28
derived controls, creating, 240-241
DESC keyword, 210
Description property, 37, 345
design guidelines, accessibility, 323
designing objects (Server Explorer), 156
development tools, .NET, 25-27
dialog boxes
  Add Item, 207
  Add New Item, 31, 45, 152
  Add Project Output Group, 374
  Add Reference, 233, 303-304
  Add Style Rule, 79
  Add Web Reference, 260
  Add/Remove Programs, 365
  Customize Toolbox, 239-241, 298
  Data Link Properties, 153, 156
  Exceptions, 350
  Generate DataSet, 160
  Insert Table, 45
  New Breakpoint, 349
  New Project, 30
  Processes, 351-352
  Select Item in Project, 374
  Style Builder, 79
digest authentication, IIS, 415
digital signing, 368
dir property, 286
directives, 347
  ASP.NET pages, 35-38
  Assembly, 36
  Cache, 420
  Control, 36
  Implements, 36
  Import, 36, 48
  OutputCache, 36, 419-420
  Page, 36-38
  Reference, 36
  Register, 36
directories, Web applications, 30
Disco protocol, 259, 262
disco.exe (Web Services Discovery Tool), 262-263
discovering Web services, 262-263
disk files
  backing stores, 191
  streams, 191
    BinaryReader class, 195-196
    BinaryWriter class, 195-196
    FileStream class, 192-194
    StreamReader class, 194-195
    StreamWriter class, 194-195
Display property, 74
displaying data, templated controls
    DataList control, 163-166
    Repeater control, 160-163

DisplayMode property, 77
DisplayName property, 345
distributed transactions (performance considerations), 392
DivideByZeroException, 128
DLL files, debugging code, 352-353
DocumentElement property, 219
double buffering, 91
downlevel browsers, ASP.NET, 59
drag-and-connect questions, exam format, 10
drag-and-drop, Server Explorer, 157-158
DropDownList control, 65-67, 147-150
DVDs, deploying Web applications, 378
dynamic assemblies, 246
dynamic controls, creating, 68-69

E

EditCommand event, 166
EditItemIndex property, 166
EditItemTemplate, 164
editors, viewing, 365
elements
    <appSettings>, 410
    <compilation>, 348
    <configSections>, 410
    <section>, 410
    sessionState, 422
    <trace>, 340
    XML, 216
#Else preprocessing directive, 347
#ElseIf preprocessing directive, 347
Enable property, 60
EnableClientScript property, 74, 77
Enabled property, 74
EnableRaisingEvents property, 393-396
EnableSessionState attribute, 37
EnableViewState property, 34, 37, 60, 389
EnableViewStateMac attribute, 37, 115
Encoding class, 285
encodings, 284-285
encryption, ViewState, 107
#End ExternalSource preprocessing directive, 347
#End If preprocessing directive, 347
#End Region preprocessing directive, 347
End() method, 97
EndEdit method, 203
EnsureChildControls method, 240
entity references, 217
entries, input controls, 75
Entries property, 394
EntryWritten event, 394
environments, learning (*PrepLogic Practice Test, Preview Edition*), 536
Error event, 34
error events, 134-135

error messages, exceptions, 124
ErrorMessage property, 74, 77
ErrorPage attribute, 37, 133
ErrorPage property, 34, 133
errors. *See also* exceptions
    configuration, DCOM, 352
    data, 220-222
    HTTP, custom error pages, 132
Eval method, 162-163
event handlers, 40, 99-100
event handling, 38
    arguments, 39
    ASP.NET
        attached delegates, 41-42, 47
        AutoEventWireup attribute, 42-43
        base class, 41
    delegates, 39-40
    events, 40
    global event handlers, 99-102
    handlers, 39
    raising methods, 40
    Web server controls, 64-65
    Web user controls, 236
event logs, 394-396
Event Viewer utility, 394
EventArgs type, 40
EventLog class, 394-396
EventLogEntryCollection object, 395
EventLogTraceListener class, 343
events
    Application.Error, 134-135
    bubbling, 65
    Calendar class, 73
    CheckedChanged, 63
    Click, 64
    ColumnChanged, 202
    ColumnChanging, 202
    Command, 64
    DataBinding, 152
    DayRender, 73
    EditCommand, 166
    EntryWritten, 394
    error, 34, 134-135
    event handling, 40
    Exited, 393
    Init, 34, 41
    Load, 34
    objects, 27
    Page.Error, 134-135
    PreRender, 34
    publisher-subscriber model, 40
    RowChanged, 202
    RowChanging, 202
    RowDeleted, 202
    RowDeleting, 202
    SelectedIndexChanged, 66
    SelectionChanged, 73
    ServerValidate, 77

TextChanged, 62
triggering, 38
Unload, 34
VisibleMonthChanged, 73
evolutionary testing, 334-336
Examination Score Report screen, *PrepLogic Practice Tests, Preview Edition*, 540
exams
adaptive exams, strategies, 17
build-list-and-reorder questions, 6-8
case studies, 4, 15
create-a-tree questions, 8-9
drag-and-connect questions, 10
fixed-length exams, strategies, 15-16
formats, 12-14
hot area questions, 12
multiple-choice questions, 5-6
practice exams, taking, 19
question handling, strategies, 18
readiness, assessing, 2
resources, 19-21
select-and-place questions, 11
short-form exams, strategies, 15-16
simulations, *PrepLogic Practice Test, Preview Edition*, 535
testing centers, 3-4
Exception class, properties, 127-128
exceptions
ArithmeticException, 128
custom, 131
debugging, 350-351
DivideByZeroException, 128
error messages, 124
Exception, 128
generating, 130
handling, 127-130
languages, throwing, 129
objects, 126-127
SystemException, 128
throwing, 390
unhandled, 128, 131
custom error pages, 132-133
error events, 134-135
Exceptions dialog box, 350
Excite Web site, 21
Execute() method, 98
ExecuteNonQuery method, 189, 199
ExecuteReader method, 199
ExecuteScalar method, 199
ExecuteXmlReader method, 199
Exhibit button, 539
exhibits, 4
Exists method, 394
ExitCode property, 393
Exited event, 393
ExitTime property, 393
Expires property, 96-97
ExpiresAbsolute property, 96-97

Explicit attribute, 37
Explorer (Internet Explorer) search pane, 319-320
Explorer (Windows), GAC (Global Assembly Cache), 369
expressions
data binding, 151
filter, 209
sort, 210
Extensible Markup Language. *See* XML
extensions. *See* file extensions
#ExternalSource preprocessing directive, 347

F

Fail method, 342
False, AutoEventWireup, 47
FCL (Framework Class Library), namespaces, 25
FieldOffset attribute, 308
fields
hidden, 104
objects, 27
file extensions
.asp, 296-297
.aspx, 297
FrontPage Server, 423-424
.msm, 370
.resx, 248
File menu commands
Build MyCustomer.dll, 302
New, Project, 30
File System Editor, 365
File Types Editor, 366
FilePath property, 93
files. *See also* configuration files; disk files; flat files
backing up, 192
configuration files, machine.config, 409-412
DLL, debugging, 352-353
global.asax, global event handling, 99-102
machine.config, 409-412
resource, 281-284
web.config
authentication providers, selecting, 415
impersonation settings, 417
modifying, 411-412
tracing, enabling, 340
WSDL, Web service messages, 259
XML files, 216-219
Files property, HttpRequest class, 93
FileStream class, 192-194
Fill method, 201, 212
filter expressions, 209

Filter property, 93, 96
filtering data, 159
Finally block, 129-130
Find method, 204
FindControl method, 166
FindRows method, 204
FirstChild property, 218
FirstDayOfWeek property, 71
fixed-length exams, 12-16
Flash Review Mode, *PrepLogic Practice Tests, Preview Edition*, 537-538
Flash Review radio button, 538
flat files
    backing stores, 191
    streams, 191-196
floppy disks, deploying Web applications, 378
Flush() method, 97, 193, 342
Font property, 60
FooterTemplate, 162
ForeColor property, 60, 74, 77
Form Collection table (ASP.NET), 340
Form property, 93
formats
    adaptive exams, strategies, 17
    case studies, strategies, 15
    exams, 12-14
    fixed-length exams, strategies, 15-16
    short-form exams, strategies, 15-16
formatting options (accessibility guidelines), 323
forms, Web Forms, 286. *See also* Web Forms
Forms authentication providers, 415
forms-based authentication, 416
fragment caching, 419
frames (accessibility guidelines), 323
Framework Class Library (FCL), namespaces, 25
FrontPage Server Extensions, 423-424
FTP, deploying Web applications, 362
fully qualified names, 179
functions
    AVG(), 183
    COUNT(), 183
    DataLoad, 149
    MAX(), 183
    MIN(), 183
    SUM(), 183

G

GAC (Global Assembly Cache), 246-247, 367-370
GacUtil.exe (Global Assembly Cache Tool), adding assemblies, 370
Generate DataSet dialog box, 160
Generate Dataset link, 160, 207

Get method, 112
GetBytes method, 285
GetChanges method, 201
GetChars method, 285
GetElementsByTagName method, 219
GetEnumerator method, 111
GetEventLogs method, 394
GetKey method, 112
GetLastError() method, 98, 135
GetObject method, 284
GetProcessById method, 393
GetProcesses method, 393
GetProcessesByName method, 393
GetString method, 284
GetTextElementEnumerator method, 288
GetXml method, 201
GetXmlSchema method, 201
Global Assembly Cache (GAC), 246-247, 367-370
Global Assembly Cache Tool (GacUtil.exe), adding assemblies, 370
Global class, 99
global event handlers, 99-102
global procedures, declaring, 297
global variables, declaring, 297
global.asax file, global event handling, 99-102
globalization, 272-274
Google Web site, 21
Grade Exam button, 539
graphics, loading randomly, 70
GridLines property, 69
GroupName property, 62-63

H

handlers, event handling, 39
handling exceptions, 127-130
HasExited property, 393
Headers Collection table (ASP.NET), 340
Headers property, 93
HeaderTemplate, 162
HeaderText property, 77
Height property, 60
help
    accessibility features, 322-326
    user assistance, 318-321
/help option (Type Library Importer), 304
HelpLink property, 127
hidden fields, 104
hierarchies
    exception handling, 128
    namespaces, 28-29
HorizontalAlign property, 68-70
hosts, runtime (ASP.NET), 29
hot area questions, exam format, 12
HTML controls, 58-59
HTML tab, 58

HtmlDecode() method, 98
HtmlEncode() method, 98
HtmlInputHidden control, 104
HtmlInputText object, 166
HTTP (Hypertext Transfer Protocol), 29, 90, 132
HTTP Response object, 31
HttpApplication class, 99
HttpApplication object, 99
HttpApplicationState class, 112
HttpApplicationState object, 111
HttpCookieCollection object, 104
HttpMethod property, 94
HttpRequest object, 93-95, 103-104
HttpResponse class, 95-97
HttpResponse object, 95-97
HttpServerUtility, 98
HttpSessionState class, 110-111
Hypertext Transfer Protocol (HTTP), 29, 90, 132

I

IComponent interface, 232
ID property, 60, 393
IDE (Integrated Development Environment), 26
identity columns, SQL Server, 190
@@IDENTITY variable, 190-191
IE. See Internet Explorer
#If preprocessing directive, 347
IIdentify interface, 418
IIS (Internet Information Services), 414
    configuring, 415-416, 423
    installing, 423
Image control, properties, 62
ImageAlign property, 62
ImageButton control, 63-64
imagemaps (accessibility guidelines), 323
images, loading randomly, 70
ImageUrl property, 62
impersonation, 416-417
Implements directive, 36
Import directive, 36, 48
Increment method, 397
incremental testing, 334-336
IncrementBy method, 397
Indent method, 342
IndentLevel property, 342
IndentSize property, 342
indexing, strings, 287
inheritance, 28, 41
Inherits attribute, 38, 43-44
Init event, 34, 41
Initial Catalog (connection strings), 198
InitialValue property, 75
INNER JOIN keyword, 180
InnerException property, 127

InnerText property, 218
InnerXml property, 218
input, text, 61
input controls, entries, 75
input methods, accessibility, 322
input server controls, 73, 76
InputStream property, 94
Insert, Table command (Table menu), 45
INSERT statement, 184-185
Insert Table dialog box, 45
InsertAfter method, 218
InsertBefore method, 218
InsertCommand property, 201
Install method(), 372
Installation Wizard, 537
installations
    .NET Framework, 24
    PrepLogic Practice Test, Preview Edition, 537
    server services, 422-424
    Web applications. See deploying Web applications
    zero-impact, 362
Installer class, 372, 375
Installer Tool (InstallUtil.exe), 372, 375
Installers property, 372
InstallUtil.exe (Installer Tool), 372, 375
InstanceName property, 397
instances. See objects
instantiating Web services, 263-264
InstMsiA.exe, 364
InstMsiW.exe, 364
Integrated Development Environment (IDE), 26
integration testing, 336
interfaces
    IComponent, 232
    IIdentity, 418
    IPrincipal, 418
    user (UI), business logic, separating, 43-48
international applications, testing, 272-274, 336-337
Internet Explorer (IE)
    ActiveX controls, 298
    search pane, 319-320
Internet Information Services (IIS), 414
    configuring, 415-416, 423
    installing, 423
    node, 424
interoperability (ASP and ASP.NET), 296-297
intranet, smart navigation, 92
intrinsic objects, 92
    HttpApplicationState, 111
    HttpRequest, 93-95
    HttpResponse, 95-97
    HttpServerUtility, 98

invariant cultures, 276
invoking Web services, 263-264
IPrincipal interface, 418
IsAuthenticated property, 94
IsClientConnected property, 96
IsCookieless property, 110
IsEnabled property, 337
IsInRole method, 418
IsNewSession property, 110
IsNull method, 203
IsPostBack property, 34, 67, 91
IsReadOnly property, 110
IsSecureConnection property, 94
IsSynchronized property, 110
IsValid property, 34, 74-75, 77
Item property, 66, 203-204
Item Review button, 538-539
ItemTemplate, 162

J-K

Just-In-Time (JIT) compilation, 389-390

keyboard navigation (accessibility
  guidelines), 323
keyboard shortcuts
  Ctrl+Shift+F8, 349
  Debug menu step execution options, 349
  F8, 348
  Shift+F8, 348
/keycontainer option (Type Library
  Importer), 304
/keyfile option (Type Library Importer),
  304
Keys property, 110-112
keywords
  ASC, 210
  CREATE PROCEDURE, 187
  DESC, 210
  INNER JOIN, 180
  Let, 297
  Me, 40
  SET, 185, 297
  UPDATE, 185
  uppercase, 177
Kill method, 392-393

L

Label control, 61, 146
Language attribute, 32, 38
language compilers, .NET Framework, 24
languages. *See also* XML (Extensible
  Markup Language)
  exceptions, throwing, 129
  MSIL (Microsoft Intermediate
    Language), 389-390

programming, Visual Basic .NET, 27
SQL (Structured Query Language), 176
WSDL (Web Services Description
  Language), 259
"last one wins" concurrency control, 221
LastChild property, 218
late-bound COM components, 297-298
Launch Conditions Editor, 367
LCID property, 38, 110
learning environment, *PrepLogic Practice
  Test, Preview Edition*, 536
left-to-right mirroring, 285-286
legacy code
  ActiveX controls, 298-300
  COM components
    calling, 304-305
    late-bound, 297-298
    runtime-callable wrappers, 300-302
    TLBIMP (Type Library Importer),
      302-304
  COM+ components, 305
  converting ASP pages to ASP.NET, 297
  PInvoke (platform invoke), 306-308
  running ASP and ASP.NET pages, 296
Length property, 193
Let keyword, 297
Level property, 346
libraries
  COM, 301
  Control Library, 237
  mscorlib.dll, 390
  System.Drawing.dll, 390
  System.Windows.Forms.dll, 390
link text (accessibility guidelines), 323
LinkButton control, 63-64
linking UI (user interface) and business
  logic, 43
links
  Add Installer, 373
  Generate Dataset, 160, 207
List controls, 65-67
ListBox control, 65-67, 147-150
ListControl class, 65-66
listeners, 343-344
Listeners property, 342-343
Load event, 34
Load method, 219
loading image (randomly), 70
LoadXml method, 219
localization, 272
  calendars, 279-280
  cultures, 274
    culture codes, 275
    CultureInfoclass, 275-276
    CurrentCulture property, 276
    CurrentUICulture property, 276
    invariant culture, 276
    localized calendars, 279-280
    properties, setting, 278-279
    resource files, 281-284

encodings, 284-285
identifying resources, 273-274
information (localized), displaying, 277-278
mirroring, 285-286
non-Latin user input, validating, 287-288
process, 273
runtime, 284
threads, 276
Lock method, 112
Log property, 394
LogDisplayName property, 395
logging exceptions, 394-396
logic, business
    UI (user interface), separating, 43-48
    Web Forms, analyzing, 47-48
logins, SQL Server, 153
LogNameFromSourceName method, 395
logos, Windows, 322

M

Machine Debug Manager (mdm.exe), 352
machine.config file, 408-412
MachineName property, 98, 395-397
managed providers, optimized, 390-391
MapImageCoordinates() method, 95
MapPath() method, 34, 95, 98
maps, imagemaps (accessibility guidelines), 323
Mark Item button, 539
MAX() function, 183
MaximumValue property, 76
MaxLength property, 61, 204
mdm.exe (Machine Debug Manager), 352
Me keyword, 40
members
    BaseValidator, 74
    Button control, 64
    Checkbox control, 63
    classes, 27
    ImageButton control, 64
    LinkButton control, 64
    ListControl class, 65-66
    Page class, 33-34
    public, simple data binding, 145-146
    RadioButton control, 63
    TextBox control, 61-62
Merge method, 201
Merge Module projects, 363
merge modules, shared assemblies, 370-371
Message property, 127
messages, error, 124
methods
    Abandon, 110
    AcceptChanges, 201
    Add, 111-112

AddCacheItemDependencies(), 97
AddCacheItemDependency(), 97
AddFileDependencies(), 97
AddFileDependency(), 97
AddHeader(), 97
AddNew, 204
AddRange, 389
AppendChild, 218
AppendHeader(), 97
AppendToLog(), 97
Assert, 342
BeginEdit, 203
BeginTransaction, 198
BinaryRead(), 95
BinaryWrite(), 97
CancelEdit, 203
Clear(), 97, 111-112, 201-202
ClearContent(), 97
ClearError(), 98, 135
ClearHeaders(), 97
Close(), 97, 193, 198, 342, 397
CloseMainWindow, 392-393
Commit(), 372
Compare, 288
conditional compilation, 347
CopyTo, 111
CreateAttribute, 218
CreateChildControls, 240
CreateCommand, 198
CreateElement, 218
CreateEventSource, 394
CreateNode, 218
CreateObject(), 98, 297
CreateObjectFromClsid(), 98
CreateParameter, 199
DataBind(), 146, 151-152
Decrement, 397
Delete, 203-204, 394
DeleteEventSource, 394
End(), 97
EndEdit, 203
EnsureChildControls, 240
Eval, 162-163
Execute(), 98
ExecuteNonQuery, 189, 199
ExecuteReader, 199
ExecuteScalar, 199
ExecuteXmlReader, 199
Exists, 394
Fail, 342
Fill, 201, 212
Find, 204
FindControl, 166
FindRows, 204
Flush(), 97, 193, 342
Get, 112
GetBytes, 285
GetChanges, 201

GetChars, 285
GetElementsByTagName, 219
GetEnumerator, 111
GetEventLog, 394
GetKey, 112
GetLastError(), 98, 135
GetObject, 284
GetProcessById, 393
GetProcesses, 393
GetProcessesByName, 393
GetString, 284
GetTextElementEnumerator, 288
GetXml, 201
GetXmlSchema, 201
HtmlDecode(), 98
HtmlEncode(), 98
Increment, 397
IncrementBy, 397
Indent, 342
InsertAfter, 218
InsertBefore, 218
Install(), 372
IsInRole, 418
IsNull, 203
Kill, 392-393
Load, 219
LoadXml, 219
Lock, 112
LogNameFromSourceName, 395
MapImageCoordinates(), 95
MapPath(), 34, 95, 98
Merge, 201
MoveNext, 288
NewRow, 202, 214
NextSample, 397
NextValue, 397
objects, 27
OnInit(), 41
OnPreRender(), 40
Open, 198
Peek, 195
Pics(), 97
PrependChild, 218
PreviousSibling, 218
raising, event handling, 40
Read, 193-195, 200
ReadByte, 193
ReadLine, 195
ReadToEnd, 195
ReadXml, 201
ReadXmlSchema, 201, 220
Redirect(), 97
references, storing, 39
Remove, 111-112
RemoveAll, 111-112, 218
RemoveAt, 111-112
RemoveChild, 218
RemoveInstance, 397

RemoveOutputCacheItem(), 97
Render, 243
RenderBeginTag, 243
RenderControl, 34
RenderEndTag, 243
ReplaceChild, 218
Response.Output.Write, 31
Response.Redirect(), 113
Response.Write, 31
Rollback(), 372
Save, 219
SaveAs(), 95
Seek, 193
Select, 202, 208
Server.Execute(), 114-115
Server.Transfer(), 113-114
Set, 112
SetCacheability, 420
SetExpire, 420
SetValidUntilExpires(true), 420
Sort, 204, 288
SourceExists, 395
Start, 392-393
Transfer(), 98
Unindent, 342
Uninstall(), 372
Unlock, 112
Update, 201, 210-213
UrlDecode(), 98
UrlEncode(), 98
UrlPathEncode(), 98
virtual protected methods, ASP.NET
    pages, 41
WaitForExit, 393
WaitForInputIdle, 393
Warn, 338
Write(), 97, 193-195, 338, 342
WriteByte, 193
WriteEntry, 395
WriteFile(), 97
WriteIf, 342
WriteLine, 195, 342
WriteLineIf, 342
WriteTo, 219
WriteXml, 202
WriteXmlSchema, 202
Microsoft certification exams
    adaptive exams, strategies, 17
    build-list-and-reorder questions, 6-8
    case studies, 4, 15
    create-a-tree questions, 8-9
    drag-and-connect questions, 10
    fixed-length exams, strategies, 15-16
    formats, 12-14
    hot area questions, 12
    multiple-choice questions, 5-6
    practice exams, taking, 19
    question handling, strategies, 18

readiness, assessing, 2
resources, 19-21
select-and-place questions, 11
short-form exams, strategies, 15-16
testing centers, 3-4
Microsoft Certified Professional pages,
19-21
Microsoft Data Engine (MSDE) databases,
26
Microsoft Intermediate Language (MSIL),
389-390
Microsoft Passport, 416
Microsoft Web site, 19, 416
Microsoft Windows Installer, 363, 369
MIN() function, 183
Mindreef SOAPScope, 265
MinimumValue property, 76
mirroring, 285-286
Mode property, 110
models, publisher-subscriber, 40
modes, Release (performance
considerations), 390
modifiers, Auto, 307
monitoring
event logs, 395-396
Web applications, 388
MoveNext method, 288
mscorcfg.msc (.NET Framework
Configuration Tool), adding assemblies,
369
mscorlib.dll library, 390
MSDE (Microsoft Data Engine) databases,
26
.msi packages, 363
MSIL (Microsoft Intermediate Language),
389-390
.msm file extension, 370
multicultural test data, 272-274, 336-337
multifile assemblies, 245
multiline text input, 61
multiple Catch blocks, 128
multiple check boxes, selecting, 66
multiple tables (DataSets), 207-208
multiple-choice questions, exam format, 5-6
multiple-table data forms, 154

N

Name property, 218
/namespace option (Type Library Importer),
304
namespaces
classes, 28
FCL (Framework Class Library), 25
hierarchies, 28-29
root namespaces, finding, 283
System.Component, 232
System.Configuration.Install, 371

System.Data, 201
System.Data.OleDb, 197
System.Data.SqlClient, 158, 220
System.Diagnositics, 341, 388, 392
System.IO, 192
System.Reflection.Emit, 246
System.Text, 285
System.Xml, 217
XML namespaces, 216-217
NameValueCollection object, 103
naming resource files, 283
navigation between pages, 113-115
NetTool, 265
Network Load Balancing (NLB), 377
New, Project command (File menu), 30
New Breakpoint dialog box, 349
New Connection button, 153
New Project button, 30
New Project command (Add menu), 364
New Project dialog box, 30
NewRow method, 202, 214
.NET assemblies. *See* assemblies
.NET components, creating, 232-235
.NET development tools, 25-27
.NET Framework
ASP.NET
classes, 29
Page class, 33-34
pages, 30-38
runtime hosts, 29
Web requests, 29-30
classes, 27
CLR (Common Language Runtime), 24
FCL (Framework Class Library),
namespaces, 25
inheritance, 28
installing, 24
language compilers, 24
namespaces, 28-29
.NET Framework Configuration Tool
(mscorcfg.msc), GAC (Global Assembly
Cache), 369
.NET Framework SDK (Software
Development Kit), 25-26, 263
.NET WebService Studio Tool, 265
Next Item button, 539
NextMonthText property, 71
NextPrevFormat property, 71
NextPrevStyle property, 71
NextSample method, 397
NextSibling property, 218
NextValue method, 397
NLB (Network Load Balancing), 377
nodes
Data Connections, 156
Default Web Server Site, 424
Internet Information Services, 424
NodeType property, 218

non-Latin user input, validating, 287-288
numbers, formatting, 276-279
NUnit, 335

O

Object data type, 297
Object type, 40
objects
    Cache, 419-420
    classes, 27
    CompareInfo, 288
    ConfigurationSettings, 413
    CounterCreationData, 399
    CounterCreationDataCollection, 399
    DataBinder, Eval method, 162
    DataColumn, 149
    DataRelation, 159
    DataRow, 149
    DataTable, 149, 159, 202
    DataView, 149, 159
    designing (Server Explorer), 156
    EventLogEntryCollection, 395
    exceptions, 126-127
    HtmlInputText, 166
    HTTP Response, 31
    HttpApplication, 99
    HttpCookieCollection, 104
    intrinsic objects, 92
        HttpApplicationState, 111
        HttpRequest, 93-95
        HttpResponse, 95-97
        HttpServerUtility, 98
    members, 27
    NameValueCollection, 103
    Page, DataBind method, 151
    PerformanceCounterCategory, 399
    ResourceManager, 283
    SqlCommand, 157
    SqlConnection, 157, 197-198
    SqlDataAdapter, 157, 200-201
    SqlDataReader, 199-200
    SqlParameter, 199
    TextWriter, 115
    WindowsIdentity, 418
    WindowsPrincipal, 418
    XmlNode, members, 218
ODBC data provider, 197
Off setting, 126
OLE DB data provider, 197
OleDbCommandBuilder class, 392
On setting, 126
OnInit() method, 41
online user assistance, 318-321
OnPreRender() method, 40
Open method, 198
Operator property, 76
optimistic concurrency controls, 221

optimized managed providers, 390-391
optimizing performance, 388-392
Oracle data provider, 197
organization classes, namespaces, 28
Other Windows, Output command
    (View menu), 343
OtherMonthDayStyle property, 71
/out option (Type Library Importer), 304
OuterXml property, 218
output caching, 419
output methods, accessibility, 322
Output property, 96
OutputCache directive, 36, 419-420
OutputStream property, 96

P

Page class, 27
    Application property, 111
    members, 33-34
    Response property, 95
    Server property, 98
    Session property, 110
    ViewState property, 105
Page Cleanup stage, ASP.NET page
    processing, 35
Page control, 74
Page directive, 36-38
Page Initialization stage, ASP.NET page
    processing, 35
Page object, DataBind method, 151
page postback, 90-92
page-level tracing, 341
Page.Error event, 134-135
pages
    ASP.NET
        code, 297
        creating, 30-31
        directives, 35-38
        executing, 32
        inheritance, 41
        processing, 35
        virtual protected methods, 41
    custom error, 132-133
    Web pages, 67-69
pairs, surrogate (Unicode), 287
Panel control, 67-69
panes, search (Internet Explorer), 319-320
Parameter object, 196-199
parameterized stored procedures, 189-190
parameters, passing, 297
Parameters property, 199
Params property, 94
Parent property, 60
ParentColumns property, 203
ParentKeyConstraint property, 203
ParentNode properties, 218
ParentTable property, 203

passing parameters, 297
Passport (Microsoft), 415-416
passport authentication, 389
Passport Software Development Kit (SDK), 416
Path property, 94
PathInfo property, 94
Peek method, 195
per-request event handlers, 100-102
perfmon.exe, 397-399
performance
    improving, 392
    optimizing, 388-392
performance counters, 396-399
Performance Monitor (perfmon.exe), 397-399
PerformanceCounter class, 397-399
PerformanceCounterCategory object, 399
PhysicalApplicationPath property, 94
PhysicalPath property, 94
PIA (Primary Interop Assembly), 305
Pics() method, 97
PInvoke (platform invoke), 306-308
PlaceHolder control, 67-69
platform invoke (PInvoke), 306-308
plus signs (+), 47
Position property, 193
postback, 65, 90-92
postback controls, 104-105
practice exams, taking, 19
Practice Test Mode, *PrepLogic Practice Tests, Preview Edition*, 538-539
Practice Test radio button, 538
PrependChild method, 218
PrepLogic Practice Tests, Preview Edition
    Competency Score, 540
    contact information, 541
    exam review, 540
    exam simulations, 535
    Examination Score Report screen, 540
    Flash Review Mode, 537-538
    installing, 537
    learning environments, 536
    options, 539
    Practice Test Mode, 538-539
    questions, 535
    removing, 537
    software requirements, 536
    time remaining, 540
PrepLogic.com Web site, 535
preprocessing directives, 347
PreRender event, 34
PreRender stage, ASP.NET page processing, 35
Previous Item button, 539
PreviousSibling method, 218
PrevMonthText property, 71
Primary Interop Assembly (PIA), 305

/primary option (Type Library Importer), 304
PrimaryKey property, 202
private assemblies, 246-247
private keys, 368
private UDDI registries, 262
procedures
    global, declaring, 297
    stored, 176, 186
        creating, 187
        @@IDENTITY variable, 190-191
        parameters, 189-190
        running, 187-189
Process class, 392
processes
    remote processes, debugging, 352
    running processes, debugging, 351-352
    session state variables, storing, 421
    starting, 392-393
    stopping, 392-393
Processes dialog box, 351-352
processModel element, 376-377, 408
Profiler and Index Tuning Wizard (SQL Server), 391
programming languages, Visual Basic .NET, 27
Project menu commands
    Add HTML Page, 133
    Add New Item, 281
Project Output command (Add menu), 374
ProjectInstaller class, 374
projects, solutions, 30. *See also* setup and deployment projects
properties
    AcceptTypes, 93
    AccessKey, 60
    AllKeys, 111
    AllowDbNull, 204
    allowDefinition, 410
    AllowDelete, 204
    AllowEdit, 204
    allowLocation, 410
    AllowNew, 204
    AlternateText, 62
    Application, 33, 111
    ApplicationPath, 93
    AspCompat, 36
    Attributes, 218
    AutoEventWireUp, 37, 42-43, 47
    AutoFlush, 342
    AutoIncrement, 204
    AutoPostBack, 61-65
    BackColor, 60
    BackImageUrl, 68-69
    Bindable, 243
    BorderColor, 60
    BorderStyle, 60
    BorderWidth, 60

How can we make this index more useful? Email us at indexes@quepublishing.com

Browser, 93
Buffer, 37, 96
BufferOutput, 96
Cache, 33, 96
CacheControl, 96-97
Calendar class, 71-72
CanRead, 193
CanSeek, 193
CanWrite, 193
CategoryName, 397
CausesValidation, 64
CellPadding, 69-71
Cells, 69
CellSpacing, 69-71
CharSet, 96
Checked, 63
ChildColumns, 203
ChildKeyConstraint, 203
ChildNodes, 218
ChildTable, 203
ClassName, 37
ClientCertificate, 93
ClientTarget, 37
ClientValidationFunction, 77
Codebehind, 47
CodePage, 37, 110
ColumnName, 204
Columns, 61
ColumnSpan, 70
CommandArgument, 64
CommandName, 64
CommandText, 199
CommandType, 199
CompareValidator class, 76
CompilerOptions, 37
complex data binding, 146-150
composite controls, 240
Condition, 367
Connection, 199
ConnectionString, 198
ContentEncoding, 93, 96
ContentLength, 93
Contents, 110-112
ContentType, 37, 93, 96
control, simple data binding, 146
Controls, 33, 60
ControlToCompare, 76
ControlToValidate, 74
Cookies, 93, 96, 104
Count, 110-112, 204
CounterHelp, 397
CounterName, 397
CounterType, 397
cpuMask, 377
CssClass, 60
Culture, 37
culture properties, setting, 278-279
Current, 288

CurrentCulture, 276-281
CurrentExecutionFilePath, 93-95
CurrentUICulture, 276-279
CustomActionData, 376
DataType, 204
DayHeaderStyle, 71
DayNameFormat, 71
DayStyle, 71
Debug, 37
DefaultProperty, 243
DefaultValue, 204, 243
DeleteCommand, 200
Description, 37, 345
dir, 286
Display, 74
DisplayMode, 77
DisplayName, 345
DocumentElement, 219
EditItemIndex, 166
EnableClientScript, 74, 77
Enabled, 60, 74
EnableRaisingEvents, 393-396
EnableSessionState, 37
EnableViewState, 34, 37, 60, 389
EnableViewStateMac, 37, 115
Entries, 394
ErrorMessage, 74, 77
ErrorPage, 34, 37, 133
Exception class, 127
ExitCode, 393
ExitTime, 393
Expires, 96-97
ExpiresAbsolute, 96-97
Explicit, 37
FieldOffset, 308
FilePath, 93
Files, 93
Filter, 93, 96
FirstChild, 218
FirstDayOfWeek, 71
Font, 60
ForeColor, 60, 74, 77
Form, 93
GridLines, 69
GroupName, 62-63
HasExited, 393
Headers, 93
HeaderText, 77
Height, 60
HelpLink, 127
HorizontalAlign, 68-70
HttpMethod, 94
ID, 60, 393
Image control, 62
ImageAlign, 62
ImageUrl, 62
IndentLevel, 342
IndentSize, 342

Inherit, 38, 43-44
InitialValue, 75
InnerException, 127
InnerText, 218
InnerXml, 218
InputStream, 94
InsertCommand, 201
Installers, 372
InstanceName, 397
IsAuthenticated, 94
IsClientConnected, 96
IsCookieless, 110
IsEnable, 337
IsNewSession, 110
IsPostBack, 34, 67, 91
IsReadOnly, 110
IsSecureConnection, 94
IsSynchronized, 110
IsValid, 34, 74-77
Item, 66, 203-204
Keys, 110-112
Language, 32, 38
LastChild, 218
LCID, 38, 110
Length, 193
Level, 346
Listener, 342-343
Log, 394
LogDisplayName, 395
MachineName, 98, 395-397
MaximumValue, 76
MaxLength, 61, 204
Message, 127
MinimumValue, 76
Mode, 110
Name, 218
NextMonthText, 71
NextPrevFormat, 71
NextPrevStyle, 71
NextSibling, 218
NodeType, 218
objects, 27
Operator, 76
OtherMonthDayStyle, 71
OuterXml, 218
Output, 96
OutputStream, 96
Page directive, 36-38
Panel control, 68
Parameters, 199
Params, 94
Parent, 60
ParentColumns, 203
ParentKeyConstraint, 203
ParentNode, 218
ParentTable, 203
Path, 94
PathInfo, 94

PhysicalApplicationPath, 94
PhysicalPath, 94
Position, 193
PrevMonthText, 71
QueryString, 94, 103
RangeValidator class, 76
RawUrl, 94
RawValue, 397
ReadOnly, 61, 397
redirect, 132
RelationName, 203
Relations, 201
RepeatColumns, 163
Request, 34
RequestType, 94
Response, 31, 34
ResponseEncoding, 38
Rows, 61, 66, 69, 202
RowSpan, 70
RowState, 203
ScriptTimeout, 98
SelectCommand, 201
SelectedDate, 72
SelectedDates, 72
SelectedDayStyle, 72
SelectedIndex, 66-67
SelectedItem, 66-67
SelectionMode, 66, 72
SelectMonthText, 72
SelectorStyle, 72
SelectWeekText, 72
Server, 34, 98
ServerVariables, 94
Session, 34
SessionID, 110
ShowDayHeader, 72
ShowGridLines, 72
ShowMessageBox, 77
ShowNextPrevMonth, 72
ShowSummary, 77
ShowTitle, 72
simple data binding, 144-146
SmartNavigation, 34, 38, 91-92
Source, 127, 395
sqlConnectionString, 422
Src, 38, 43-44
StackTrace, 127
StartInfo, 392-393
StaticObjects, 110-112
Status, 96
StatusCode, 96, 132
StatusDescription, 96
Strict, 38
StrucLayout, 308
Style, 60
SuppressContent, 96
SyncRoot, 110
TabIndex, 60

Table class, 69
TableCell class, 70
TableName, 202
TableRow class, 69
Tables, 201
TargetSite, 127
Text, 61-64, 70, 74, 77
TextAlign, 63
TextMode, 62
Timeout, 110
TITLE, 320
TitleFormat, 72
TitleStyle, 72
TodayDayStyle, 72
TodaysDate, 72
ToolboxData, 243
ToolTip, 60, 320
TotalBytes, 94
Trace, 34, 38
<trace> element, 340
TraceError, 346
TraceInfo, 346
TraceMode, 38, 337
TraceVerbose, 346
TraceWarning, 346
Transaction, 38
Type, 76
UICulture, 38
Unique, 204
UpdateCommand, 201, 221
Url, 94
UrlReferrer, 94
UserAgent, 94
UserHostAddress, 94
UserHostName, 94
UserLanguages, 94
Validate, 74
ValidationExpression, 75
ValidationSummary class, 77
Validators, 34
Value, 77, 218
ValueToCompare, 76
VaryByParam, 420
VerticalAlign, 69-70
ViewState, 105
Visible, 34, 60
VisibleDate, 72
WarningLevel, 38
Web user controls, 236
WebControl class, 60
webGarden, 377
WeekendDayStyle, 72
Width, 60
Wrap, 62, 68-70
XML, 216
protocols
    Disco, 259, 262
    HTTP (Hypertext Transfer Protocol),
        90

SOAP (Simple Object Access Protocol),
    258
UDDI (Universal Description, Discover,
    and Integration), 259, 262
prototypes, references, 39
proxy classes, 263-264
public keys, 368
public members, simple data binding,
    145-146
public UDDI registries, 262
/publickey option (Type Library Importer),
    304
publisher-subscriber model, events, 40
publishing performance data, 399

Q

queries
    ad hoc, 176
        DELETE statement, 186
        INSERT statement, 184-185
        running, 177-178
        SELECT statement, 178-184
        UPDATE statement, 185-186
    cross-product, 179
Query Analyzer (SQL Server), 391
query strings, 102-103
Querystring Collection table (ASP.NET),
    340
QueryString property, 94, 103
question mark (?), 102
question-handling strategies, 18
questions, *PrepLogic Practice Test, Preview
    Edition*, 535

R

radio buttons
    Class Name, 79
    Flash Review, 539
    Practice Test, 539
    selecting, 67
RadioButton control, 62-63
RadioButtonList control, 65-66, 150
raising methods, event handling, 40
RangeValidator class, properties, 76
RangeValidator control, 76
RawUrl property, 94
RawValue property, 397
Read method, 193-195, 200
ReadByte method, 193
reading event logs, 395-396
reading performance counter data, 397-399
ReadLine method, 195
ReadOnly property, 61, 397
ReadToEnd method, 195
ReadXml method, 201
ReadXmlSchema method, 201, 220

redirect attribute, 132
Redirect() method, 97
Reference directive, 36
reference option (Type Library Importer), 304
references
    methods, storing, 39
    Web, 264
#Region preprocessing directive, 347
Register directive, 36
registries, UDDI, 262
Registry Editor, 366
regression testing, 336
RegularExpressionValidator control, 75
Rehabilitative Act, Section 508, 325-326
relational data (XML), 219-220
relational databases, ADO.NET object model
    adding data, 213-214
    data editing, 210
    data providers, 196-201
    data updates, 211-212
    DataSet classes, 201-210
    DataTable object, 202
    deleting data, 214-215
RelationName property, 203
Relations collection, 159
Relations property, 201
Release configurations, 341
Release mode (performance considerations), 390
remote processes, debugging, 352
RemoteOnly setting, 126
removable media, Web application deployment, 378
Remove method, 111-112
RemoveAll method, 111-112, 218
RemoveAt method, 111-112
RemoveChild method, 218
RemoveInstance method, 397
RemoveOutputCacheItem() method, 97
Render method, 243
RenderBeginTag method, 243
RenderControl method, 34
RenderEndTag method, 243
RepeatColumns property, 163
Repeater control, 160-163
ReplaceChild method, 218
Request Details table (ASP.NET), 339
Request property, 34
requests, Web (ASP.NET), 29-30
RequestType property, 94
RequiredFieldValidator control, 75
resource files, 281-284
Resource Generator tool, 248
resource-only assemblies, 247-248
ResourceManager class, 284
ResourceManager object, 283

resources
    exam strategies, 19-21
    localizable, 273-274
Response property, 31, 34, 95
Response.Output.Write() method, 31
Response.Redirect() method, 113
Response.Write() method, 31
ResponseEncoding attribute, 38
resultsets, retrieving, 199
.resx file extension, 248
right-to-left mirroring, 285-286
role-based authorization, 417-418
role-based security, 413, 418
Rollback() method, 372
root namespaces, finding, 283
round-trip, 90-92
RowChanged event, 202
RowChanging event, 202
RowDeleted event, 202
RowDeleting event, 202
rows, tables, 184
Rows property, 61, 66, 69, 202
RowSpan property, 70
RowState property, 203
running processes, debugging, 351-352
runtime, resources, 284
runtime hosts, ASP.NET, 29
Runtime Callable Wrappers, 300-302

S

sampling performance counters, 397-399
satellite assemblies, 248
Save button, 68
Save method, 219
SaveAs() method, 95
scalability, Web farms, 377
ScriptTimeout property, 98
scroll position, 91
search panes (Internet Explorer), 319-320
Section 508 standards (Rehabilitative Act), 325-326
<section> element, 410
security
    authentication, 413-416
    authorization, 416-418
    role-based, 413
    ViewState, 107-108
Security event logs, 394-395
Seek method, 193
Select Item in Project dialog box, 374
Select method, 202, 208
SELECT statement, 178-184, 188
select-and-place questions, exam format, 11
SelectCommand property, 201
SelectedDate property, 72
SelectedDates property, 72
SelectedDayStyle property, 72

SelectedIndex property, 66-67
SelectedIndexChanged event, 66
SelectedItem property, 66-67
SelectionChanged event, 73
SelectionMode property, 66, 72
SelectMonthText property, 72
SelectorStyle property, 72
SelectWeekText property, 72
SeparatorTemplate, 162
server code, Web server controls, 65
Server Explorer
    Data Connections, 156
    drag-and-drop, 157-158
    object design, 156
    predefined installation components,
    372-373
Server Extensions Wizard, 424
Server object, 113-115
Server property, 34, 98
server services, 422-424
Server Variables table (ASP.NET), 340
server-side custom validations, 77
server-side state management, 109-112
server-side validations, 73
Server.Execute() method, 114-115
Server.Transfer() method, 113-114
servers. *See also* SQL Server
    data filtering, 159
    FrontPage Server Extensions,
    configuring/installing, 423-424
ServerValidate event, 77
ServerVariables property, 94
services. *See* IIS (Internet Information
    Services); server services; Web services
Session property, 34, 110
session state, 109-110
session state information, application per-
    formance, 388
Session State table (ASP.NET), 339
session state variables, 408, 420-422
session-level global event handling, 99-100
Session_End() event handler, 100
Session_Start event handler, 100
SessionIDs, 109-110
sessionState element, 422
SET keyword, 185, 297
Set method, 112
SetCacheability method, 420
SetExpires method, 420
setup and deployment projects, 363
    configuration settings, 365
    creating, 364, 379
    Custom Actions Editor, 366
    File System Editor, 365
    File Types Editor, 366
    Launch Conditions Editor, 367
    Registry Editor, 366
    User Interface Editor, 366

Setup projects, installation components,
    374-375
Setup.exe bootstrapper (Windows Installer),
    364
SetValidUntilExpires(true) method, 420
shared assemblies, 246-247, 367
    delay signing, 370
    GAC (Global Assembly Cache), 369-370
    merge modules, 370-371
    strong names, 368
shfusion.dll (Assembly Cache Viewer Shell
    Extension), 369
short-form exams, 12-16
Show All Files button, 264
Show Answer button, 537-539
ShowDayHeader property, 72
ShowGridLines property, 72
ShowMessageBox property, 77
ShowNextPrevMonth property, 72
ShowSummary property, 77
ShowTitle property, 72
/silent option (Type Library Importer), 304
simple data binding, 144-146
Simple Object Access Protocol (SOAP), 258
simulations, 12, 535
single line text input, 61
single-file assemblies, 245
single-table data forms, 152-154
Single-Threaded Apartment (STA) model,
    298
sites. *See* Web sites
SmartNavigation property, 34, 38, 91-92
sn.exe (Strong Name tool), 368
SOAP (Simple Object Access Protocol), 258
software, *PrepLogic Practice Test, Preview
    Edition*, 536
Software NLB (Network Load Balancing),
    377
sort expressions, 210
Sort method, 204, 288
sorting data, 288
Source property, 127, 395
SourceExists method, 395
specifications, custom, 76
SQL (Structured Query Language), 176.
    See also T-SQL
SQL Server
    connection pooling, 197-198, 391
    data
        ad hoc queries, 176-186
        stored procedures, 176, 186-191
    data providers, 196
    DataSet objects, DataTable, 202
    identity columns, 190
    keywords, uppercase, 177
    logging on, 153
    Profiler and Index Tuning Wizard, 391

Query Analyzer, 391
session state variables, storing, 422
TDS (Tabular Data Stream), 390
SQL statements, versus stored procedures, 391
SqlCommand object, 157
SqlCommandBuilder class, 392
SqlConnection object, 157, 197-198
sqlConnectionString attribute, 422
SqlDataAdapter object, 157, 200-201
SqlDataReader object, 199-200
SqlError class, 220
SqlException class, 220
SqlParameter object, 199
Src attribute, 38, 43-44
STA (Single-Threaded Apartment) model, 298
StackTrace property, 127
Start menu (Debug menu), 68
Start method, 392-393
Start Without Debugging command (Debug menu), 46
StartInfo property, 392-393
state constants, 210
state management
    client-side techniques, 102-108
    server-side techniques, 109-112
State Service, session state variables, 421
state variables, configuration file changes, 408
statements
    Declare, 307
    DELETE, 186
    INSERT, 184-185
    SELECT, 178-184, 188
    SQL, versus stored procedures, 391
    Throw, 130
    UPDATE, 185-186
static assemblies, 246
static members, classes, 27
StaticObjects property, 110-112
Status property, 96
StatusCode property, 96, 132
StatusDescription property, 96
Step Into command (Debug menu), 348
Step Out command (Debug menu), 349
Step Over command (Debug menu), 348
stepping, debugging Web applications, 348-349
stored procedures, 176, 186
    creating, 187
    parameters, 189-191
    running, 187-189
    versus SQL statements, 391
storing
    references, methods, 39
    session state variables, 421-422

StreamReader class, 194-195
streams, 191-196
StreamWriter class, 194-195
Strict attribute, 38
/strictref option (Type Library Importer), 304
string comparison rules, localization, 276
string indexing, 287-288
StringBuilder class, 389
StringInfo class, 287-288
strings
    comparing, 288
    connection, 198
    modifying, 389
    sorting, 288
Strong Name tool (sn.exe), 368
strong names
    assemblies, 247
    shared assemblies, 368
strongly typed DataSets, 206-207
StructLayout attribute, 308
Structured Query Language (SQL), 176
Style Builder dialog box, 79
Style property, 60
style sheets (accessibility guidelines), 323
subtract sign (-), 47
SUM() function, 183
SuppressContent property, 96
surrogate pairs, Unicode, 287
symbols, DEBUG or TRACE, 341
synchronization, 220
SyncRoot property, 110
syntax. *See also* code; legacy code
/sysarray option (Type Library Importer), 304
System event logs, 394
System.Component namespace, 232
System.Configuration.Install namespace, 371
System.Data namespace, 201
System.Data.OleDb namespace, 197
System.Data.SqlClient, 158, 220, 390
System.Diagnostics namespace, 341, 388, 392
System.Drawing.dll library, 390
System.IO namespace, 192
System.Reflection.Emit namespace, 246
System.Text namespace, 285
System.Windows.Forms.dll library, 390
System.Xml namespace, 217
SystemException, 126, 128

T

T-SQL, ad hoc queries, 176
    DELETE statement, 186
    INSERT statement, 184-185
    running, 177-178

SELECT statement, 178-184
UPDATE statement, 185-186
TabIndex property, 60
Table class, properties, 69
Table control, 69-70
Table menu commands, Insert, Table, 45
TableCell class, properties, 70
TableCell control, 69-70
TableName property, 202
TableRow class, properties, 69
TableRow control, 69-70
tables
    accessibility guidelines, 323
    creating, 69
    DataTable object, 202
    multiple (DataSets), 207-208
    rows, adding, 184
Tables collection, 159
Tables property, 201
tabs
    Background, 79
    COM components, 298
    Components, 239
    Connection, 153
    HTML, 58
    Text, 79
Tabular Data Stream (TDS), 390
tags
    CommandName, 166
    XML, 215-216
tamper-proofing, ViewState, 107
TargetSite property, 127
TDS (Tabular Data Stream), 390
templated controls, data displays
    DataList control, 163-166
    Repeater control, 160-163
templates
    AlternatingTemplate, 162
    Assembly Resource File, 281
    Code File, 44
    EditItemTemplate, 164
    FooterTemplate, 162
    HeaderTemplate, 162
    ItemTemplate, 162
    SeparatorTemplate, 162
    Text File, 31
test drivers, 335
test plans, 334
testing
    application accessibility, 326
    Web applications
        incremental testing, 334-335
        integration tests, 336
        international applications, 336-337.
            See also globalization
        regression tests, 336
        test plans, 334
        unit tests, 335-336
    Web services, 264

testing centers, environment, 3-4
tests. See exams
text, accessibility guidelines, 323
Text File template, 31
text input, 61
Text property, 61-64, 70, 74, 77
text strings, 287-288
Text tab, 79
TextAlign property, 63
TextBox control, members, 61-62
TextChanged event, 62
TextMode property, 62
TextWriter object, 115
TextWriterTraceListener class, 343
threads, localization, 276
Throw statement, 130
throwing exceptions, 129, 390
Timeout property, 110
times, formatting, 276-279
TITLE attribute, 320
TitleFormat property, 72
TitleStyle property, 72
TLBIMP (Type Library Importer), 302-304
TodayDayStyle property, 72
TodaysDate property, 72
toolbar buttons, Show All Files, 264
Toolbox
    ActiveX controls, adding, 299
    HTML controls, 58
ToolboxData attribute, 243
tools
    Installer Tool (InstallUtil.exe), 372, 375
    Mindreef SOAPScope, 265
    .NET development tools, 25-27
    .NET Framework Configuration Tool
        (mscorcfg.msc), adding assemblies, 369
    .NET WebService Studio Tool, 265
    NetTool, 265
    Resource Generator, 248
    Strong Name (sn.exe), 368
    Web Service Discovery Tool (disco.exe),
        262-263
    Web Services Description Language
        Tool (wsdl.exe), 263-264
    XML Spy, 265
Tools menu commands, Debug Processes,
    351
ToolTip property, 60
ToolTips, 320
top-down integration testing, 336
TotalBytes property, 94
Trace attribute, 38
Trace class, 341-343
<trace> element, 340
Trace Information table (ASP.NET), 339
Trace property, 34
trace switches, 345-346
TRACE symbol, 341
TraceContext class, 337-341

TraceError property, 346
TraceInfo property, 346
TraceMode property, 38, 337
TraceSwitch class, 345
TraceVerbose property, 346
TraceWarning property, 346
tracing
    application-level, 341
    conditional compilation, 347
    Debug class, 341-343
    enabling, 338
    page-level, 341
    Trace class, 341-343
    trace listeners, 343-344
    trace switches, 345-346
    TraceContext class, 337-341
    writing trace messages to trace logs, 338
Transaction attribute, 38
transactions, distributed (performance
    considerations), 392
Transfer() method, 98
triggering events, 38
True, AutoEventWireup attribute, 42
Try block, 127
type, inheritance, 28
Type Library Importer (TLBIMP), 302-304
Type property, 76
types, 40

U

UDDI (Universal Description, Discover,
    and Integration), 259, 262
UI (user interface), business logic, 43-48
UICulture attribute, 38
umbrella integration testing, 336
unboxing, 389
unhandled exceptions, 128, 131
    custom error pages, 132-133
    error events, 134-135
Unicode, 284-285
    combining character sequence, 287
    international applications, 336
    surrogate pairs, 287
UnicodeEncoding class, 285
Unindent method, 342
Uninstall() method, 372
Unique property, 204
unit testing, 335-336
Universal Description, Discovery, and
    Integration (UDDI), 259, 262
Unload event, 34
Unlock method, 112
unmanaged code, performance
    considerations, 390
/unsafe option (Type Library Importer), 304
UPDATE
    keyword, 185
    statement, 185-186

Update method, 201, 210-213
UpdateCommand property, 201, 221
updating data (ADO.NET), 211-212
uplevel browsers, ASP.NET, 59
Url property, 94
UrlDecode() method, 98
UrlEncode() method, 98
UrlPathEncode() method, 98
UrlReferrer property, 94
user assistance, 318-321
User Code Initialization stage, ASP.NET
    page processing, 35
user input, non-Latin, 287-288
user interface (UI), business logic, 43-48
User Interface Editor, 366
user interfaces, data binding
    complex, 146-150
    Data Form Wizard, 152-154
    DataBind method, 151-152
    simple, 144-146
UserAgent property, 94
UserHostAddress property, 94
UserHostName property, 94
UserLanguages property, 94
UTF-16. *See* Unicode
UTF7Encoding class, 285
UTF8Encoding class, 285

V

Validate property, 74
validating non-Latin user input, 287-288
validation controls, 73-77
ValidationExpression property, 75
validations, 73
ValidationSummary class, properties, 77
ValidationSummary control, 77
Validators property, 34
Value property, 77, 218
values, input server controls, 76
ValueToCompare property, 76
variables
    global, declaring, 297
    @@IDENTITY, 190-191
    session state, 408, 420-422
Variant data type, 297
VaryByParam attribute, 420
/verbose option (Type Library Importer),
    304
VerticalAlign property, 69-70
video (accessibility guidelines), 323
View Items button, 539
View menu commands, Other Windows,
    Output, 343
viewing editors, 365
ViewState
    application performance, 389
    disabling, 106-107

encrypting, 107
non-postback controls, 105
page-level values, 105
postback controls, 104-105
security, 107-108
tamper-proof, 107
ViewState container, 240
ViewState property, 105
virtual directories, Web applications, 30
virtual protected methods, ASP.NET pages, 41
Visible property, 34, 60
VisibleDate property, 72
VisibleMonthChanged event, 73
Visual Basic .NET, 27
Visual Studio .NET, 26-27
  ASP.NET pages, creating, 30
  code outlining, 47
  solutions, 30
  Web Forms, creating, 44-46

W

W3C (World Wide Web Consortium), Web Accessibility Initiative guidelines, 324-325
WaitForExit method, 393
WaitForInputIdle method, 393
Warn method, 338
WarningLevel attribute, 38
Web Accessibility Initiative guidelines, 324-325
Web applications
  accessibility features, 322-326
  configuring, 408-412
  debugging, 348-353
  deploying
    clusters, 378
    deployment planning, 376
    FTP deployment, 362
    Microsoft Windows Installer, 363
    setup and deployment projects.
      See setup and deployment projects
    shared assemblies, 367-371
    via removable media, 378
    Web farms, 377
    Web gardens, 376-377
    Web-based deployment, 379
    XCOPY deployment, 362
  event logs, 394-396
  improving, 392
  installation, 371-375
  managing and monitoring, 388
  navigating between pages, 113-115
  performance, optimizing, 388-392
  performance counters, 396-399
  processes, starting/stopping, 392-393
  testing, 334-337

tracing
  application-level, 341
  conditional compilation, 347
  Debug class, 341-343
  page-level, 341
  Trace class, 341-343
  trace listeners, 343-344
  trace switches, 345-346
  TraceContext class, 337-341
user assistance, 318-321
virtual directories, 30
Web browsers, ActiveX support, 298
Web custom controls
  choosing, 243-244
  composite controls, 237-240
  creating, 237, 241-243
  derived controls, 240-241
Web farms, 377, 421
Web Forms
  ad hoc queries, 178
  ASP.NET
    event handling, 41-43, 47
    UI (user interface) and business logic, 43-48
  business logic, analyzing, 47-48
  creating, 44-48
  event handling, 38-40
  mirroring, 286
  .NET Framework, 24, 29-30
  Page class, 33-34
    ASP.NET, 29-38
    classes, 27
    CLR (Common Language Runtime), 24
    FCL (Framework Class Library), namespaces, 25
    inheritance, 28
    installing, 24
    language compilers, 24
    namespaces, 28-29
Web gardens, 376-377, 421
Web Matrix Project (ASP.NET), 26
Web pages, 67-69
Web references, 264
Web requests, ASP.NET, 29-30
Web server controls
  AdRotator controls, 70
  AutoPostBack property, 65
  Button control, 63-64
  Calendar controls, 71-73
  CheckBox control, 62-63
  client code, 65
  DataGrid control, 65
  declaring, 59
  event handling, 64-65
  Image control, 62
  ImageButton control, 63-64
  Label control, 61

LinkButton control, 63-64
List controls, 65-67
Panel controls, 67-69
PlaceHolder controls, 67-69
RadioButton control, 62-63
server code, 65
Table controls, 69-70
TableCell controls, 69-70
TableRow controls, 69-70
TextBox control, 61-62
WebControl class, 60
Web services, 258
   Airport Weather, 259-261
   Disco protocol, 259, 262
   discovering, 262-263
   instantiating, 263-264
   invoking, 259-264
   SOAP (Simple Object Access Protocol),
      258
   testing, 264
   UDDI (Universal Description,
      Discovery, and Integration), 259, 262
   WSDL (Web Services Description
      Language), 259
Web Services Description Language
   (WSDL), 259
Web Services Description Language Tool
   (wsdl.exe), 263-264
Web Services Discovery Tool (disco.exe),
   262-263
Web Setup projects, 363
Web sites
   Altavista, 21
   Excite, 21
   Google, 21
   Microsoft, 19, 416
   PrepLogic.com, 535
Web user controls, 235-236
Web-based deployment, 379
Web-based resources, 20-21
web.config file
   authentication providers, selecting, 415
   impersonation settings, 417
   modifying, 411-412
   processModel element, 376-377
   tracing, enabling, 340
WebControl class, properties, 60
WebCustomControl class, 241-243
webGarden attribute, 377
WeekendDayStyle property, 72
WHERE clause, 222
whitespace, trimming, 75
Width property, 60
windows, browsers, 318
Windows authentication providers, 415
Windows Component Wizard, 423
Windows Explorer, GAC (Global Assembly
   Cache), 369

Windows Installer, 363-364, 369
Windows integrated authentication, IIS,
   415
Windows logo, 322
WindowsIdentity object, 418
WindowsPrincipal object, 418
wizards
   Data Form Wizard, 152-154
   Installation, 536
   Profile and Index Tuning Wizard, 391
   Server Extensions Wizard, 424
   Windows Component Wizard, 423
Wrap property, 62, 68-70
wrappers, Runtime Callable Wrappers,
   300-302
Write() method, 97, 193-196, 338, 342
WriteByte method, 193
WriteEntry method, 395
WriteFile() method, 97
WriteIf method, 342
WriteLine method, 195, 342
WriteLineIf method, 342
WriteTo method, 219
WriteXml method, 202
WriteXmlSchema method, 202
writing
   code, 129
   to event logs, 395
WSDL (Web Services Description
   Language), 259
wsdl.exe (Web Services Description
   Language Tool), 263-264

X-Z

XCOPY command, 362
XML (Extensible Markup Language)
   attributes, 216
   data, 215-220
   elements, 216
   entity references, 217
   files, 216-219
   tags, 215-216
   Web server controls, 59
XML Spy, 265
XmlDataDocument class, 219-220
XmlDocument class, 218-219
XmlNode class, 217-219
XmlNode objects, members, 218

zero-impact installations, 362